D1488576

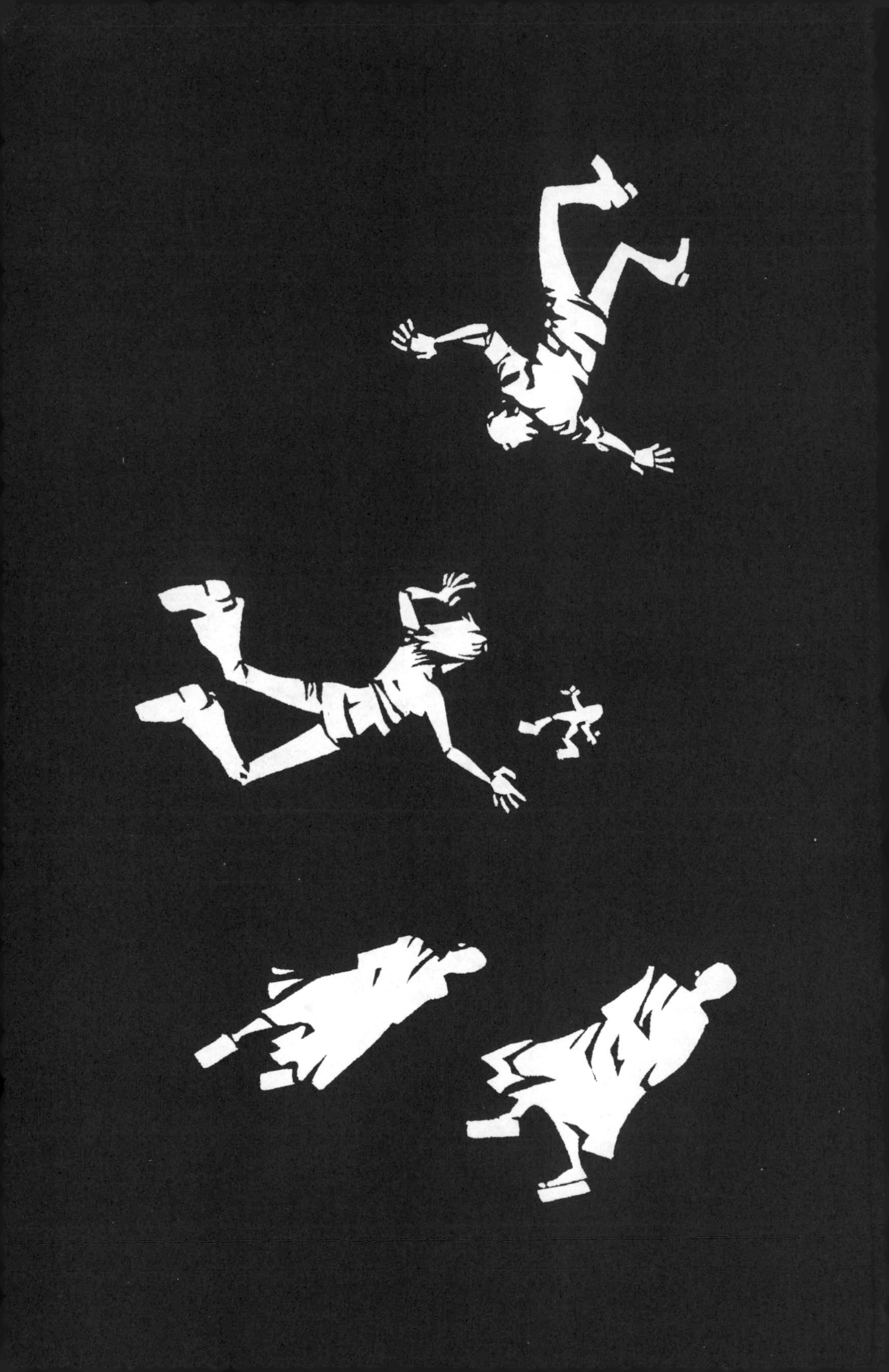

MAXWELL STRANGEWELL

story and art by
THE FILLBACH BROTHERS

DARK HORSE BOOKS®

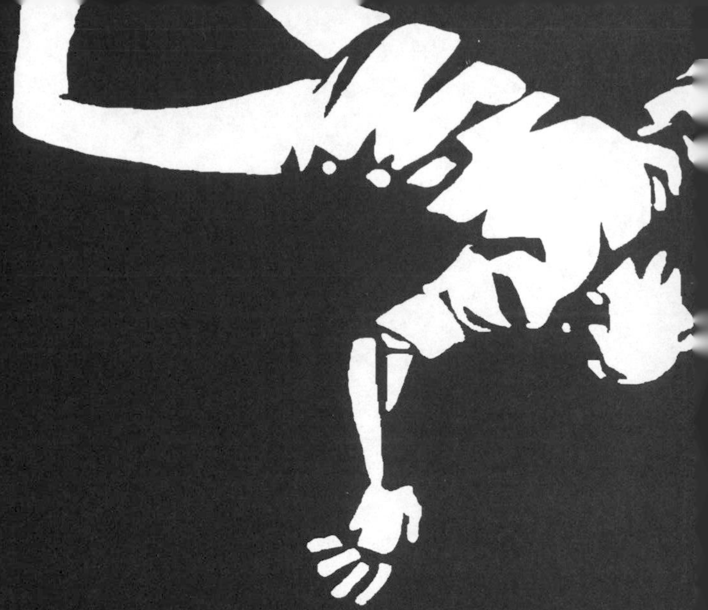

publisher - **MIKE RICHARDSON**
art director - **LIA RIBACCHI**
designer - **DARIN FABRICK**
logo designer - **KEITH WOOD**
assistant editor - **KATIE MOODY**
editor - **DAVE LAND**

MAXWELL STRANGEWELL™

Published by
Dark Horse Books
A division of Dark Horse Comics, Inc.
10956 SE Main Street
Milwaukie, OR 97222

darkhorse.com

To find a comic shop in your area call the Comic Shop Locator Service
toll-free at (888) 266-4226

First edition: June 2007
ISBN-10: 1-59307-794-7
ISBN-13: 978-1-59307-794-5

10 9 8 7 6 5 4 3 2 1

PRINTED IN U.S.A.

CHAPTER·ONE

FALLING TO EARTH

TWO ROADS DIVERGED IN A WOOD, AND I --
I TOOK THE ONE LESS TRAVELED BY,
AND THAT HAS MADE ALL THE DIFFERENCE.
(ROBERT FROST, "The Road Not Taken")

"I MAY NOT HAVE GONE WHERE I INTENDED TO GO, BUT I
THINK I HAVE ENDED UP WHERE I INTENDED TO BE."
- DOUGLAS ADAMS

DARKNESS.

WHITE LIGHT.

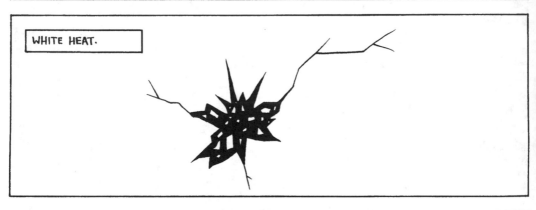

WHITE HEAT.

A JOLTING PUNCH.

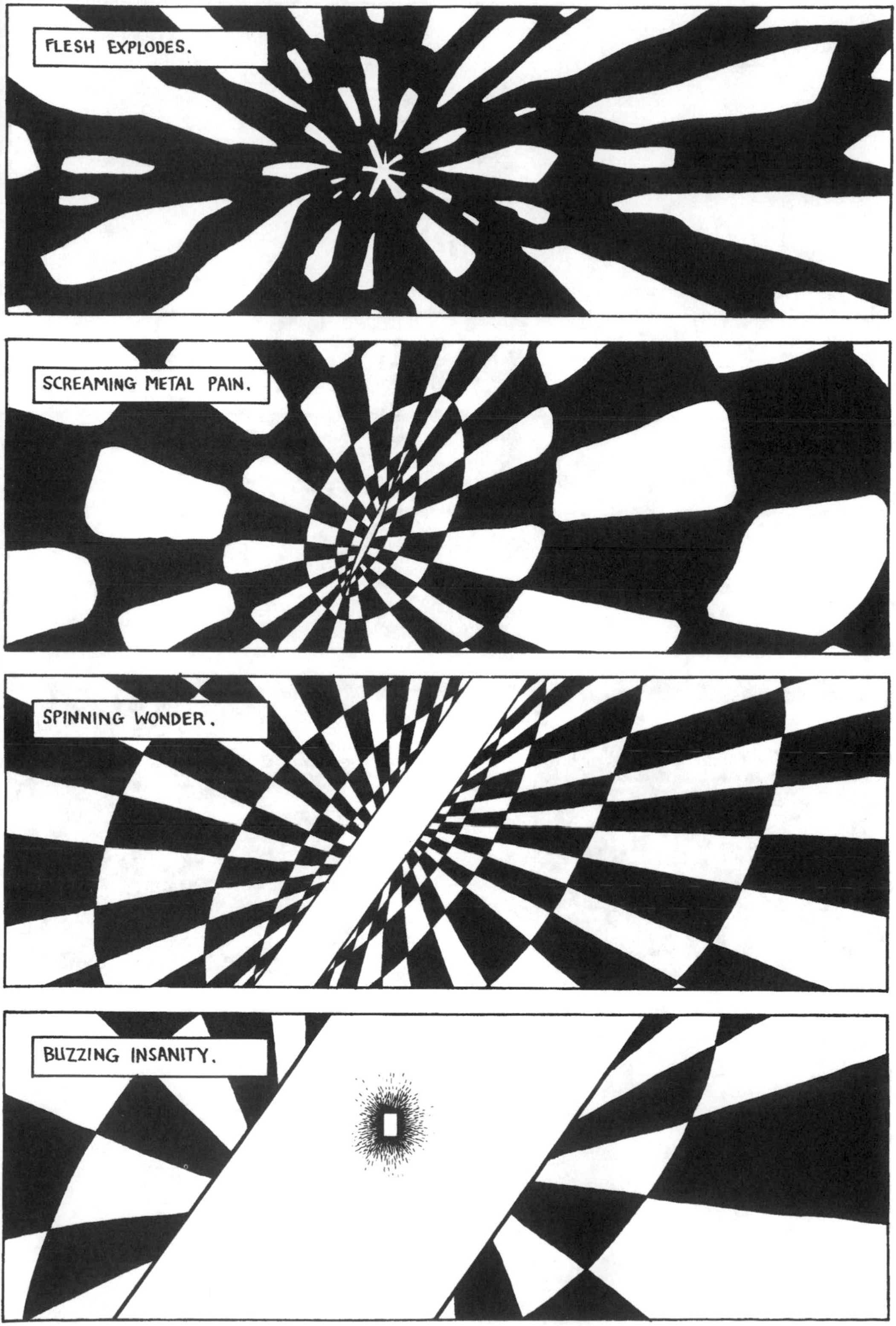
FLESH EXPLODES.
SCREAMING METAL PAIN.
SPINNING WONDER.
BUZZING INSANITY.

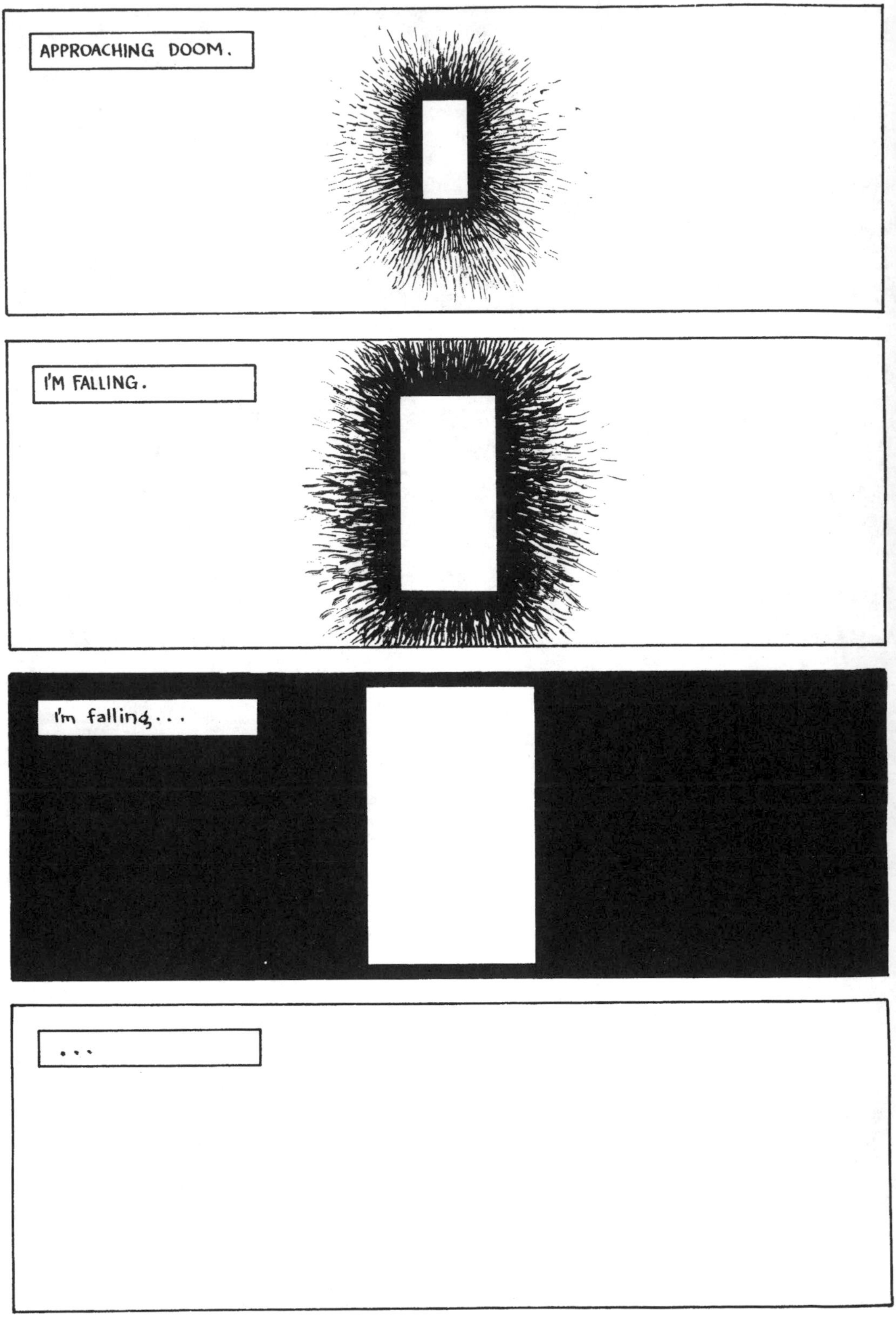
APPROACHING DOOM.
I'M FALLING.
I'm falling...
...

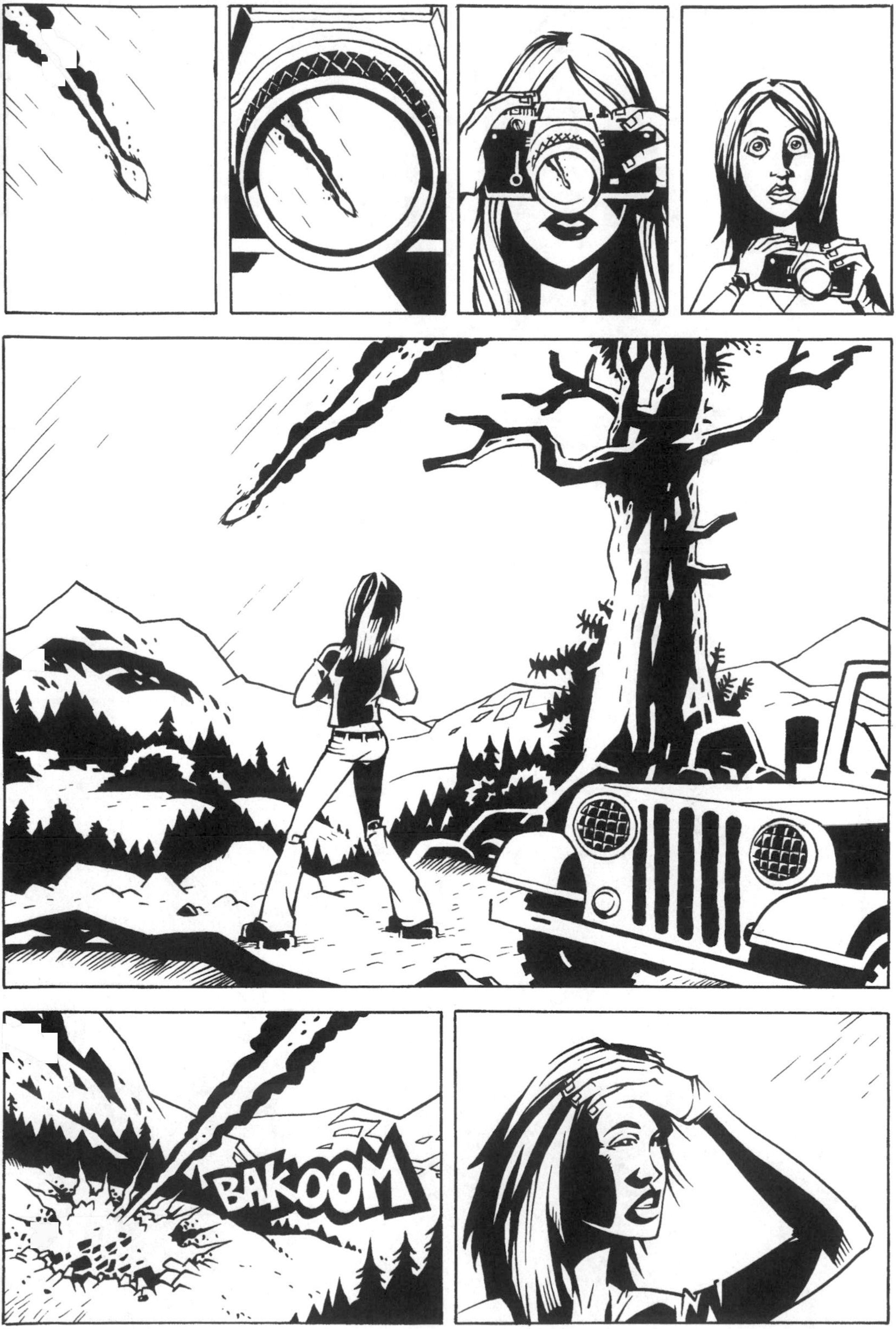
BAKOOM

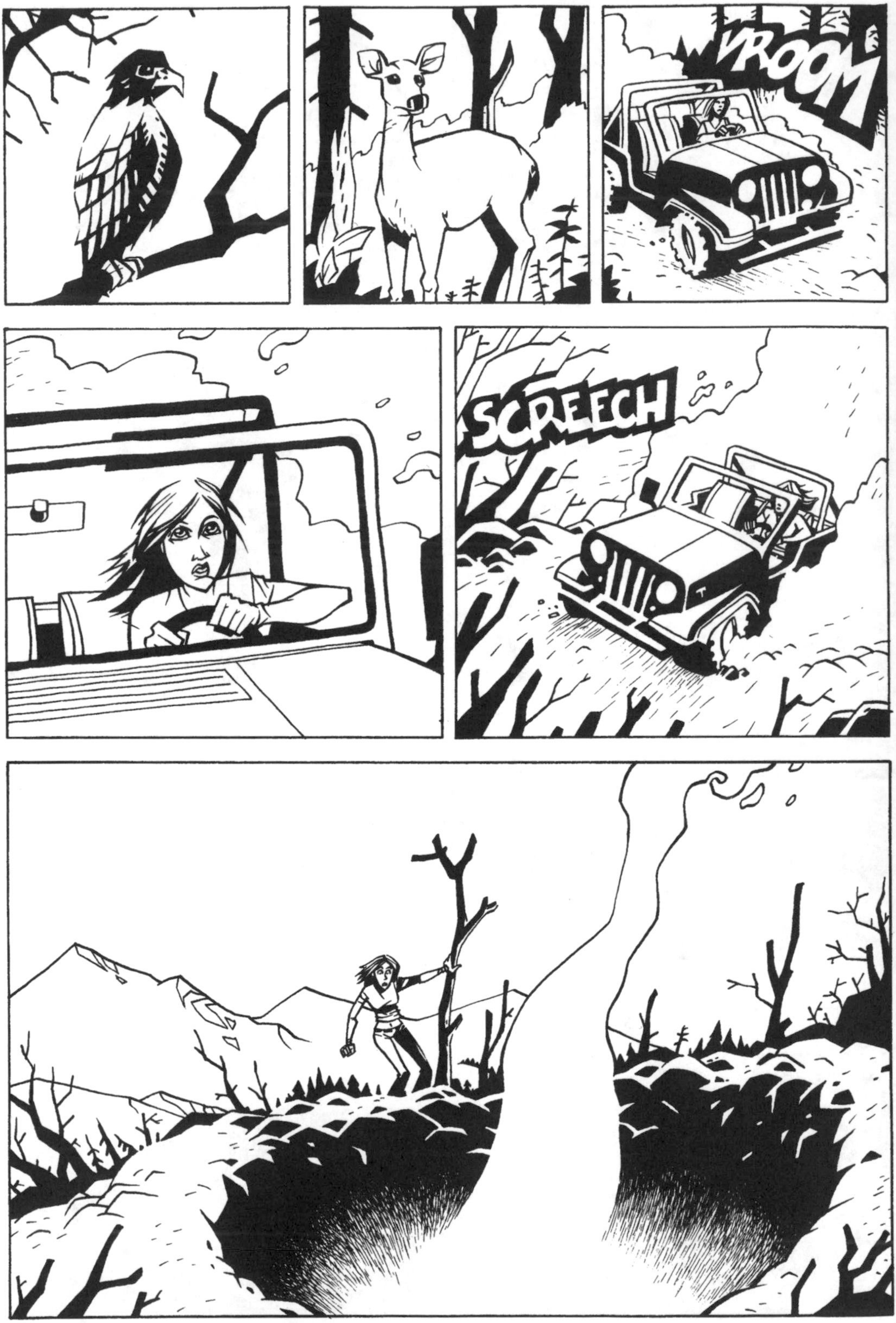
VROOM
SCREECH

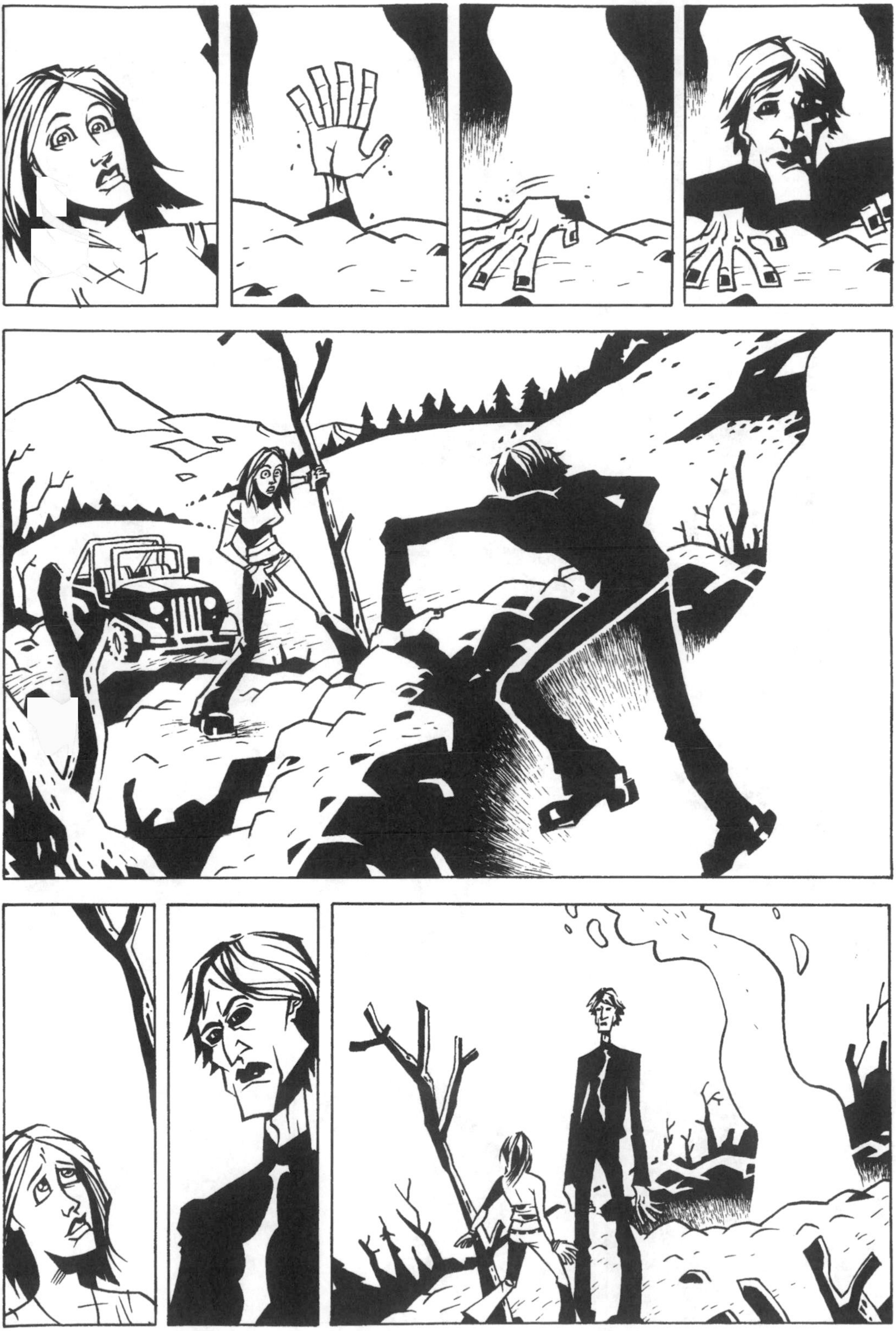

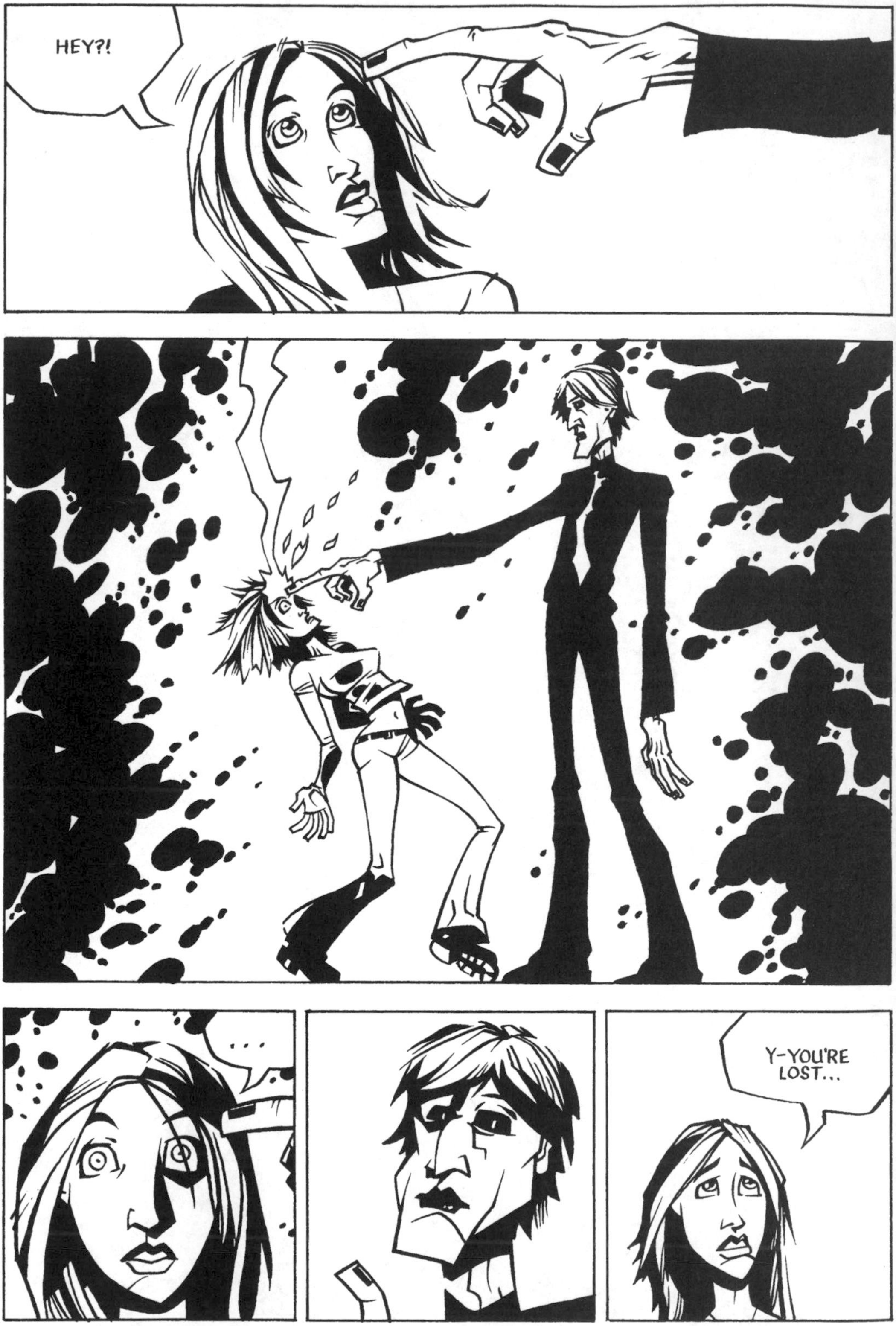
HEY?!
...
Y-YOU'RE LOST...

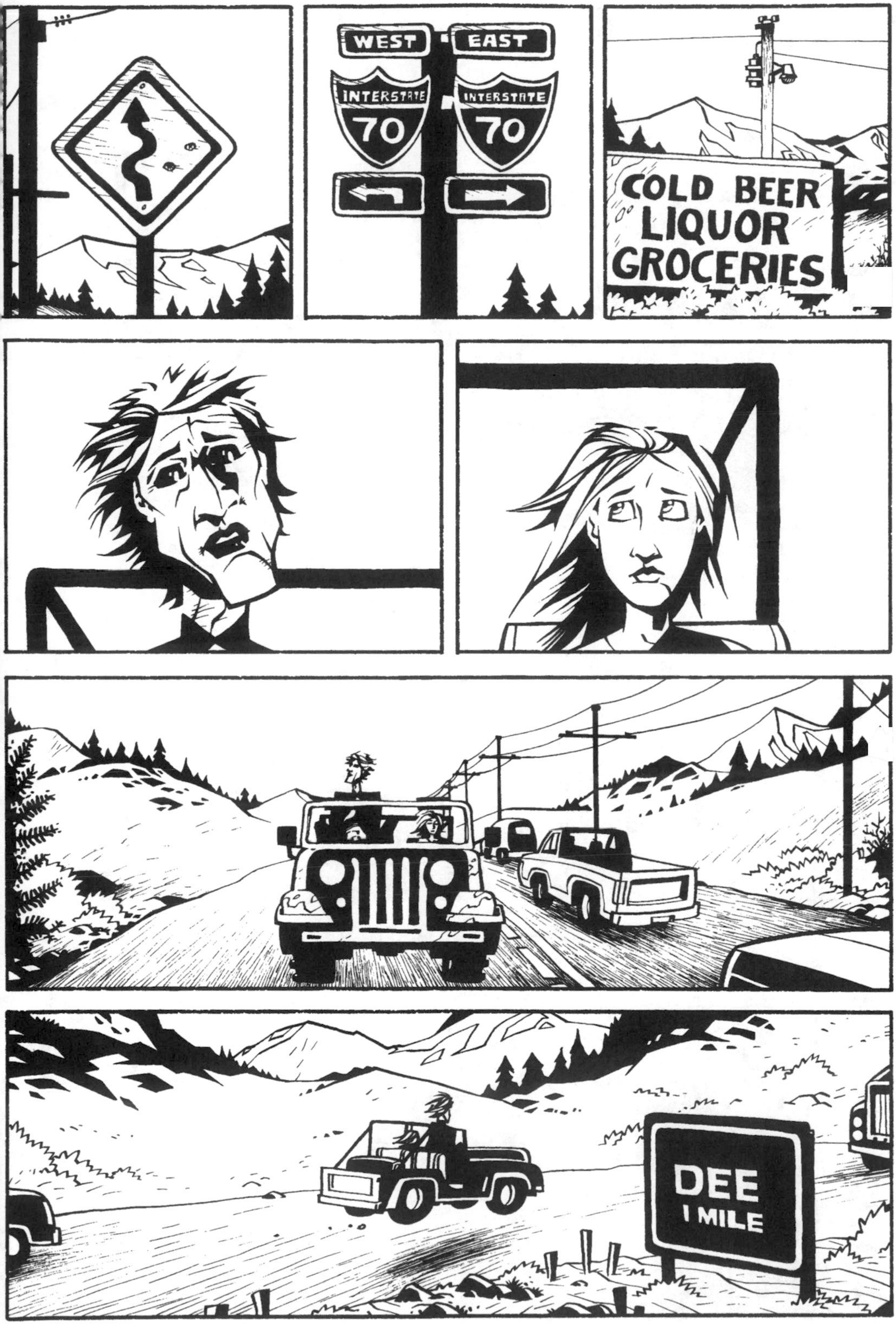
WEST
EAST
INTERSTATE
70
INTERSTATE
70
COLD BEER
LIQUOR
GROCERIES
DEE
1 MILE

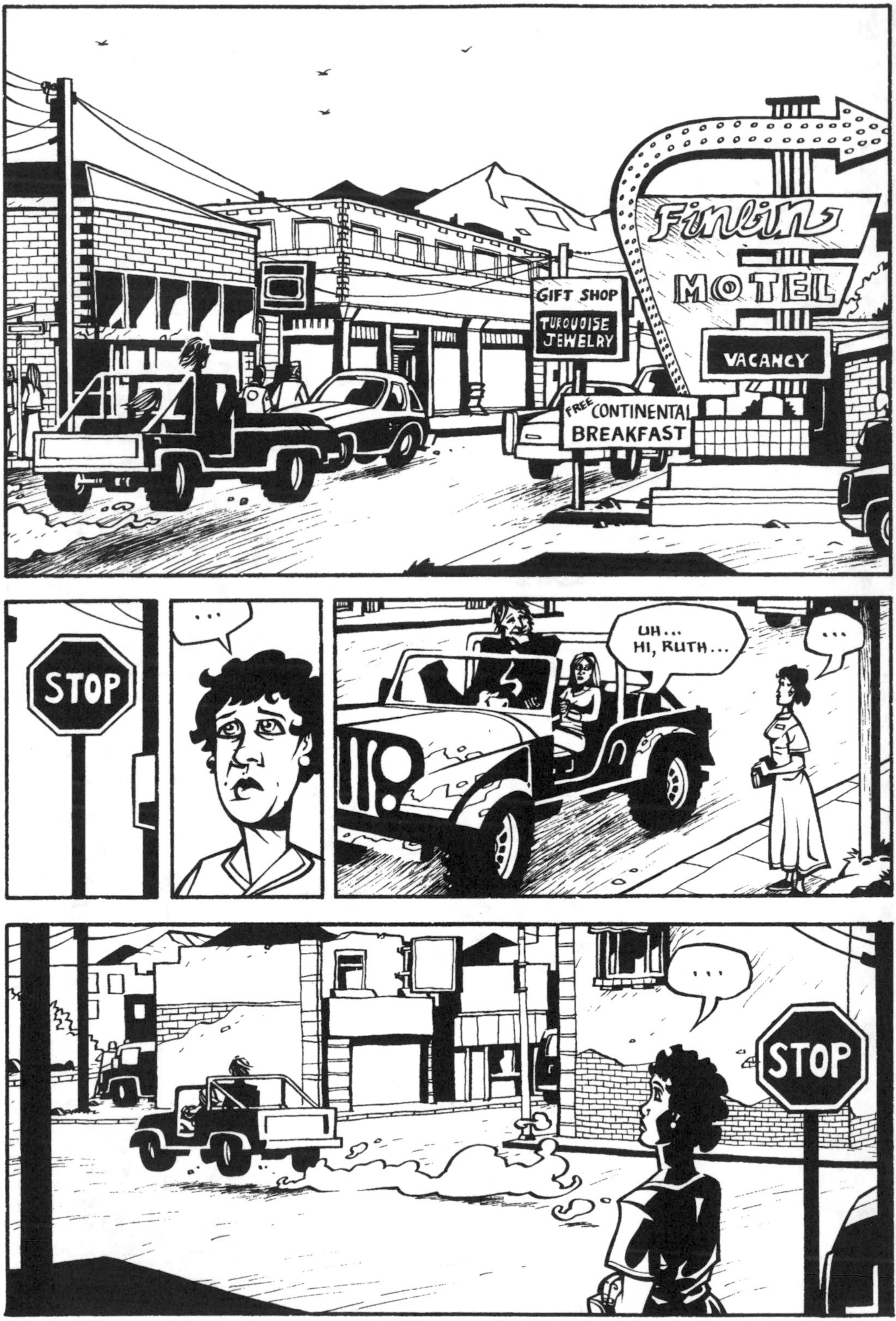

FINLIN MOTEL
GIFT SHOP
TURQUOISE JEWELRY
VACANCY
FREE CONTINENTAL BREAKFAST
STOP
...
UH... HI, RUTH...
...
...
STOP

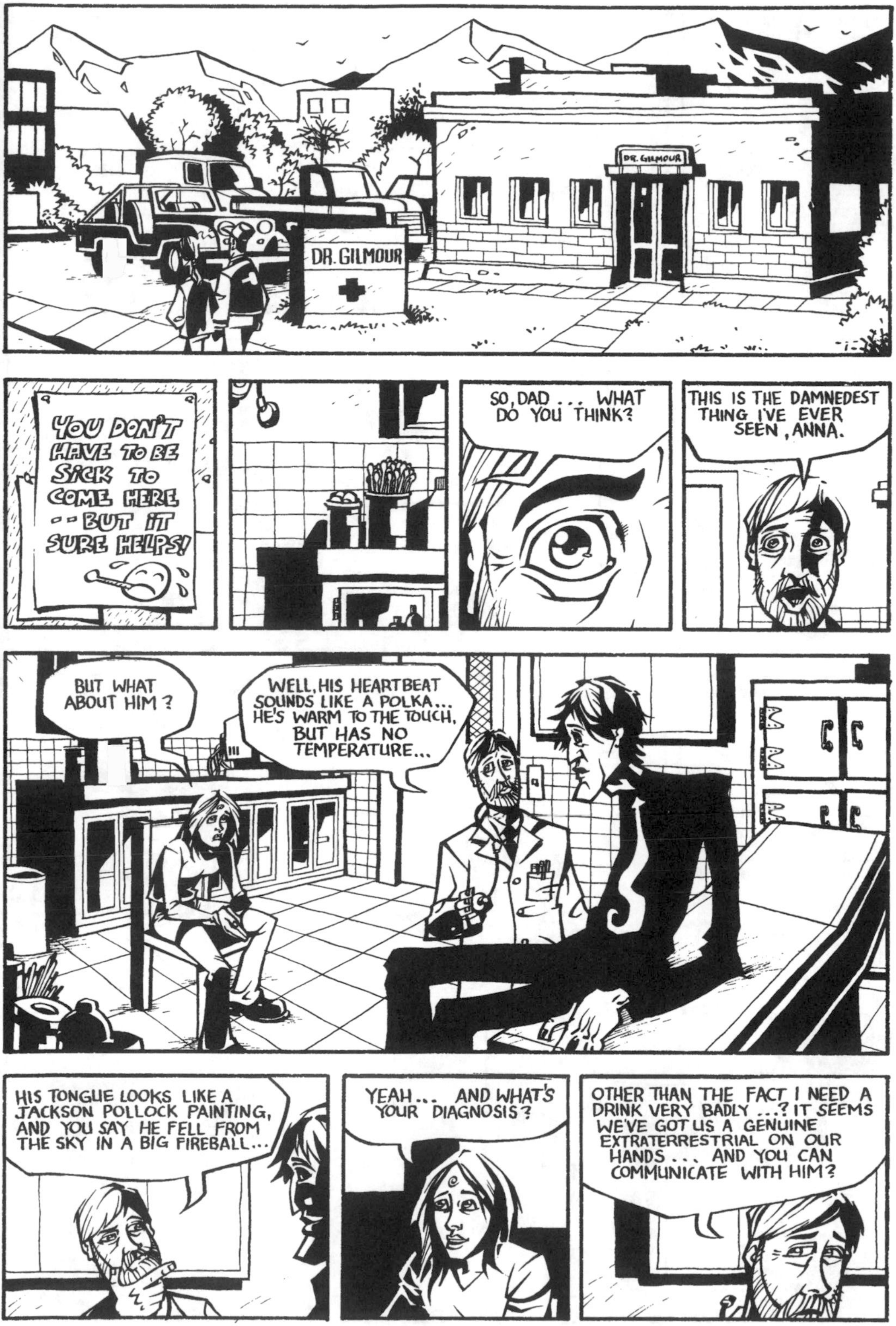
DR. GILMOUR
DR. GILMOUR
YOU DON'T HAVE TO BE SICK TO COME HERE -- BUT IT SURE HELPS!
SO, DAD ... WHAT DO YOU THINK?
THIS IS THE DAMNEDEST THING I'VE EVER SEEN, ANNA.
BUT WHAT ABOUT HIM?
WELL, HIS HEARTBEAT SOUNDS LIKE A POLKA... HE'S WARM TO THE TOUCH, BUT HAS NO TEMPERATURE...
HIS TONGUE LOOKS LIKE A JACKSON POLLOCK PAINTING, AND YOU SAY HE FELL FROM THE SKY IN A BIG FIREBALL...
YEAH... AND WHAT'S YOUR DIAGNOSIS?
OTHER THAN THE FACT I NEED A DRINK VERY BADLY ...? IT SEEMS WE'VE GOT US A GENUINE EXTRATERRESTRIAL ON OUR HANDS ... AND YOU CAN COMMUNICATE WITH HIM?

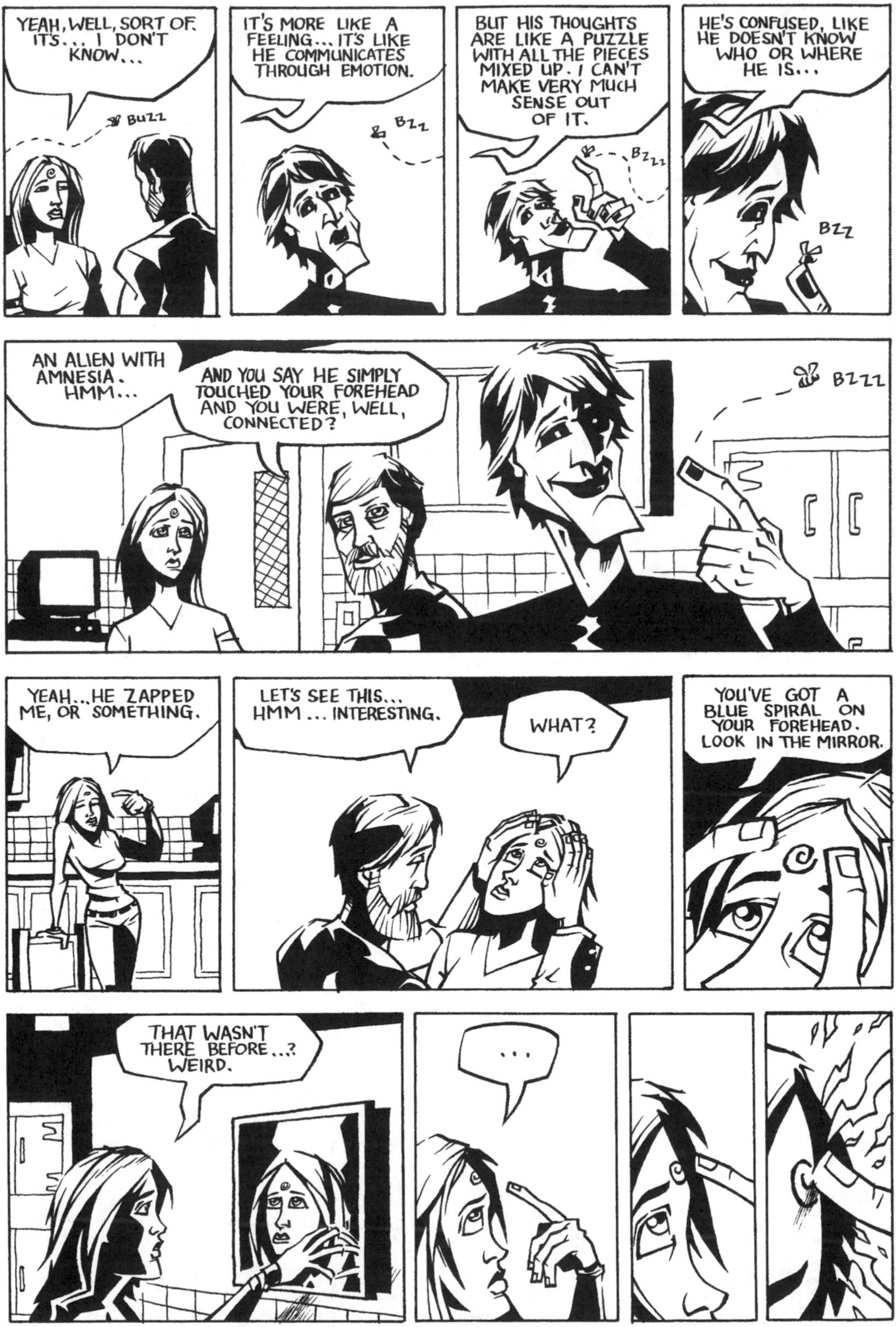
YEAH, WELL, SORT OF. IT'S... I DON'T KNOW...
BUZZ
IT'S MORE LIKE A FEELING... IT'S LIKE HE COMMUNICATES THROUGH EMOTION.
BZZ
BUT HIS THOUGHTS ARE LIKE A PUZZLE WITH ALL THE PIECES MIXED UP. I CAN'T MAKE VERY MUCH SENSE OUT OF IT.
BZZZ
HE'S CONFUSED, LIKE HE DOESN'T KNOW WHO OR WHERE HE IS...
BZZ
AN ALIEN WITH AMNESIA. HMM...
AND YOU SAY HE SIMPLY TOUCHED YOUR FOREHEAD AND YOU WERE, WELL, CONNECTED?
BZZZ
YEAH...HE ZAPPED ME, OR SOMETHING.
LET'S SEE THIS... HMM ... INTERESTING.
WHAT?
YOU'VE GOT A BLUE SPIRAL ON YOUR FOREHEAD. LOOK IN THE MIRROR.
THAT WASN'T THERE BEFORE...? WEIRD.
...

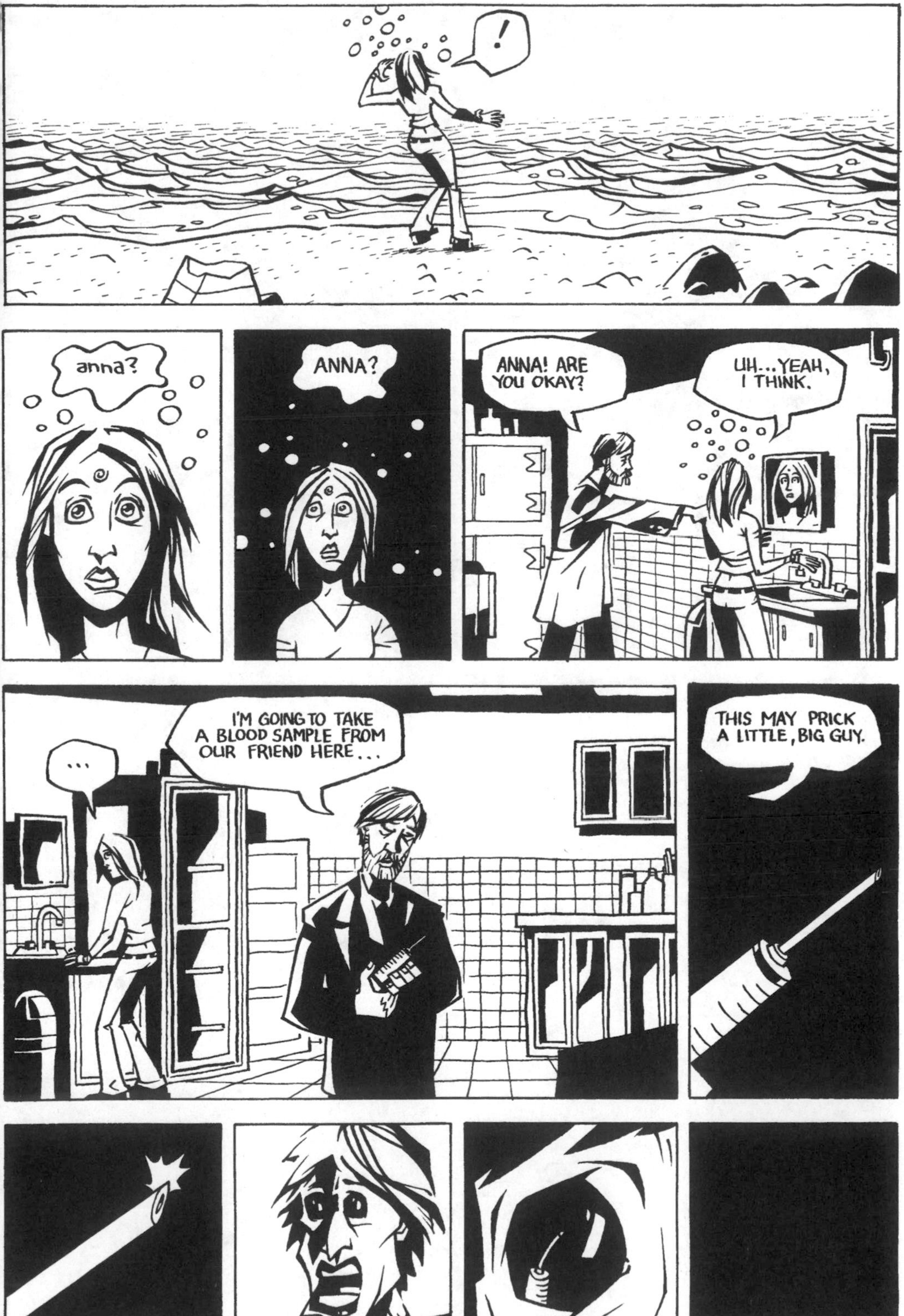
!
anna?
ANNA?
ANNA! ARE YOU OKAY?
UH...YEAH, I THINK.
...
I'M GOING TO TAKE A BLOOD SAMPLE FROM OUR FRIEND HERE...
THIS MAY PRICK A LITTLE, BIG GUY.

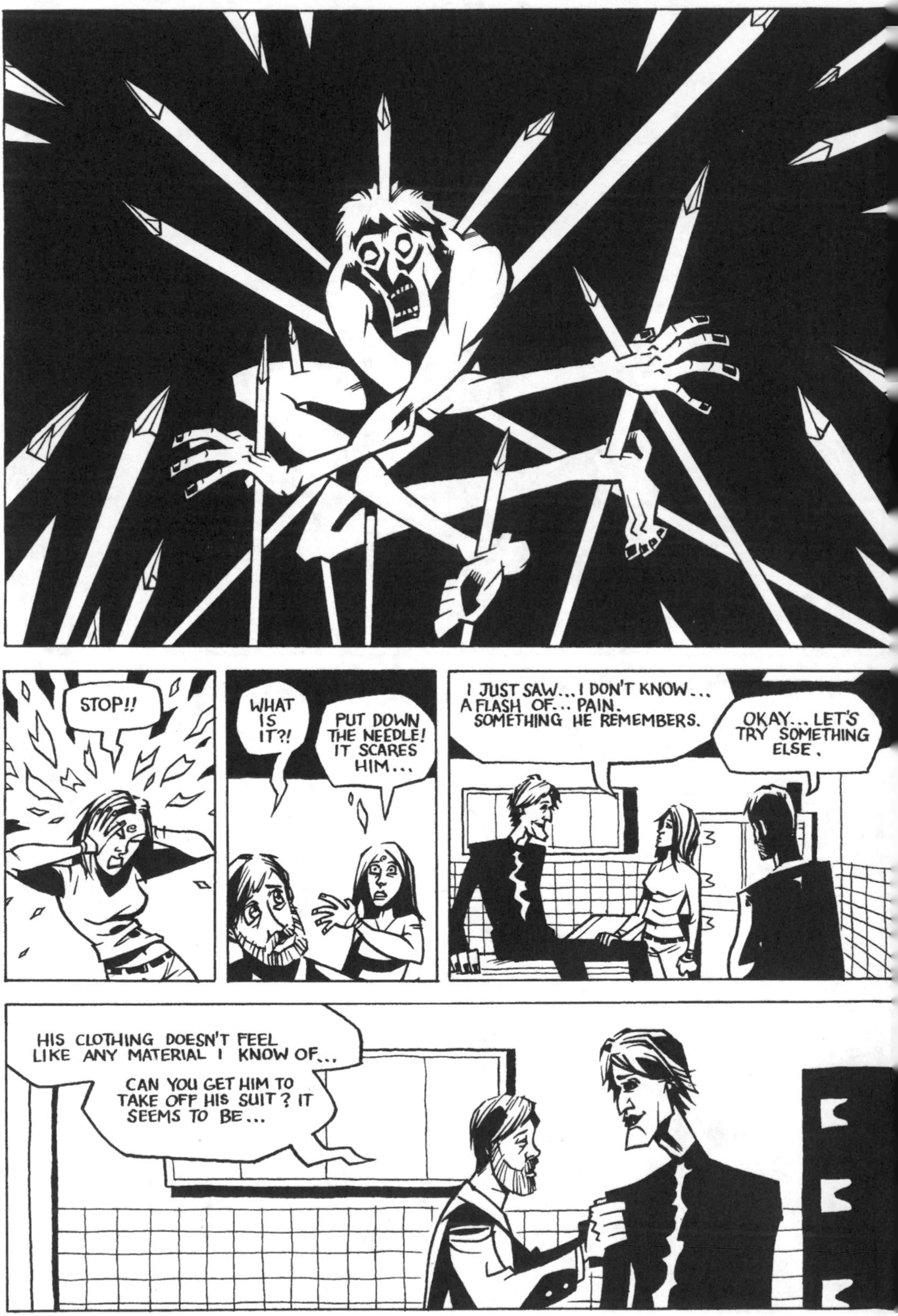
STOP!!
WHAT IS IT?!
PUT DOWN THE NEEDLE! IT SCARES HIM...
I JUST SAW... I DON'T KNOW... A FLASH OF... PAIN. SOMETHING HE REMEMBERS.
OKAY... LET'S TRY SOMETHING ELSE.
HIS CLOTHING DOESN'T FEEL LIKE ANY MATERIAL I KNOW OF...
CAN YOU GET HIM TO TAKE OFF HIS SUIT? IT SEEMS TO BE...

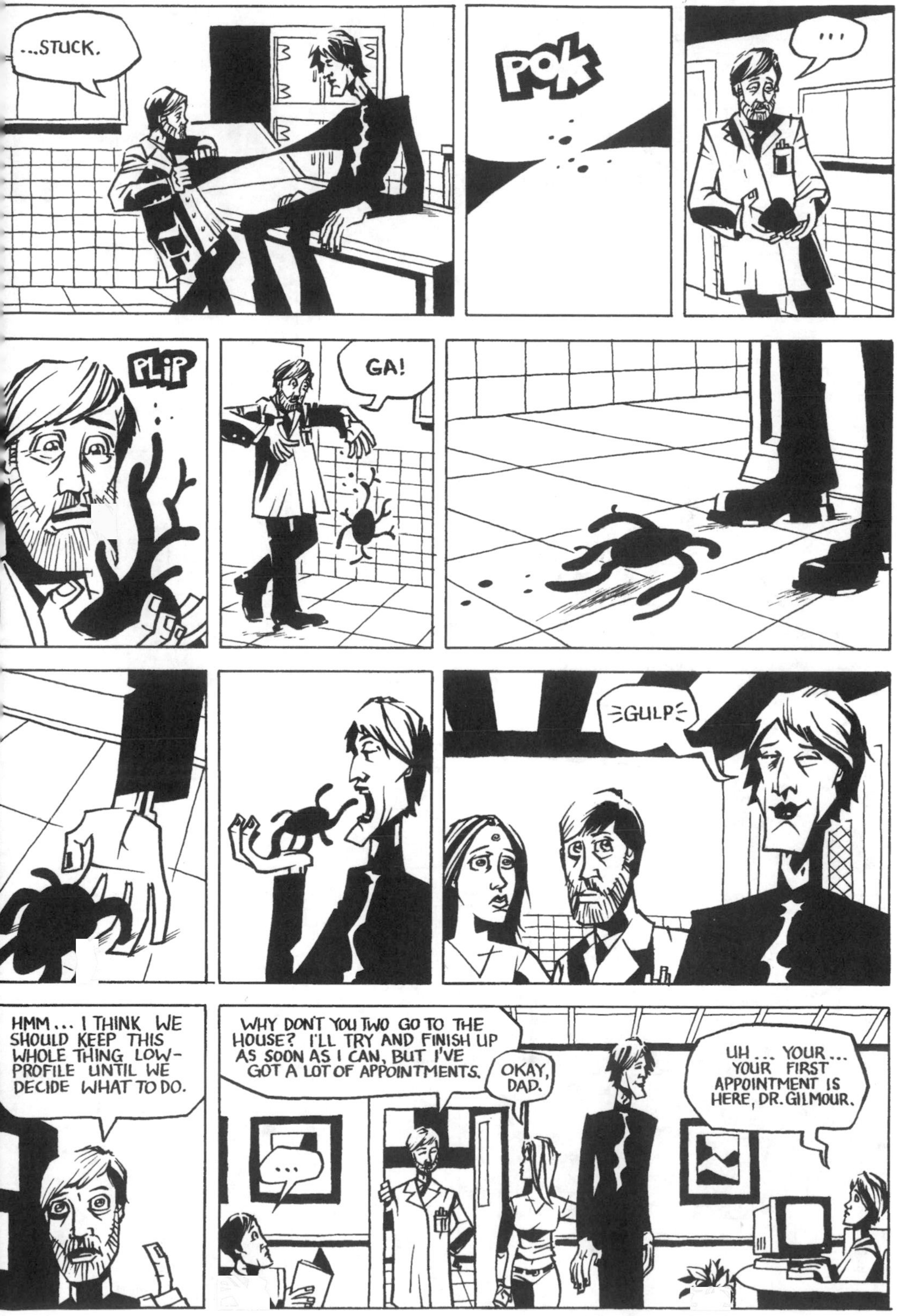
...STUCK.
POK
...
PLIP
GA!
GULP
HMM... I THINK WE SHOULD KEEP THIS WHOLE THING LOW-PROFILE UNTIL WE DECIDE WHAT TO DO.
WHY DON'T YOU TWO GO TO THE HOUSE? I'LL TRY AND FINISH UP AS SOON AS I CAN, BUT I'VE GOT A LOT OF APPOINTMENTS.
OKAY, DAD.
...
UH... YOUR... YOUR FIRST APPOINTMENT IS HERE, DR. GILMOUR.

EDDIE·BURNS
ACCOUNTANT
COUNTANT
...HE'S HERE...
BY THE GREAT GROGLAR OF ESPAR-ESPUS...
HE'S HERE...
DR. GILMOUR
...I SUPPOSE IT'S MY DUTY TO REPORT TO THE HEAD OFFICE IMMEDIATELY...
SIGH
POKE
I WAS REALLY BEGINNING TO LIKE IT HERE... AND HE'S GOT TO SHOW UP...
PLOP
shit.

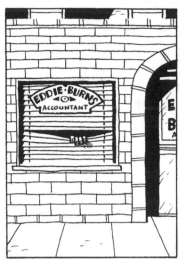

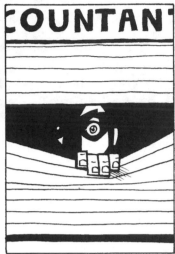

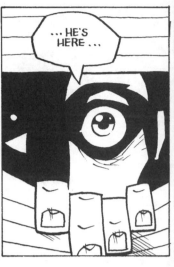

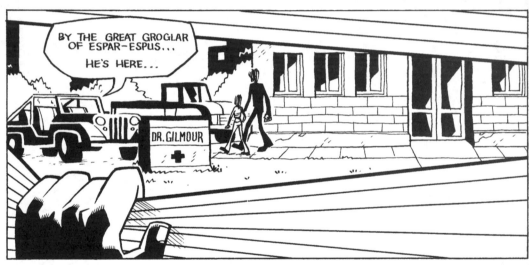

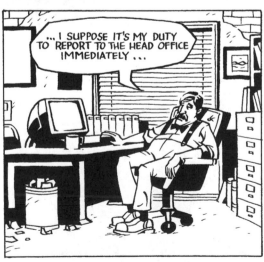

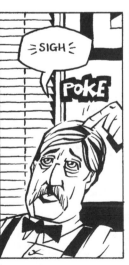

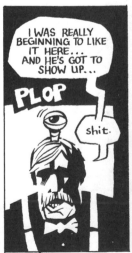

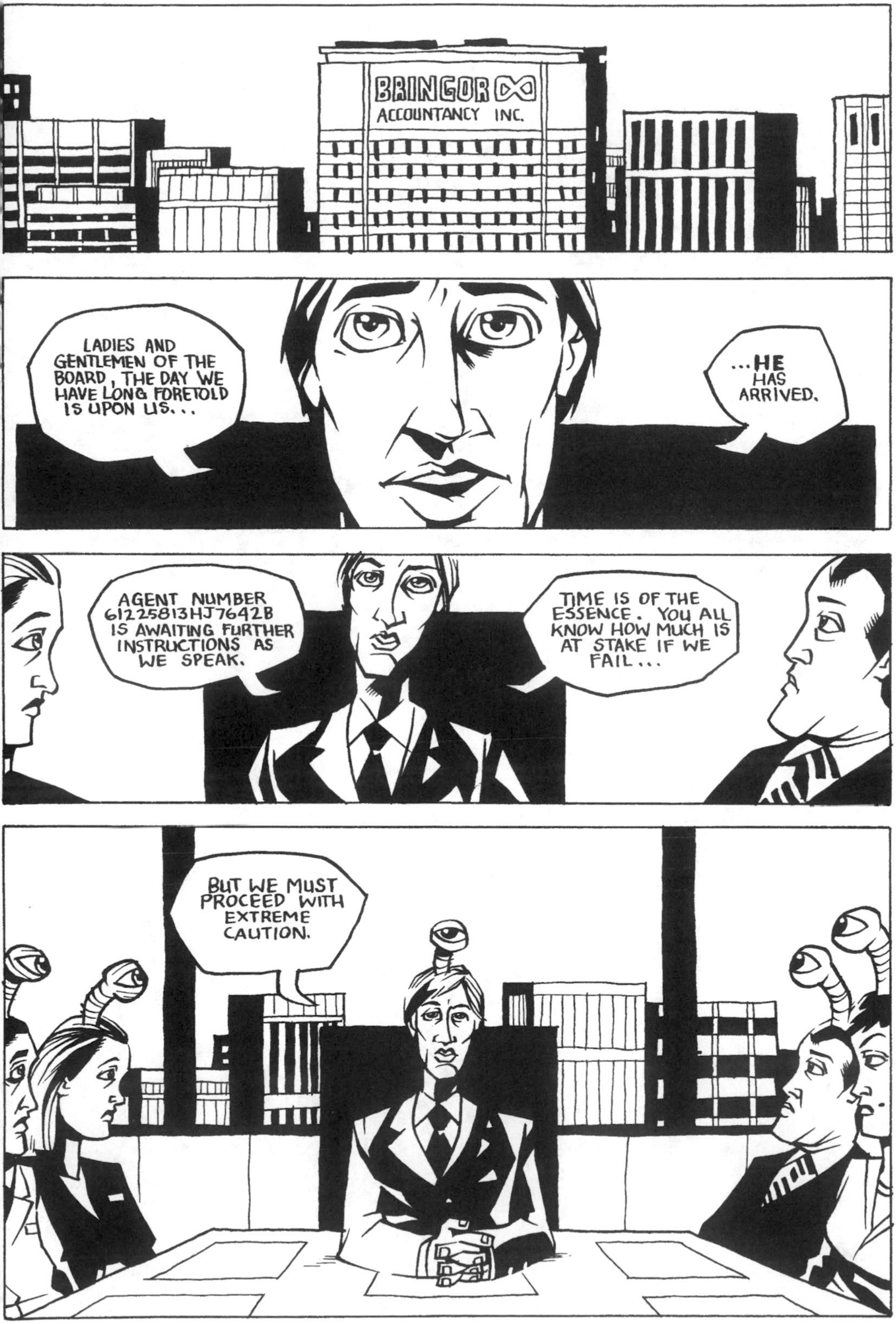
BRINGOR
ACCOUNTANCY INC.
LADIES AND GENTLEMEN OF THE BOARD, THE DAY WE HAVE LONG FORETOLD IS UPON US...
...HE HAS ARRIVED.
AGENT NUMBER 61225813HJ7642B IS AWAITING FURTHER INSTRUCTIONS AS WE SPEAK.
TIME IS OF THE ESSENCE. YOU ALL KNOW HOW MUCH IS AT STAKE IF WE FAIL...
BUT WE MUST PROCEED WITH EXTREME CAUTION.

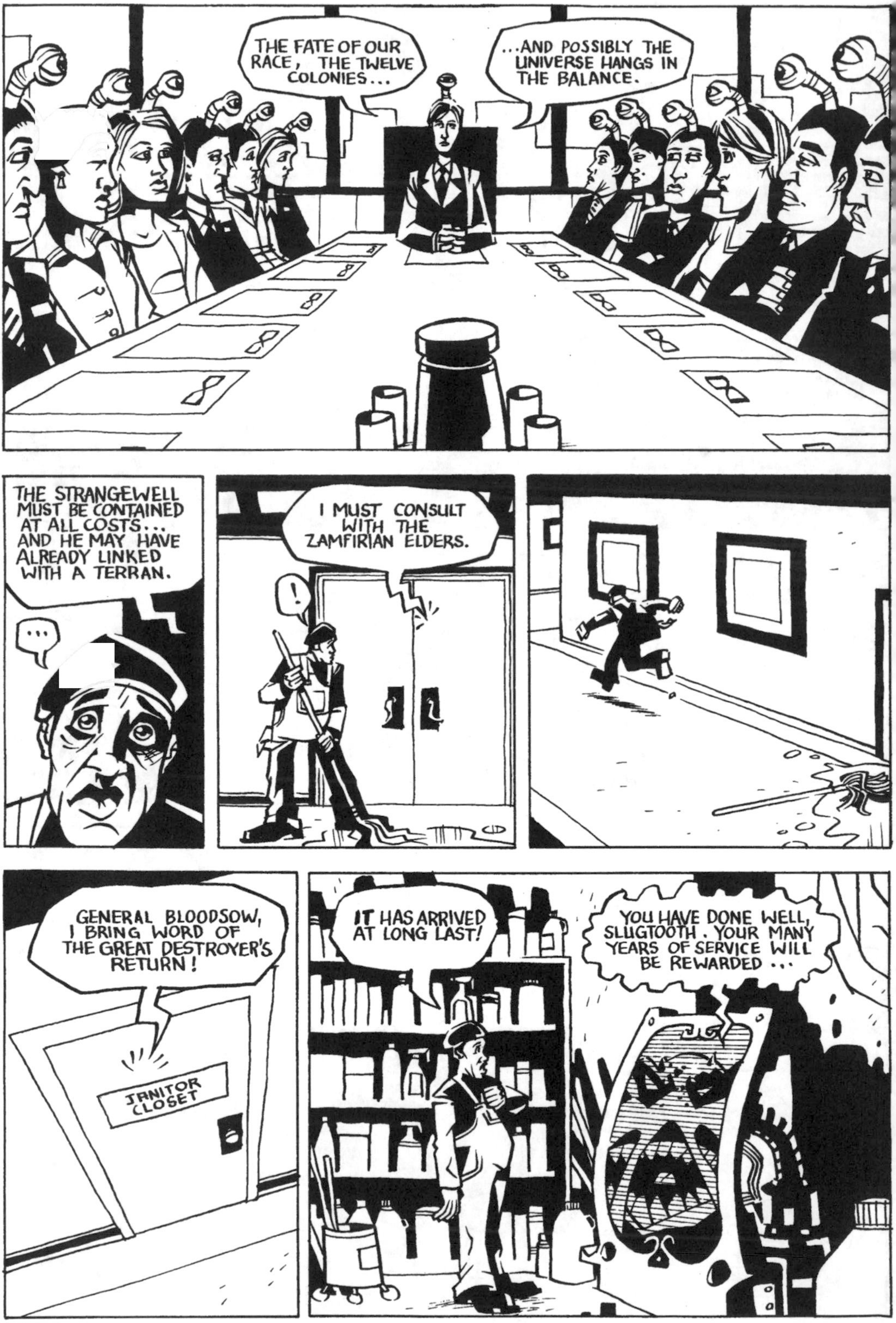
THE FATE OF OUR RACE, THE TWELVE COLONIES...
...AND POSSIBLY THE UNIVERSE HANGS IN THE BALANCE.
THE STRANGEWELL MUST BE CONTAINED AT ALL COSTS... AND HE MAY HAVE ALREADY LINKED WITH A TERRAN.
...
I MUST CONSULT WITH THE ZAMFIRIAN ELDERS.
!
GENERAL BLOODSOW, I BRING WORD OF THE GREAT DESTROYER'S RETURN!
JANITOR CLOSET
IT HAS ARRIVED AT LONG LAST!
YOU HAVE DONE WELL, SLUGTOOTH. YOUR MANY YEARS OF SERVICE WILL BE REWARDED...

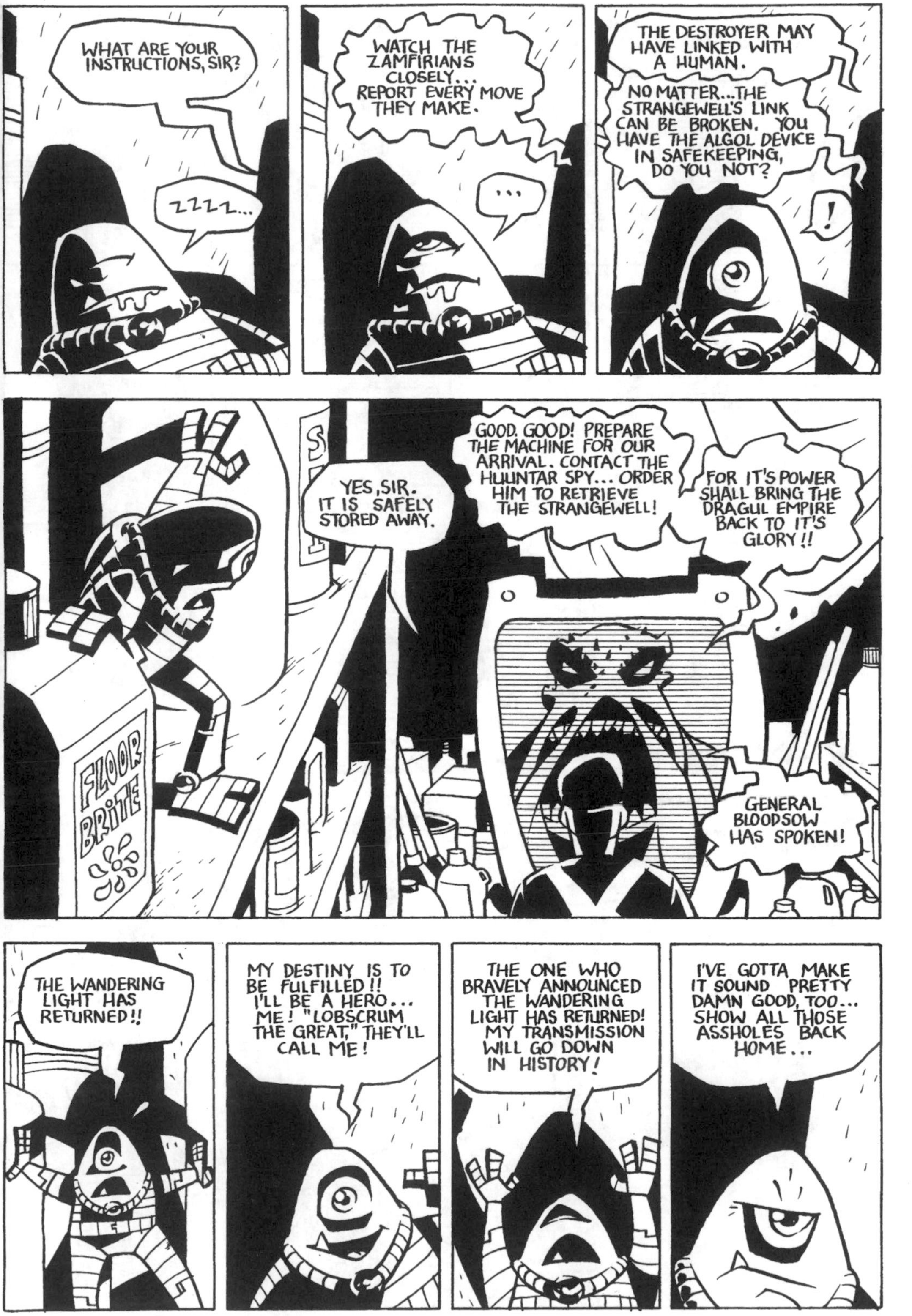
WHAT ARE YOUR INSTRUCTIONS, SIR?
ZZZZ...
WATCH THE ZAMFIRIANS CLOSELY... REPORT EVERY MOVE THEY MAKE.
...
THE DESTROYER MAY HAVE LINKED WITH A HUMAN.
NO MATTER...THE STRANGEWELL'S LINK CAN BE BROKEN. YOU HAVE THE ALGOL DEVICE IN SAFEKEEPING, DO YOU NOT?
!
YES, SIR. IT IS SAFELY STORED AWAY.
GOOD. GOOD! PREPARE THE MACHINE FOR OUR ARRIVAL. CONTACT THE HUUNTAR SPY... ORDER HIM TO RETRIEVE THE STRANGEWELL!
FOR IT'S POWER SHALL BRING THE DRAGUL EMPIRE BACK TO IT'S GLORY!!
GENERAL BLOODSOW HAS SPOKEN!
FLOOR BRITE
THE WANDERING LIGHT HAS RETURNED!!
MY DESTINY IS TO BE FULFILLED!! I'LL BE A HERO... ME! "LOBSCRUM THE GREAT," THEY'LL CALL ME!
THE ONE WHO BRAVELY ANNOUNCED THE WANDERING LIGHT HAS RETURNED! MY TRANSMISSION WILL GO DOWN IN HISTORY!
I'VE GOTTA MAKE IT SOUND PRETTY DAMN GOOD, TOO... SHOW ALL THOSE ASSHOLES BACK HOME...

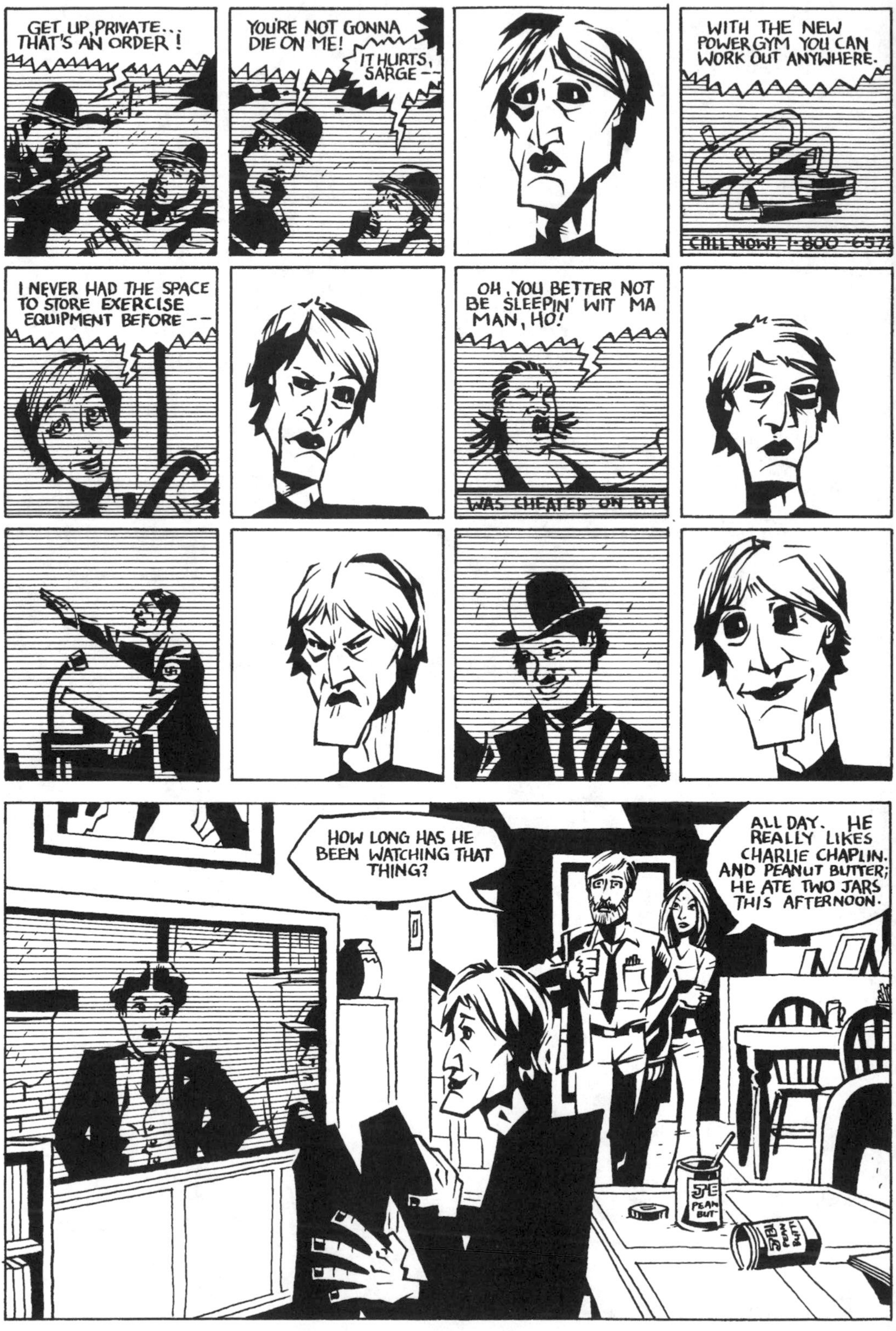
GET UP, PRIVATE... THAT'S AN ORDER!
YOU'RE NOT GONNA DIE ON ME!
IT HURTS, SARGE--
WITH THE NEW POWERGYM YOU CAN WORK OUT ANYWHERE.
CALL NOW! 1-800-657
I NEVER HAD THE SPACE TO STORE EXERCISE EQUIPMENT BEFORE--
OH, YOU BETTER NOT BE SLEEPIN' WIT MA MAN, HO!
WAS CHEATED ON BY
HOW LONG HAS HE BEEN WATCHING THAT THING?
ALL DAY. HE REALLY LIKES CHARLIE CHAPLIN. AND PEANUT BUTTER; HE ATE TWO JARS THIS AFTERNOON.

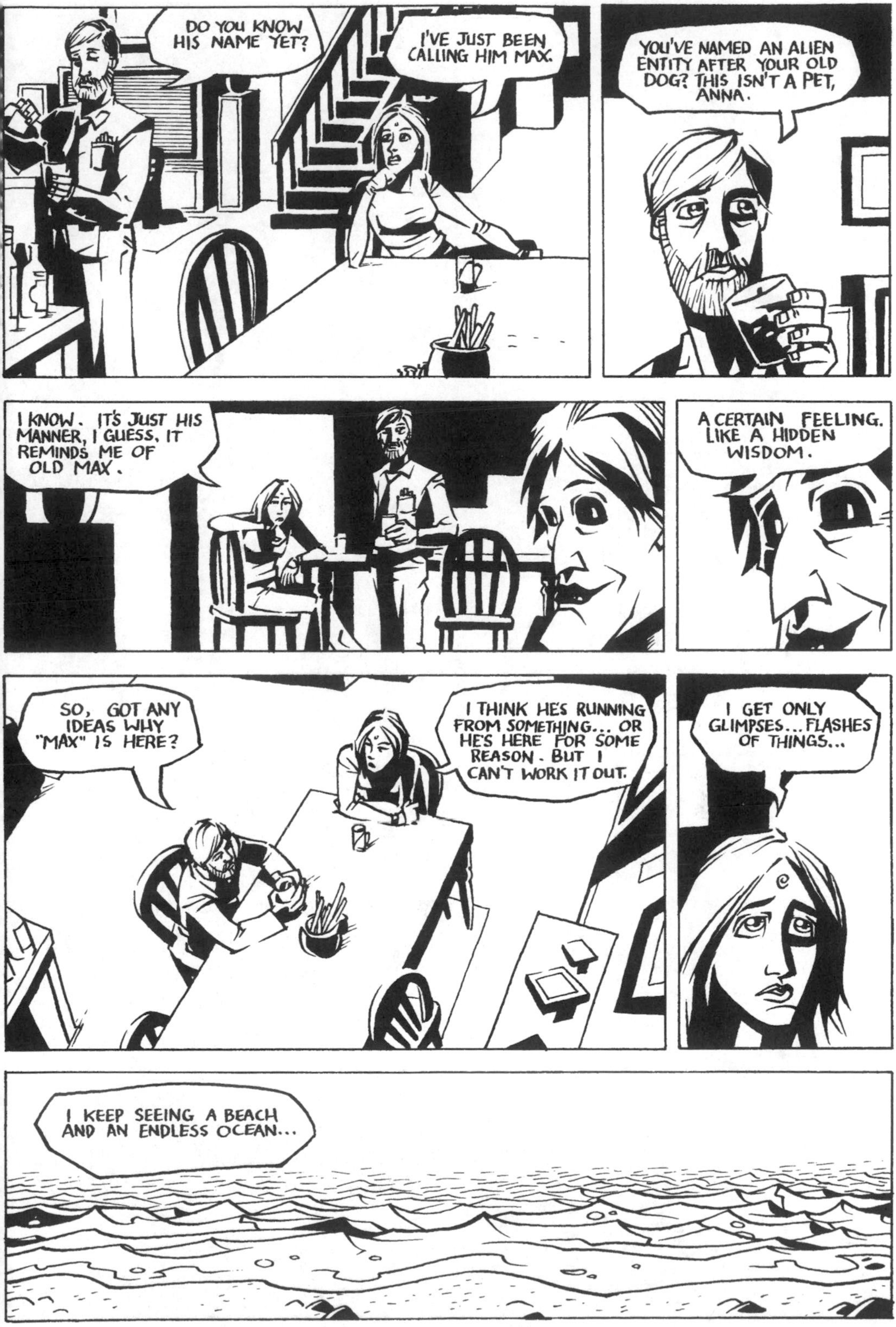
DO YOU KNOW HIS NAME YET?
I'VE JUST BEEN CALLING HIM MAX.
YOU'VE NAMED AN ALIEN ENTITY AFTER YOUR OLD DOG? THIS ISN'T A PET, ANNA.
I KNOW. IT'S JUST HIS MANNER, I GUESS. IT REMINDS ME OF OLD MAX.
A CERTAIN FEELING. LIKE A HIDDEN WISDOM.
SO, GOT ANY IDEAS WHY "MAX" IS HERE?
I THINK HE'S RUNNING FROM SOMETHING... OR HE'S HERE FOR SOME REASON. BUT I CAN'T WORK IT OUT.
I GET ONLY GLIMPSES... FLASHES OF THINGS...
I KEEP SEEING A BEACH AND AN ENDLESS OCEAN...

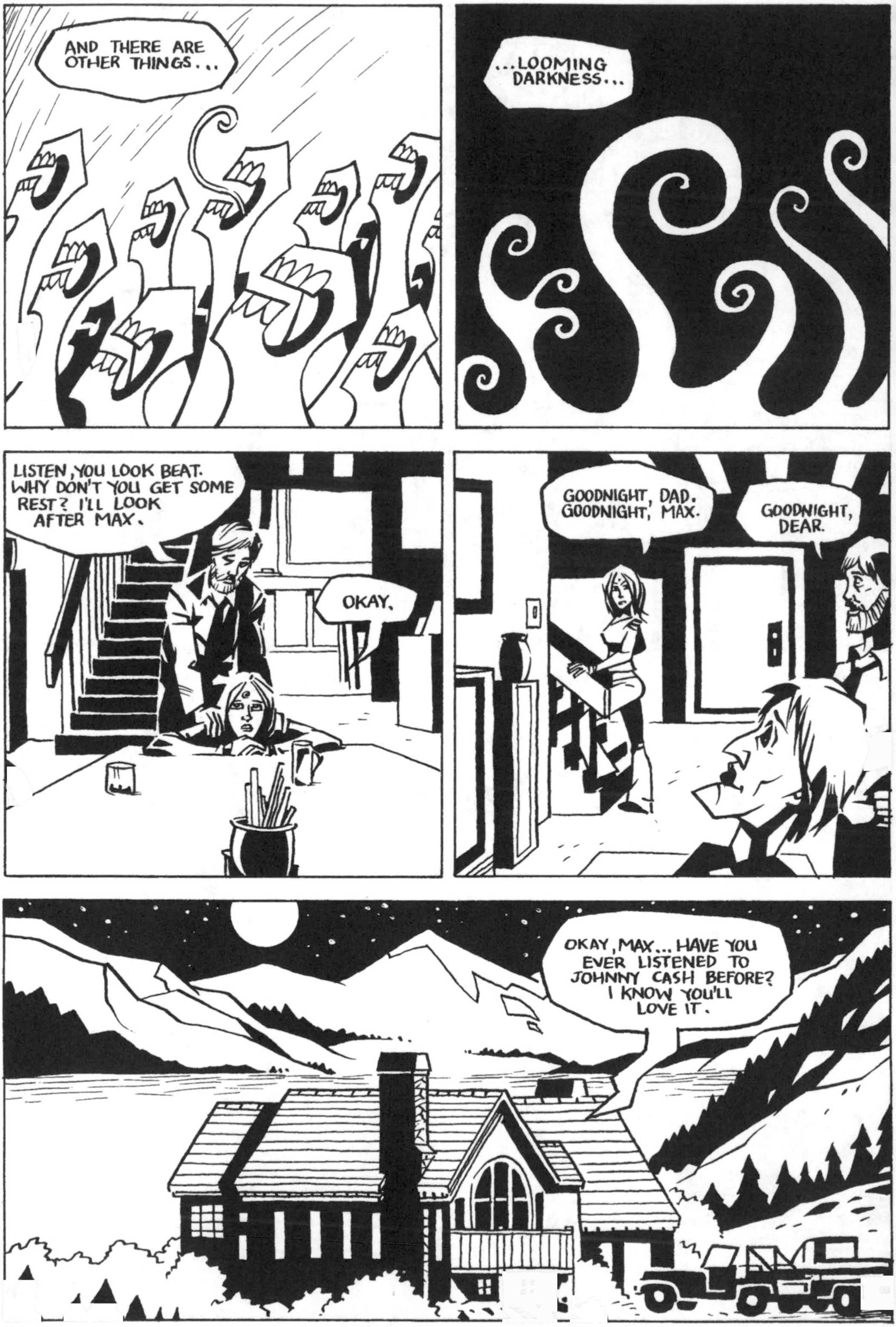
AND THERE ARE OTHER THINGS...
...LOOMING DARKNESS...
LISTEN, YOU LOOK BEAT. WHY DON'T YOU GET SOME REST? I'LL LOOK AFTER MAX.
OKAY.
GOODNIGHT, DAD. GOODNIGHT, MAX.
GOODNIGHT, DEAR.
OKAY, MAX... HAVE YOU EVER LISTENED TO JOHNNY CASH BEFORE? I KNOW YOU'LL LOVE IT.

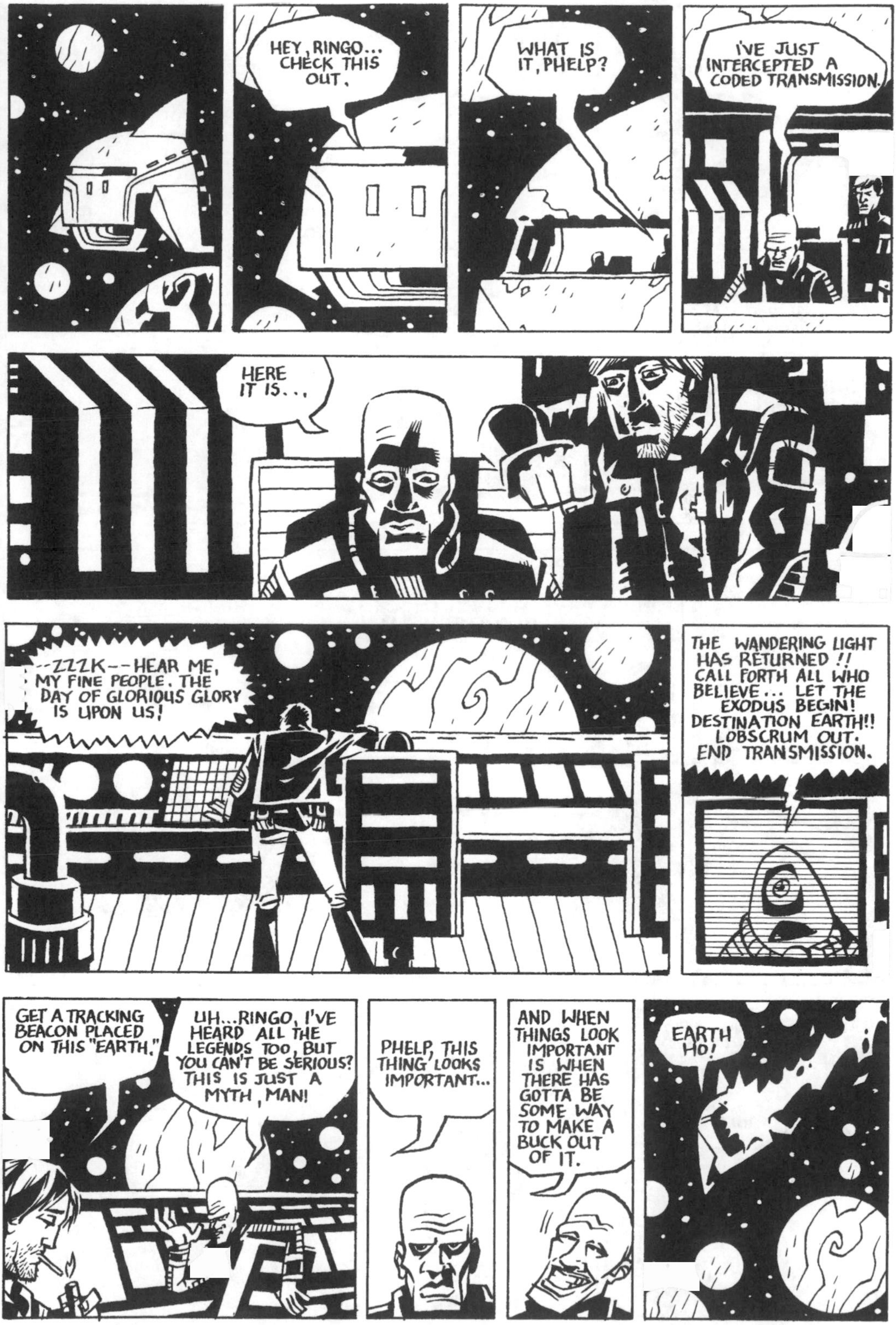
HEY, RINGO... CHECK THIS OUT.
WHAT IS IT, PHELP?
I'VE JUST INTERCEPTED A CODED TRANSMISSION.
HERE IT IS...
--ZZZK--HEAR ME, MY FINE PEOPLE. THE DAY OF GLORIOUS GLORY IS UPON US!
THE WANDERING LIGHT HAS RETURNED!! CALL FORTH ALL WHO BELIEVE... LET THE EXODUS BEGIN! DESTINATION EARTH!! LOBSCRUM OUT. END TRANSMISSION.
GET A TRACKING BEACON PLACED ON THIS "EARTH."
UH...RINGO, I'VE HEARD ALL THE LEGENDS TOO, BUT YOU CAN'T BE SERIOUS? THIS IS JUST A MYTH, MAN!
PHELP, THIS THING LOOKS IMPORTANT...
AND WHEN THINGS LOOK IMPORTANT IS WHEN THERE HAS GOTTA BE SOME WAY TO MAKE A BUCK OUT OF IT.
EARTH HO!

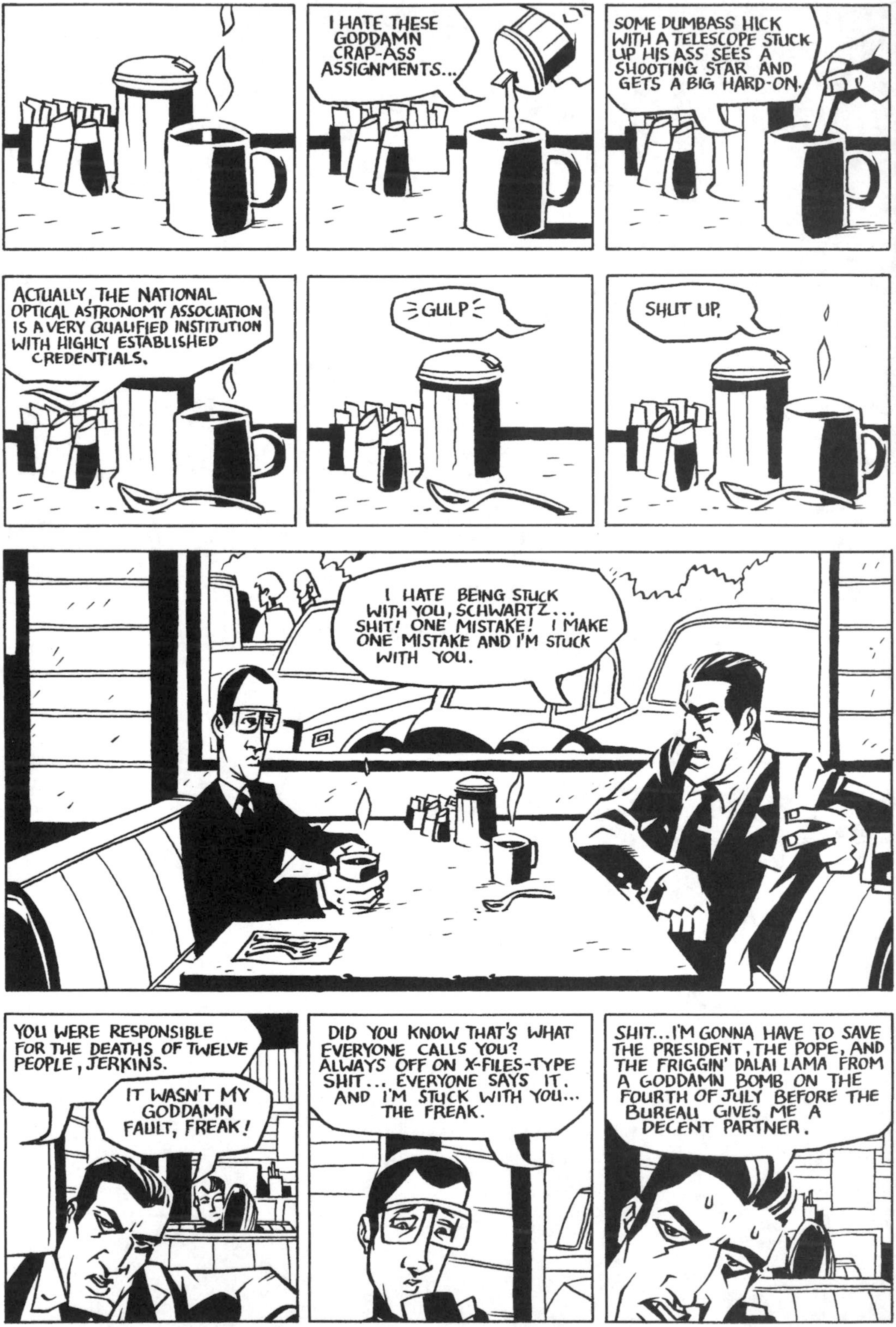
I HATE THESE GODDAMN CRAP-ASS ASSIGNMENTS...
SOME DUMBASS HICK WITH A TELESCOPE STUCK UP HIS ASS SEES A SHOOTING STAR AND GETS A BIG HARD-ON.
ACTUALLY, THE NATIONAL OPTICAL ASTRONOMY ASSOCIATION IS A VERY QUALIFIED INSTITUTION WITH HIGHLY ESTABLISHED CREDENTIALS.
GULP
SHUT UP.
I HATE BEING STUCK WITH YOU, SCHWARTZ... SHIT! ONE MISTAKE! I MAKE ONE MISTAKE AND I'M STUCK WITH YOU.
YOU WERE RESPONSIBLE FOR THE DEATHS OF TWELVE PEOPLE, JERKINS.
IT WASN'T MY GODDAMN FAULT, FREAK!
DID YOU KNOW THAT'S WHAT EVERYONE CALLS YOU? ALWAYS OFF ON X-FILES-TYPE SHIT... EVERYONE SAYS IT. AND I'M STUCK WITH YOU... THE FREAK.
SHIT...I'M GONNA HAVE TO SAVE THE PRESIDENT, THE POPE, AND THE FRIGGIN' DALAI LAMA FROM A GODDAMN BOMB ON THE FOURTH OF JULY BEFORE THE BUREAU GIVES ME A DECENT PARTNER.

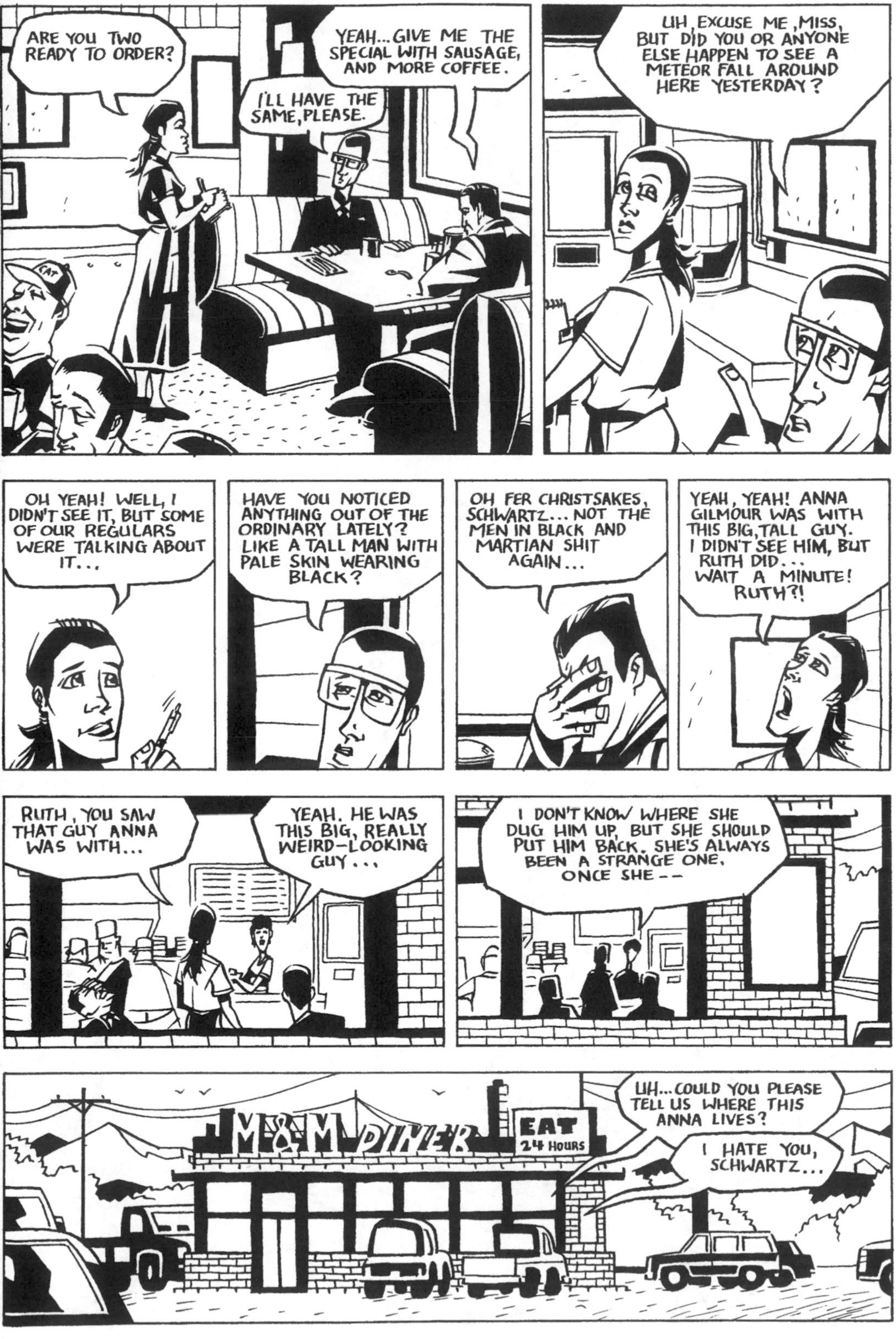
ARE YOU TWO READY TO ORDER?
YEAH... GIVE ME THE SPECIAL WITH SAUSAGE, AND MORE COFFEE.
I'LL HAVE THE SAME, PLEASE.
UH, EXCUSE ME, MISS, BUT DID YOU OR ANYONE ELSE HAPPEN TO SEE A METEOR FALL AROUND HERE YESTERDAY?
OH YEAH! WELL, I DIDN'T SEE IT, BUT SOME OF OUR REGULARS WERE TALKING ABOUT IT...
HAVE YOU NOTICED ANYTHING OUT OF THE ORDINARY LATELY? LIKE A TALL MAN WITH PALE SKIN WEARING BLACK?
OH FER CHRISTSAKES, SCHWARTZ... NOT THE MEN IN BLACK AND MARTIAN SHIT AGAIN...
YEAH, YEAH! ANNA GILMOUR WAS WITH THIS BIG, TALL GUY. I DIDN'T SEE HIM, BUT RUTH DID... WAIT A MINUTE! RUTH?!
RUTH, YOU SAW THAT GUY ANNA WAS WITH...
YEAH. HE WAS THIS BIG, REALLY WEIRD-LOOKING GUY...
I DON'T KNOW WHERE SHE DUG HIM UP, BUT SHE SHOULD PUT HIM BACK. SHE'S ALWAYS BEEN A STRANGE ONE. ONCE SHE--
M&M DINER
EAT
24 HOURS
UH... COULD YOU PLEASE TELL US WHERE THIS ANNA LIVES?
I HATE YOU, SCHWARTZ...

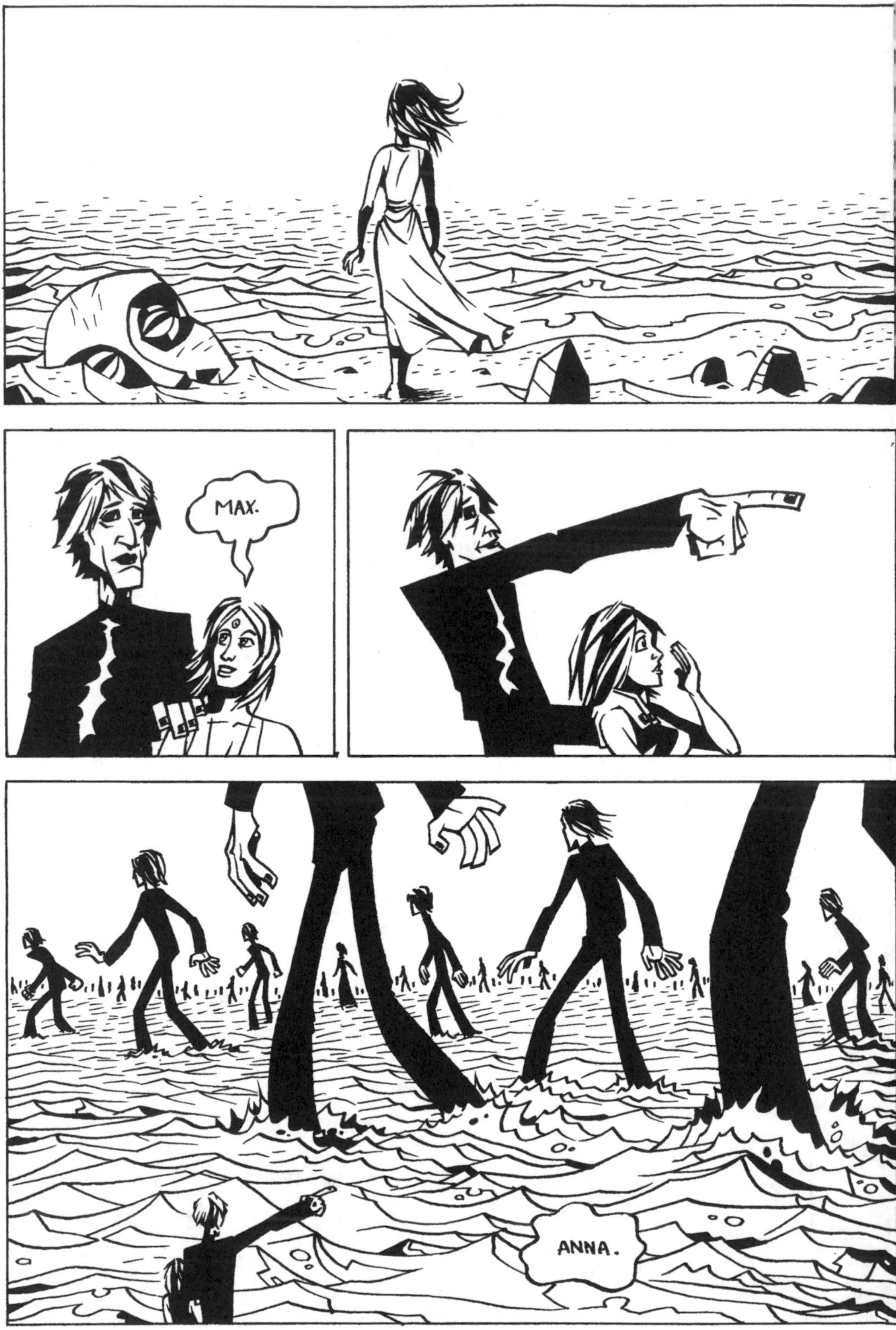
MAX.
ANNA.

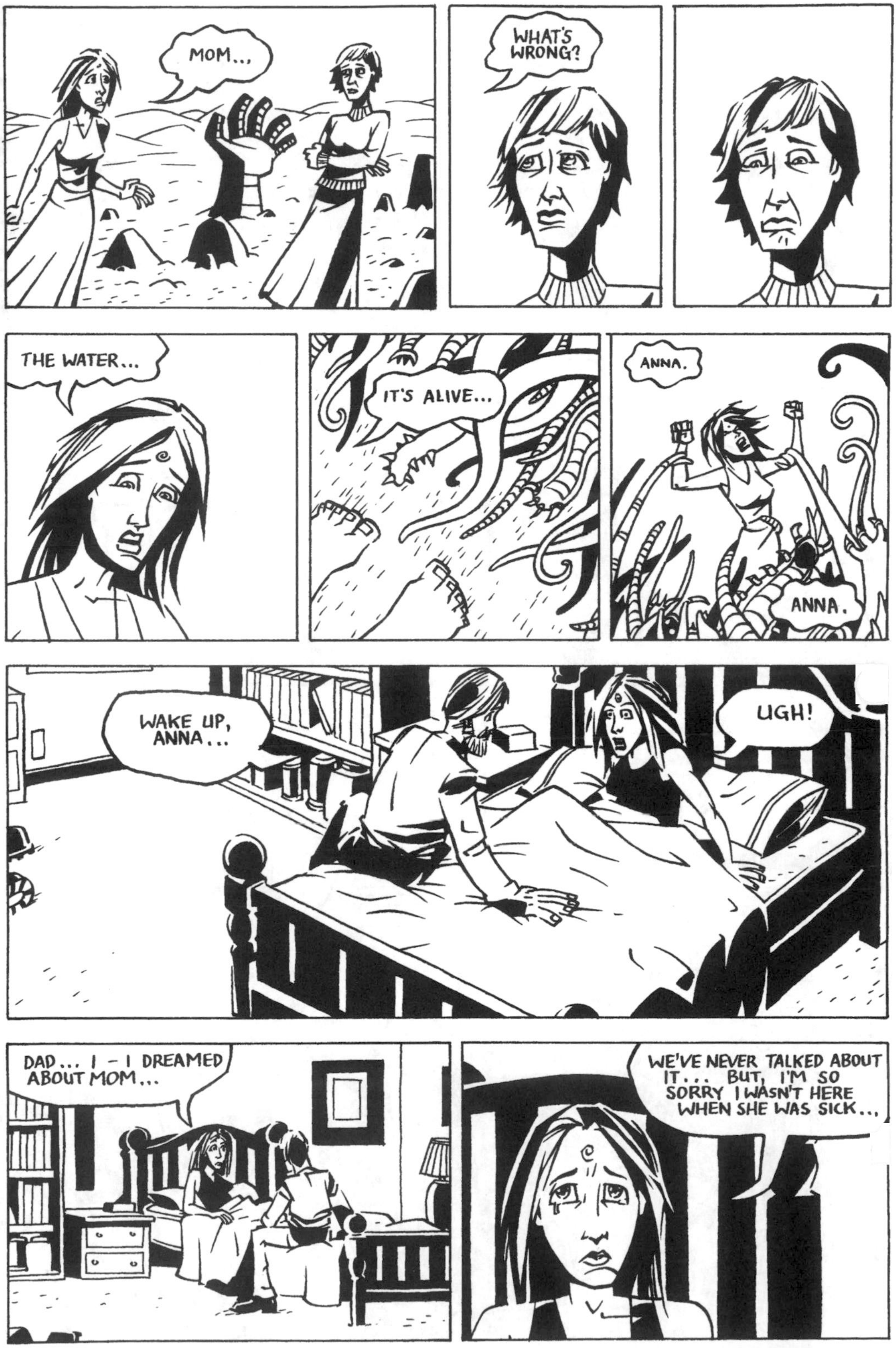
MOM...
WHAT'S WRONG?
THE WATER...
IT'S ALIVE...
ANNA.
ANNA.
WAKE UP, ANNA...
UGH!
DAD... I - I DREAMED ABOUT MOM...
WE'VE NEVER TALKED ABOUT IT... BUT, I'M SO SORRY I WASN'T HERE WHEN SHE WAS SICK...

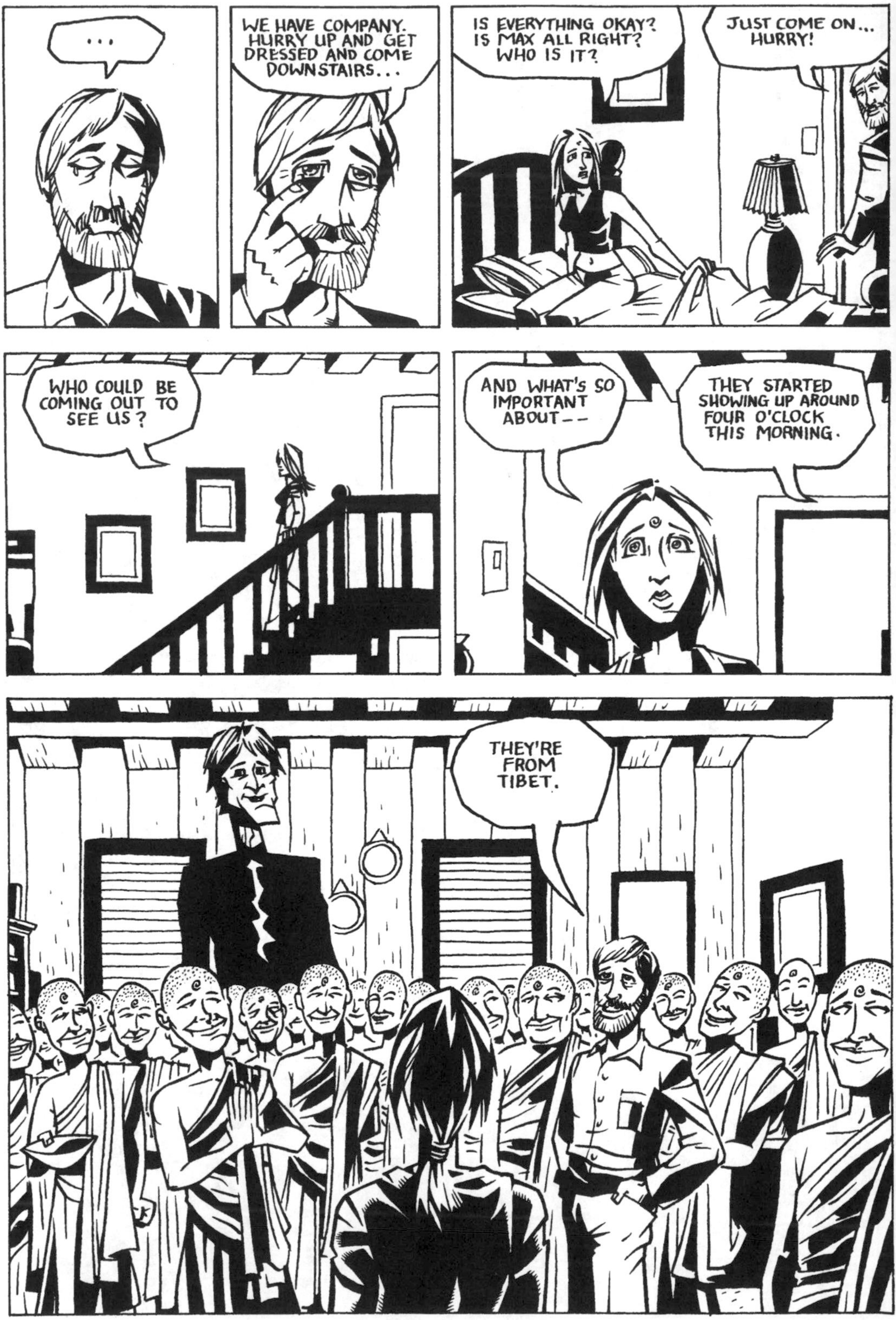
...
WE HAVE COMPANY. HURRY UP AND GET DRESSED AND COME DOWNSTAIRS...
IS EVERYTHING OKAY? IS MAX ALL RIGHT? WHO IS IT?
JUST COME ON... HURRY!
WHO COULD BE COMING OUT TO SEE US?
AND WHAT'S SO IMPORTANT ABOUT--
THEY STARTED SHOWING UP AROUND FOUR O'CLOCK THIS MORNING.
THEY'RE FROM TIBET.

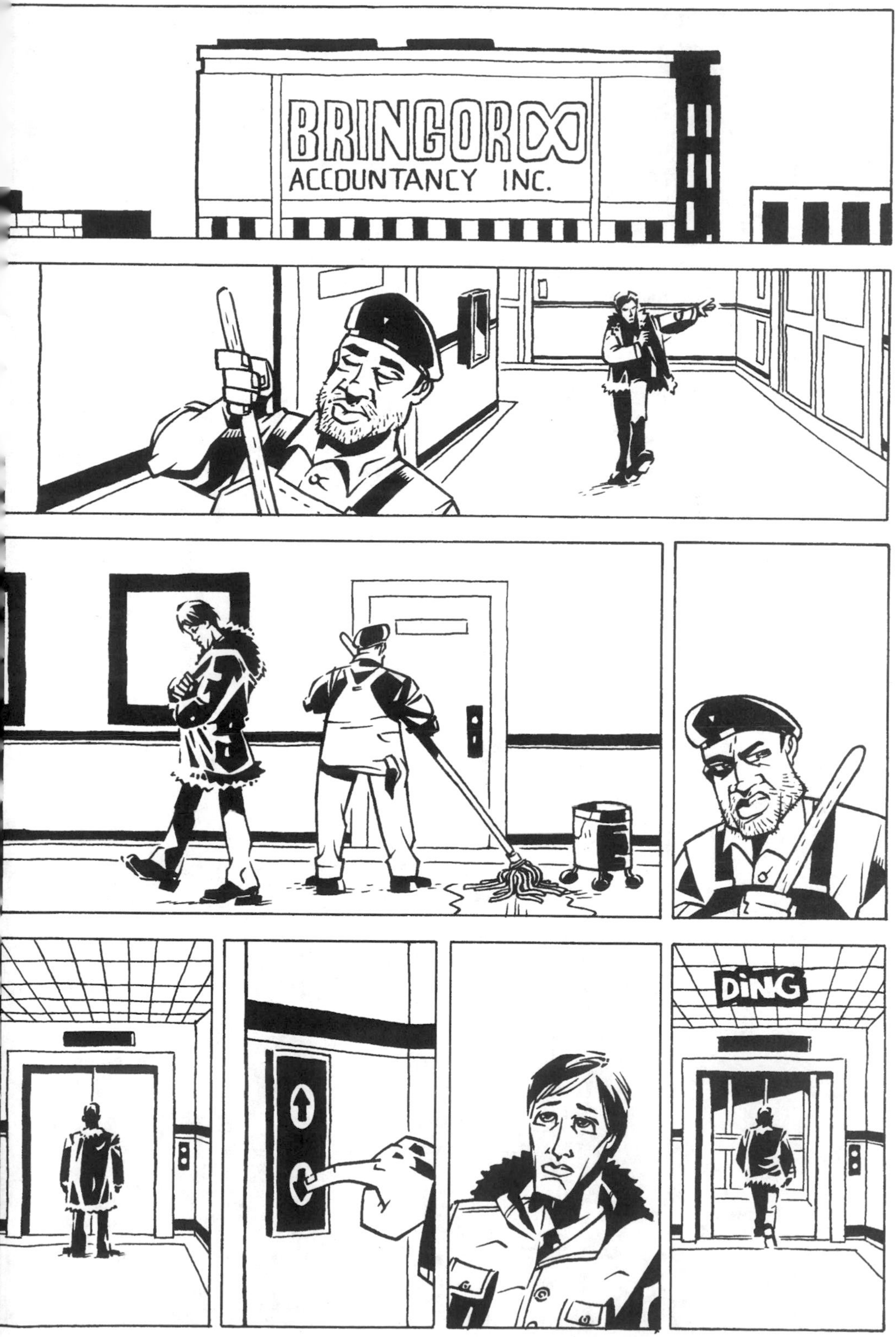
BRINGORCO
ACCOUNTANCY INC.
DiNG

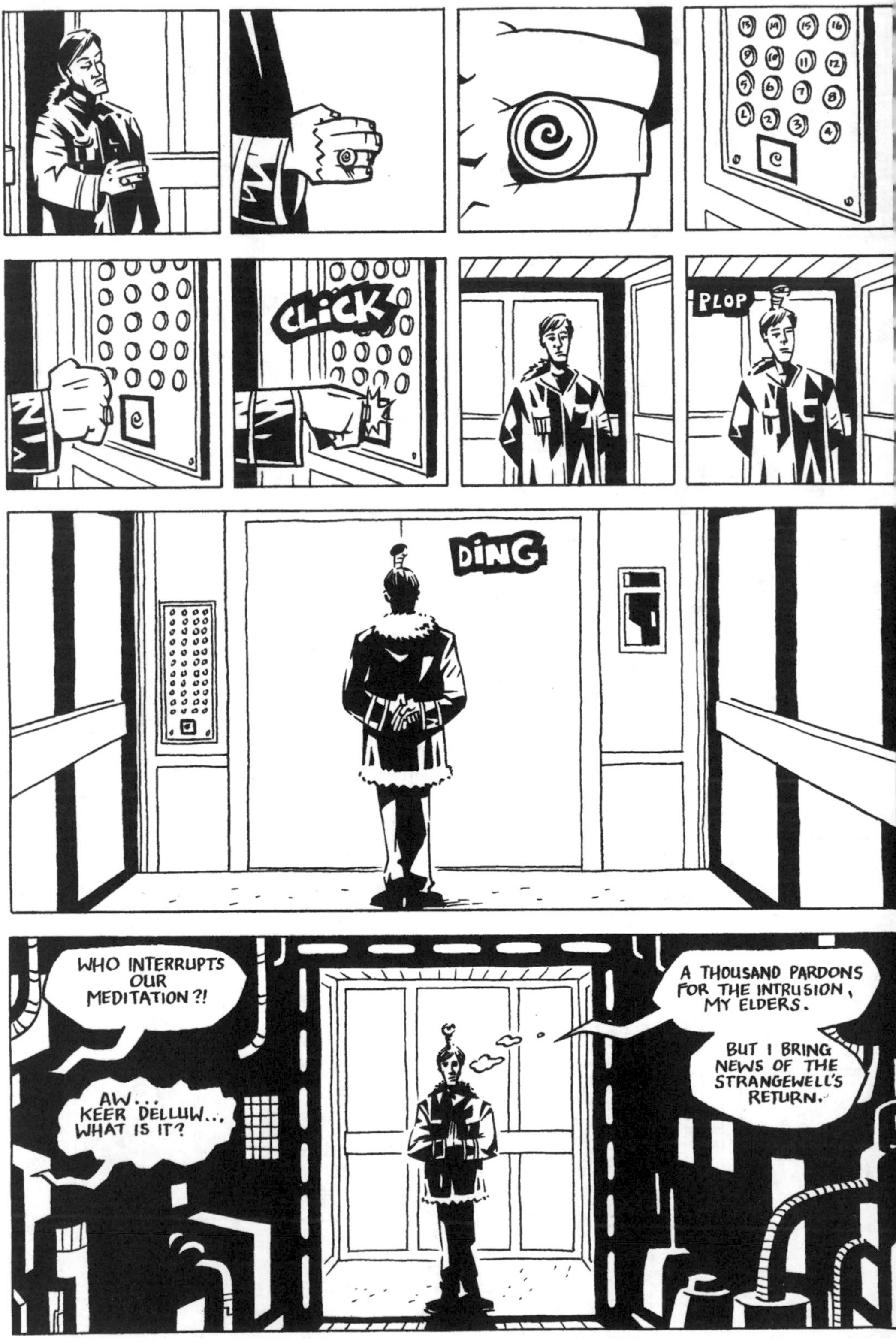
CLICK
PLOP
DING
WHO INTERRUPTS OUR MEDITATION?!
AW... KEER DELLUW... WHAT IS IT?
A THOUSAND PARDONS FOR THE INTRUSION, MY ELDERS.
BUT I BRING NEWS OF THE STRANGEWELL'S RETURN.

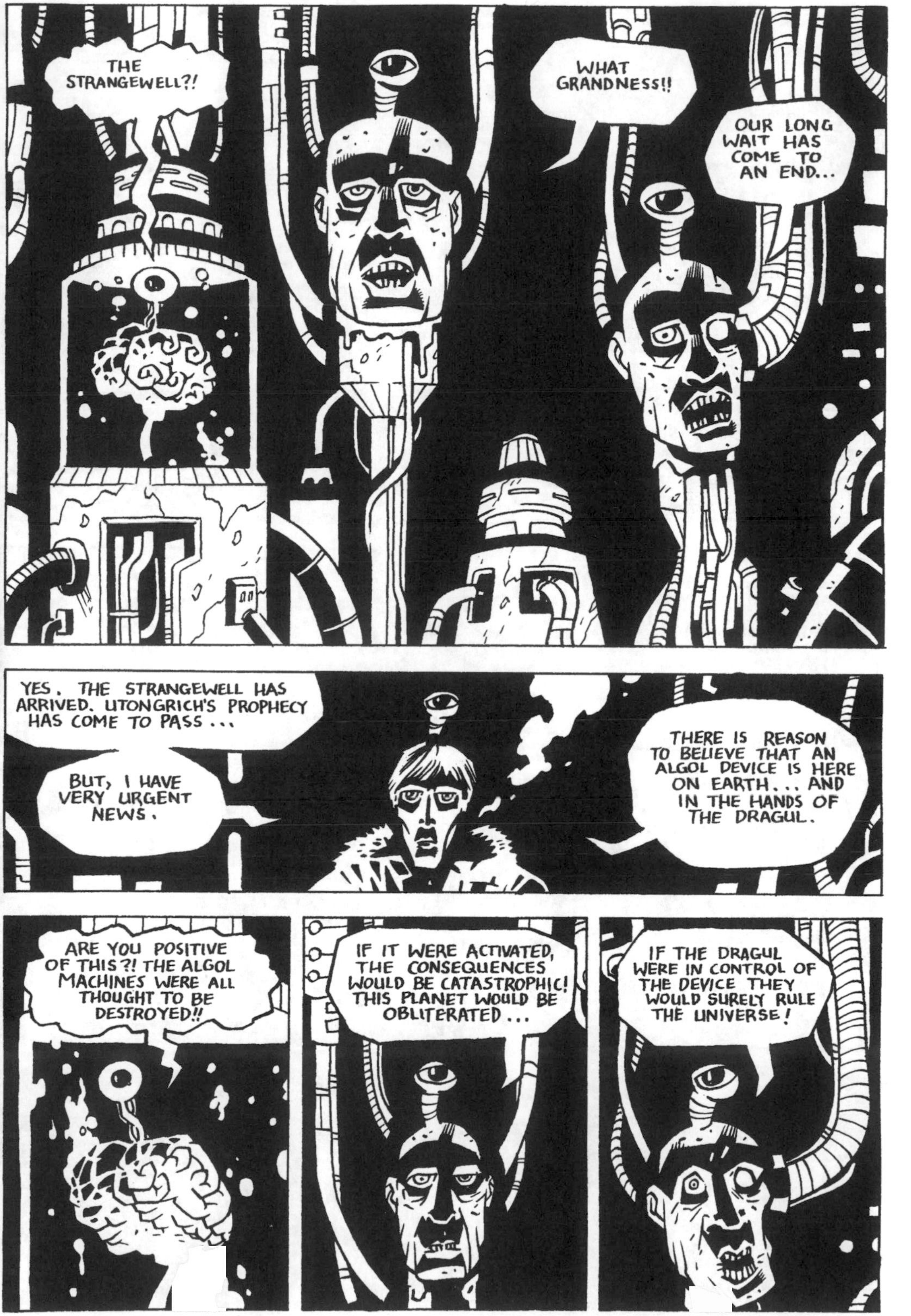
THE STRANGEWELL?!
WHAT GRANDNESS!!
OUR LONG WAIT HAS COME TO AN END...
YES. THE STRANGEWELL HAS ARRIVED. UTONGRICH'S PROPHECY HAS COME TO PASS...
BUT, I HAVE VERY URGENT NEWS.
THERE IS REASON TO BELIEVE THAT AN ALGOL DEVICE IS HERE ON EARTH... AND IN THE HANDS OF THE DRAGUL.
ARE YOU POSITIVE OF THIS?! THE ALGOL MACHINES WERE ALL THOUGHT TO BE DESTROYED!!
IF IT WERE ACTIVATED, THE CONSEQUENCES WOULD BE CATASTROPHIC! THIS PLANET WOULD BE OBLITERATED...
IF THE DRAGUL WERE IN CONTROL OF THE DEVICE THEY WOULD SURELY RULE THE UNIVERSE!

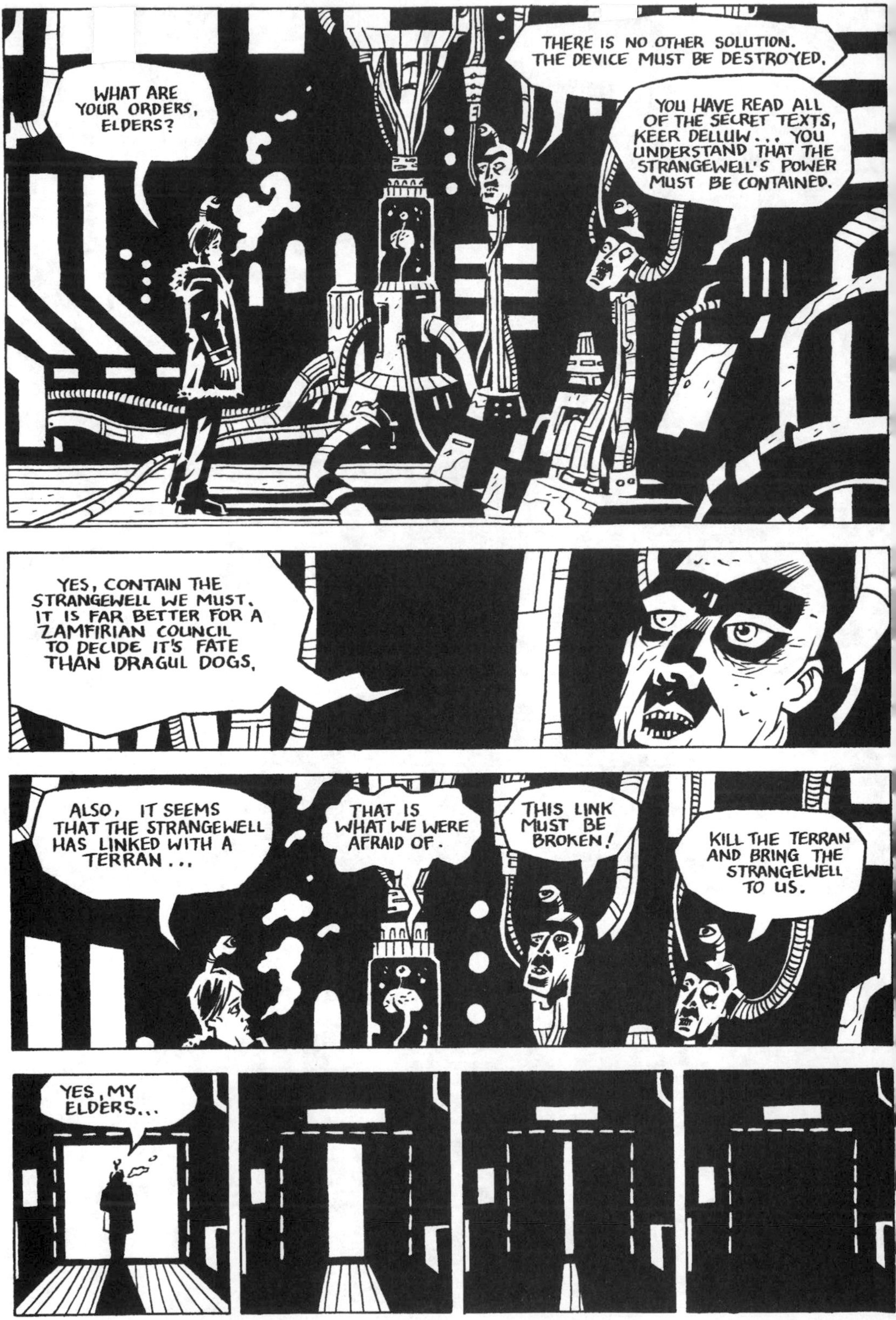
WHAT ARE YOUR ORDERS, ELDERS?
THERE IS NO OTHER SOLUTION. THE DEVICE MUST BE DESTROYED.
YOU HAVE READ ALL OF THE SECRET TEXTS, KEER DELLUW... YOU UNDERSTAND THAT THE STRANGEWELL'S POWER MUST BE CONTAINED.
YES, CONTAIN THE STRANGEWELL WE MUST. IT IS FAR BETTER FOR A ZAMFIRIAN COUNCIL TO DECIDE IT'S FATE THAN DRAGUL DOGS.
ALSO, IT SEEMS THAT THE STRANGEWELL HAS LINKED WITH A TERRAN...
THAT IS WHAT WE WERE AFRAID OF.
THIS LINK MUST BE BROKEN!
KILL THE TERRAN AND BRING THE STRANGEWELL TO US.
YES, MY ELDERS...

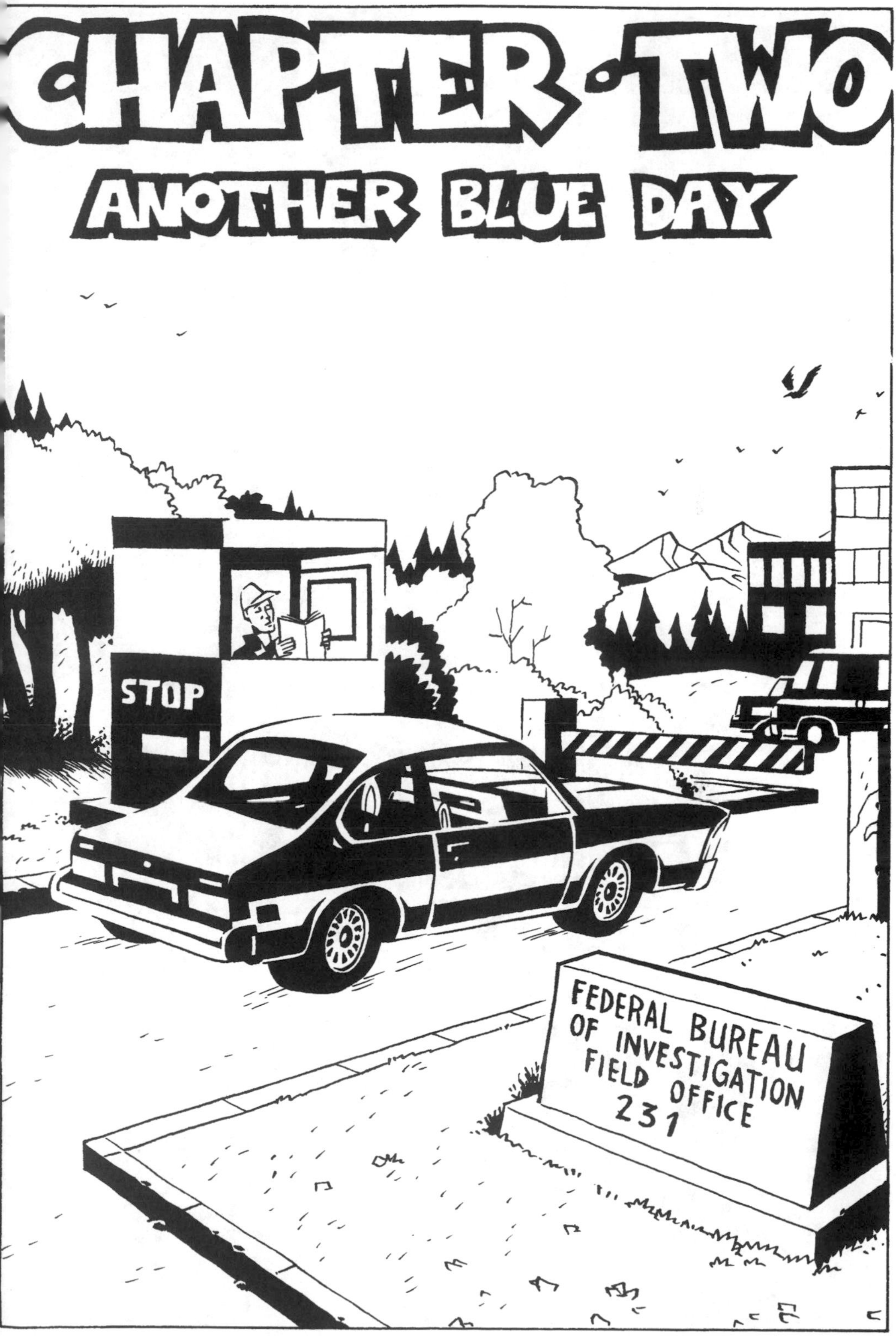
CHAPTER · TWO
ANOTHER BLUE DAY
STOP
FEDERAL BUREAU
OF INVESTIGATION
FIELD OFFICE
231

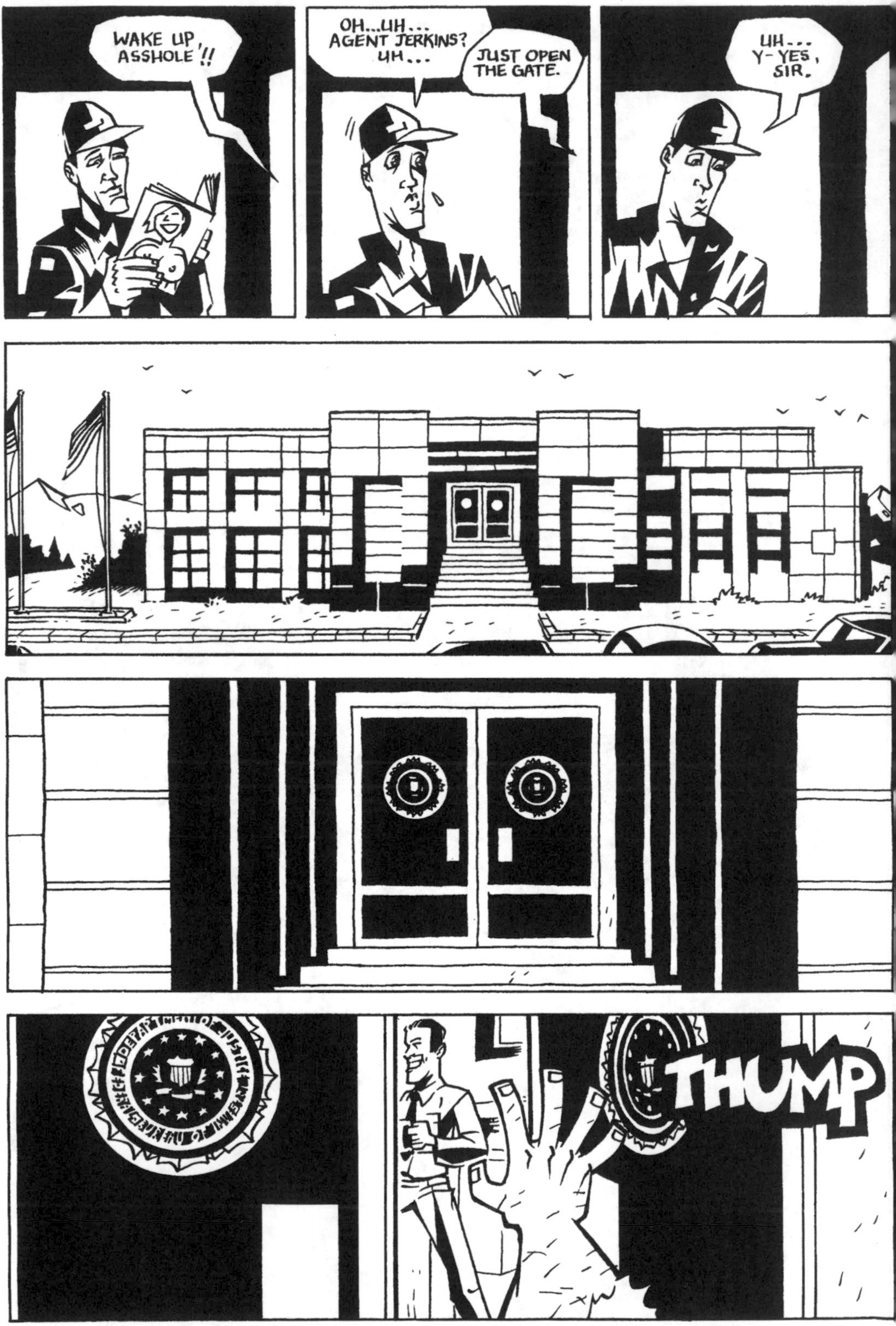
WAKE UP, ASSHOLE!!
OH...UH... AGENT JERKINS? UH...
JUST OPEN THE GATE.
UH... Y-YES, SIR.
THUMP

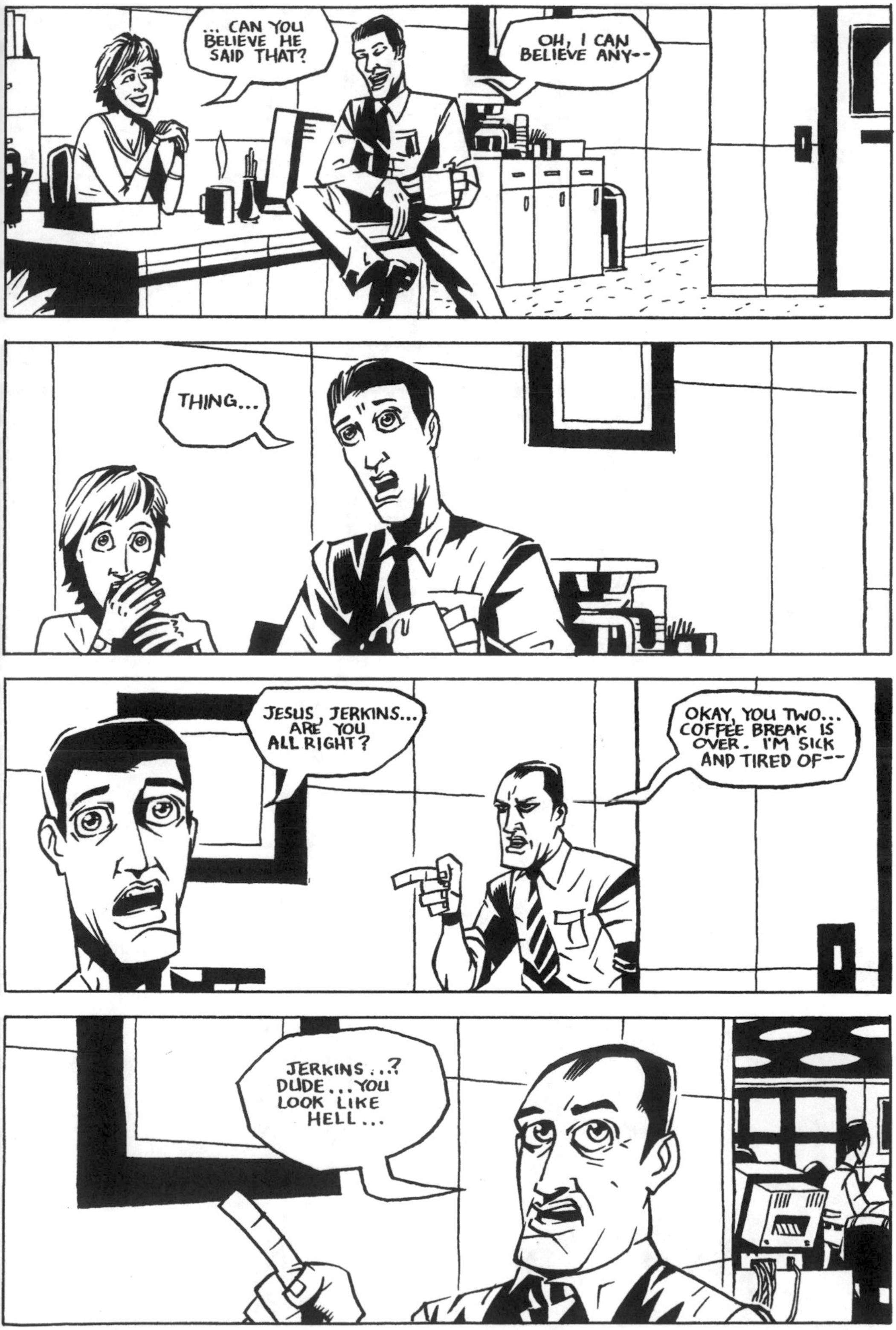
... CAN YOU BELIEVE HE SAID THAT?
OH, I CAN BELIEVE ANY--
THING...
JESUS, JERKINS... ARE YOU ALL RIGHT?
OKAY, YOU TWO... COFFEE BREAK IS OVER. I'M SICK AND TIRED OF--
JERKINS...? DUDE... YOU LOOK LIKE HELL...

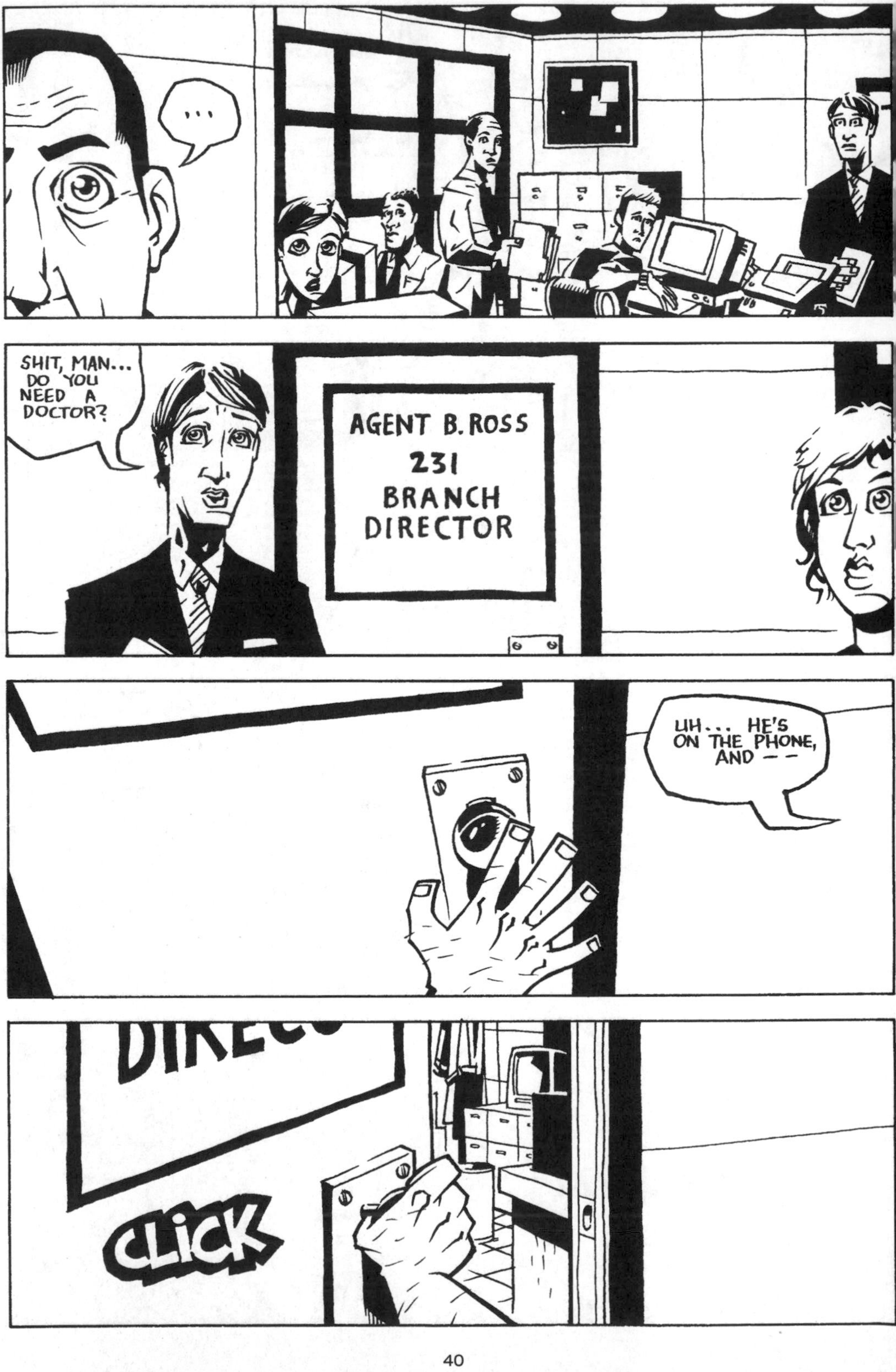
...
SHIT, MAN... DO YOU NEED A DOCTOR?
AGENT B. ROSS
231
BRANCH
DIRECTOR
UH... HE'S ON THE PHONE, AND --
DIREC
CLICK

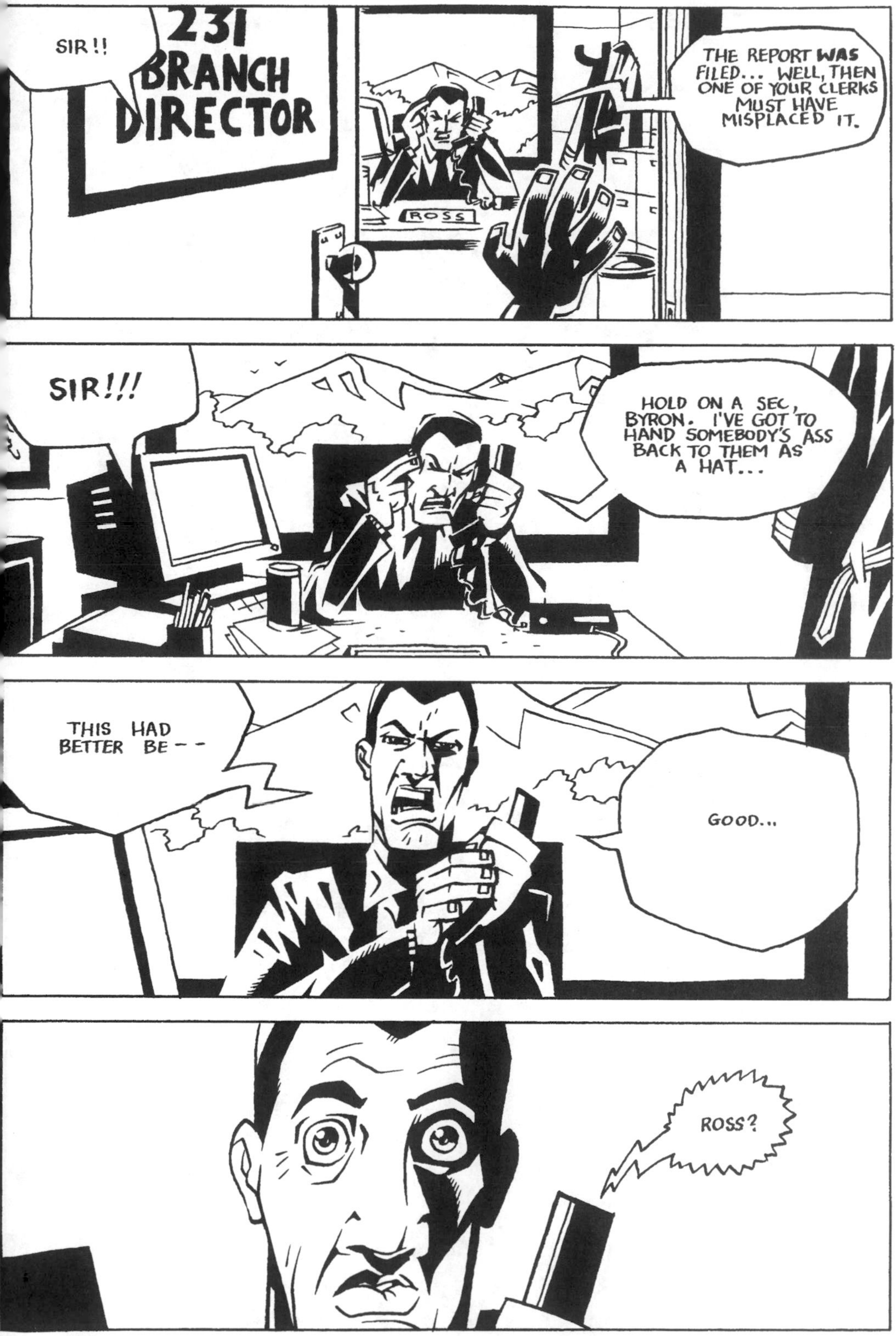
231
BRANCH
DIRECTOR
SIR!!
ROSS
THE REPORT WAS FILED... WELL, THEN ONE OF YOUR CLERKS MUST HAVE MISPLACED IT.
SIR!!!
HOLD ON A SEC, BYRON. I'VE GOT TO HAND SOMEBODY'S ASS BACK TO THEM AS A HAT...
THIS HAD BETTER BE--
GOOD...
ROSS?

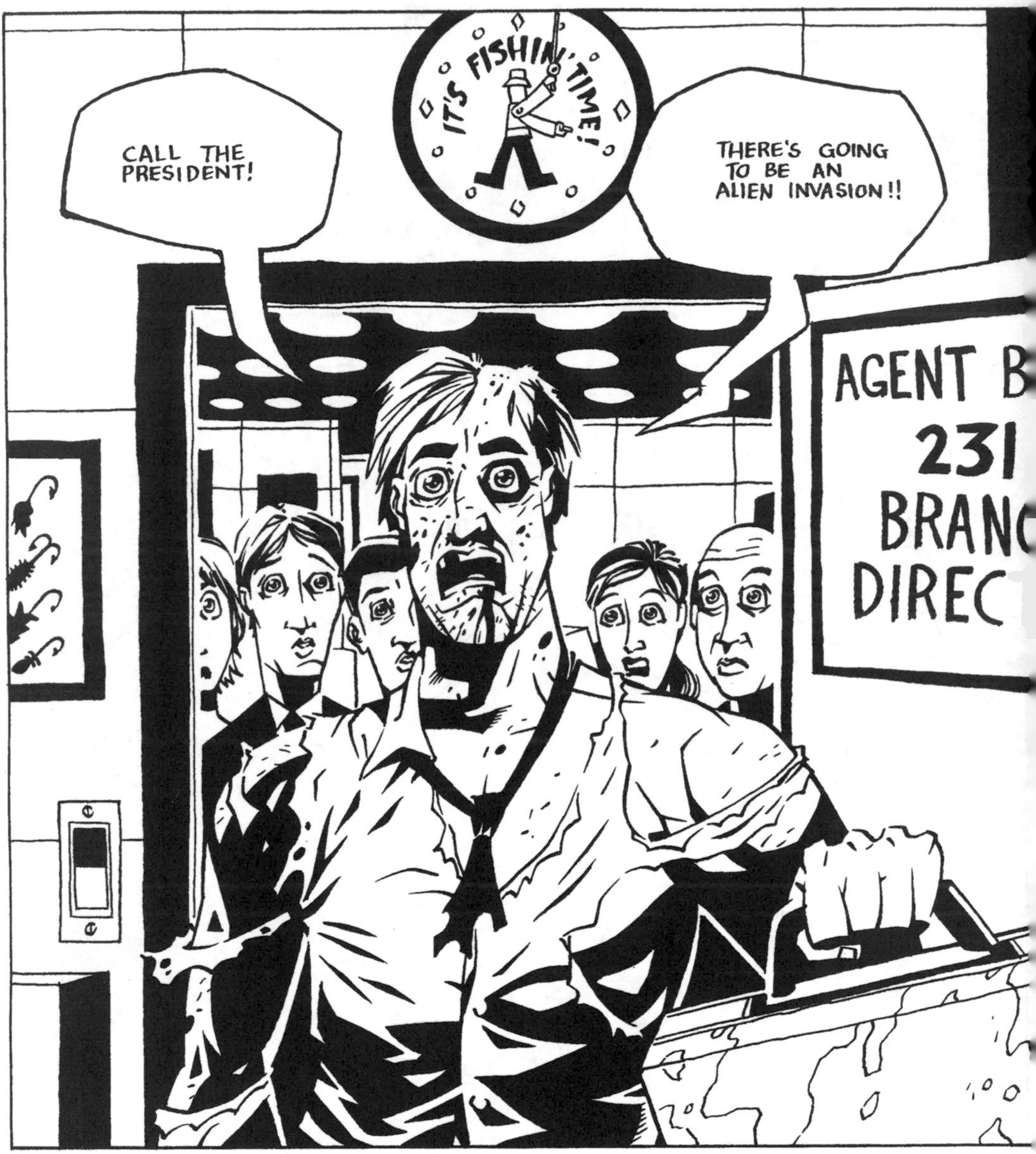
IT'S FISHIN' TIME!
CALL THE PRESIDENT!
THERE'S GOING TO BE AN ALIEN INVASION!!
AGENT B
231
BRANC
DIREC

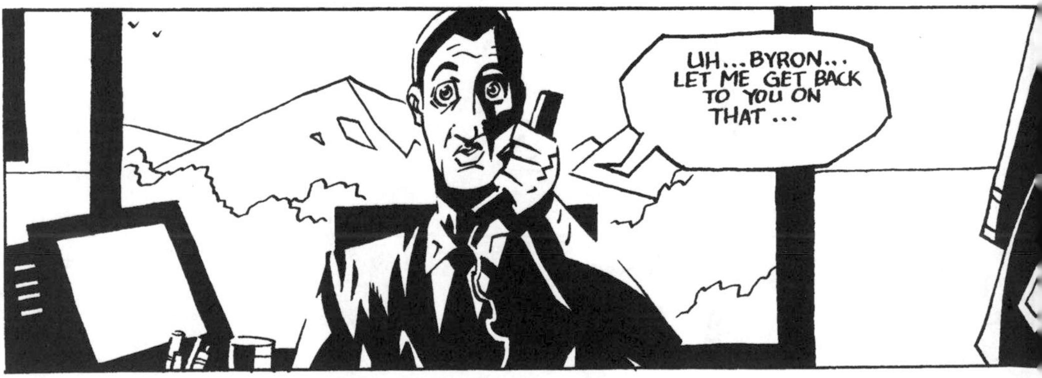
UH... BYRON... LET ME GET BACK TO YOU ON THAT...

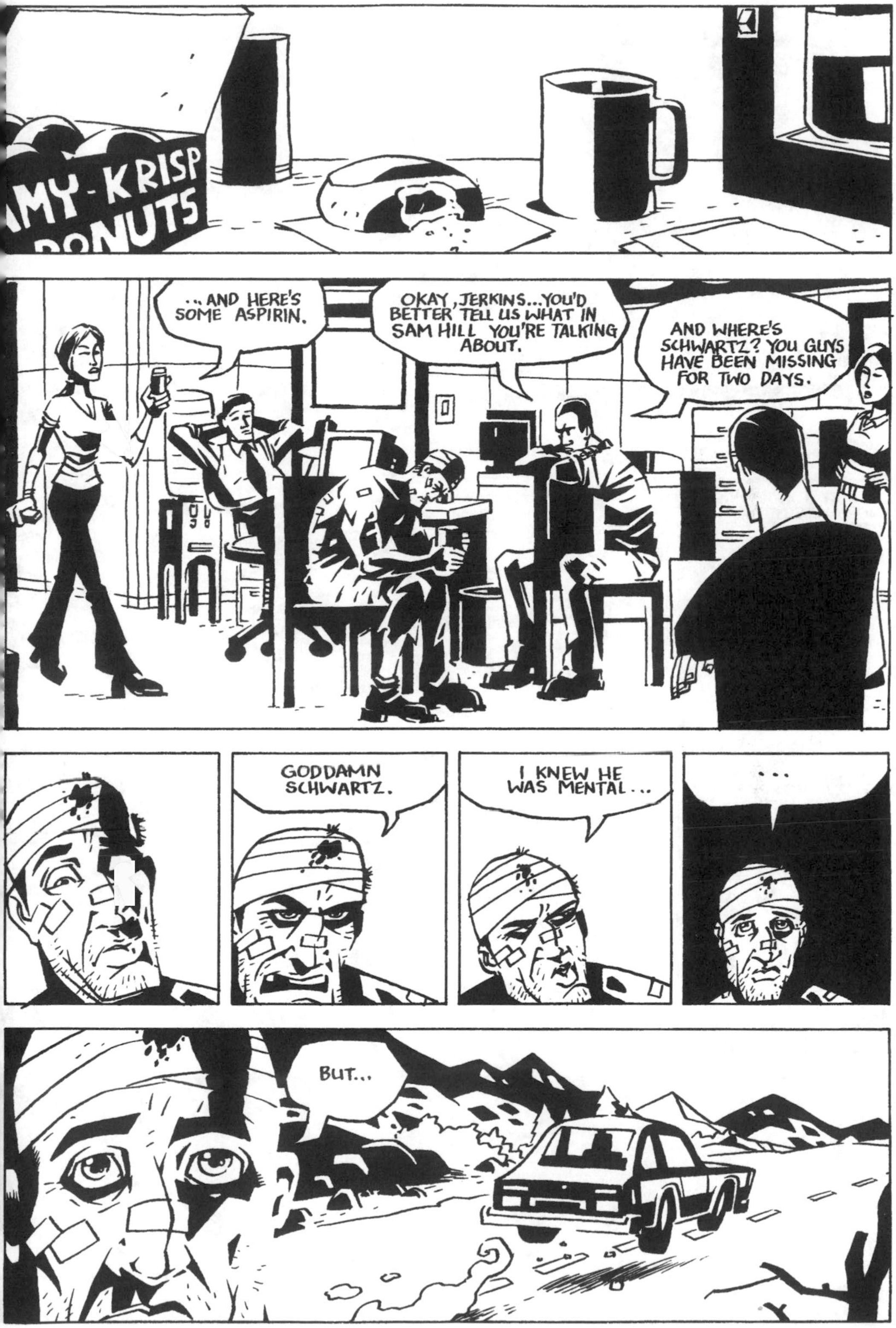

AMY-KRISP DONUTS
...AND HERE'S SOME ASPIRIN.
OKAY, JERKINS... YOU'D BETTER TELL US WHAT IN SAM HILL YOU'RE TALKING ABOUT.
AND WHERE'S SCHWARTZ? YOU GUYS HAVE BEEN MISSING FOR TWO DAYS.
GODDAMN SCHWARTZ.
I KNEW HE WAS MENTAL...
...
BUT...

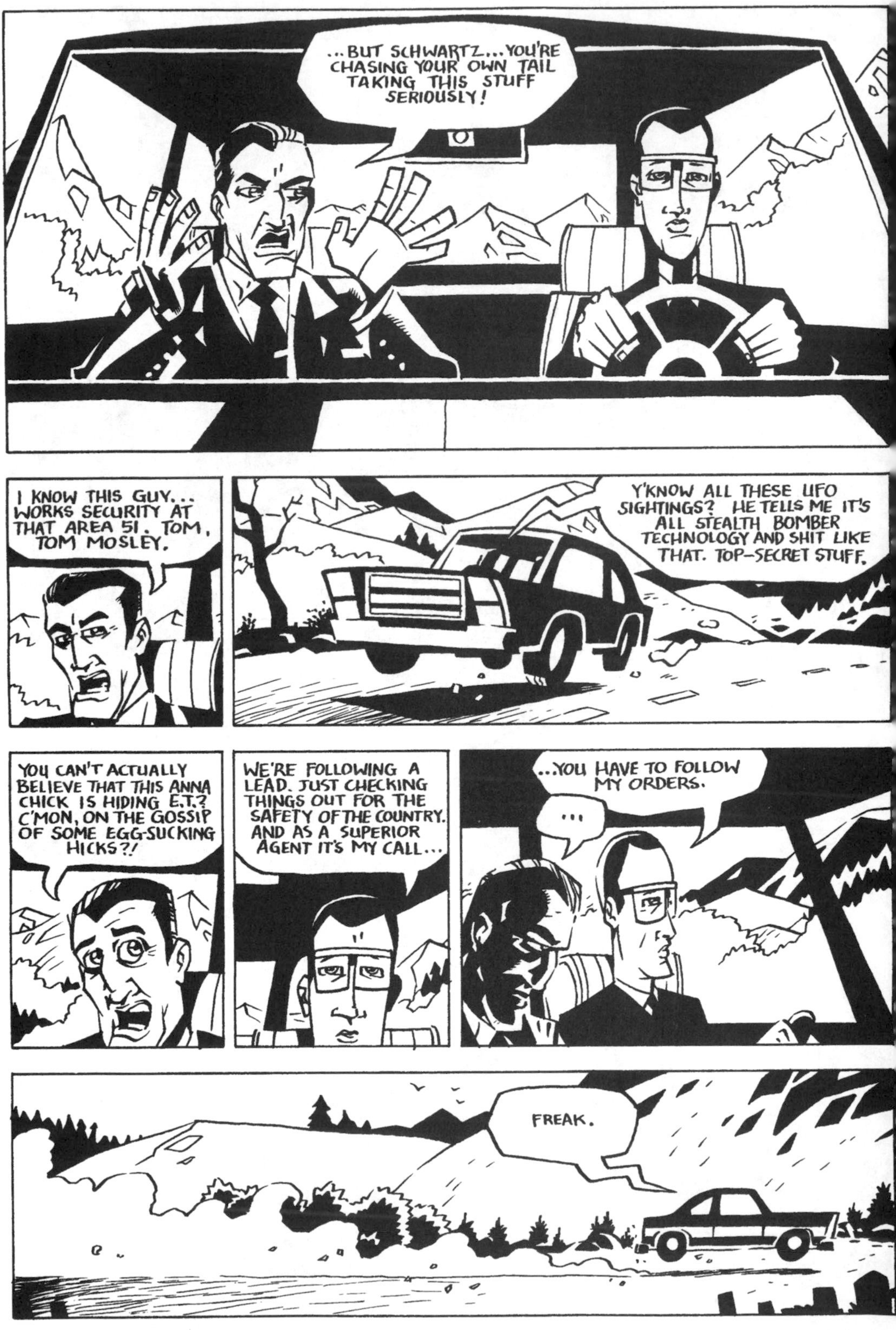
...BUT SCHWARTZ...YOU'RE CHASING YOUR OWN TAIL TAKING THIS STUFF SERIOUSLY!
I KNOW THIS GUY... WORKS SECURITY AT THAT AREA 51. TOM, TOM MOSLEY.
Y'KNOW ALL THESE UFO SIGHTINGS? HE TELLS ME IT'S ALL STEALTH BOMBER TECHNOLOGY AND SHIT LIKE THAT. TOP-SECRET STUFF.
YOU CAN'T ACTUALLY BELIEVE THAT THIS ANNA CHICK IS HIDING E.T.? C'MON, ON THE GOSSIP OF SOME EGG-SUCKING HICKS?!
WE'RE FOLLOWING A LEAD. JUST CHECKING THINGS OUT FOR THE SAFETY OF THE COUNTRY. AND AS A SUPERIOR AGENT IT'S MY CALL...
...YOU HAVE TO FOLLOW MY ORDERS.
...
FREAK.

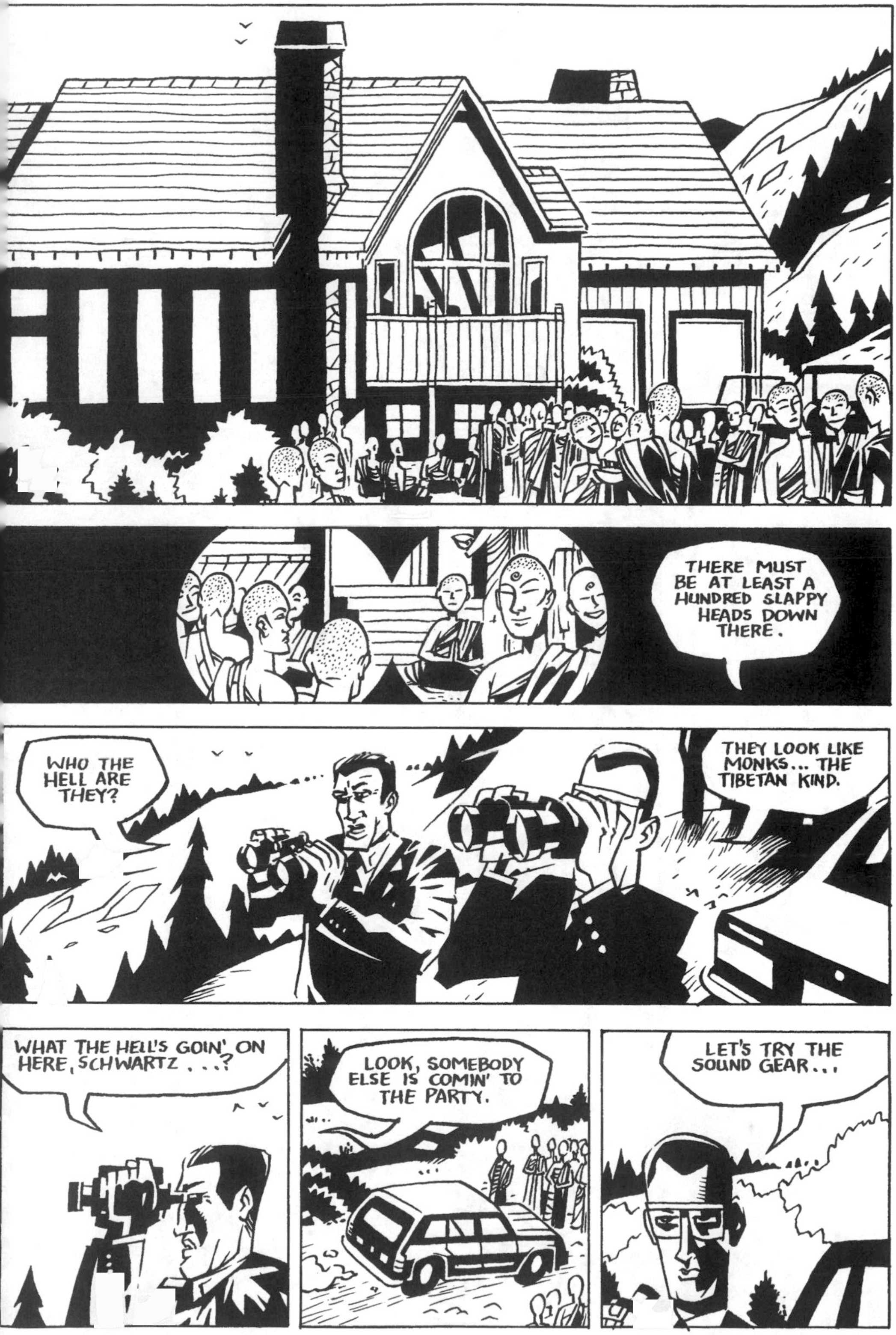
THERE MUST BE AT LEAST A HUNDRED SLAPPY HEADS DOWN THERE.
WHO THE HELL ARE THEY?
THEY LOOK LIKE MONKS... THE TIBETAN KIND.
WHAT THE HELL'S GOIN' ON HERE, SCHWARTZ...?
LOOK, SOMEBODY ELSE IS COMIN' TO THE PARTY.
LET'S TRY THE SOUND GEAR...

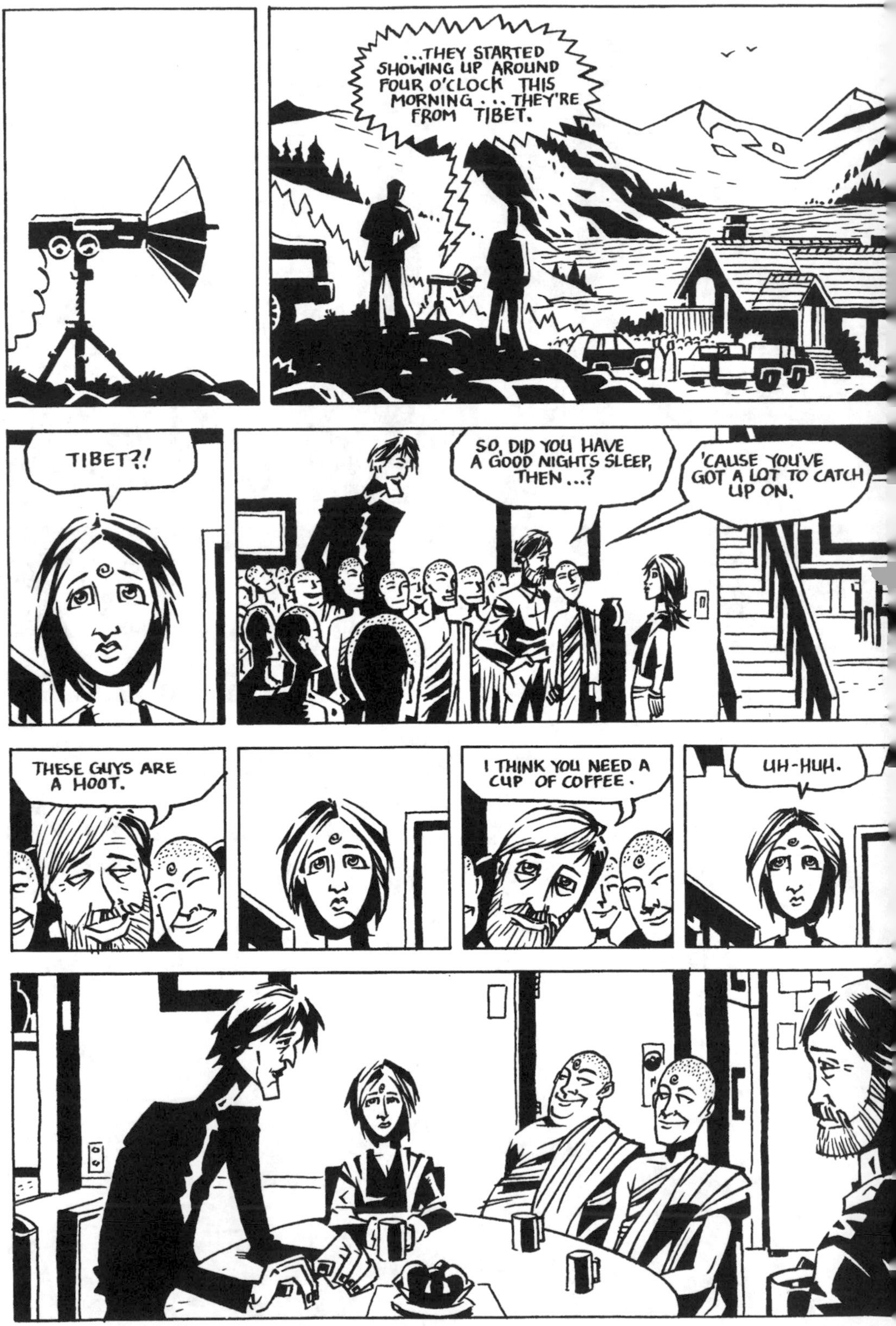
...THEY STARTED SHOWING UP AROUND FOUR O'CLOCK THIS MORNING ... THEY'RE FROM TIBET.
TIBET?!
SO, DID YOU HAVE A GOOD NIGHTS SLEEP, THEN ...?
'CAUSE YOU'VE GOT A LOT TO CATCH UP ON.
THESE GUYS ARE A HOOT.
I THINK YOU NEED A CUP OF COFFEE.
UH-HUH.

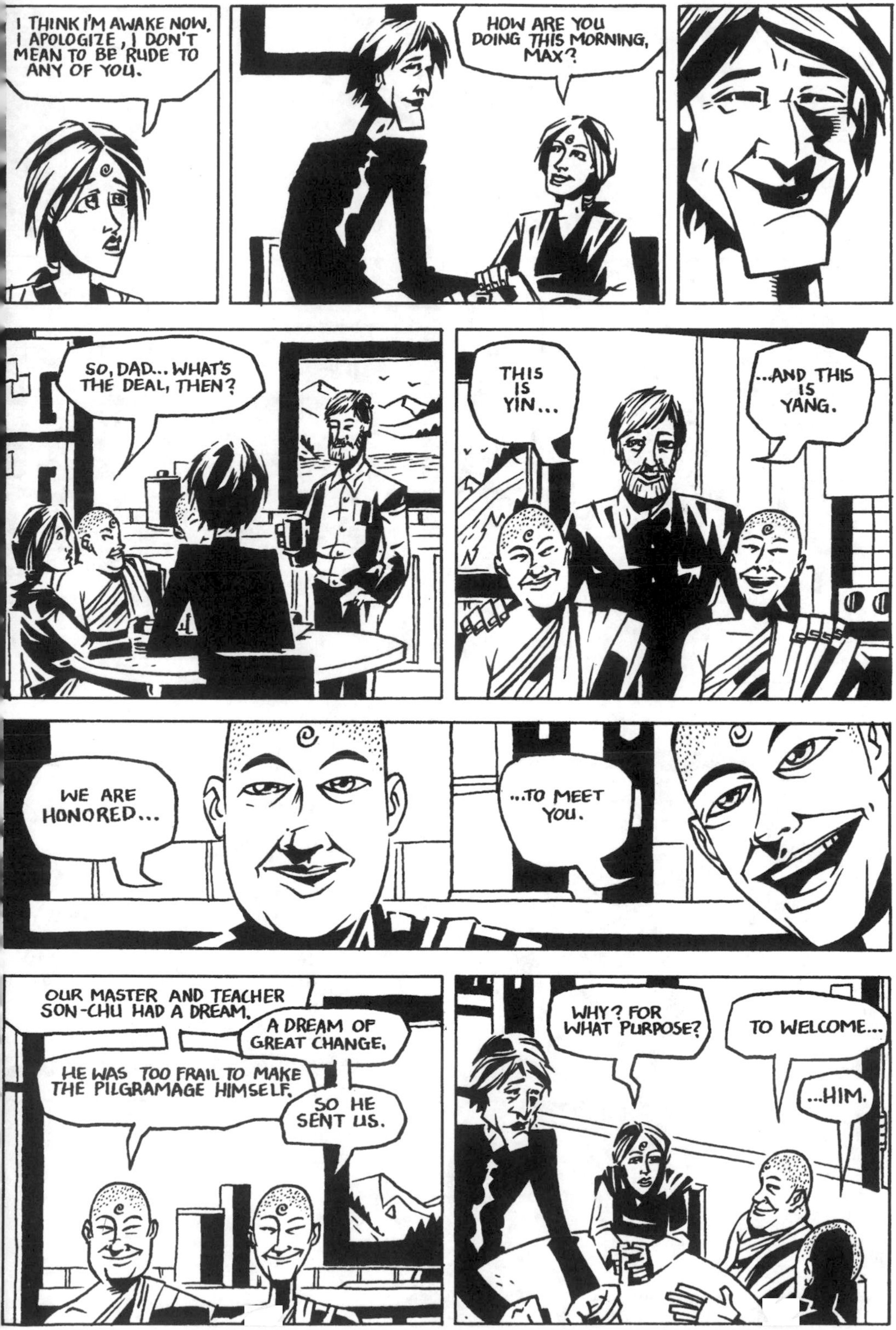
I THINK I'M AWAKE NOW. I APOLOGIZE, I DON'T MEAN TO BE RUDE TO ANY OF YOU.
HOW ARE YOU DOING THIS MORNING, MAX?
SO, DAD... WHAT'S THE DEAL, THEN?
THIS IS YIN...
...AND THIS IS YANG.
WE ARE HONORED...
...TO MEET YOU.
OUR MASTER AND TEACHER SON-CHU HAD A DREAM.
A DREAM OF GREAT CHANGE.
HE WAS TOO FRAIL TO MAKE THE PILGRAMAGE HIMSELF.
SO HE SENT US.
WHY? FOR WHAT PURPOSE?
TO WELCOME...
...HIM.

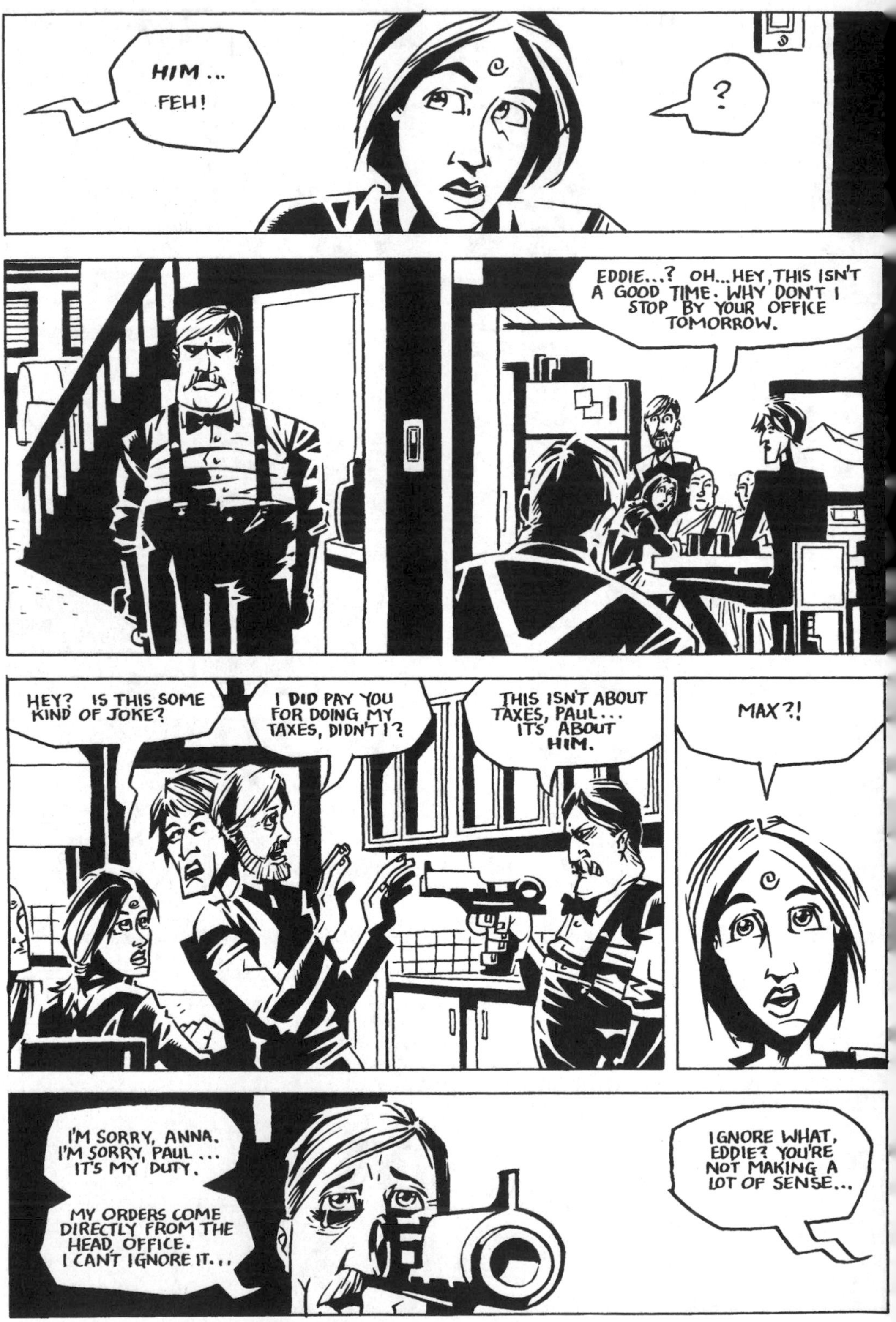
HIM... FEH!
?
EDDIE...? OH... HEY, THIS ISN'T A GOOD TIME. WHY DON'T I STOP BY YOUR OFFICE TOMORROW.
HEY? IS THIS SOME KIND OF JOKE?
I DID PAY YOU FOR DOING MY TAXES, DIDN'T I?
THIS ISN'T ABOUT TAXES, PAUL... IT'S ABOUT HIM.
MAX?!
I'M SORRY, ANNA. I'M SORRY, PAUL... IT'S MY DUTY.
MY ORDERS COME DIRECTLY FROM THE HEAD OFFICE. I CAN'T IGNORE IT...
IGNORE WHAT, EDDIE? YOU'RE NOT MAKING A LOT OF SENSE...

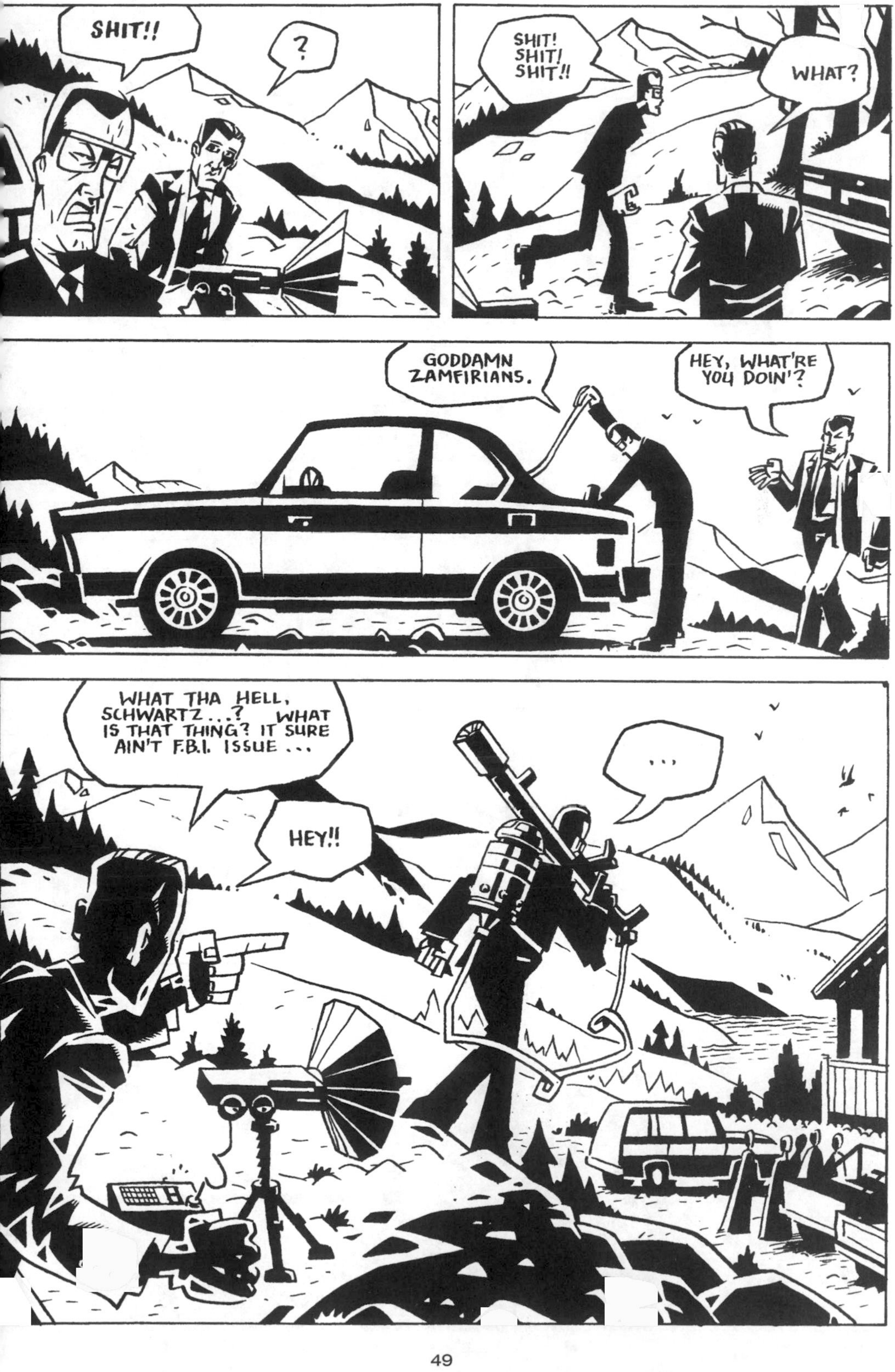
SHIT!!
?
SHIT!
SHIT!
SHIT!!
WHAT?
GODDAMN ZAMFIRIANS.
HEY, WHAT'RE YOU DOIN'?
WHAT THA HELL, SCHWARTZ...? WHAT IS THAT THING? IT SURE AIN'T F.B.I. ISSUE...
...
HEY!!

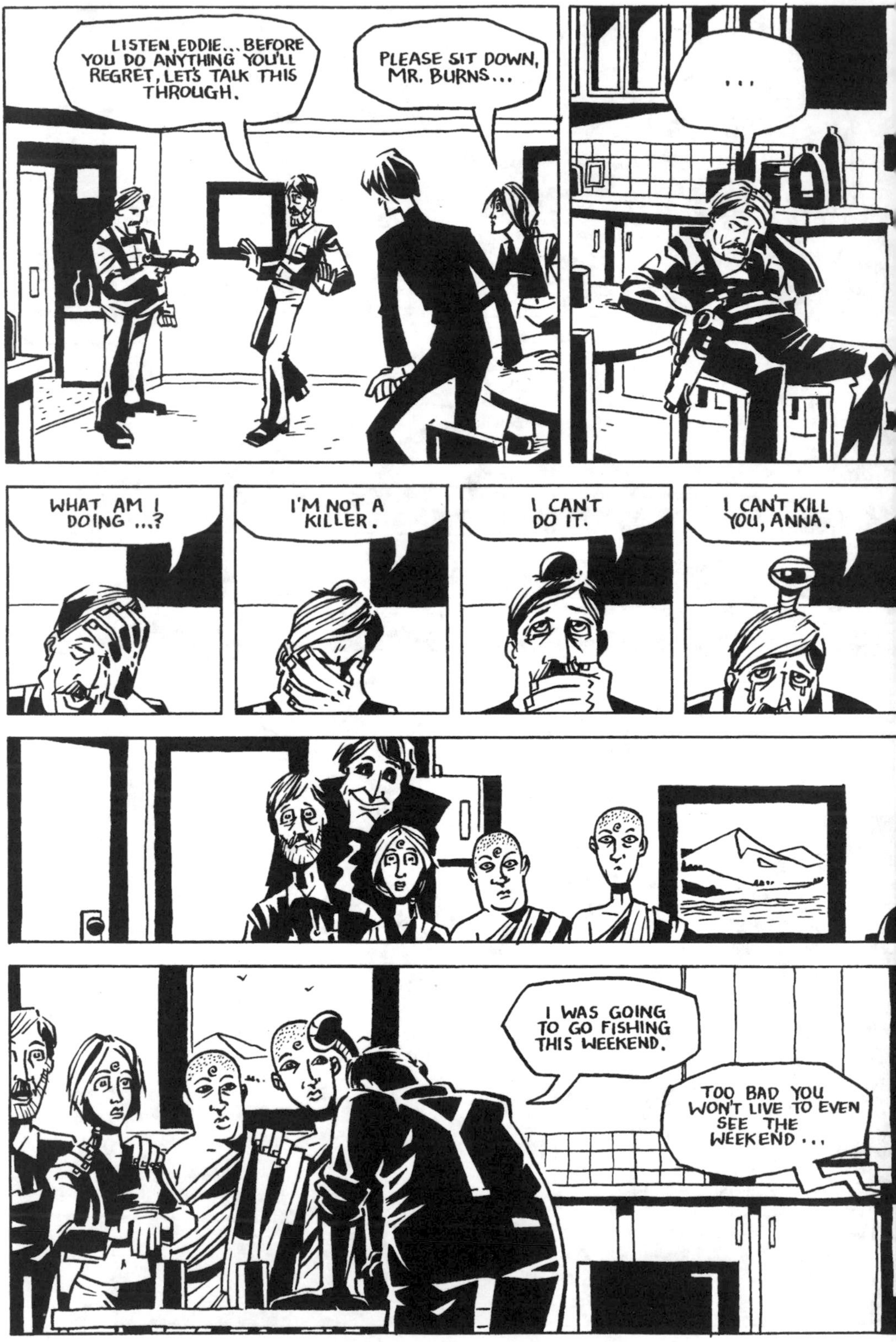
LISTEN, EDDIE... BEFORE YOU DO ANYTHING YOU'LL REGRET, LET'S TALK THIS THROUGH.
PLEASE SIT DOWN, MR. BURNS...
...
WHAT AM I DOING ...?
I'M NOT A KILLER.
I CAN'T DO IT.
I CAN'T KILL YOU, ANNA.
I WAS GOING TO GO FISHING THIS WEEKEND.
TOO BAD YOU WON'T LIVE TO EVEN SEE THE WEEKEND...

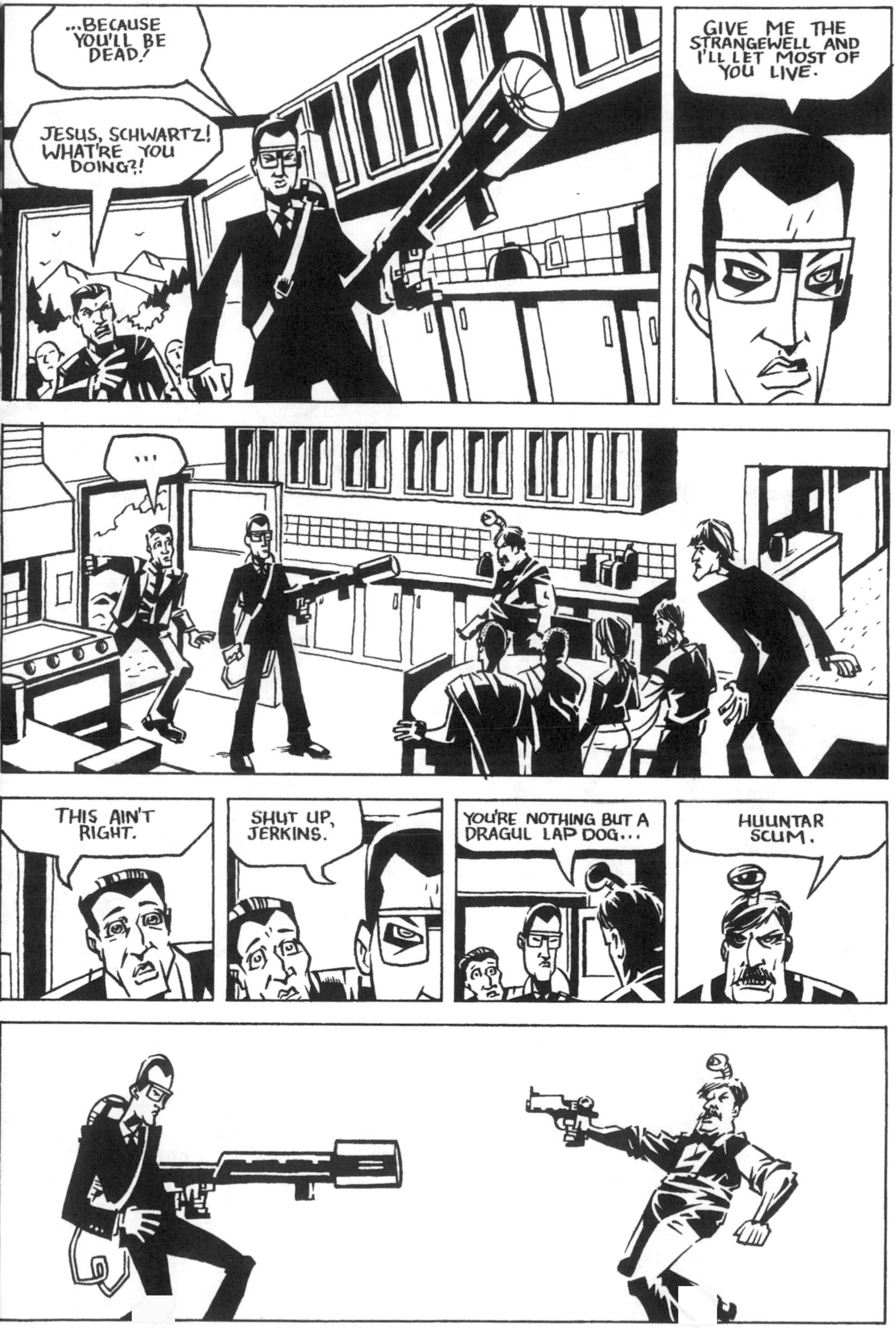
...BECAUSE YOU'LL BE DEAD!
JESUS, SCHWARTZ! WHAT'RE YOU DOING?!
GIVE ME THE STRANGEWELL AND I'LL LET MOST OF YOU LIVE.
...
THIS AIN'T RIGHT.
SHUT UP, JERKINS.
YOU'RE NOTHING BUT A DRAGUL LAP DOG...
HUUNTAR SCUM.

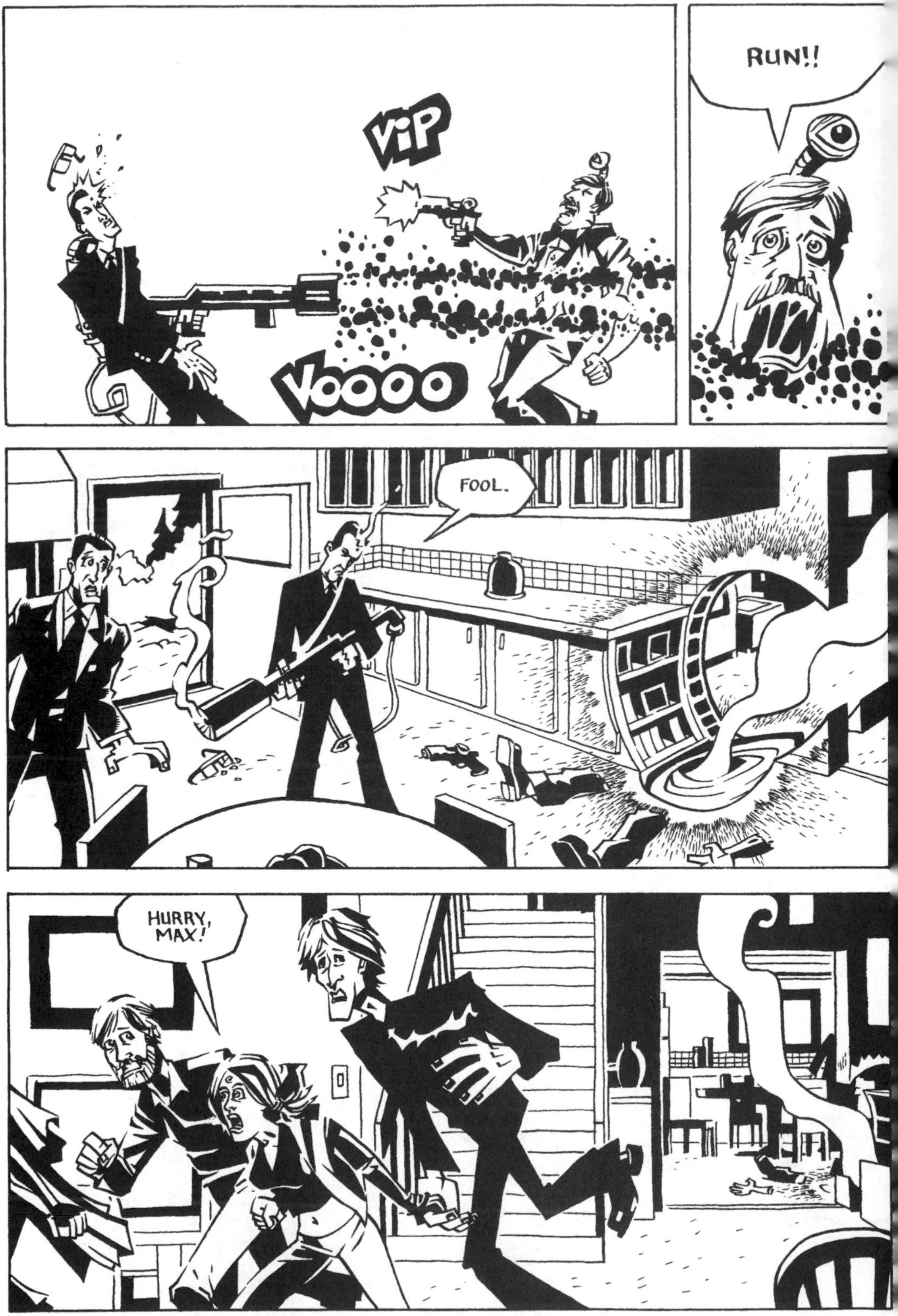

ViP
VOOOO
RUN!!
FOOL.
HURRY, MAX!

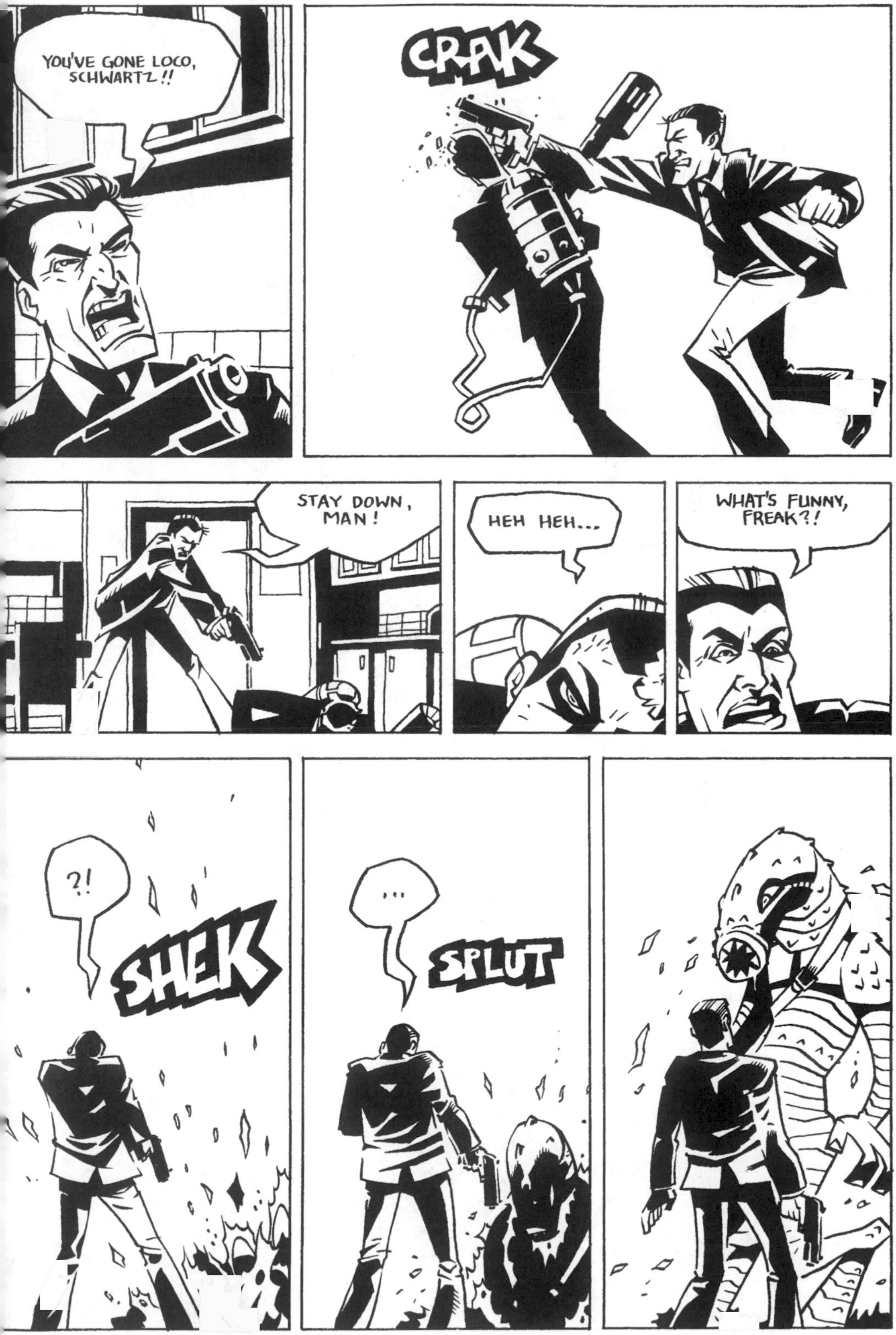
YOU'VE GONE LOCO, SCHWARTZ!!
CRAK
STAY DOWN, MAN!
HEH HEH...
WHAT'S FUNNY, FREAK?!
?!
SHEK
...
SPLUT

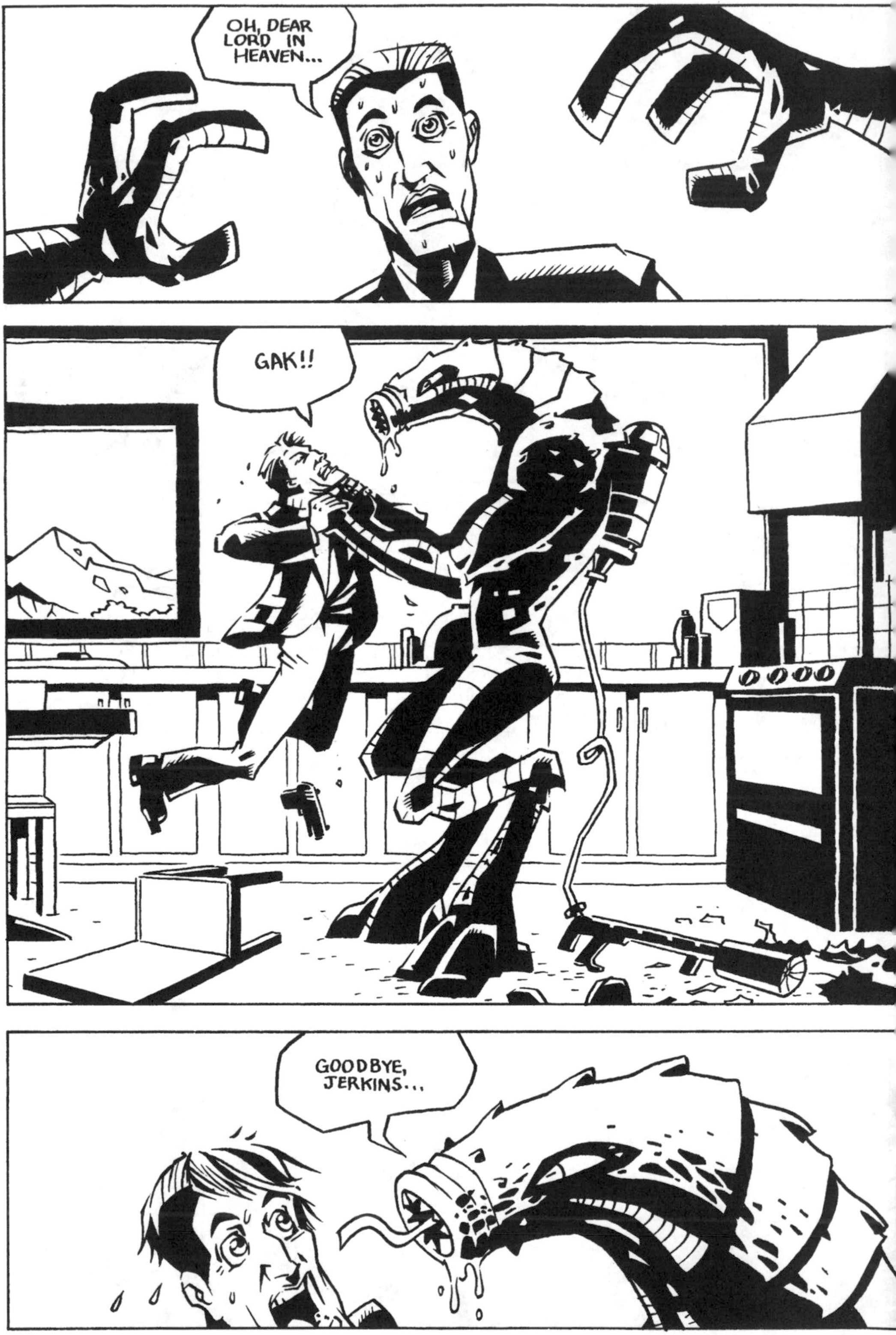
OH, DEAR LORD IN HEAVEN...
GAK!!
GOODBYE, JERKINS...

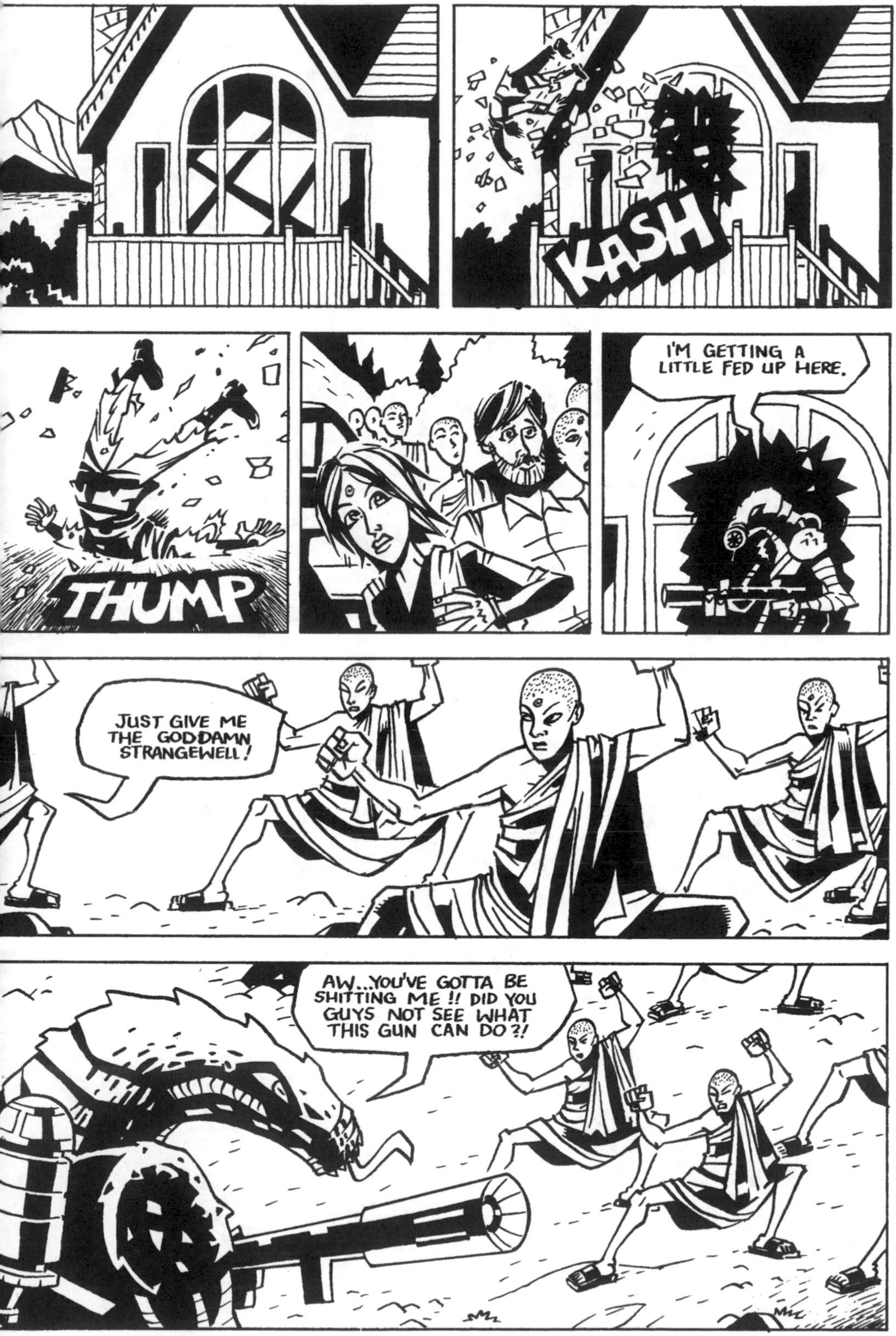
KASH
THUMP
I'M GETTING A LITTLE FED UP HERE.
JUST GIVE ME THE GODDAMN STRANGEWELL!
AW...YOU'VE GOTTA BE SHITTING ME!! DID YOU GUYS NOT SEE WHAT THIS GUN CAN DO?!

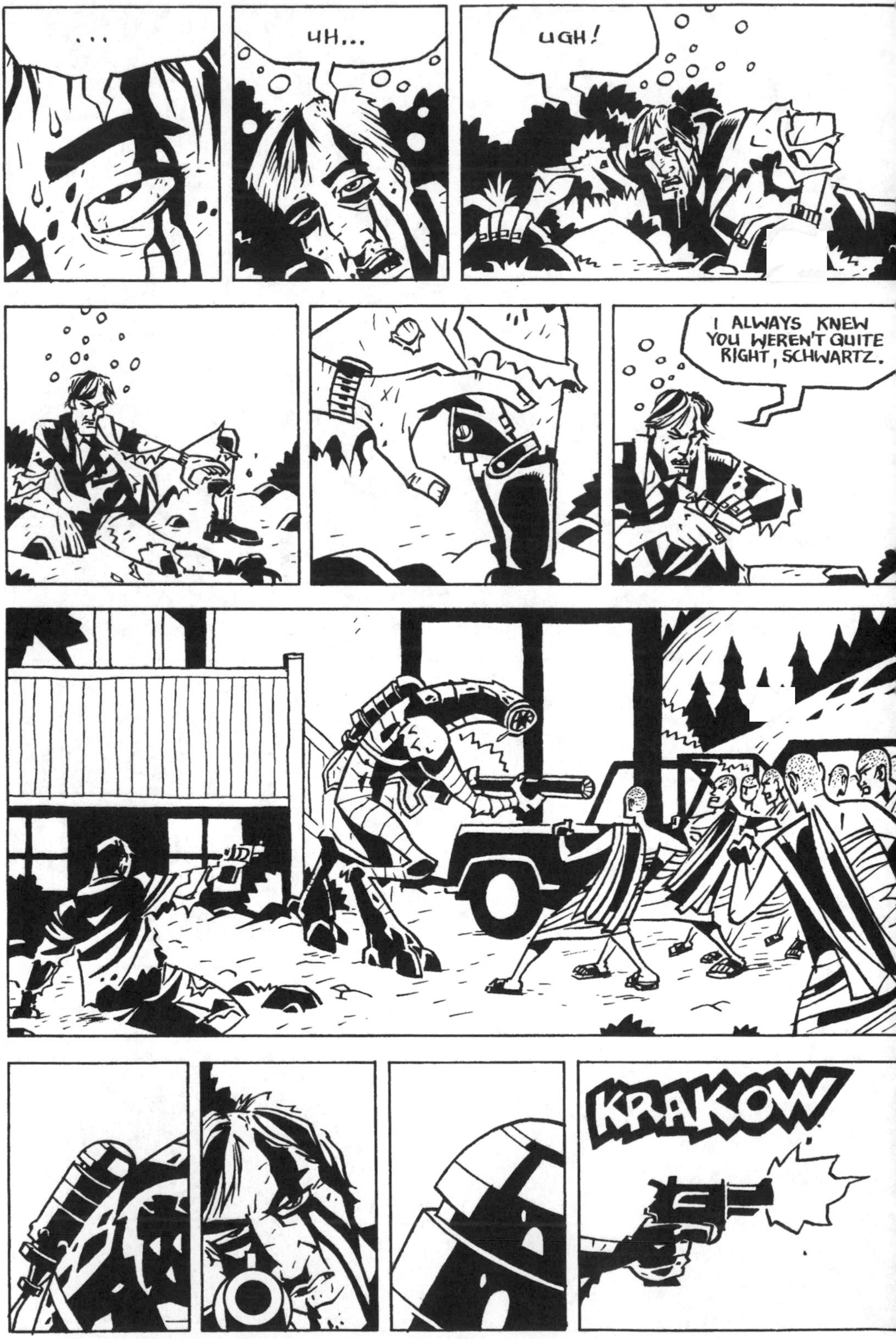
...
UH...
UGH!
I ALWAYS KNEW YOU WEREN'T QUITE RIGHT, SCHWARTZ.
KRAKOW

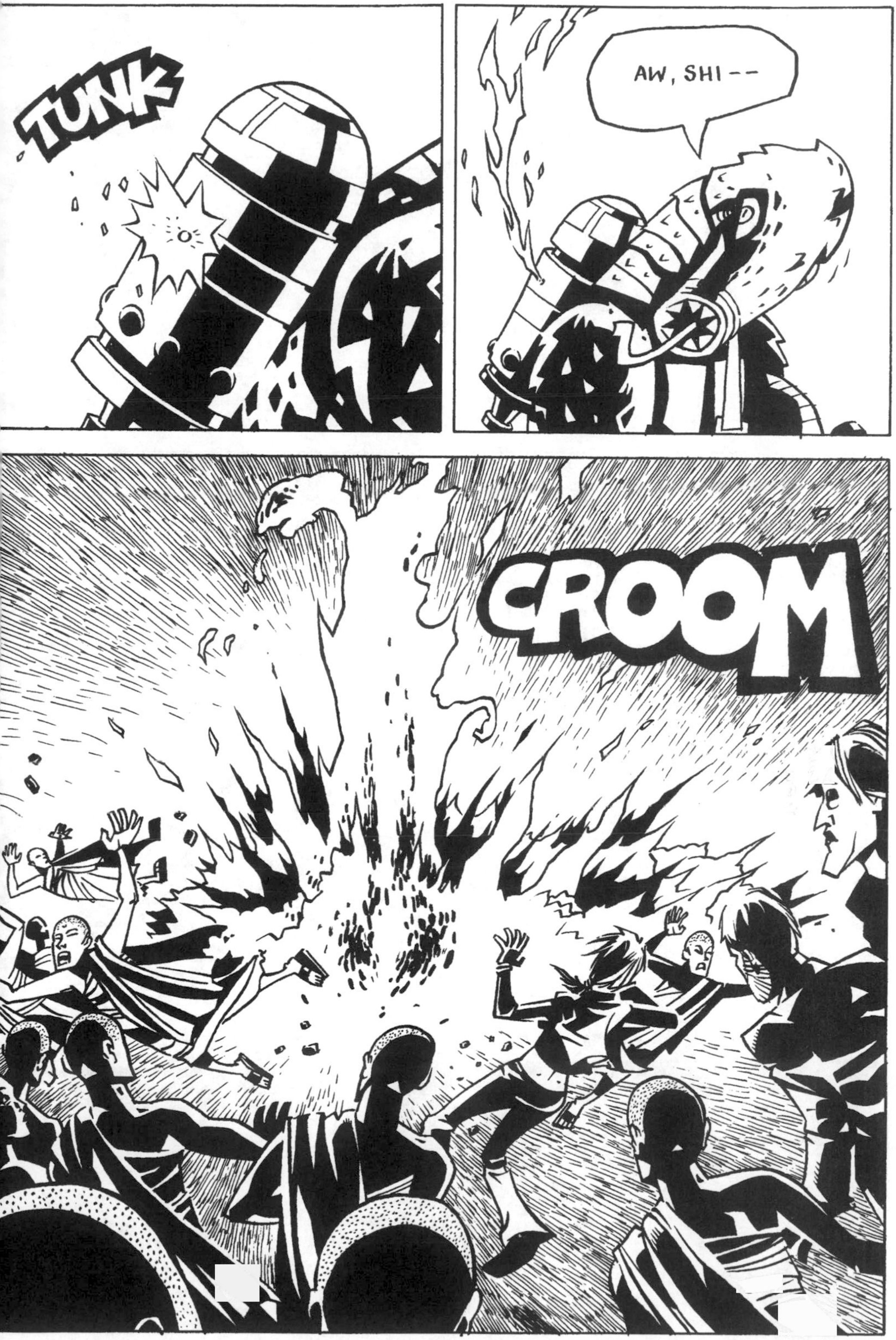
TUNK
AW, SHI--
CROOM

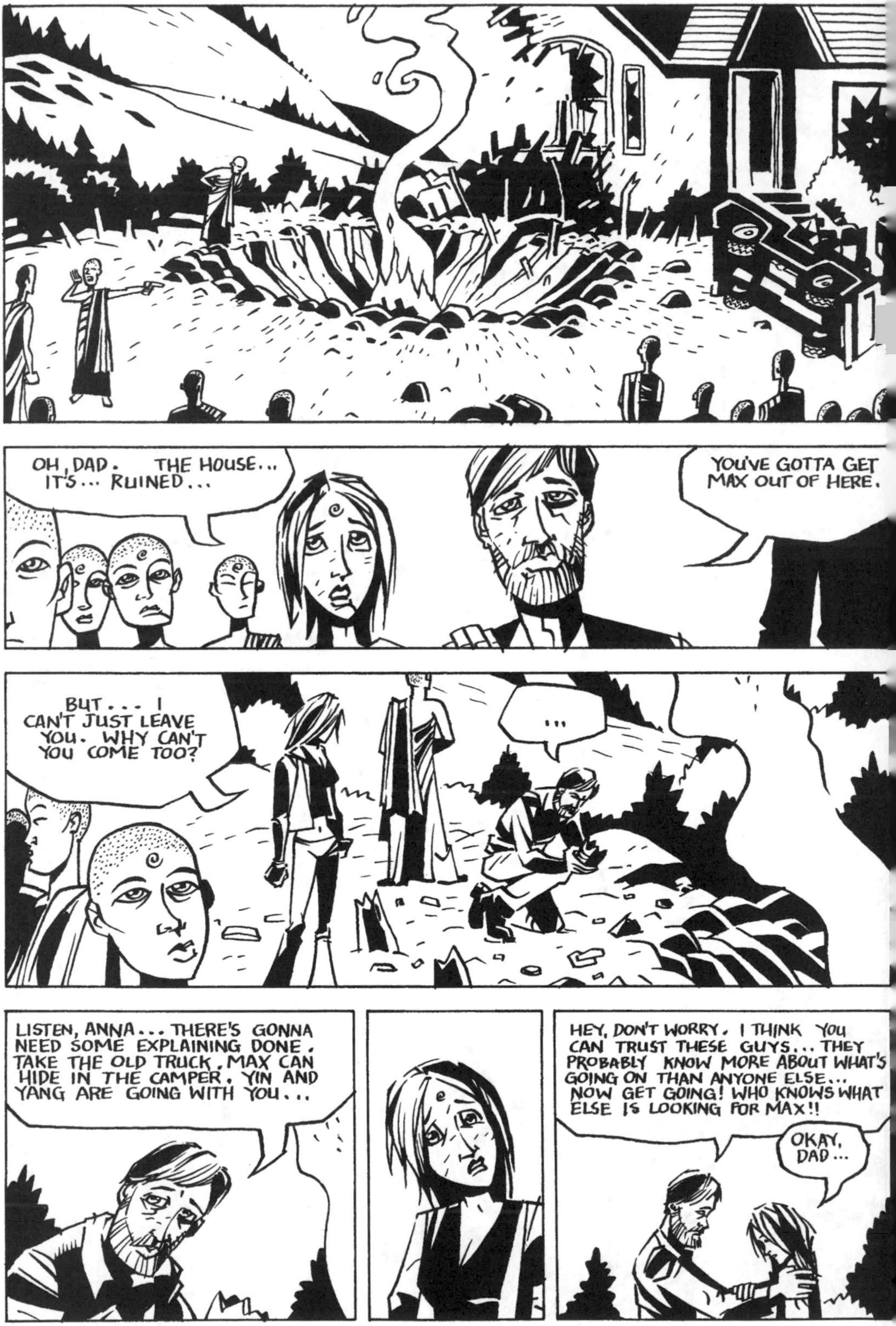
OH, DAD. THE HOUSE... IT'S... RUINED...
YOU'VE GOTTA GET MAX OUT OF HERE.
BUT... I CAN'T JUST LEAVE YOU. WHY CAN'T YOU COME TOO?
...
LISTEN, ANNA... THERE'S GONNA NEED SOME EXPLAINING DONE. TAKE THE OLD TRUCK, MAX CAN HIDE IN THE CAMPER. YIN AND YANG ARE GOING WITH YOU...
HEY, DON'T WORRY. I THINK YOU CAN TRUST THESE GUYS... THEY PROBABLY KNOW MORE ABOUT WHAT'S GOING ON THAN ANYONE ELSE... NOW GET GOING! WHO KNOWS WHAT ELSE IS LOOKING FOR MAX!!
OKAY, DAD...

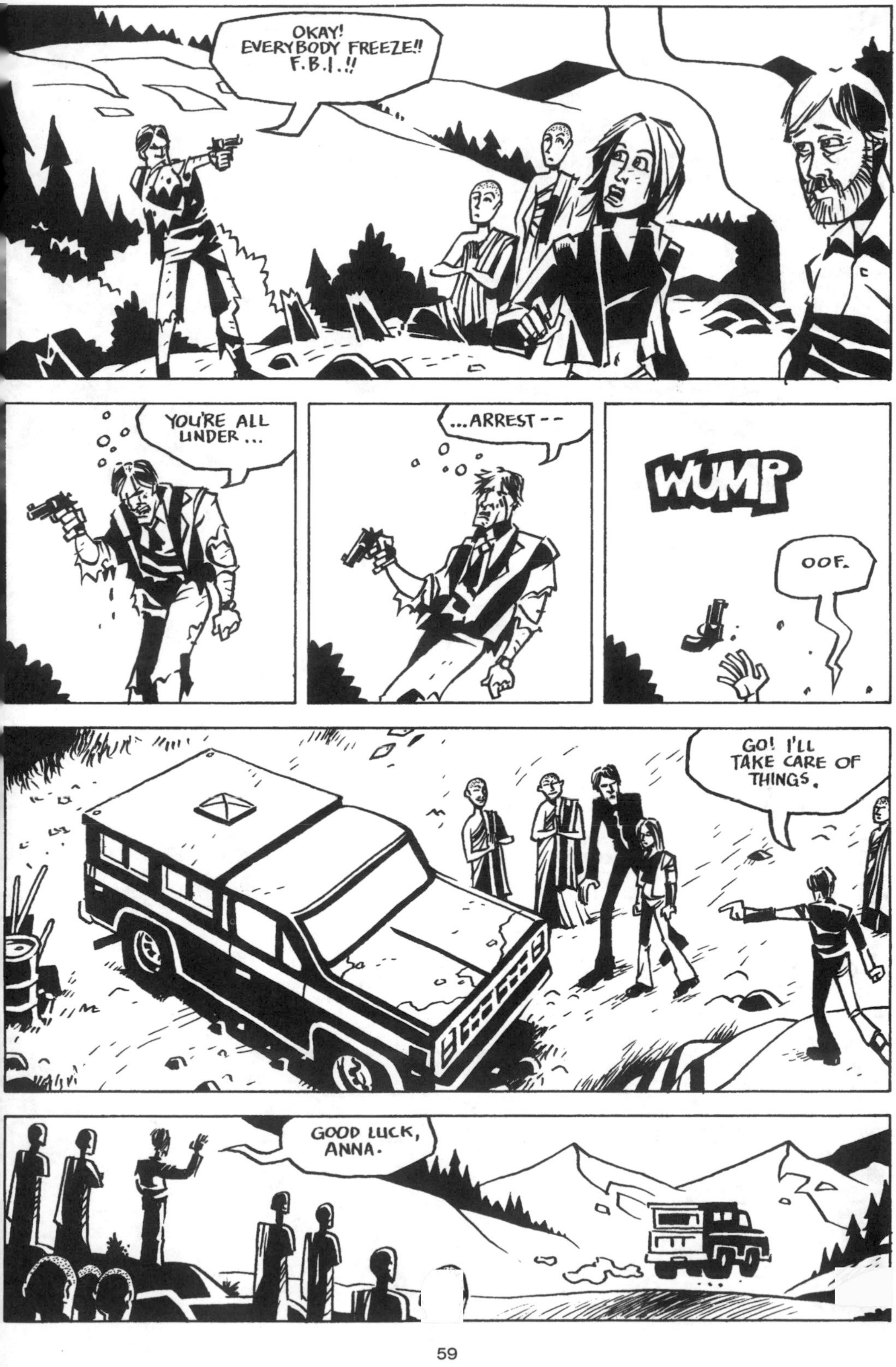
OKAY! EVERYBODY FREEZE!! F.B.I..!!
YOU'RE ALL UNDER...
...ARREST--
WUMP
OOF.
GO! I'LL TAKE CARE OF THINGS.
GOOD LUCK, ANNA.

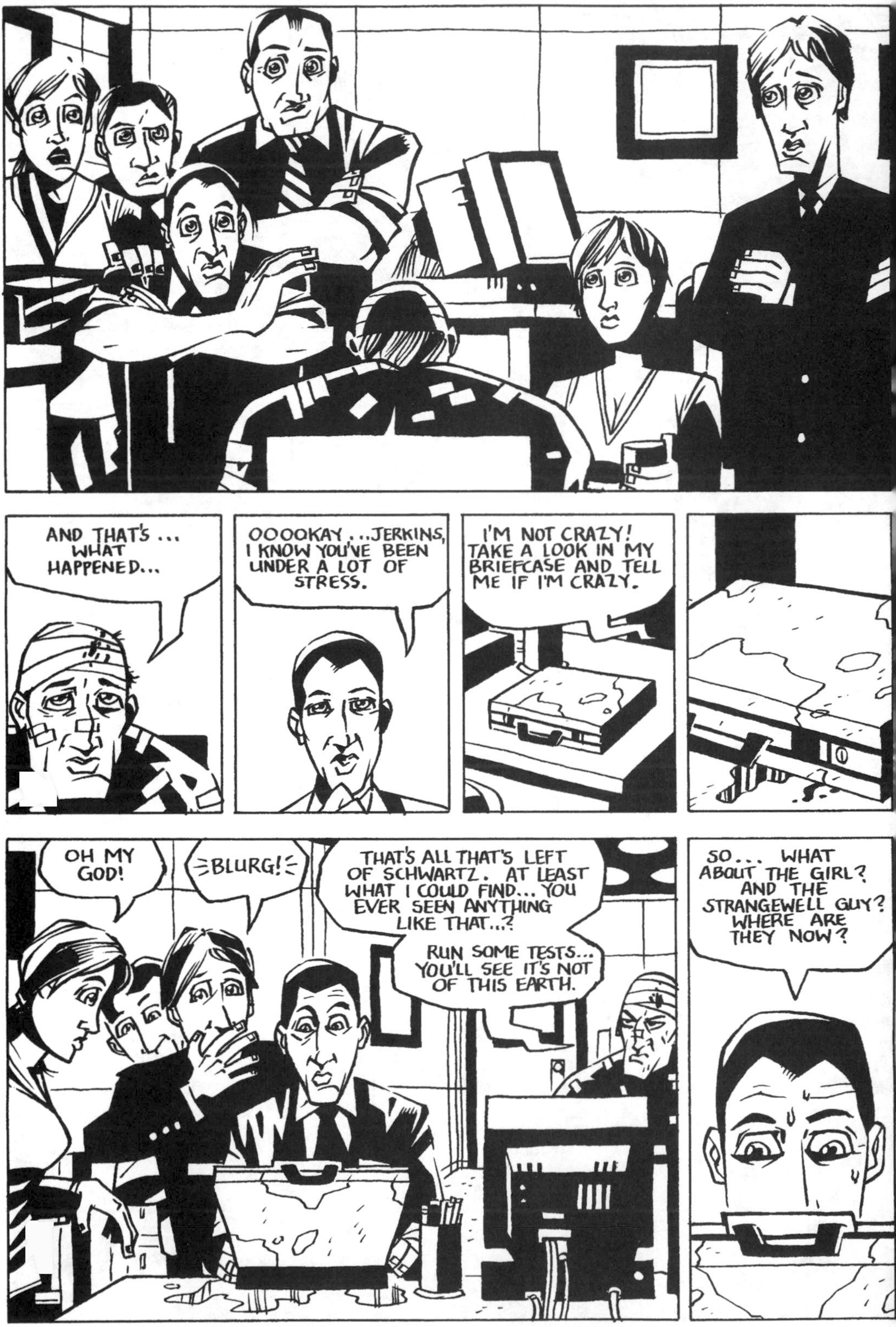
AND THAT'S ... WHAT HAPPENED...
OOOOKAY ...JERKINS, I KNOW YOU'VE BEEN UNDER A LOT OF STRESS.
I'M NOT CRAZY! TAKE A LOOK IN MY BRIEFCASE AND TELL ME IF I'M CRAZY.
OH MY GOD!
BLURG!
THAT'S ALL THAT'S LEFT OF SCHWARTZ. AT LEAST WHAT I COULD FIND... YOU EVER SEEN ANYTHING LIKE THAT...?
RUN SOME TESTS... YOU'LL SEE IT'S NOT OF THIS EARTH.
SO... WHAT ABOUT THE GIRL? AND THE STRANGEWELL GUY? WHERE ARE THEY NOW?

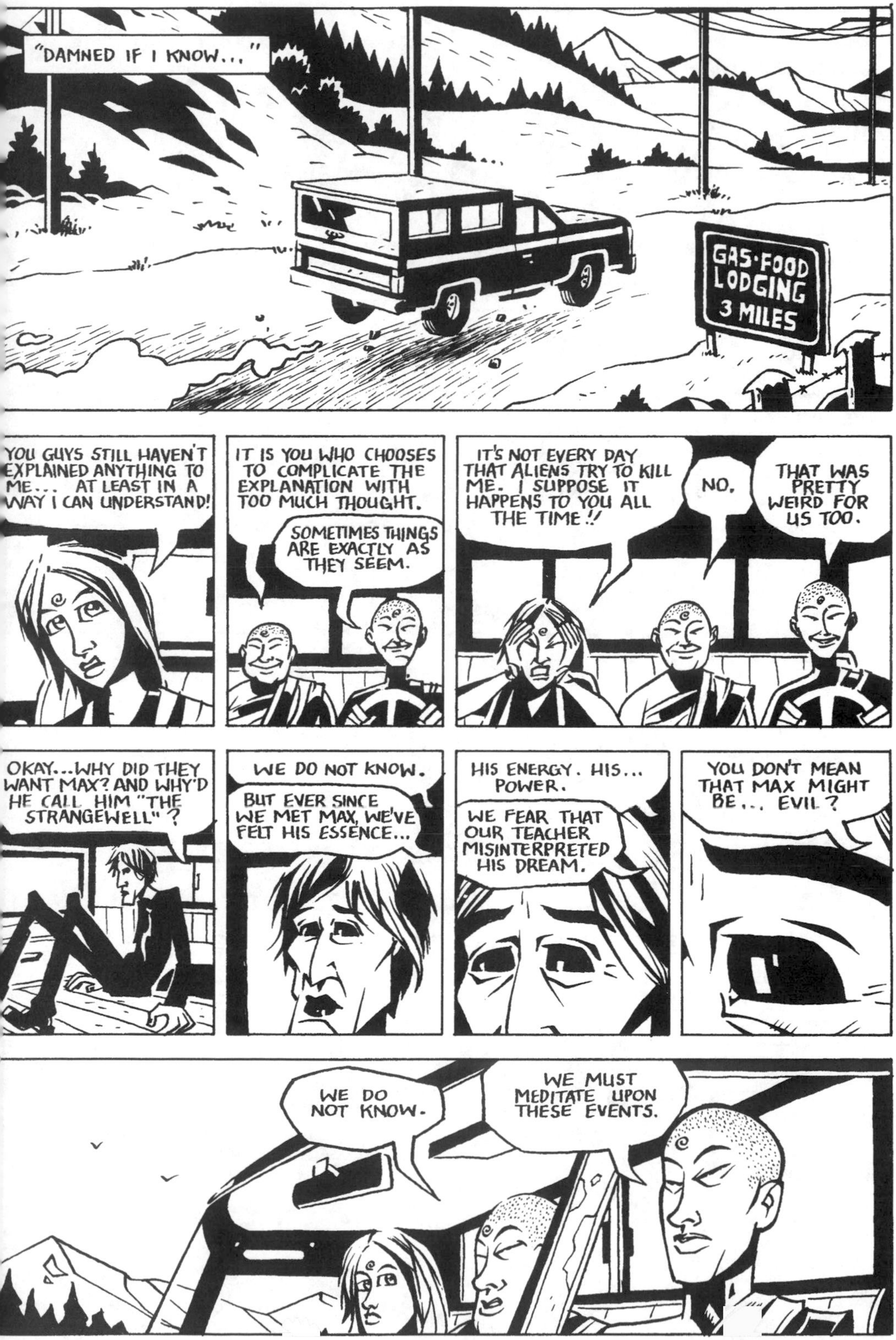
"DAMNED IF I KNOW..."
GAS·FOOD LODGING 3 MILES
YOU GUYS STILL HAVEN'T EXPLAINED ANYTHING TO ME... AT LEAST IN A WAY I CAN UNDERSTAND!
IT IS YOU WHO CHOOSES TO COMPLICATE THE EXPLANATION WITH TOO MUCH THOUGHT.
SOMETIMES THINGS ARE EXACTLY AS THEY SEEM.
IT'S NOT EVERY DAY THAT ALIENS TRY TO KILL ME. I SUPPOSE IT HAPPENS TO YOU ALL THE TIME!!
NO.
THAT WAS PRETTY WEIRD FOR US TOO.
OKAY...WHY DID THEY WANT MAX? AND WHY'D HE CALL HIM "THE STRANGEWELL"?
WE DO NOT KNOW.
BUT EVER SINCE WE MET MAX, WE'VE FELT HIS ESSENCE...
HIS ENERGY. HIS... POWER.
WE FEAR THAT OUR TEACHER MISINTERPRETED HIS DREAM.
YOU DON'T MEAN THAT MAX MIGHT BE... EVIL?
WE DO NOT KNOW.
WE MUST MEDITATE UPON THESE EVENTS.

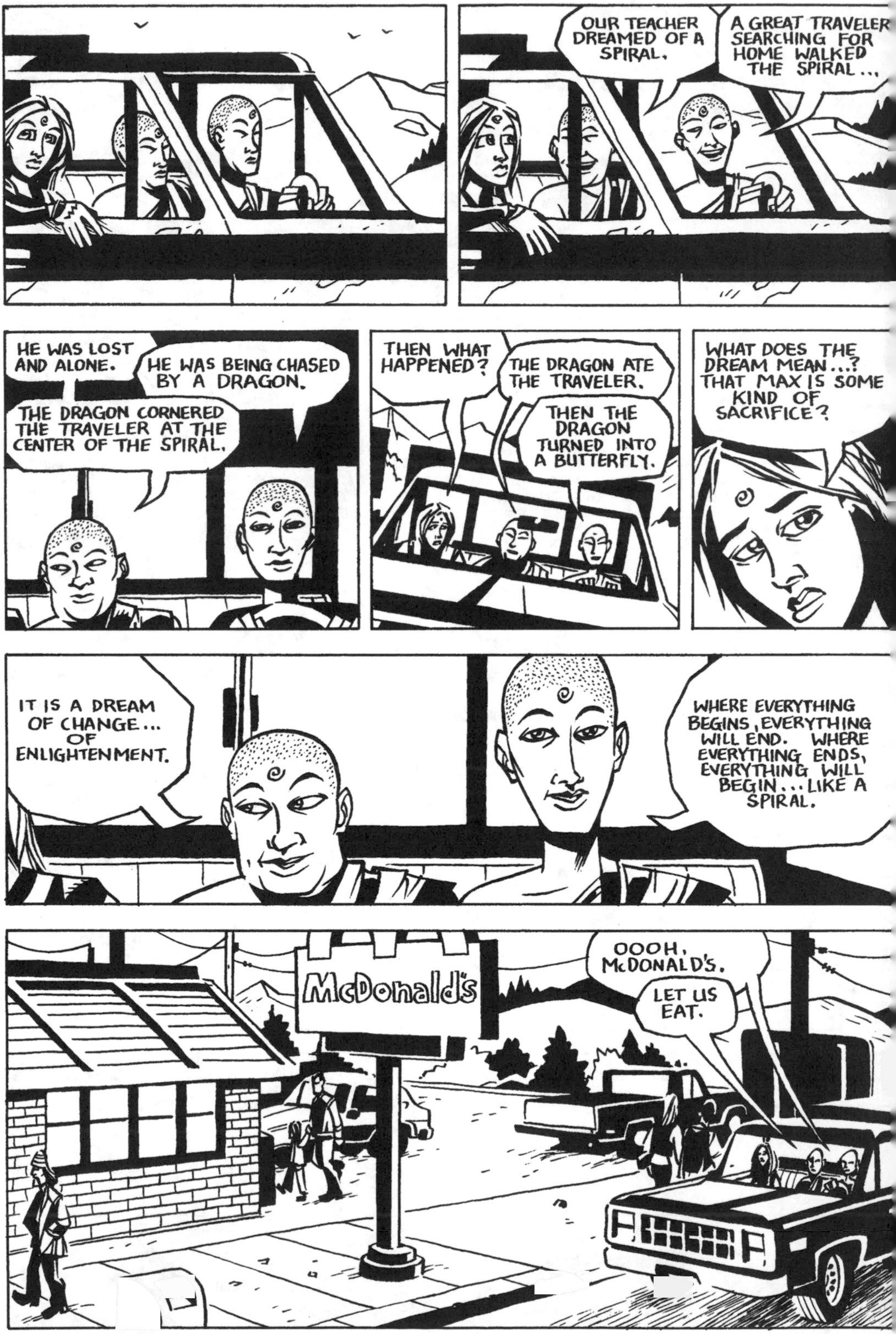
OUR TEACHER DREAMED OF A SPIRAL.
A GREAT TRAVELER SEARCHING FOR HOME WALKED THE SPIRAL...
HE WAS LOST AND ALONE.
HE WAS BEING CHASED BY A DRAGON.
THE DRAGON CORNERED THE TRAVELER AT THE CENTER OF THE SPIRAL.
THEN WHAT HAPPENED?
THE DRAGON ATE THE TRAVELER.
THEN THE DRAGON TURNED INTO A BUTTERFLY.
WHAT DOES THE DREAM MEAN...? THAT MAX IS SOME KIND OF SACRIFICE?
IT IS A DREAM OF CHANGE... OF ENLIGHTENMENT.
WHERE EVERYTHING BEGINS, EVERYTHING WILL END. WHERE EVERYTHING ENDS, EVERYTHING WILL BEGIN... LIKE A SPIRAL.
McDonald's
OOOH, McDONALD'S.
LET US EAT.

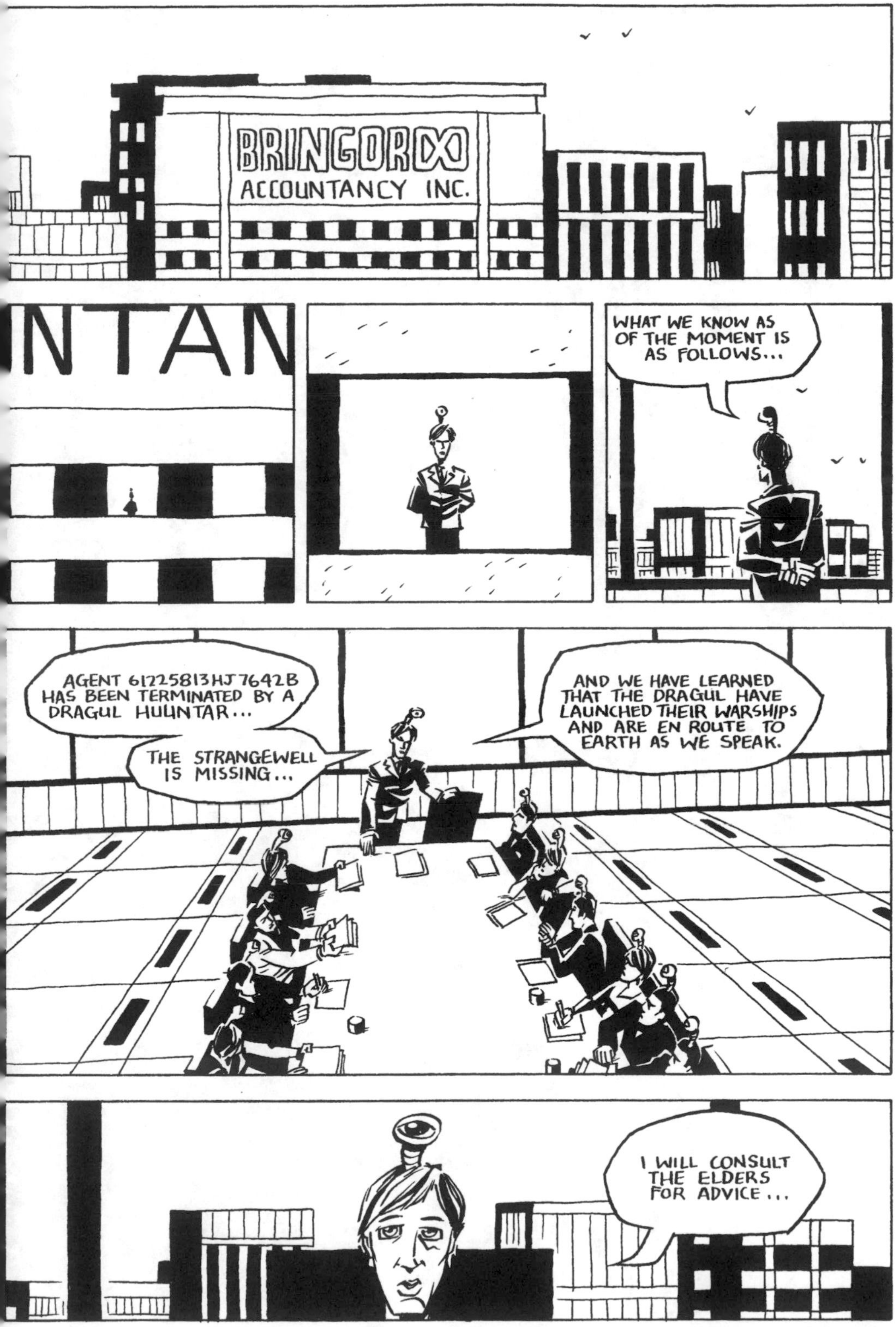
BRINGORD
ACCOUNTANCY INC.
NTAN
WHAT WE KNOW AS OF THE MOMENT IS AS FOLLOWS...
AGENT 61225813HJ7642B HAS BEEN TERMINATED BY A DRAGUL HUUNTAR...
THE STRANGEWELL IS MISSING...
AND WE HAVE LEARNED THAT THE DRAGUL HAVE LAUNCHED THEIR WARSHIPS AND ARE EN ROUTE TO EARTH AS WE SPEAK.
I WILL CONSULT THE ELDERS FOR ADVICE...

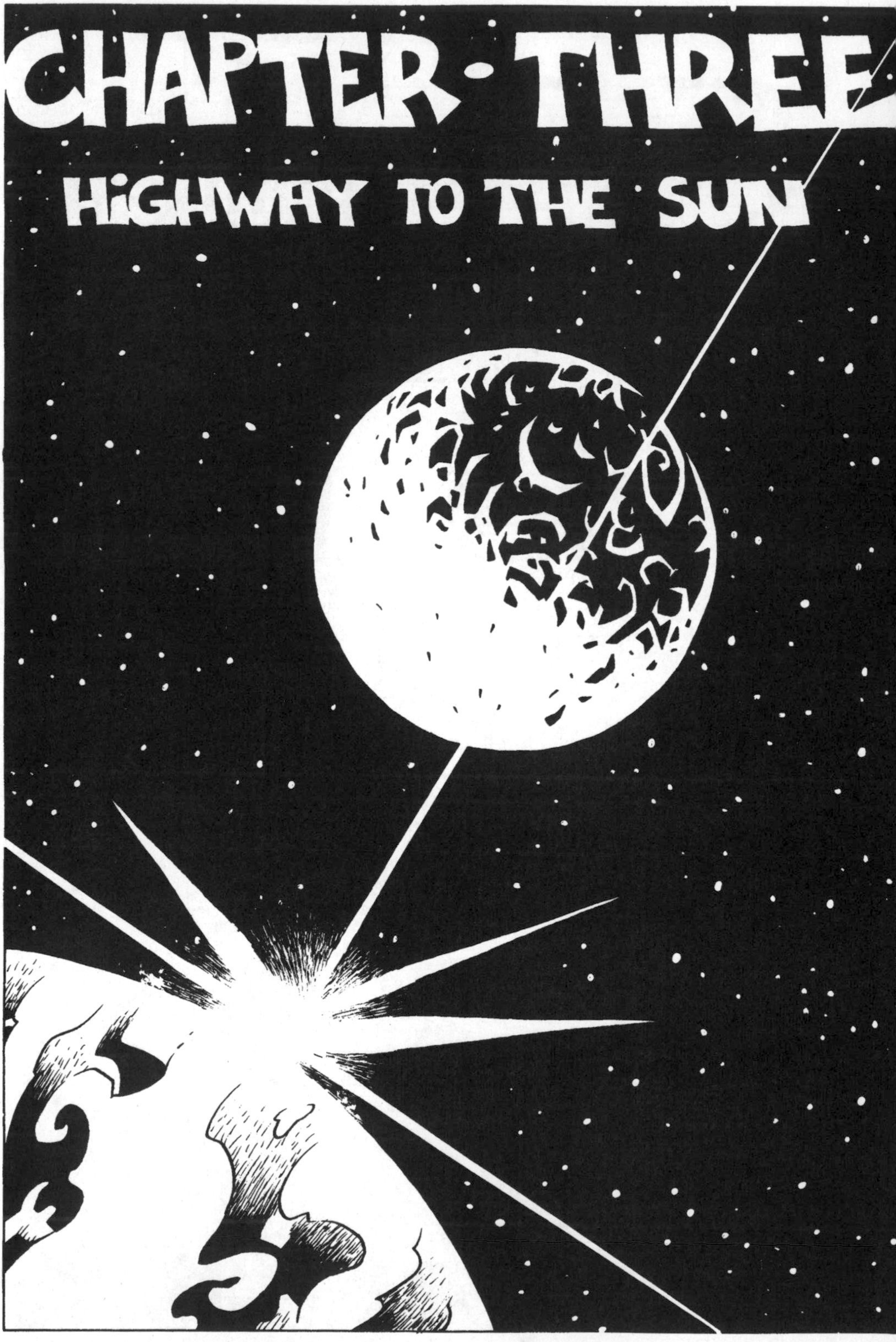
CHAPTER · THREE
HIGHWAY TO THE SUN

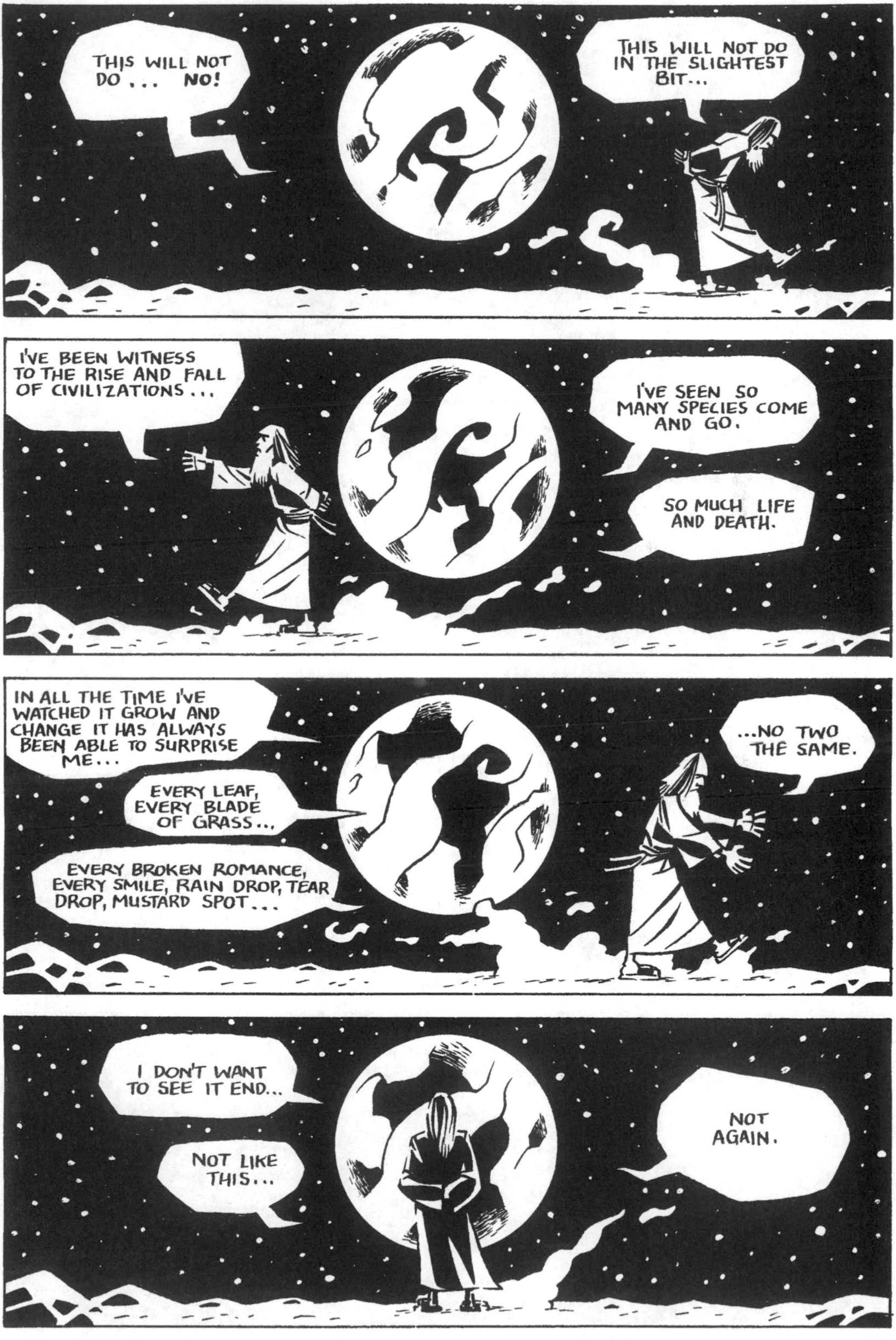
THIS WILL NOT DO... NO!
THIS WILL NOT DO IN THE SLIGHTEST BIT...
I'VE BEEN WITNESS TO THE RISE AND FALL OF CIVILIZATIONS...
I'VE SEEN SO MANY SPECIES COME AND GO.
SO MUCH LIFE AND DEATH.
IN ALL THE TIME I'VE WATCHED IT GROW AND CHANGE IT HAS ALWAYS BEEN ABLE TO SURPRISE ME...
EVERY LEAF, EVERY BLADE OF GRASS...
EVERY BROKEN ROMANCE, EVERY SMILE, RAIN DROP, TEAR DROP, MUSTARD SPOT...
...NO TWO THE SAME.
I DON'T WANT TO SEE IT END...
NOT LIKE THIS...
NOT AGAIN.

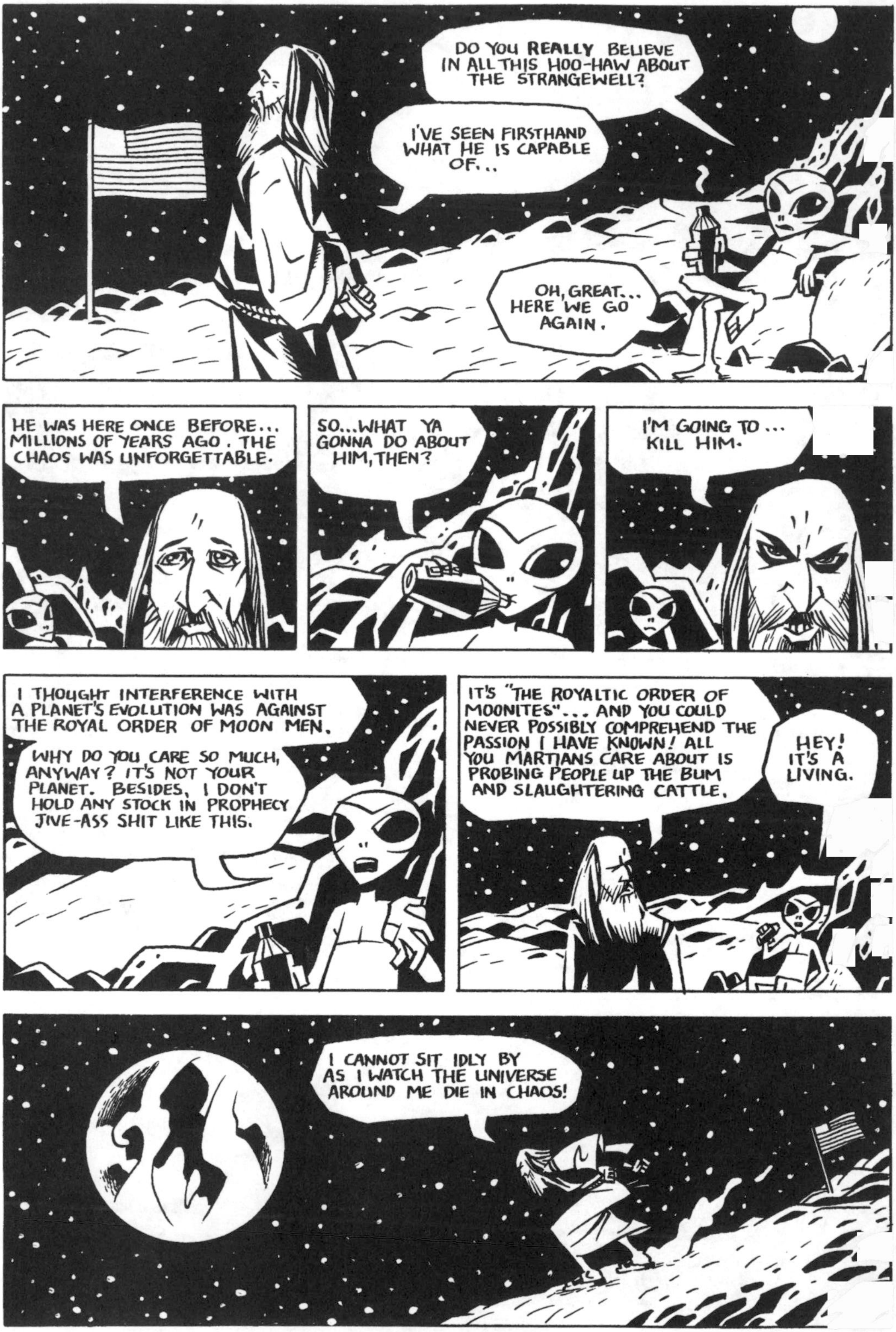

DO YOU REALLY BELIEVE IN ALL THIS HOO-HAW ABOUT THE STRANGEWELL?
I'VE SEEN FIRSTHAND WHAT HE IS CAPABLE OF...
OH, GREAT... HERE WE GO AGAIN.
HE WAS HERE ONCE BEFORE... MILLIONS OF YEARS AGO. THE CHAOS WAS UNFORGETTABLE.
SO...WHAT YA GONNA DO ABOUT HIM, THEN?
I'M GOING TO... KILL HIM.
I THOUGHT INTERFERENCE WITH A PLANET'S EVOLUTION WAS AGAINST THE ROYAL ORDER OF MOON MEN.
WHY DO YOU CARE SO MUCH, ANYWAY? IT'S NOT YOUR PLANET. BESIDES, I DON'T HOLD ANY STOCK IN PROPHECY JIVE-ASS SHIT LIKE THIS.
IT'S "THE ROYALTIC ORDER OF MOONITES"... AND YOU COULD NEVER POSSIBLY COMPREHEND THE PASSION I HAVE KNOWN! ALL YOU MARTIANS CARE ABOUT IS PROBING PEOPLE UP THE BUM AND SLAUGHTERING CATTLE.
HEY! IT'S A LIVING.
I CANNOT SIT IDLY BY AS I WATCH THE UNIVERSE AROUND ME DIE IN CHAOS!

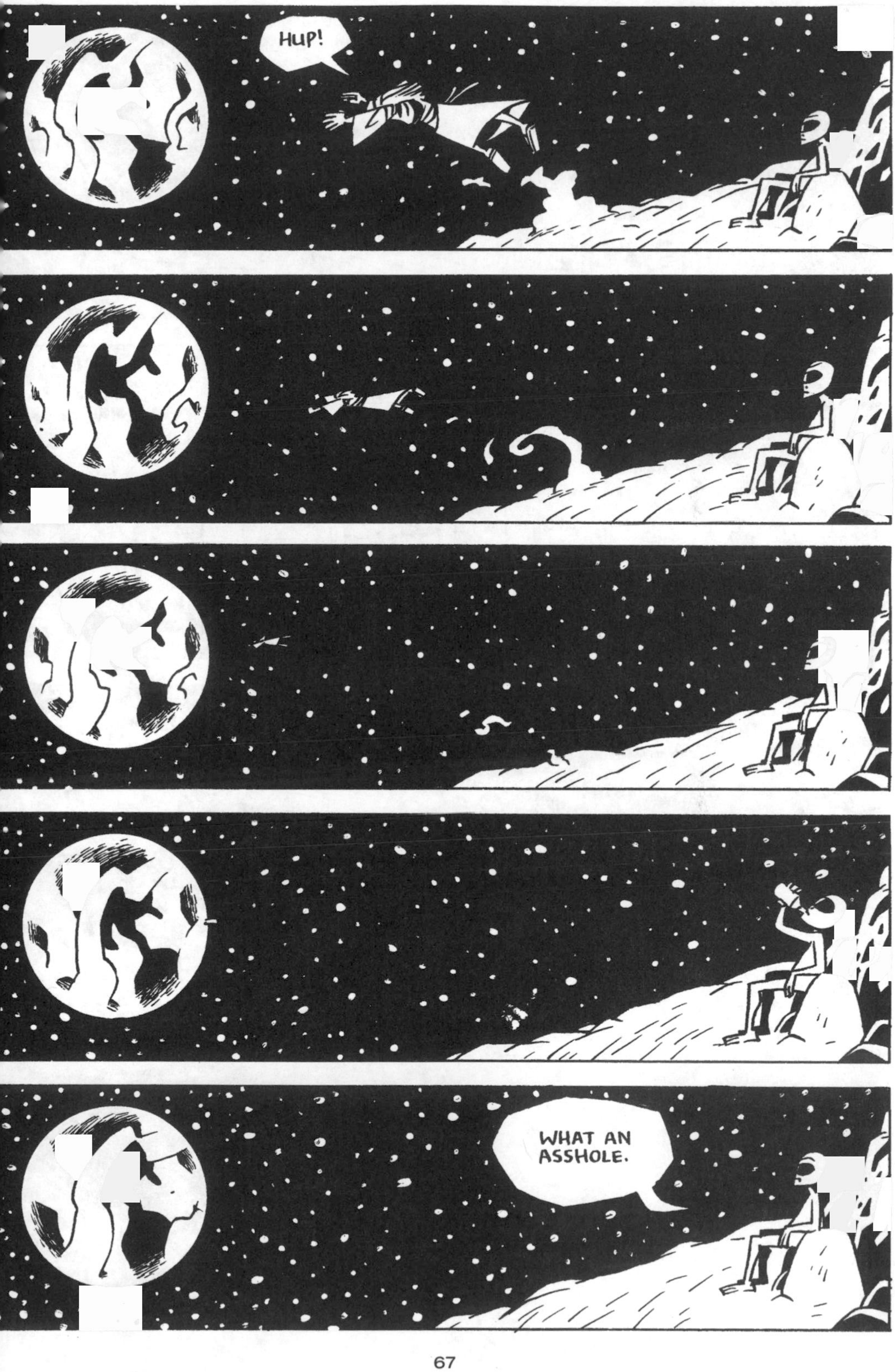
HUP!
WHAT AN ASSHOLE.

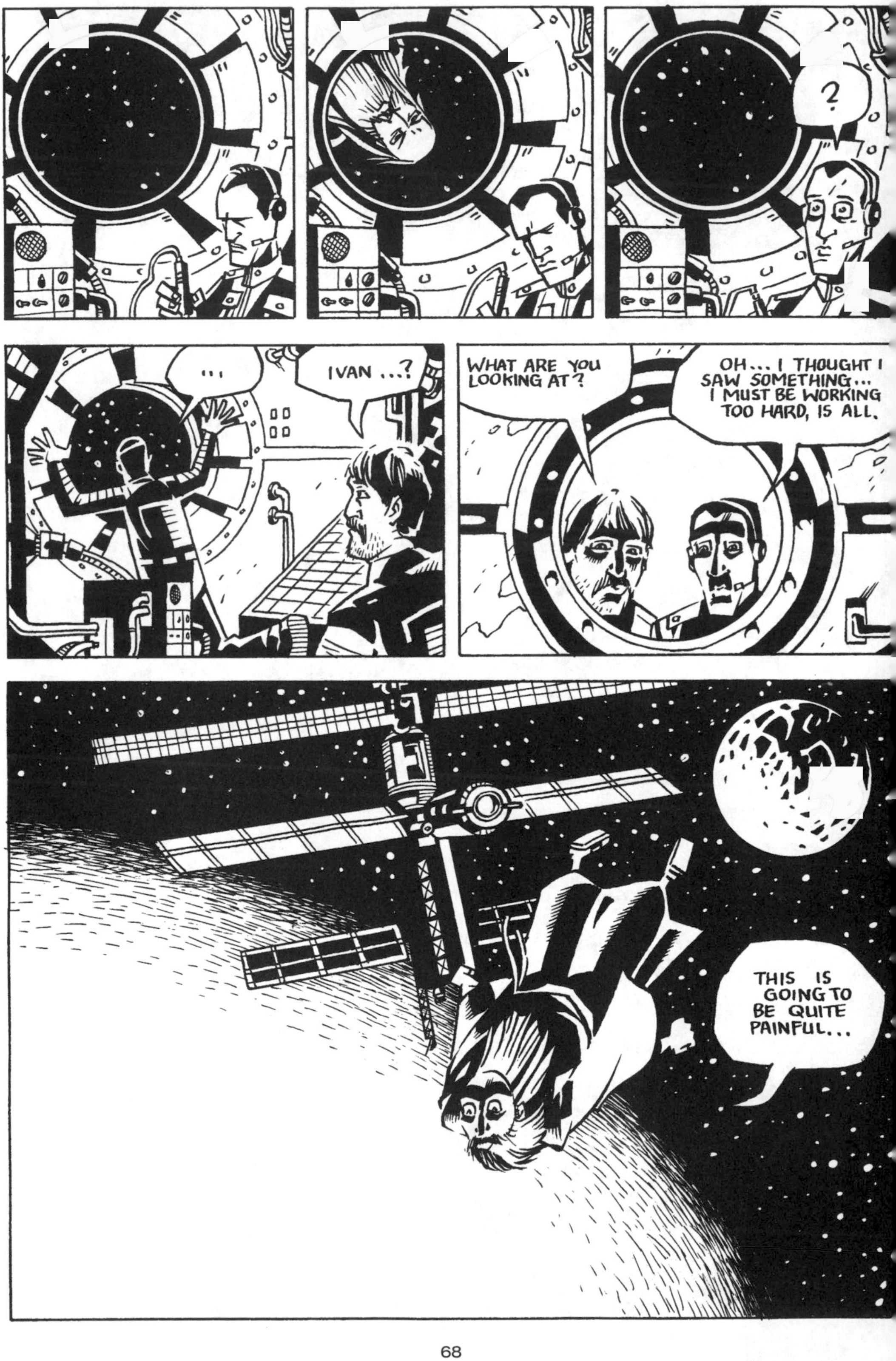
?
...
IVAN ...?
WHAT ARE YOU LOOKING AT?
OH... I THOUGHT I SAW SOMETHING... I MUST BE WORKING TOO HARD, IS ALL.
THIS IS GOING TO BE QUITE PAINFUL...

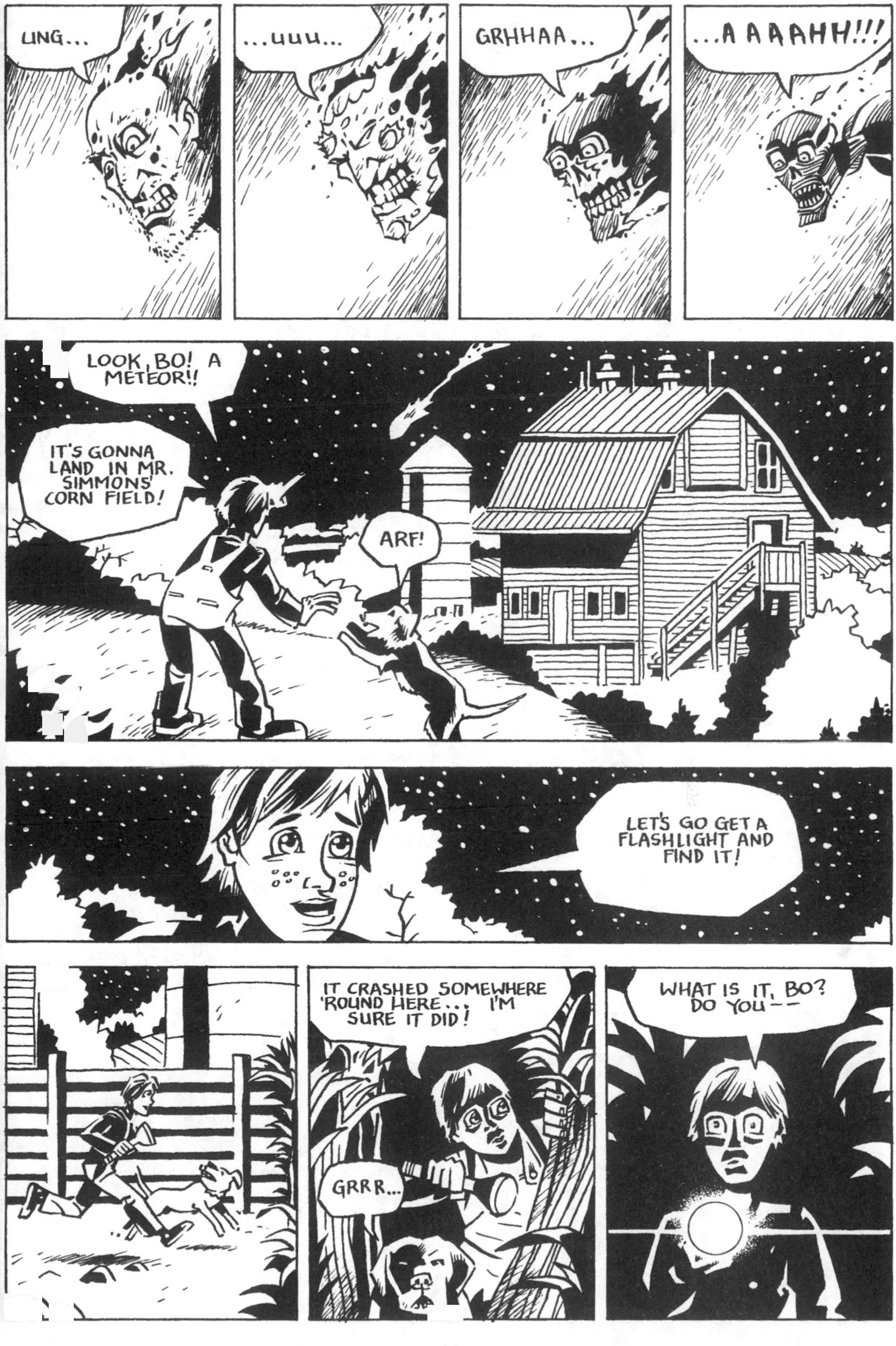
UNG...
...uuu...
GRHHAA...
...AAAAHH!!!
LOOK, BO! A METEOR!!
IT'S GONNA LAND IN MR. SIMMONS' CORN FIELD!
ARF!
LET'S GO GET A FLASHLIGHT AND FIND IT!
IT CRASHED SOMEWHERE 'ROUND HERE... I'M SURE IT DID!
GRRR...
WHAT IS IT, BO? DO YOU--

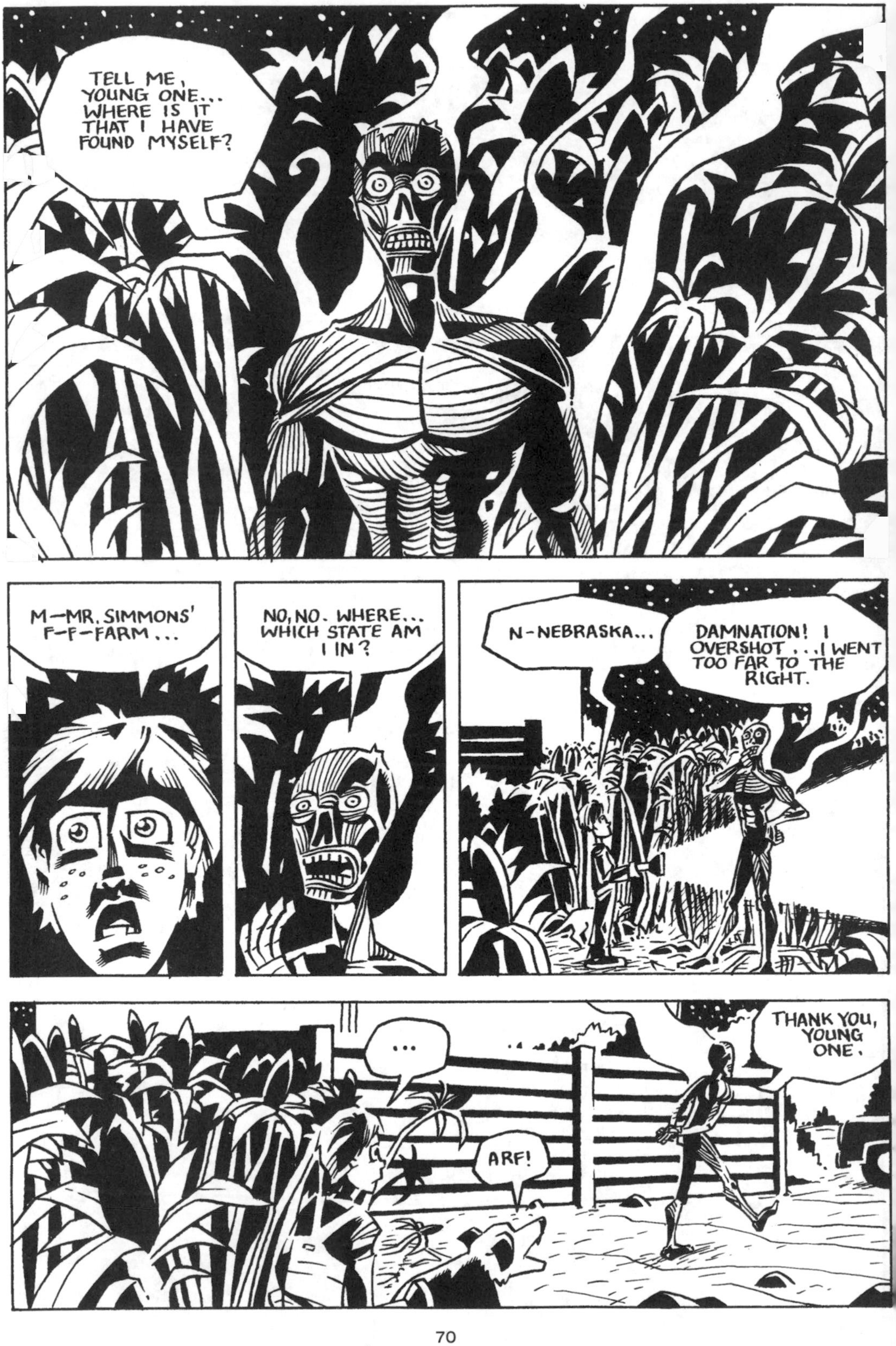
TELL ME, YOUNG ONE... WHERE IS IT THAT I HAVE FOUND MYSELF?
M—MR. SIMMONS' F-F-FARM...
NO, NO. WHERE... WHICH STATE AM I IN?
N-NEBRASKA...
DAMNATION! I OVERSHOT ...I WENT TOO FAR TO THE RIGHT.
...
ARF!
THANK YOU, YOUNG ONE.

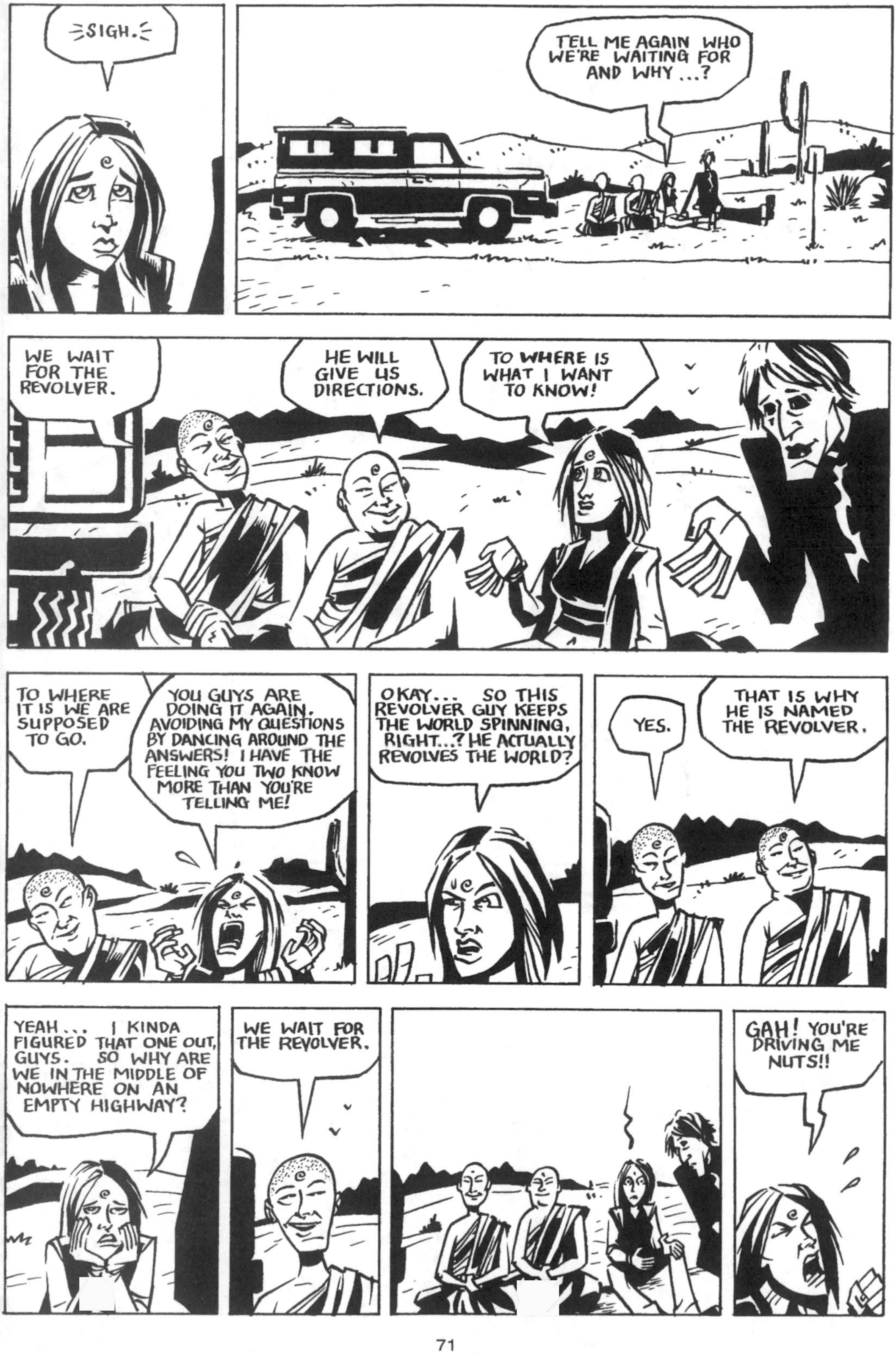
SIGH.
TELL ME AGAIN WHO WE'RE WAITING FOR AND WHY...?
WE WAIT FOR THE REVOLVER.
HE WILL GIVE US DIRECTIONS.
TO WHERE IS WHAT I WANT TO KNOW!
TO WHERE IT IS WE ARE SUPPOSED TO GO.
YOU GUYS ARE DOING IT AGAIN. AVOIDING MY QUESTIONS BY DANCING AROUND THE ANSWERS! I HAVE THE FEELING YOU TWO KNOW MORE THAN YOU'RE TELLING ME!
OKAY... SO THIS REVOLVER GUY KEEPS THE WORLD SPINNING, RIGHT...? HE ACTUALLY REVOLVES THE WORLD?
YES.
THAT IS WHY HE IS NAMED THE REVOLVER.
YEAH... I KINDA FIGURED THAT ONE OUT, GUYS. SO WHY ARE WE IN THE MIDDLE OF NOWHERE ON AN EMPTY HIGHWAY?
WE WAIT FOR THE REVOLVER.
GAH! YOU'RE DRIVING ME NUTS!!

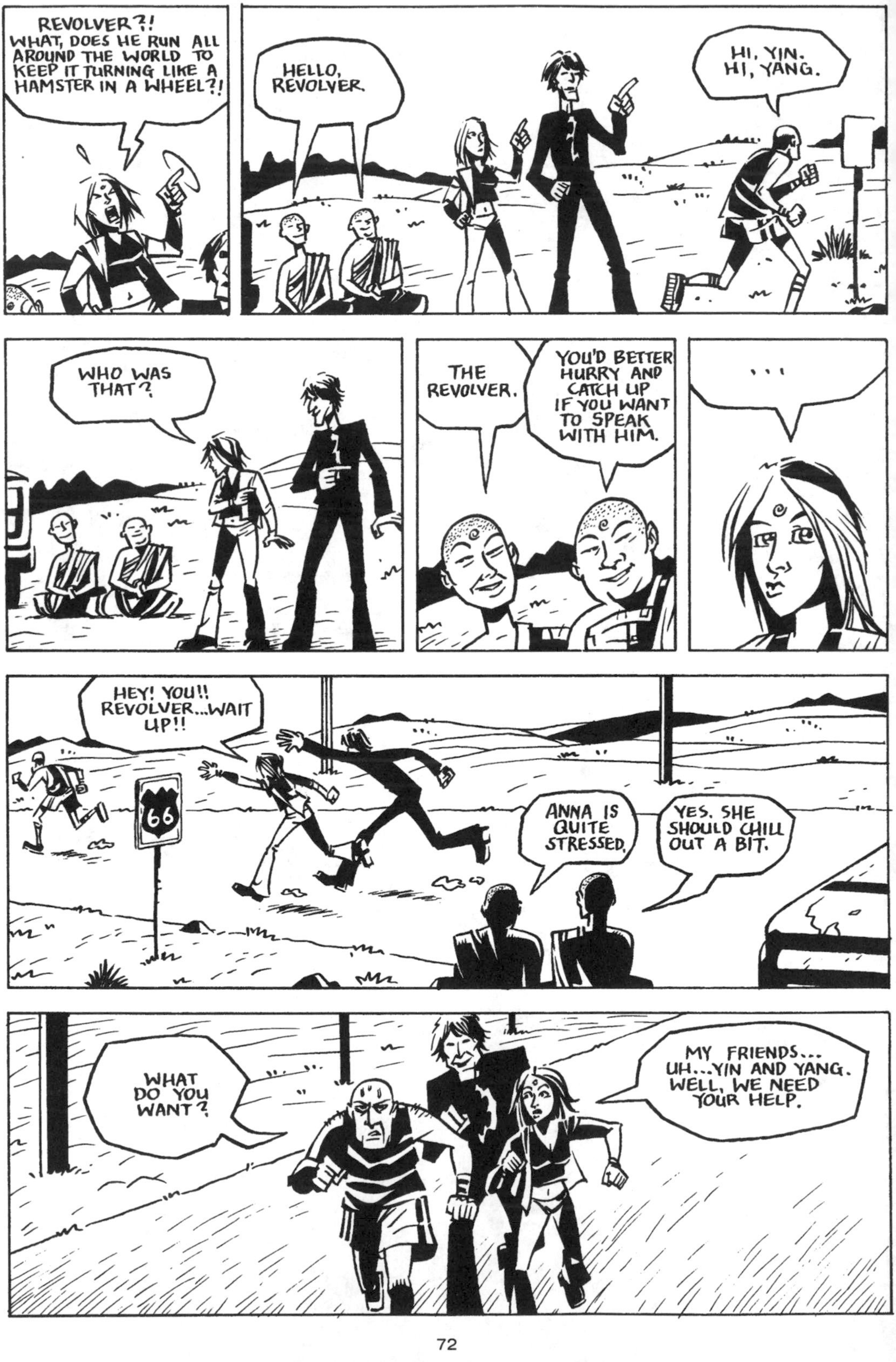
REVOLVER?! WHAT, DOES HE RUN ALL AROUND THE WORLD TO KEEP IT TURNING LIKE A HAMSTER IN A WHEEL?!
HELLO, REVOLVER.
HI, YIN. HI, YANG.
WHO WAS THAT?
THE REVOLVER.
YOU'D BETTER HURRY AND CATCH UP IF YOU WANT TO SPEAK WITH HIM.
...
HEY! YOU!! REVOLVER...WAIT UP!!
66
ANNA IS QUITE STRESSED.
YES. SHE SHOULD CHILL OUT A BIT.
WHAT DO YOU WANT?
MY FRIENDS... UH...YIN AND YANG. WELL, WE NEED YOUR HELP.

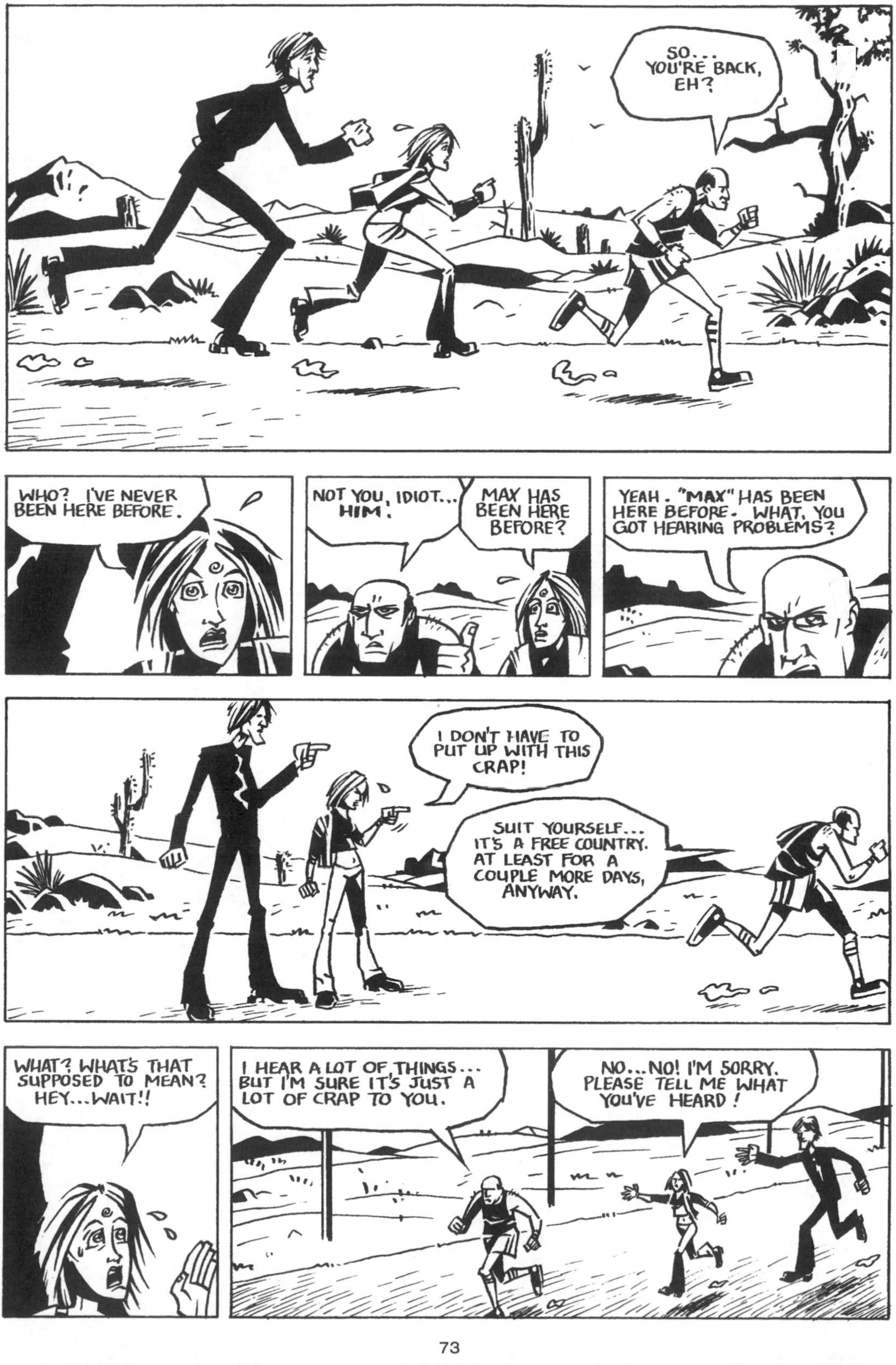
SO... YOU'RE BACK, EH?
WHO? I'VE NEVER BEEN HERE BEFORE.
NOT YOU, IDIOT... HIM.
MAX HAS BEEN HERE BEFORE?
YEAH. "MAX" HAS BEEN HERE BEFORE. WHAT, YOU GOT HEARING PROBLEMS?
I DON'T HAVE TO PUT UP WITH THIS CRAP!
SUIT YOURSELF... IT'S A FREE COUNTRY. AT LEAST FOR A COUPLE MORE DAYS, ANYWAY.
WHAT? WHAT'S THAT SUPPOSED TO MEAN? HEY...WAIT!!
I HEAR A LOT OF THINGS... BUT I'M SURE IT'S JUST A LOT OF CRAP TO YOU.
NO...NO! I'M SORRY. PLEASE TELL ME WHAT YOU'VE HEARD!

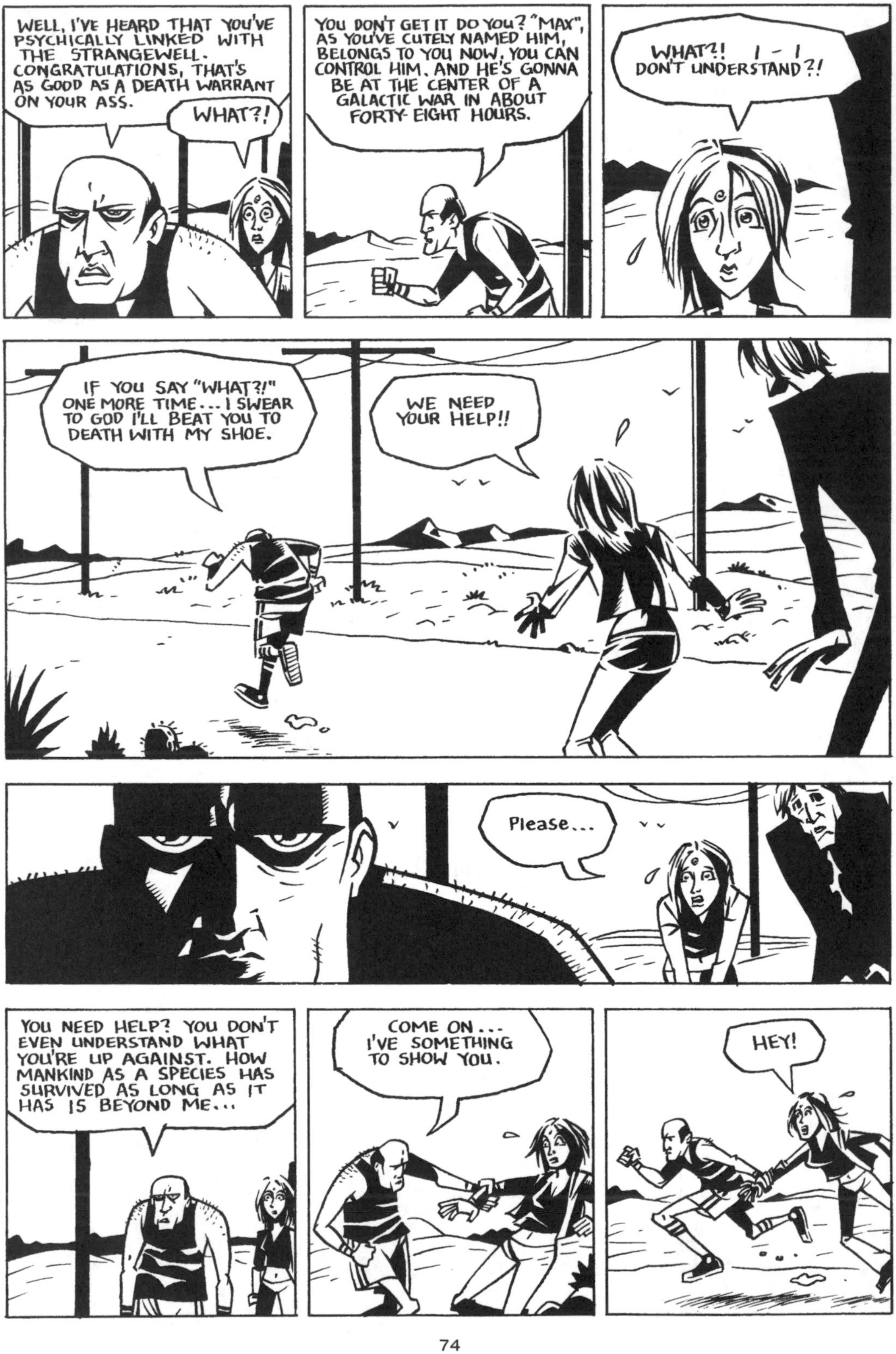
WELL, I'VE HEARD THAT YOU'VE PSYCHICALLY LINKED WITH THE STRANGEWELL. CONGRATULATIONS, THAT'S AS GOOD AS A DEATH WARRANT ON YOUR ASS.
WHAT?!
YOU DON'T GET IT DO YOU? "MAX", AS YOU'VE CUTELY NAMED HIM, BELONGS TO YOU NOW. YOU CAN CONTROL HIM. AND HE'S GONNA BE AT THE CENTER OF A GALACTIC WAR IN ABOUT FORTY-EIGHT HOURS.
WHAT?! I - I DON'T UNDERSTAND?!
IF YOU SAY "WHAT?!" ONE MORE TIME... I SWEAR TO GOD I'LL BEAT YOU TO DEATH WITH MY SHOE.
WE NEED YOUR HELP!!
Please...
YOU NEED HELP? YOU DON'T EVEN UNDERSTAND WHAT YOU'RE UP AGAINST. HOW MANKIND AS A SPECIES HAS SURVIVED AS LONG AS IT HAS IS BEYOND ME...
COME ON... I'VE SOMETHING TO SHOW YOU.
HEY!

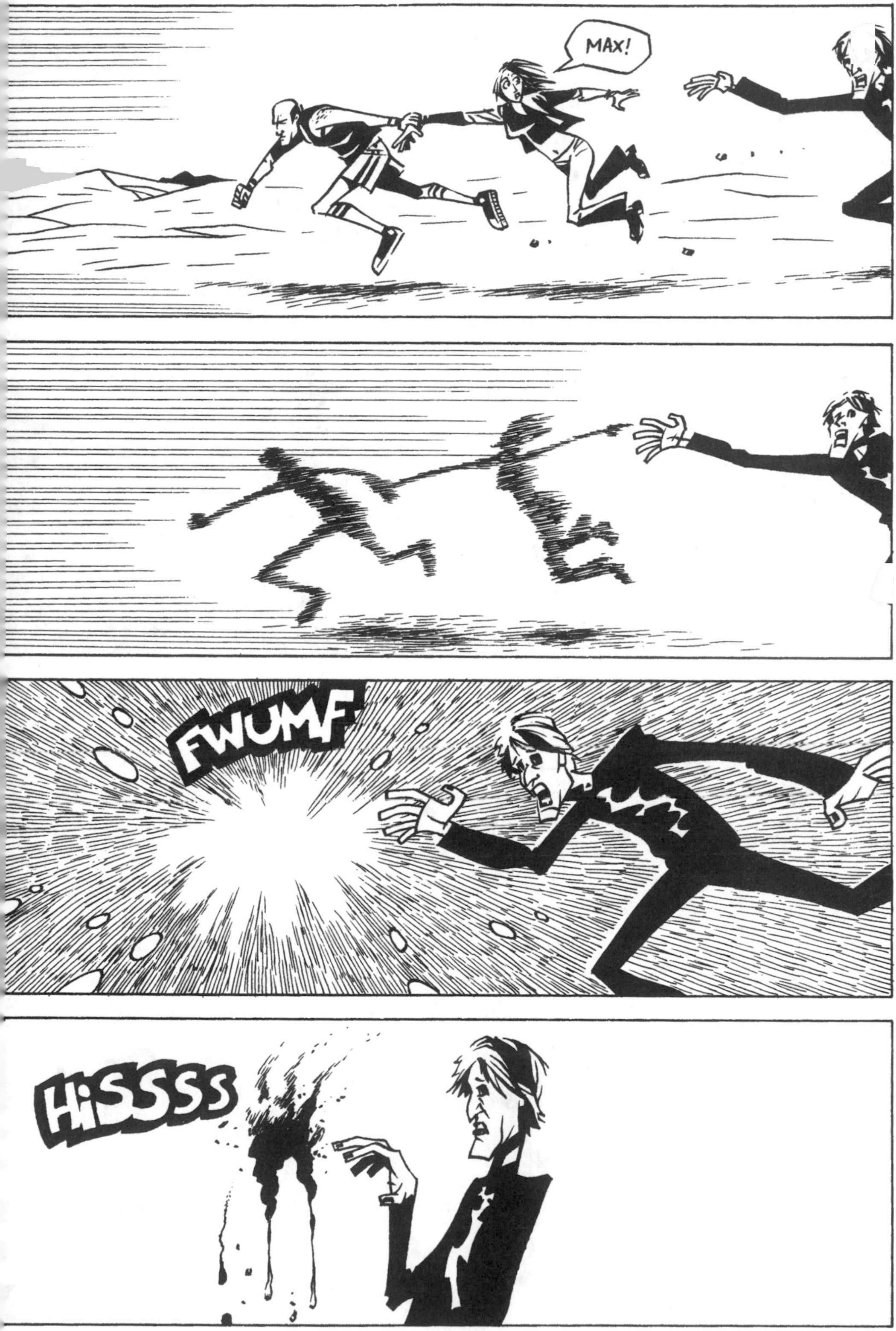
MAX!
FWUMF
HiSSSS

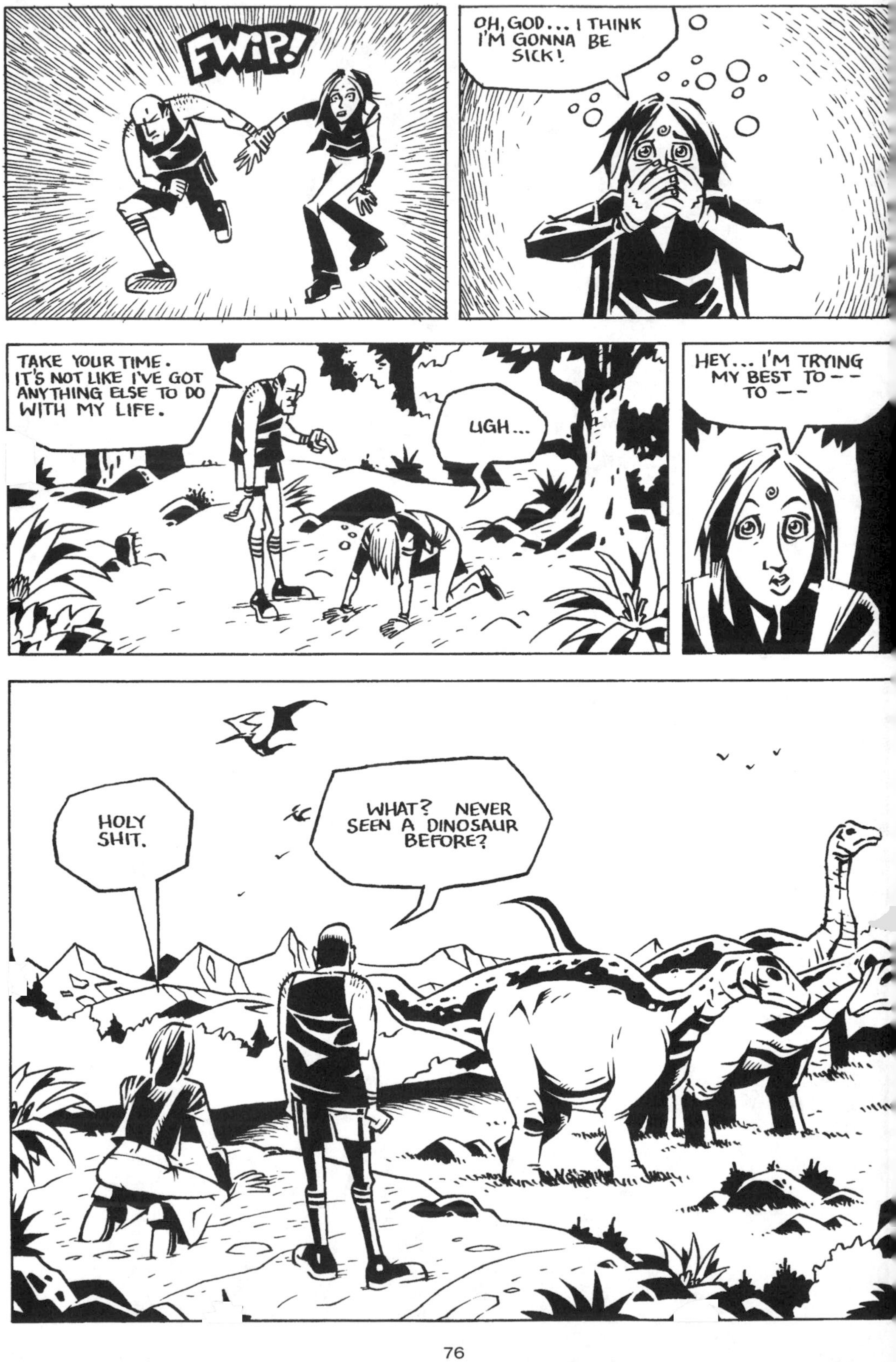
FWIP!
OH, GOD... I THINK I'M GONNA BE SICK!
TAKE YOUR TIME. IT'S NOT LIKE I'VE GOT ANYTHING ELSE TO DO WITH MY LIFE.
UGH...
HEY... I'M TRYING MY BEST TO -- TO --
HOLY SHIT.
WHAT? NEVER SEEN A DINOSAUR BEFORE?

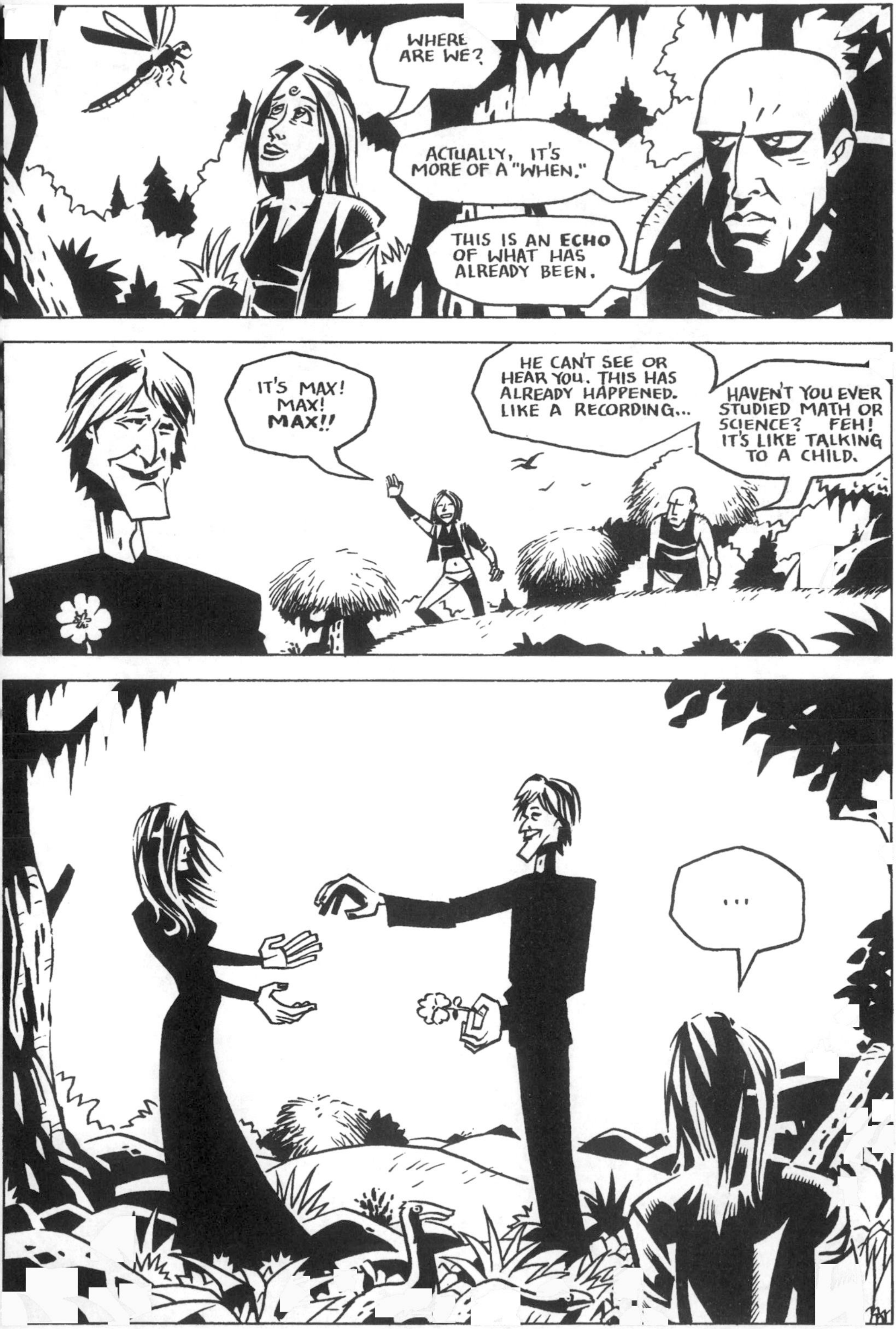
WHERE ARE WE?
ACTUALLY, IT'S MORE OF A "WHEN."
THIS IS AN ECHO OF WHAT HAS ALREADY BEEN.
IT'S MAX! MAX! MAX!!
HE CAN'T SEE OR HEAR YOU. THIS HAS ALREADY HAPPENED. LIKE A RECORDING...
HAVEN'T YOU EVER STUDIED MATH OR SCIENCE? FEH! IT'S LIKE TALKING TO A CHILD.
...

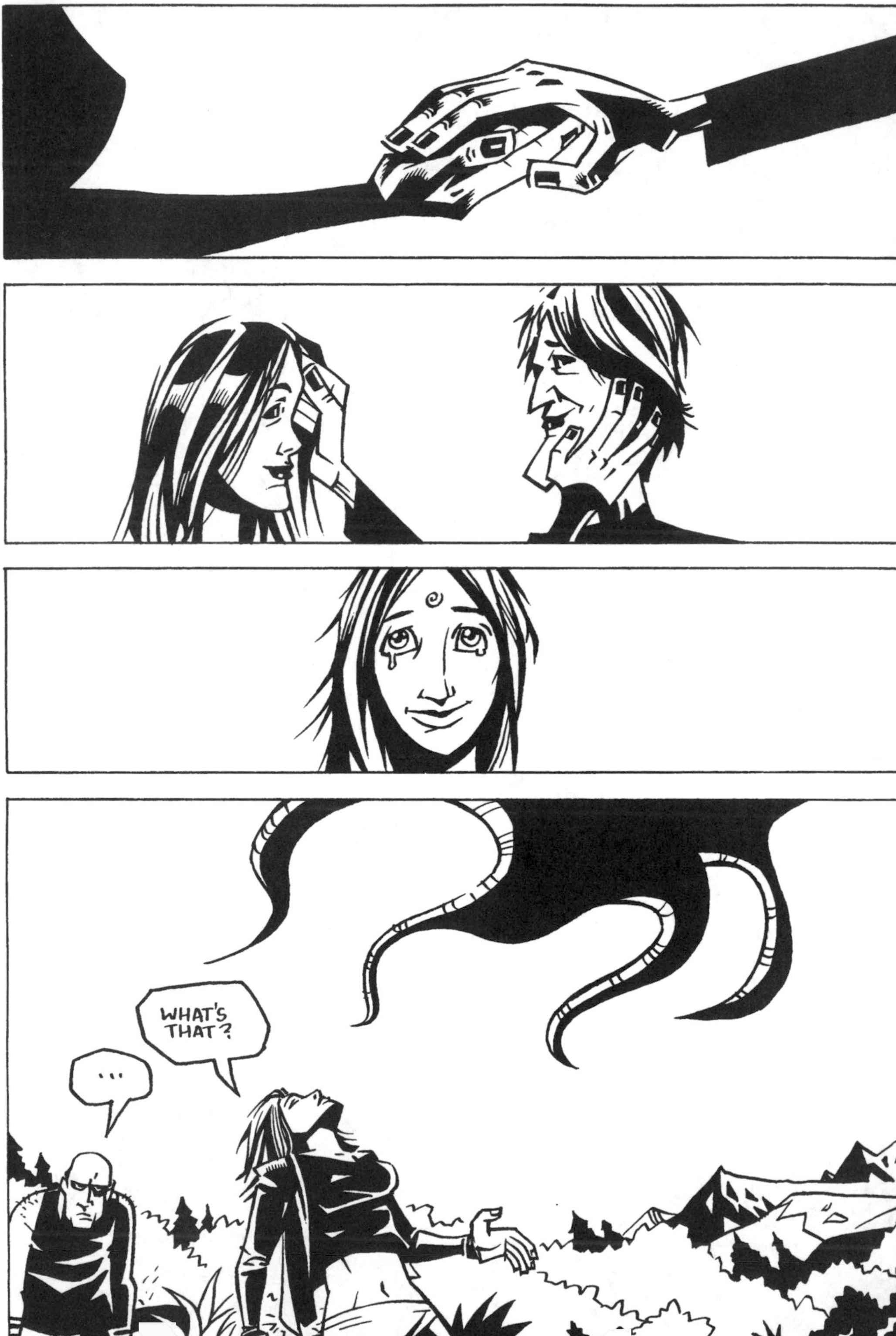
...
WHAT'S THAT?

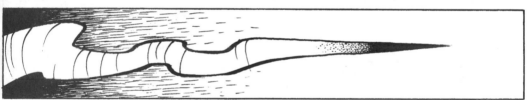

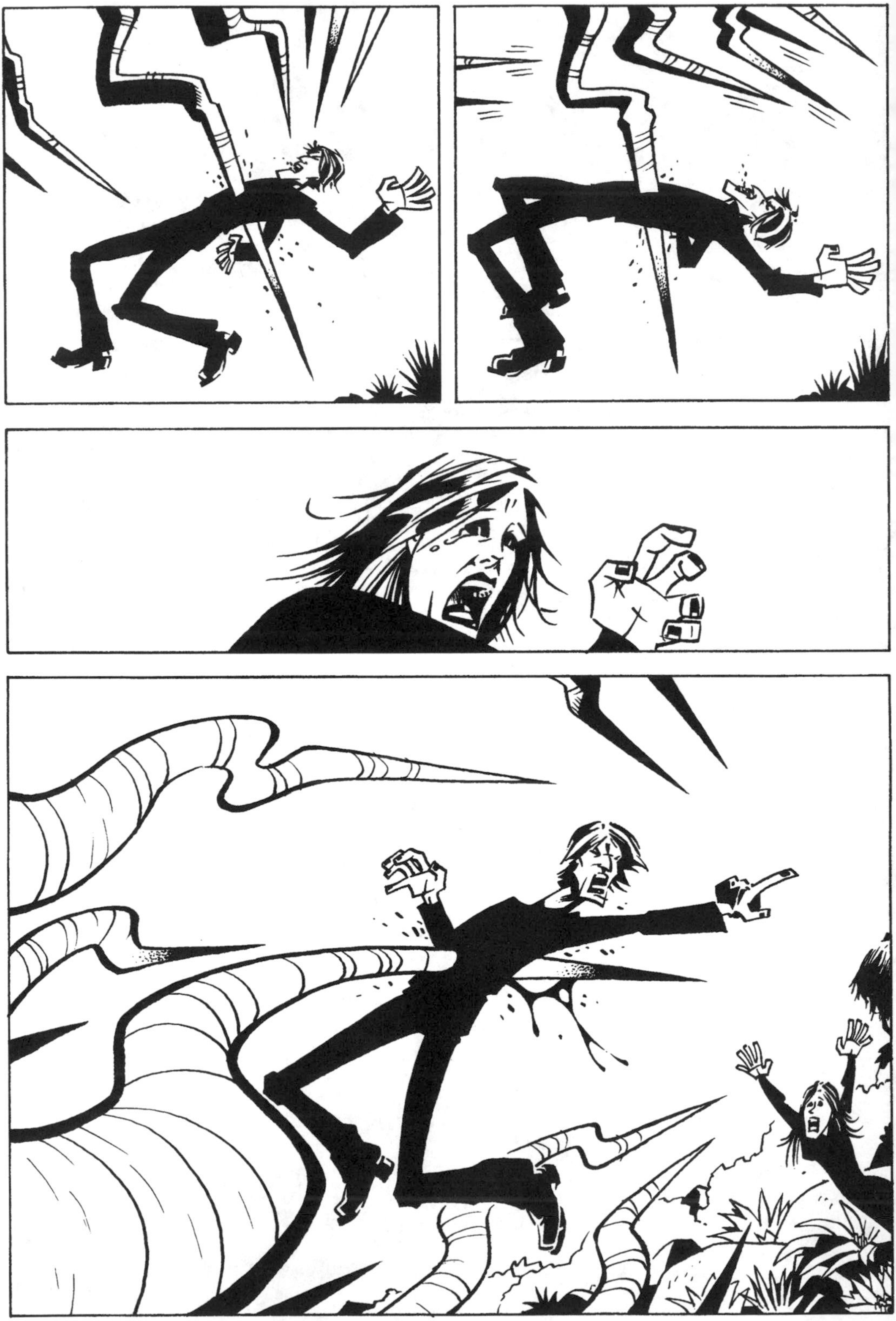

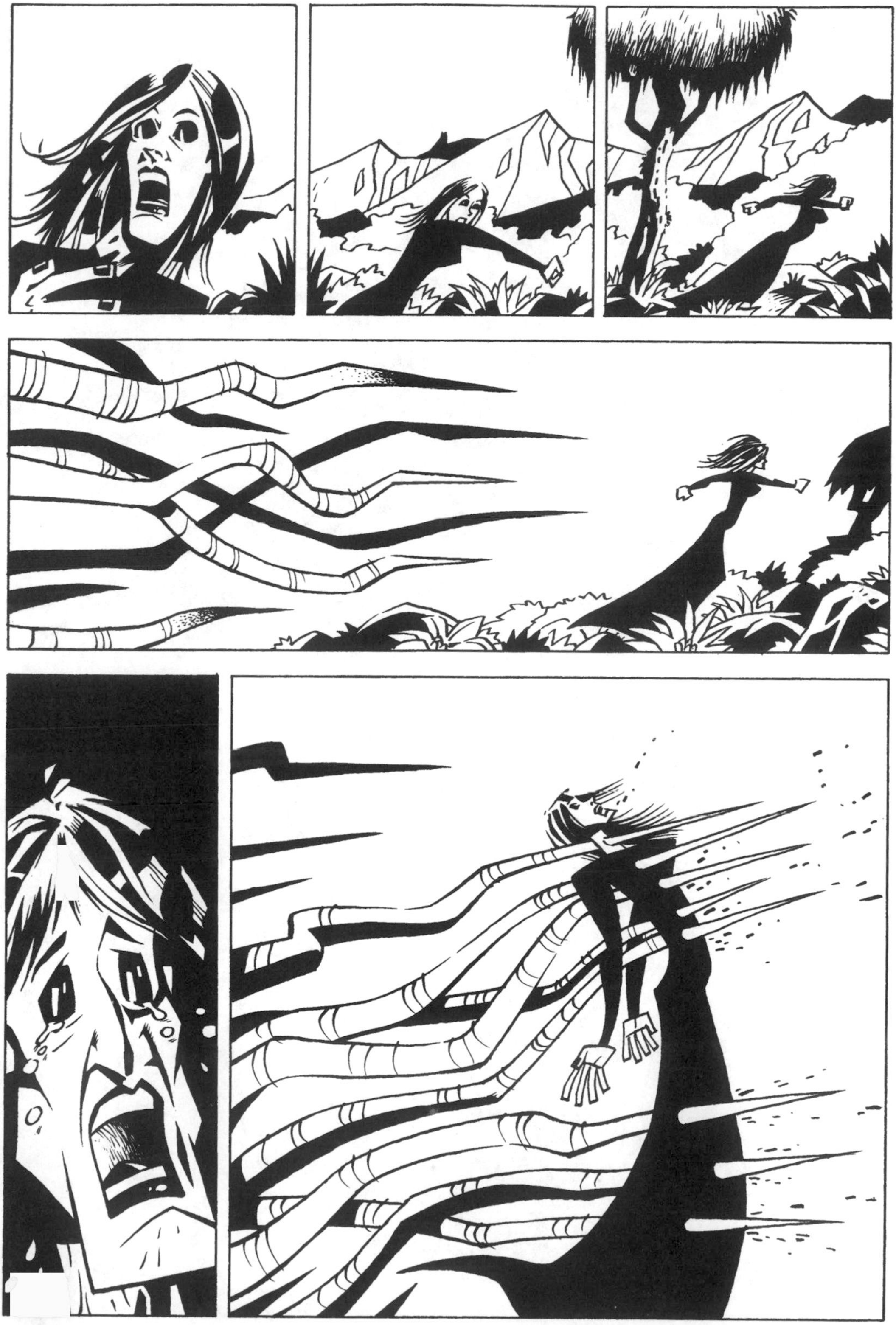

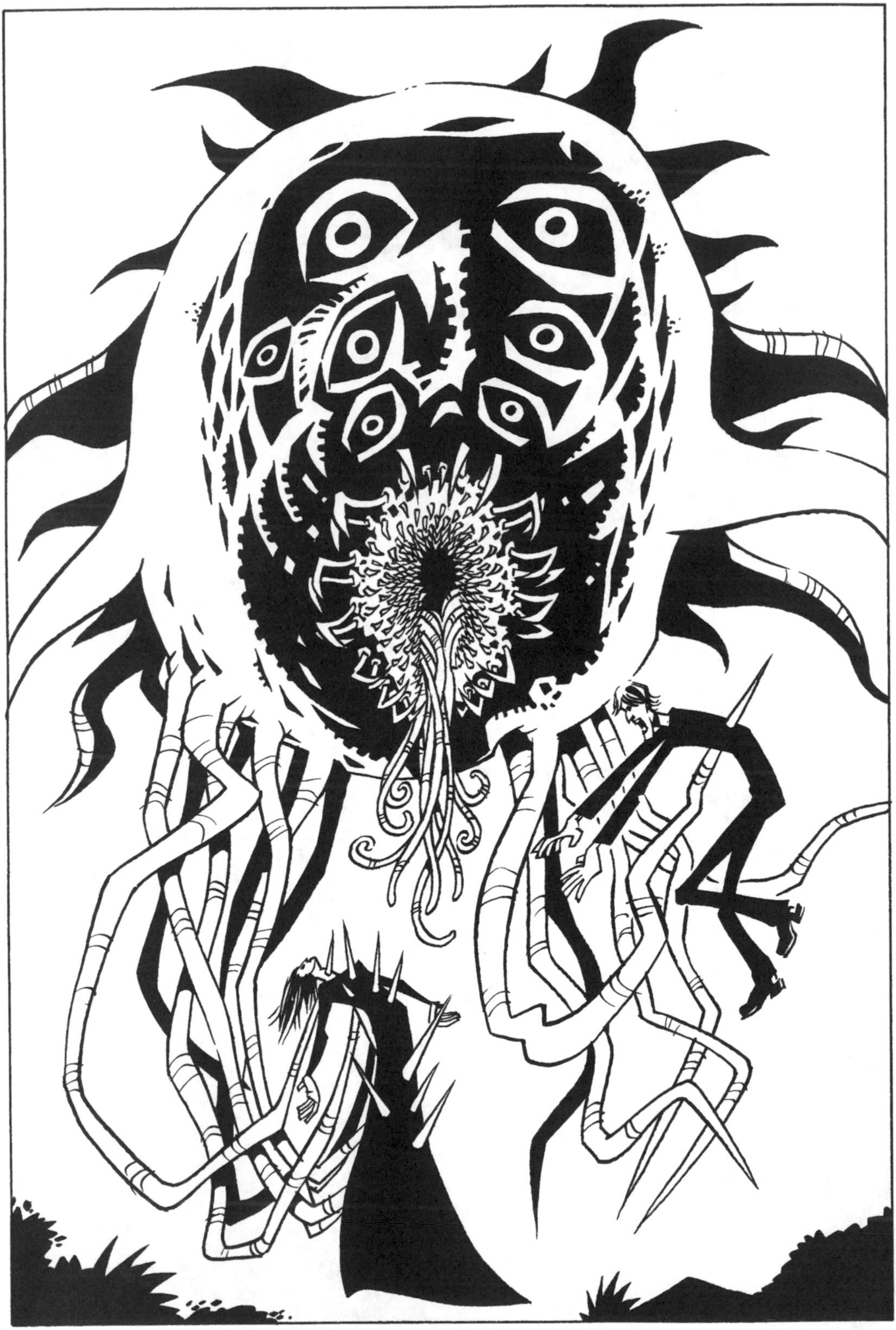

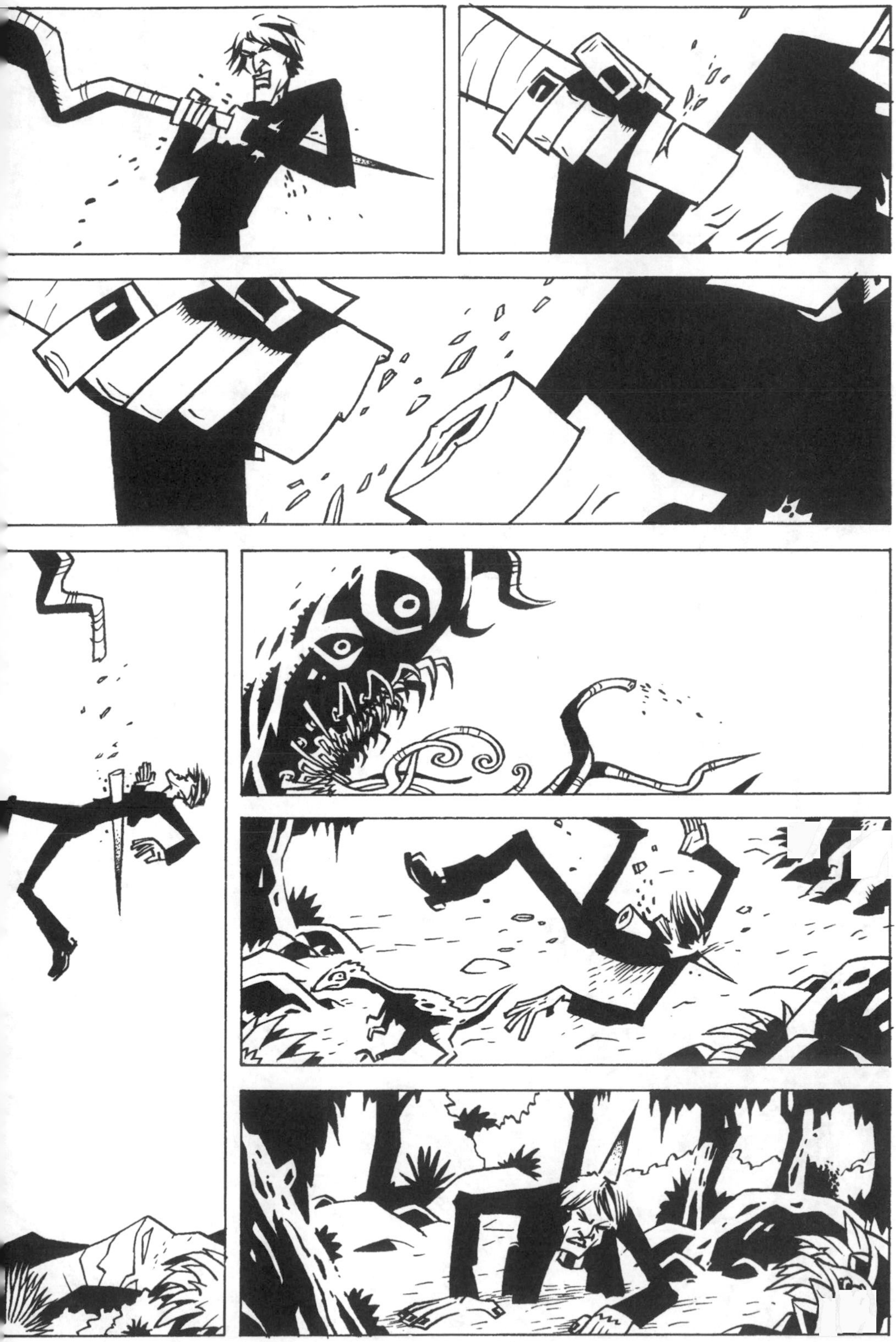

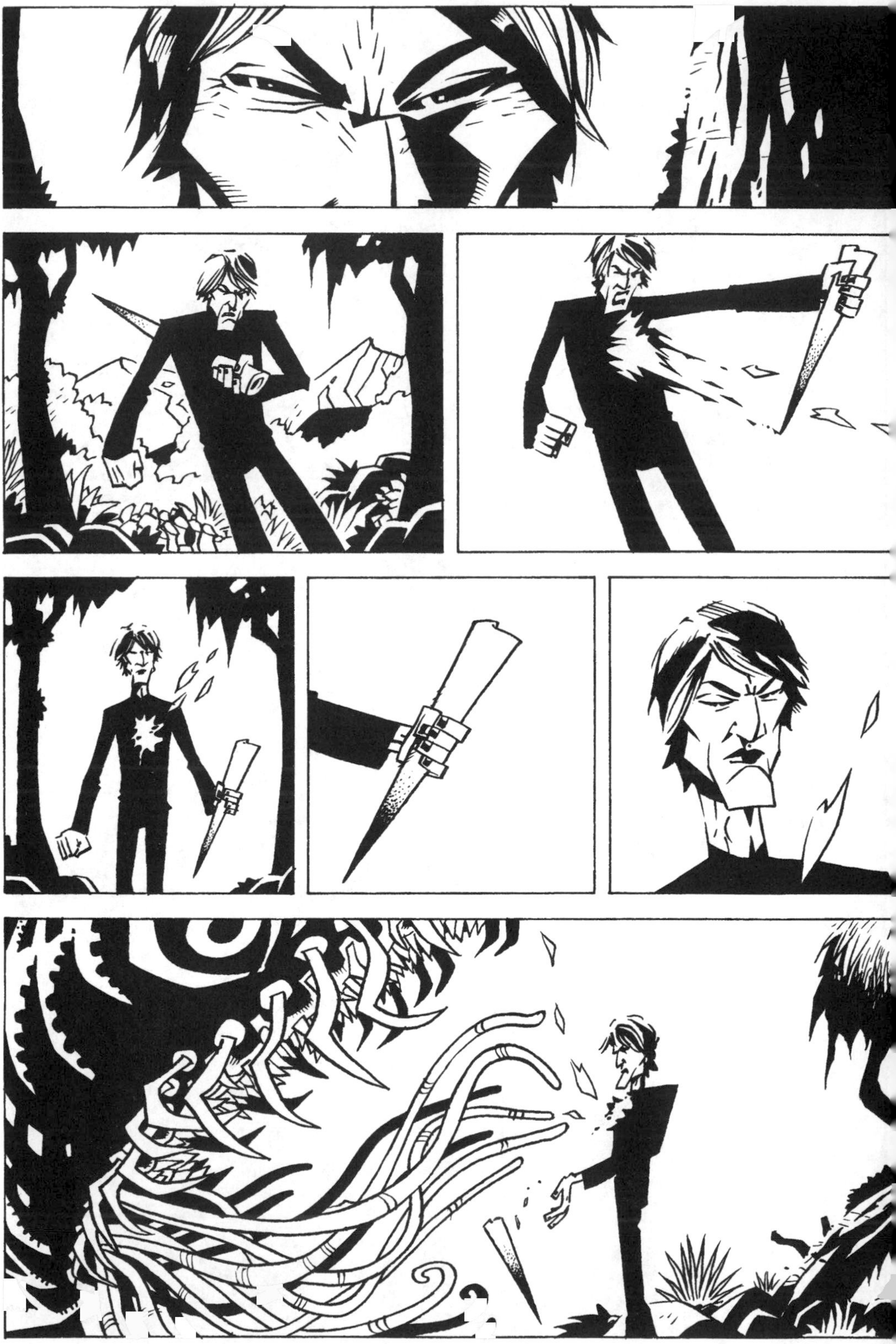

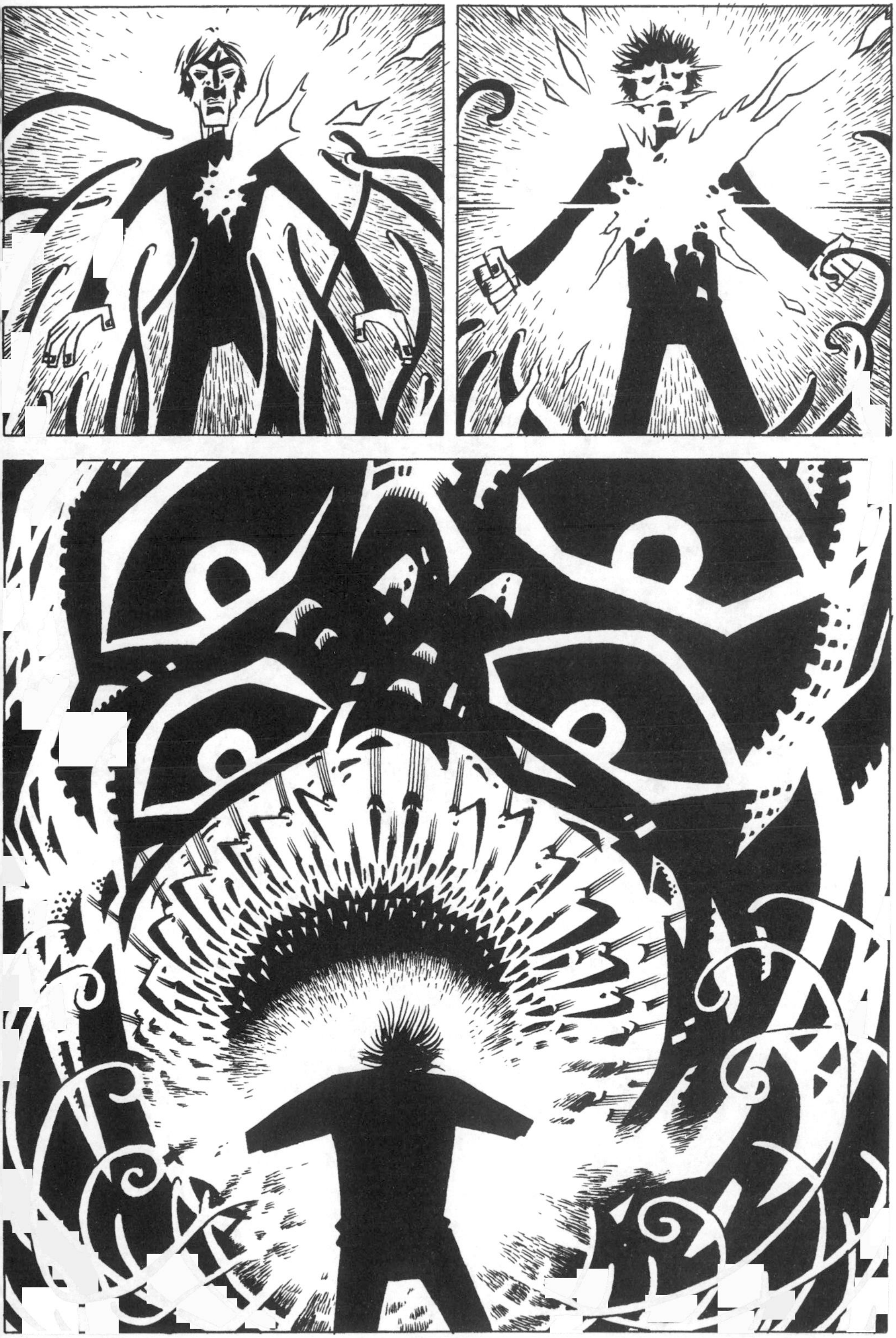

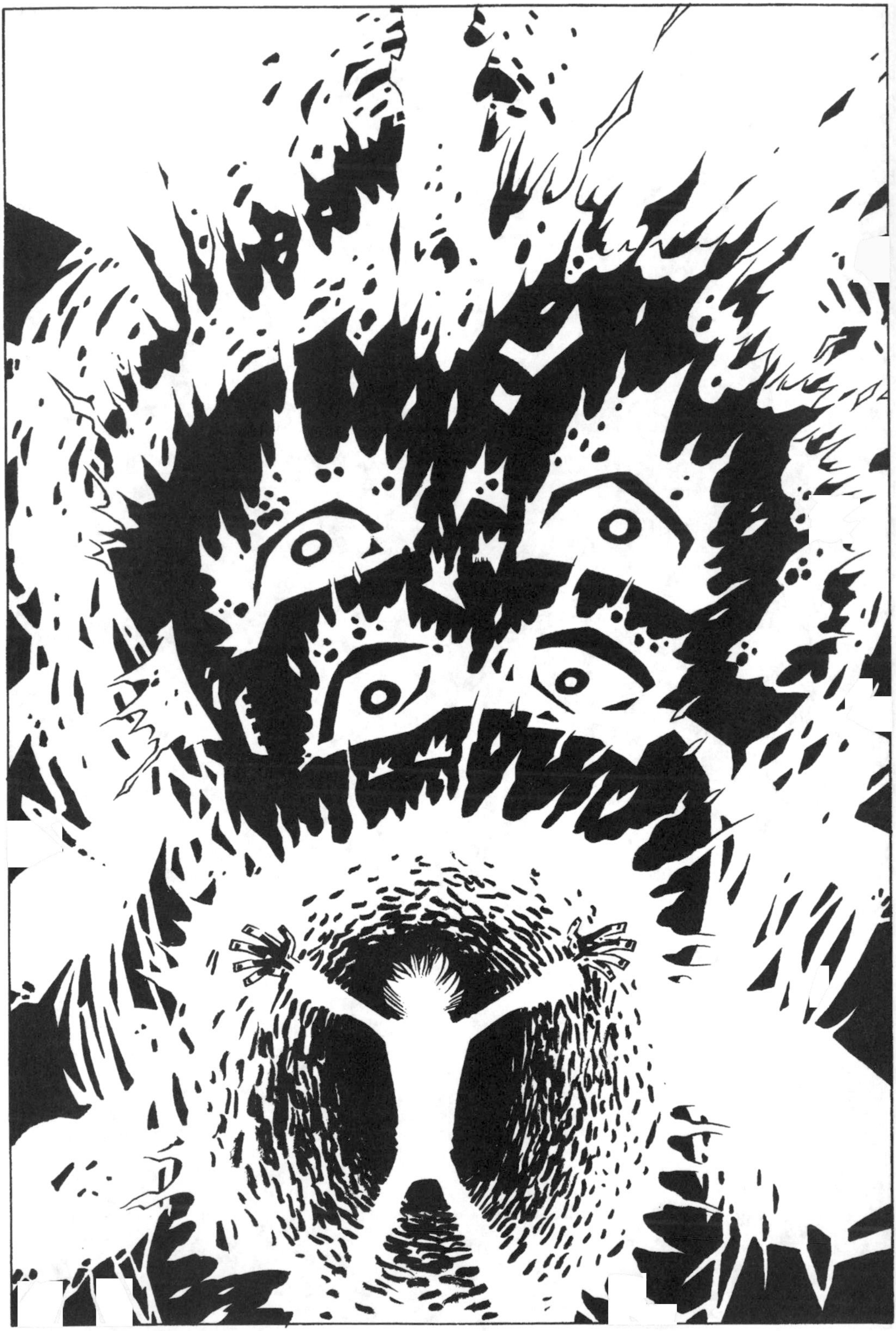

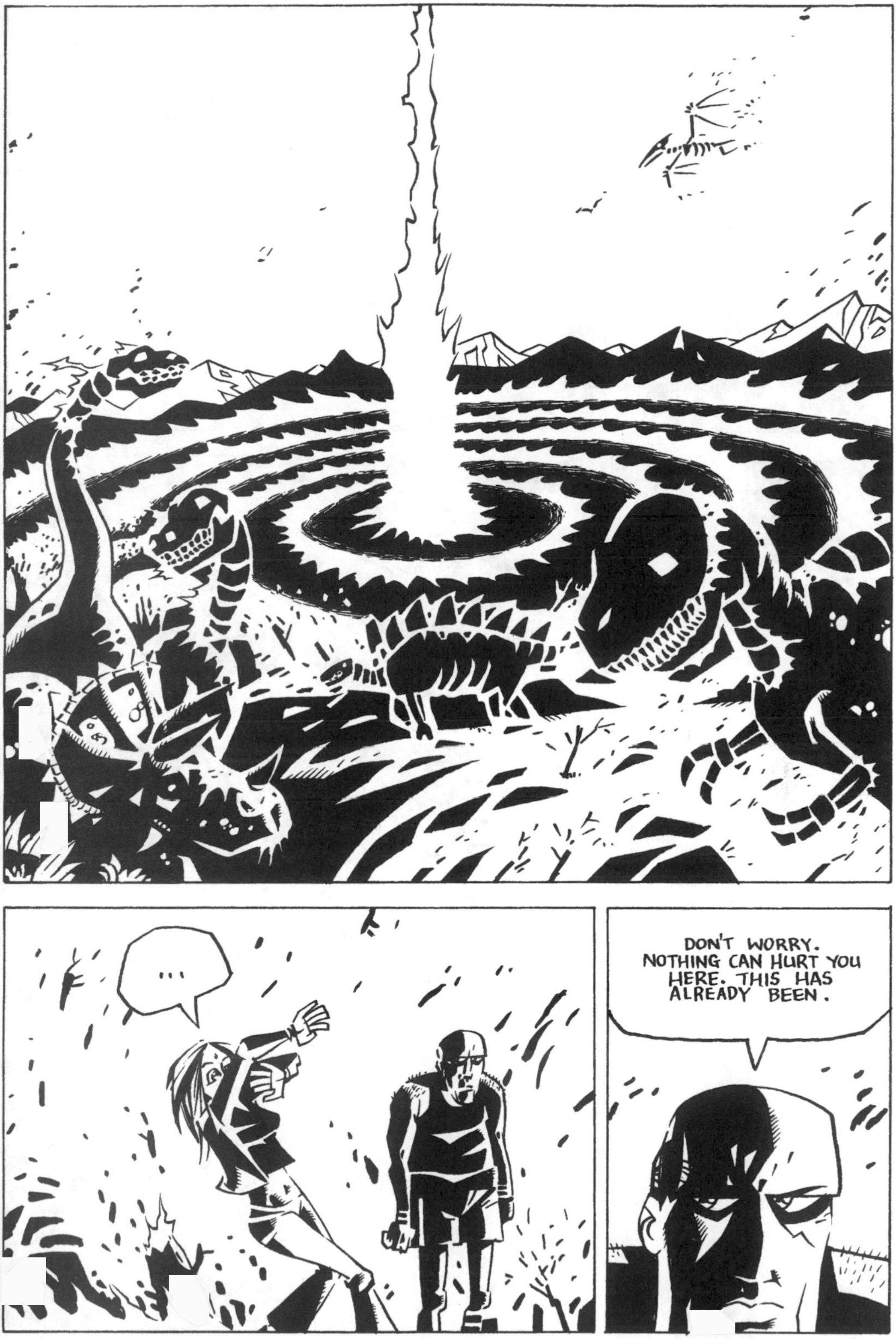
...
DON'T WORRY. NOTHING CAN HURT YOU HERE. THIS HAS ALREADY BEEN.

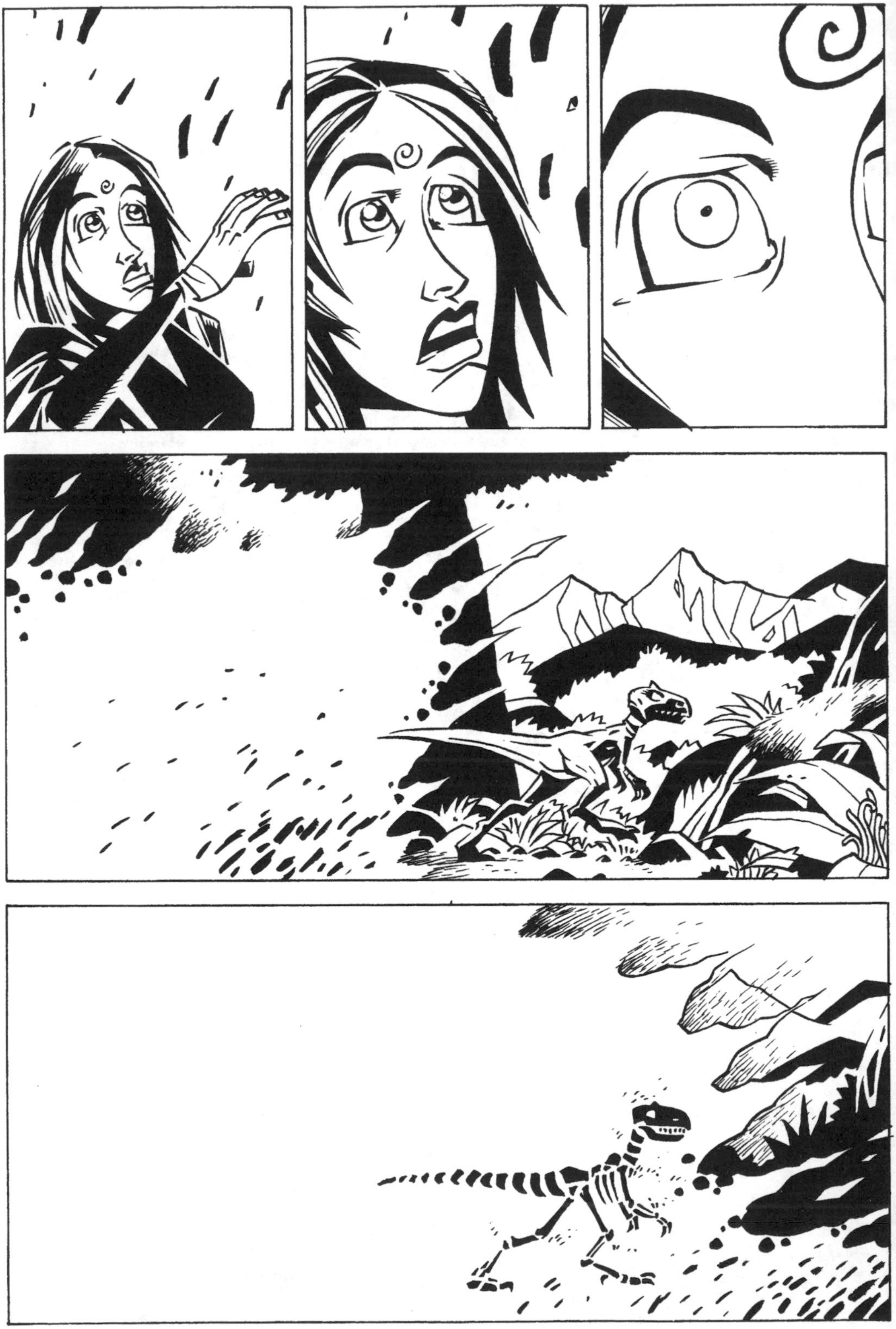

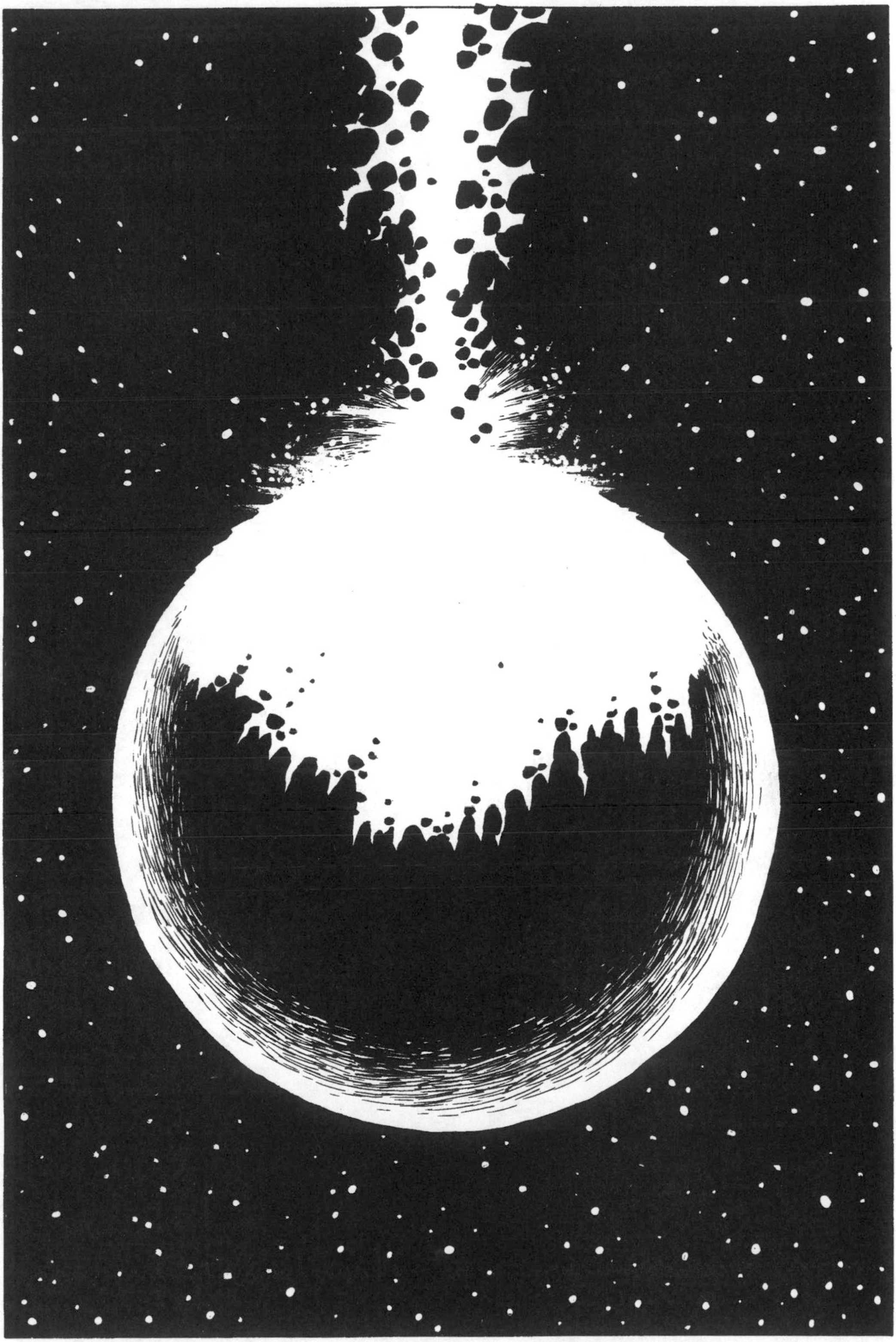

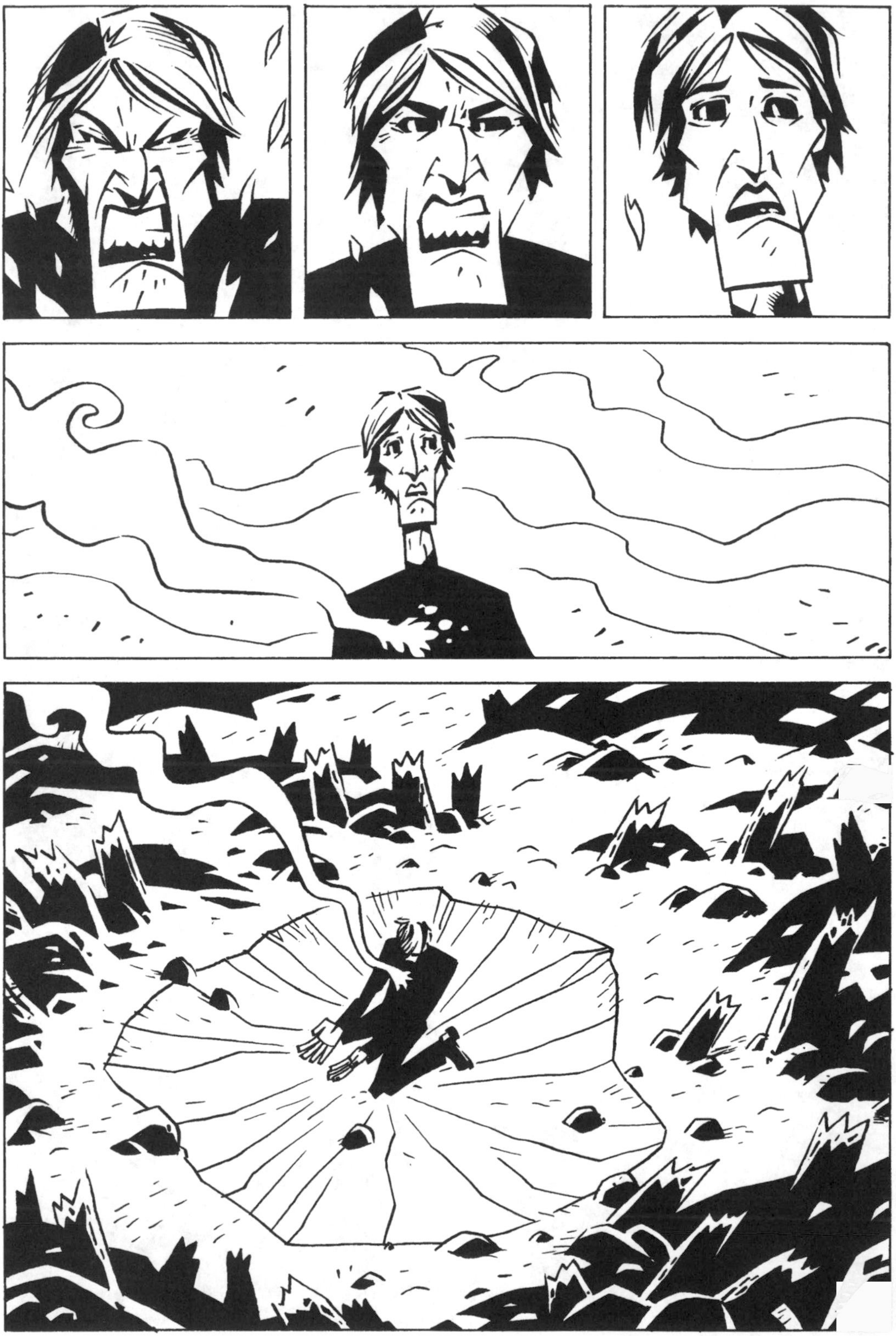

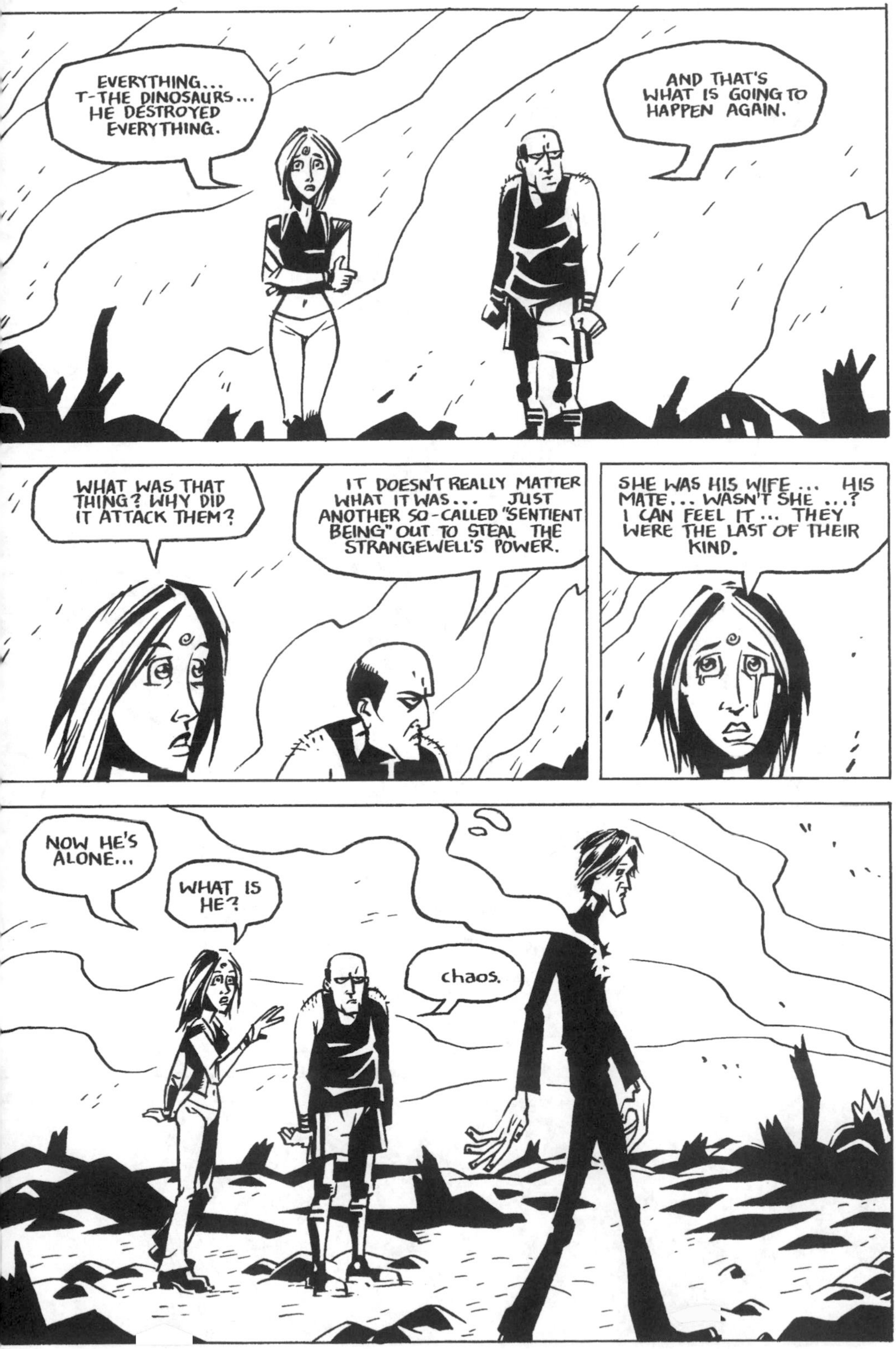

EVERYTHING... T-THE DINOSAURS... HE DESTROYED EVERYTHING.
AND THAT'S WHAT IS GOING TO HAPPEN AGAIN.
WHAT WAS THAT THING? WHY DID IT ATTACK THEM?
IT DOESN'T REALLY MATTER WHAT IT WAS... JUST ANOTHER SO-CALLED "SENTIENT BEING" OUT TO STEAL THE STRANGEWELL'S POWER.
SHE WAS HIS WIFE... HIS MATE... WASN'T SHE ...? I CAN FEEL IT... THEY WERE THE LAST OF THEIR KIND.
NOW HE'S ALONE...
WHAT IS HE?
chaos.

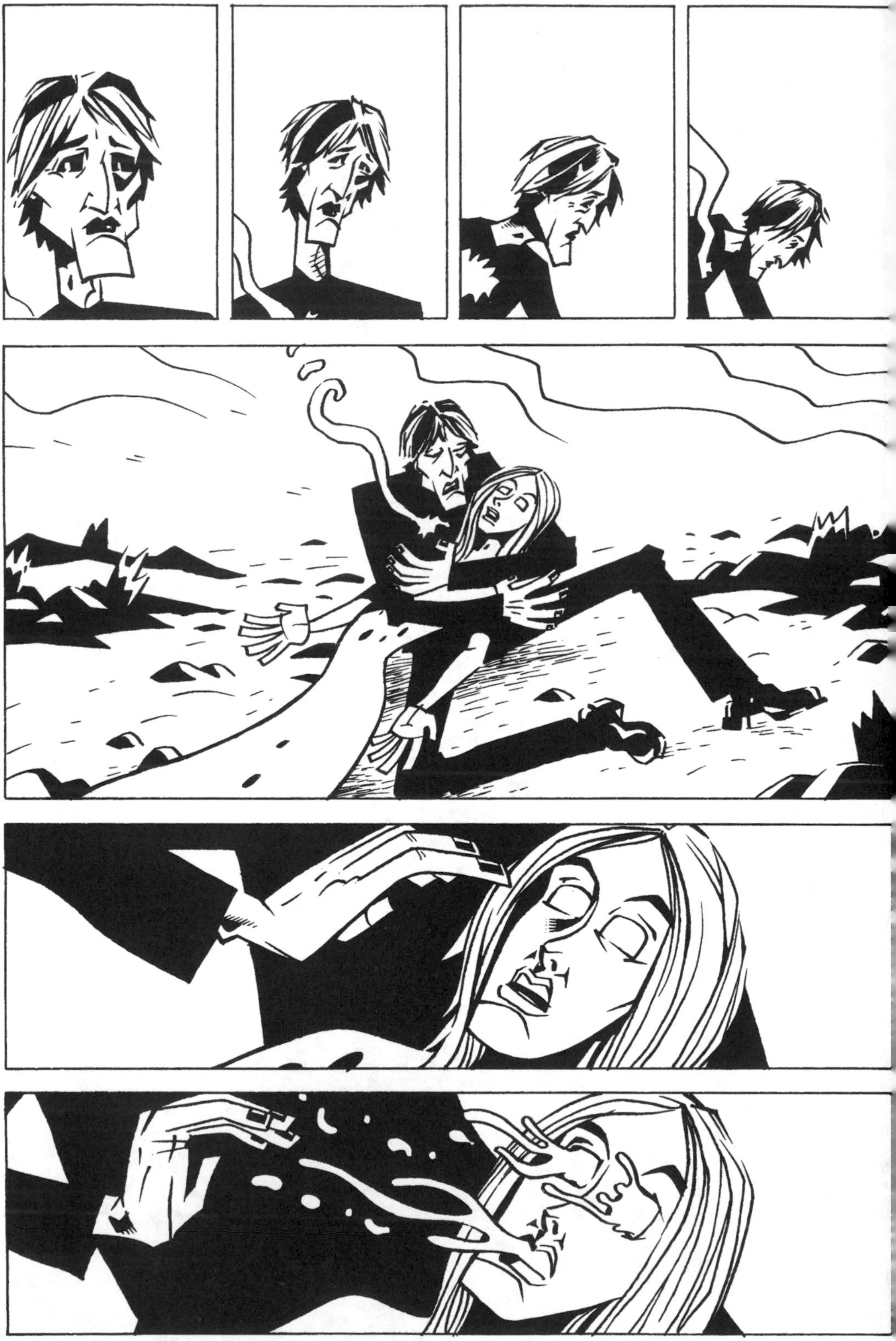

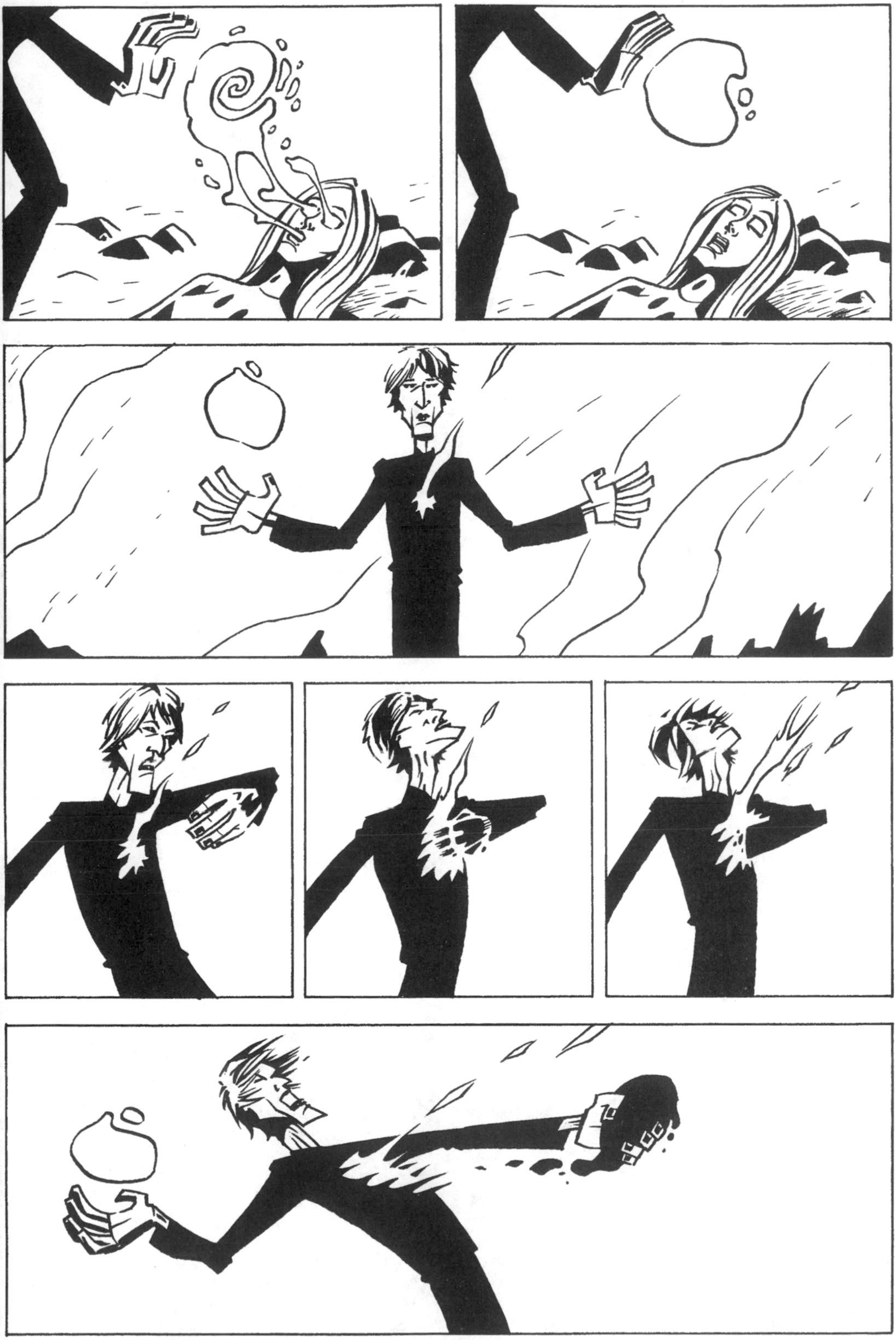

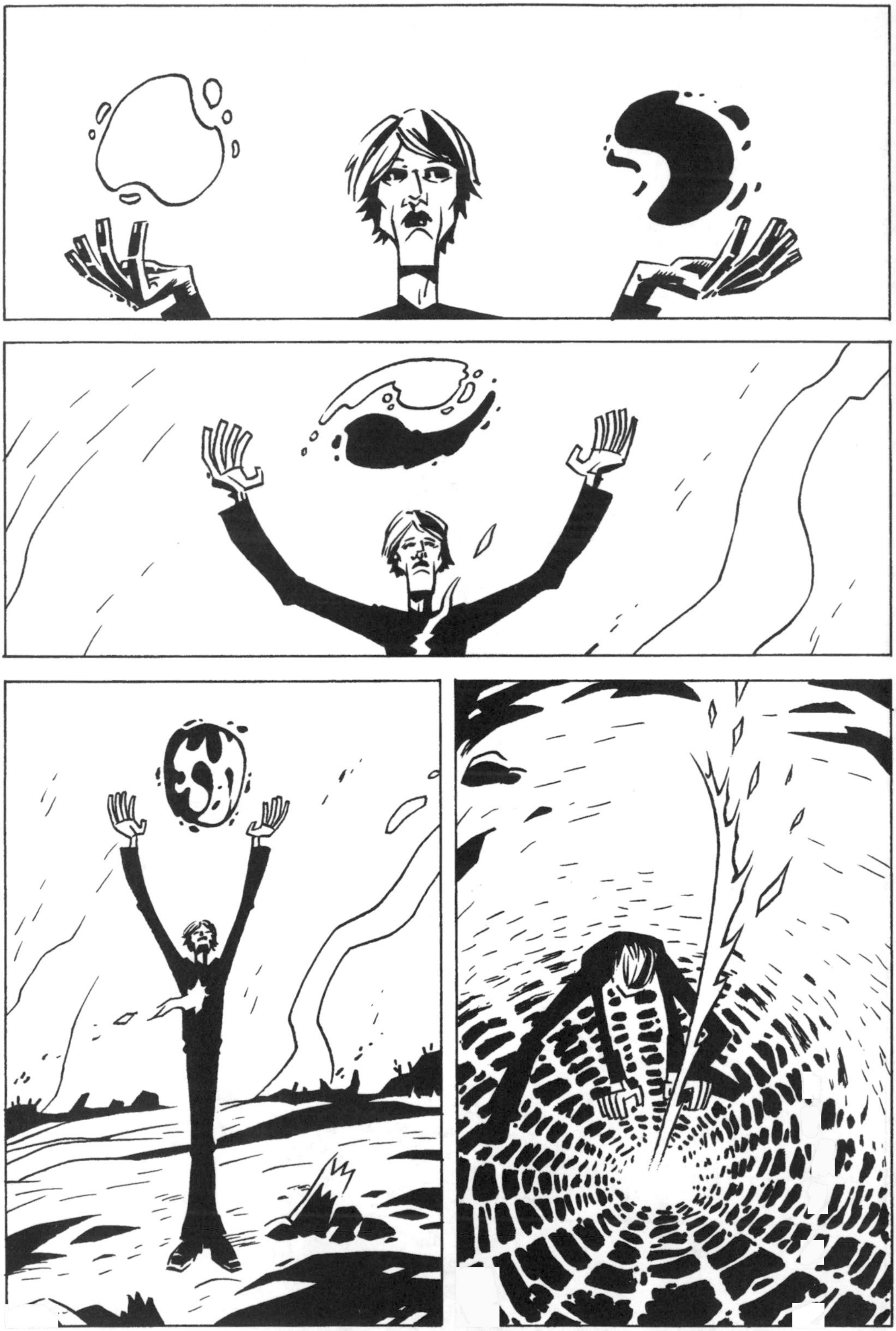

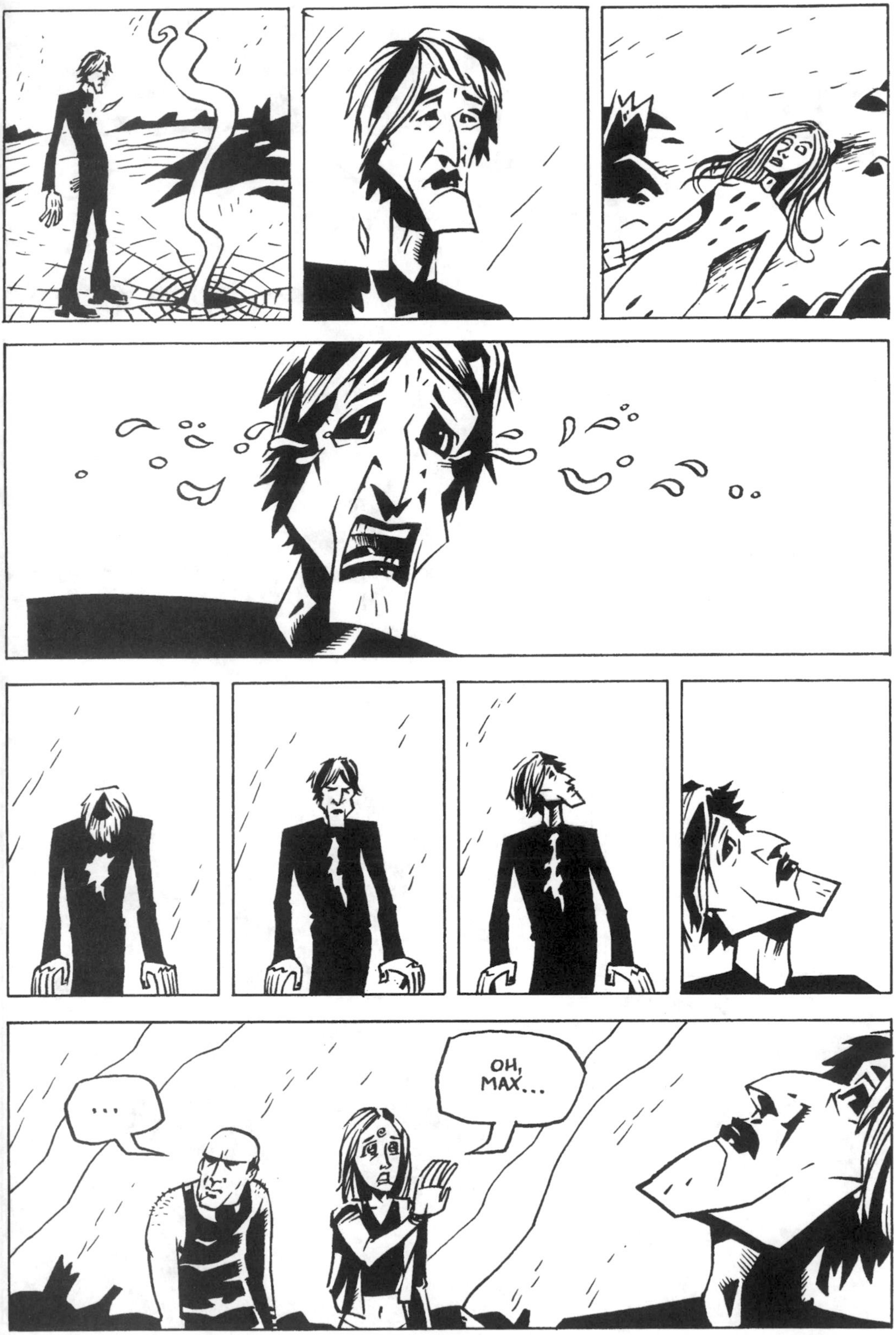
...
OH, MAX...

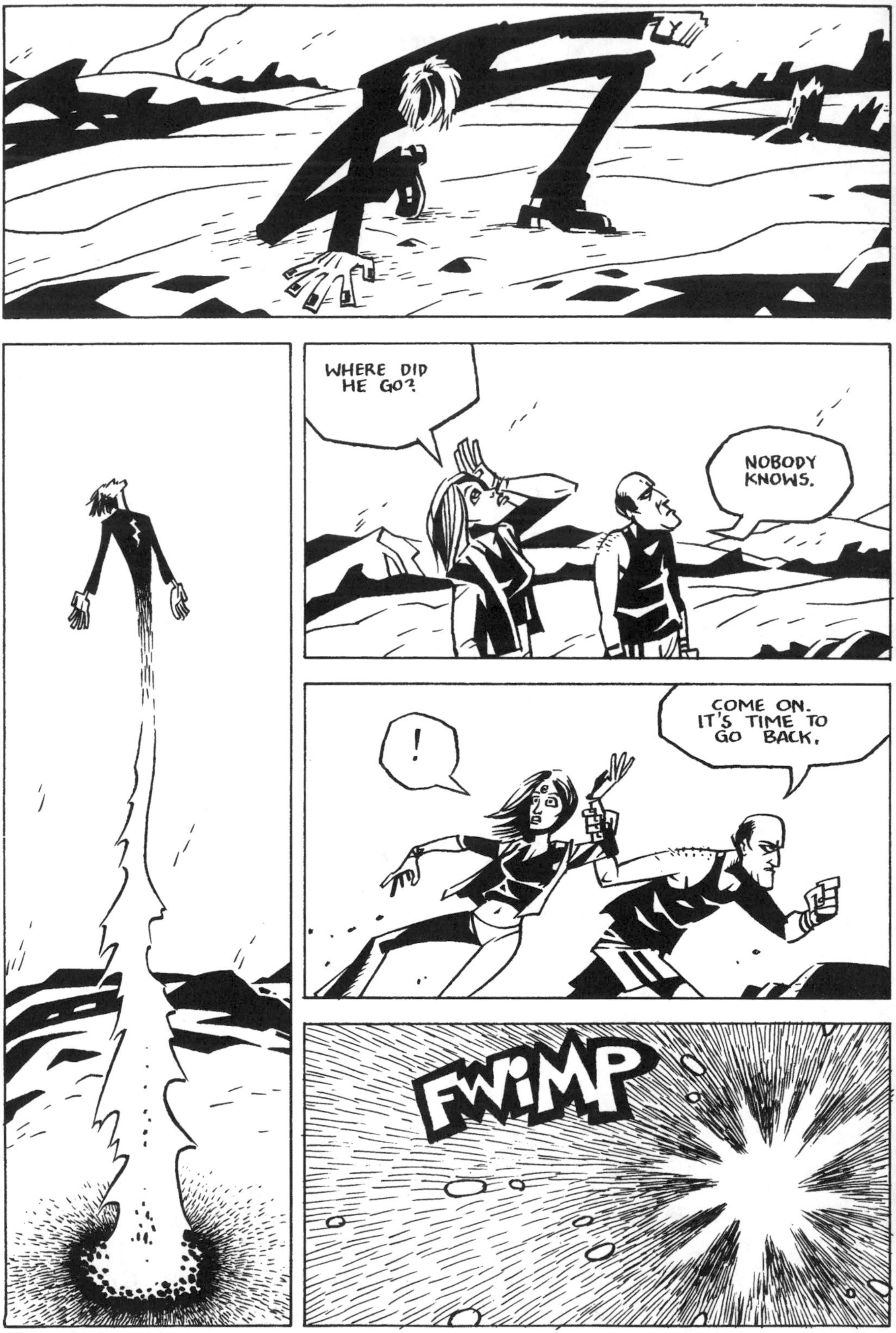
WHERE DID HE GO?
NOBODY KNOWS.
!
COME ON. IT'S TIME TO GO BACK.
FWIMP

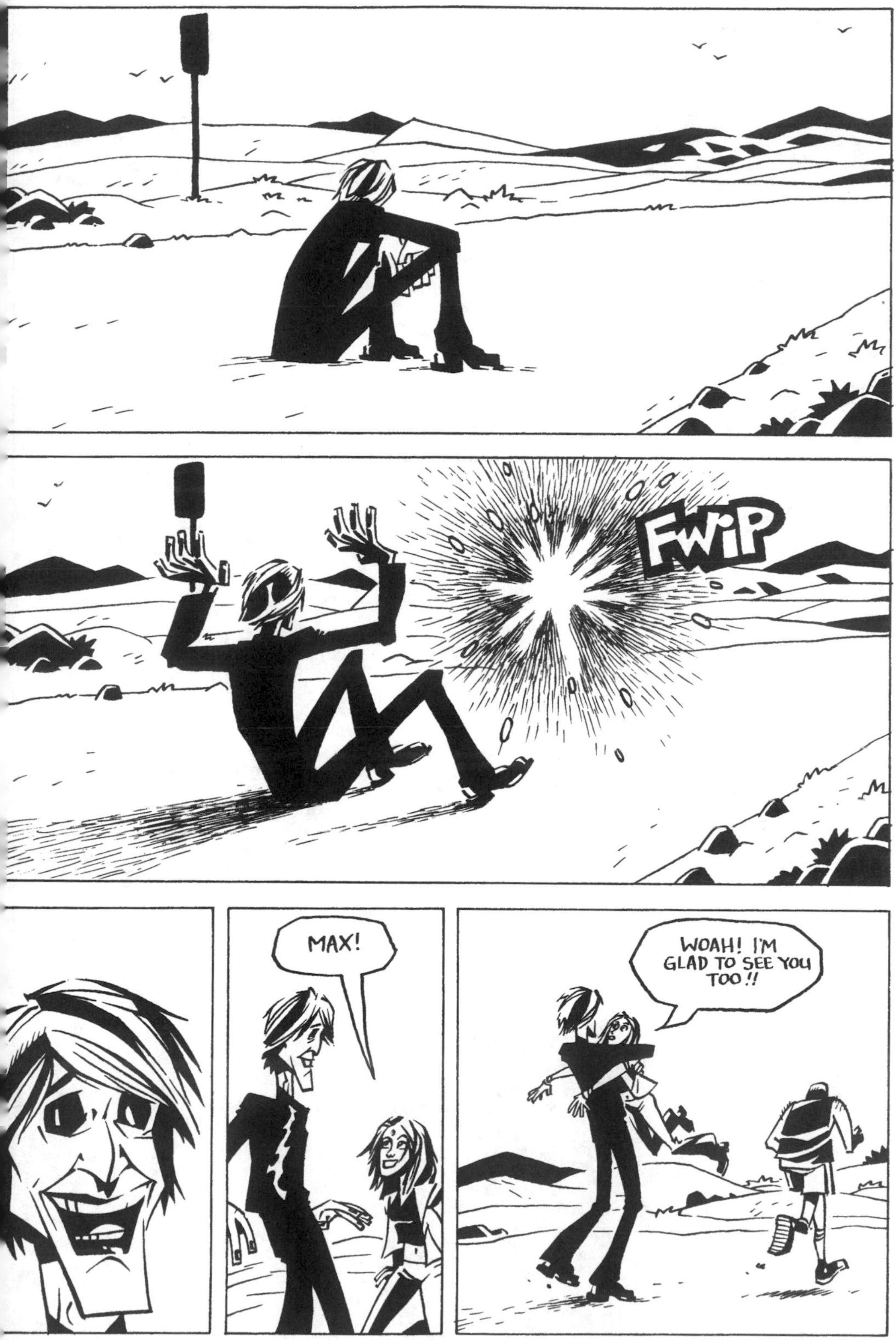
FWIP
MAX!
WOAH! I'M GLAD TO SEE YOU TOO!!

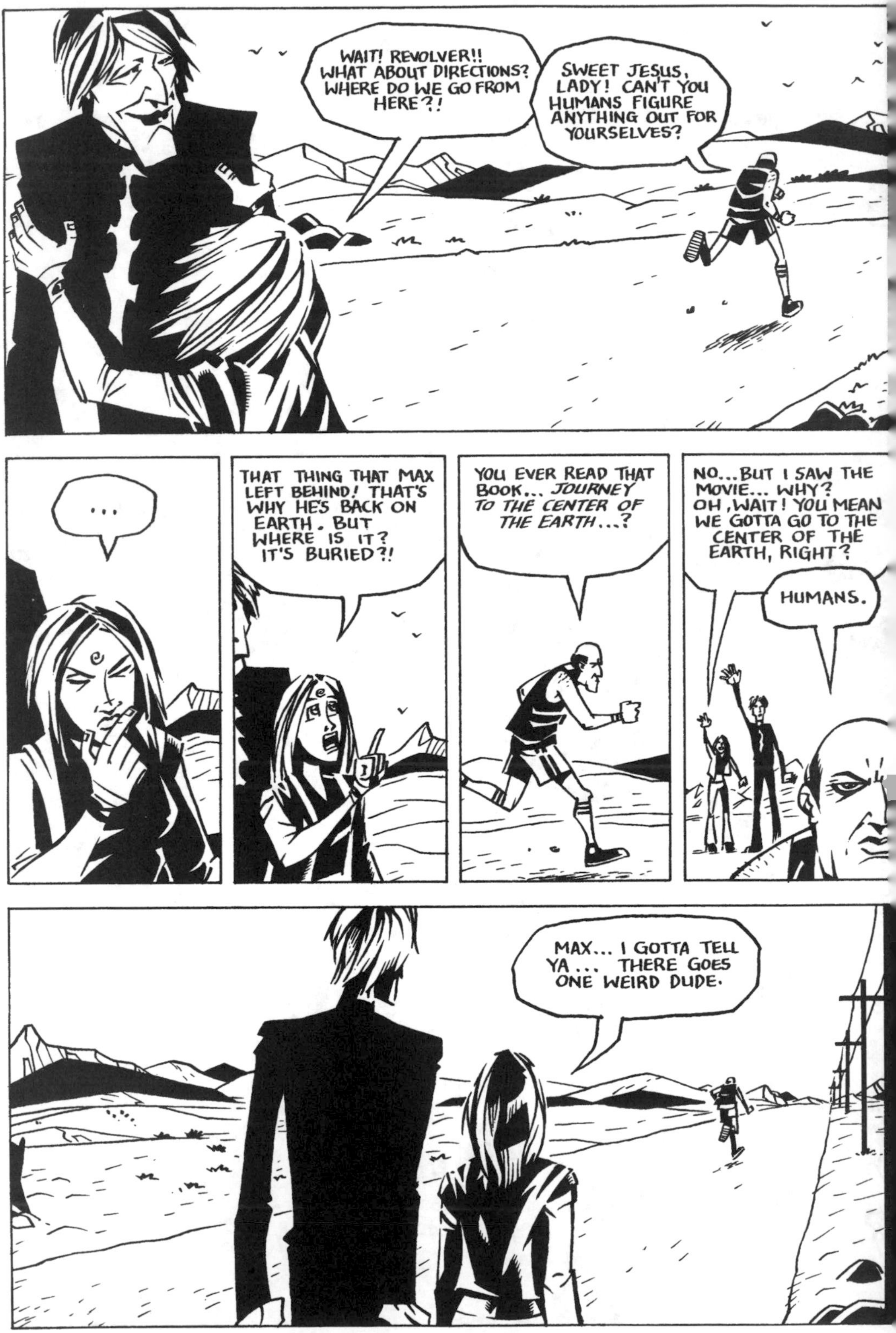
WAIT! REVOLVER!! WHAT ABOUT DIRECTIONS? WHERE DO WE GO FROM HERE?!
SWEET JESUS, LADY! CAN'T YOU HUMANS FIGURE ANYTHING OUT FOR YOURSELVES?
...
THAT THING THAT MAX LEFT BEHIND! THAT'S WHY HE'S BACK ON EARTH. BUT WHERE IS IT? IT'S BURIED?!
YOU EVER READ THAT BOOK... *JOURNEY TO THE CENTER OF THE EARTH*...?
NO...BUT I SAW THE MOVIE... WHY? OH, WAIT! YOU MEAN WE GOTTA GO TO THE CENTER OF THE EARTH, RIGHT?
HUMANS.
MAX... I GOTTA TELL YA... THERE GOES ONE WEIRD DUDE.

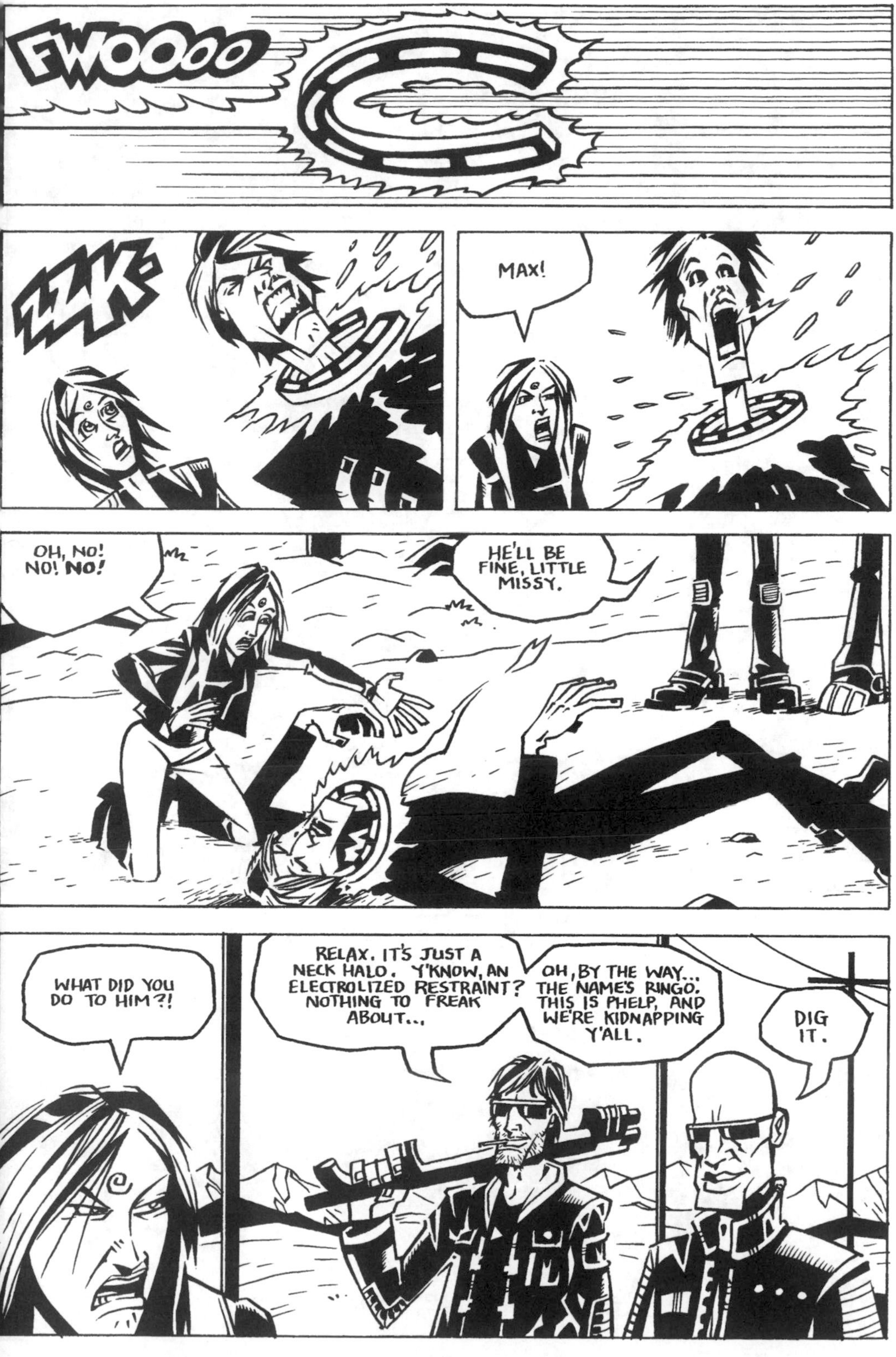
FWOOOO
ZZK-
MAX!
OH, NO! NO! NO!
HE'LL BE FINE, LITTLE MISSY.
WHAT DID YOU DO TO HIM?!
RELAX. IT'S JUST A NECK HALO. Y'KNOW, AN ELECTROLIZED RESTRAINT? NOTHING TO FREAK ABOUT...
OH, BY THE WAY... THE NAME'S RINGO. THIS IS PHELP, AND WE'RE KIDNAPPING Y'ALL.
DIG IT.

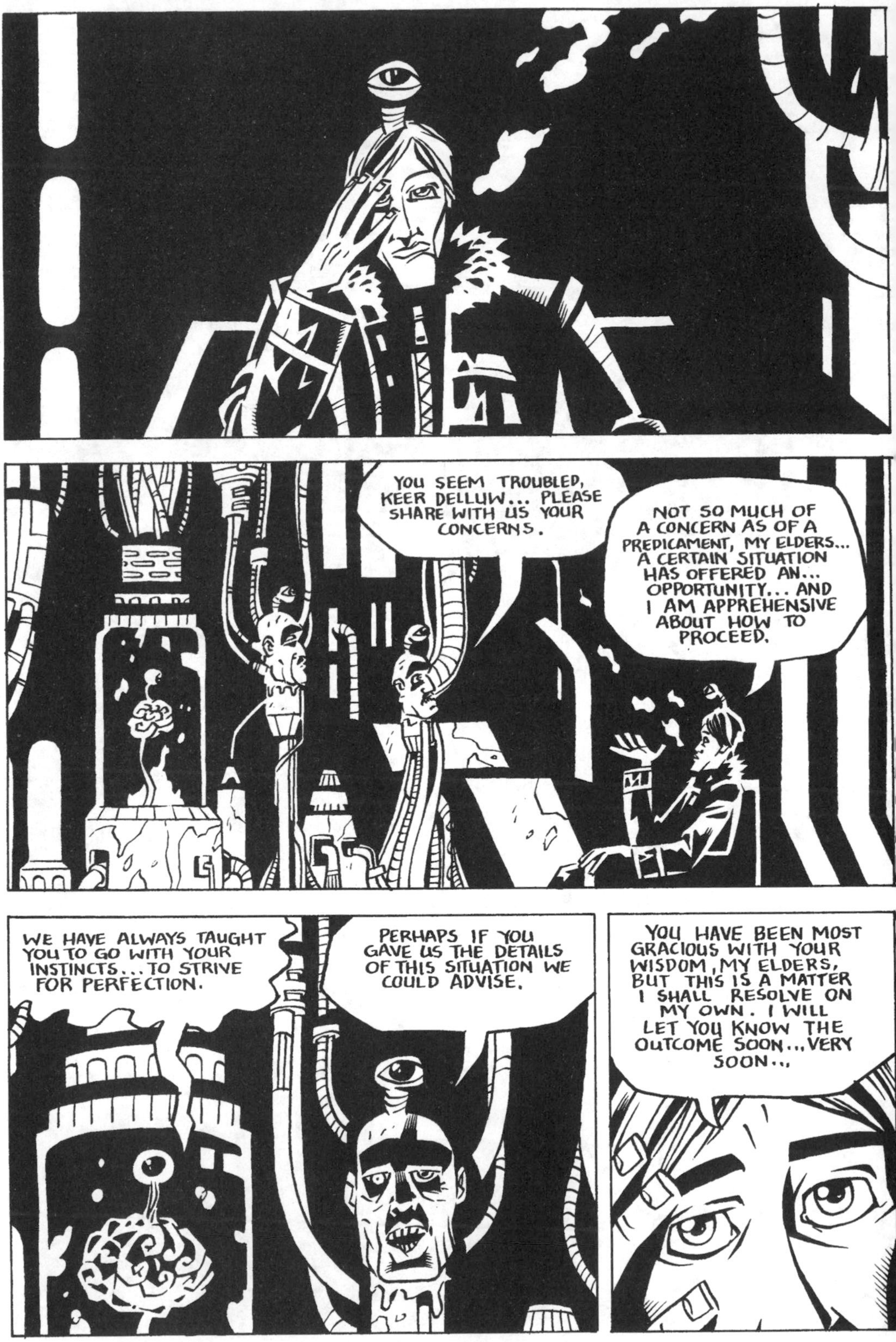
YOU SEEM TROUBLED, KEER DELLUW... PLEASE SHARE WITH US YOUR CONCERNS.
NOT SO MUCH OF A CONCERN AS OF A PREDICAMENT, MY ELDERS... A CERTAIN SITUATION HAS OFFERED AN... OPPORTUNITY... AND I AM APPREHENSIVE ABOUT HOW TO PROCEED.
WE HAVE ALWAYS TAUGHT YOU TO GO WITH YOUR INSTINCTS... TO STRIVE FOR PERFECTION.
PERHAPS IF YOU GAVE US THE DETAILS OF THIS SITUATION WE COULD ADVISE.
YOU HAVE BEEN MOST GRACIOUS WITH YOUR WISDOM, MY ELDERS, BUT THIS IS A MATTER I SHALL RESOLVE ON MY OWN. I WILL LET YOU KNOW THE OUTCOME SOON..., VERY SOON...,

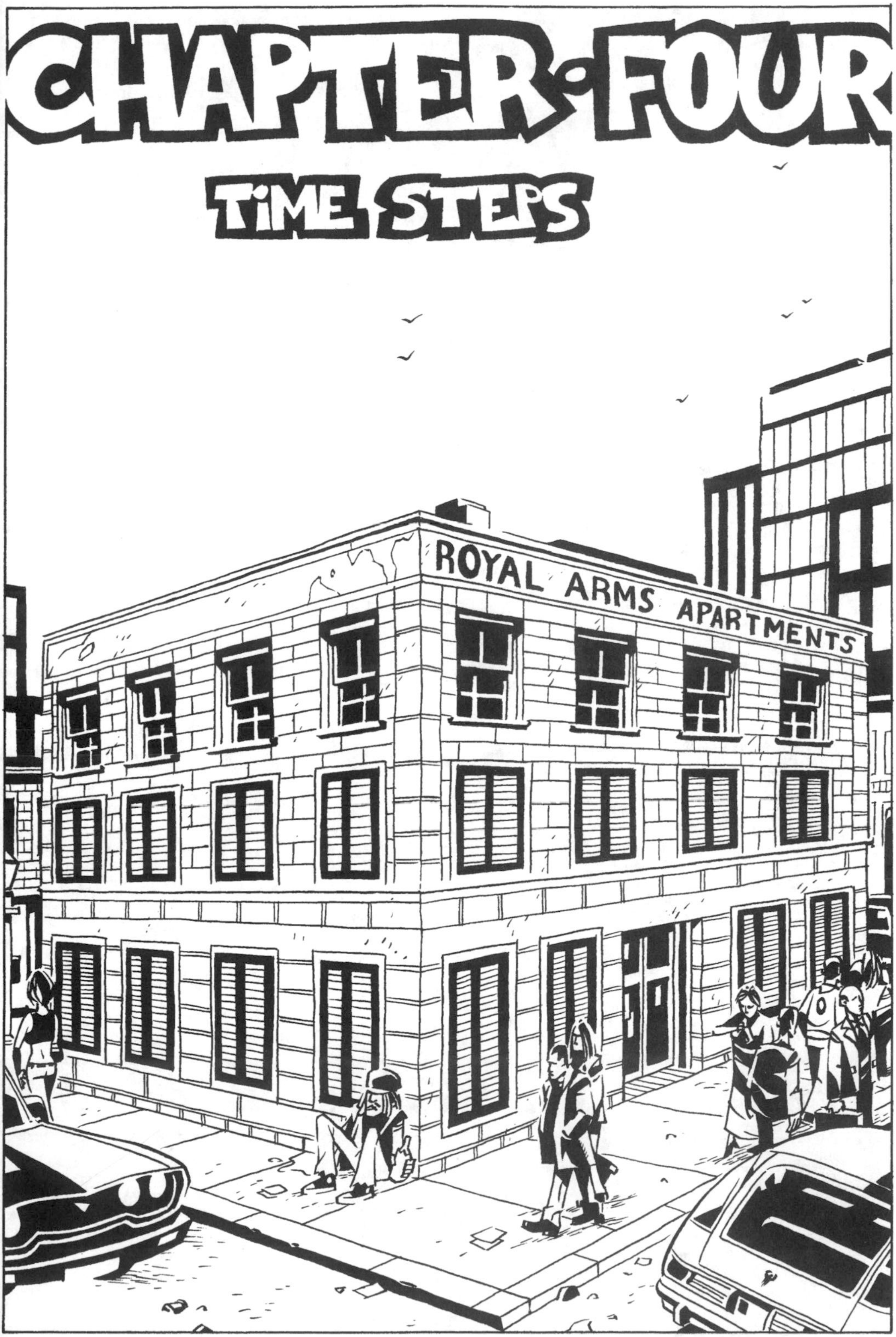
CHAPTER FOUR
TIME STEPS
ROYAL ARMS APARTMENTS

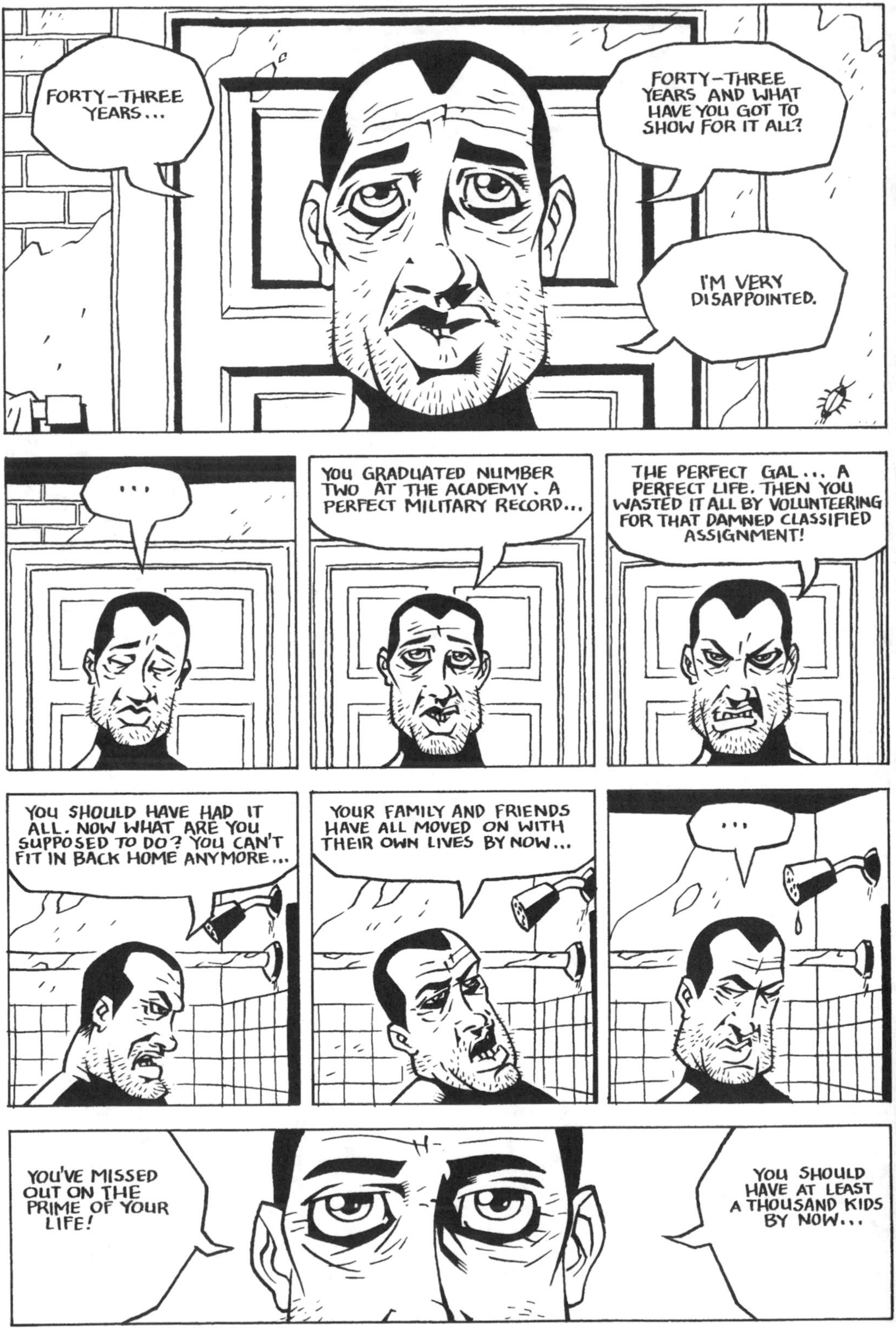
FORTY-THREE YEARS...
FORTY-THREE YEARS AND WHAT HAVE YOU GOT TO SHOW FOR IT ALL?
I'M VERY DISAPPOINTED.
...
YOU GRADUATED NUMBER TWO AT THE ACADEMY. A PERFECT MILITARY RECORD...
THE PERFECT GAL... A PERFECT LIFE. THEN YOU WASTED IT ALL BY VOLUNTEERING FOR THAT DAMNED CLASSIFIED ASSIGNMENT!
YOU SHOULD HAVE HAD IT ALL. NOW WHAT ARE YOU SUPPOSED TO DO? YOU CAN'T FIT IN BACK HOME ANYMORE...
YOUR FAMILY AND FRIENDS HAVE ALL MOVED ON WITH THEIR OWN LIVES BY NOW...
...
YOU'VE MISSED OUT ON THE PRIME OF YOUR LIFE!
YOU SHOULD HAVE AT LEAST A THOUSAND KIDS BY NOW...

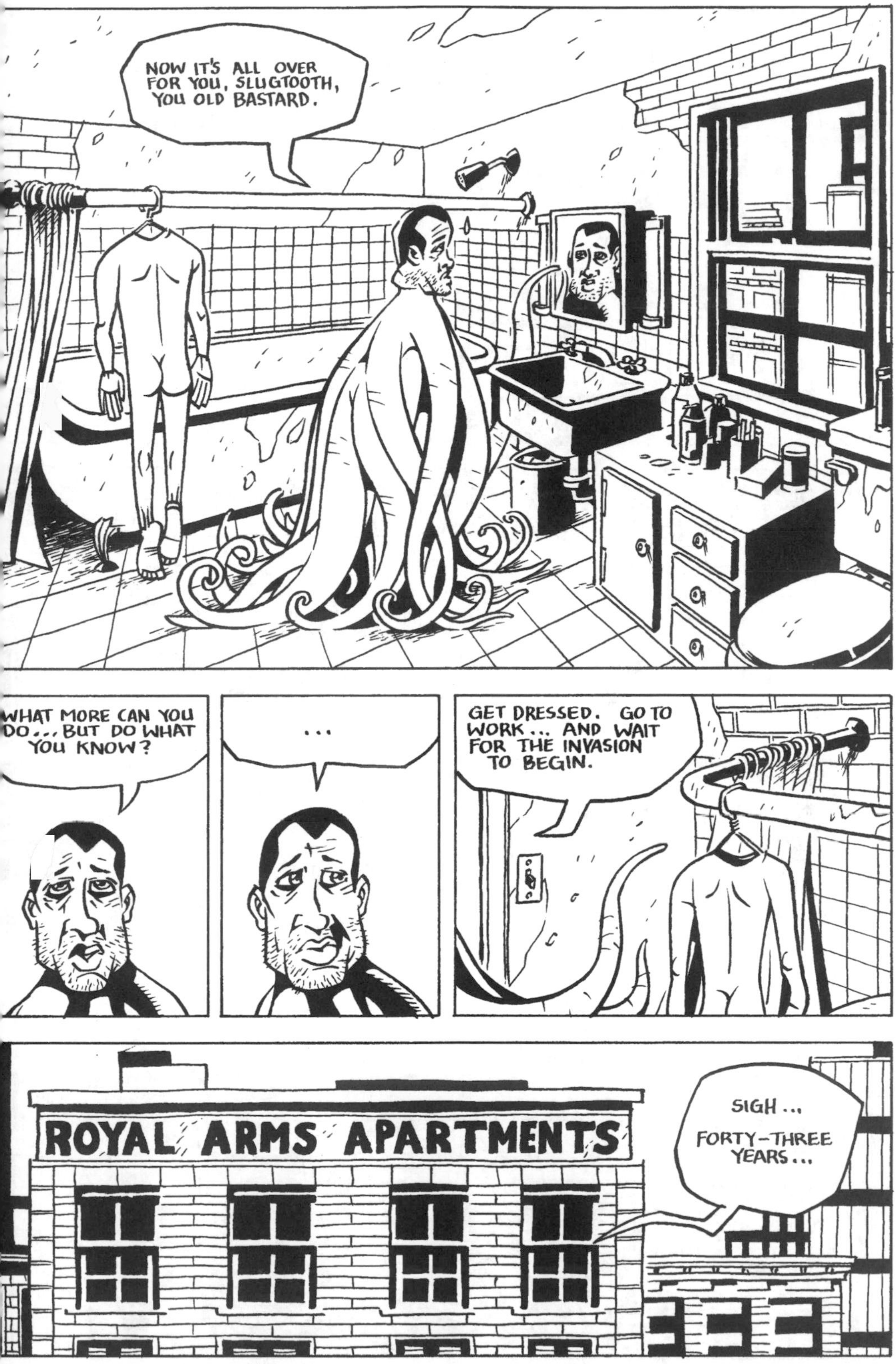
NOW IT'S ALL OVER FOR YOU, SLUGTOOTH, YOU OLD BASTARD.
WHAT MORE CAN YOU DO... BUT DO WHAT YOU KNOW?
...
GET DRESSED. GO TO WORK... AND WAIT FOR THE INVASION TO BEGIN.
ROYAL ARMS APARTMENTS
SIGH...
FORTY-THREE YEARS...

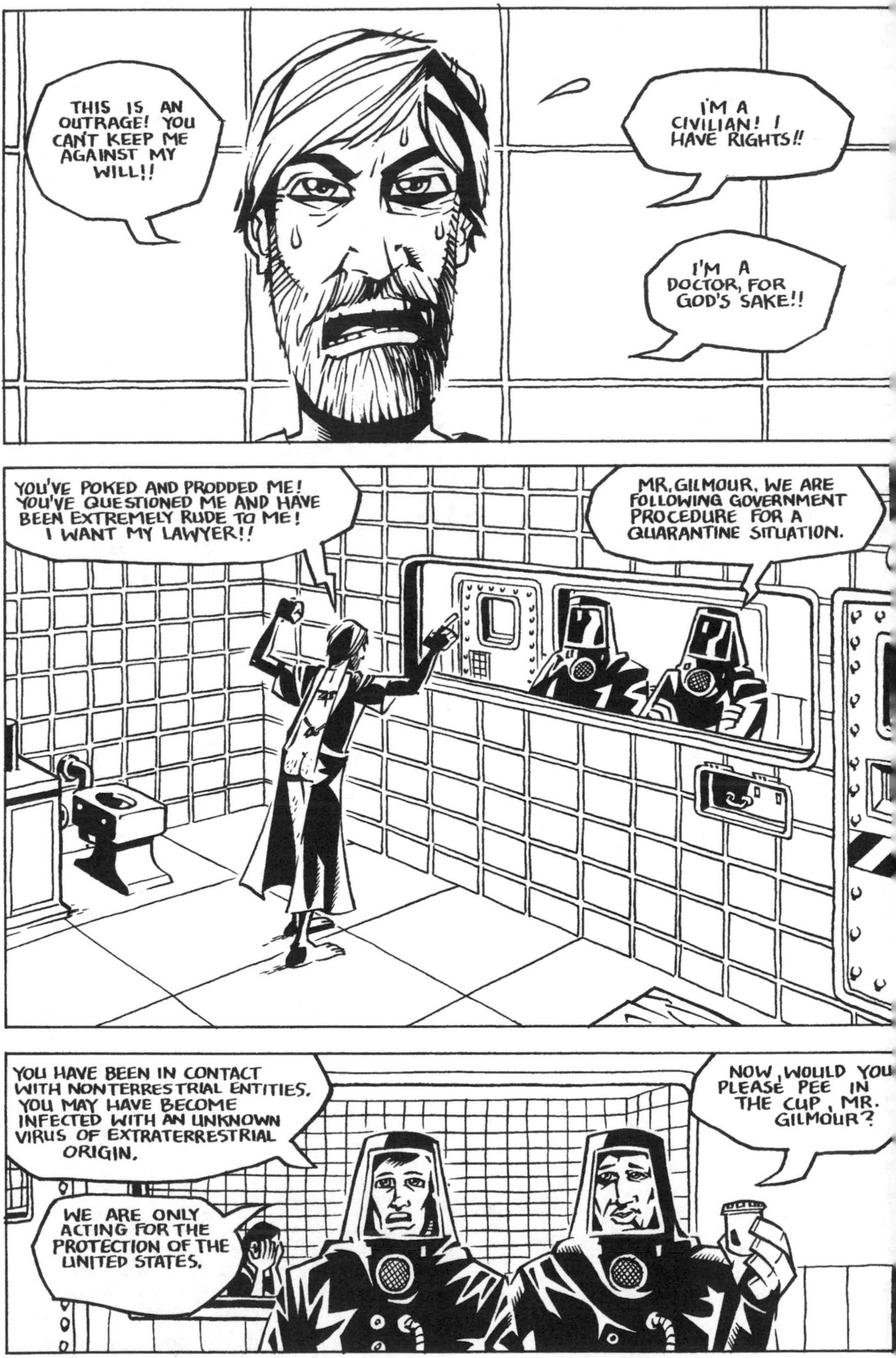
THIS IS AN OUTRAGE! YOU CAN'T KEEP ME AGAINST MY WILL!!
I'M A CIVILIAN! I HAVE RIGHTS!!
I'M A DOCTOR, FOR GOD'S SAKE!!
YOU'VE POKED AND PRODDED ME! YOU'VE QUESTIONED ME AND HAVE BEEN EXTREMELY RUDE TO ME! I WANT MY LAWYER!!
MR. GILMOUR, WE ARE FOLLOWING GOVERNMENT PROCEDURE FOR A QUARANTINE SITUATION.
YOU HAVE BEEN IN CONTACT WITH NONTERRESTRIAL ENTITIES. YOU MAY HAVE BECOME INFECTED WITH AN UNKNOWN VIRUS OF EXTRATERRESTRIAL ORIGIN.
WE ARE ONLY ACTING FOR THE PROTECTION OF THE UNITED STATES.
NOW, WOULD YOU PLEASE PEE IN THE CUP, MR. GILMOUR?

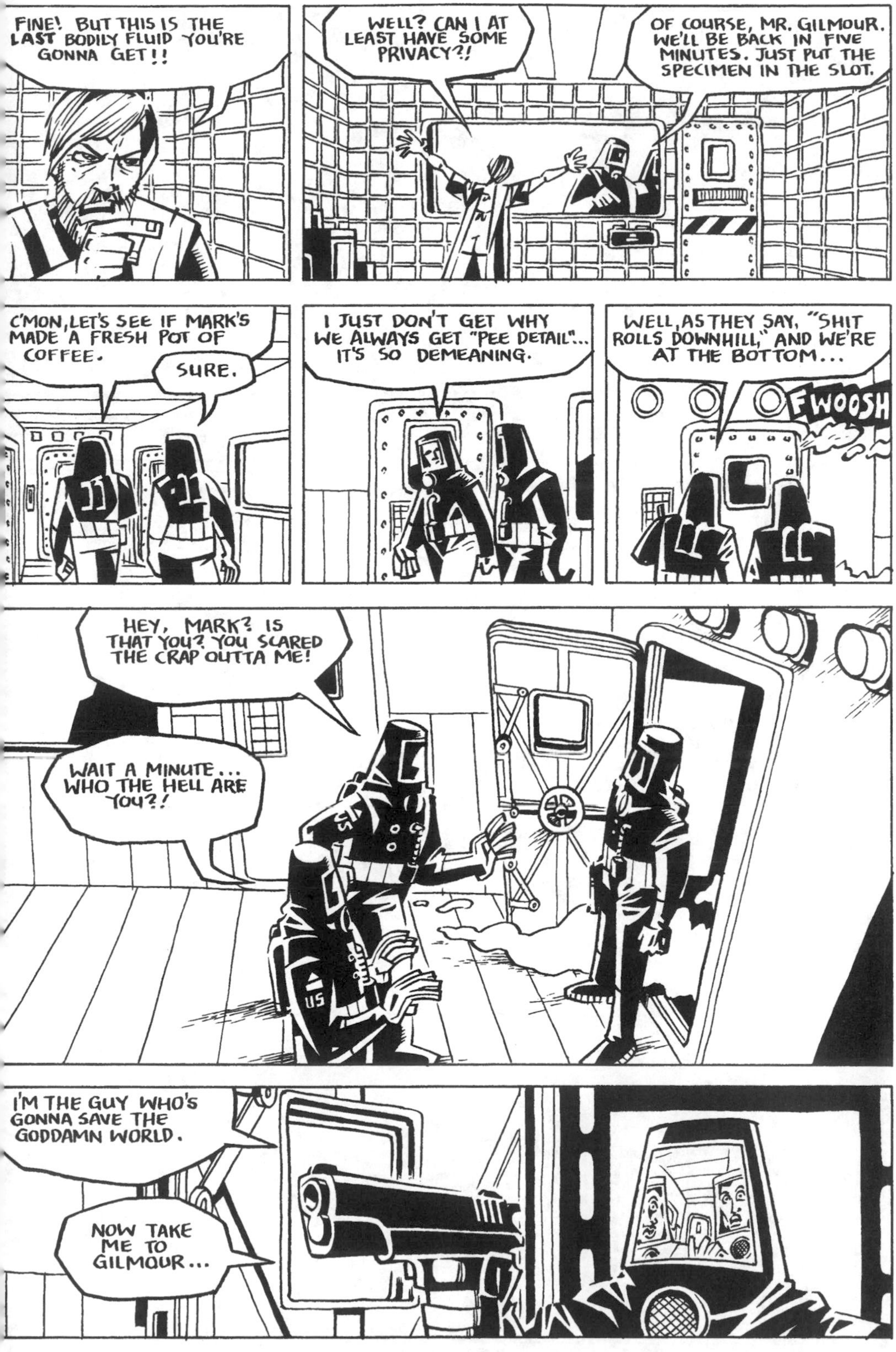

FINE! BUT THIS IS THE LAST BODILY FLUID YOU'RE GONNA GET!!
WELL? CAN I AT LEAST HAVE SOME PRIVACY?!
OF COURSE, MR. GILMOUR. WE'LL BE BACK IN FIVE MINUTES. JUST PUT THE SPECIMEN IN THE SLOT.
C'MON, LET'S SEE IF MARK'S MADE A FRESH POT OF COFFEE.
SURE.
I JUST DON'T GET WHY WE ALWAYS GET "PEE DETAIL"... IT'S SO DEMEANING.
WELL, AS THEY SAY, "SHIT ROLLS DOWNHILL," AND WE'RE AT THE BOTTOM...
FWOOSH
HEY, MARK? IS THAT YOU? YOU SCARED THE CRAP OUTTA ME!
WAIT A MINUTE... WHO THE HELL ARE YOU?!
US
I'M THE GUY WHO'S GONNA SAVE THE GODDAMN WORLD.
NOW TAKE ME TO GILMOUR...

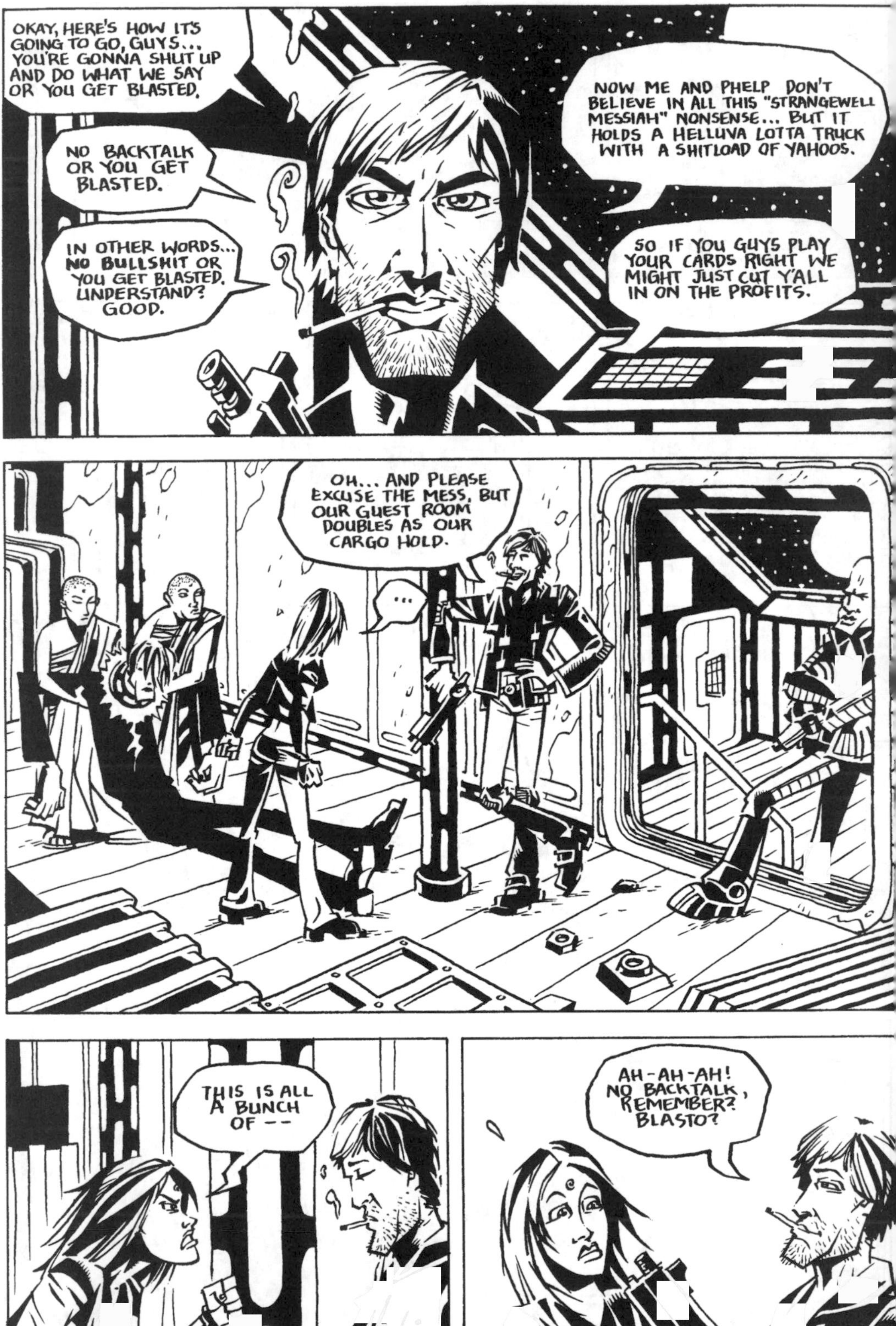
OKAY, HERE'S HOW IT'S GOING TO GO, GUYS... YOU'RE GONNA SHUT UP AND DO WHAT WE SAY OR YOU GET BLASTED.
NO BACKTALK OR YOU GET BLASTED.
IN OTHER WORDS... NO BULLSHIT OR YOU GET BLASTED. UNDERSTAND? GOOD.
NOW ME AND PHELP DON'T BELIEVE IN ALL THIS "STRANGEWELL MESSIAH" NONSENSE... BUT IT HOLDS A HELLUVA LOTTA TRUCK WITH A SHITLOAD OF YAHOOS.
SO IF YOU GUYS PLAY YOUR CARDS RIGHT WE MIGHT JUST CUT Y'ALL IN ON THE PROFITS.
OH... AND PLEASE EXCUSE THE MESS, BUT OUR GUEST ROOM DOUBLES AS OUR CARGO HOLD.
...
THIS IS ALL A BUNCH OF --
AH-AH-AH! NO BACKTALK, REMEMBER? BLASTO?

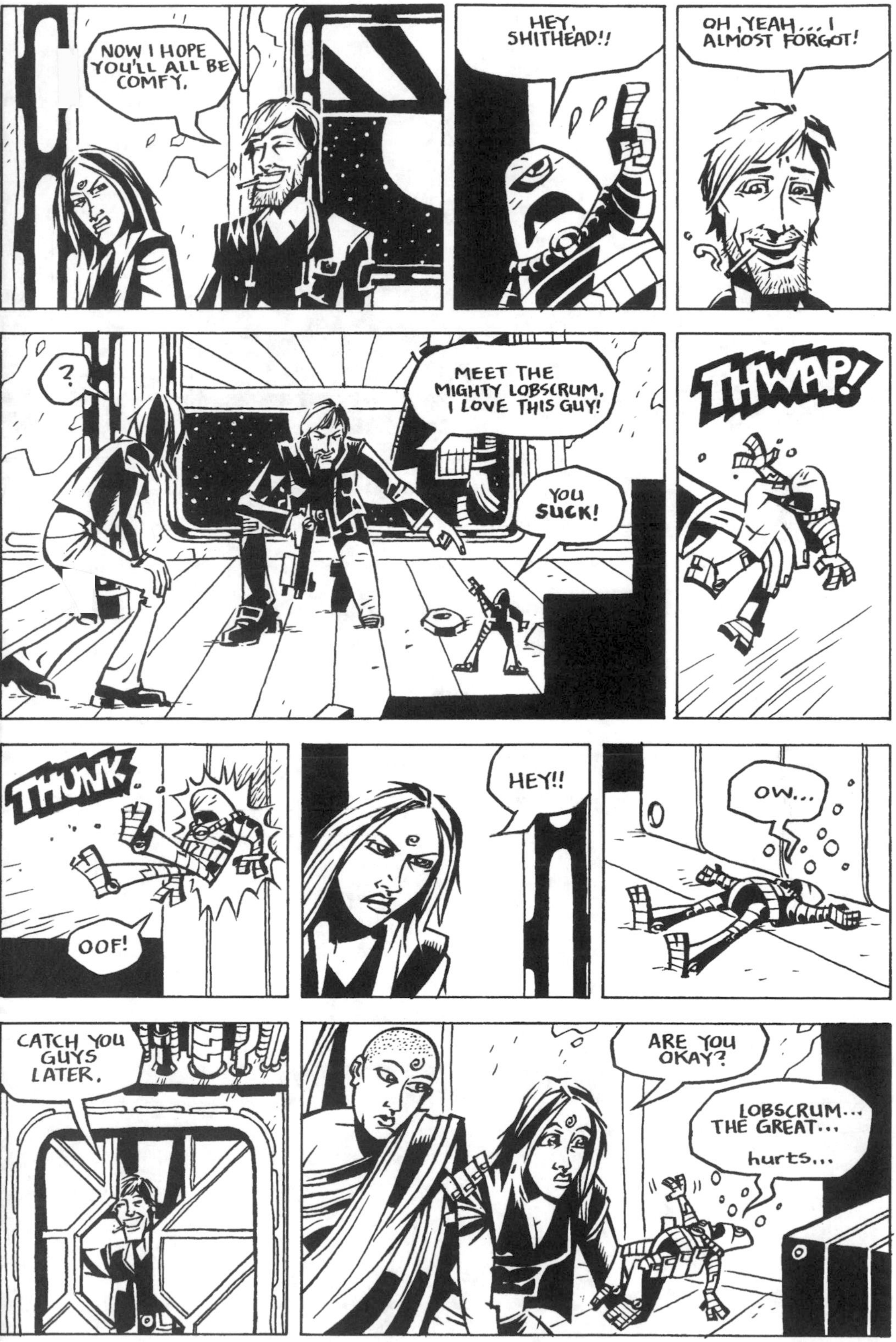
NOW I HOPE YOU'LL ALL BE COMFY.
HEY, SHITHEAD!!
OH, YEAH... I ALMOST FORGOT!
?
MEET THE MIGHTY LOBSCRUM. I LOVE THIS GUY!
YOU SUCK!
THWAP!
THUNK
OOF!
HEY!!
OW...
CATCH YOU GUYS LATER.
ARE YOU OKAY?
LOBSCRUM... THE GREAT...
hurts...

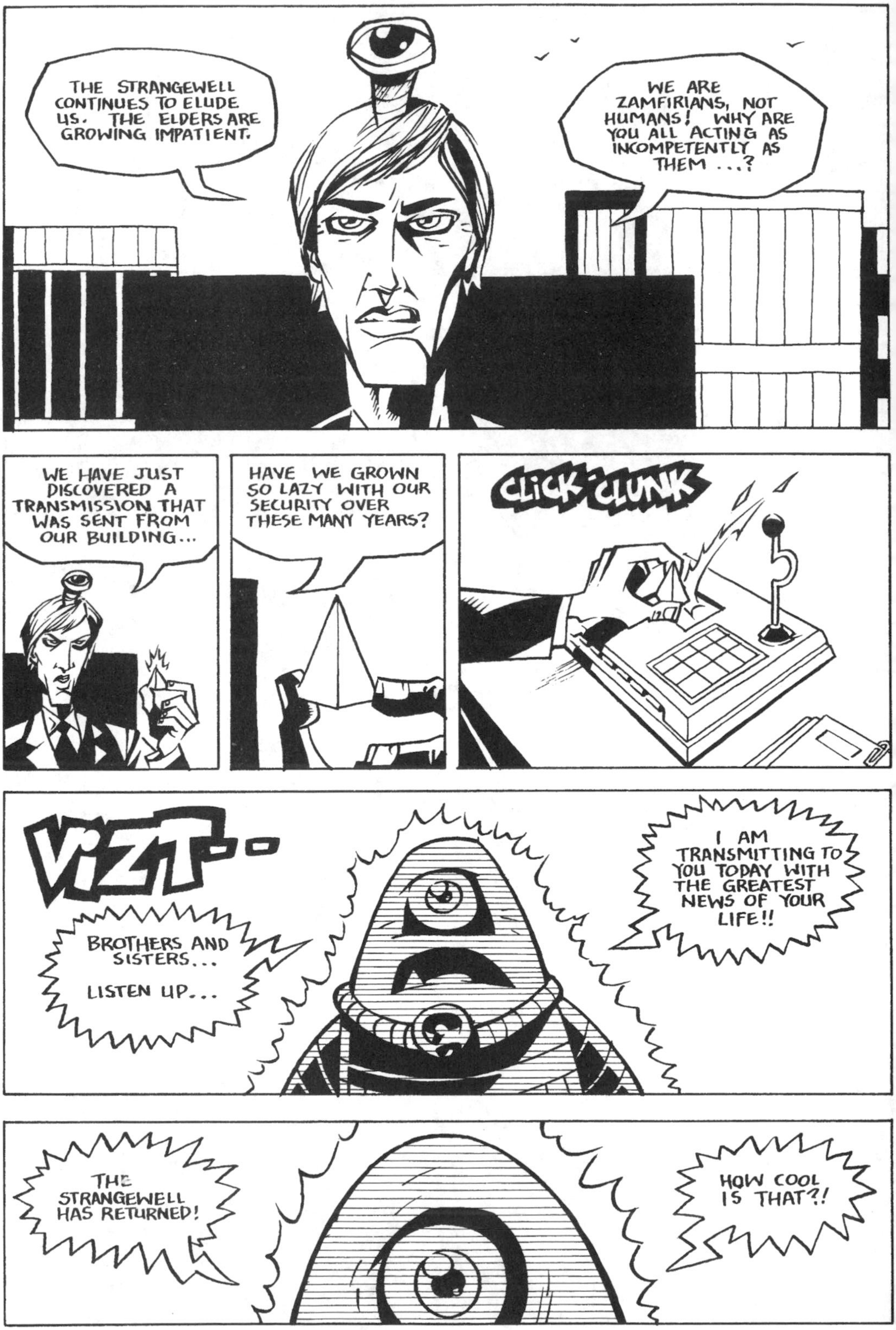
THE STRANGEWELL CONTINUES TO ELUDE US. THE ELDERS ARE GROWING IMPATIENT.
WE ARE ZAMFIRIANS, NOT HUMANS! WHY ARE YOU ALL ACTING AS INCOMPETENTLY AS THEM ...?
WE HAVE JUST DISCOVERED A TRANSMISSION THAT WAS SENT FROM OUR BUILDING...
HAVE WE GROWN SO LAZY WITH OUR SECURITY OVER THESE MANY YEARS?
CLICK CLUNK
VIZT--
BROTHERS AND SISTERS... LISTEN UP...
I AM TRANSMITTING TO YOU TODAY WITH THE GREATEST NEWS OF YOUR LIFE!!
THE STRANGEWELL HAS RETURNED!
HOW COOL IS THAT?!

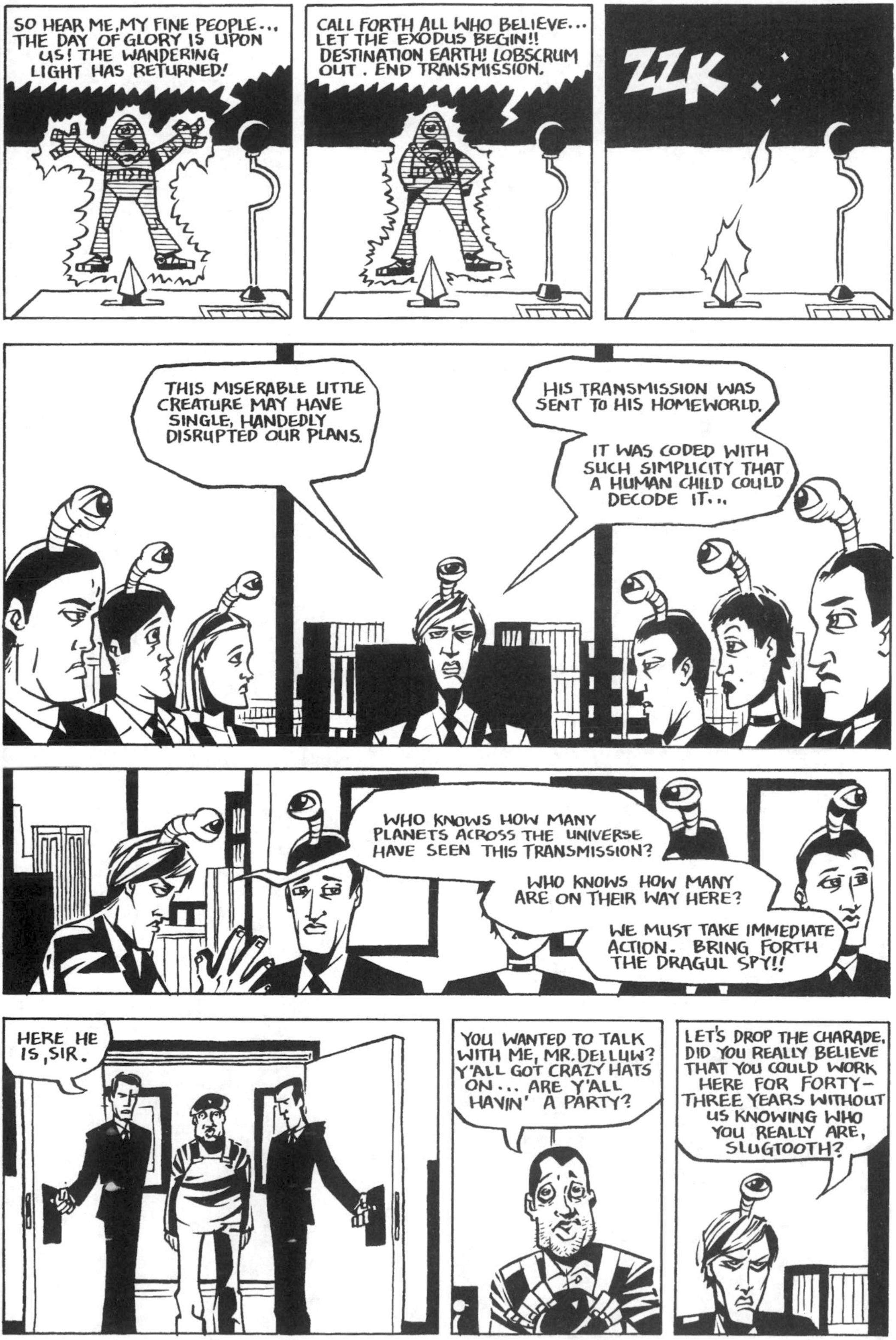
SO HEAR ME, MY FINE PEOPLE... THE DAY OF GLORY IS UPON US! THE WANDERING LIGHT HAS RETURNED!
CALL FORTH ALL WHO BELIEVE... LET THE EXODUS BEGIN!! DESTINATION EARTH! LOBSCRUM OUT. END TRANSMISSION.
ZZK
THIS MISERABLE LITTLE CREATURE MAY HAVE SINGLE, HANDEDLY DISRUPTED OUR PLANS.
HIS TRANSMISSION WAS SENT TO HIS HOMEWORLD.
IT WAS CODED WITH SUCH SIMPLICITY THAT A HUMAN CHILD COULD DECODE IT...
WHO KNOWS HOW MANY PLANETS ACROSS THE UNIVERSE HAVE SEEN THIS TRANSMISSION?
WHO KNOWS HOW MANY ARE ON THEIR WAY HERE?
WE MUST TAKE IMMEDIATE ACTION. BRING FORTH THE DRAGUL SPY!!
HERE HE IS, SIR.
YOU WANTED TO TALK WITH ME, MR. DELLUW? Y'ALL GOT CRAZY HATS ON... ARE Y'ALL HAVIN' A PARTY?
LET'S DROP THE CHARADE. DID YOU REALLY BELIEVE THAT YOU COULD WORK HERE FOR FORTY-THREE YEARS WITHOUT US KNOWING WHO YOU REALLY ARE, SLUGTOOTH?

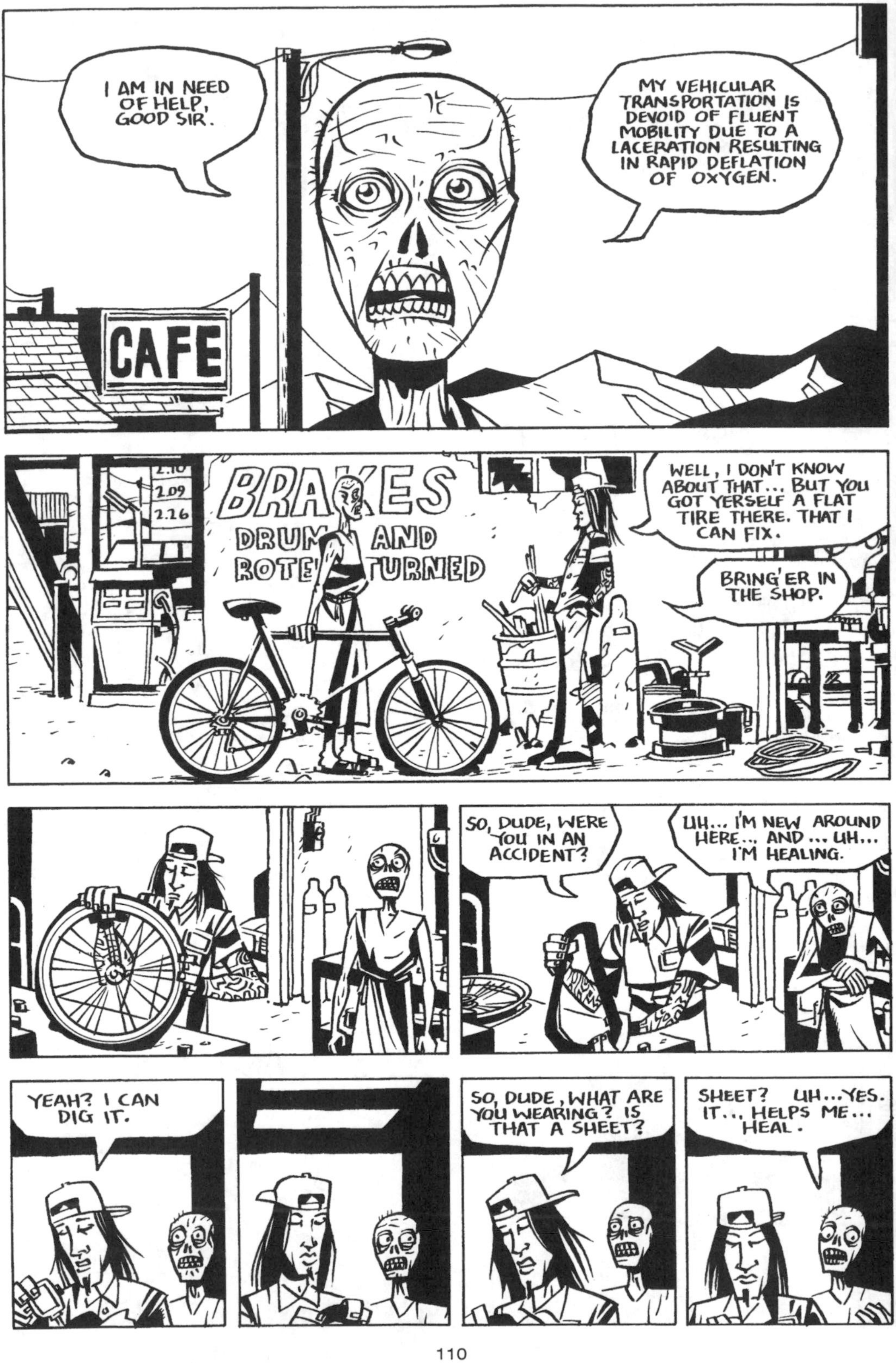
I AM IN NEED OF HELP, GOOD SIR.
MY VEHICULAR TRANSPORTATION IS DEVOID OF FLUENT MOBILITY DUE TO A LACERATION RESULTING IN RAPID DEFLATION OF OXYGEN.
CAFE
BRAKES
DRUM AND ROTE TURNED
2.09
2.26
WELL, I DON'T KNOW ABOUT THAT... BUT YOU GOT YERSELF A FLAT TIRE THERE. THAT I CAN FIX.
BRING'ER IN THE SHOP.
SO, DUDE, WERE YOU IN AN ACCIDENT?
UH... I'M NEW AROUND HERE... AND... UH... I'M HEALING.
YEAH? I CAN DIG IT.
SO, DUDE, WHAT ARE YOU WEARING? IS THAT A SHEET?
SHEET? UH...YES. IT... HELPS ME... HEAL.

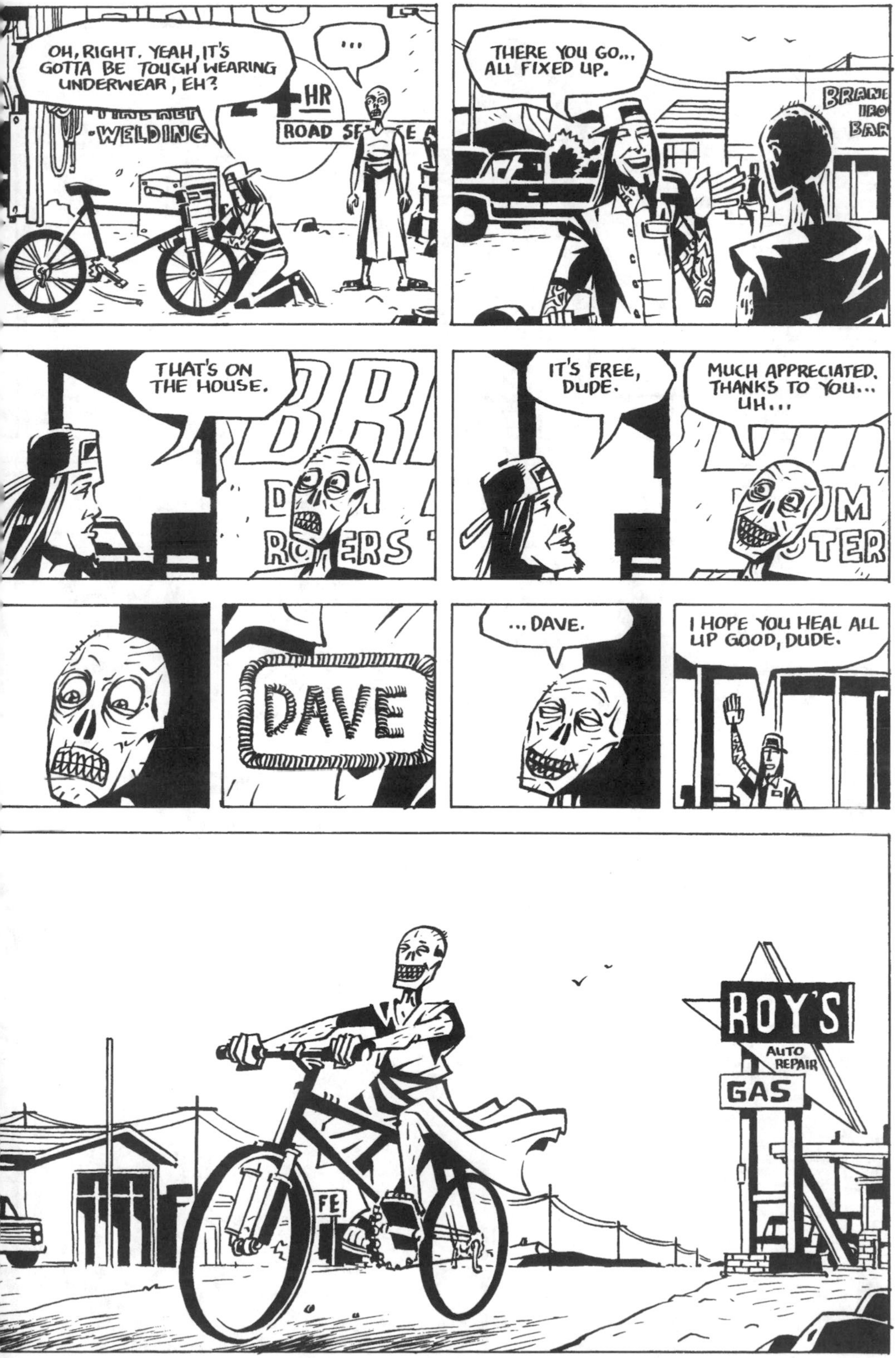
OH, RIGHT. YEAH, IT'S GOTTA BE TOUGH WEARING UNDERWEAR, EH?
...
-WELDING
24 HR
THERE YOU GO... ALL FIXED UP.
THAT'S ON THE HOUSE.
IT'S FREE, DUDE.
MUCH APPRECIATED. THANKS TO YOU... UH...
DAVE
...DAVE.
I HOPE YOU HEAL ALL UP GOOD, DUDE.
ROY'S
AUTO REPAIR
GAS

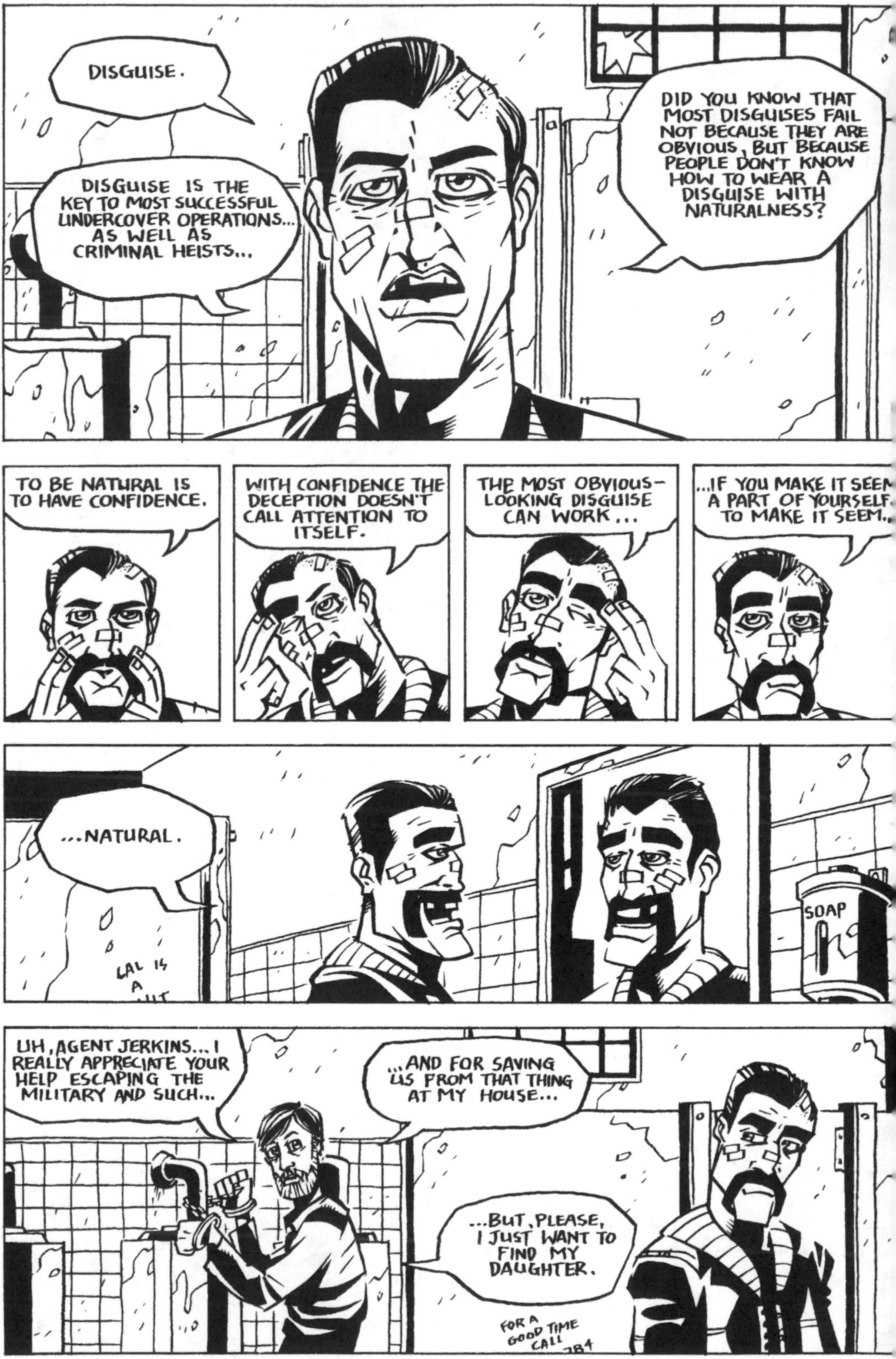
DISGUISE.
DISGUISE IS THE KEY TO MOST SUCCESSFUL UNDERCOVER OPERATIONS... AS WELL AS CRIMINAL HEISTS...
DID YOU KNOW THAT MOST DISGUISES FAIL NOT BECAUSE THEY ARE OBVIOUS, BUT BECAUSE PEOPLE DON'T KNOW HOW TO WEAR A DISGUISE WITH NATURALNESS?
TO BE NATURAL IS TO HAVE CONFIDENCE.
WITH CONFIDENCE THE DECEPTION DOESN'T CALL ATTENTION TO ITSELF.
THE MOST OBVIOUS-LOOKING DISGUISE CAN WORK...
...IF YOU MAKE IT SEEM A PART OF YOURSELF. TO MAKE IT SEEM...
...NATURAL.
SOAP
UH, AGENT JERKINS... I REALLY APPRECIATE YOUR HELP ESCAPING THE MILITARY AND SUCH...
...AND FOR SAVING US FROM THAT THING AT MY HOUSE...
...BUT, PLEASE, I JUST WANT TO FIND MY DAUGHTER.
FOR A GOOD TIME CALL

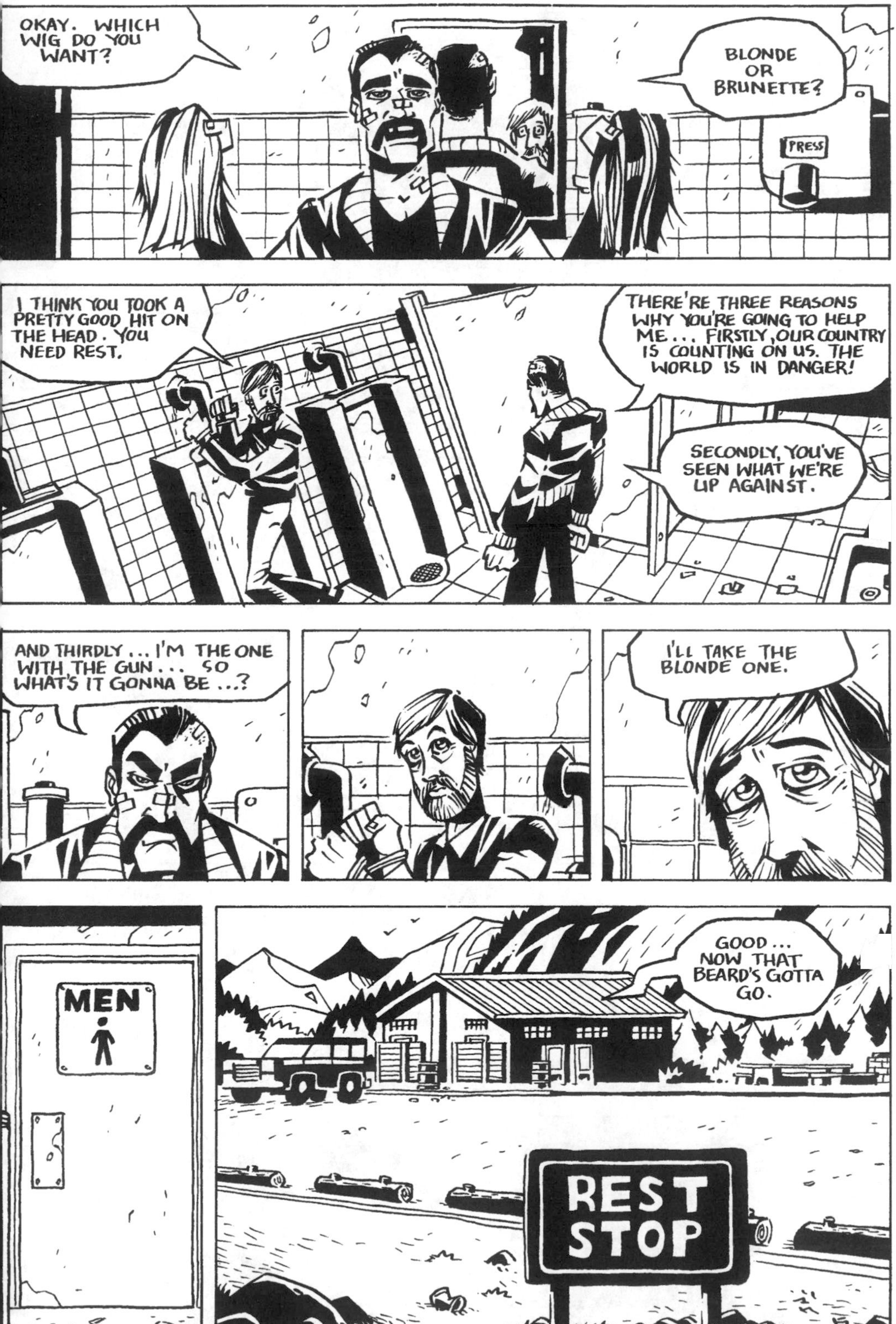
OKAY. WHICH WIG DO YOU WANT?
BLONDE OR BRUNETTE?
PRESS
I THINK YOU TOOK A PRETTY GOOD HIT ON THE HEAD. YOU NEED REST.
THERE'RE THREE REASONS WHY YOU'RE GOING TO HELP ME... FIRSTLY, OUR COUNTRY IS COUNTING ON US. THE WORLD IS IN DANGER!
SECONDLY, YOU'VE SEEN WHAT WE'RE UP AGAINST.
AND THIRDLY... I'M THE ONE WITH THE GUN... SO WHAT'S IT GONNA BE...?
I'LL TAKE THE BLONDE ONE.
MEN
GOOD... NOW THAT BEARD'S GOTTA GO.
REST STOP

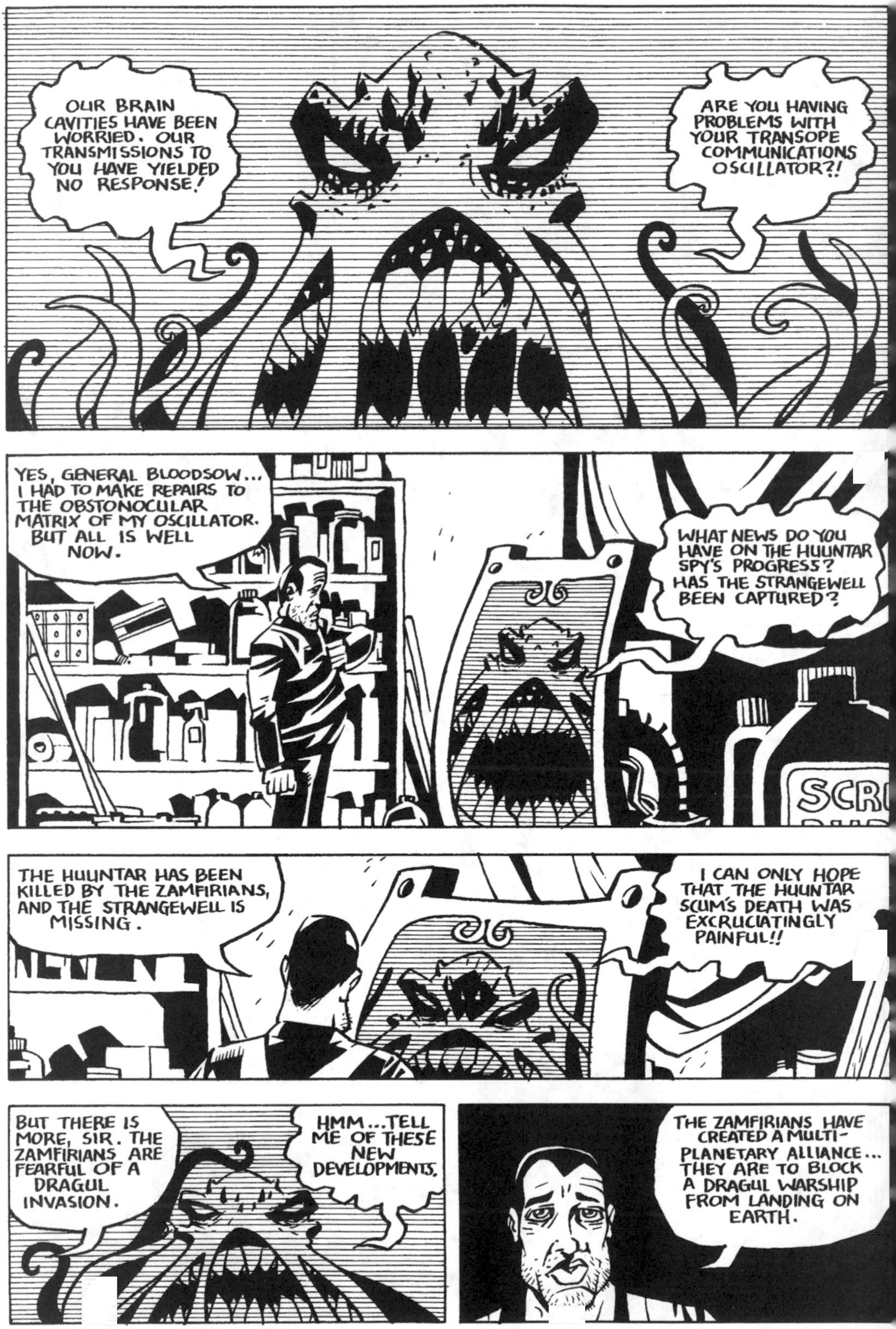
OUR BRAIN CAVITIES HAVE BEEN WORRIED. OUR TRANSMISSIONS TO YOU HAVE YIELDED NO RESPONSE!
ARE YOU HAVING PROBLEMS WITH YOUR TRANSOPE COMMUNICATIONS OSCILLATOR?!
YES, GENERAL BLOODSOW... I HAD TO MAKE REPAIRS TO THE OBSTONOCULAR MATRIX OF MY OSCILLATOR. BUT ALL IS WELL NOW.
WHAT NEWS DO YOU HAVE ON THE HUUNTAR SPY'S PROGRESS? HAS THE STRANGEWELL BEEN CAPTURED?
SCR
THE HUUNTAR HAS BEEN KILLED BY THE ZAMFIRIANS, AND THE STRANGEWELL IS MISSING.
I CAN ONLY HOPE THAT THE HUUNTAR SCUM'S DEATH WAS EXCRUCIATINGLY PAINFUL!!
BUT THERE IS MORE, SIR. THE ZAMFIRIANS ARE FEARFUL OF A DRAGUL INVASION.
HMM... TELL ME OF THESE NEW DEVELOPMENTS.
THE ZAMFIRIANS HAVE CREATED A MULTI-PLANETARY ALLIANCE... THEY ARE TO BLOCK A DRAGUL WARSHIP FROM LANDING ON EARTH.

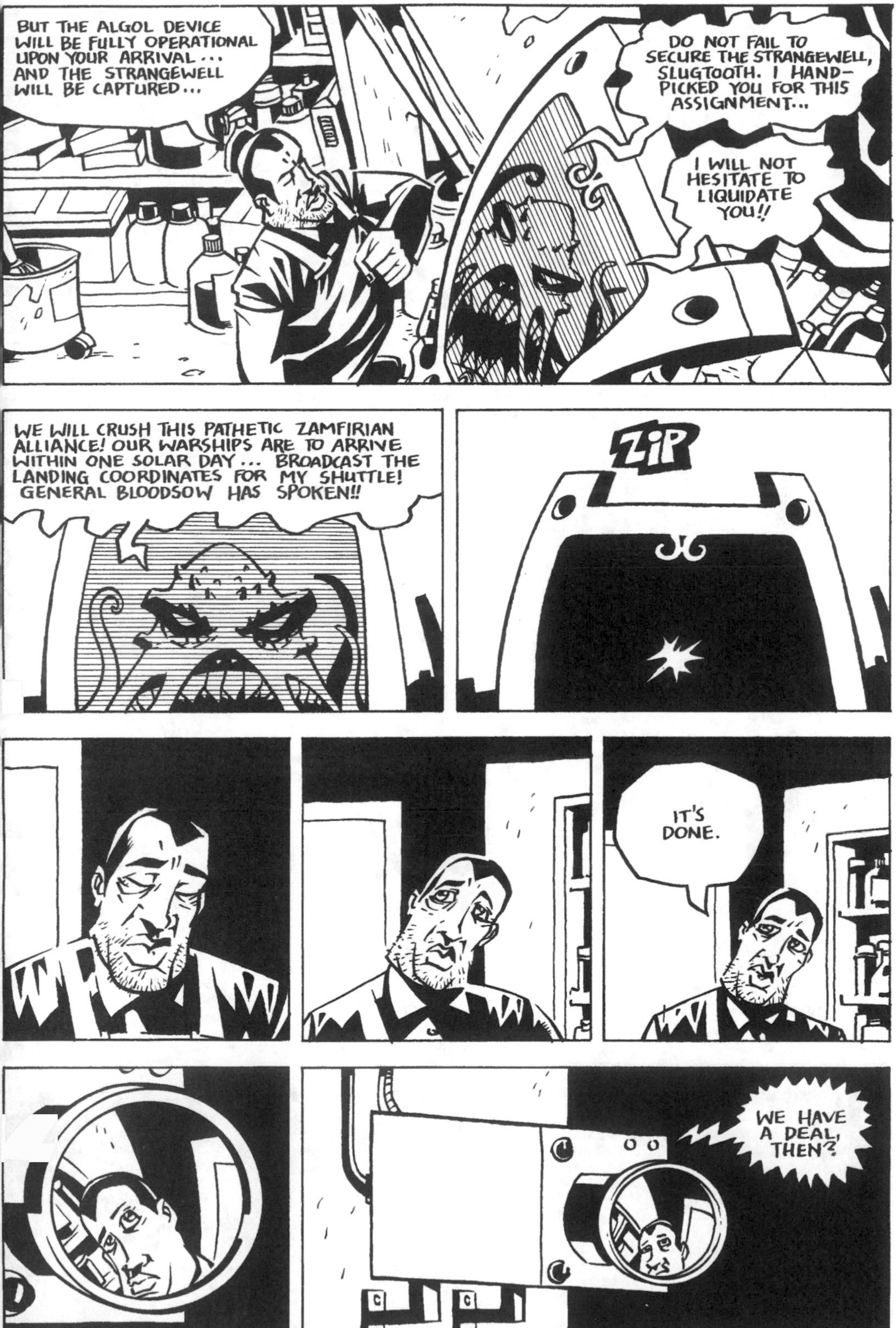
BUT THE ALGOL DEVICE WILL BE FULLY OPERATIONAL UPON YOUR ARRIVAL... AND THE STRANGEWELL WILL BE CAPTURED...
DO NOT FAIL TO SECURE THE STRANGEWELL, SLUGTOOTH. I HAND-PICKED YOU FOR THIS ASSIGNMENT...
I WILL NOT HESITATE TO LIQUIDATE YOU!!
WE WILL CRUSH THIS PATHETIC ZAMFIRIAN ALLIANCE! OUR WARSHIPS ARE TO ARRIVE WITHIN ONE SOLAR DAY... BROADCAST THE LANDING COORDINATES FOR MY SHUTTLE! GENERAL BLOODSOW HAS SPOKEN!!
ZIP
IT'S DONE.
WE HAVE A DEAL, THEN?

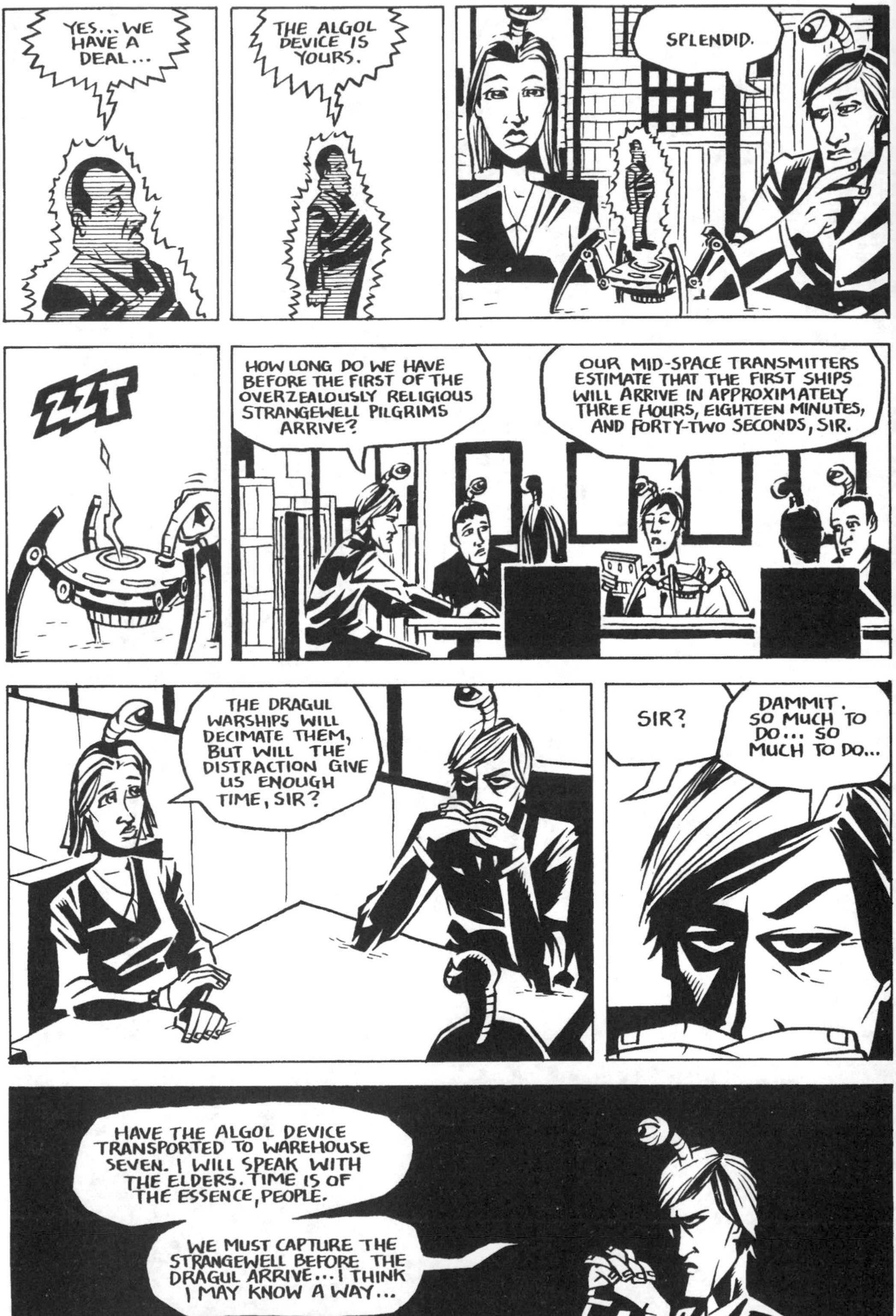
YES... WE HAVE A DEAL...
THE ALGOL DEVICE IS YOURS.
SPLENDID.
ZZT
HOW LONG DO WE HAVE BEFORE THE FIRST OF THE OVERZEALOUSLY RELIGIOUS STRANGEWELL PILGRIMS ARRIVE?
OUR MID-SPACE TRANSMITTERS ESTIMATE THAT THE FIRST SHIPS WILL ARRIVE IN APPROXIMATELY THREE HOURS, EIGHTEEN MINUTES, AND FORTY-TWO SECONDS, SIR.
THE DRAGUL WARSHIPS WILL DECIMATE THEM, BUT WILL THE DISTRACTION GIVE US ENOUGH TIME, SIR?
SIR?
DAMMIT. SO MUCH TO DO... SO MUCH TO DO...
HAVE THE ALGOL DEVICE TRANSPORTED TO WAREHOUSE SEVEN. I WILL SPEAK WITH THE ELDERS. TIME IS OF THE ESSENCE, PEOPLE.
WE MUST CAPTURE THE STRANGEWELL BEFORE THE DRAGUL ARRIVE... I THINK I MAY KNOW A WAY...

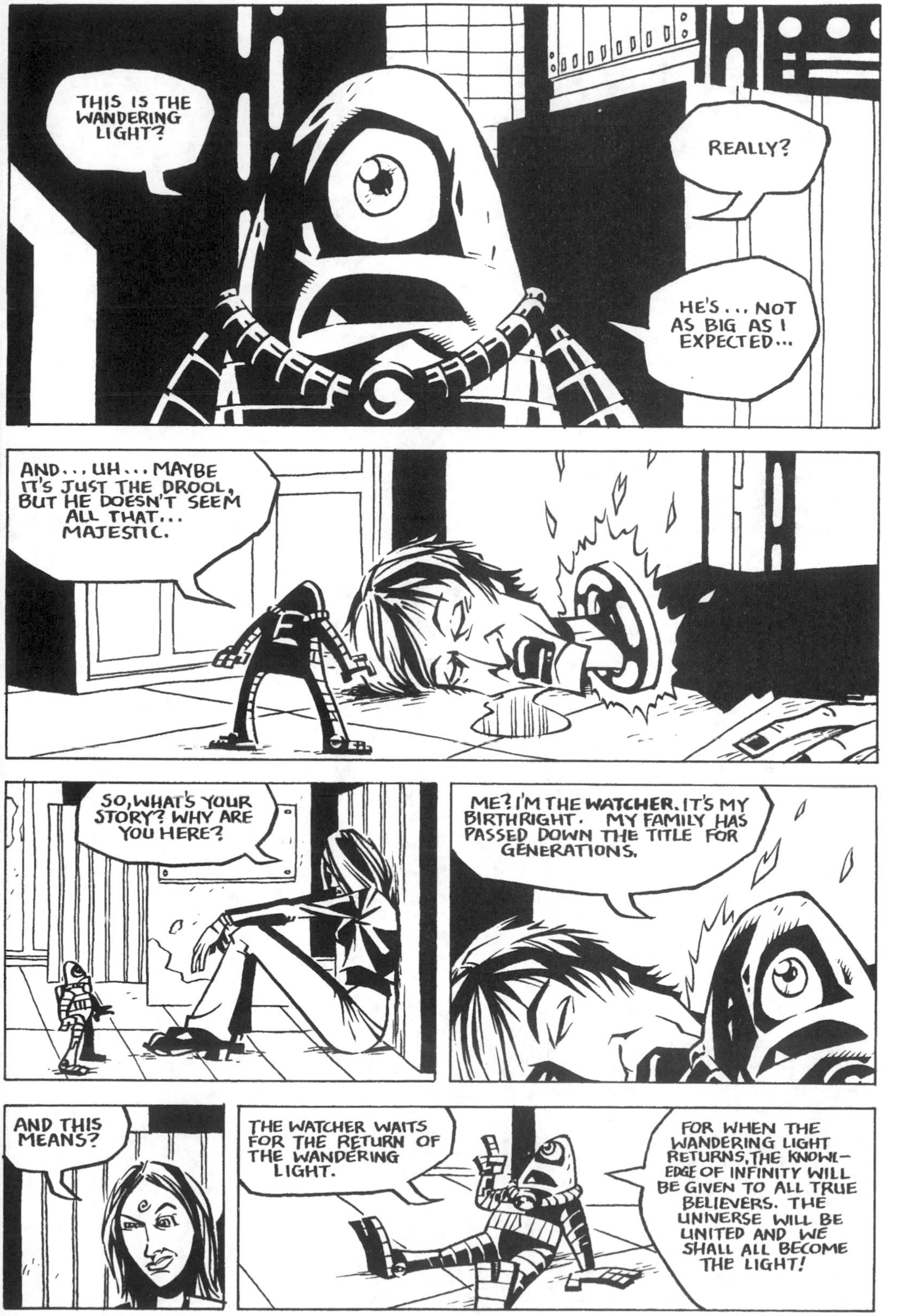
THIS IS THE WANDERING LIGHT?
REALLY?
HE'S... NOT AS BIG AS I EXPECTED...
AND... UH... MAYBE IT'S JUST THE DROOL, BUT HE DOESN'T SEEM ALL THAT... MAJESTIC.
SO, WHAT'S YOUR STORY? WHY ARE YOU HERE?
ME? I'M THE WATCHER. IT'S MY BIRTHRIGHT. MY FAMILY HAS PASSED DOWN THE TITLE FOR GENERATIONS.
AND THIS MEANS?
THE WATCHER WAITS FOR THE RETURN OF THE WANDERING LIGHT.
FOR WHEN THE WANDERING LIGHT RETURNS, THE KNOWL-EDGE OF INFINITY WILL BE GIVEN TO ALL TRUE BELIEVERS. THE UNIVERSE WILL BE UNITED AND WE SHALL ALL BECOME THE LIGHT!

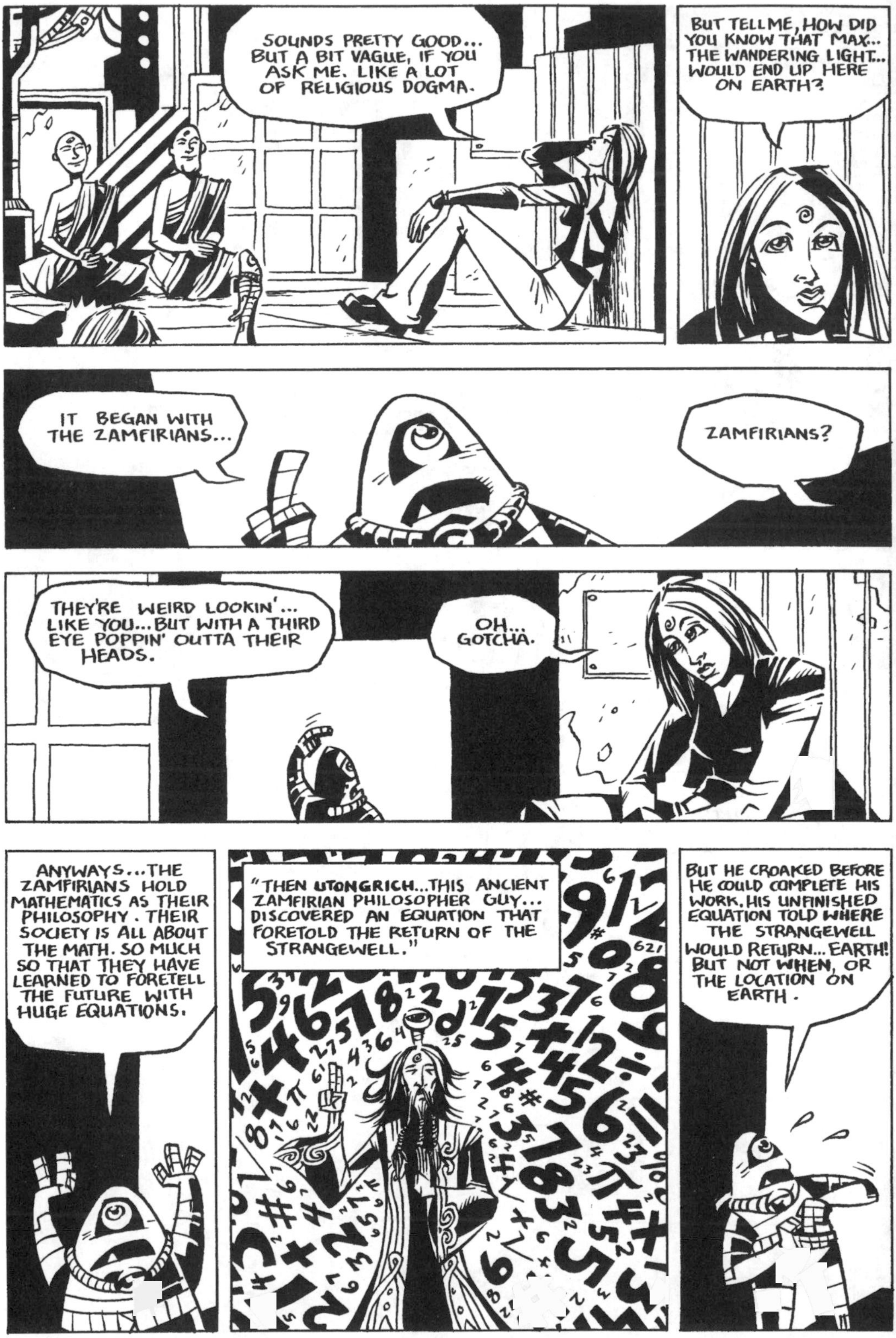
SOUNDS PRETTY GOOD... BUT A BIT VAGUE, IF YOU ASK ME. LIKE A LOT OF RELIGIOUS DOGMA.
BUT TELL ME, HOW DID YOU KNOW THAT MAX... THE WANDERING LIGHT... WOULD END UP HERE ON EARTH?
IT BEGAN WITH THE ZAMFIRIANS...
ZAMFIRIANS?
THEY'RE WEIRD LOOKIN'... LIKE YOU... BUT WITH A THIRD EYE POPPIN' OUTTA THEIR HEADS.
OH... GOTCHA.
ANYWAYS... THE ZAMFIRIANS HOLD MATHEMATICS AS THEIR PHILOSOPHY. THEIR SOCIETY IS ALL ABOUT THE MATH. SO MUCH SO THAT THEY HAVE LEARNED TO FORETELL THE FUTURE WITH HUGE EQUATIONS.
"THEN UTONGRICH... THIS ANCIENT ZAMFIRIAN PHILOSOPHER GUY... DISCOVERED AN EQUATION THAT FORETOLD THE RETURN OF THE STRANGEWELL."
BUT HE CROAKED BEFORE HE COULD COMPLETE HIS WORK. HIS UNFINISHED EQUATION TOLD WHERE THE STRANGEWELL WOULD RETURN... EARTH! BUT NOT WHEN, OR THE LOCATION ON EARTH.

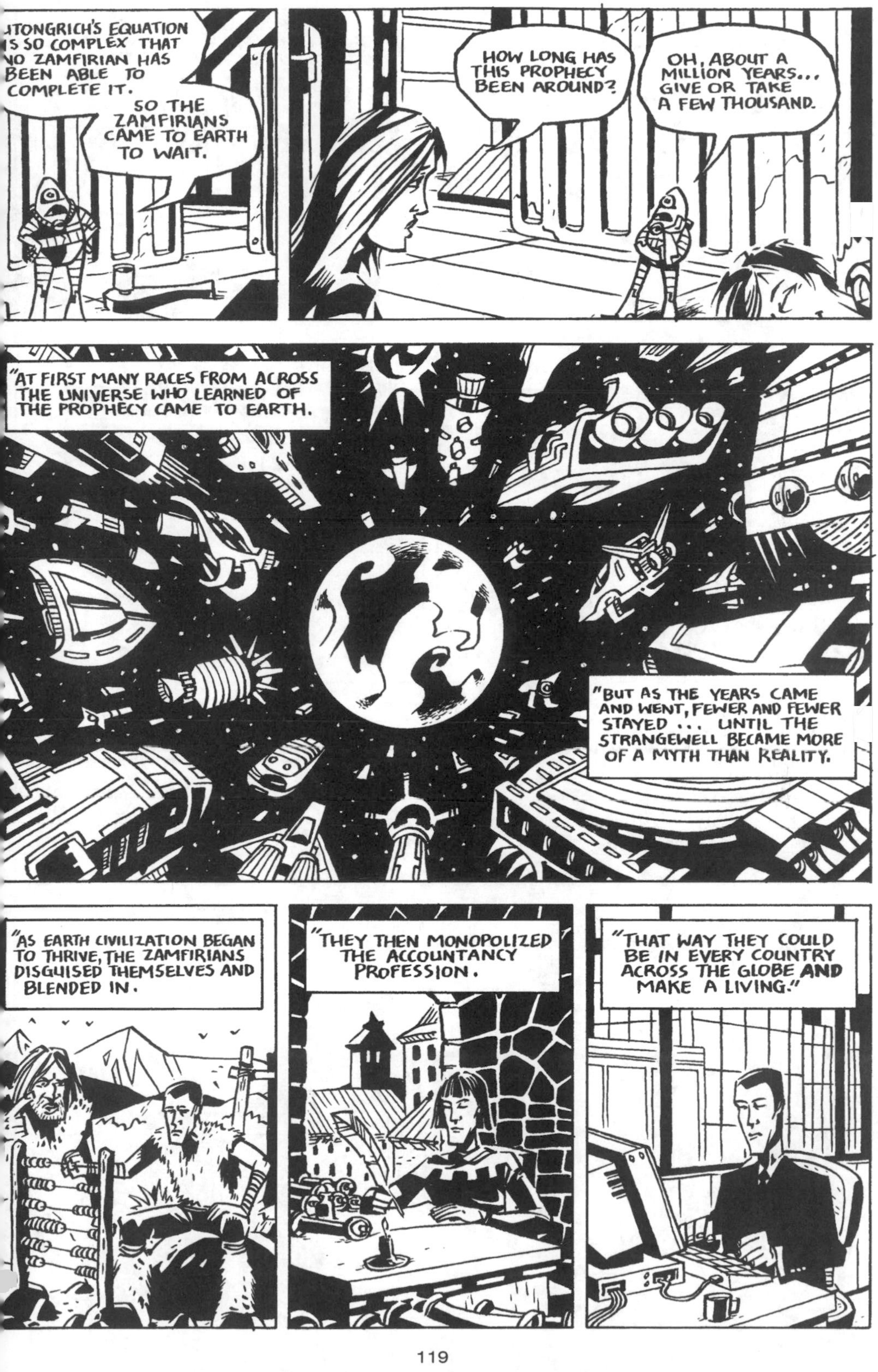

UTONGRICH'S EQUATION IS SO COMPLEX THAT NO ZAMFIRIAN HAS BEEN ABLE TO COMPLETE IT.
SO THE ZAMFIRIANS CAME TO EARTH TO WAIT.
HOW LONG HAS THIS PROPHECY BEEN AROUND?
OH, ABOUT A MILLION YEARS... GIVE OR TAKE A FEW THOUSAND.
"AT FIRST MANY RACES FROM ACROSS THE UNIVERSE WHO LEARNED OF THE PROPHECY CAME TO EARTH.
"BUT AS THE YEARS CAME AND WENT, FEWER AND FEWER STAYED ... UNTIL THE STRANGEWELL BECAME MORE OF A MYTH THAN REALITY.
"AS EARTH CIVILIZATION BEGAN TO THRIVE, THE ZAMFIRIANS DISGUISED THEMSELVES AND BLENDED IN.
"THEY THEN MONOPOLIZED THE ACCOUNTANCY PROFESSION.
"THAT WAY THEY COULD BE IN EVERY COUNTRY ACROSS THE GLOBE AND MAKE A LIVING."

THAT'S INSANE! WELL, ACTUALLY, THAT WOULD EXPLAIN A LOT ABOUT ACCOUNTANTS.

I MYSELF AM LOBSCRUM THE FIVE TOUSANDTH. MY FAMILY HAS BEEN VIGILANT IN WATCHING FOR THE STRANGEWELL... THOUGH THE LOBSCRUM NAME DOESN'T GET MUCH RESPECT ON MY HOMEWORLD, NIONA, ANYMORE.

AND NOW HE'S HERE AND THE LOBSCRUM NAME WILL BECOME LEGEND!! ESPECIALLY WHEN THE OTHERS ARRIVE!

OTHERS?!

oh, no... the galactic war.

I SENT A TRANSMISSION TO NIONA SO ALL TRUE BELIEVERS CAN COME AND WITNESS THE BIRTH OF THE NEW UNIVERSE!!

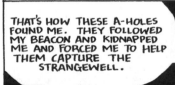

THAT'S HOW THESE A-HOLES FOUND ME. THEY FOLLOWED MY BEACON AND KIDNAPPED ME AND FORCED ME TO HELP THEM CAPTURE THE STRANGEWELL.

I JUST DON'T KNOW HOW THEY WERE ABLE TO DECODE MY TRANSMISSION! IT WAS LOCKED WITH THE MOST COMPLEX CODE I COULD THINK OF.

THIS IS ALL BLOWING MY MIND. I STILL DON'T UNDERSTAND HOW I'M LINKED WITH MAX...

AND NOW I'M FINDING OUT JUST HOW BIG THE UNIVERSE REALLY IS.

WHAT?!

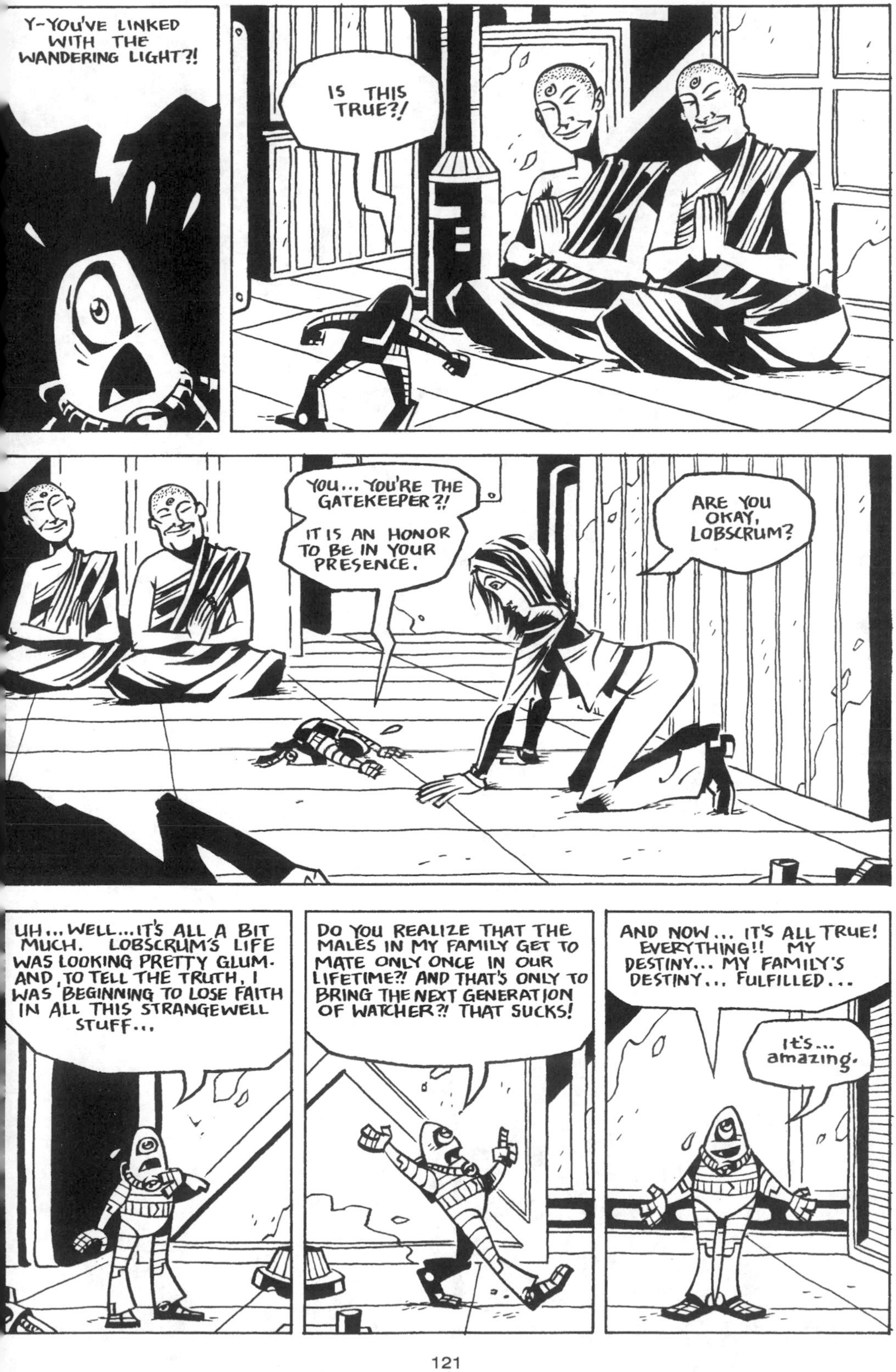
Y-YOU'VE LINKED WITH THE WANDERING LIGHT?!
IS THIS TRUE?!
YOU... YOU'RE THE GATEKEEPER?!
IT IS AN HONOR TO BE IN YOUR PRESENCE.
ARE YOU OKAY, LOBSCRUM?
UH... WELL... IT'S ALL A BIT MUCH. LOBSCRUM'S LIFE WAS LOOKING PRETTY GLUM. AND, TO TELL THE TRUTH, I WAS BEGINNING TO LOSE FAITH IN ALL THIS STRANGEWELL STUFF...
DO YOU REALIZE THAT THE MALES IN MY FAMILY GET TO MATE ONLY ONCE IN OUR LIFETIME?! AND THAT'S ONLY TO BRING THE NEXT GENERATION OF WATCHER?! THAT SUCKS!
AND NOW... IT'S ALL TRUE! EVERYTHING!! MY DESTINY... MY FAMILY'S DESTINY... FULFILLED...
It's... amazing.

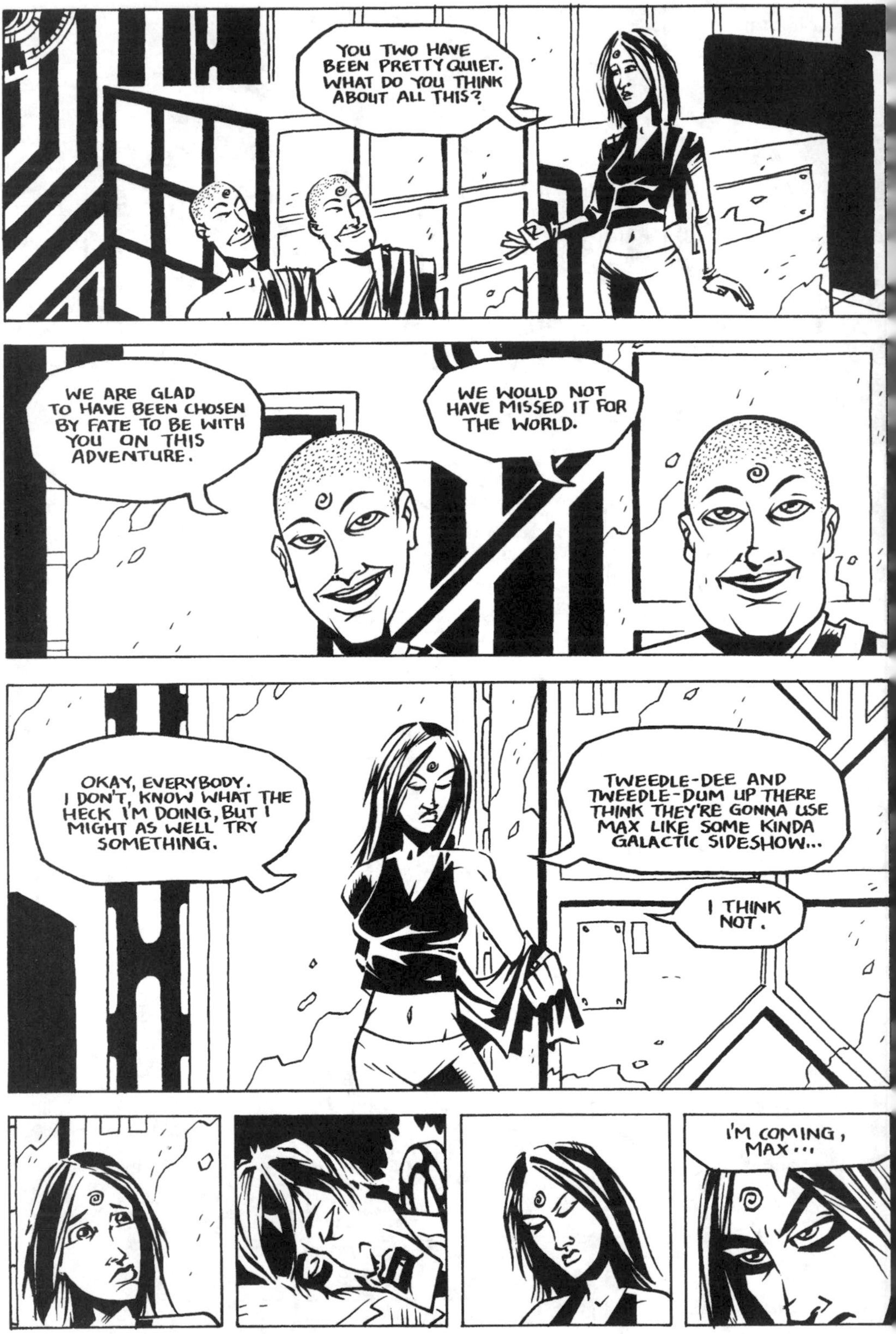

YOU TWO HAVE BEEN PRETTY QUIET. WHAT DO YOU THINK ABOUT ALL THIS?
WE ARE GLAD TO HAVE BEEN CHOSEN BY FATE TO BE WITH YOU ON THIS ADVENTURE.
WE WOULD NOT HAVE MISSED IT FOR THE WORLD.
OKAY, EVERYBODY. I DON'T KNOW WHAT THE HECK I'M DOING, BUT I MIGHT AS WELL TRY SOMETHING.
TWEEDLE-DEE AND TWEEDLE-DUM UP THERE THINK THEY'RE GONNA USE MAX LIKE SOME KINDA GALACTIC SIDESHOW...
I THINK NOT.
I'M COMING, MAX...

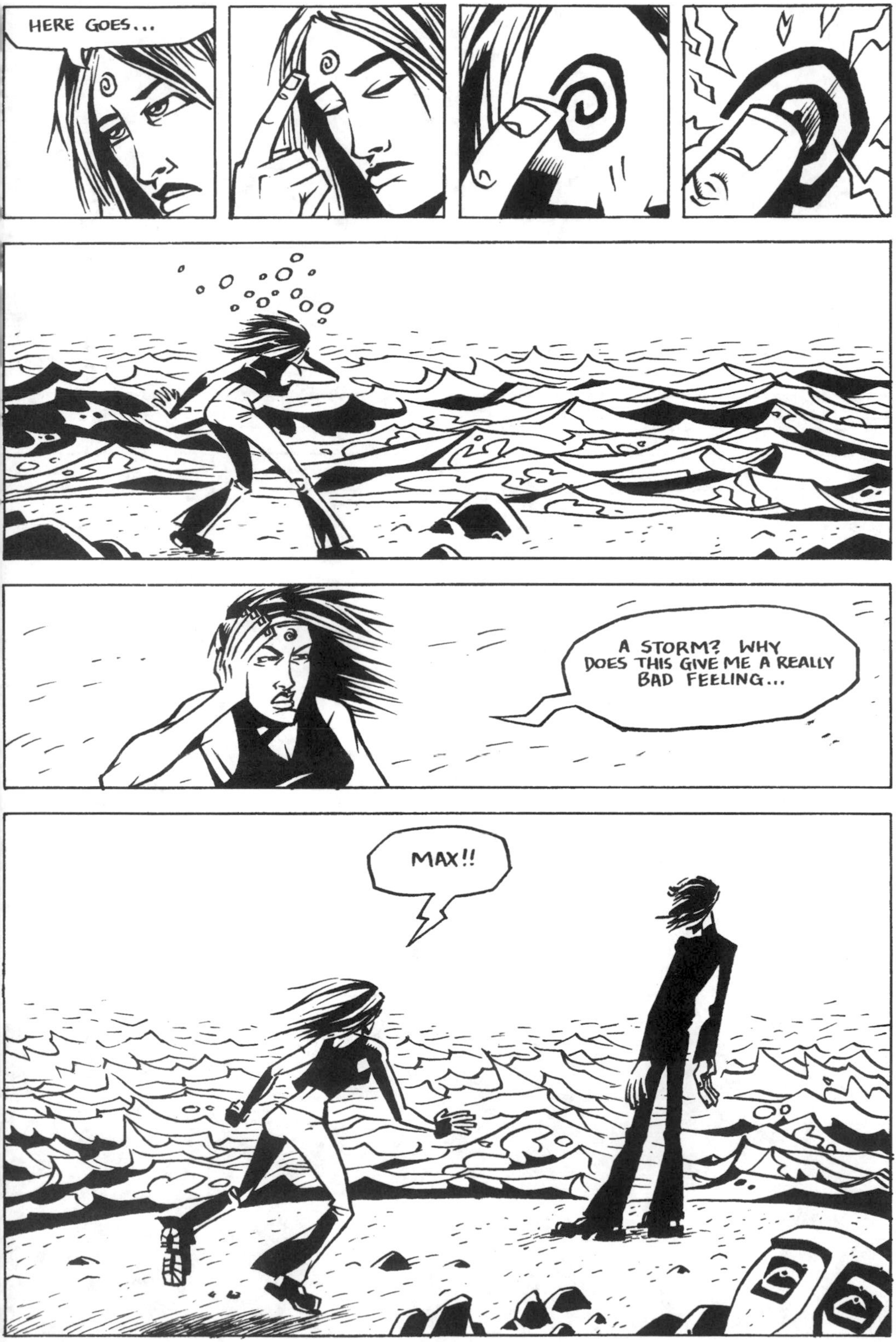
HERE GOES...
A STORM? WHY DOES THIS GIVE ME A REALLY BAD FEELING...
MAX!!

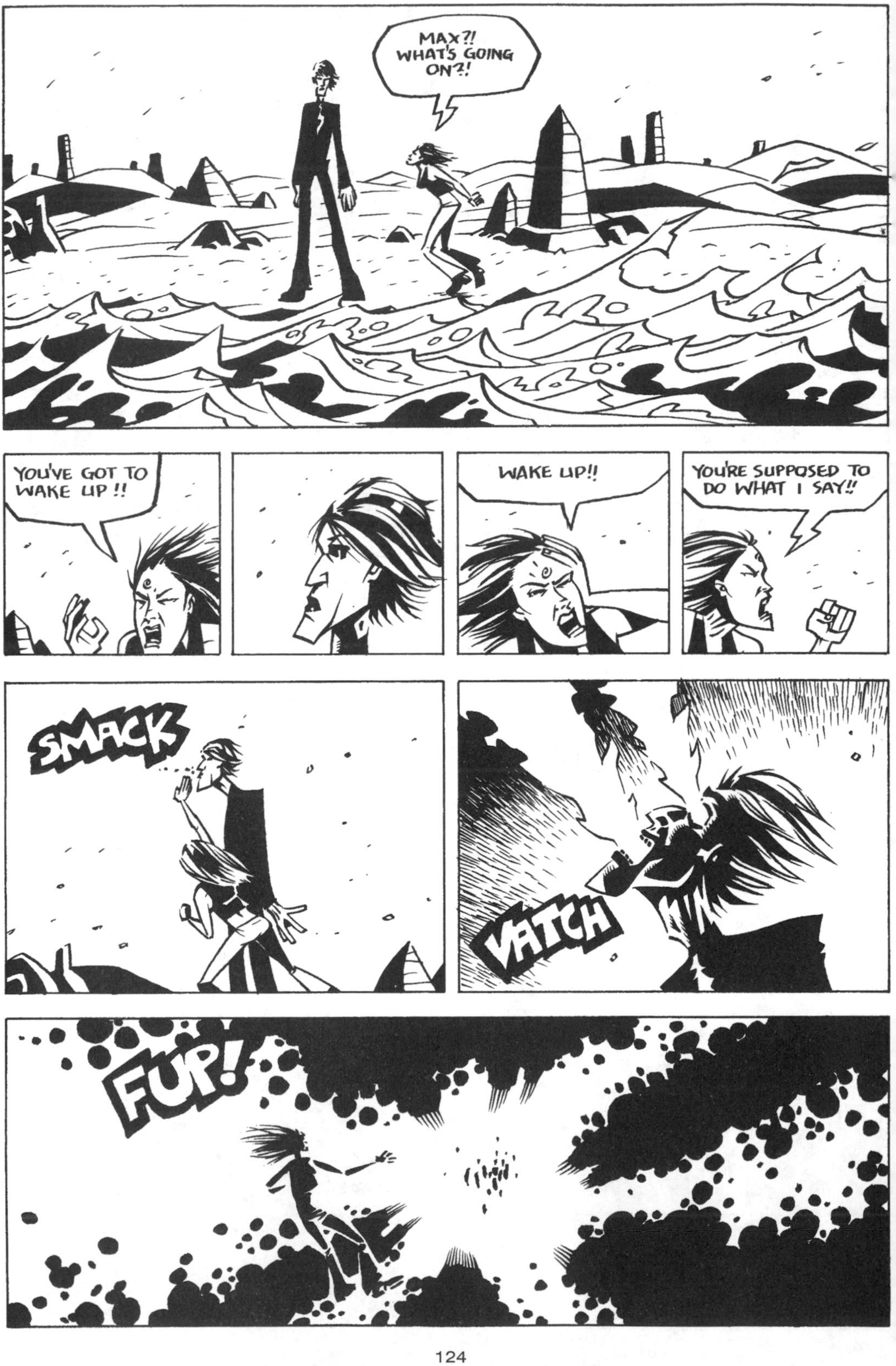
MAX?! WHAT'S GOING ON?!
YOU'VE GOT TO WAKE UP !!
WAKE UP!!
YOU'RE SUPPOSED TO DO WHAT I SAY!!
SMACK
VATCH
FUP!

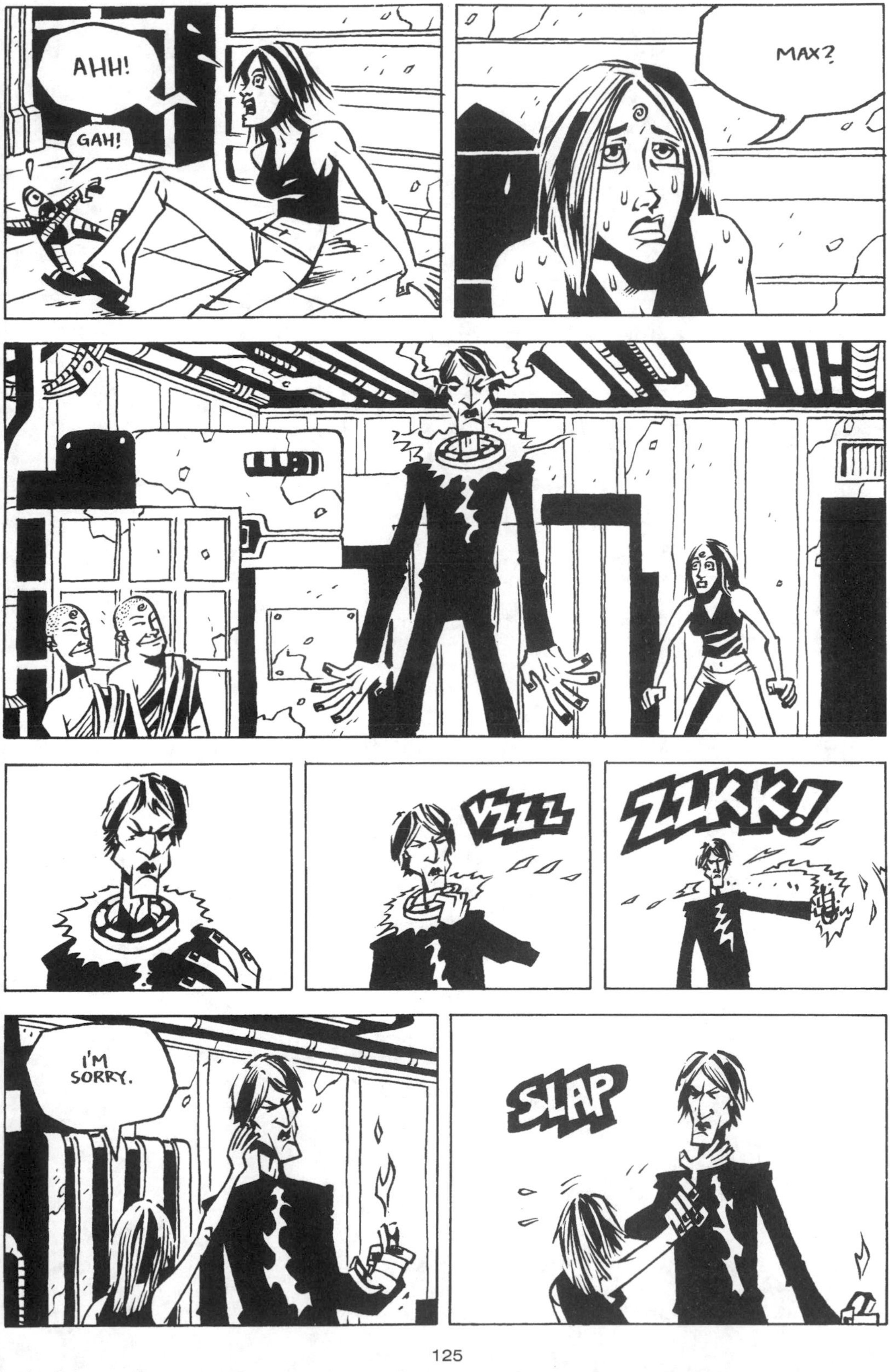
AHH!
GAH!
MAX?
VZZZ
ZZKK!
I'M SORRY.
SLAP

...

I'M SORRY. I DIDN'T KNOW WHAT TO DO...

OKAY, MAX. LET'S SHOW THESE GUYS WHAT'S WHAT.

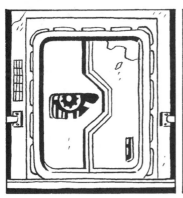

I'M GONNA GO AND CHECK ON 'EM.

RELAX, MAN...

EVERYTHING'S UNDER CONTROL. WE'LL JUST HANG IN ORBIT OF THIS EARTH PLACE AND WAIT FOR THE STRANGEWELL FREAKS TO ARRIVE. THEN WE'LL SELL THE BIG DUDE TO THE HIGHEST BIDDER...

WHAT COULD GO WRONG?

KROOM

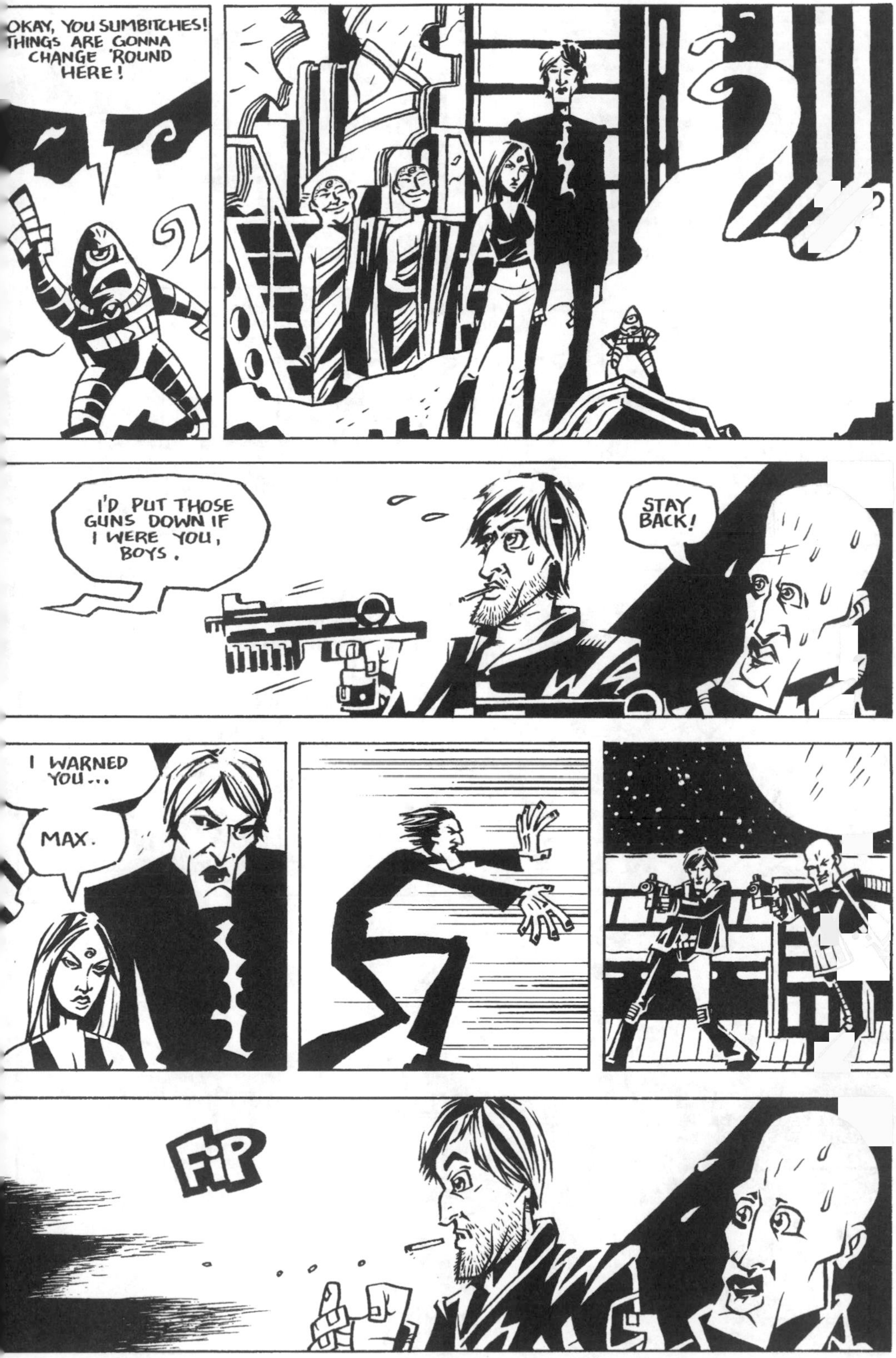
OKAY, YOU SUMBITCHES! THINGS ARE GONNA CHANGE 'ROUND HERE!
I'D PUT THOSE GUNS DOWN IF I WERE YOU, BOYS.
STAY BACK!
I WARNED YOU...
MAX.
FIP

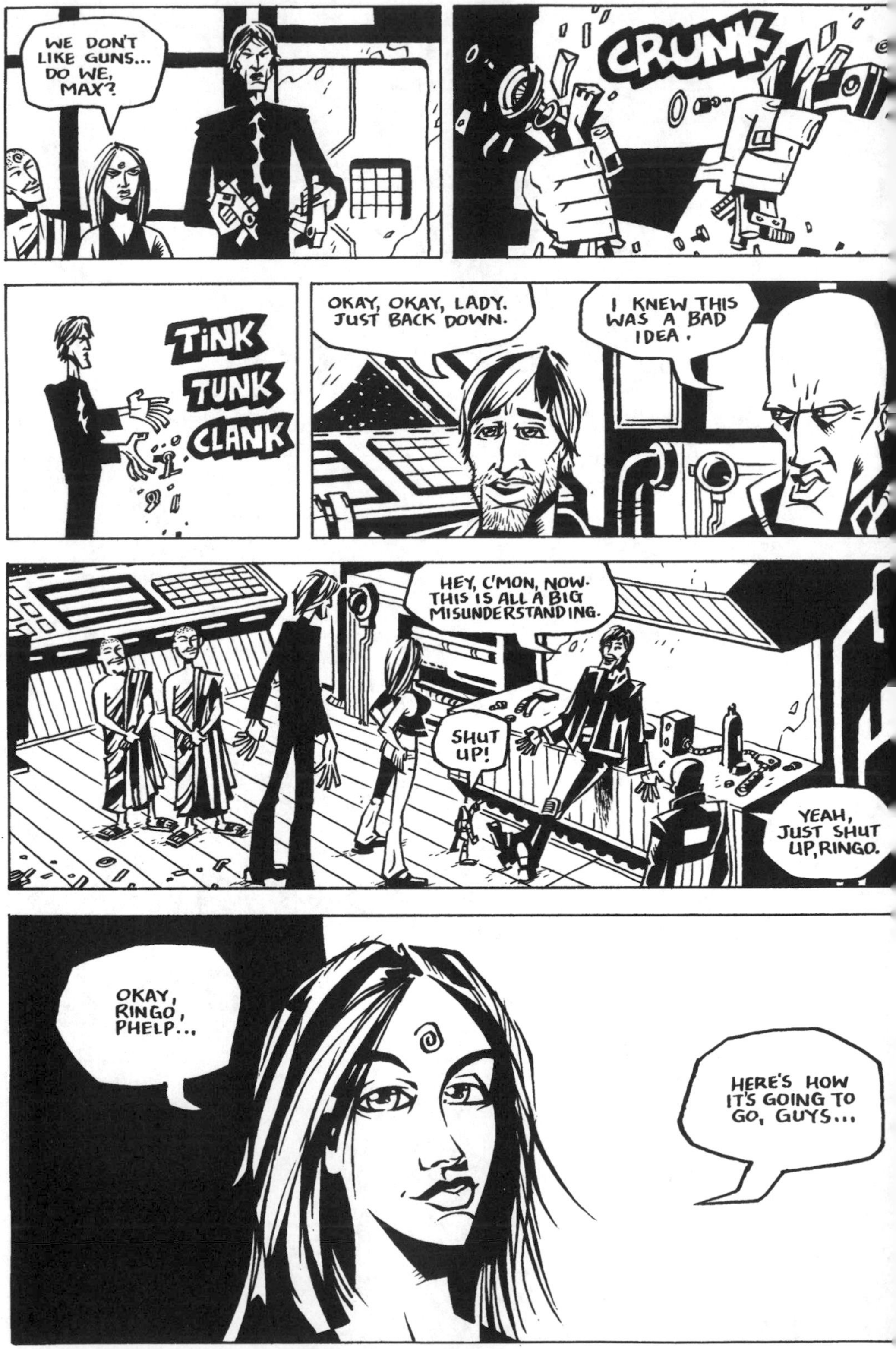
WE DON'T LIKE GUNS... DO WE, MAX?
CRUNK
TINK
TUNK
CLANK
OKAY, OKAY, LADY. JUST BACK DOWN.
I KNEW THIS WAS A BAD IDEA.
HEY, C'MON, NOW. THIS IS ALL A BIG MISUNDERSTANDING.
SHUT UP!
YEAH, JUST SHUT UP, RINGO.
OKAY, RINGO, PHELP...
HERE'S HOW IT'S GOING TO GO, GUYS...

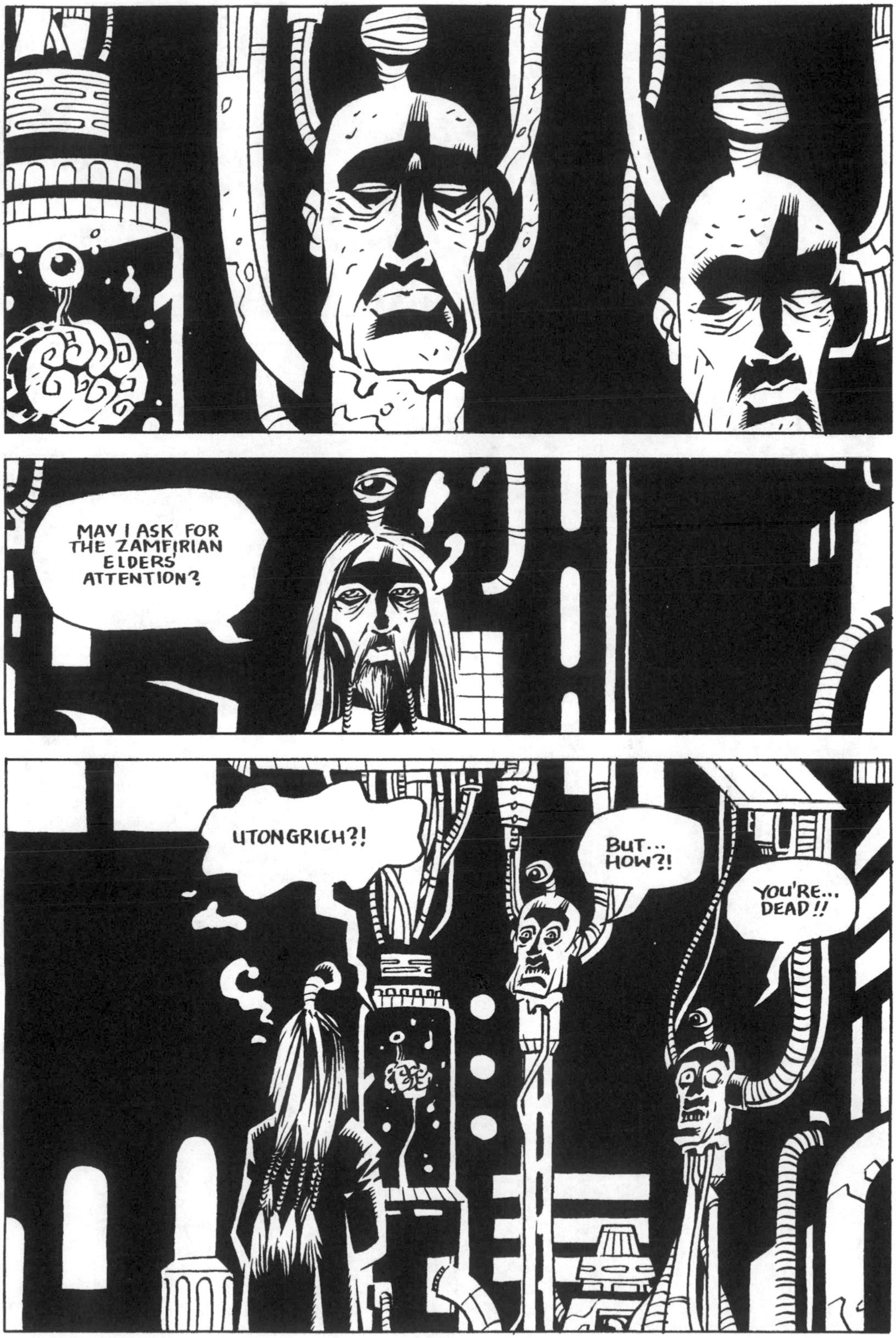

MAY I ASK FOR THE ZAMFIRIAN ELDERS' ATTENTION?
UTONGRICH?!
BUT... HOW?!
YOU'RE... DEAD!!

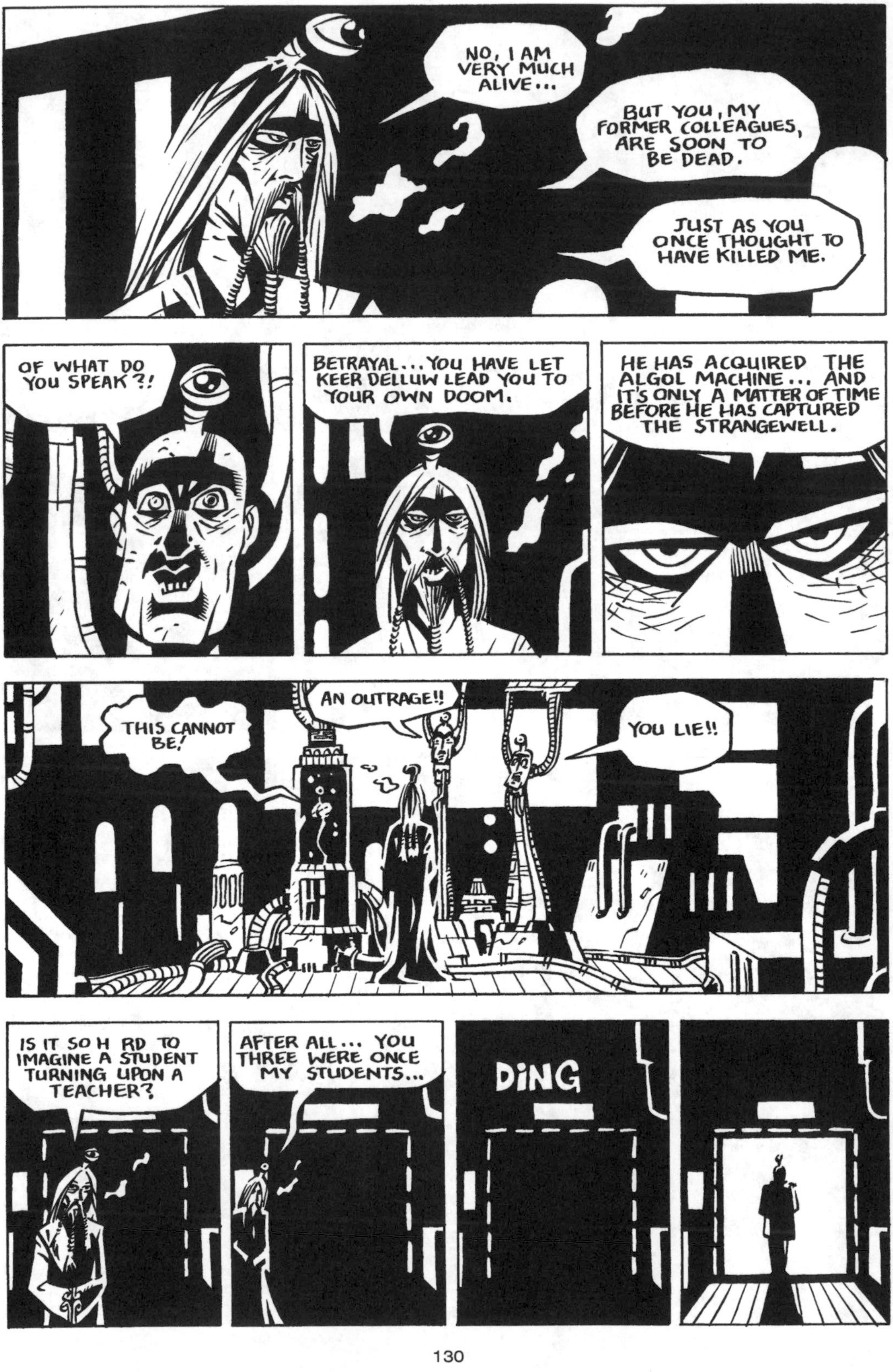
NO, I AM VERY MUCH ALIVE...
BUT YOU, MY FORMER COLLEAGUES, ARE SOON TO BE DEAD.
JUST AS YOU ONCE THOUGHT TO HAVE KILLED ME.
OF WHAT DO YOU SPEAK?!
BETRAYAL... YOU HAVE LET KEER DELLUW LEAD YOU TO YOUR OWN DOOM.
HE HAS ACQUIRED THE ALGOL MACHINE... AND IT'S ONLY A MATTER OF TIME BEFORE HE HAS CAPTURED THE STRANGEWELL.
THIS CANNOT BE!
AN OUTRAGE!!
YOU LIE!!
IS IT SO H RD TO IMAGINE A STUDENT TURNING UPON A TEACHER?
AFTER ALL... YOU THREE WERE ONCE MY STUDENTS...
DING

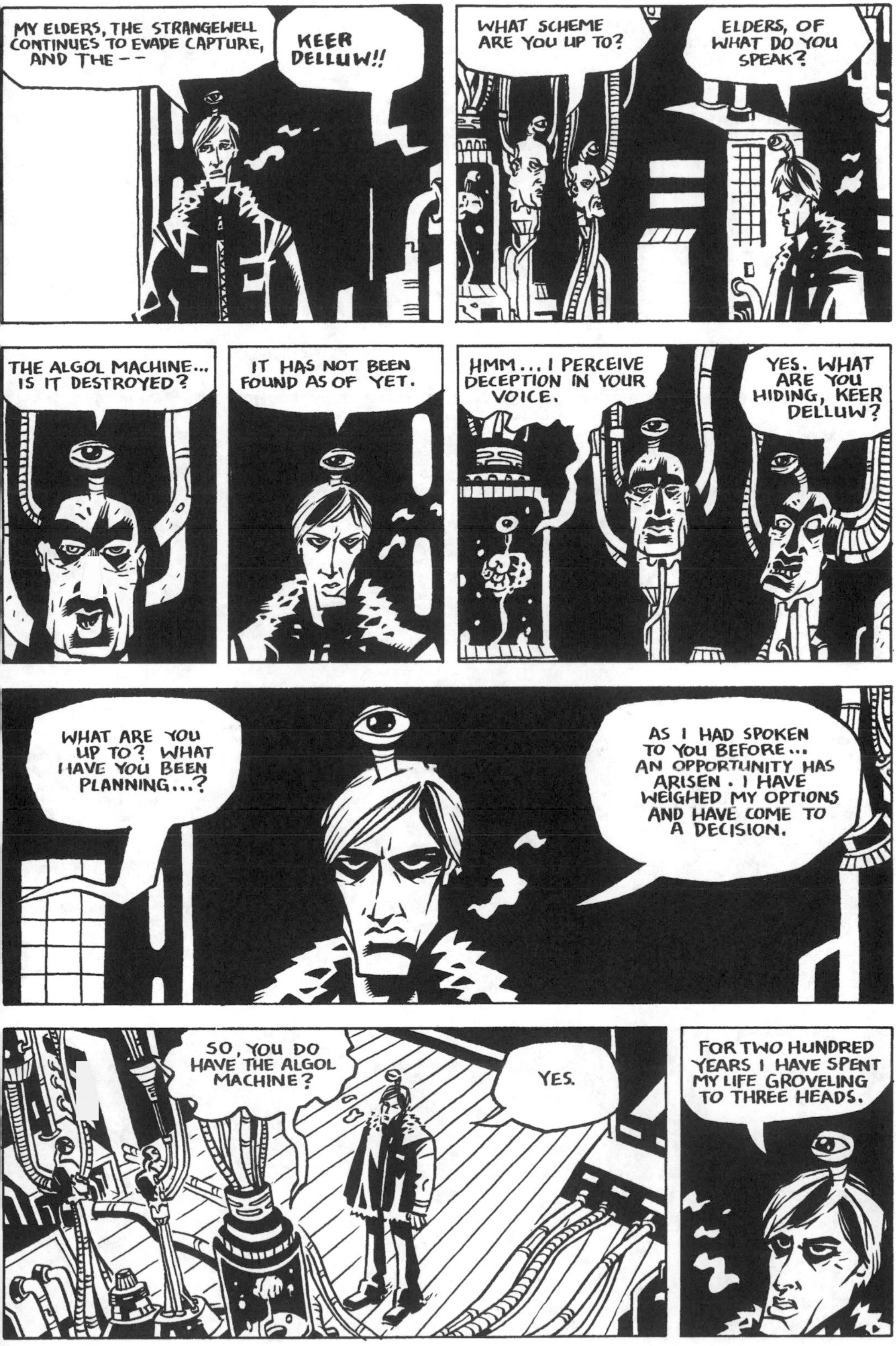
MY ELDERS, THE STRANGEWELL CONTINUES TO EVADE CAPTURE, AND THE--
KEER DELLUW!!
WHAT SCHEME ARE YOU UP TO?
ELDERS, OF WHAT DO YOU SPEAK?
THE ALGOL MACHINE... IS IT DESTROYED?
IT HAS NOT BEEN FOUND AS OF YET.
HMM... I PERCEIVE DECEPTION IN YOUR VOICE.
YES. WHAT ARE YOU HIDING, KEER DELLUW?
WHAT ARE YOU UP TO? WHAT HAVE YOU BEEN PLANNING...?
AS I HAD SPOKEN TO YOU BEFORE... AN OPPORTUNITY HAS ARISEN. I HAVE WEIGHED MY OPTIONS AND HAVE COME TO A DECISION.
SO, YOU DO HAVE THE ALGOL MACHINE?
YES.
FOR TWO HUNDRED YEARS I HAVE SPENT MY LIFE GROVELING TO THREE HEADS.

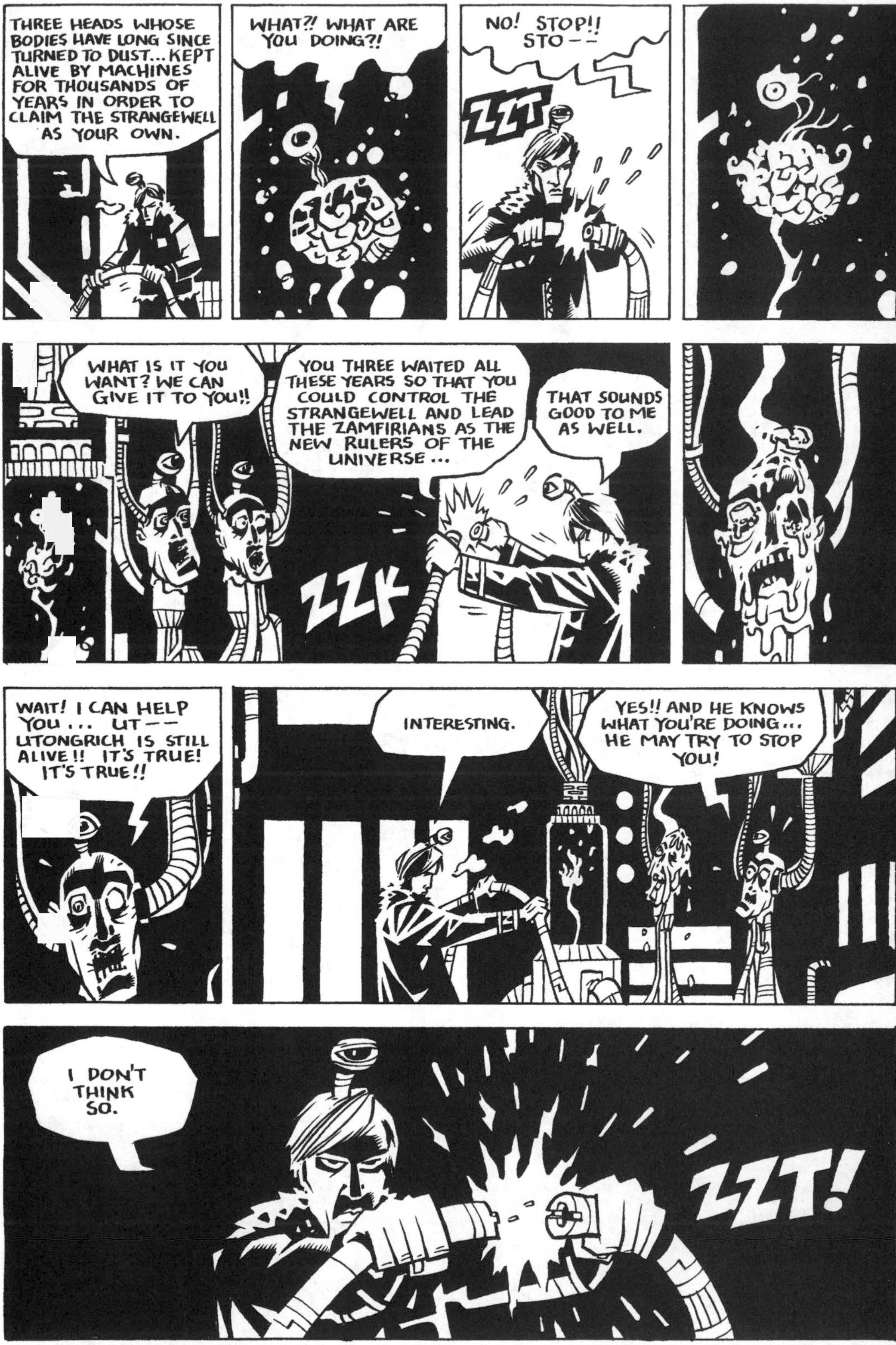
THREE HEADS WHOSE BODIES HAVE LONG SINCE TURNED TO DUST... KEPT ALIVE BY MACHINES FOR THOUSANDS OF YEARS IN ORDER TO CLAIM THE STRANGEWELL AS YOUR OWN.
WHAT?! WHAT ARE YOU DOING?!
NO! STOP!! STO--
ZZT
WHAT IS IT YOU WANT? WE CAN GIVE IT TO YOU!!
YOU THREE WAITED ALL THESE YEARS SO THAT YOU COULD CONTROL THE STRANGEWELL AND LEAD THE ZAMFIRIANS AS THE NEW RULERS OF THE UNIVERSE...
THAT SOUNDS GOOD TO ME AS WELL.
ZZK
WAIT! I CAN HELP YOU... UT-- UTONGRICH IS STILL ALIVE!! IT'S TRUE! IT'S TRUE!!
INTERESTING.
YES!! AND HE KNOWS WHAT YOU'RE DOING... HE MAY TRY TO STOP YOU!
I DON'T THINK SO.
ZZT!

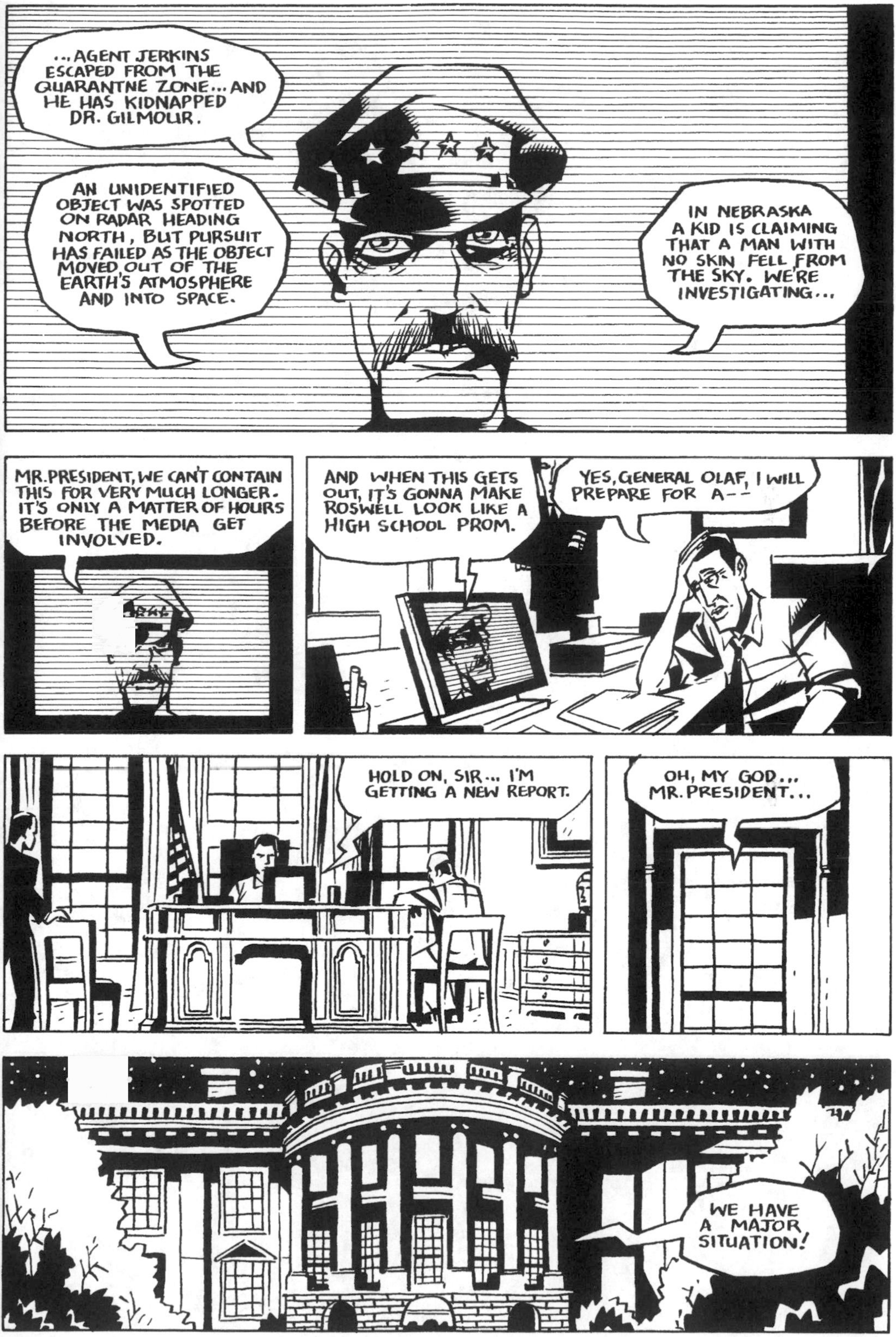
...AGENT JERKINS ESCAPED FROM THE QUARANTNE ZONE... AND HE HAS KIDNAPPED DR. GILMOUR.
AN UNIDENTIFIED OBJECT WAS SPOTTED ON RADAR HEADING NORTH, BUT PURSUIT HAS FAILED AS THE OBJECT MOVED OUT OF THE EARTH'S ATMOSPHERE AND INTO SPACE.
IN NEBRASKA A KID IS CLAIMING THAT A MAN WITH NO SKIN FELL FROM THE SKY. WE'RE INVESTIGATING...
MR. PRESIDENT, WE CAN'T CONTAIN THIS FOR VERY MUCH LONGER. IT'S ONLY A MATTER OF HOURS BEFORE THE MEDIA GET INVOLVED.
AND WHEN THIS GETS OUT, IT'S GONNA MAKE ROSWELL LOOK LIKE A HIGH SCHOOL PROM.
YES, GENERAL OLAF, I WILL PREPARE FOR A--
HOLD ON, SIR... I'M GETTING A NEW REPORT.
OH, MY GOD... MR. PRESIDENT...
WE HAVE A MAJOR SITUATION!

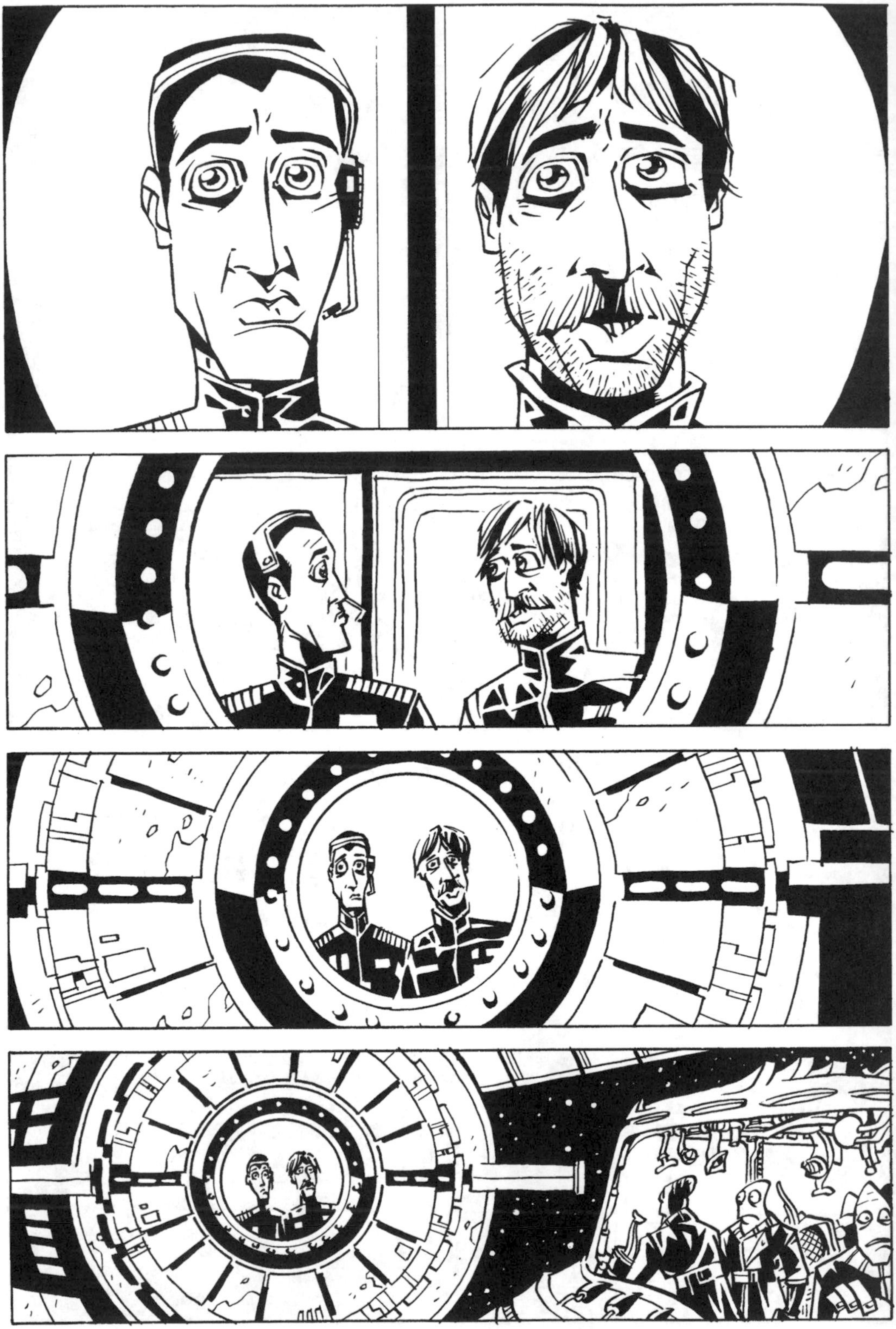

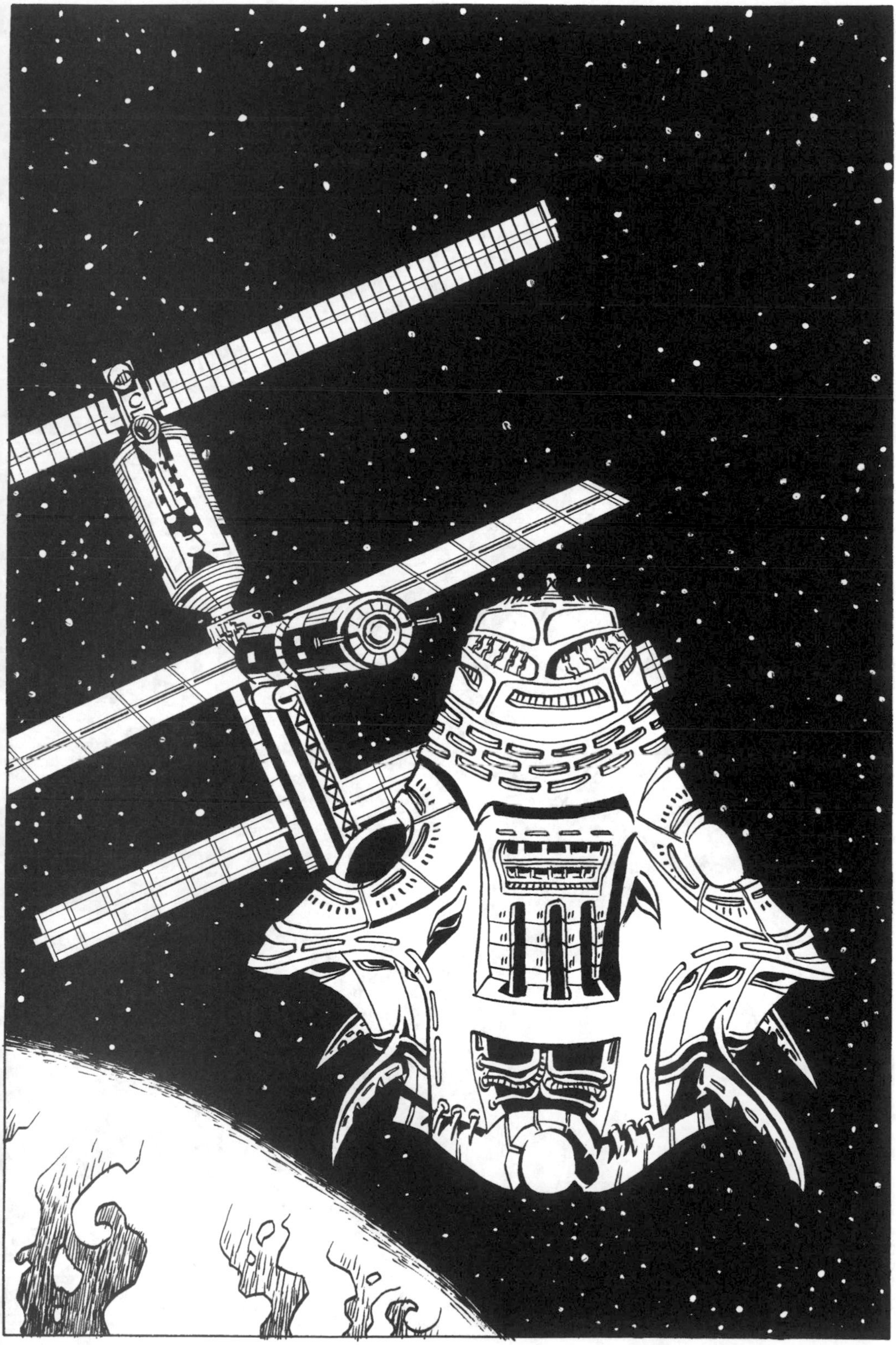

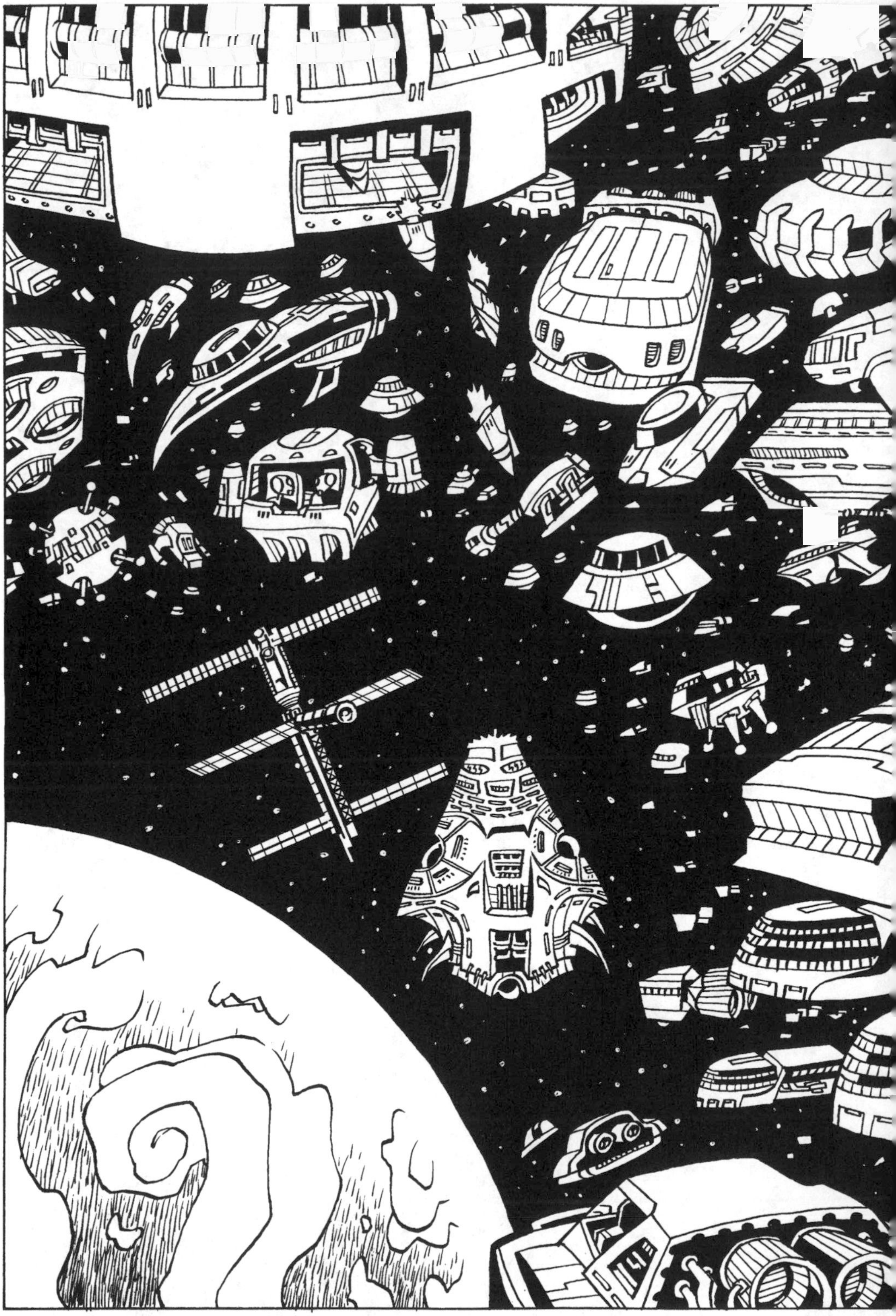

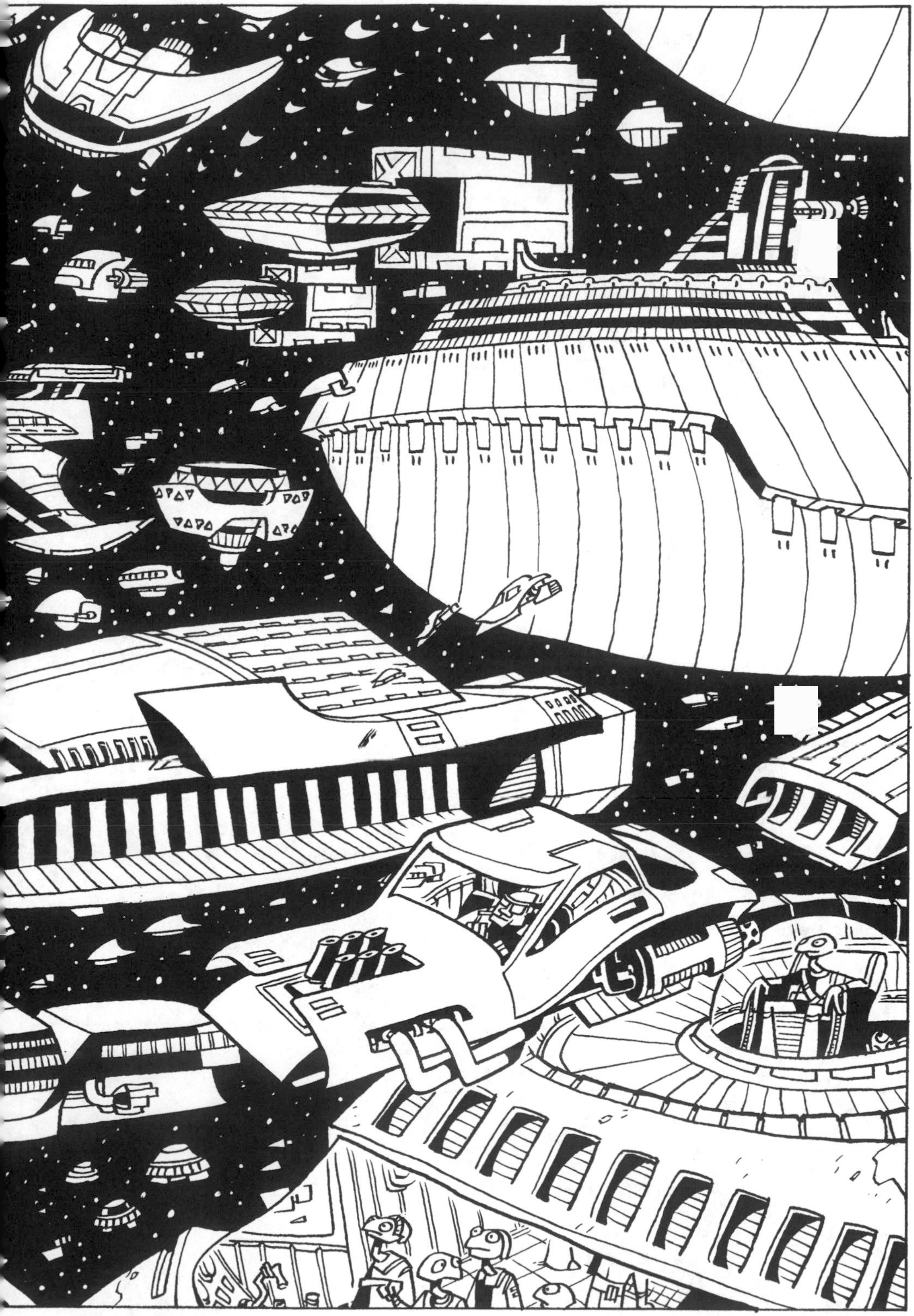

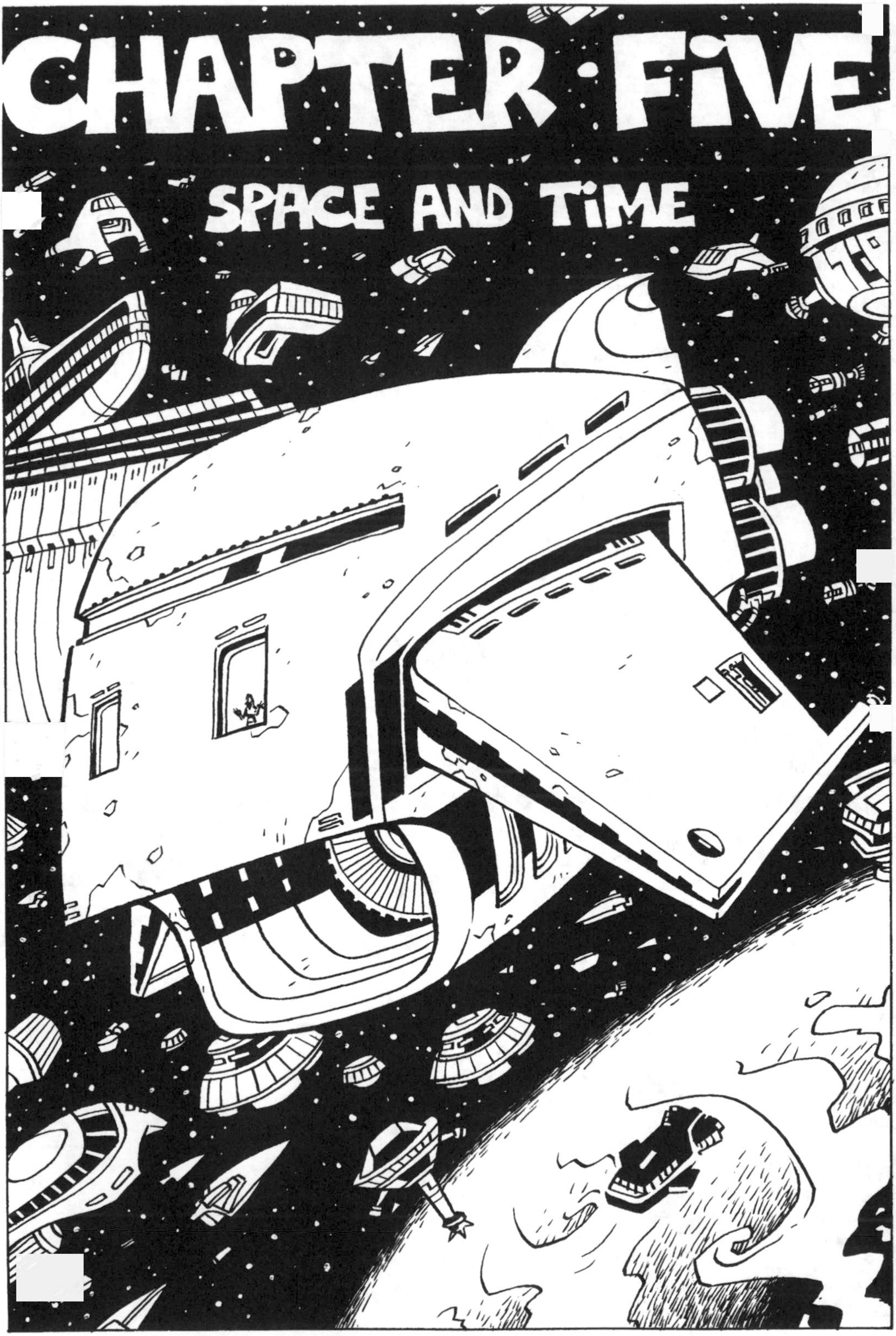
CHAPTER FIVE
SPACE AND TIME

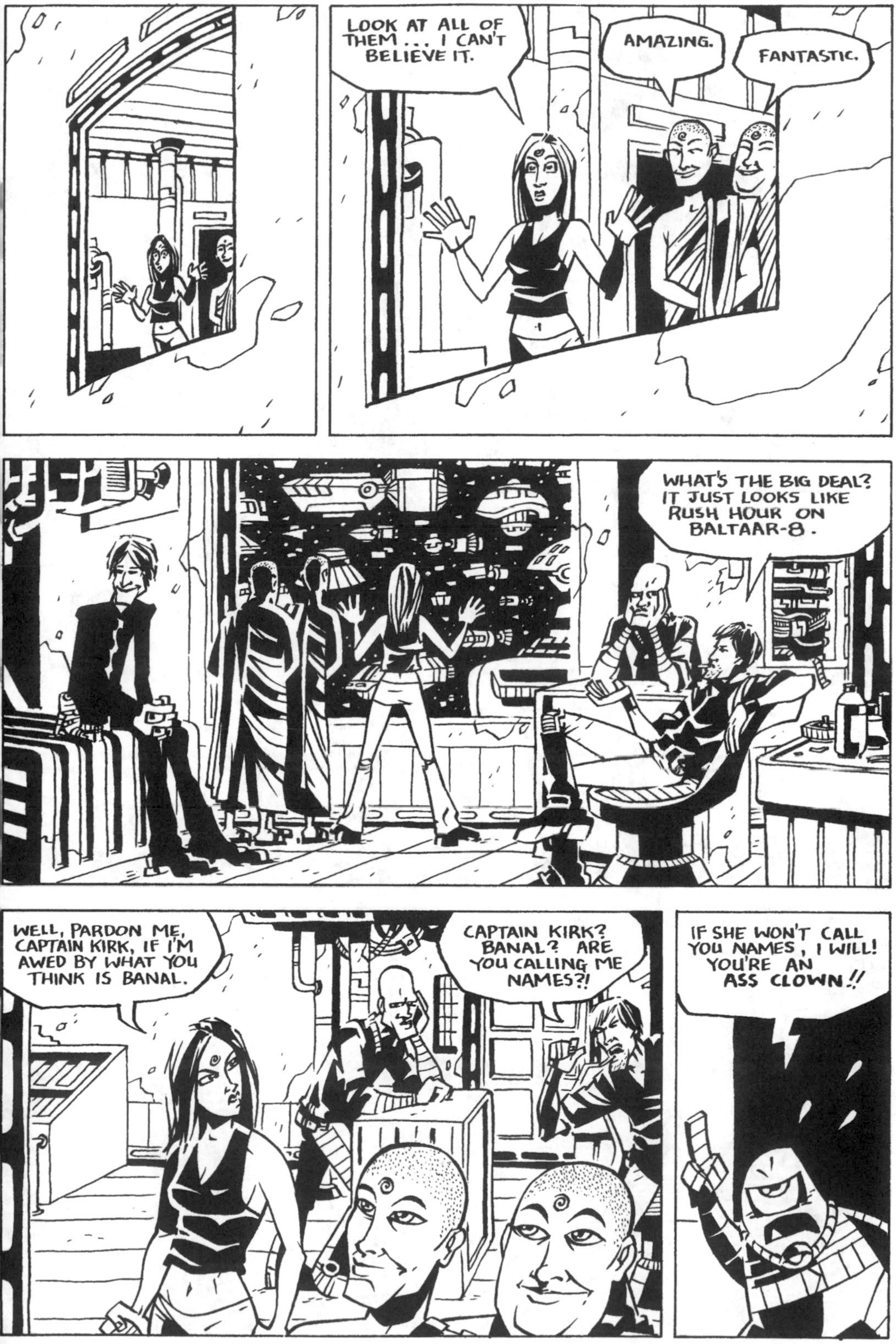
LOOK AT ALL OF THEM ... I CAN'T BELIEVE IT.
AMAZING.
FANTASTIC.
WHAT'S THE BIG DEAL? IT JUST LOOKS LIKE RUSH HOUR ON BALTAAR-8.
WELL, PARDON ME, CAPTAIN KIRK, IF I'M AWED BY WHAT YOU THINK IS BANAL.
CAPTAIN KIRK? BANAL? ARE YOU CALLING ME NAMES?!
IF SHE WON'T CALL YOU NAMES, I WILL! YOU'RE AN ASS CLOWN!!

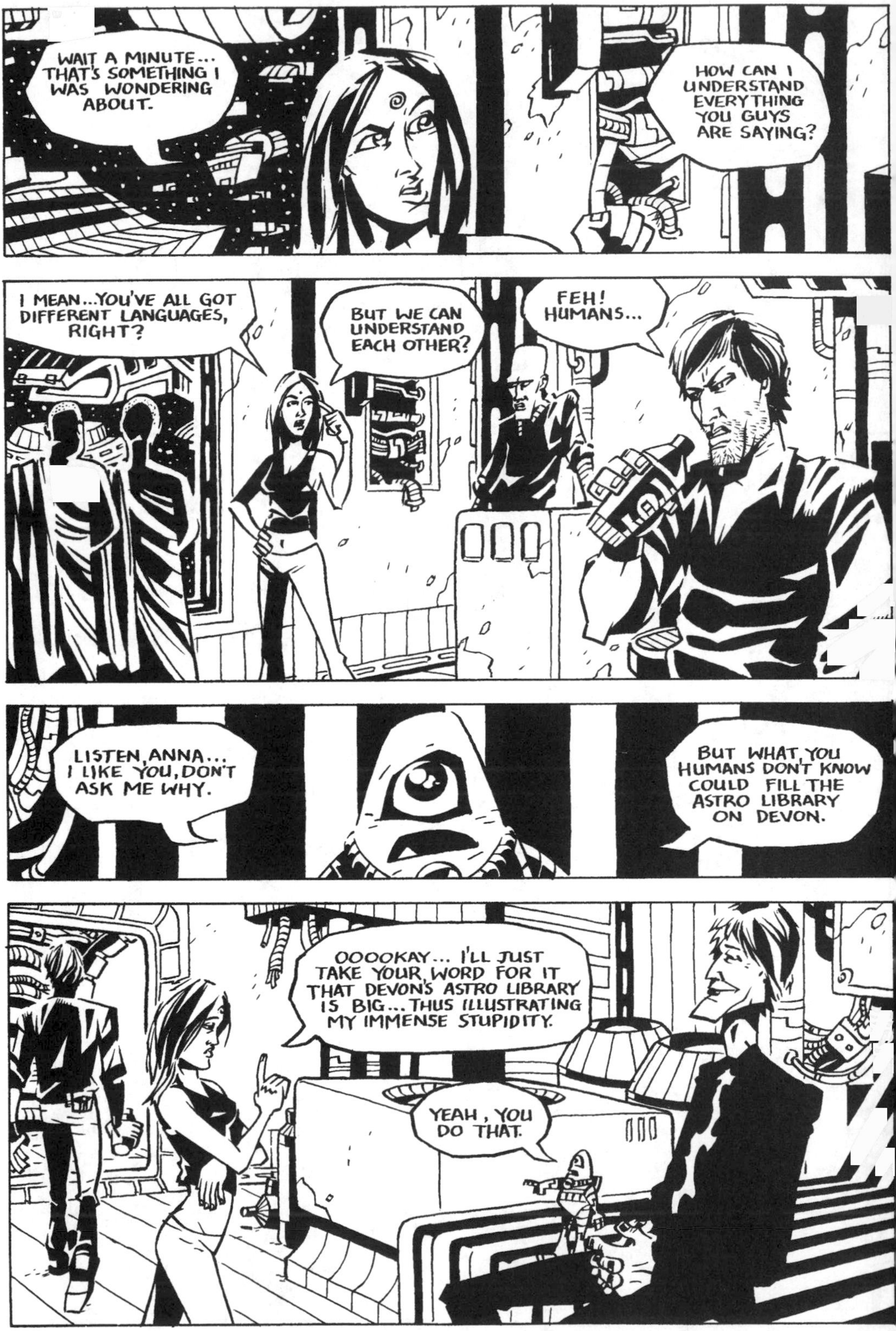
WAIT A MINUTE... THAT'S SOMETHING I WAS WONDERING ABOUT.
HOW CAN I UNDERSTAND EVERYTHING YOU GUYS ARE SAYING?
I MEAN...YOU'VE ALL GOT DIFFERENT LANGUAGES, RIGHT?
BUT WE CAN UNDERSTAND EACH OTHER?
FEH! HUMANS...
LISTEN, ANNA... I LIKE YOU, DON'T ASK ME WHY.
BUT WHAT YOU HUMANS DON'T KNOW COULD FILL THE ASTRO LIBRARY ON DEVON.
OOOOKAY... I'LL JUST TAKE YOUR WORD FOR IT THAT DEVON'S ASTRO LIBRARY IS BIG... THUS ILLUSTRATING MY IMMENSE STUPIDITY.
YEAH, YOU DO THAT.

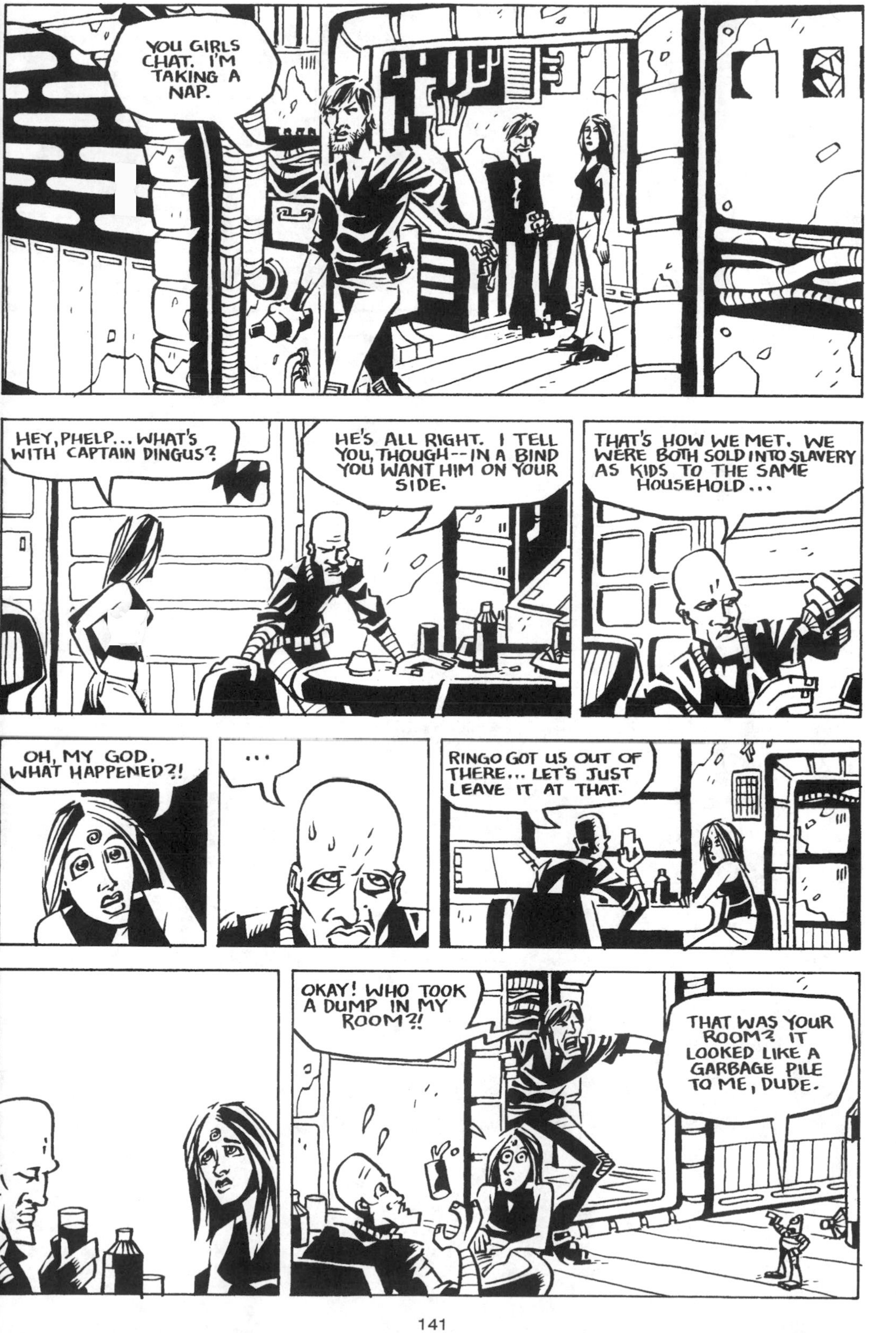
YOU GIRLS CHAT. I'M TAKING A NAP.
HEY, PHELP... WHAT'S WITH CAPTAIN DINGUS?
HE'S ALL RIGHT. I TELL YOU, THOUGH-- IN A BIND YOU WANT HIM ON YOUR SIDE.
THAT'S HOW WE MET. WE WERE BOTH SOLD INTO SLAVERY AS KIDS TO THE SAME HOUSEHOLD...
OH, MY GOD. WHAT HAPPENED?!
...
RINGO GOT US OUT OF THERE... LET'S JUST LEAVE IT AT THAT.
OKAY! WHO TOOK A DUMP IN MY ROOM?!
THAT WAS YOUR ROOM? IT LOOKED LIKE A GARBAGE PILE TO ME, DUDE.

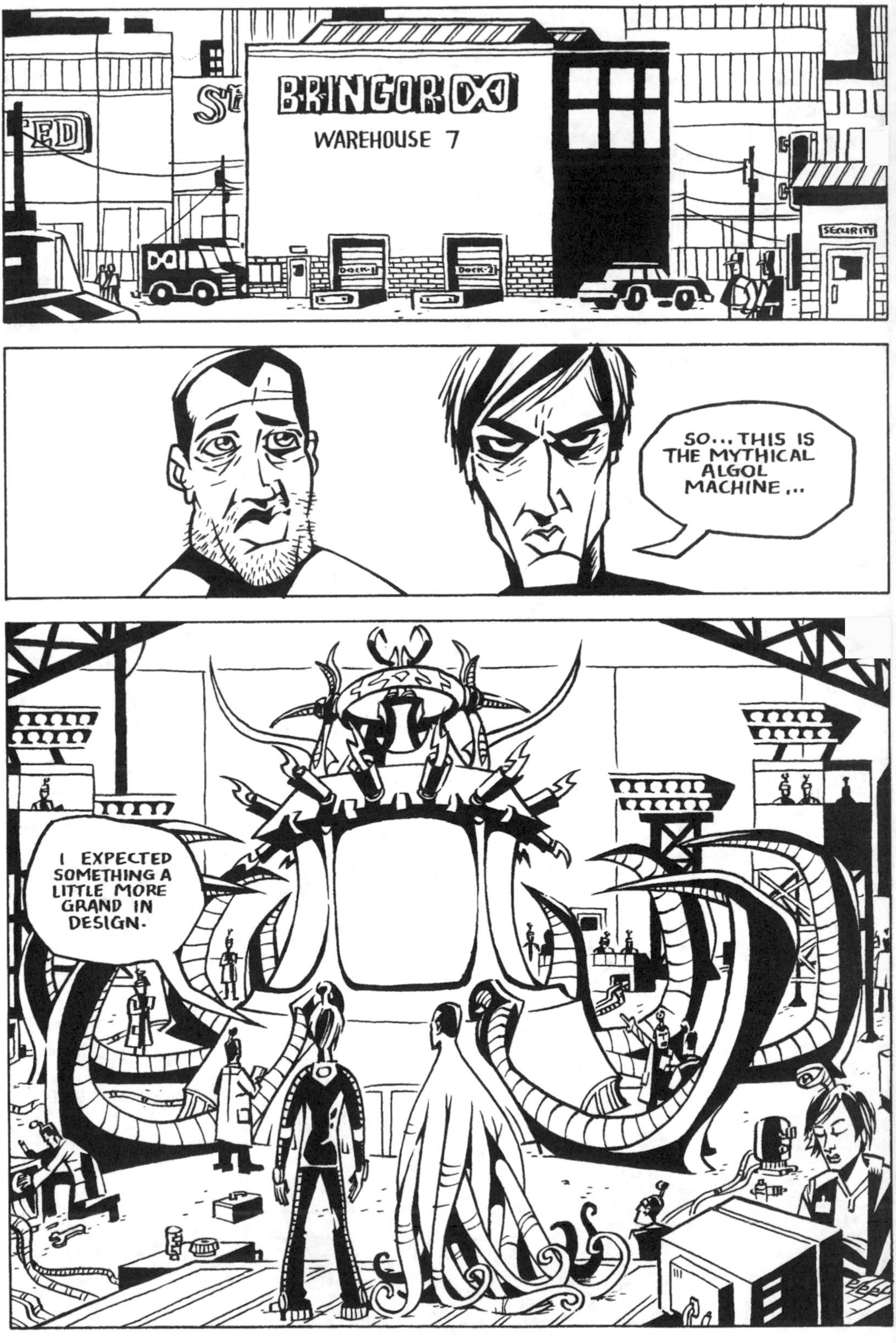
BRINGOR
WAREHOUSE 7
SECURITY
SO... THIS IS THE MYTHICAL ALGOL MACHINE...
I EXPECTED SOMETHING A LITTLE MORE GRAND IN DESIGN.

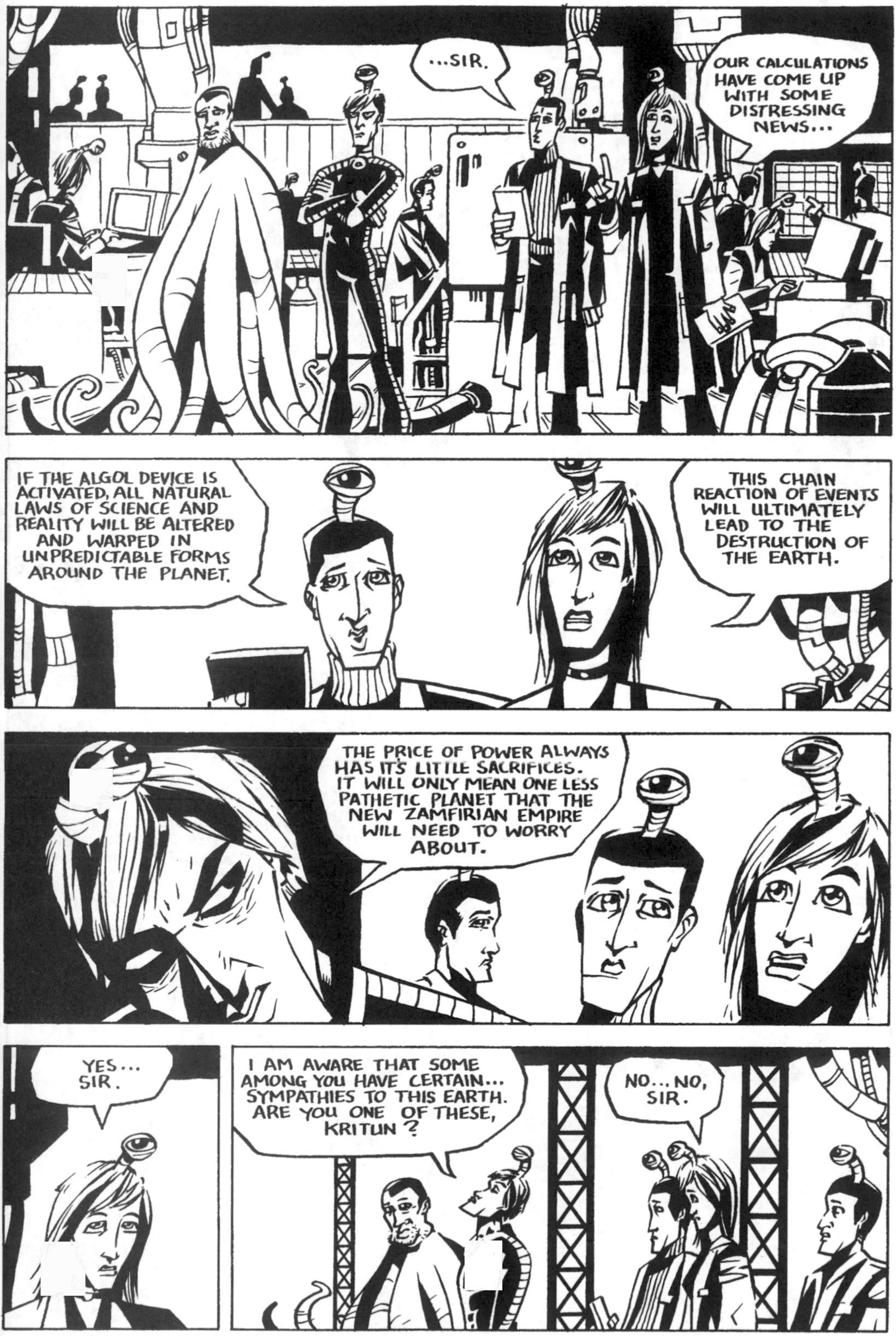

...SIR.
OUR CALCULATIONS HAVE COME UP WITH SOME DISTRESSING NEWS...
IF THE ALGOL DEVICE IS ACTIVATED, ALL NATURAL LAWS OF SCIENCE AND REALITY WILL BE ALTERED AND WARPED IN UNPREDICTABLE FORMS AROUND THE PLANET.
THIS CHAIN REACTION OF EVENTS WILL ULTIMATELY LEAD TO THE DESTRUCTION OF THE EARTH.
THE PRICE OF POWER ALWAYS HAS IT'S LITTLE SACRIFICES. IT WILL ONLY MEAN ONE LESS PATHETIC PLANET THAT THE NEW ZAMFIRIAN EMPIRE WILL NEED TO WORRY ABOUT.
YES... SIR.
I AM AWARE THAT SOME AMONG YOU HAVE CERTAIN... SYMPATHIES TO THIS EARTH. ARE YOU ONE OF THESE, KRITUN ?
NO... NO, SIR.

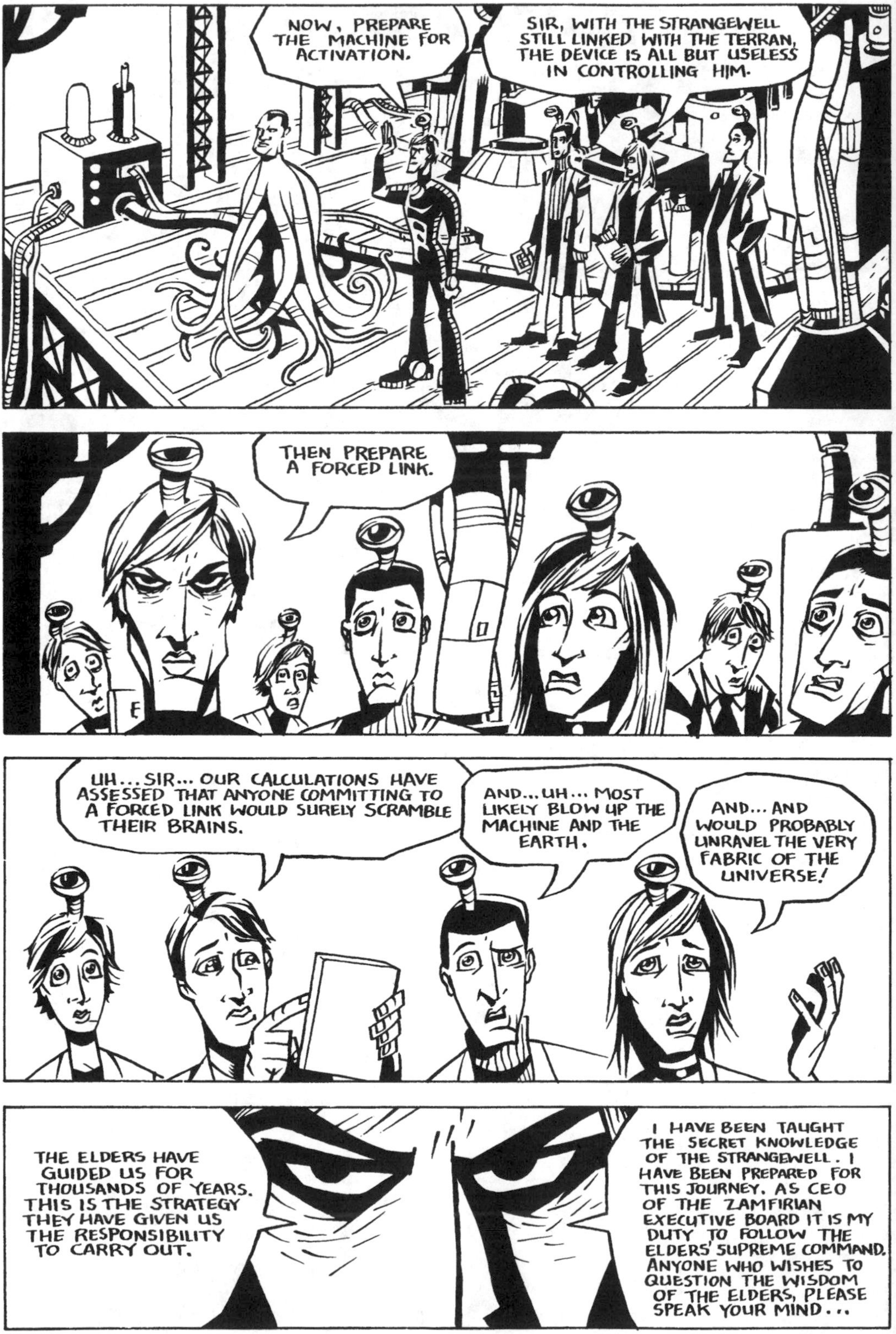
NOW, PREPARE THE MACHINE FOR ACTIVATION.
SIR, WITH THE STRANGEWELL STILL LINKED WITH THE TERRAN, THE DEVICE IS ALL BUT USELESS IN CONTROLLING HIM.
THEN PREPARE A FORCED LINK.
UH... SIR... OUR CALCULATIONS HAVE ASSESSED THAT ANYONE COMMITTING TO A FORCED LINK WOULD SURELY SCRAMBLE THEIR BRAINS.
AND... UH... MOST LIKELY BLOW UP THE MACHINE AND THE EARTH.
AND... AND WOULD PROBABLY UNRAVEL THE VERY FABRIC OF THE UNIVERSE!
THE ELDERS HAVE GUIDED US FOR THOUSANDS OF YEARS. THIS IS THE STRATEGY THEY HAVE GIVEN US THE RESPONSIBILITY TO CARRY OUT.
I HAVE BEEN TAUGHT THE SECRET KNOWLEDGE OF THE STRANGEWELL. I HAVE BEEN PREPARED FOR THIS JOURNEY. AS CEO OF THE ZAMFIRIAN EXECUTIVE BOARD IT IS MY DUTY TO FOLLOW THE ELDERS' SUPREME COMMAND. ANYONE WHO WISHES TO QUESTION THE WISDOM OF THE ELDERS, PLEASE SPEAK YOUR MIND...

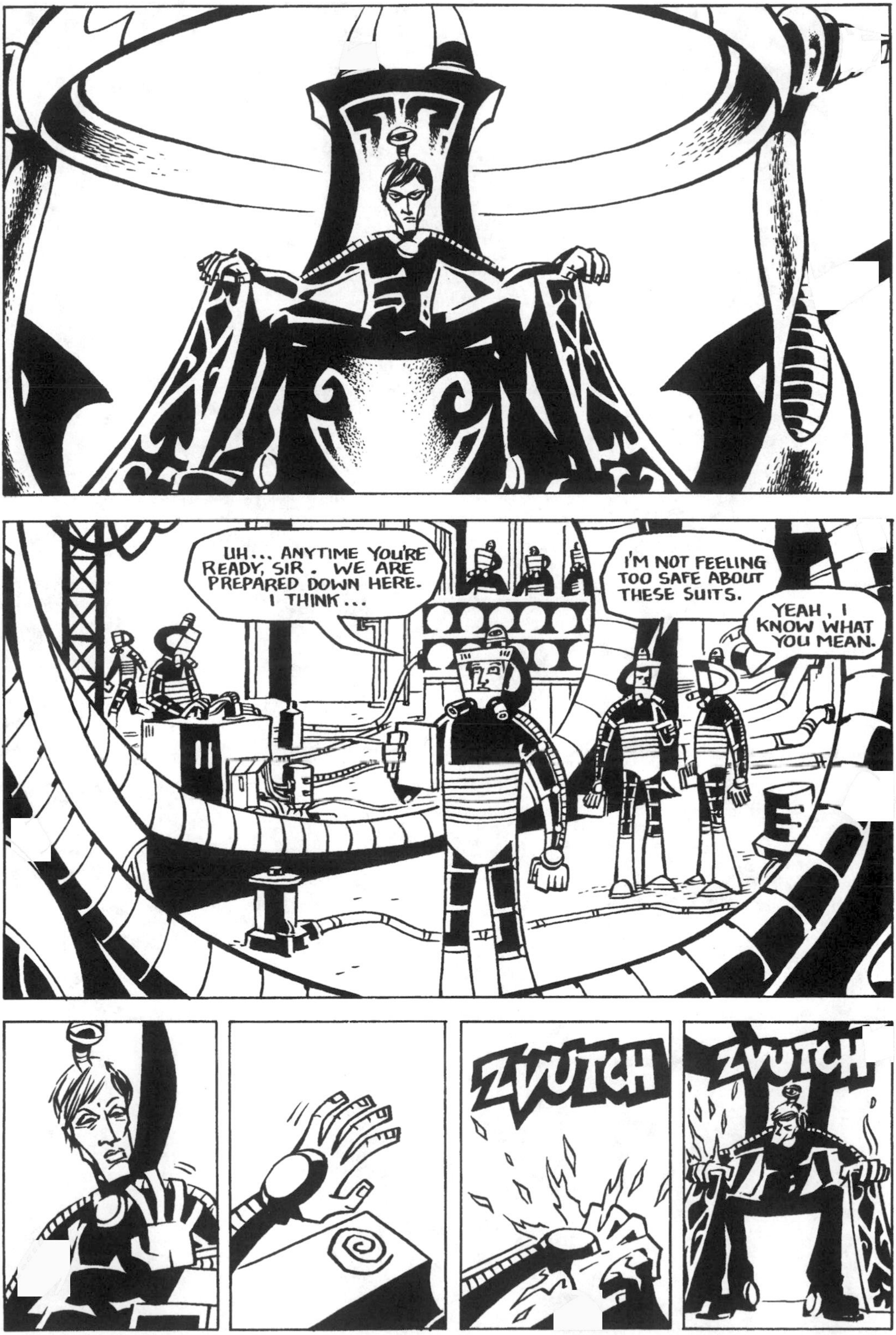
UH... ANYTIME YOU'RE READY, SIR. WE ARE PREPARED DOWN HERE. I THINK...
I'M NOT FEELING TOO SAFE ABOUT THESE SUITS.
YEAH, I KNOW WHAT YOU MEAN.
ZVUTCH
ZVUTCH

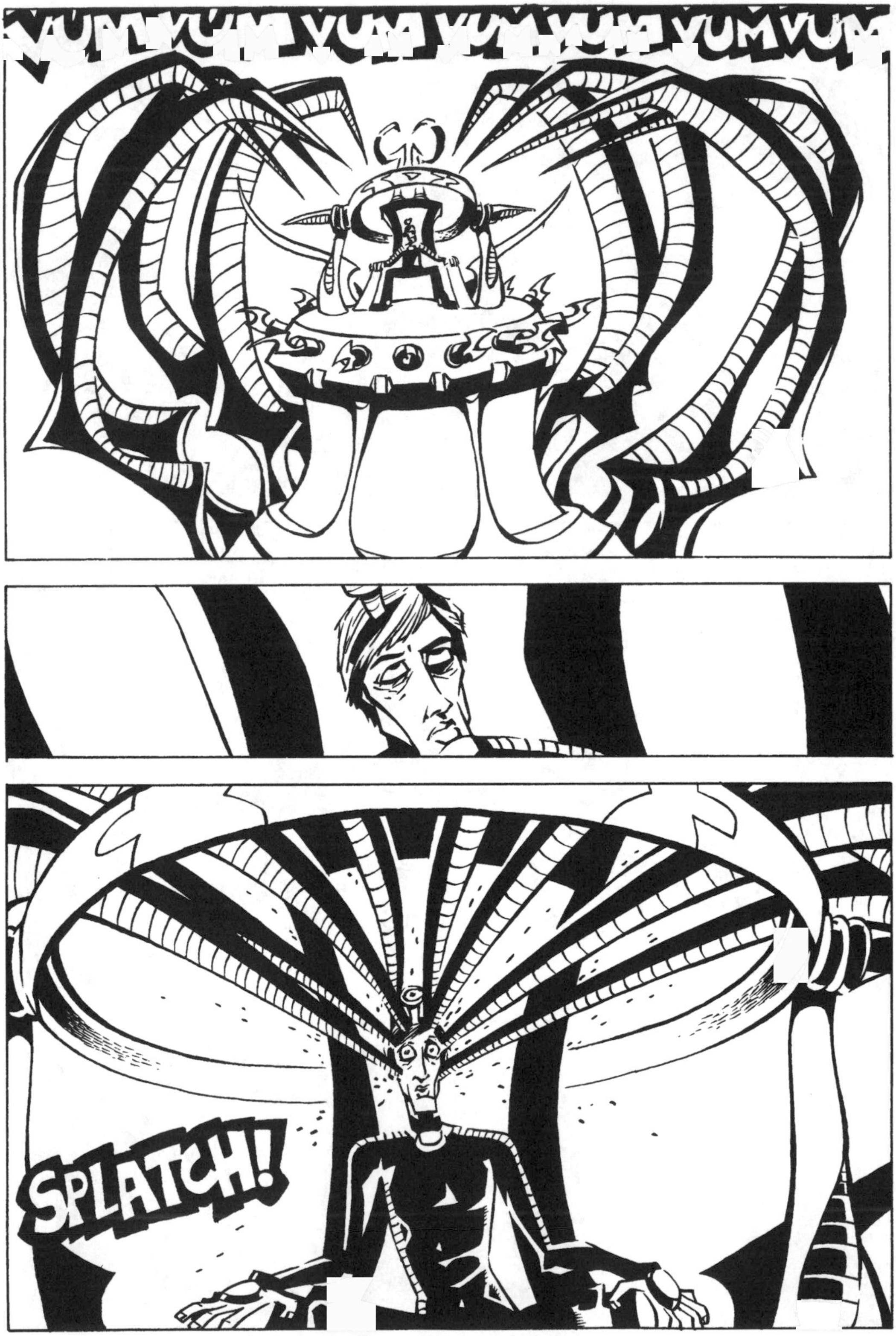
YUM YUM YUM YUM YUM YUM YUM
SPLATCH!

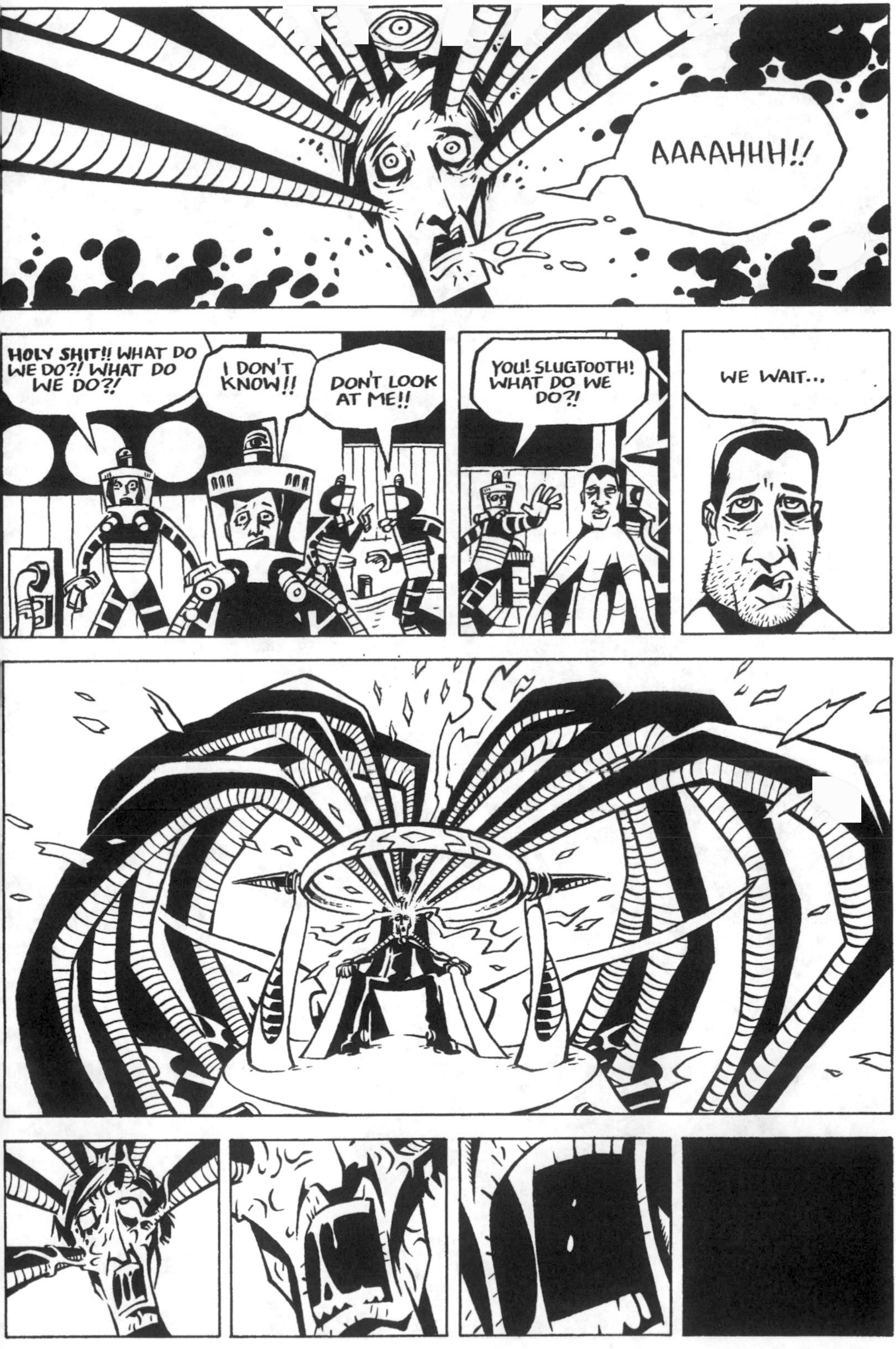
AAAAHHH!!
HOLY SHIT!! WHAT DO WE DO?! WHAT DO WE DO?!
I DON'T KNOW!!
DON'T LOOK AT ME!!
YOU! SLUGTOOTH! WHAT DO WE DO?!
WE WAIT...

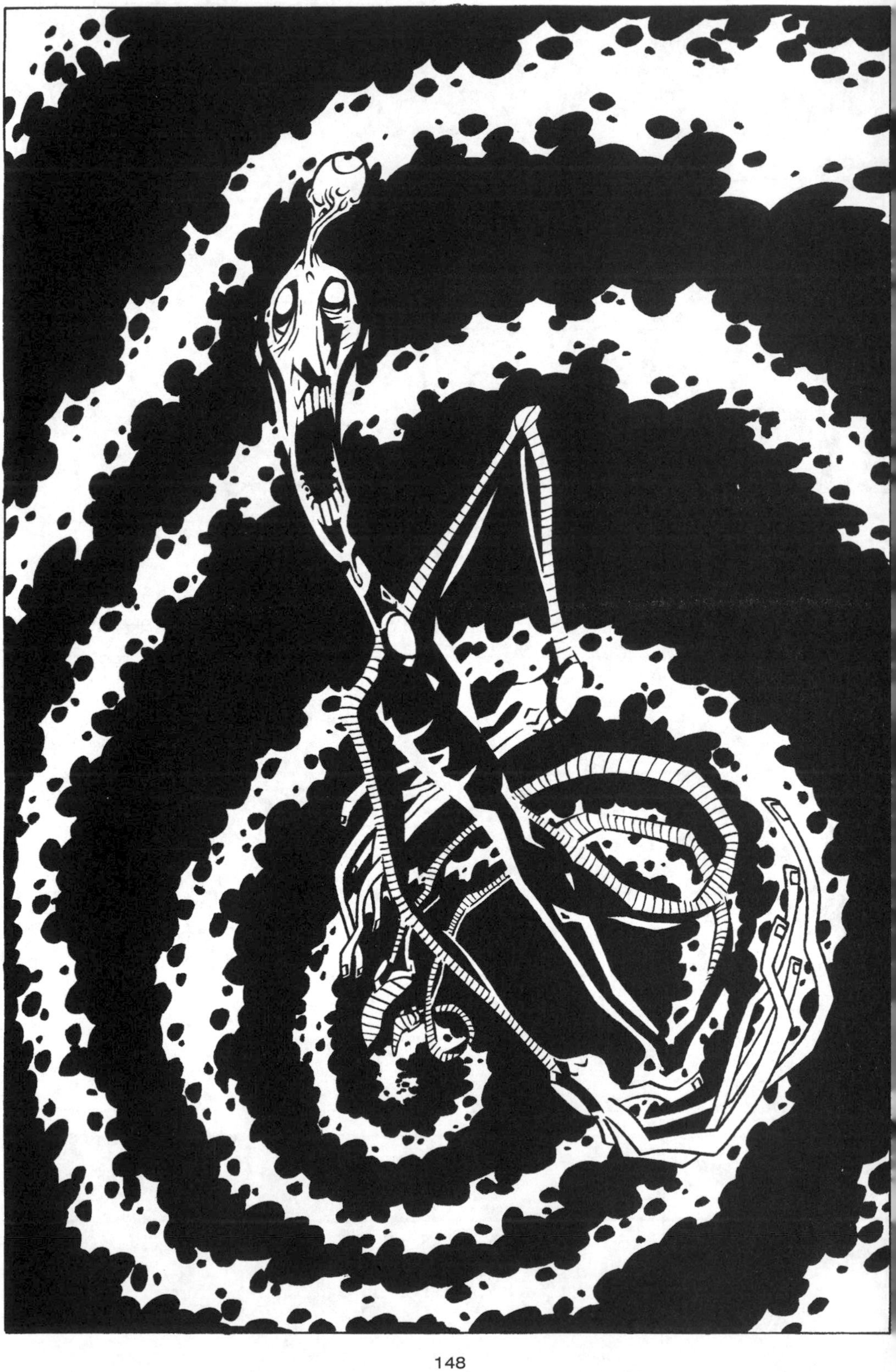

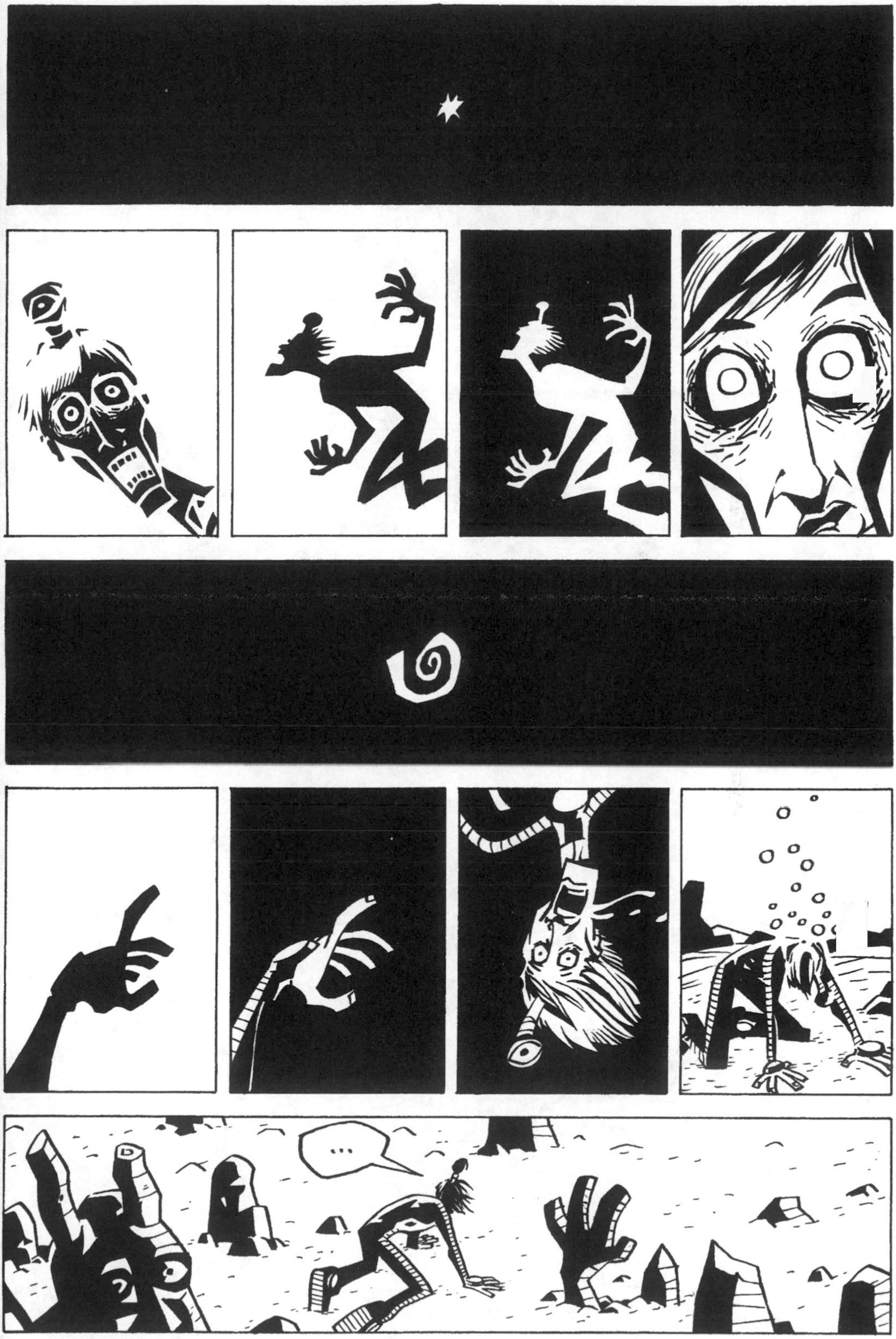
...

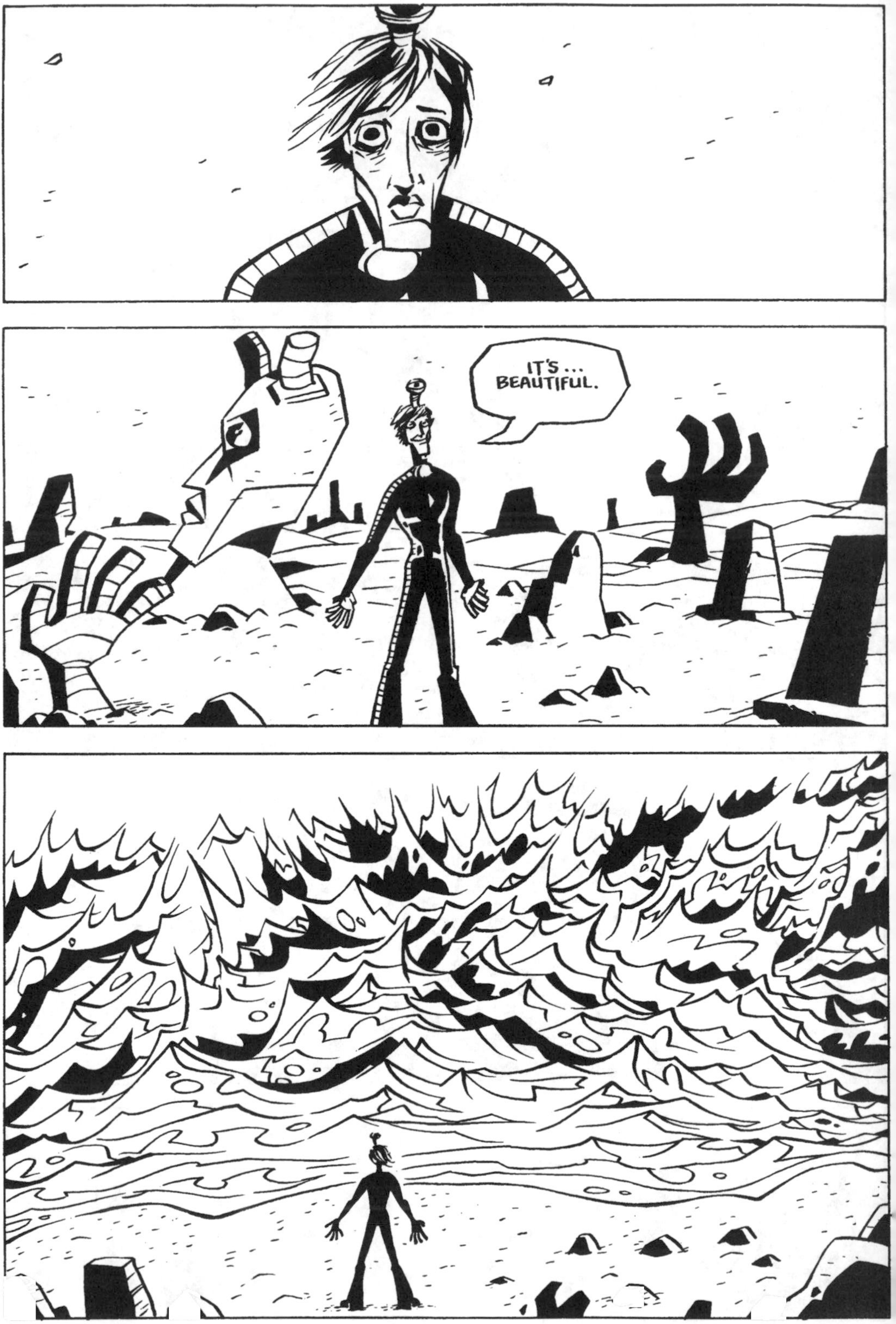
IT'S... BEAUTIFUL.

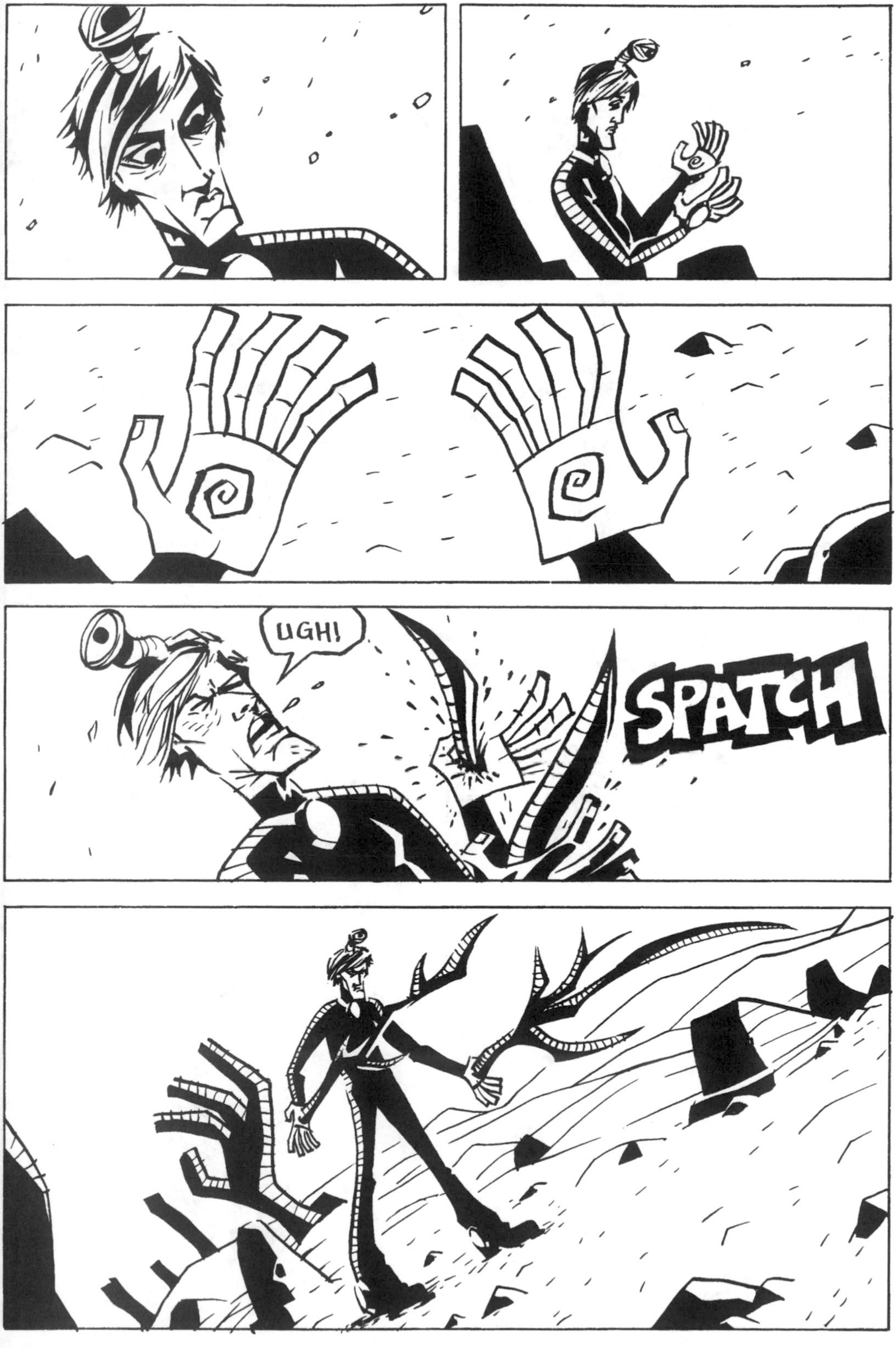
UGH!
SPATCH

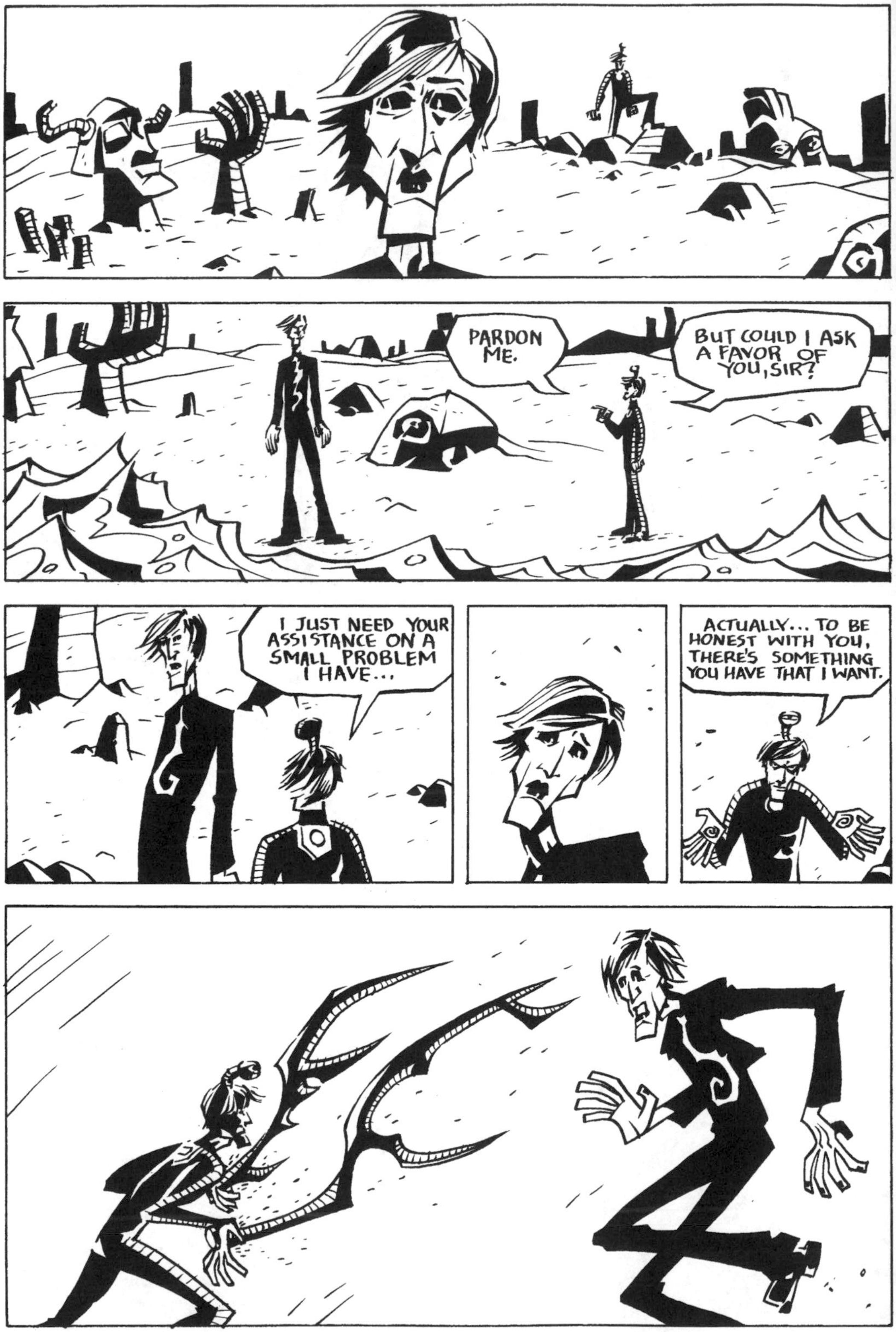
PARDON ME.
BUT COULD I ASK A FAVOR OF YOU, SIR?
I JUST NEED YOUR ASSISTANCE ON A SMALL PROBLEM I HAVE...
ACTUALLY... TO BE HONEST WITH YOU, THERE'S SOMETHING YOU HAVE THAT I WANT.

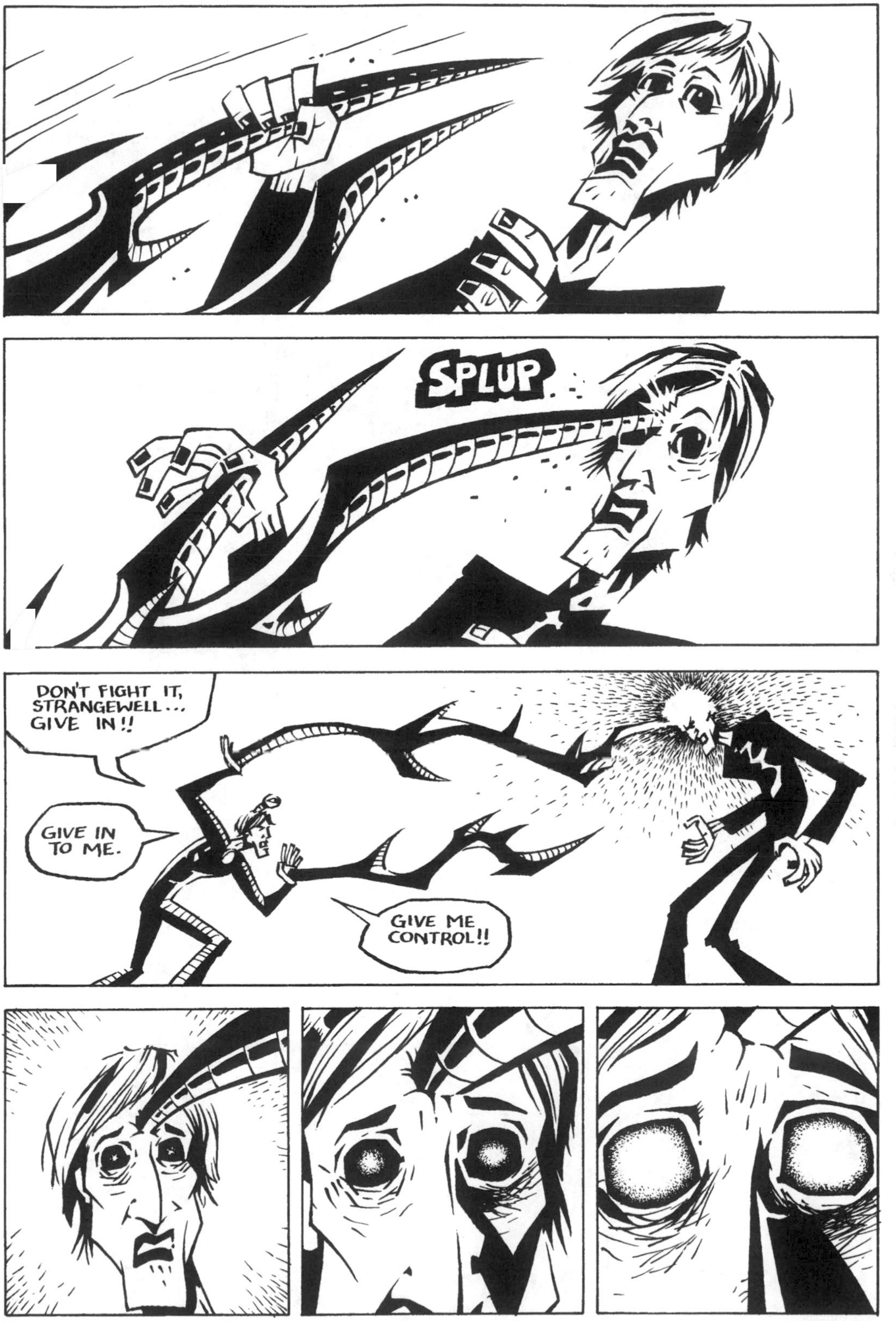
SPLUP
DON'T FIGHT IT, STRANGEWELL... GIVE IN!!
GIVE IN TO ME.
GIVE ME CONTROL!!

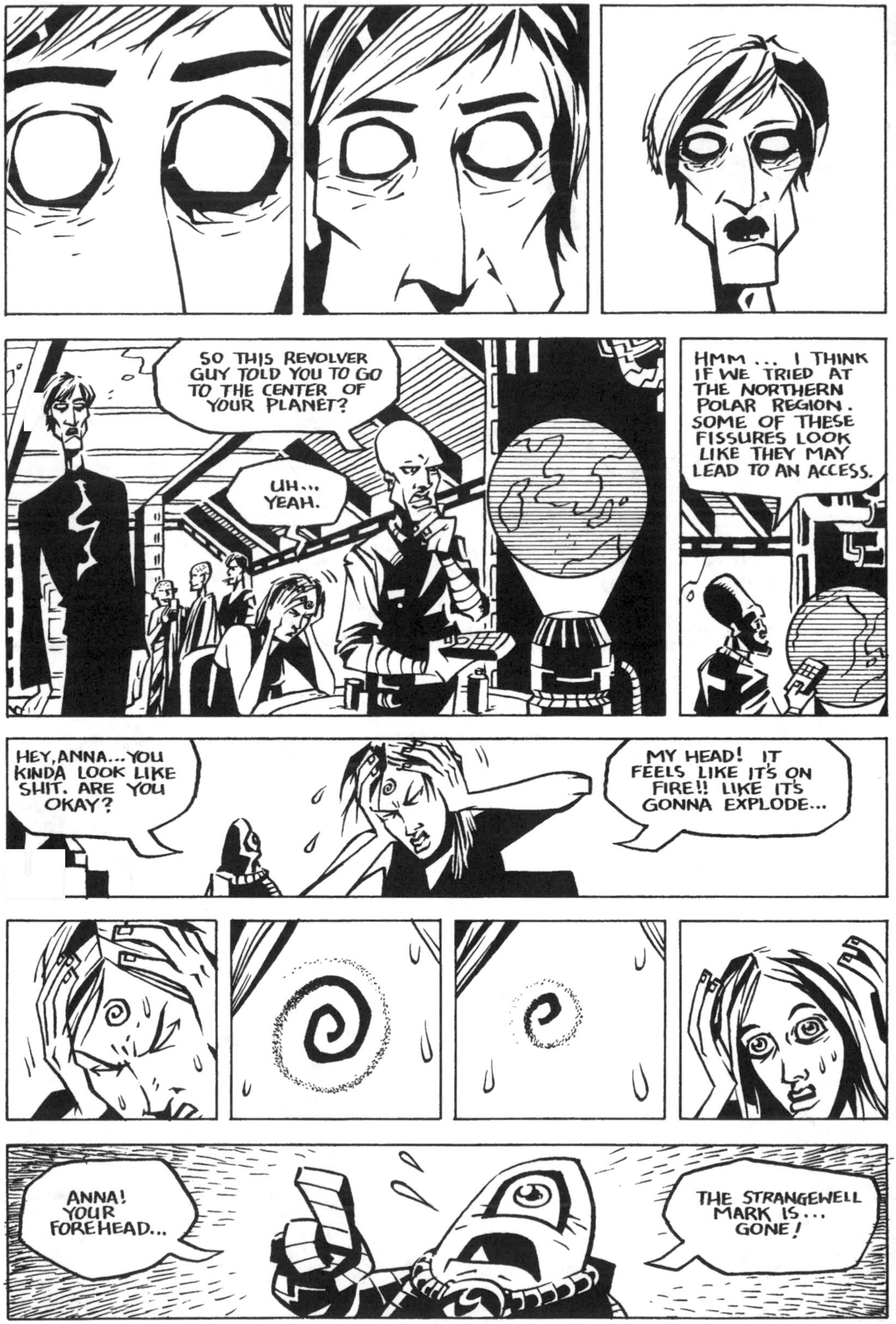
SO THIS REVOLVER GUY TOLD YOU TO GO TO THE CENTER OF YOUR PLANET?
UH... YEAH.
HMM ... I THINK IF WE TRIED AT THE NORTHERN POLAR REGION. SOME OF THESE FISSURES LOOK LIKE THEY MAY LEAD TO AN ACCESS.
HEY, ANNA... YOU KINDA LOOK LIKE SHIT. ARE YOU OKAY?
MY HEAD! IT FEELS LIKE IT'S ON FIRE!! LIKE IT'S GONNA EXPLODE...
ANNA! YOUR FOREHEAD...
THE STRANGEWELL MARK IS... GONE!

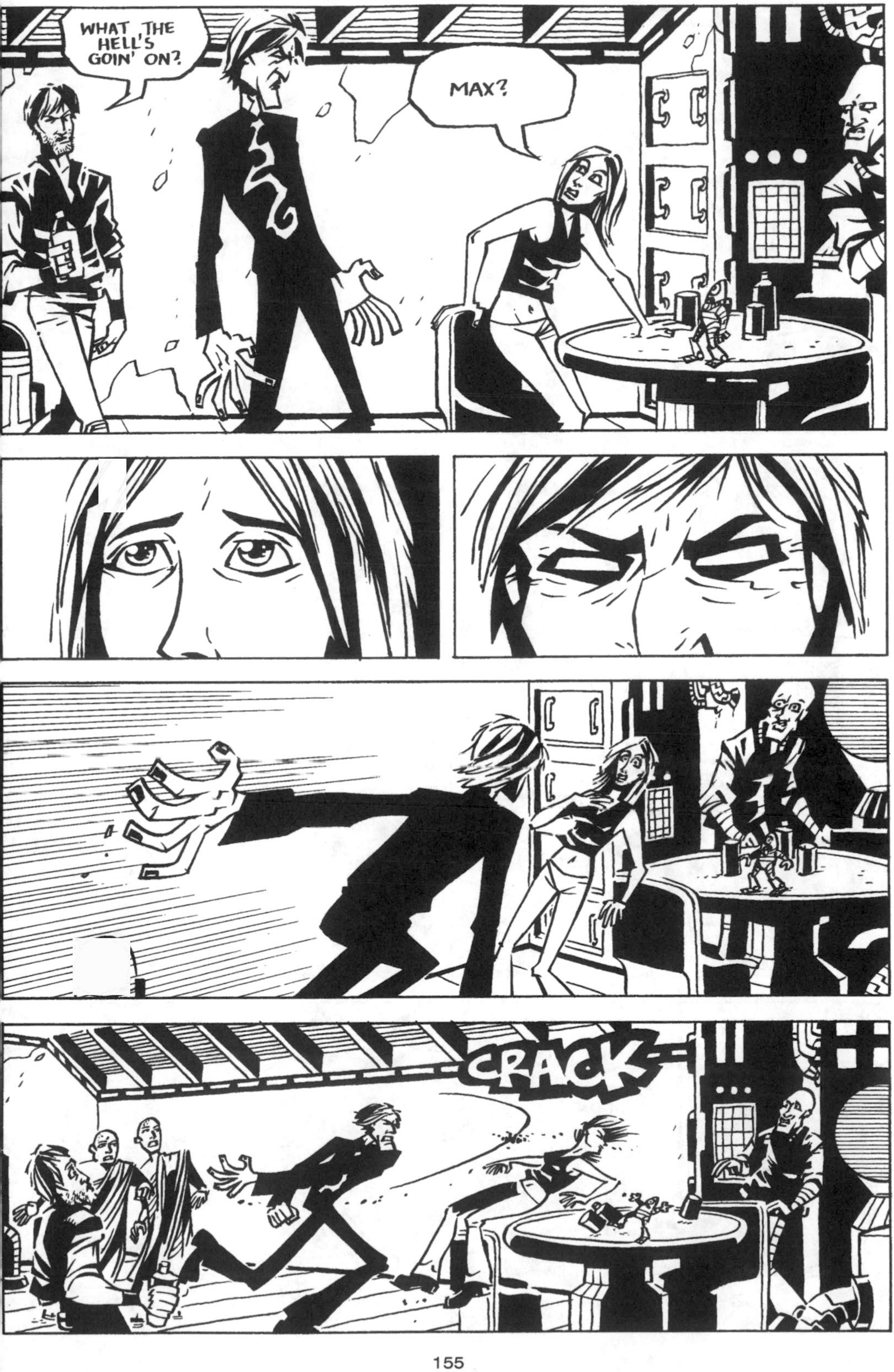
WHAT THE HELL'S GOIN' ON?
MAX?
CRACK

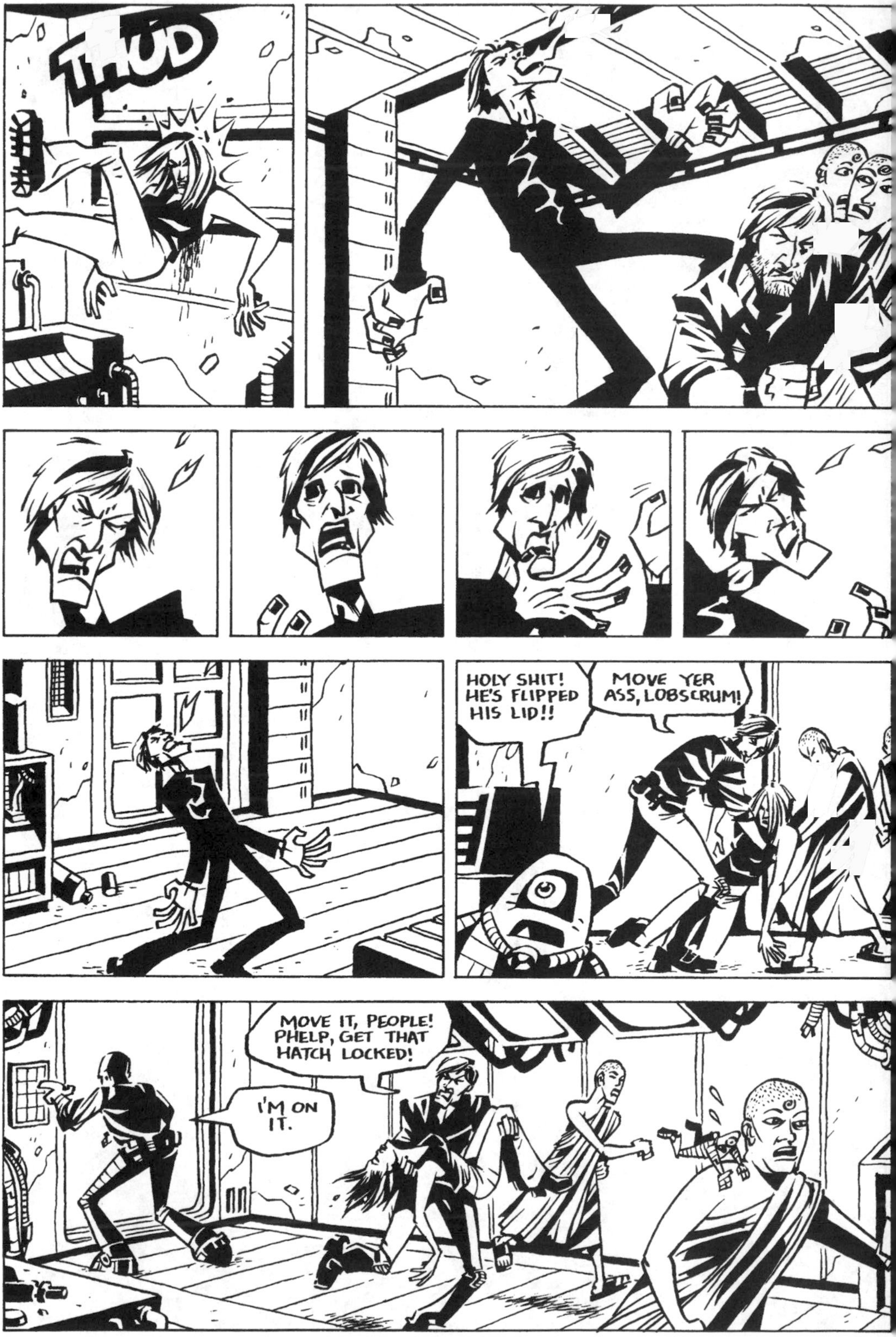
THUD
HOLY SHIT! HE'S FLIPPED HIS LID!!
MOVE YER ASS, LOBSCRUM!
MOVE IT, PEOPLE! PHELP, GET THAT HATCH LOCKED!
I'M ON IT.

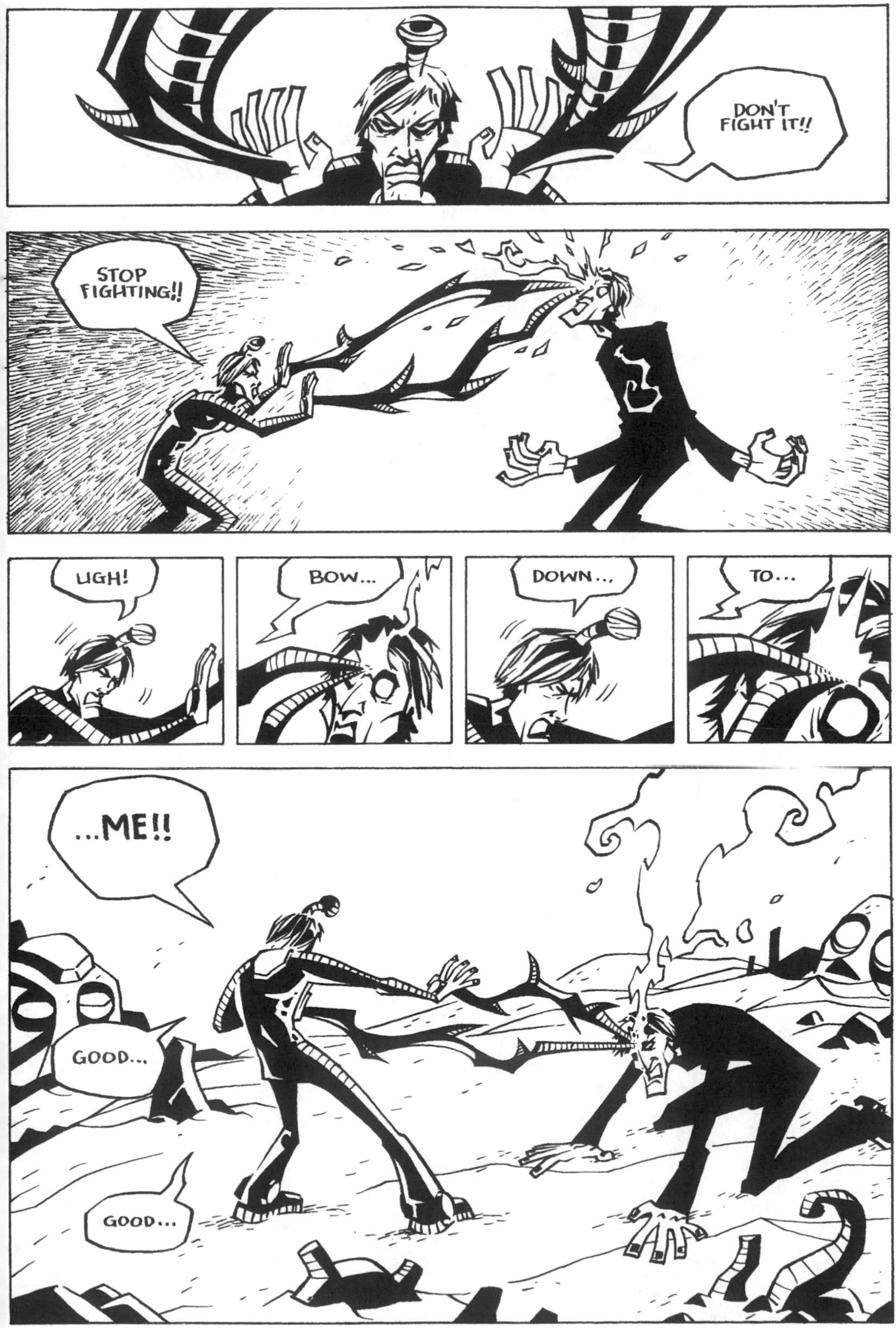
DON'T FIGHT IT!!
STOP FIGHTING!!
UGH!
BOW...
DOWN...
TO...
...ME!!
GOOD...
GOOD...

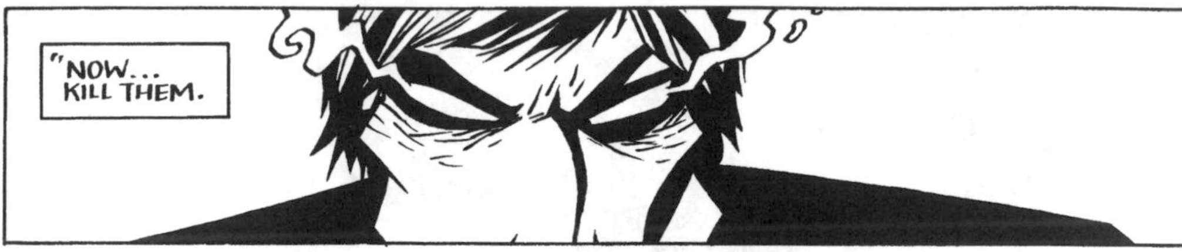
"NOW... KILL THEM.

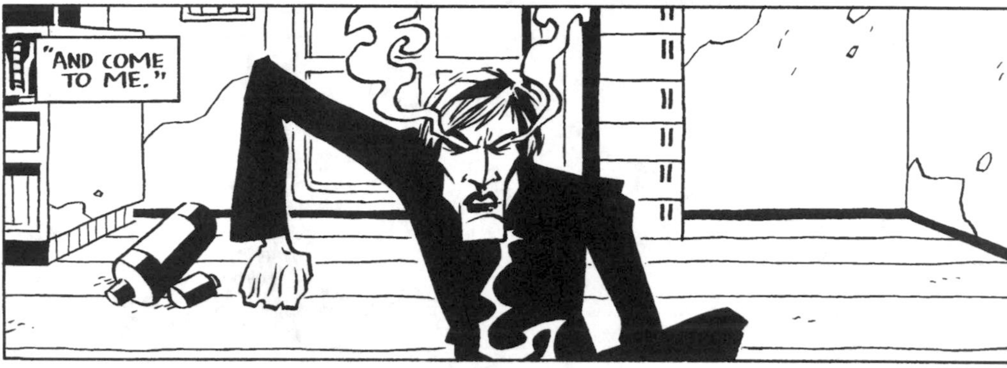
"AND COME TO ME."

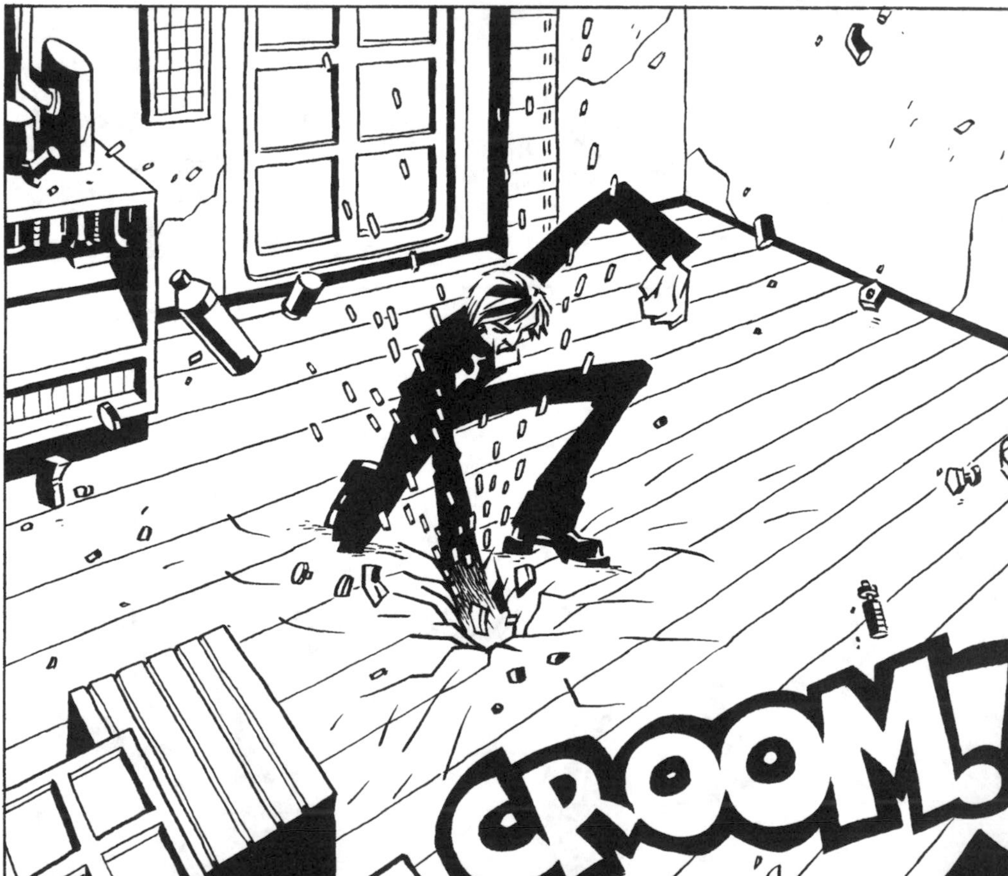
CROOM!

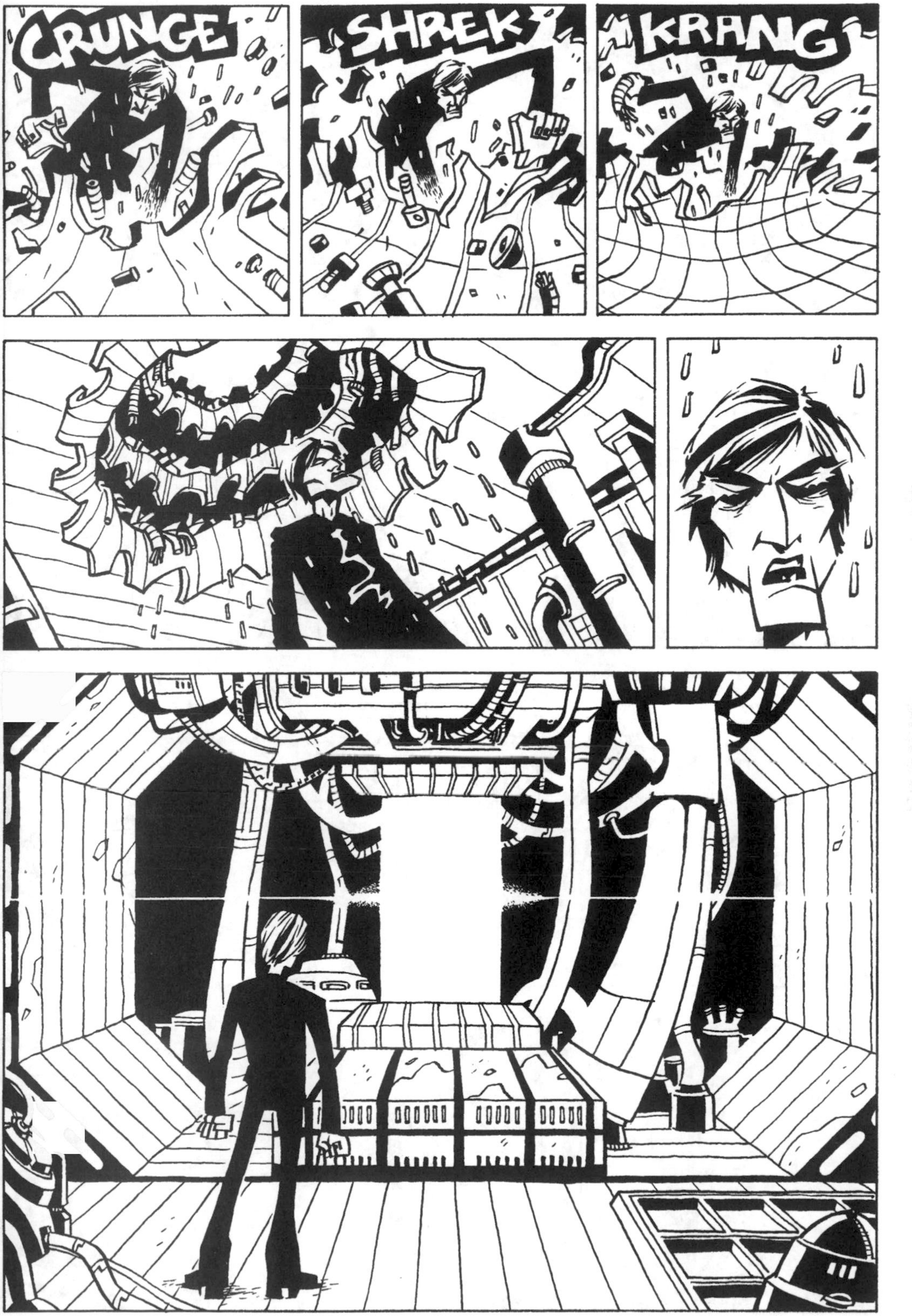
CRUNGE
SHREK
KRANG

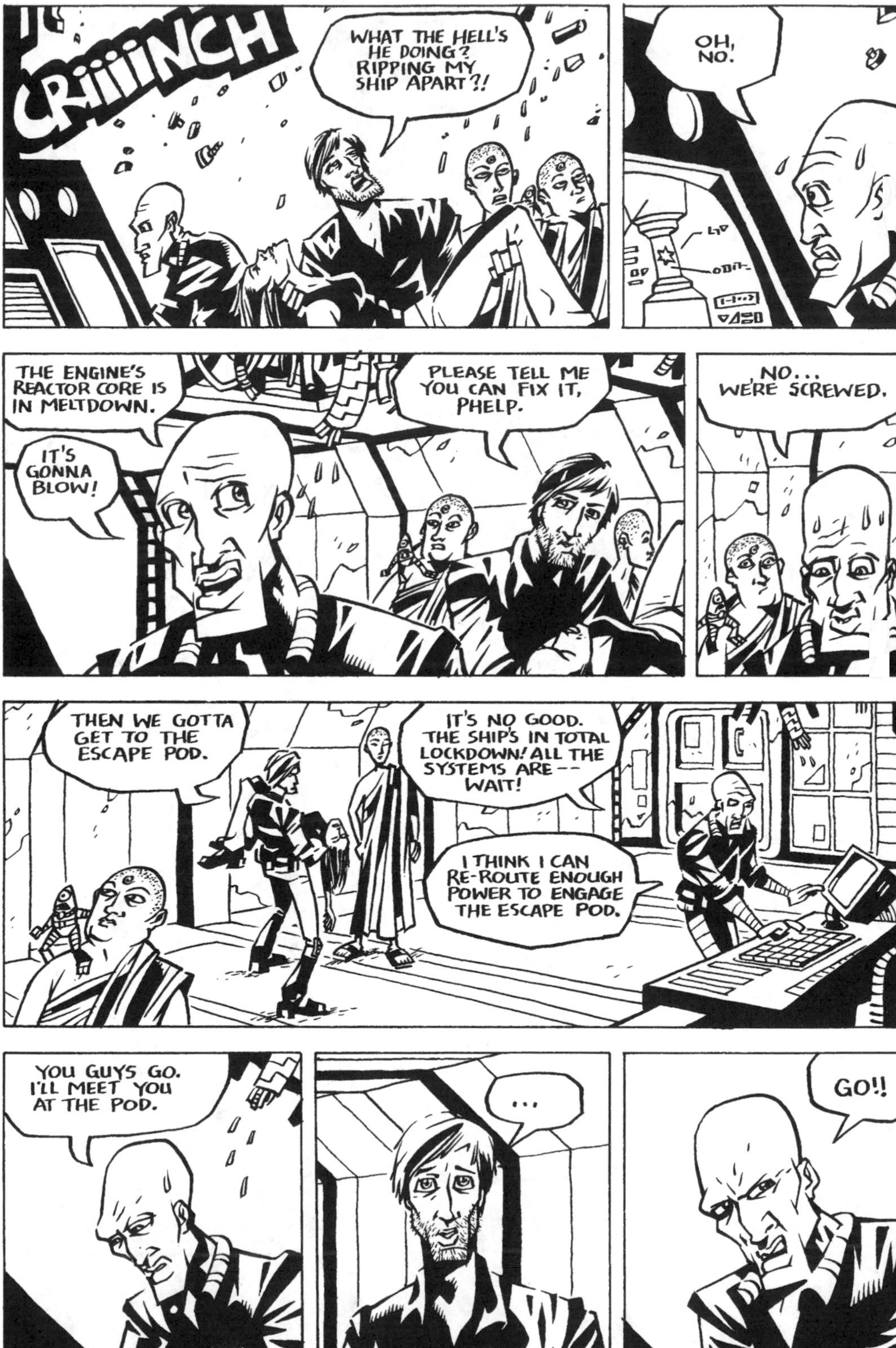
CRiiiINCH
WHAT THE HELL'S HE DOING? RIPPING MY SHIP APART?!
OH, NO.
THE ENGINE'S REACTOR CORE IS IN MELTDOWN.
IT'S GONNA BLOW!
PLEASE TELL ME YOU CAN FIX IT, PHELP.
NO... WE'RE SCREWED.
THEN WE GOTTA GET TO THE ESCAPE POD.
IT'S NO GOOD. THE SHIP'S IN TOTAL LOCKDOWN! ALL THE SYSTEMS ARE-- WAIT!
I THINK I CAN RE-ROUTE ENOUGH POWER TO ENGAGE THE ESCAPE POD.
YOU GUYS GO. I'LL MEET YOU AT THE POD.
...
GO!!

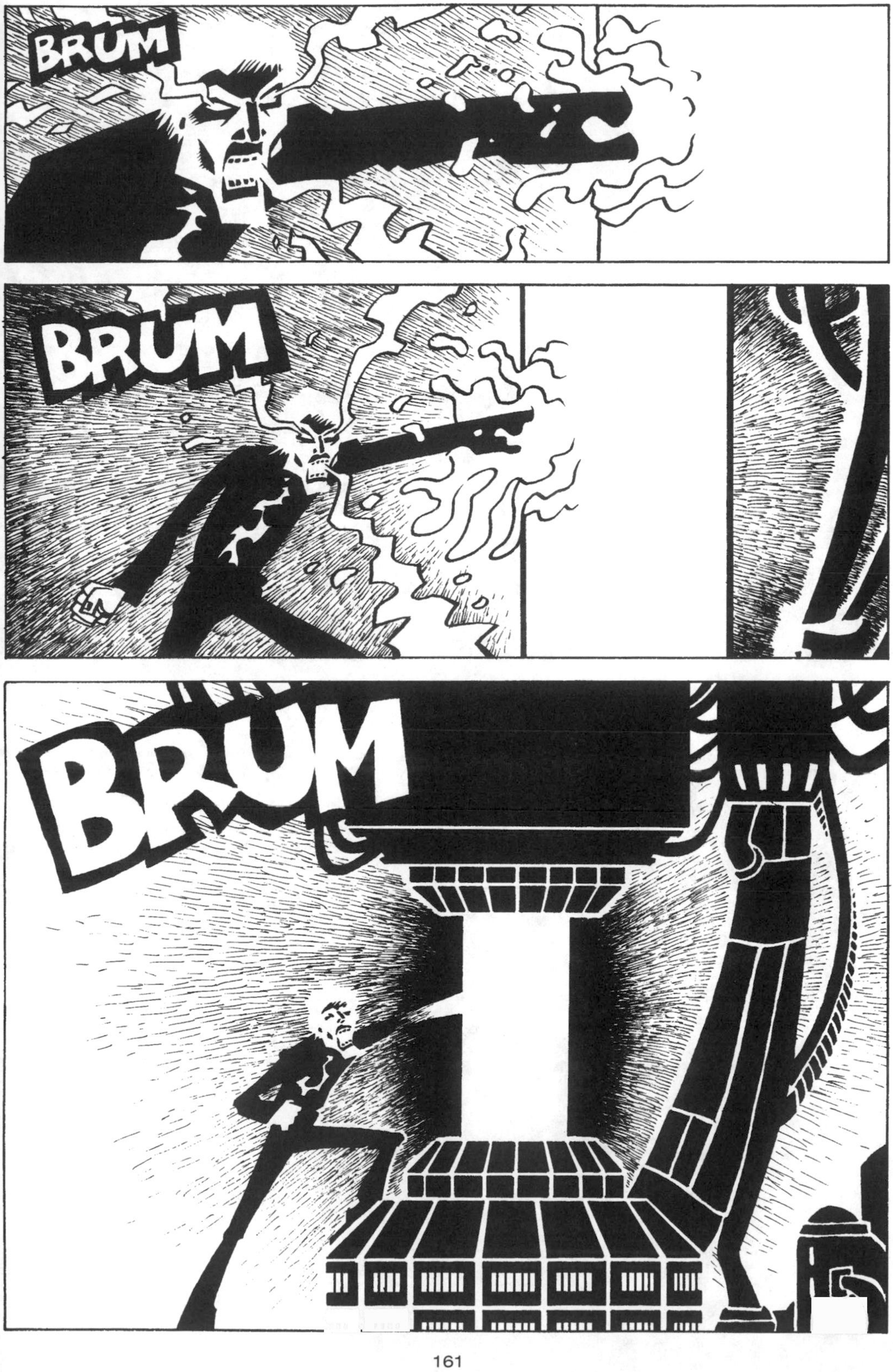
BRUM
BRUM
BRUM

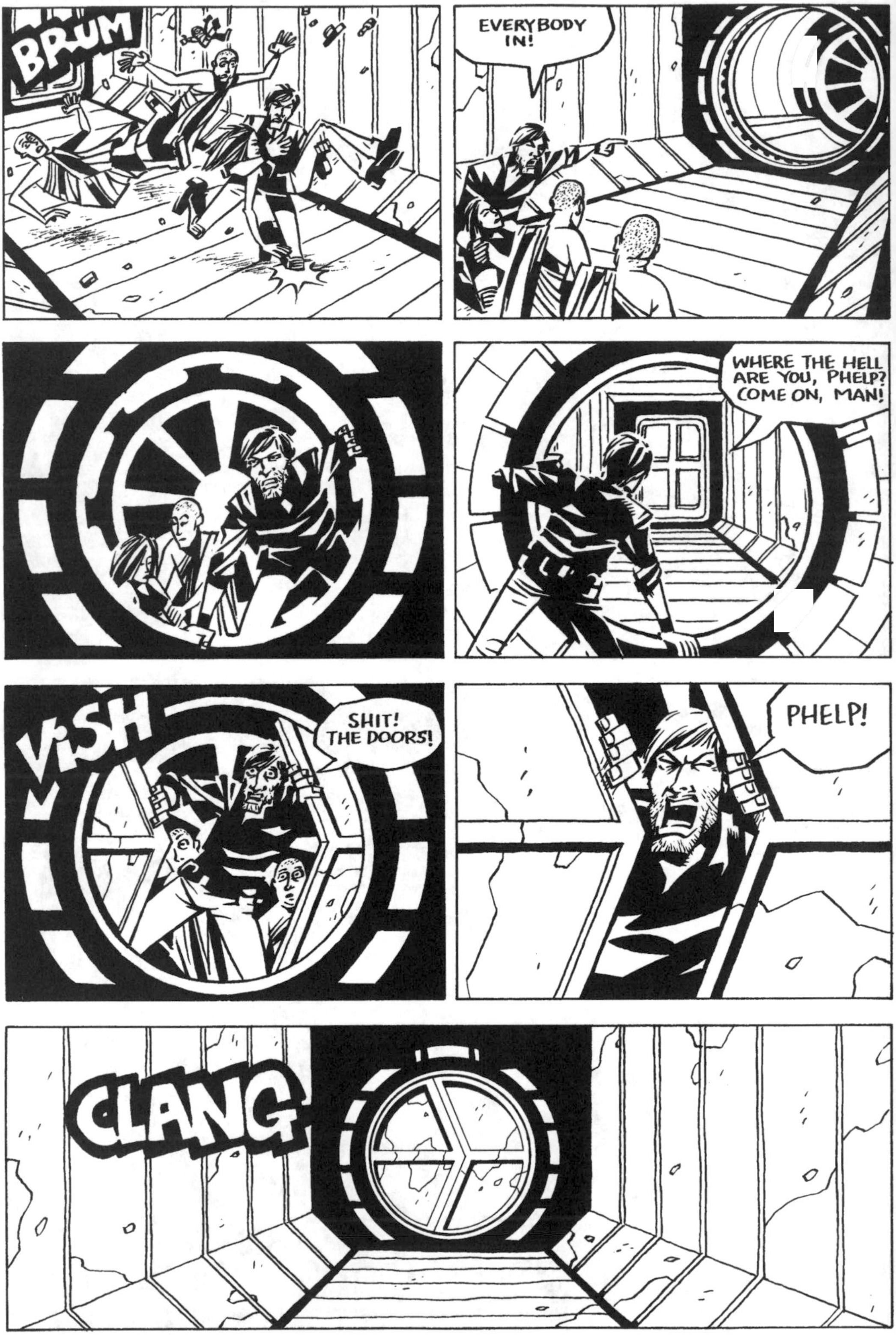
BRUM
EVERYBODY IN!
WHERE THE HELL ARE YOU, PHELP? COME ON, MAN!
VISH
SHIT! THE DOORS!
PHELP!
CLANG

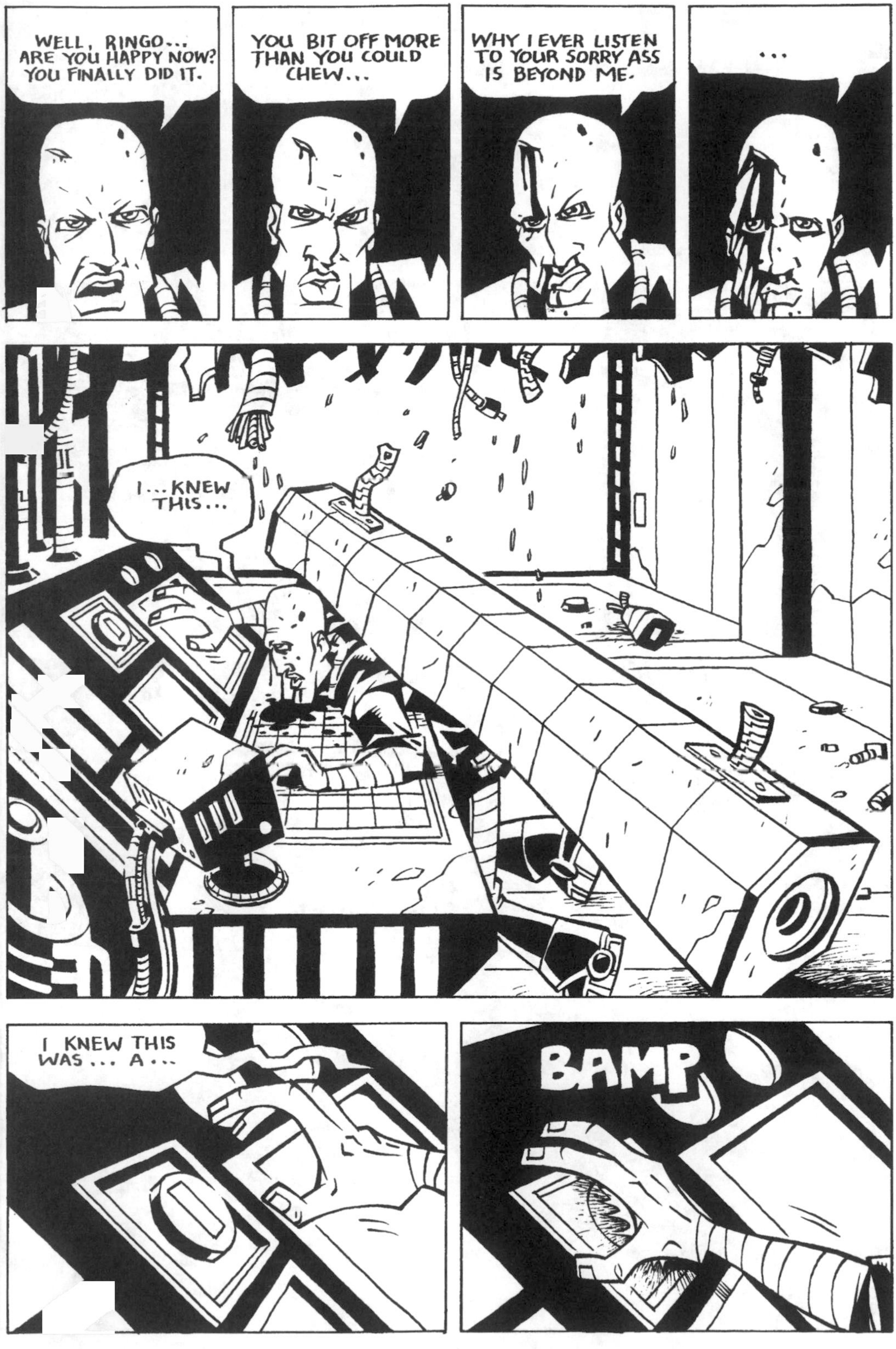
WELL, RINGO... ARE YOU HAPPY NOW? YOU FINALLY DID IT.
YOU BIT OFF MORE THAN YOU COULD CHEW...
WHY I EVER LISTEN TO YOUR SORRY ASS IS BEYOND ME.
...
I... KNEW THIS...
I KNEW THIS WAS... A...
BAMP

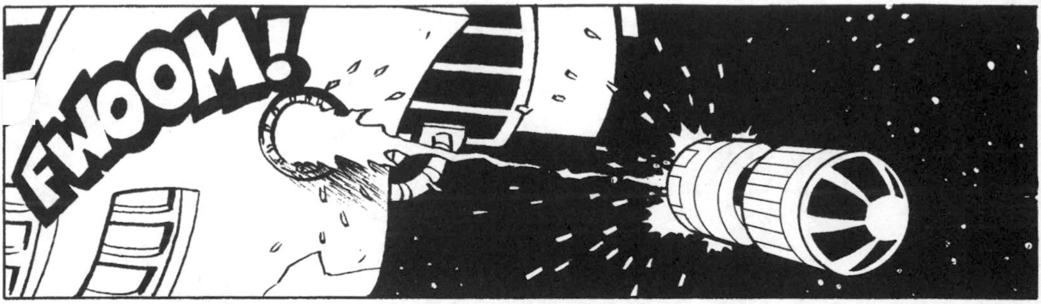
FWOOM!

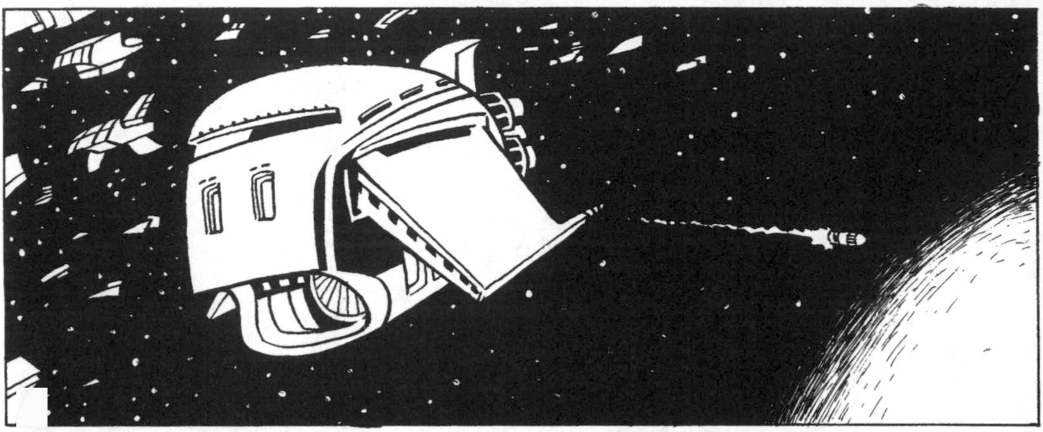

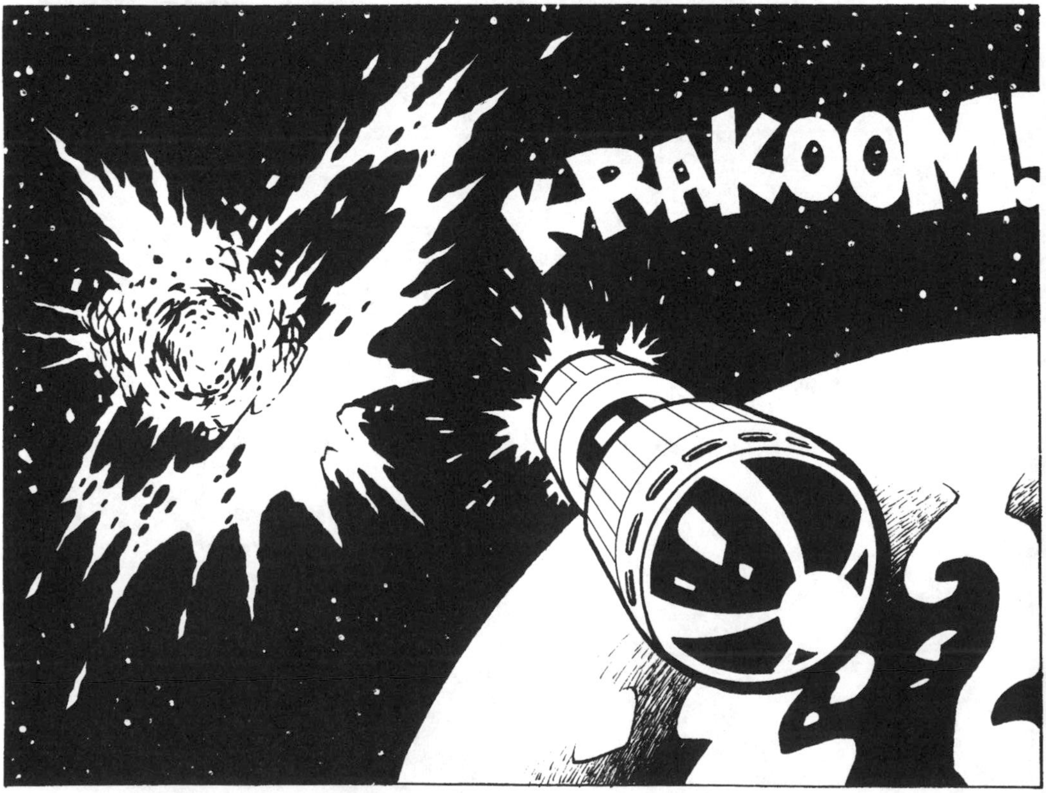
KRAKOOM!

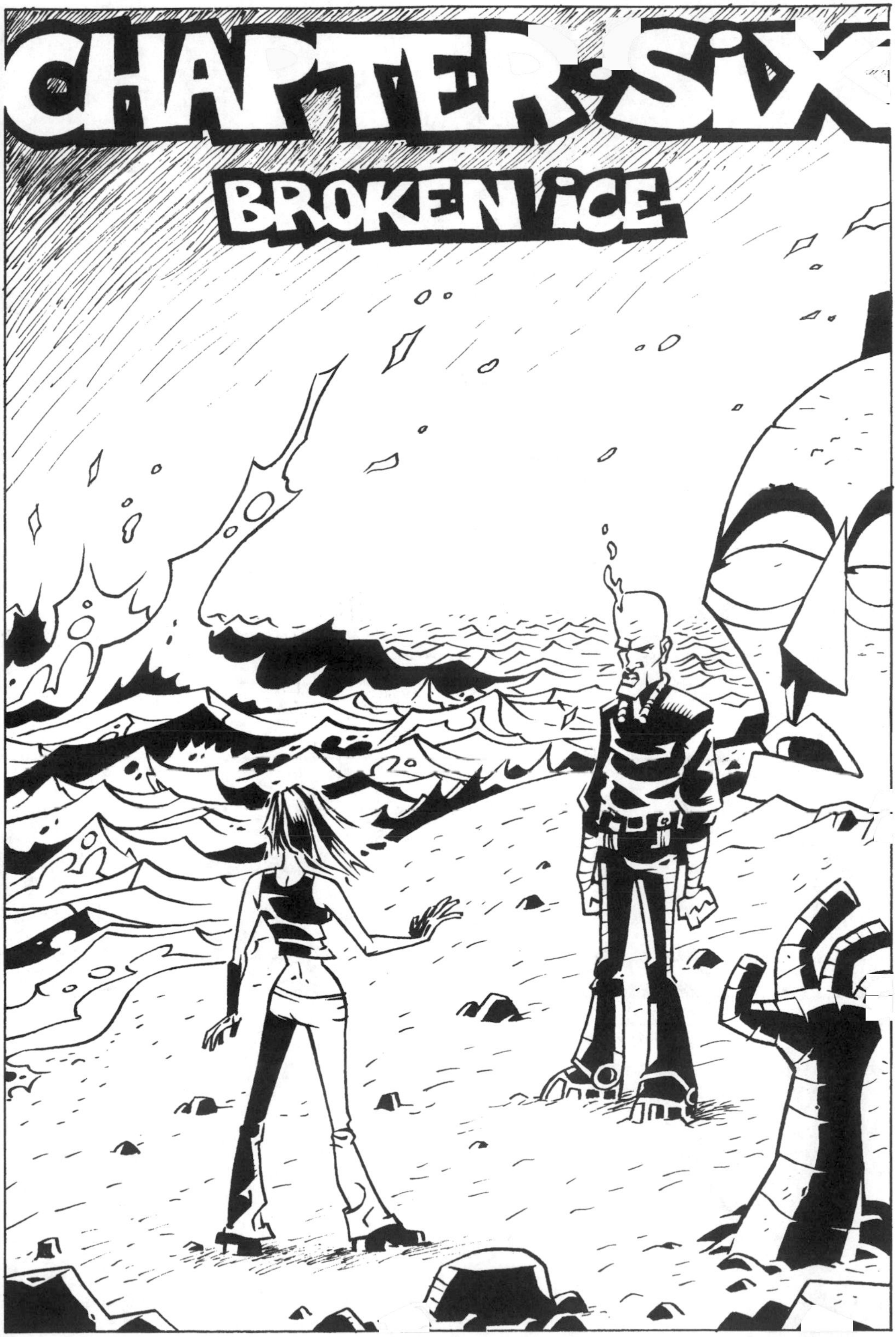
CHAPTER SIX
BROKEN ICE

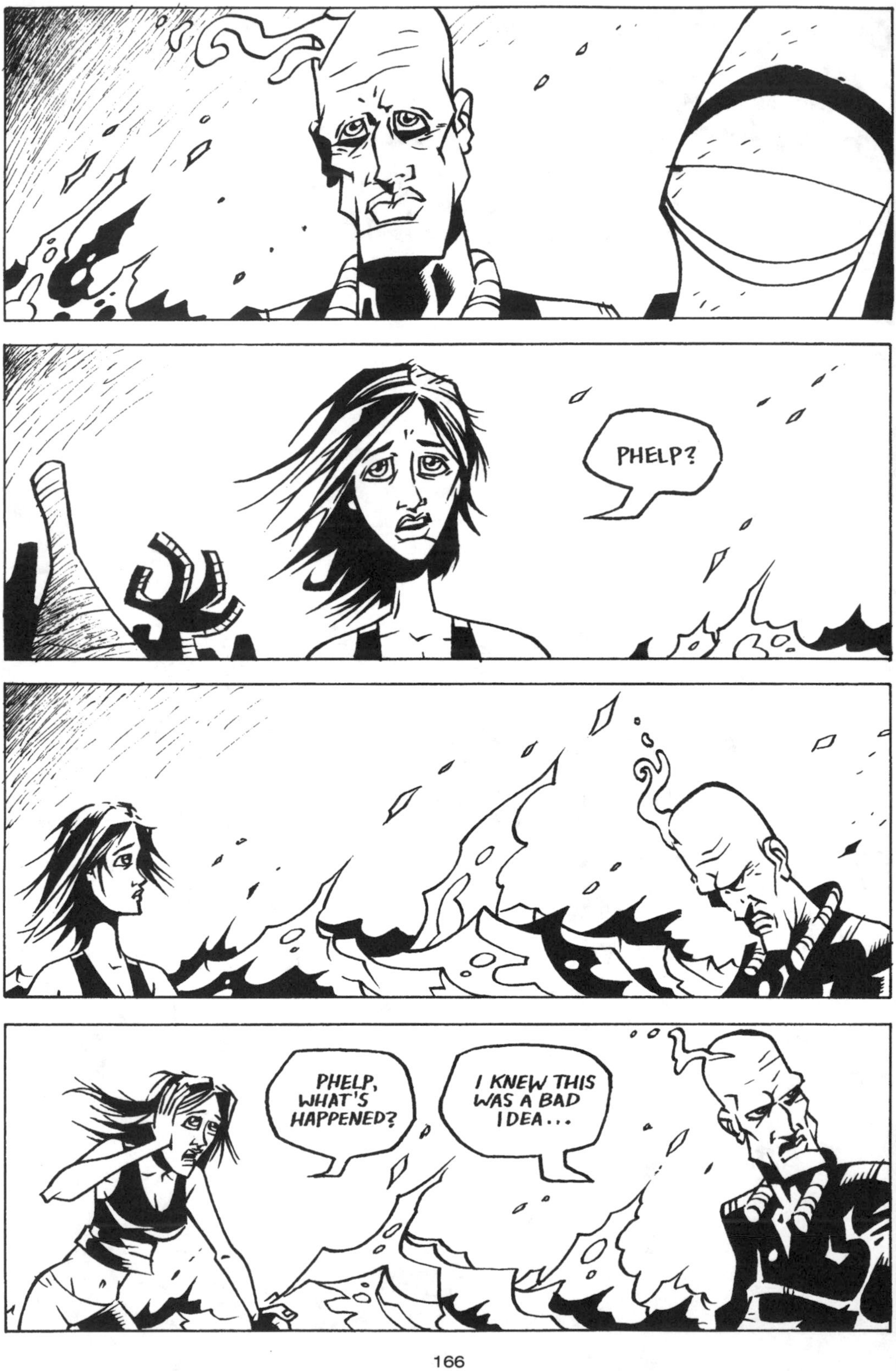
PHELP?
PHELP, WHAT'S HAPPENED?
I KNEW THIS WAS A BAD IDEA...

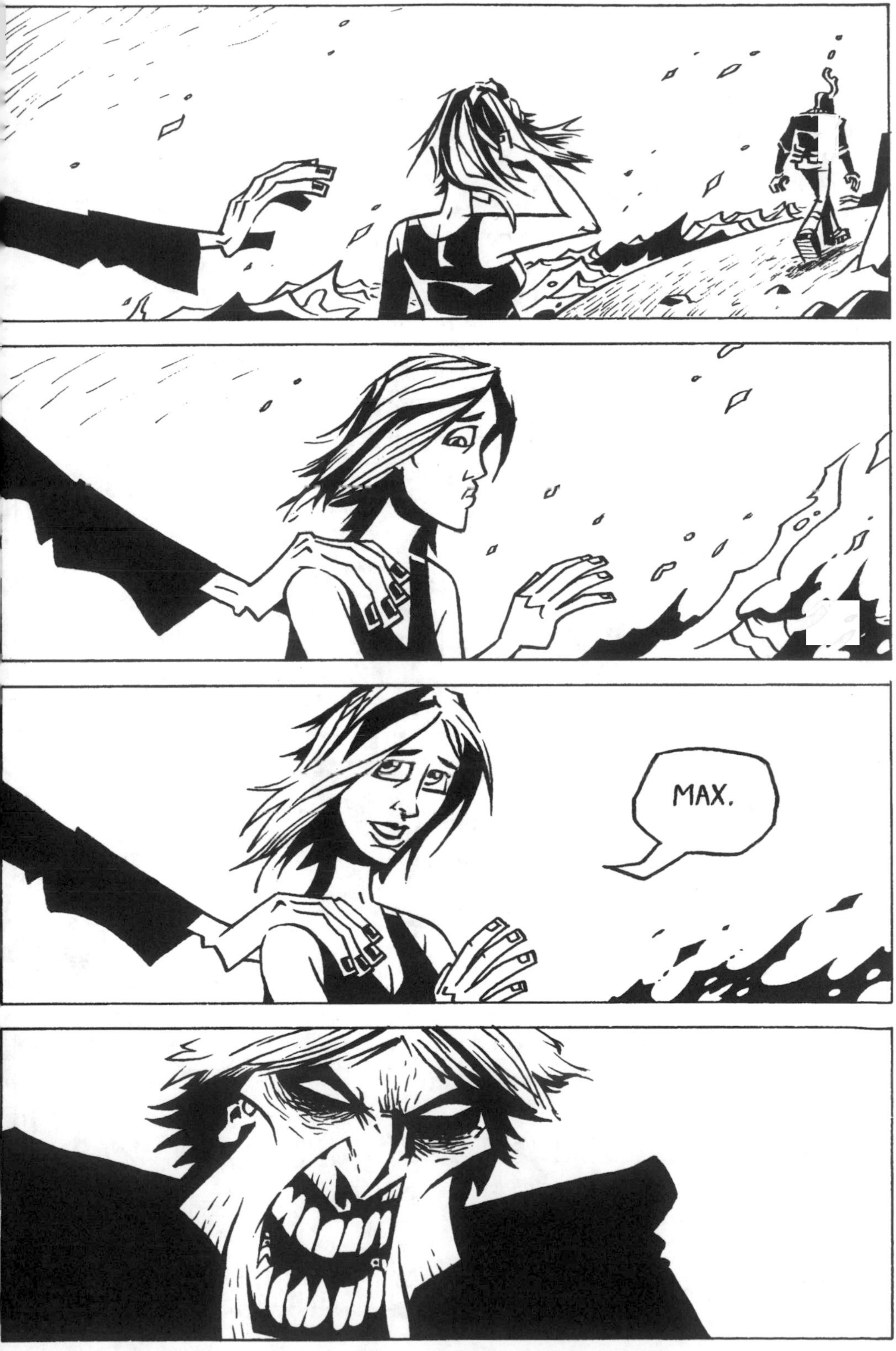
MAX.

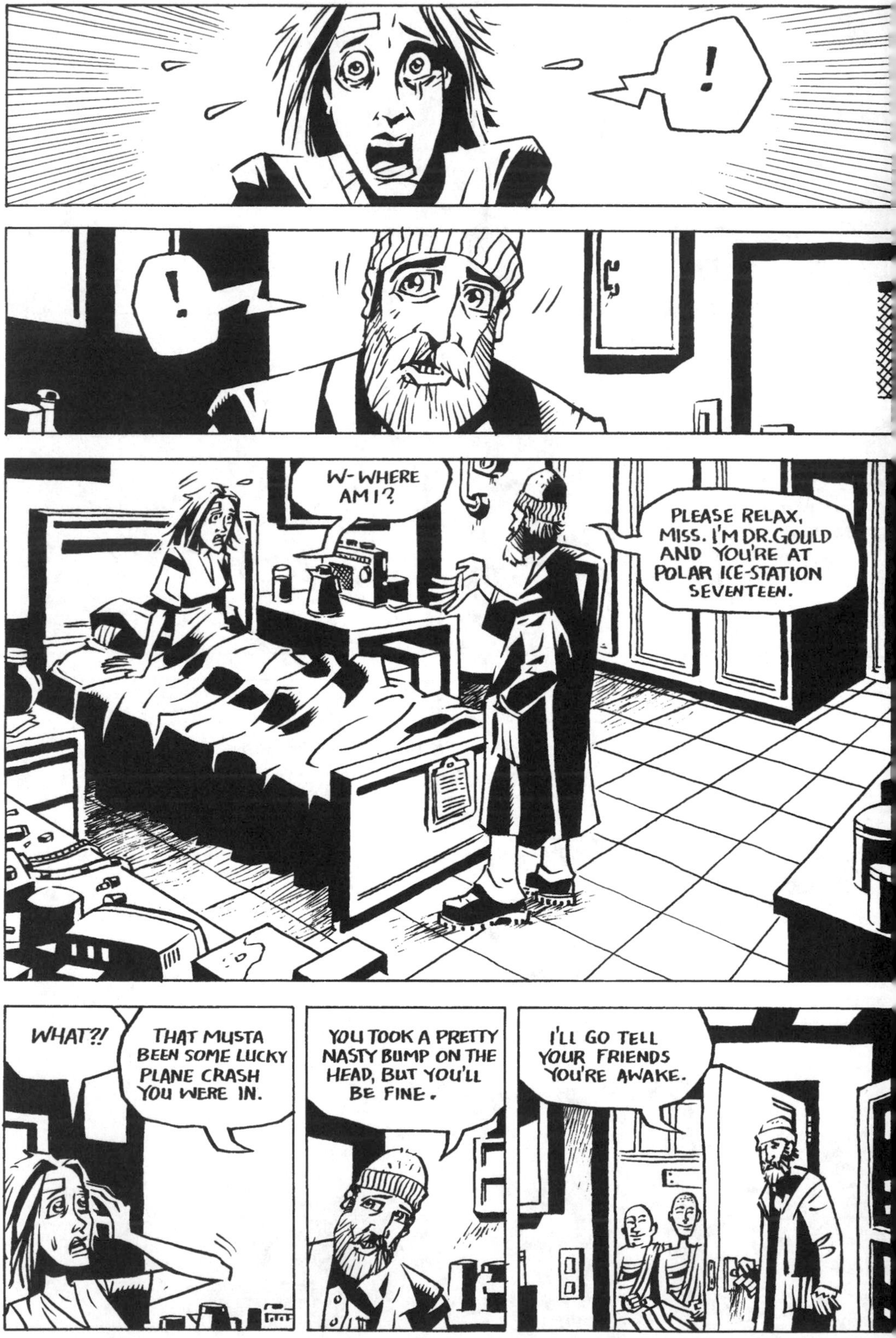
!
!
W-WHERE AM I?
PLEASE RELAX, MISS. I'M DR. GOULD AND YOU'RE AT POLAR ICE-STATION SEVENTEEN.
WHAT?!
THAT MUSTA BEEN SOME LUCKY PLANE CRASH YOU WERE IN.
YOU TOOK A PRETTY NASTY BUMP ON THE HEAD, BUT YOU'LL BE FINE.
I'LL GO TELL YOUR FRIENDS YOU'RE AWAKE.

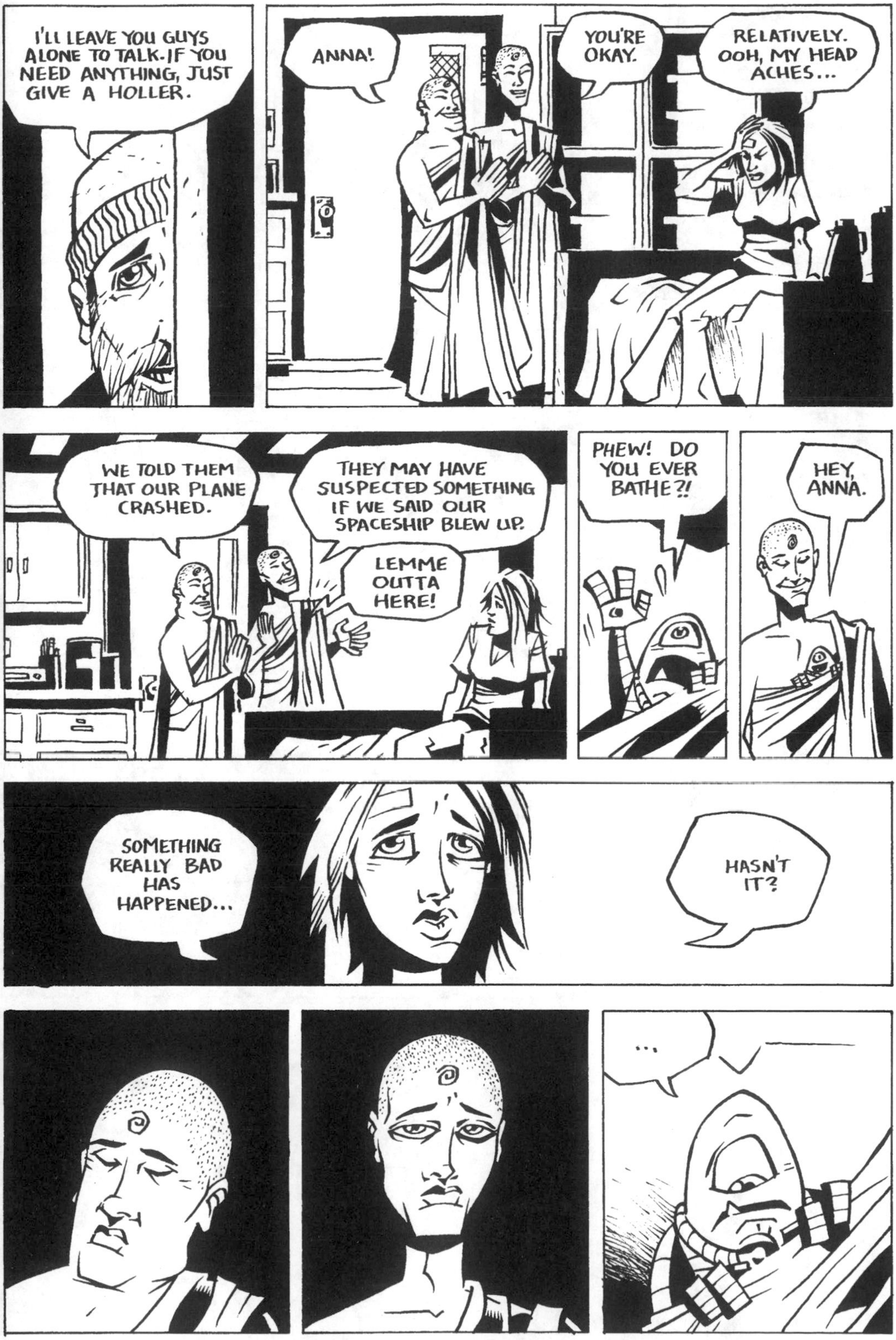
I'LL LEAVE YOU GUYS ALONE TO TALK. IF YOU NEED ANYTHING, JUST GIVE A HOLLER.
ANNA!
YOU'RE OKAY.
RELATIVELY. OOH, MY HEAD ACHES...
WE TOLD THEM THAT OUR PLANE CRASHED.
THEY MAY HAVE SUSPECTED SOMETHING IF WE SAID OUR SPACESHIP BLEW UP.
LEMME OUTTA HERE!
PHEW! DO YOU EVER BATHE?!
HEY, ANNA.
SOMETHING REALLY BAD HAS HAPPENED...
HASN'T IT?
...

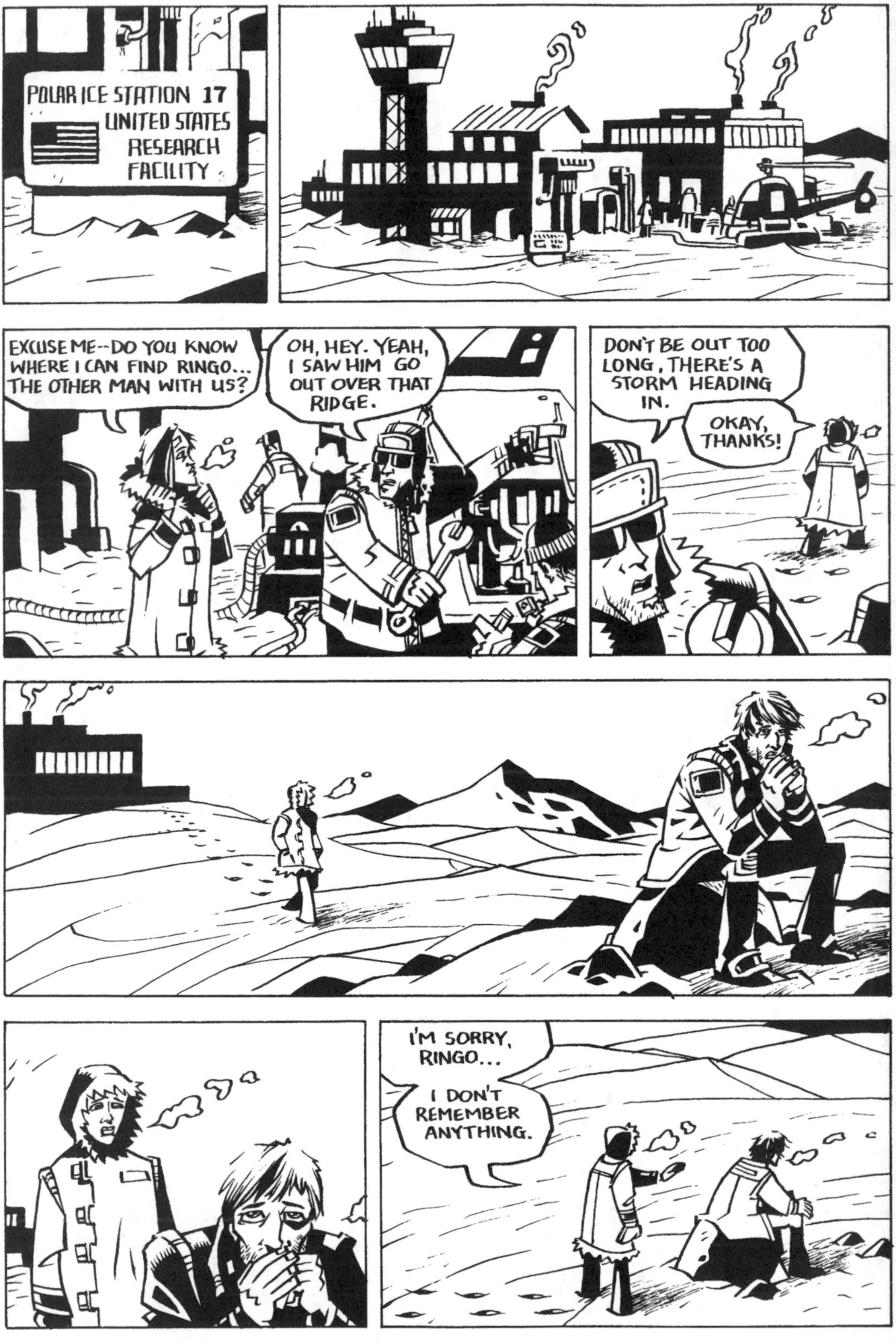
POLAR ICE STATION 17
UNITED STATES
RESEARCH
FACILITY
EXCUSE ME--DO YOU KNOW WHERE I CAN FIND RINGO... THE OTHER MAN WITH US?
OH, HEY. YEAH, I SAW HIM GO OUT OVER THAT RIDGE.
DON'T BE OUT TOO LONG, THERE'S A STORM HEADING IN.
OKAY, THANKS!
I'M SORRY, RINGO...
I DON'T REMEMBER ANYTHING.

IT'S LIKE A LIGHT SWITCH WAS TURNED OFF IN MY HEAD. I CAN'T FEEL MAX ANYMORE... OUR LINK IS BROKEN... I THINK.

I DON'T BLAME YOU.

...

GO!!

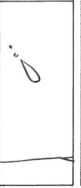

TINK

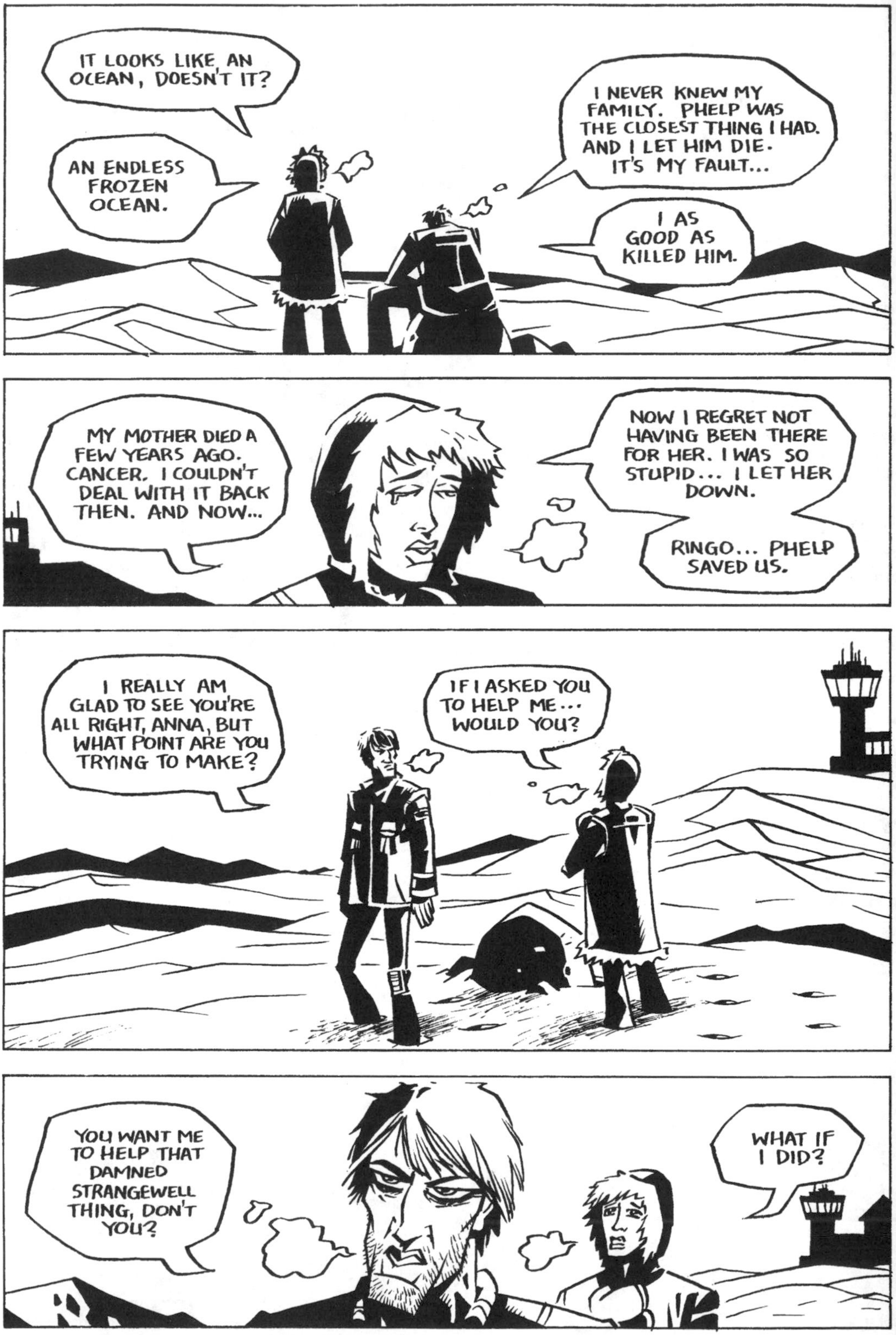
IT LOOKS LIKE AN OCEAN, DOESN'T IT?
AN ENDLESS FROZEN OCEAN.
I NEVER KNEW MY FAMILY. PHELP WAS THE CLOSEST THING I HAD. AND I LET HIM DIE. IT'S MY FAULT...
I AS GOOD AS KILLED HIM.
MY MOTHER DIED A FEW YEARS AGO. CANCER. I COULDN'T DEAL WITH IT BACK THEN. AND NOW...
NOW I REGRET NOT HAVING BEEN THERE FOR HER. I WAS SO STUPID... I LET HER DOWN.
RINGO... PHELP SAVED US.
I REALLY AM GLAD TO SEE YOU'RE ALL RIGHT, ANNA, BUT WHAT POINT ARE YOU TRYING TO MAKE?
IF I ASKED YOU TO HELP ME... WOULD YOU?
YOU WANT ME TO HELP THAT DAMNED STRANGEWELL THING, DON'T YOU?
WHAT IF I DID?

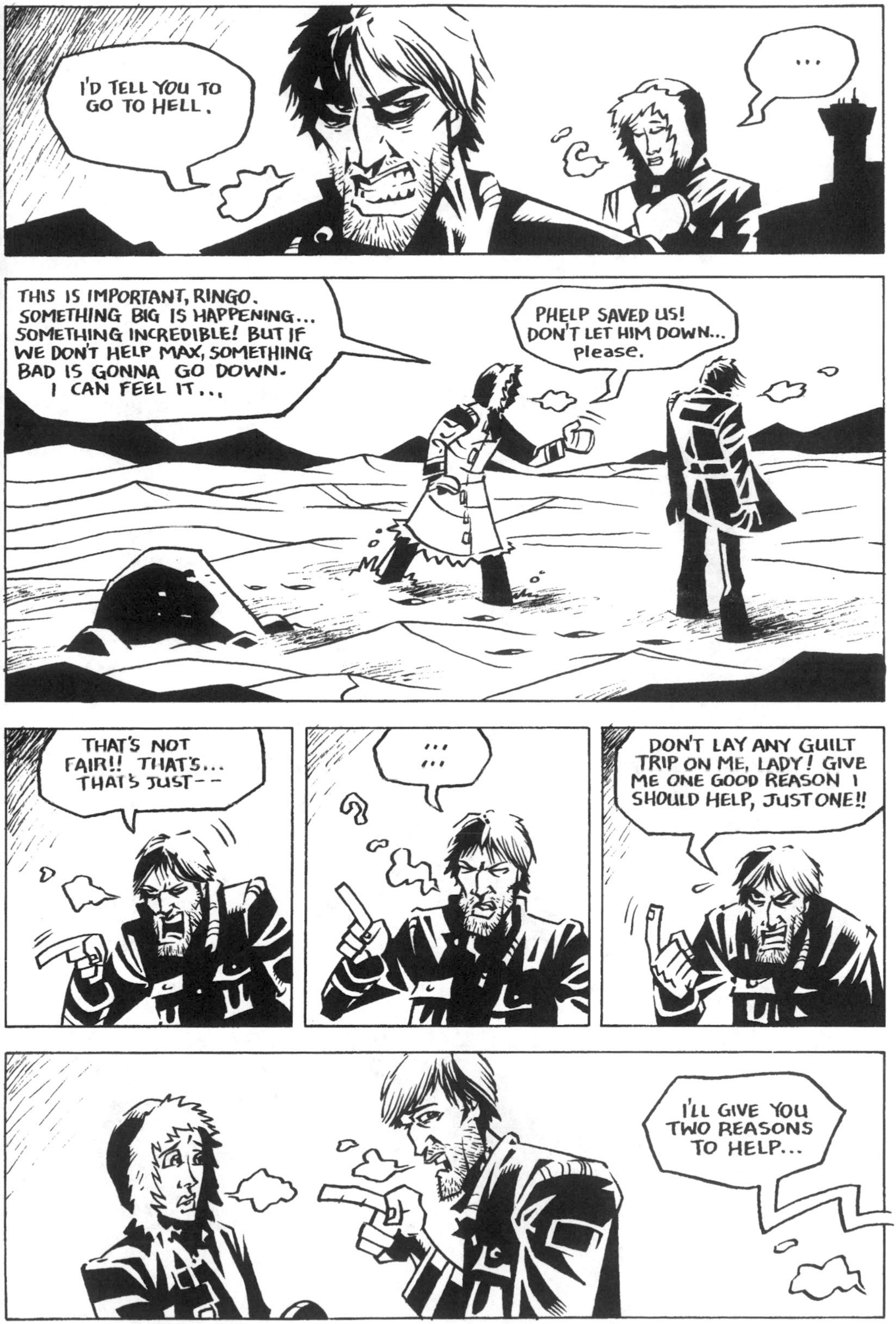
I'D TELL YOU TO GO TO HELL.
...
THIS IS IMPORTANT, RINGO. SOMETHING BIG IS HAPPENING... SOMETHING INCREDIBLE! BUT IF WE DON'T HELP MAX, SOMETHING BAD IS GONNA GO DOWN. I CAN FEEL IT...
PHELP SAVED US! DON'T LET HIM DOWN... please.
THAT'S NOT FAIR!! THAT'S... THAT'S JUST--
...
...
DON'T LAY ANY GUILT TRIP ON ME, LADY! GIVE ME ONE GOOD REASON I SHOULD HELP, JUST ONE!!
I'LL GIVE YOU TWO REASONS TO HELP...

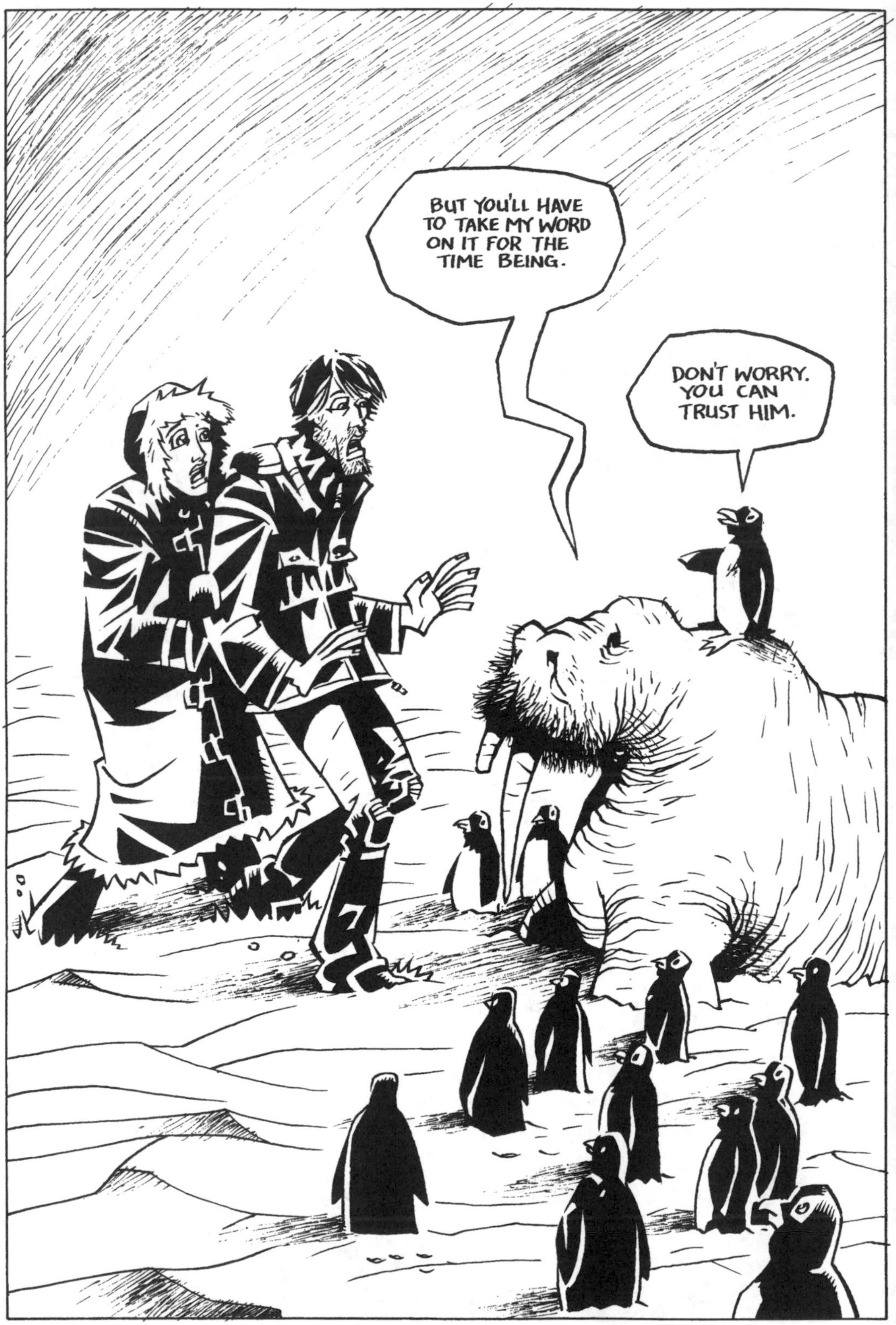
BUT YOU'LL HAVE TO TAKE MY WORD ON IT FOR THE TIME BEING.
DON'T WORRY. YOU CAN TRUST HIM.

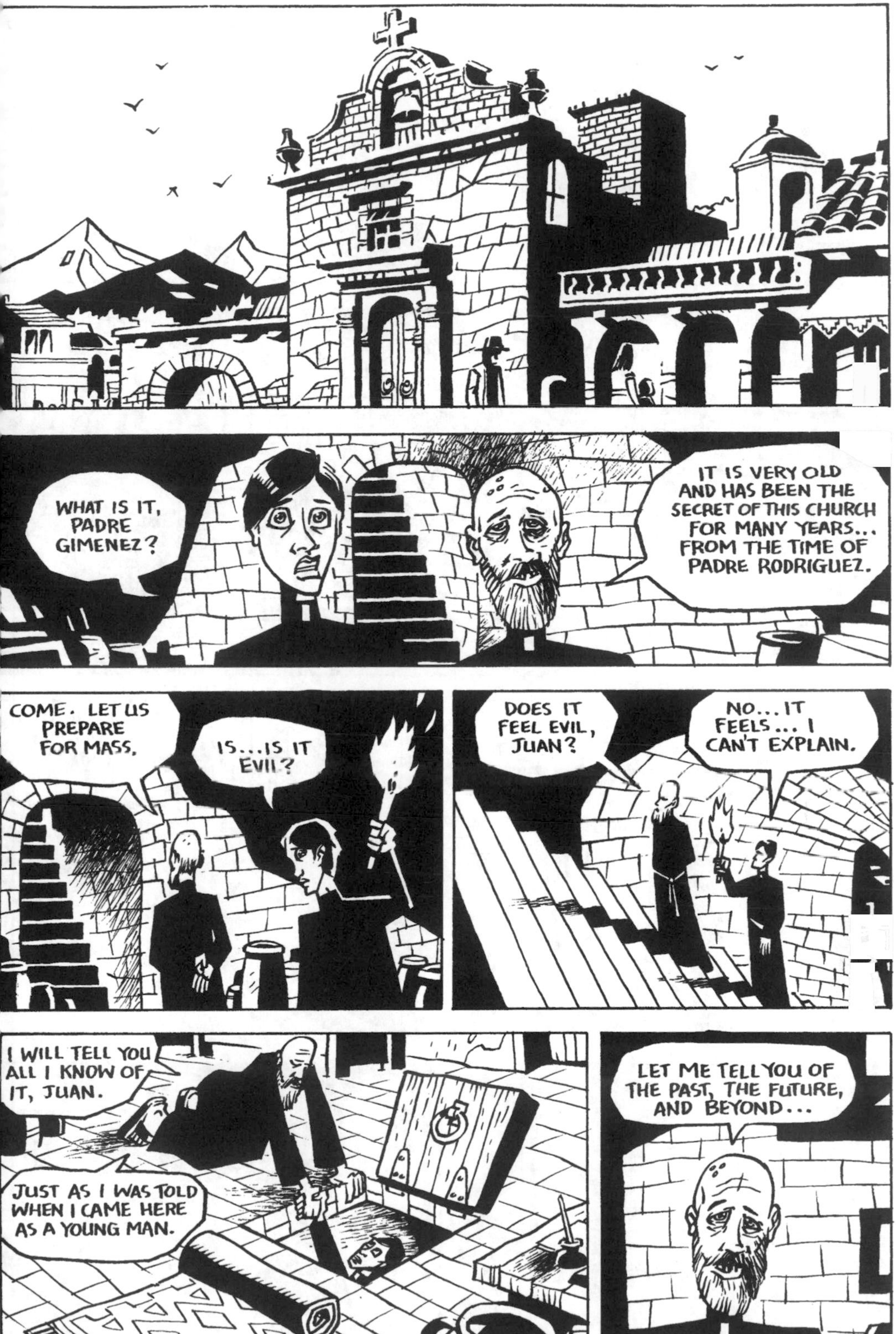
WHAT IS IT, PADRE GIMENEZ?
IT IS VERY OLD AND HAS BEEN THE SECRET OF THIS CHURCH FOR MANY YEARS... FROM THE TIME OF PADRE RODRIGUEZ.
COME. LET US PREPARE FOR MASS.
IS...IS IT EVIL?
DOES IT FEEL EVIL, JUAN?
NO...IT FEELS... I CAN'T EXPLAIN.
I WILL TELL YOU ALL I KNOW OF IT, JUAN.
JUST AS I WAS TOLD WHEN I CAME HERE AS A YOUNG MAN.
LET ME TELL YOU OF THE PAST, THE FUTURE, AND BEYOND...

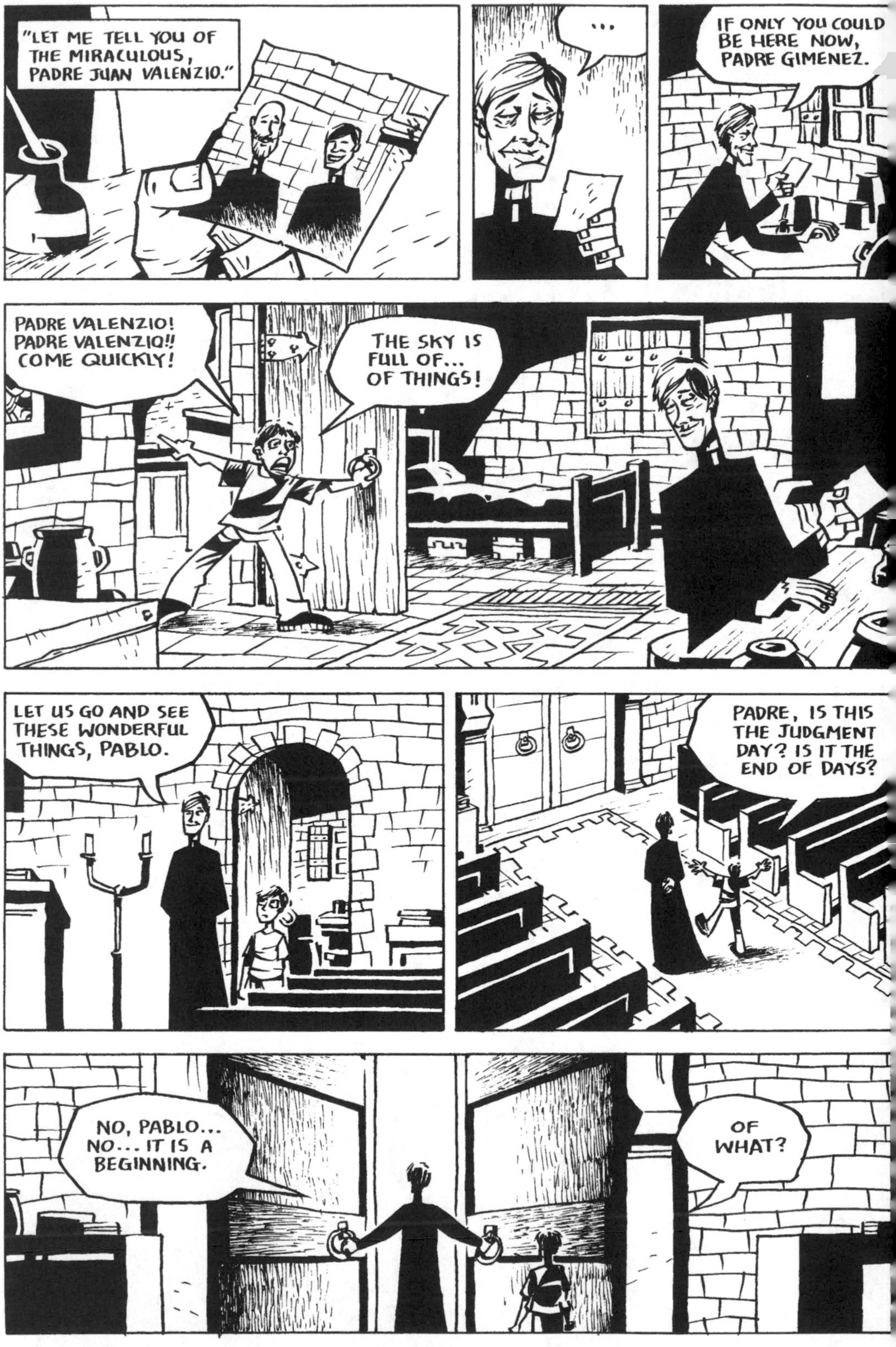
"LET ME TELL YOU OF THE MIRACULOUS, PADRE JUAN VALENZIO."
...
IF ONLY YOU COULD BE HERE NOW, PADRE GIMENEZ.
PADRE VALENZIO! PADRE VALENZIO!! COME QUICKLY!
THE SKY IS FULL OF... OF THINGS!
LET US GO AND SEE THESE WONDERFUL THINGS, PABLO.
PADRE, IS THIS THE JUDGMENT DAY? IS IT THE END OF DAYS?
NO, PABLO... NO... IT IS A BEGINNING.
OF WHAT?

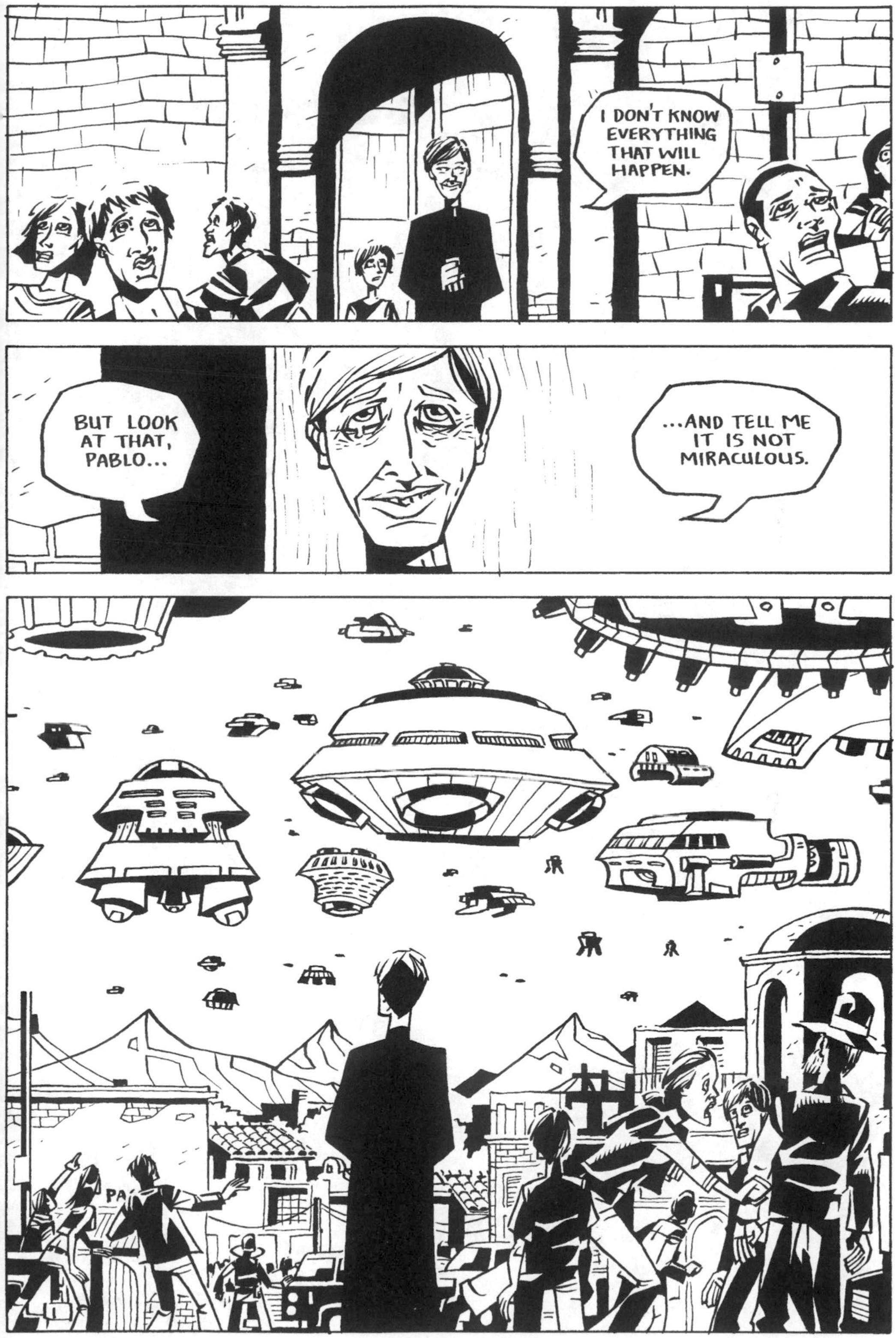
I DON'T KNOW EVERYTHING THAT WILL HAPPEN.
BUT LOOK AT THAT, PABLO...
...AND TELL ME IT IS NOT MIRACULOUS.

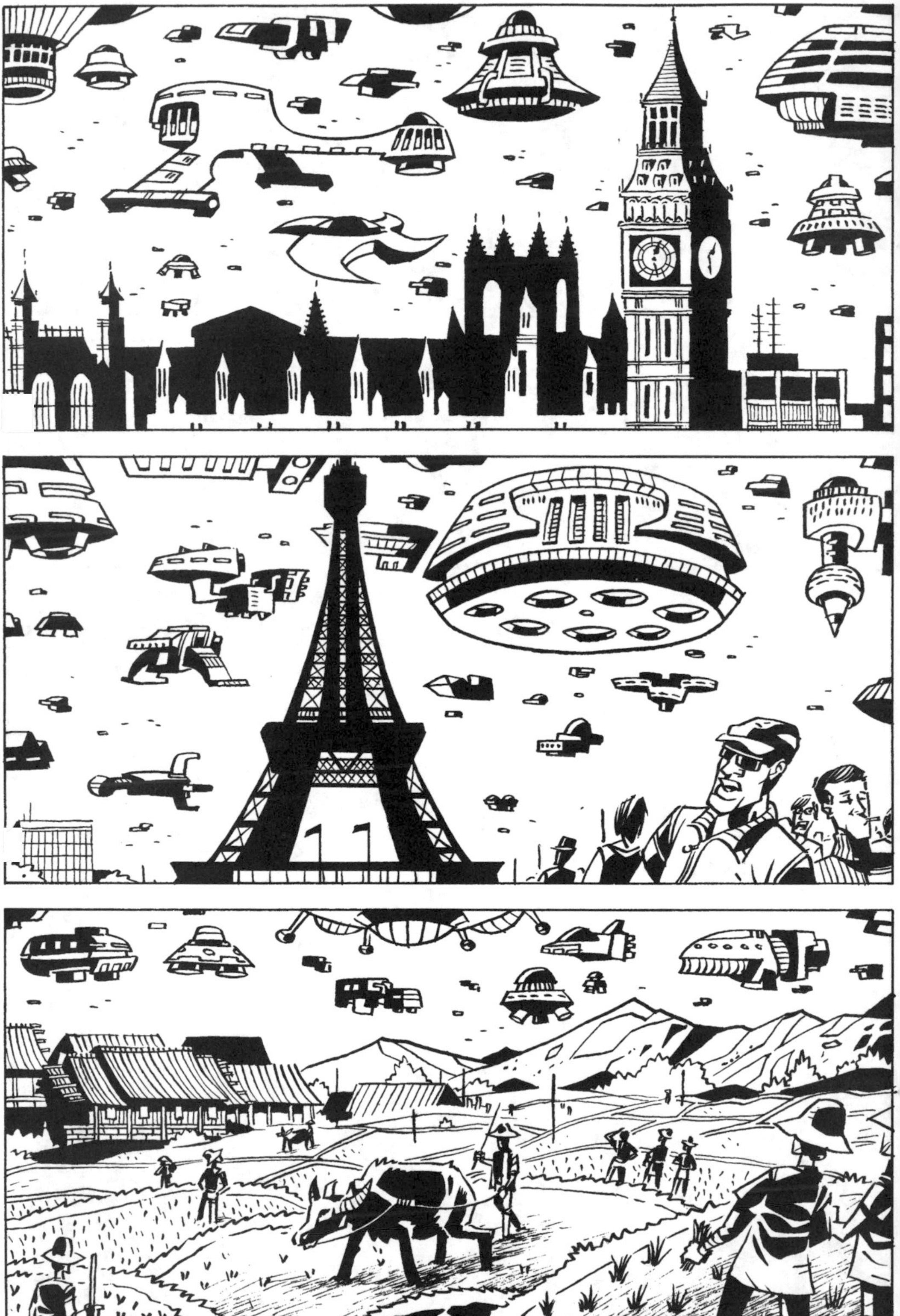

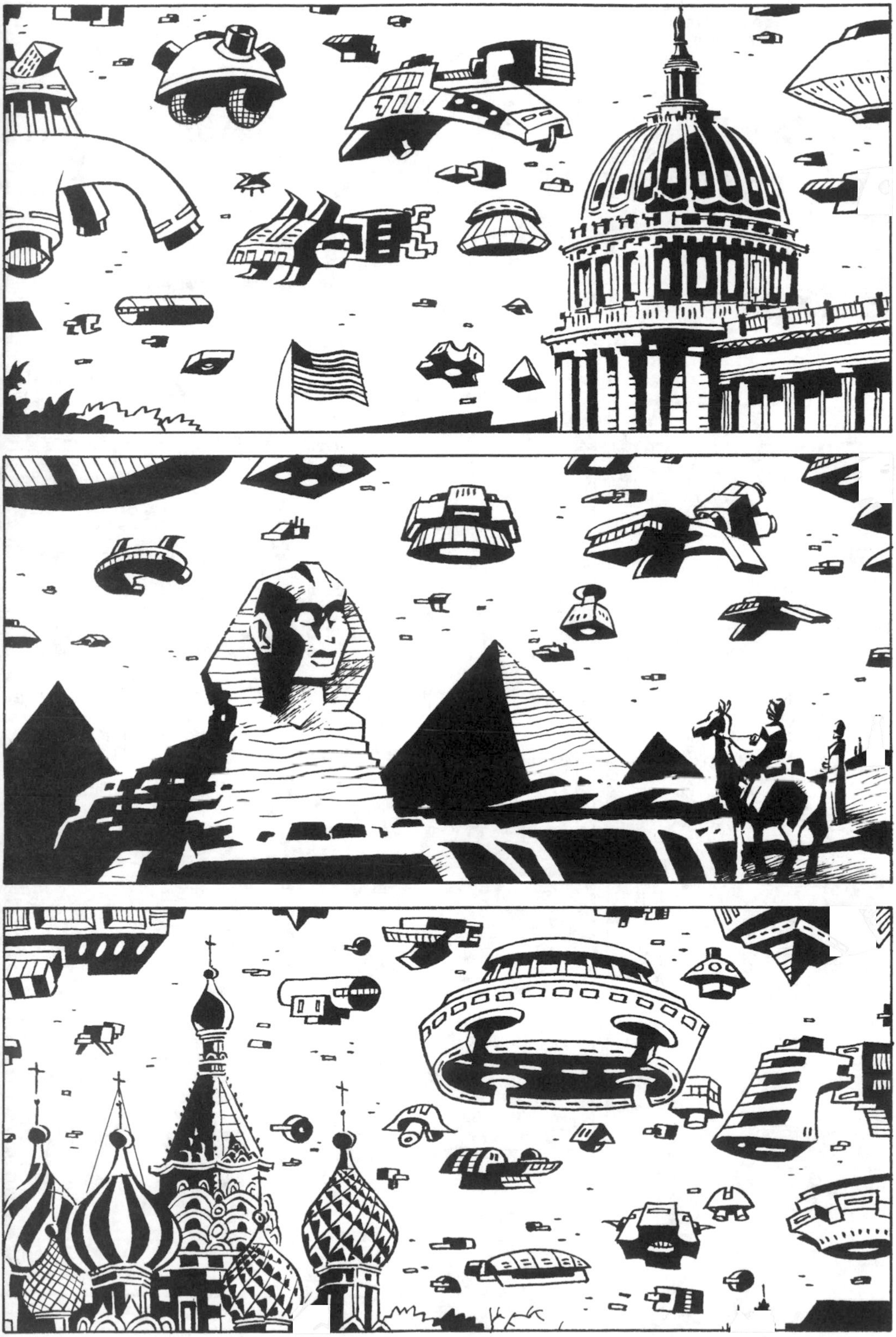

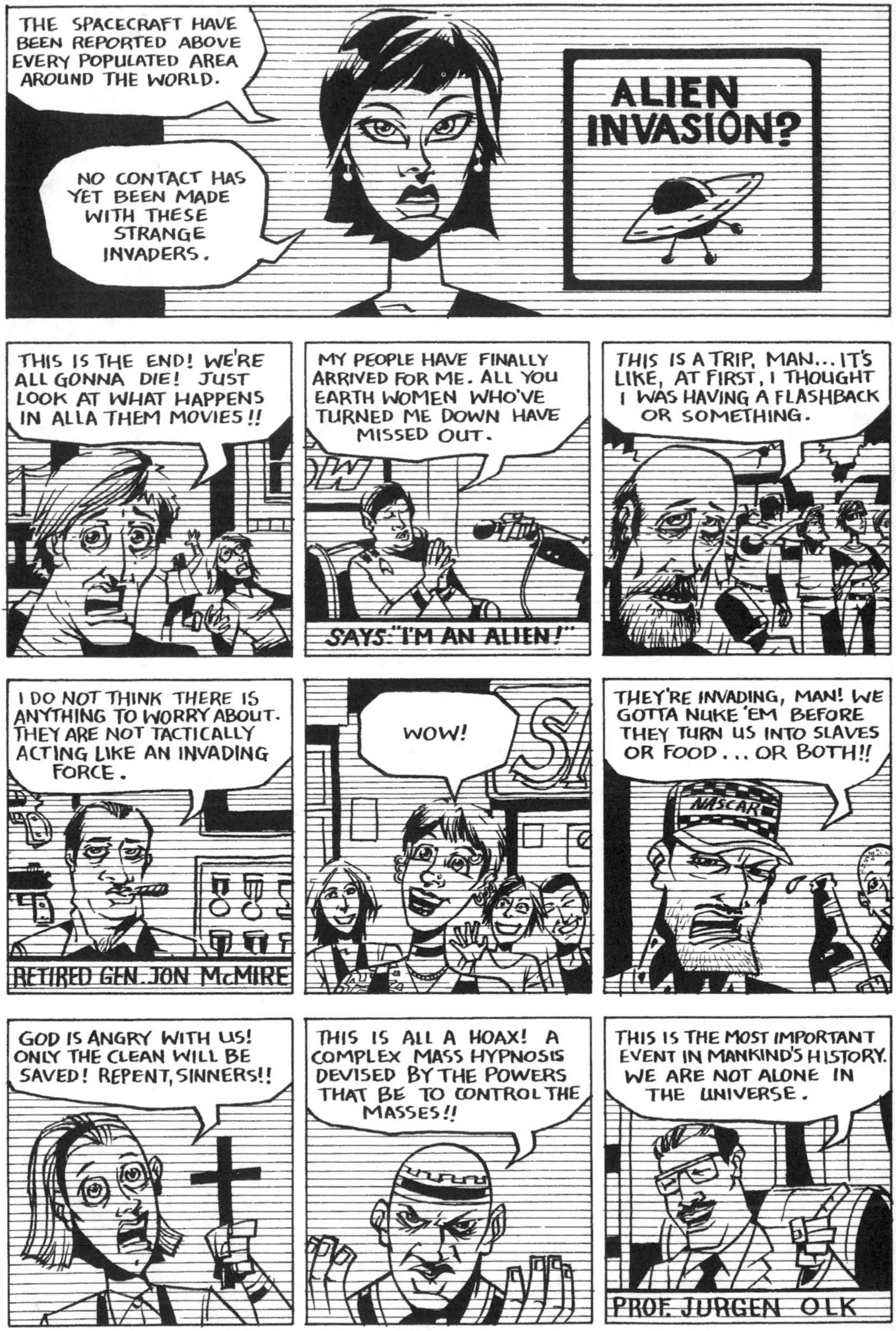
THE SPACECRAFT HAVE BEEN REPORTED ABOVE EVERY POPULATED AREA AROUND THE WORLD.
NO CONTACT HAS YET BEEN MADE WITH THESE STRANGE INVADERS.
ALIEN INVASION?
THIS IS THE END! WE'RE ALL GONNA DIE! JUST LOOK AT WHAT HAPPENS IN ALLA THEM MOVIES!!
MY PEOPLE HAVE FINALLY ARRIVED FOR ME. ALL YOU EARTH WOMEN WHO'VE TURNED ME DOWN HAVE MISSED OUT.
SAYS: "I'M AN ALIEN!"
THIS IS A TRIP, MAN... IT'S LIKE, AT FIRST, I THOUGHT I WAS HAVING A FLASHBACK OR SOMETHING.
I DO NOT THINK THERE IS ANYTHING TO WORRY ABOUT. THEY ARE NOT TACTICALLY ACTING LIKE AN INVADING FORCE.
RETIRED GEN. JON McMIRE
WOW!
THEY'RE INVADING, MAN! WE GOTTA NUKE 'EM BEFORE THEY TURN US INTO SLAVES OR FOOD... OR BOTH!!
NASCAR
GOD IS ANGRY WITH US! ONLY THE CLEAN WILL BE SAVED! REPENT, SINNERS!!
THIS IS ALL A HOAX! A COMPLEX MASS HYPNOSIS DEVISED BY THE POWERS THAT BE TO CONTROL THE MASSES!!
THIS IS THE MOST IMPORTANT EVENT IN MANKIND'S HISTORY. WE ARE NOT ALONE IN THE UNIVERSE.
PROF. JURGEN OLK

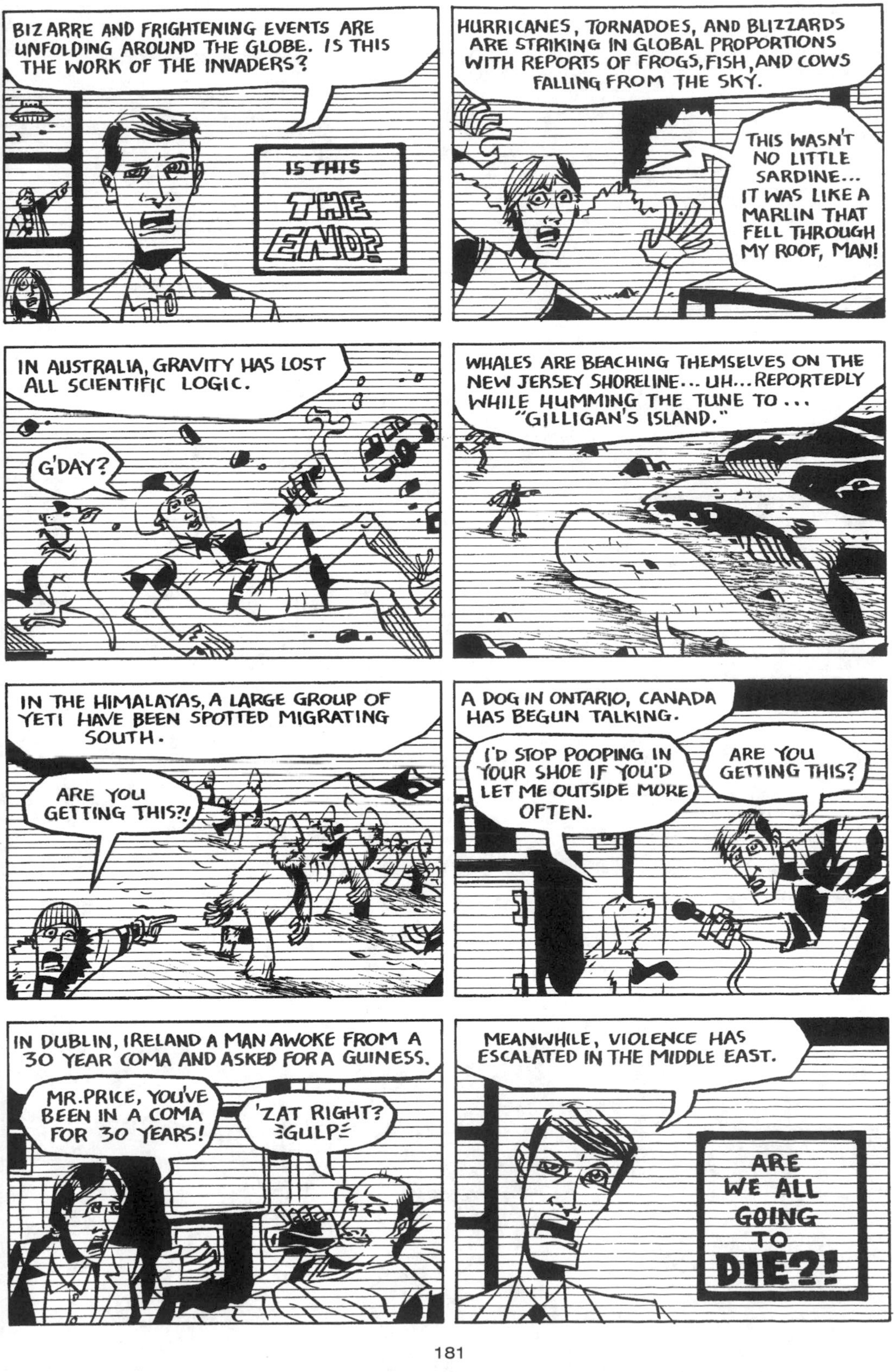
BIZARRE AND FRIGHTENING EVENTS ARE UNFOLDING AROUND THE GLOBE. IS THIS THE WORK OF THE INVADERS?
IS THIS THE END?
HURRICANES, TORNADOES, AND BLIZZARDS ARE STRIKING IN GLOBAL PROPORTIONS WITH REPORTS OF FROGS, FISH, AND COWS FALLING FROM THE SKY.
THIS WASN'T NO LITTLE SARDINE... IT WAS LIKE A MARLIN THAT FELL THROUGH MY ROOF, MAN!
IN AUSTRALIA, GRAVITY HAS LOST ALL SCIENTIFIC LOGIC.
G'DAY?
WHALES ARE BEACHING THEMSELVES ON THE NEW JERSEY SHORELINE... UH... REPORTEDLY WHILE HUMMING THE TUNE TO... "GILLIGAN'S ISLAND."
IN THE HIMALAYAS, A LARGE GROUP OF YETI HAVE BEEN SPOTTED MIGRATING SOUTH.
ARE YOU GETTING THIS?!
A DOG IN ONTARIO, CANADA HAS BEGUN TALKING.
I'D STOP POOPING IN YOUR SHOE IF YOU'D LET ME OUTSIDE MORE OFTEN.
ARE YOU GETTING THIS?
IN DUBLIN, IRELAND A MAN AWOKE FROM A 30 YEAR COMA AND ASKED FOR A GUINESS.
MR. PRICE, YOU'VE BEEN IN A COMA FOR 30 YEARS!
'ZAT RIGHT? GULP
MEANWHILE, VIOLENCE HAS ESCALATED IN THE MIDDLE EAST.
ARE WE ALL GOING TO DIE?!

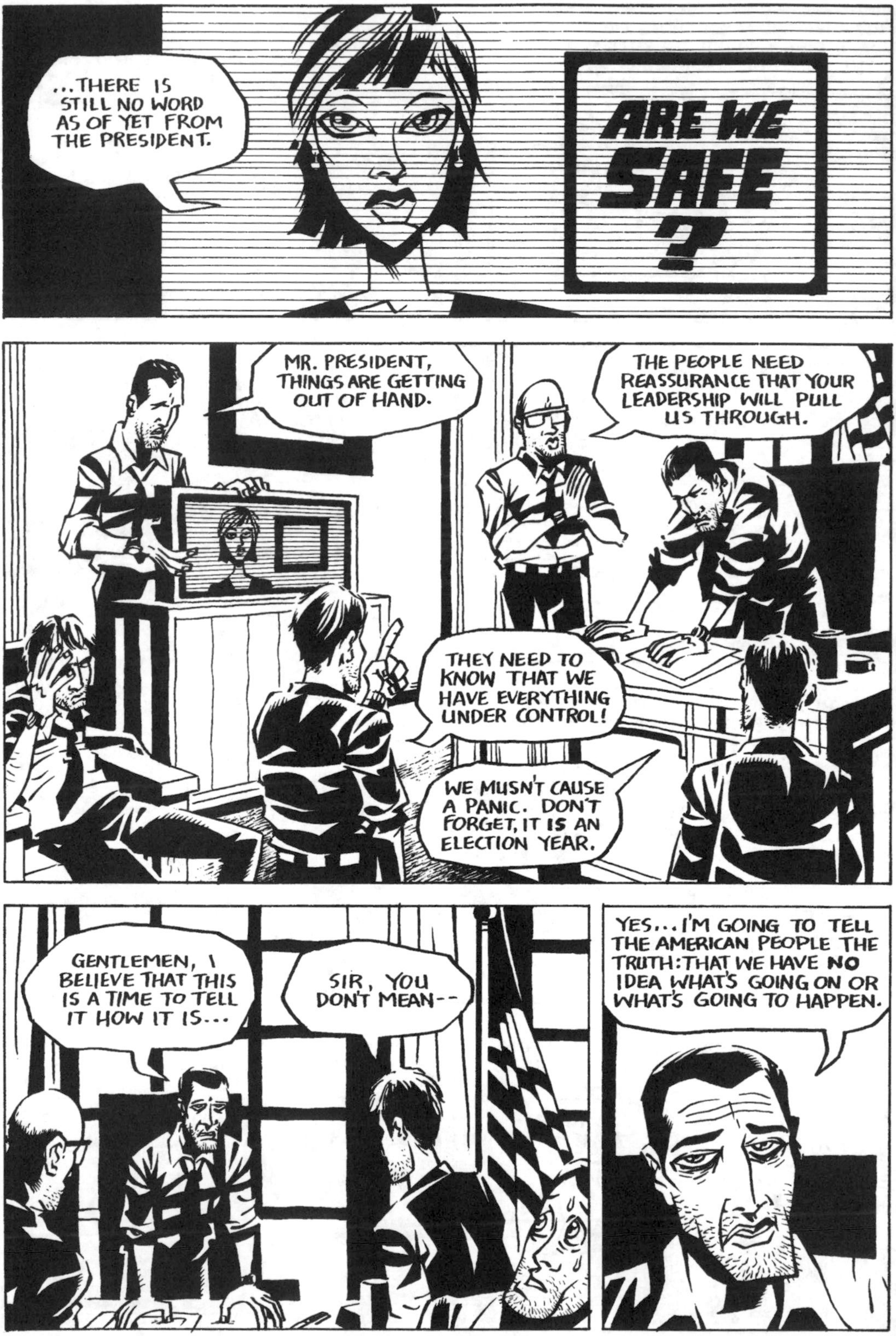
...THERE IS STILL NO WORD AS OF YET FROM THE PRESIDENT.
ARE WE SAFE ?
MR. PRESIDENT, THINGS ARE GETTING OUT OF HAND.
THE PEOPLE NEED REASSURANCE THAT YOUR LEADERSHIP WILL PULL US THROUGH.
THEY NEED TO KNOW THAT WE HAVE EVERYTHING UNDER CONTROL!
WE MUSN'T CAUSE A PANIC. DON'T FORGET, IT **IS** AN ELECTION YEAR.
GENTLEMEN, I BELIEVE THAT THIS IS A TIME TO TELL IT HOW IT IS...
SIR, YOU DON'T MEAN--
YES... I'M GOING TO TELL THE AMERICAN PEOPLE THE TRUTH: THAT WE HAVE **NO** IDEA WHAT'S GOING ON OR WHAT'S GOING TO HAPPEN.

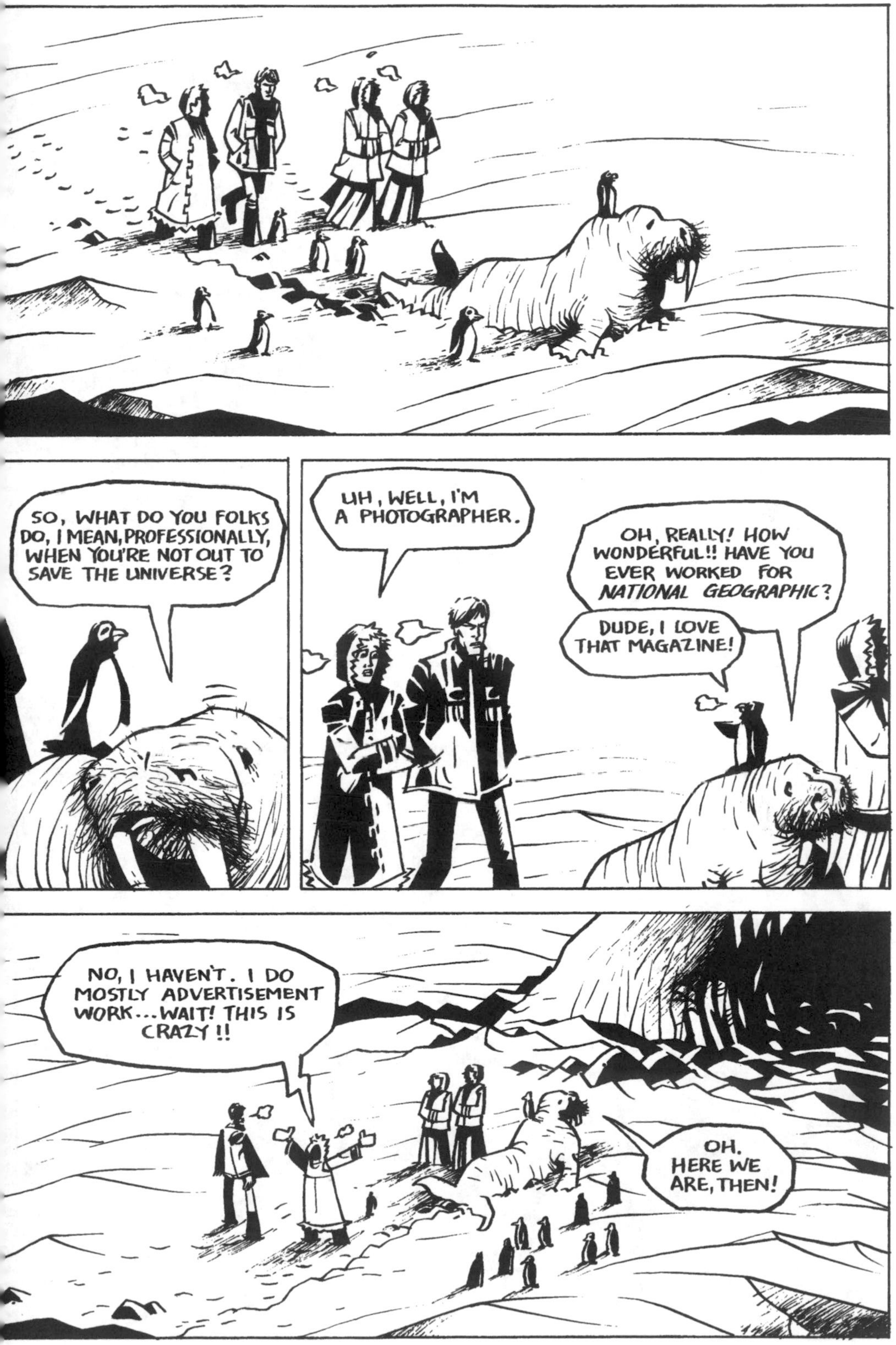
SO, WHAT DO YOU FOLKS DO, I MEAN, PROFESSIONALLY, WHEN YOU'RE NOT OUT TO SAVE THE UNIVERSE?
UH, WELL, I'M A PHOTOGRAPHER.
OH, REALLY! HOW WONDERFUL!! HAVE YOU EVER WORKED FOR NATIONAL GEOGRAPHIC?
DUDE, I LOVE THAT MAGAZINE!
NO, I HAVEN'T. I DO MOSTLY ADVERTISEMENT WORK...WAIT! THIS IS CRAZY!!
OH. HERE WE ARE, THEN!

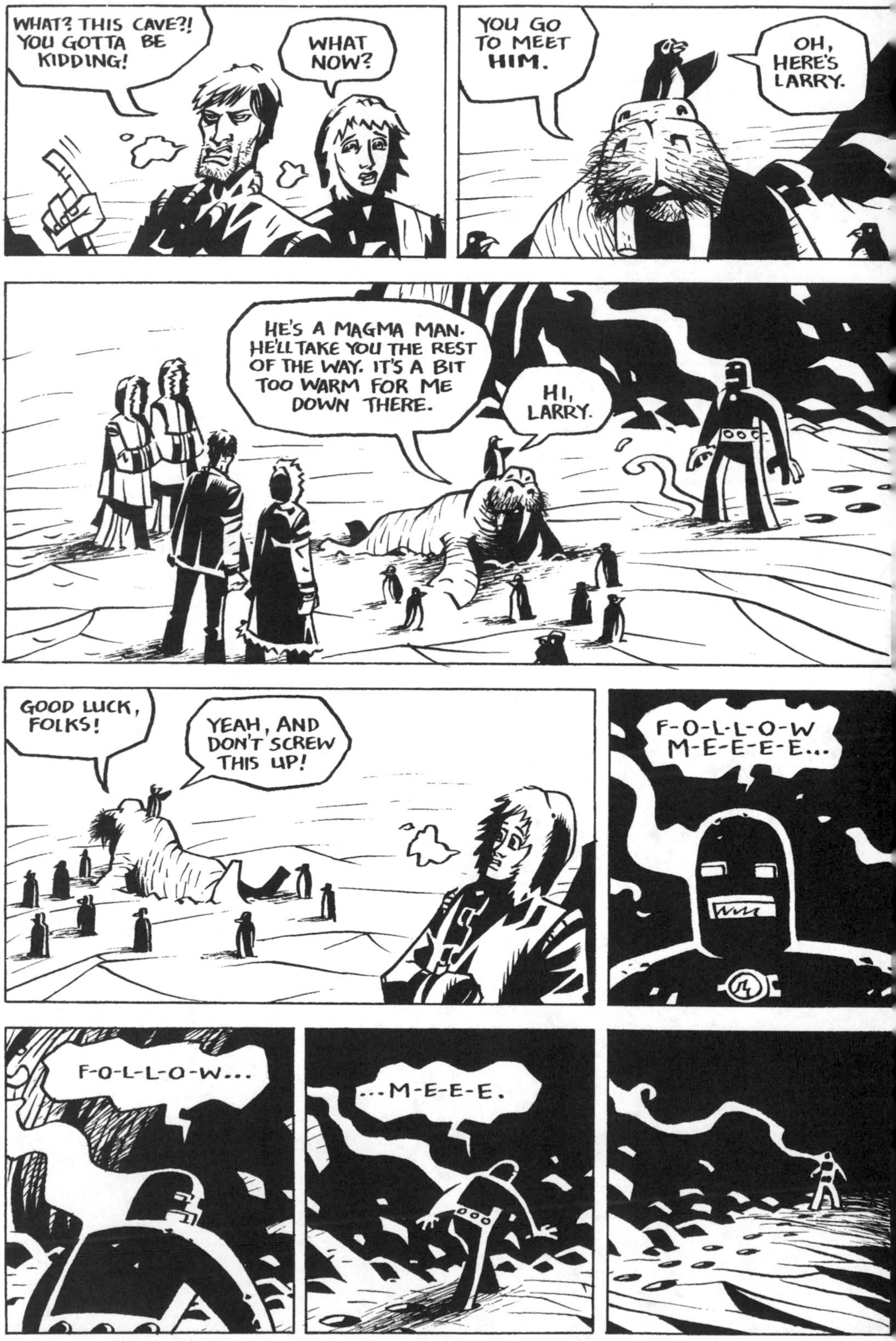
WHAT? THIS CAVE?! YOU GOTTA BE KIDDING!
WHAT NOW?
YOU GO TO MEET HIM.
OH, HERE'S LARRY.
HE'S A MAGMA MAN. HE'LL TAKE YOU THE REST OF THE WAY. IT'S A BIT TOO WARM FOR ME DOWN THERE.
HI, LARRY.
GOOD LUCK, FOLKS!
YEAH, AND DON'T SCREW THIS UP!
F-O-L-L-O-W M-E-E-E-E...
F-O-L-L-O-W...
...M-E-E-E.

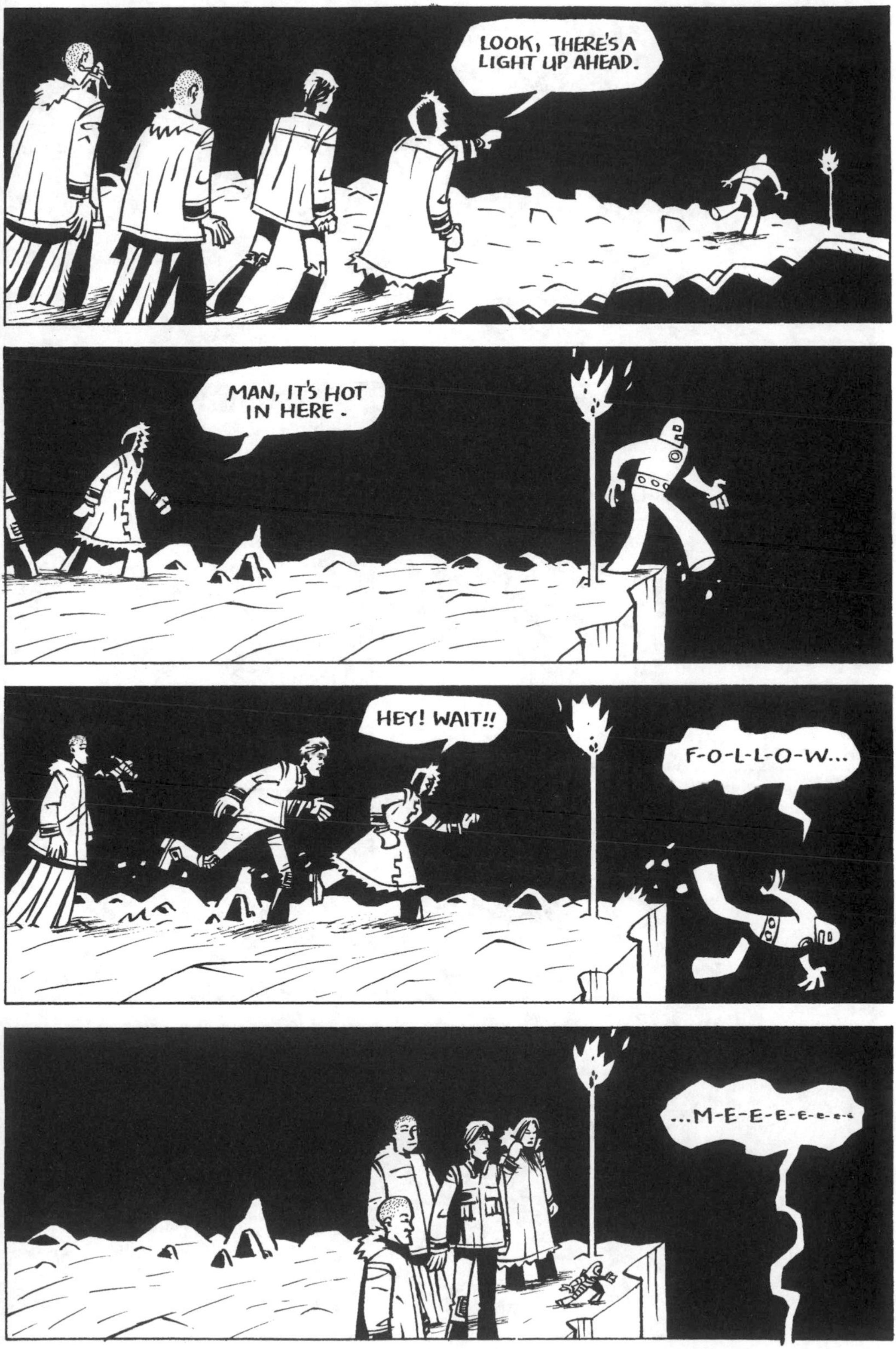
LOOK, THERE'S A LIGHT UP AHEAD.
MAN, IT'S HOT IN HERE.
HEY! WAIT!!
F-O-L-L-O-W...
...M-E-E-E-E-E-E-E

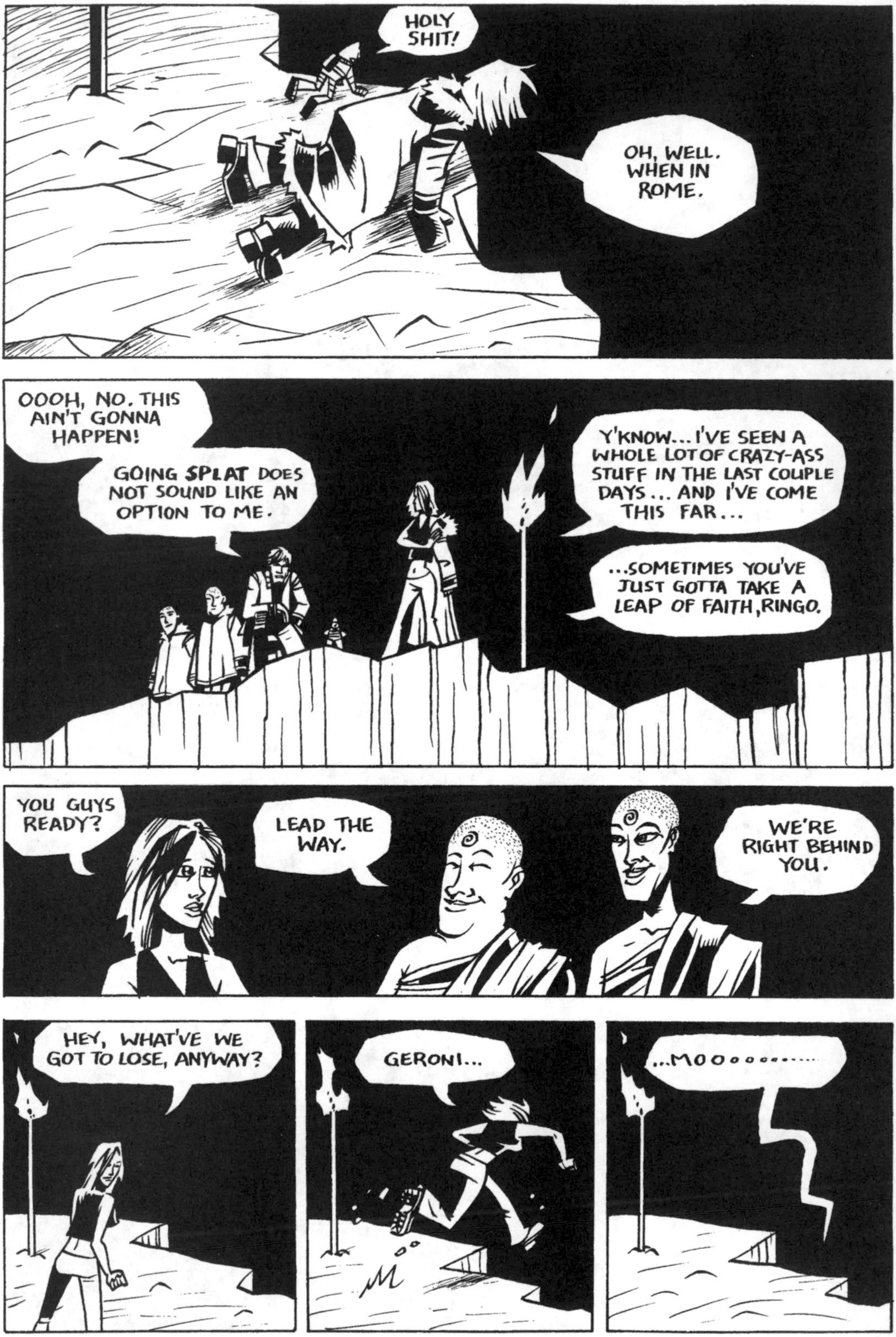
HOLY SHIT!
OH, WELL. WHEN IN ROME.
OOOH, NO. THIS AIN'T GONNA HAPPEN!
GOING SPLAT DOES NOT SOUND LIKE AN OPTION TO ME.
Y'KNOW... I'VE SEEN A WHOLE LOT OF CRAZY-ASS STUFF IN THE LAST COUPLE DAYS... AND I'VE COME THIS FAR...
...SOMETIMES YOU'VE JUST GOTTA TAKE A LEAP OF FAITH, RINGO.
YOU GUYS READY?
LEAD THE WAY.
WE'RE RIGHT BEHIND YOU.
HEY, WHAT'VE WE GOT TO LOSE, ANYWAY?
GERONI...
...MOOoooo.....

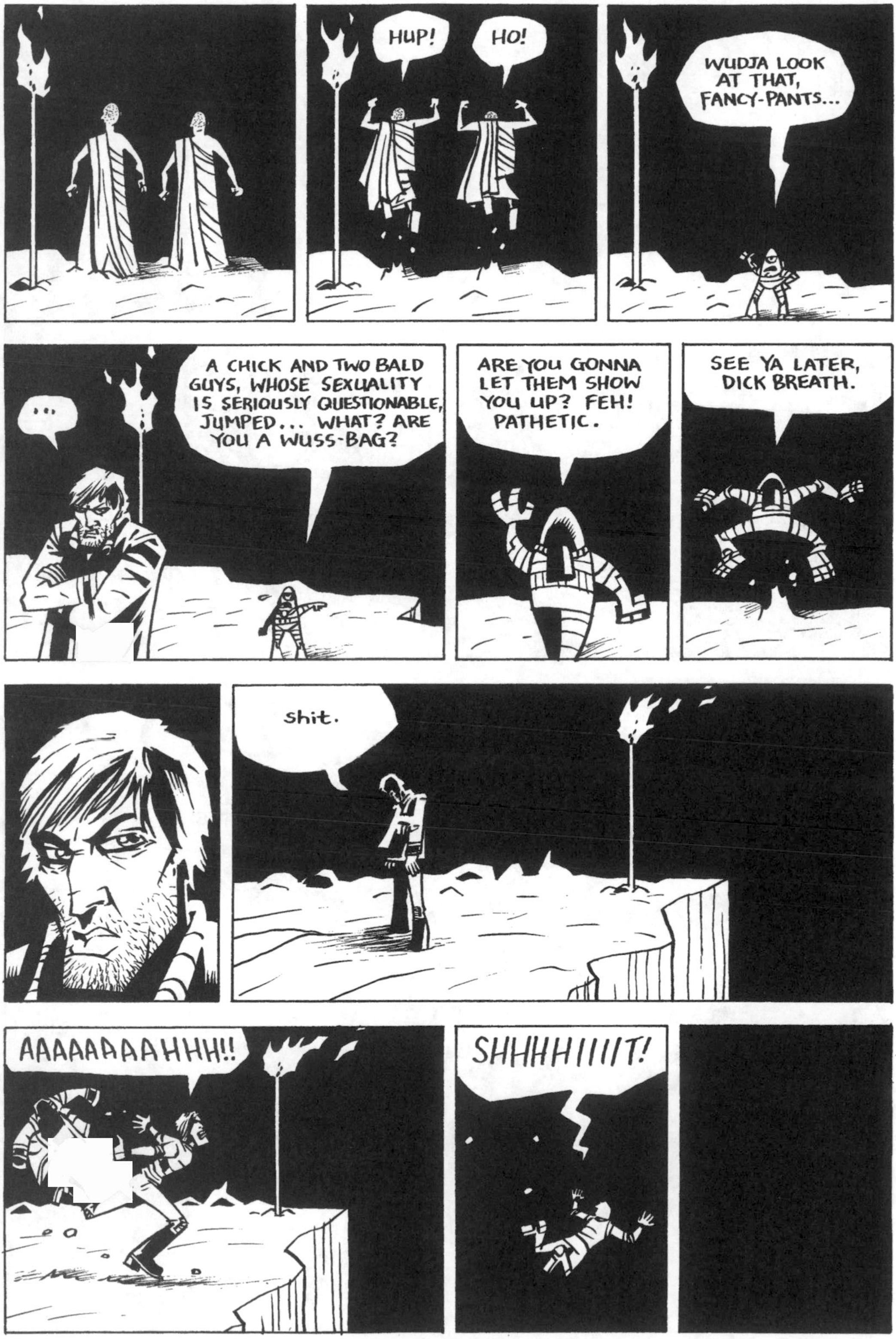
HUP!
HO!
WUDJA LOOK AT THAT, FANCY-PANTS...
...
A CHICK AND TWO BALD GUYS, WHOSE SEXUALITY IS SERIOUSLY QUESTIONABLE, JUMPED... WHAT? ARE YOU A WUSS-BAG?
ARE YOU GONNA LET THEM SHOW YOU UP? FEH! PATHETIC.
SEE YA LATER, DICK BREATH.
shit.
AAAAAAAAHHH!!
SHHHHIIIIT!

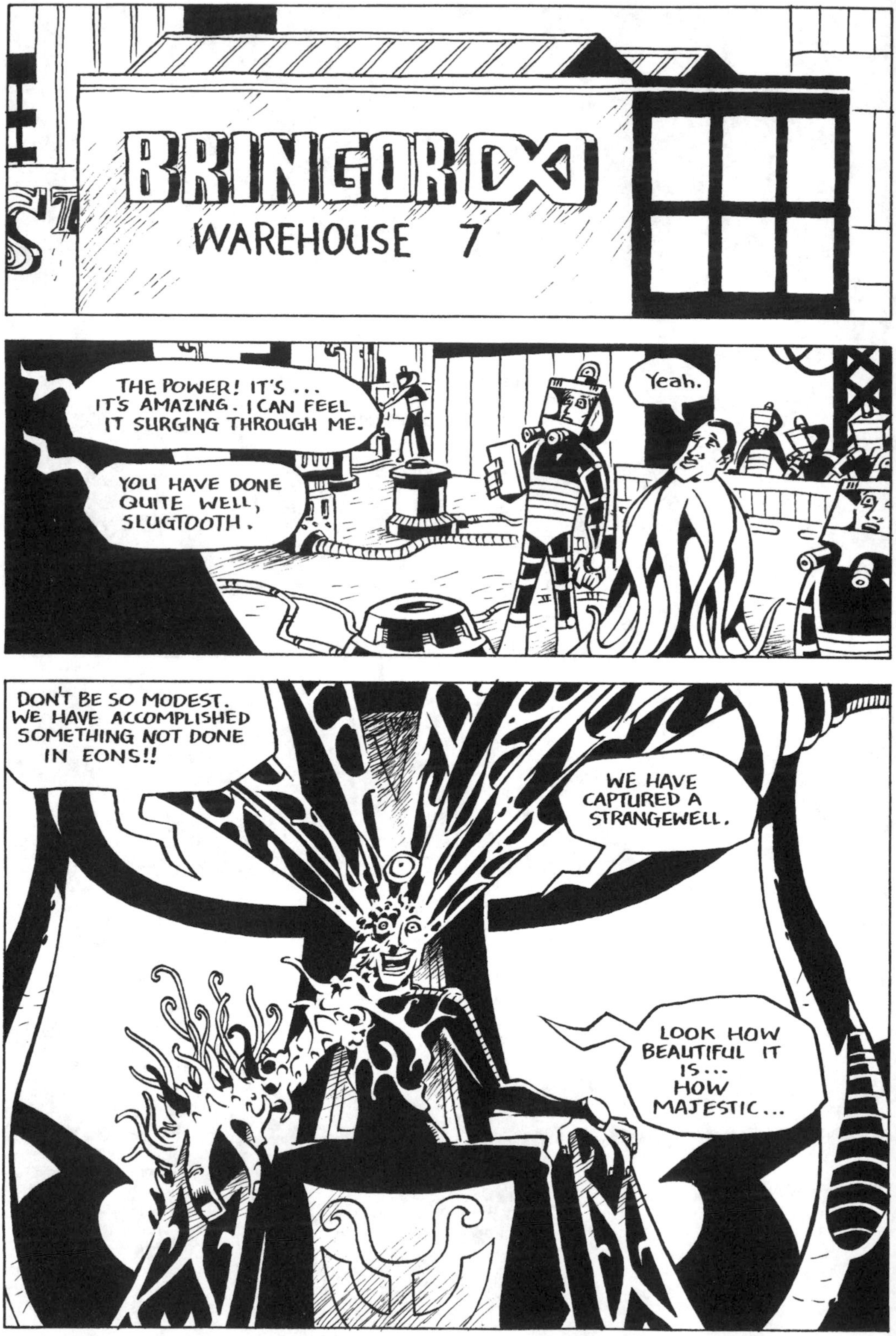
BRINGOR
WAREHOUSE 7
THE POWER! IT'S ... IT'S AMAZING. I CAN FEEL IT SURGING THROUGH ME.
YOU HAVE DONE QUITE WELL, SLUGTOOTH.
Yeah.
DON'T BE SO MODEST. WE HAVE ACCOMPLISHED SOMETHING NOT DONE IN EONS!!
WE HAVE CAPTURED A STRANGEWELL.
LOOK HOW BEAUTIFUL IT IS... HOW MAJESTIC...

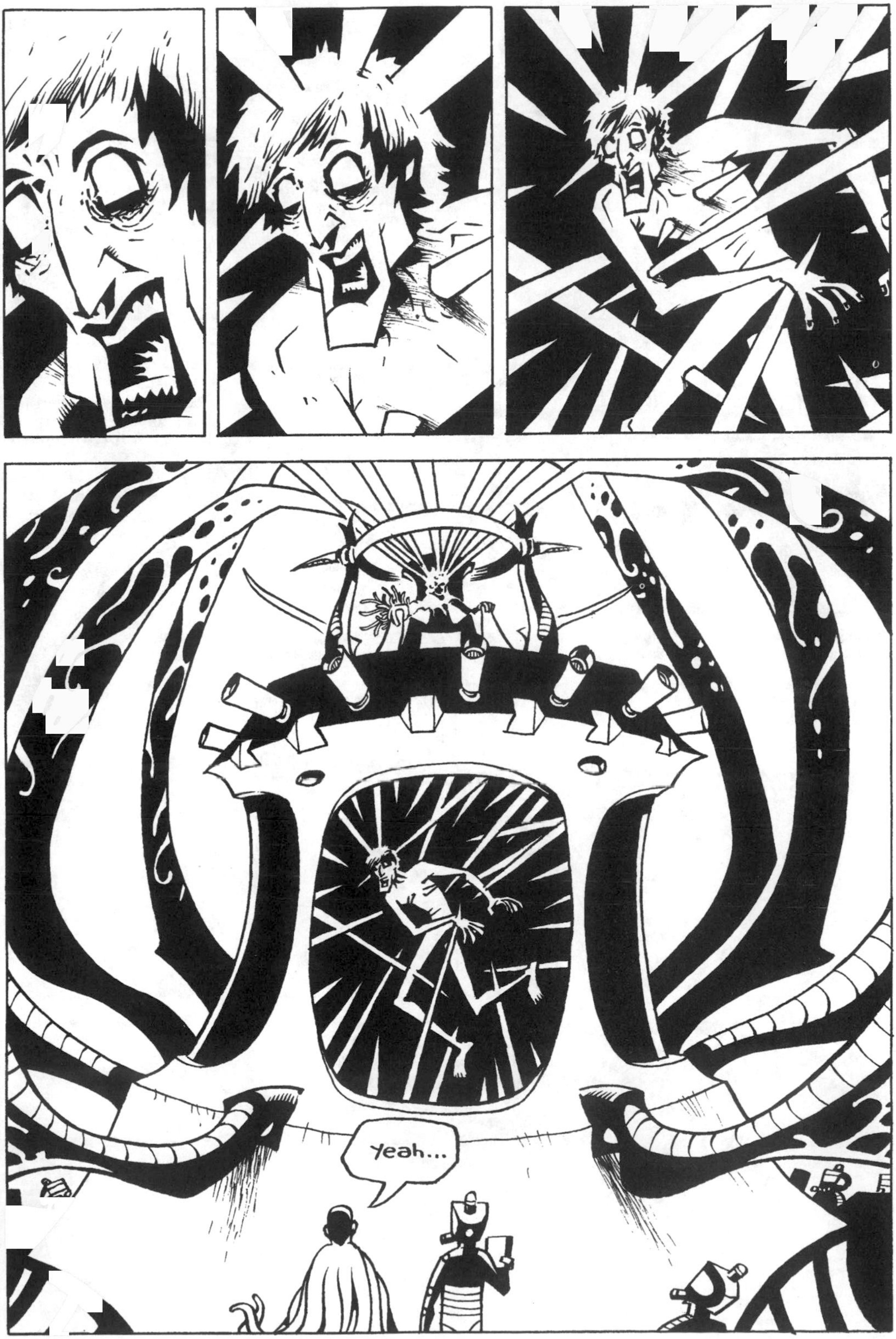
Yeah...

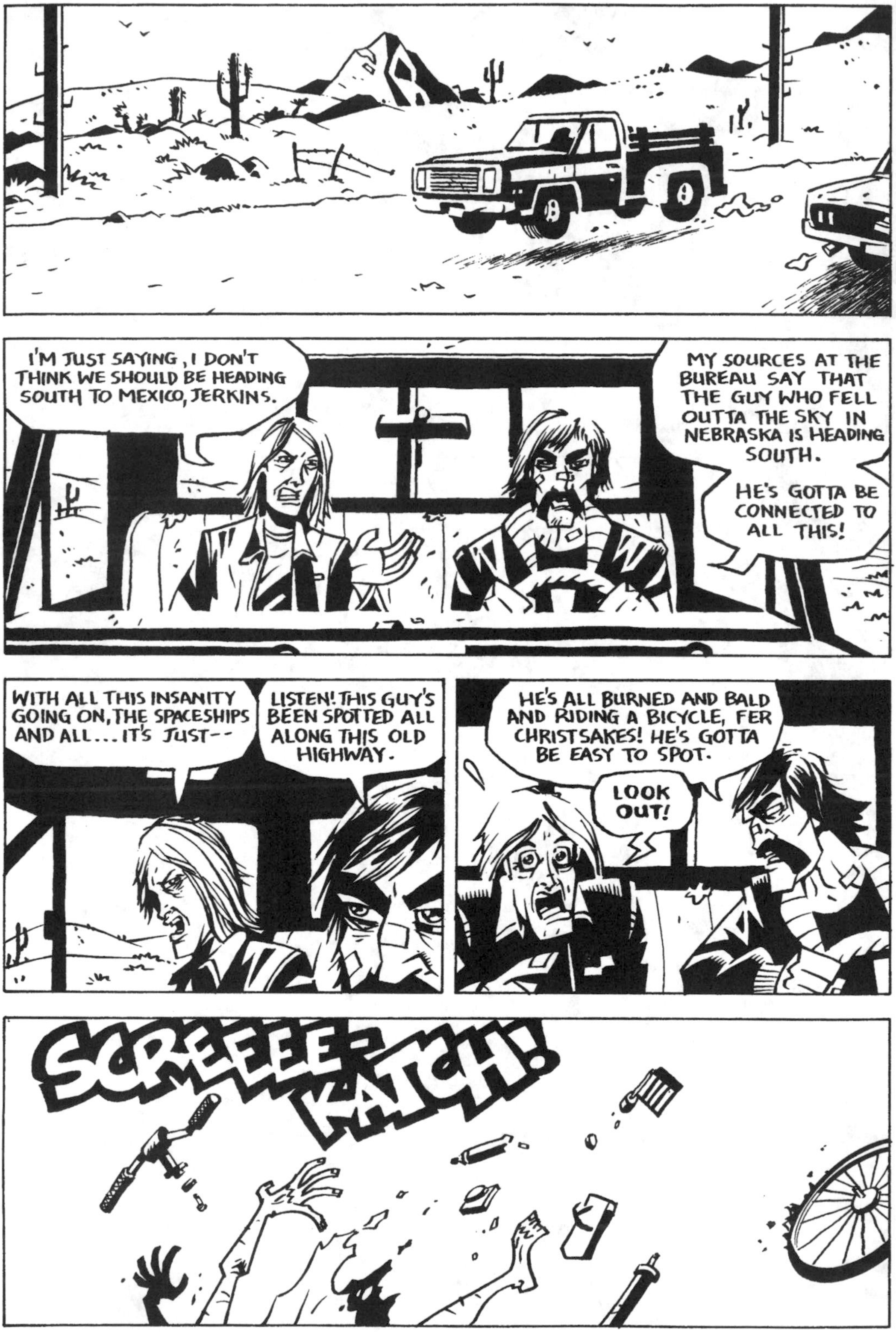
I'M JUST SAYING, I DON'T THINK WE SHOULD BE HEADING SOUTH TO MEXICO, JERKINS.
MY SOURCES AT THE BUREAU SAY THAT THE GUY WHO FELL OUTTA THE SKY IN NEBRASKA IS HEADING SOUTH.
HE'S GOTTA BE CONNECTED TO ALL THIS!
WITH ALL THIS INSANITY GOING ON, THE SPACESHIPS AND ALL... IT'S JUST--
LISTEN! THIS GUY'S BEEN SPOTTED ALL ALONG THIS OLD HIGHWAY.
HE'S ALL BURNED AND BALD AND RIDING A BICYCLE, FER CHRISTSAKES! HE'S GOTTA BE EASY TO SPOT.
LOOK OUT!
SCREEEEE-KATCH!

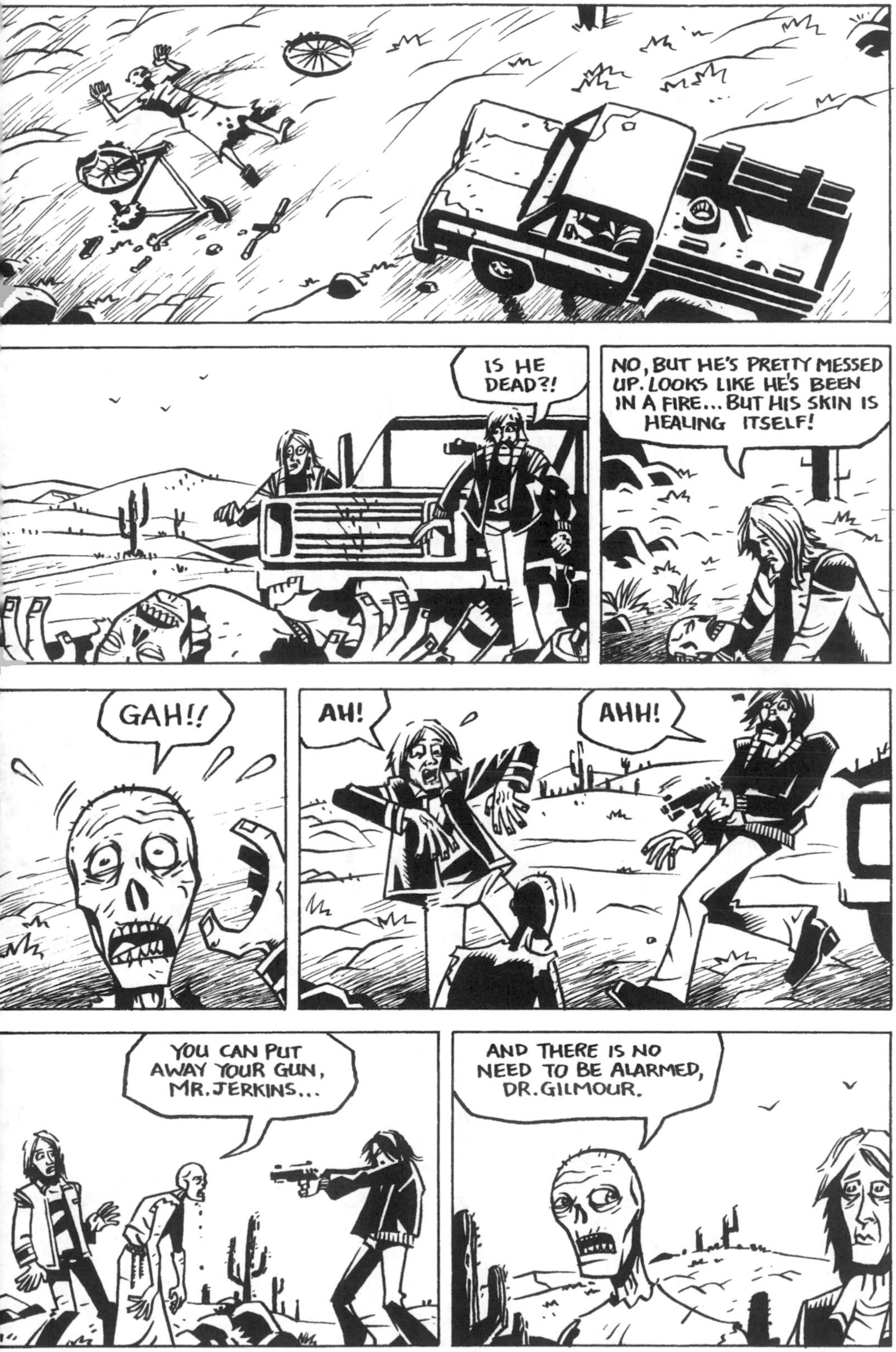
IS HE DEAD?!
NO, BUT HE'S PRETTY MESSED UP. LOOKS LIKE HE'S BEEN IN A FIRE... BUT HIS SKIN IS HEALING ITSELF!
GAH!!
AH!
AHH!
YOU CAN PUT AWAY YOUR GUN, MR. JERKINS...
AND THERE IS NO NEED TO BE ALARMED, DR. GILMOUR.

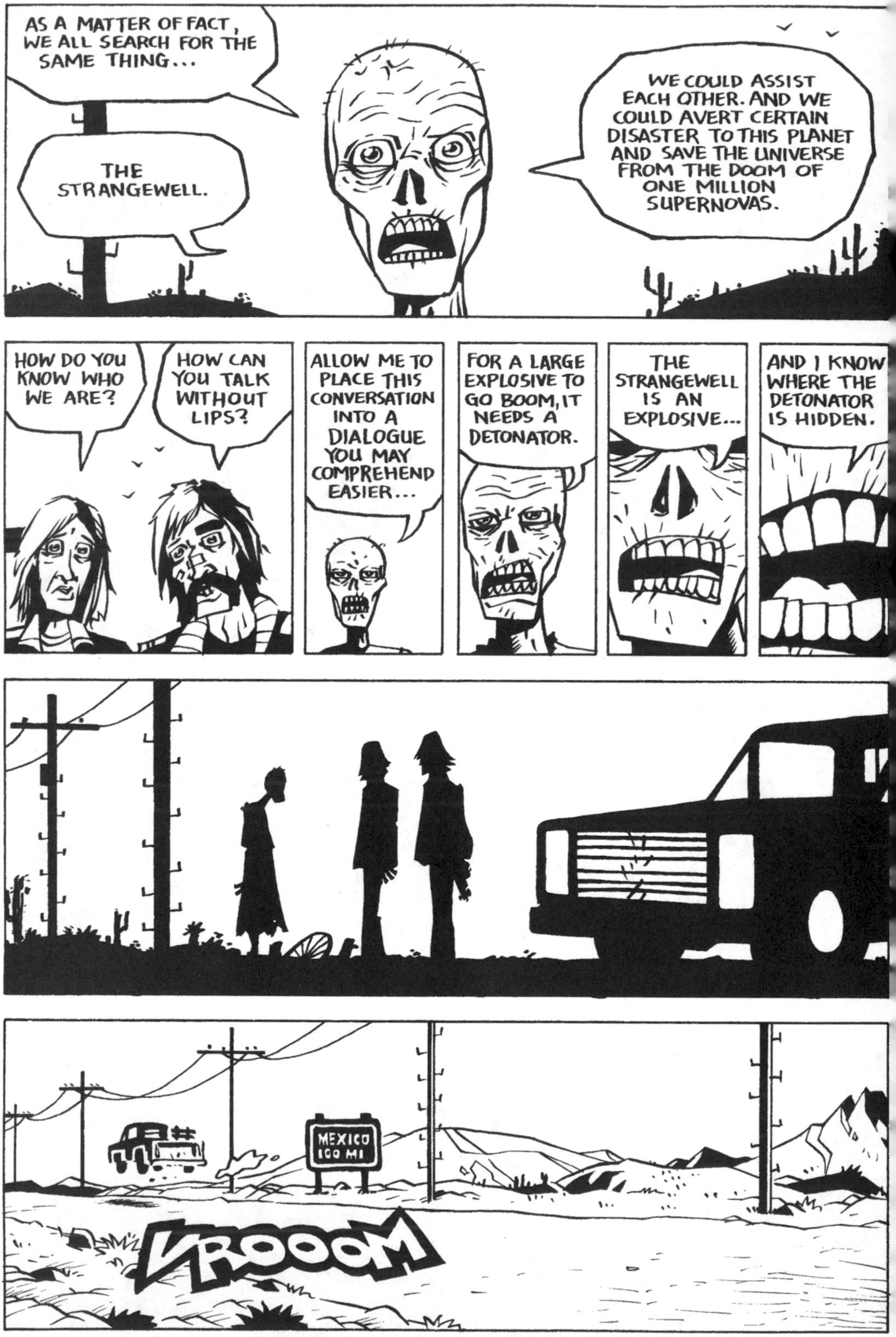
AS A MATTER OF FACT, WE ALL SEARCH FOR THE SAME THING...
THE STRANGEWELL.
WE COULD ASSIST EACH OTHER. AND WE COULD AVERT CERTAIN DISASTER TO THIS PLANET AND SAVE THE UNIVERSE FROM THE DOOM OF ONE MILLION SUPERNOVAS.
HOW DO YOU KNOW WHO WE ARE?
HOW CAN YOU TALK WITHOUT LIPS?
ALLOW ME TO PLACE THIS CONVERSATION INTO A DIALOGUE YOU MAY COMPREHEND EASIER...
FOR A LARGE EXPLOSIVE TO GO BOOM, IT NEEDS A DETONATOR.
THE STRANGEWELL IS AN EXPLOSIVE...
AND I KNOW WHERE THE DETONATOR IS HIDDEN.
MEXICO
100 MI
VROOOM

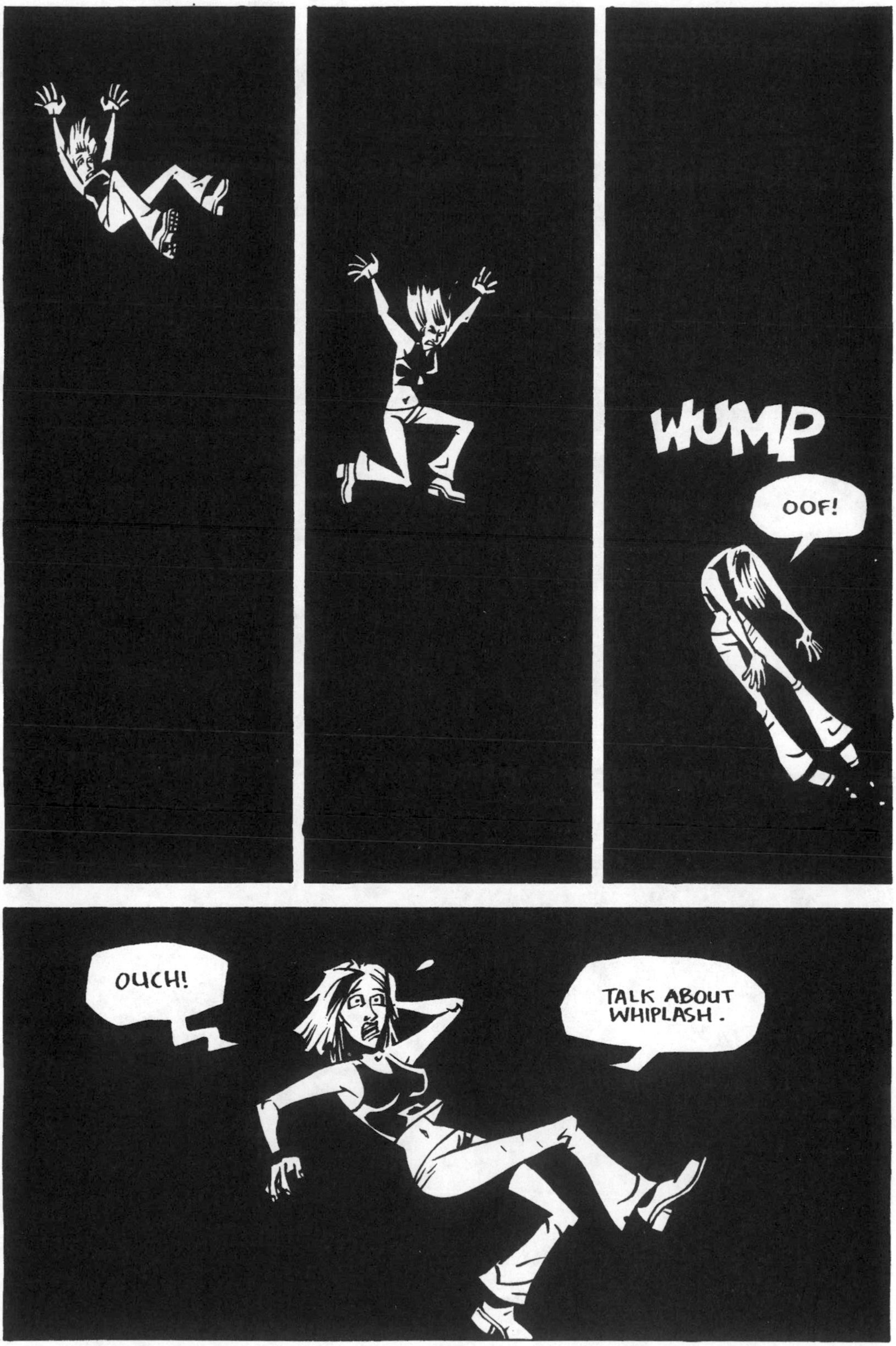
WUMP
OOF!
OUCH!
TALK ABOUT WHIPLASH.

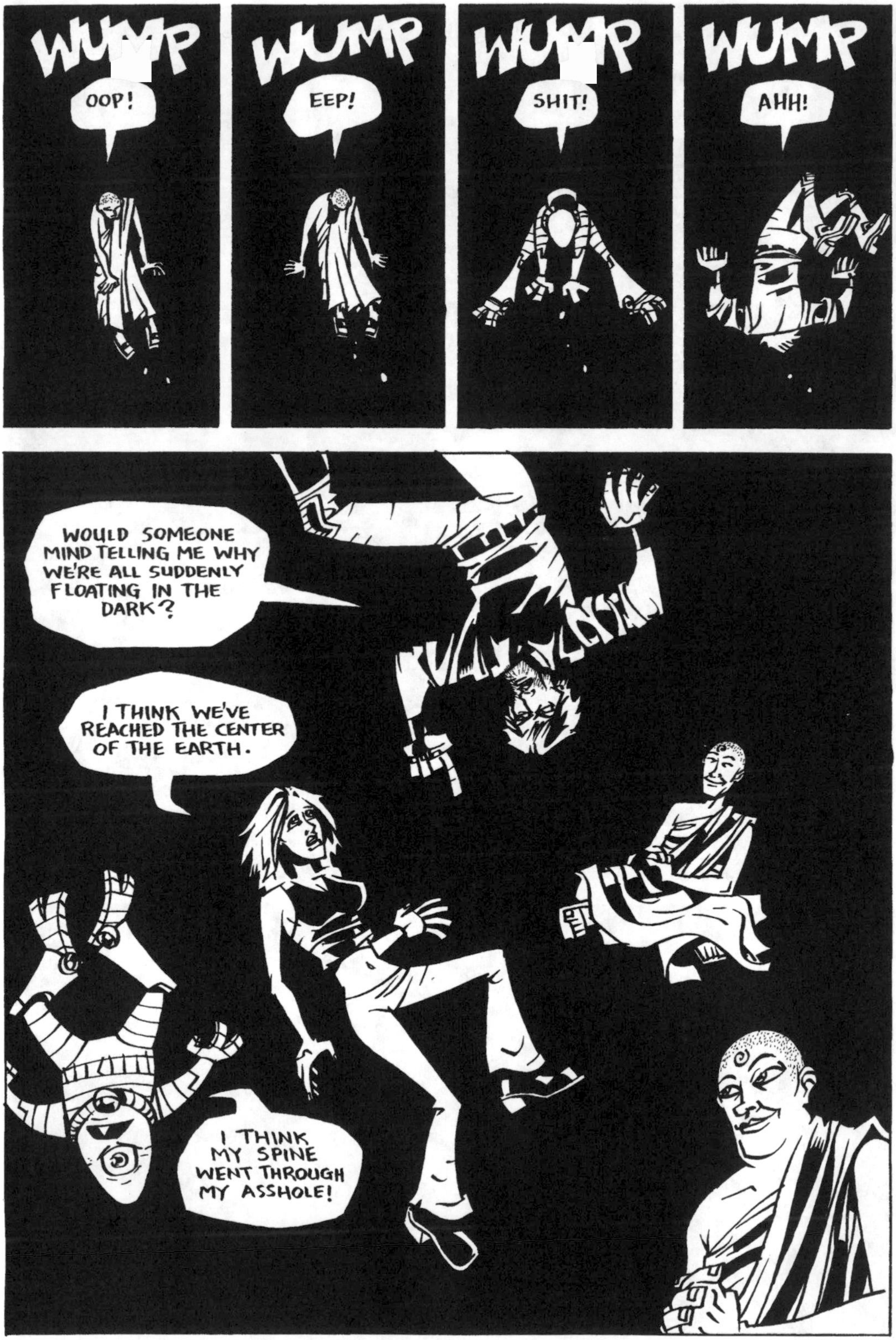

WUMP
OOP!
WUMP
EEP!
WUMP
SHIT!
WUMP
AHH!
WOULD SOMEONE MIND TELLING ME WHY WE'RE ALL SUDDENLY FLOATING IN THE DARK?
I THINK WE'VE REACHED THE CENTER OF THE EARTH.
I THINK MY SPINE WENT THROUGH MY ASSHOLE!

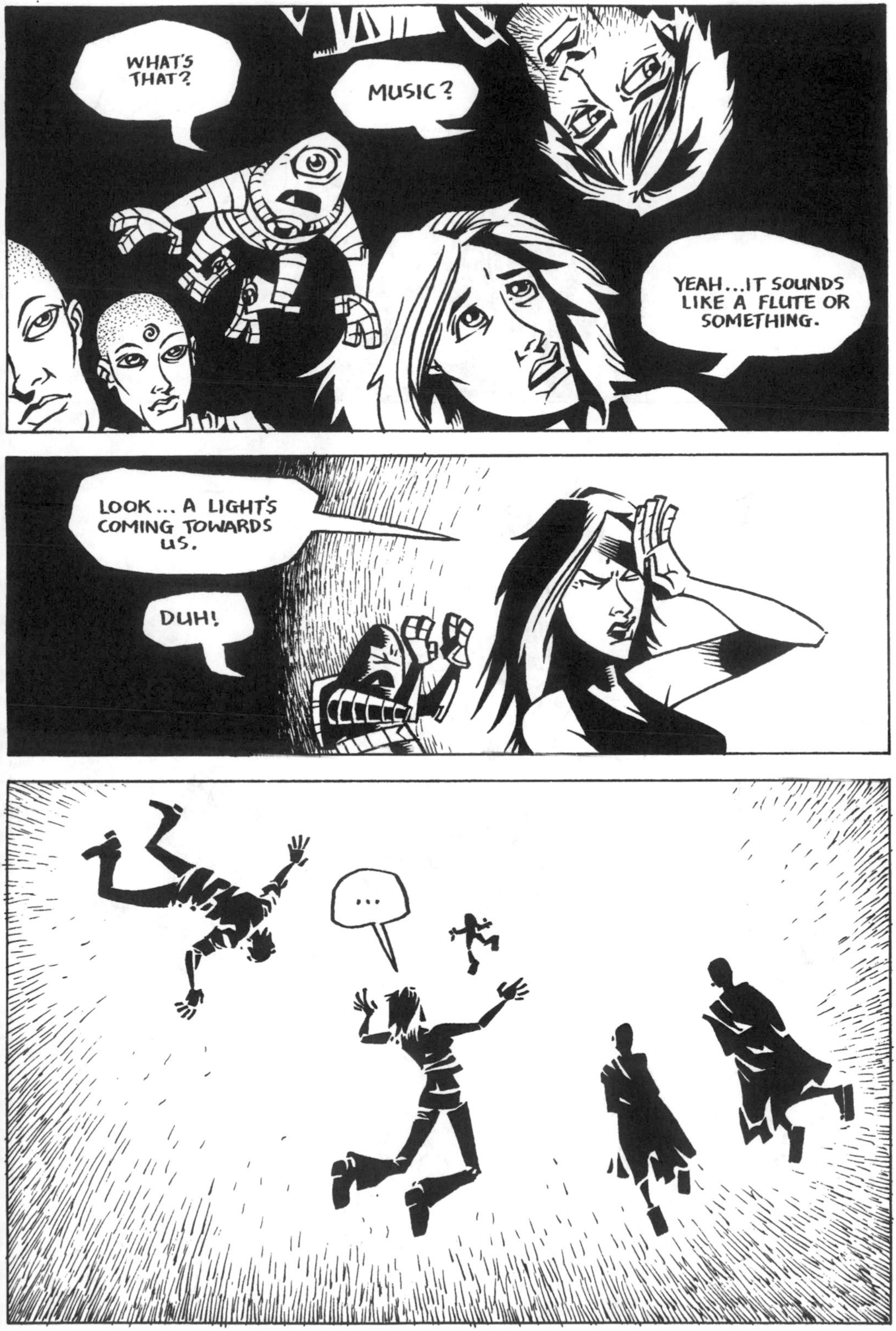
WHAT'S THAT?
MUSIC?
YEAH...IT SOUNDS LIKE A FLUTE OR SOMETHING.
LOOK... A LIGHT'S COMING TOWARDS US.
DUH!
...

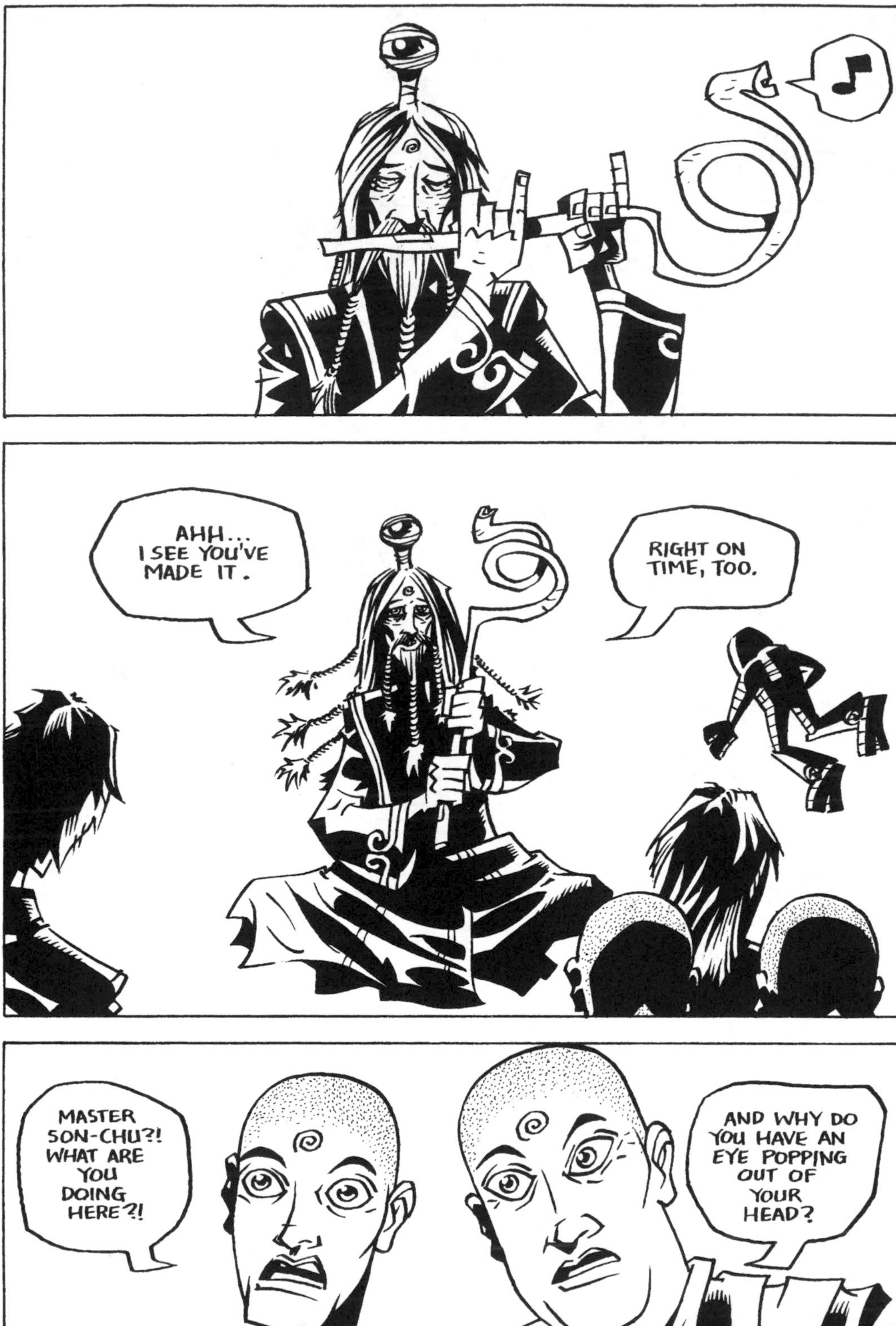
AHH...
I SEE YOU'VE
MADE IT.
RIGHT ON
TIME, TOO.
MASTER
SON-CHU?!
WHAT ARE
YOU
DOING
HERE?!
AND WHY DO
YOU HAVE AN
EYE POPPING
OUT OF
YOUR
HEAD?

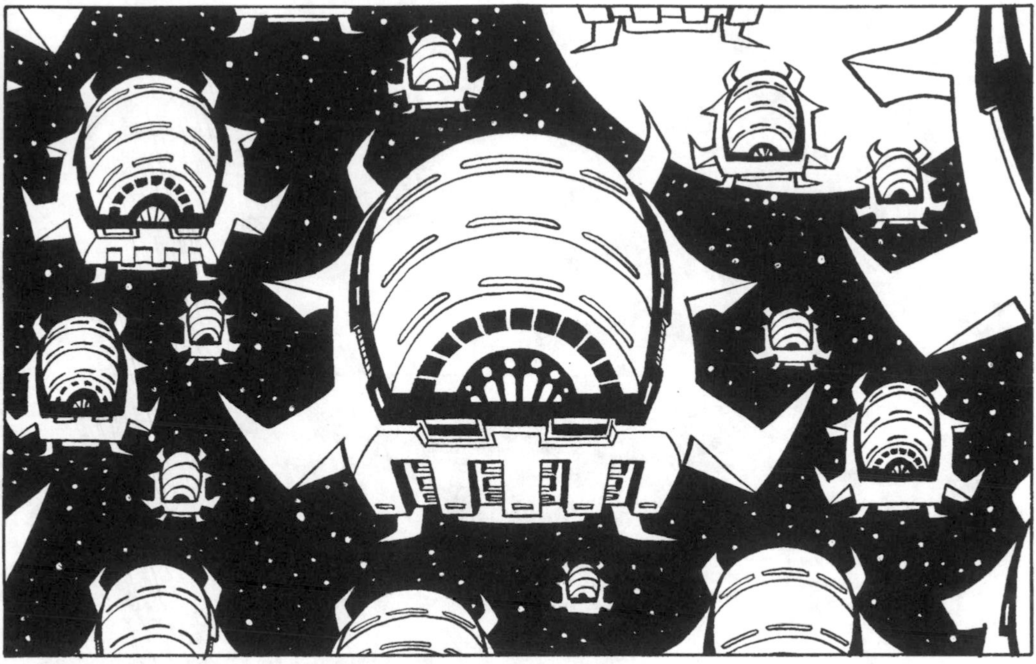

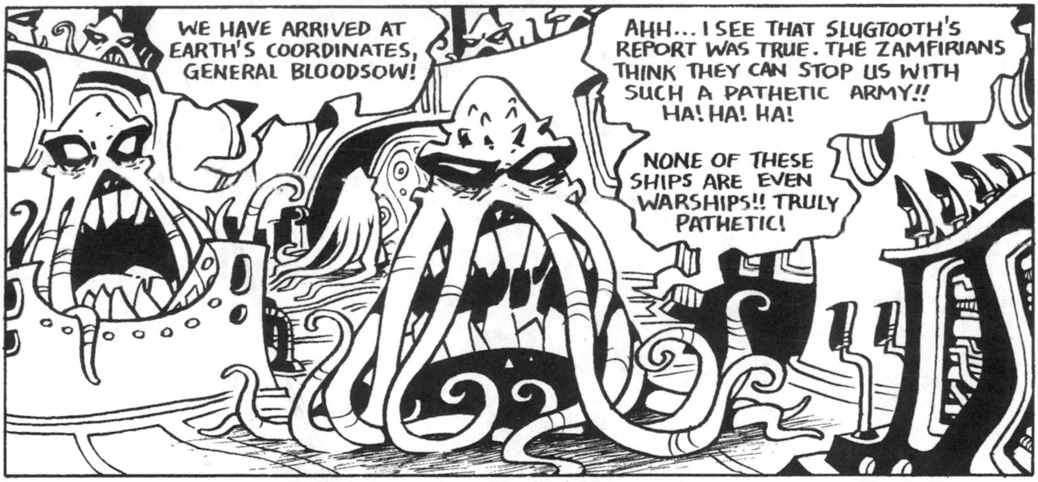

WE HAVE ARRIVED AT EARTH'S COORDINATES, GENERAL BLOODSOW!
AHH... I SEE THAT SLUGTOOTH'S REPORT WAS TRUE. THE ZAMFIRIANS THINK THEY CAN STOP US WITH SUCH A PATHETIC ARMY!! HA! HA! HA!
NONE OF THESE SHIPS ARE EVEN WARSHIPS!! TRULY PATHETIC!

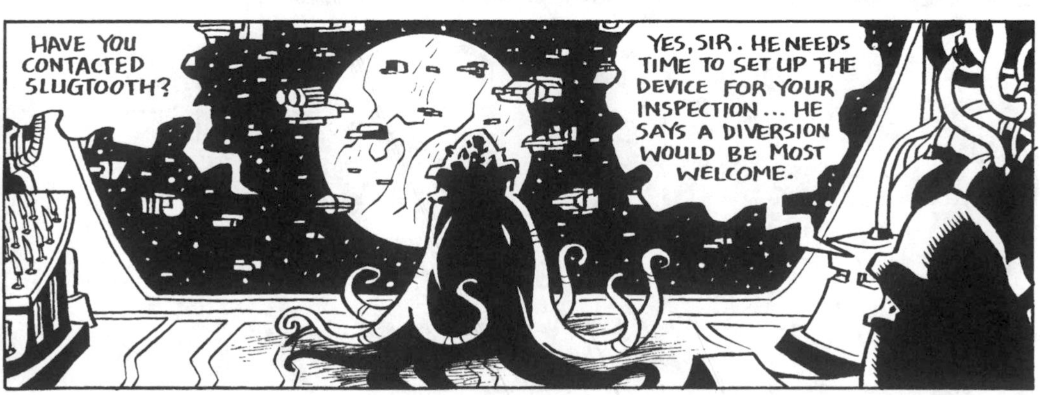

HAVE YOU CONTACTED SLUGTOOTH?
YES, SIR. HE NEEDS TIME TO SET UP THE DEVICE FOR YOUR INSPECTION... HE SAYS A DIVERSION WOULD BE MOST WELCOME.

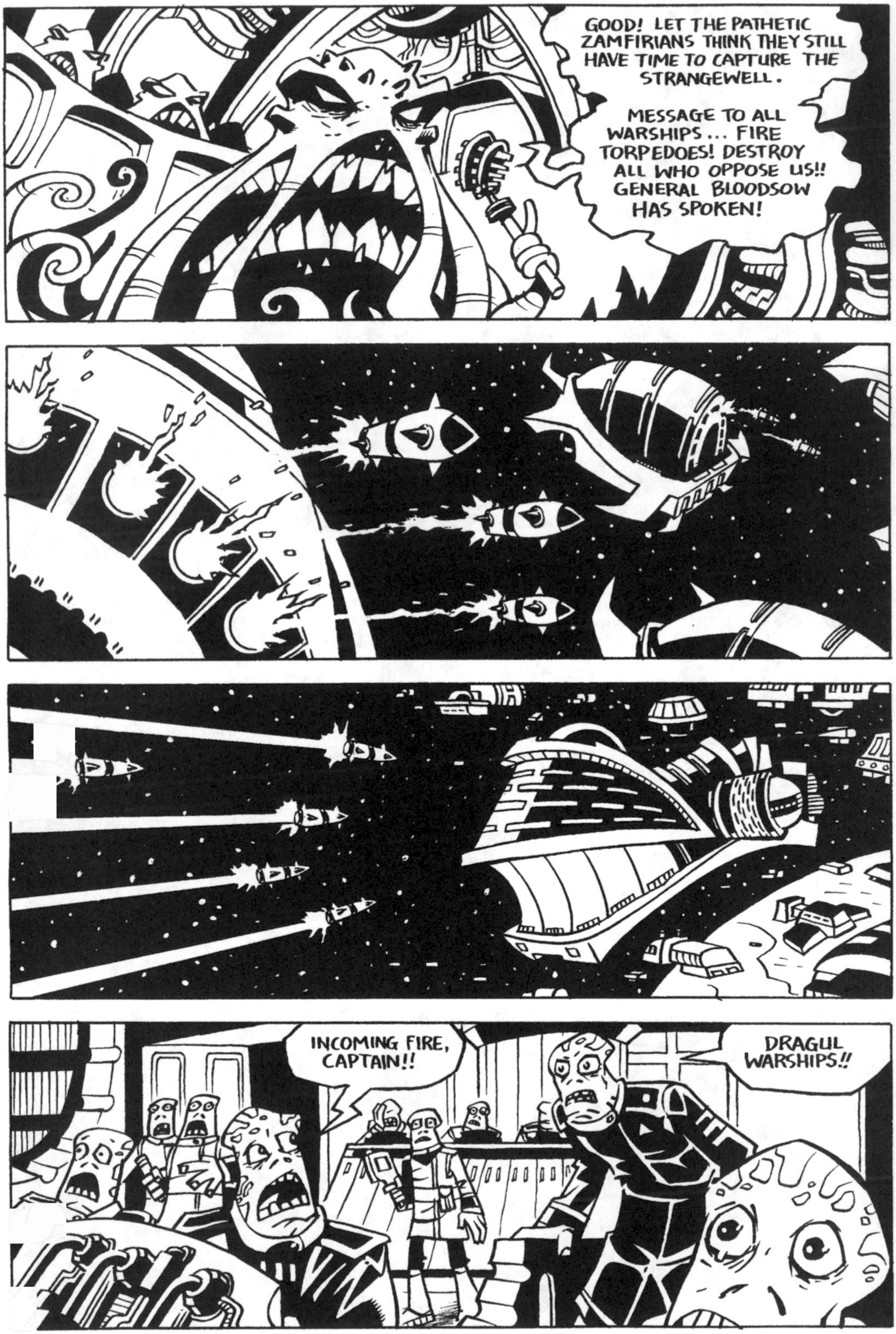
GOOD! LET THE PATHETIC ZAMFIRIANS THINK THEY STILL HAVE TIME TO CAPTURE THE STRANGEWELL.
MESSAGE TO ALL WARSHIPS... FIRE TORPEDOES! DESTROY ALL WHO OPPOSE US!! GENERAL BLOODSOW HAS SPOKEN!
INCOMING FIRE, CAPTAIN!!
DRAGUL WARSHIPS!!

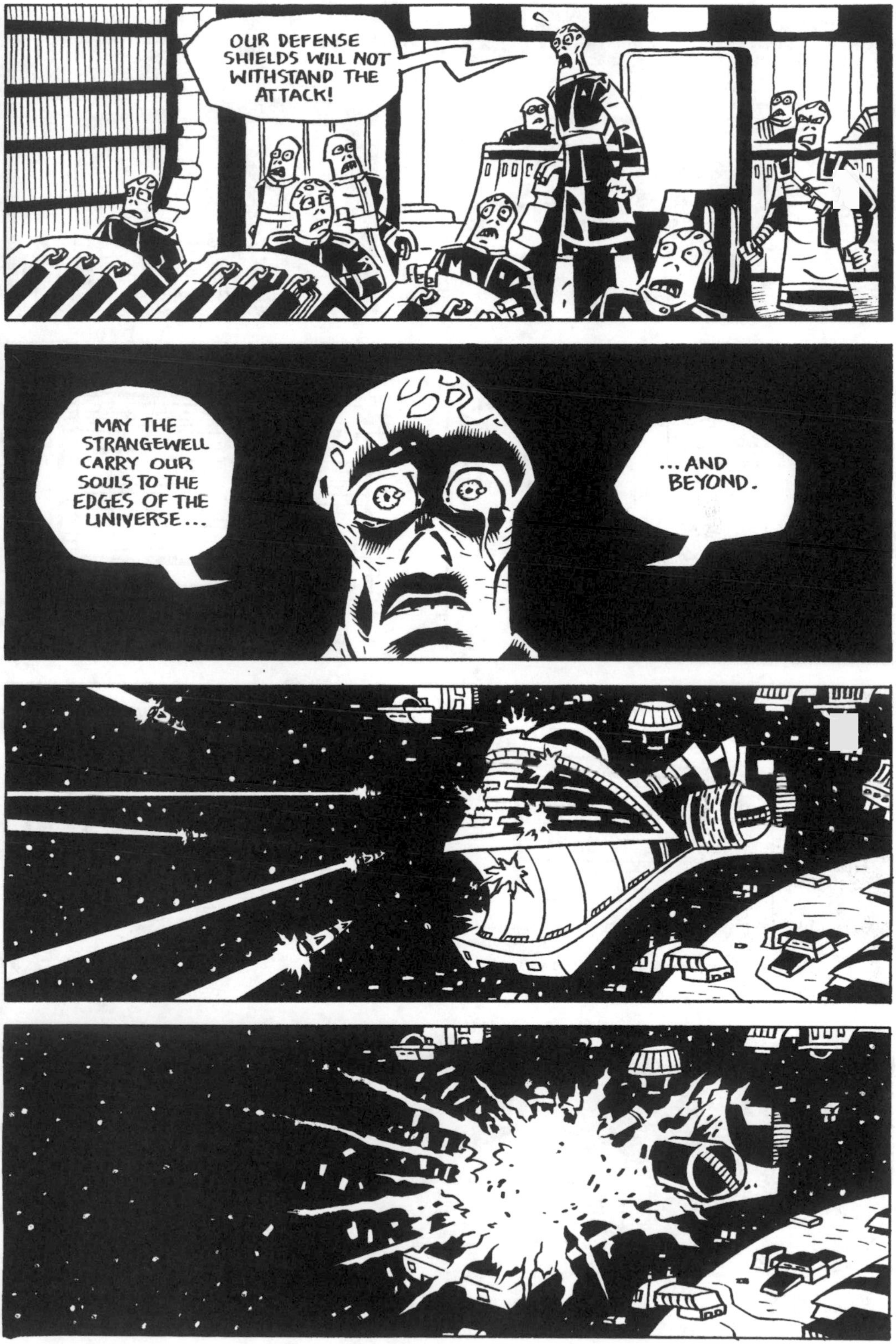
OUR DEFENSE SHIELDS WILL NOT WITHSTAND THE ATTACK!
MAY THE STRANGEWELL CARRY OUR SOULS TO THE EDGES OF THE UNIVERSE...
...AND BEYOND.

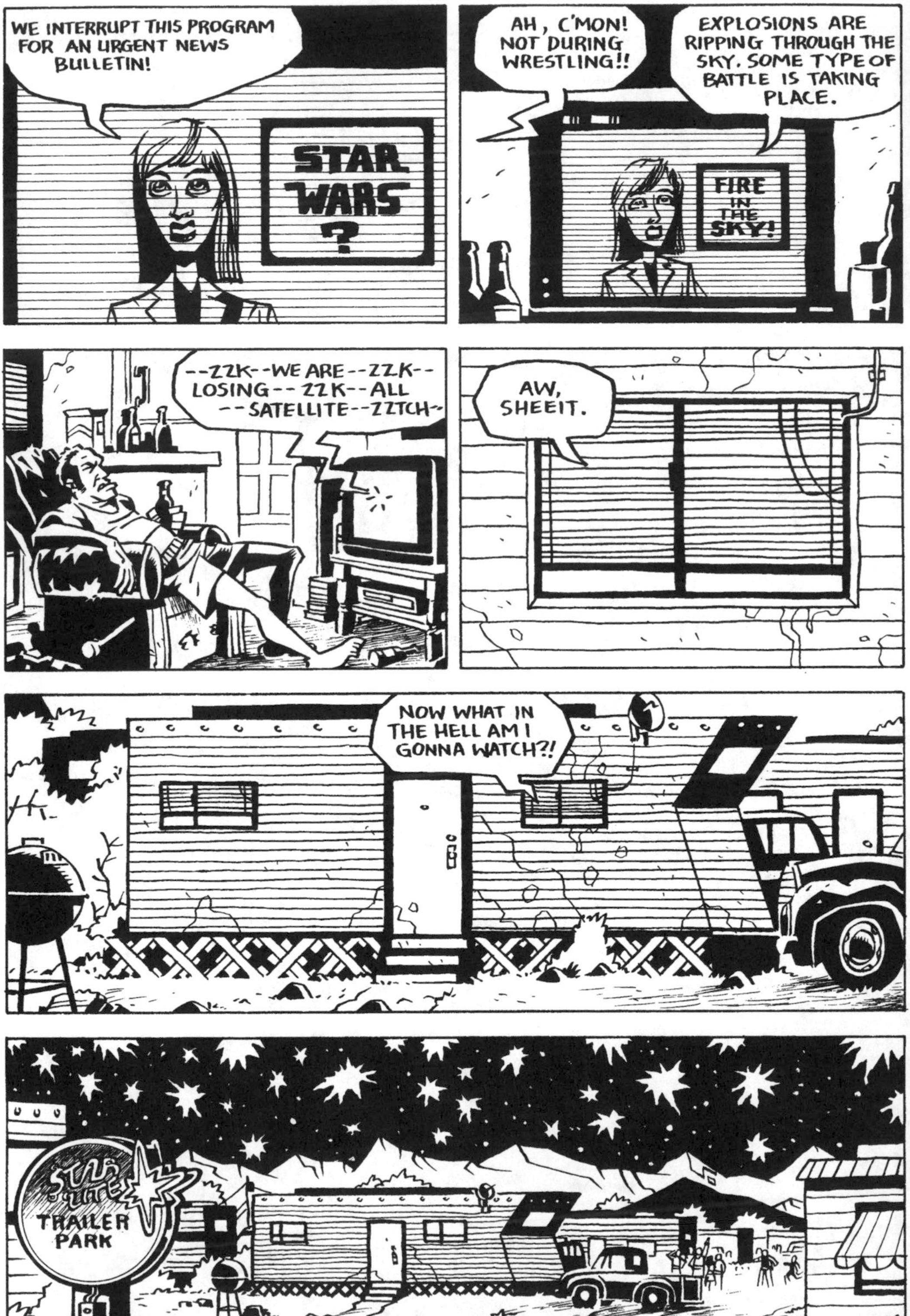
WE INTERRUPT THIS PROGRAM FOR AN URGENT NEWS BULLETIN!
STAR WARS ?
AH, C'MON! NOT DURING WRESTLING!!
EXPLOSIONS ARE RIPPING THROUGH THE SKY. SOME TYPE OF BATTLE IS TAKING PLACE.
FIRE IN THE SKY!
--ZZK--WE ARE--ZZK--LOSING--ZZK--ALL --SATELLITE--ZZTCH--
AW, SHEEIT.
NOW WHAT IN THE HELL AM I GONNA WATCH?!
TRAILER PARK

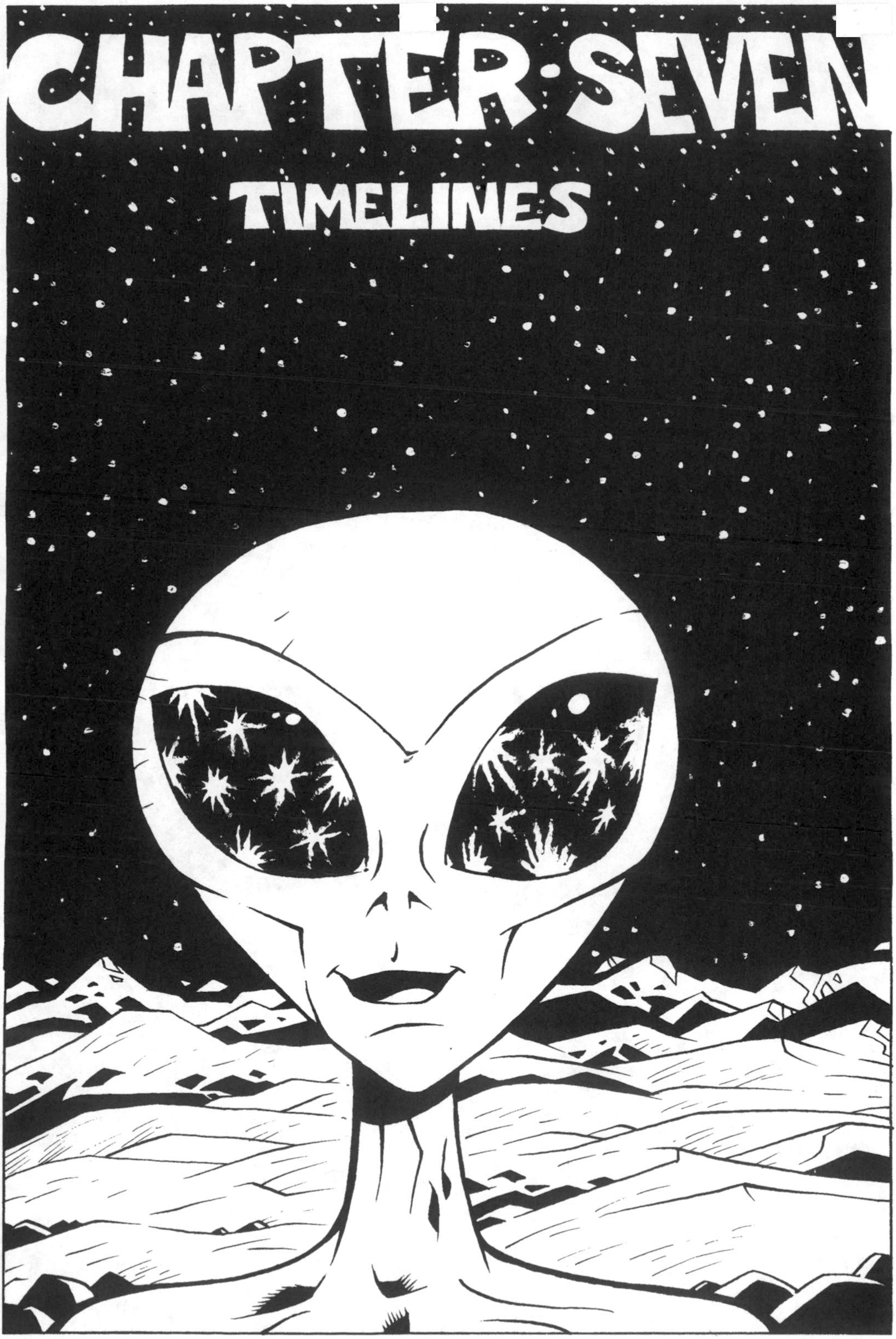
CHAPTER SEVEN
TIMELINES

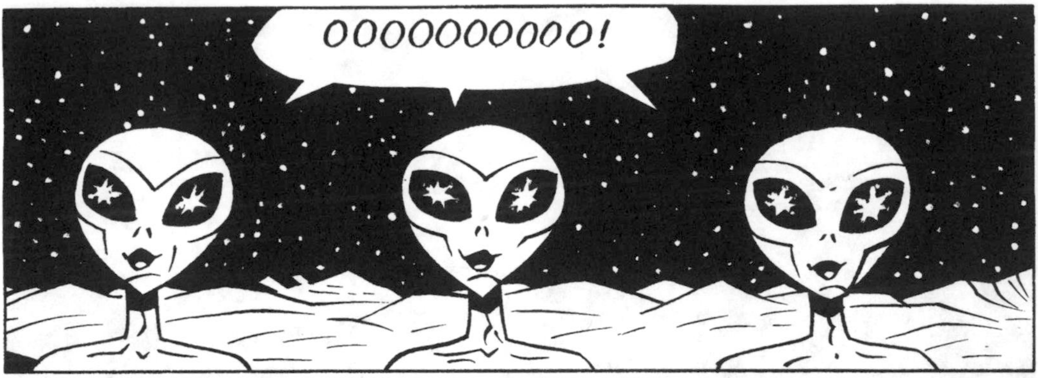
OOOOOOOOOO!

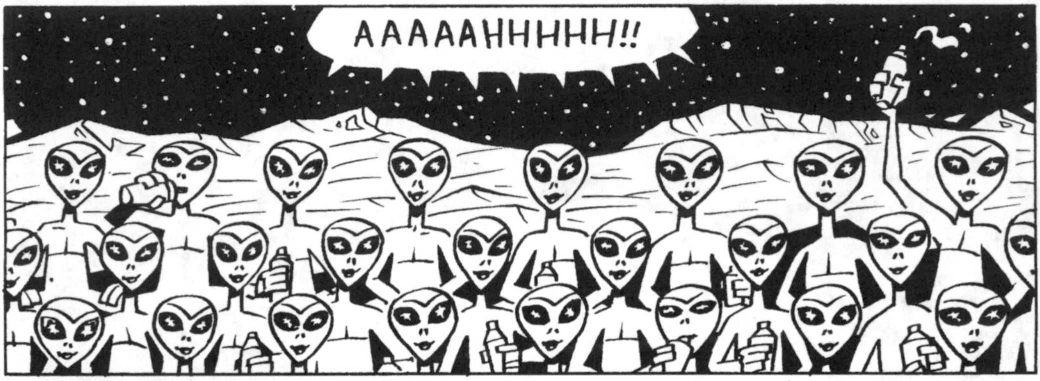
AAAAAHHHHH!!

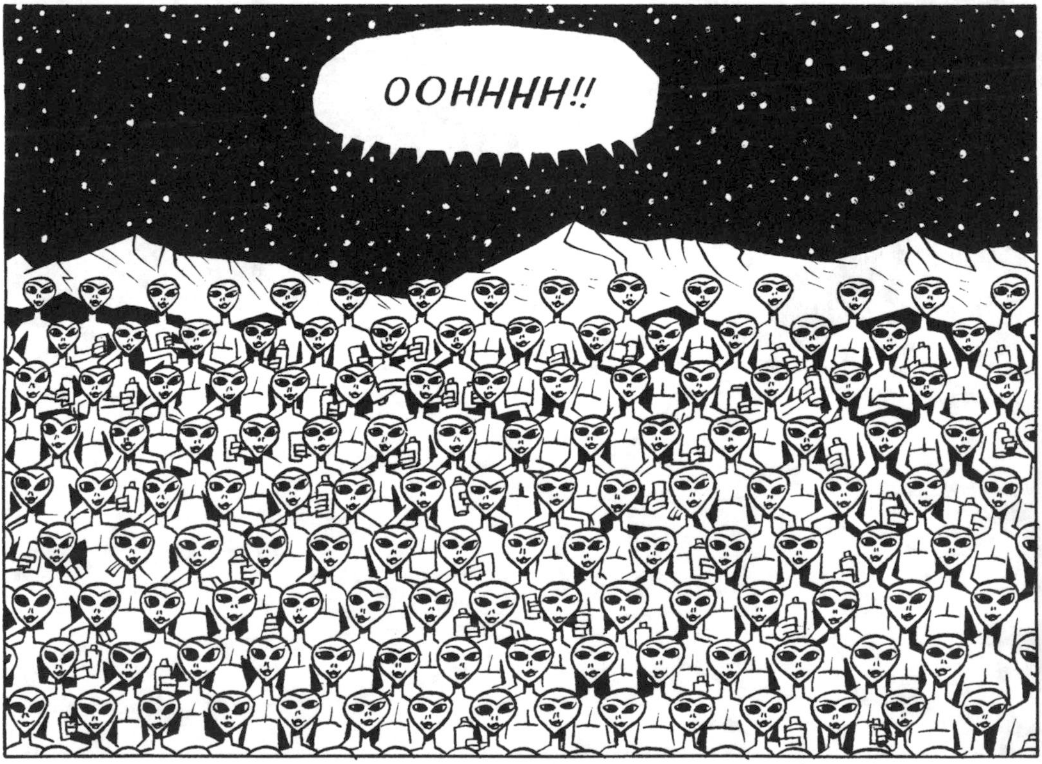
OOHHHH!!

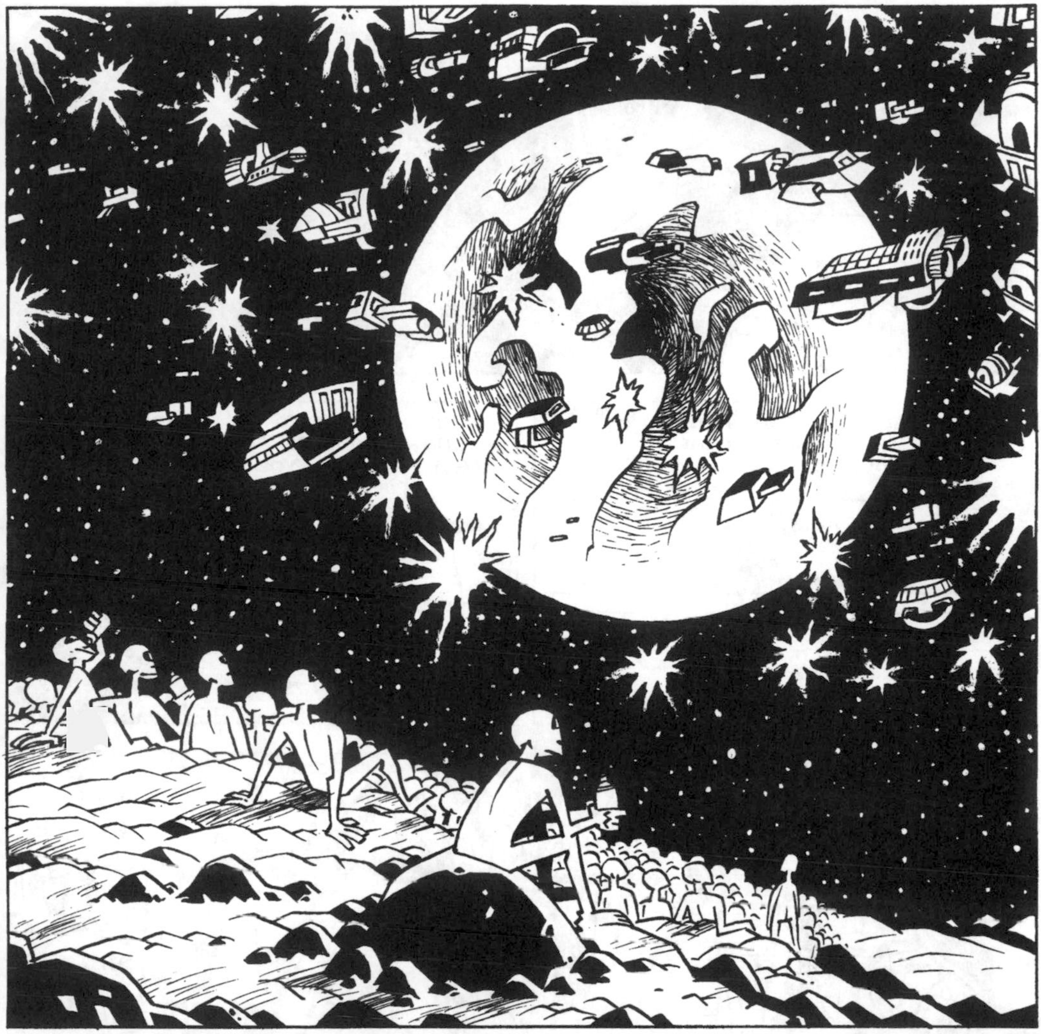

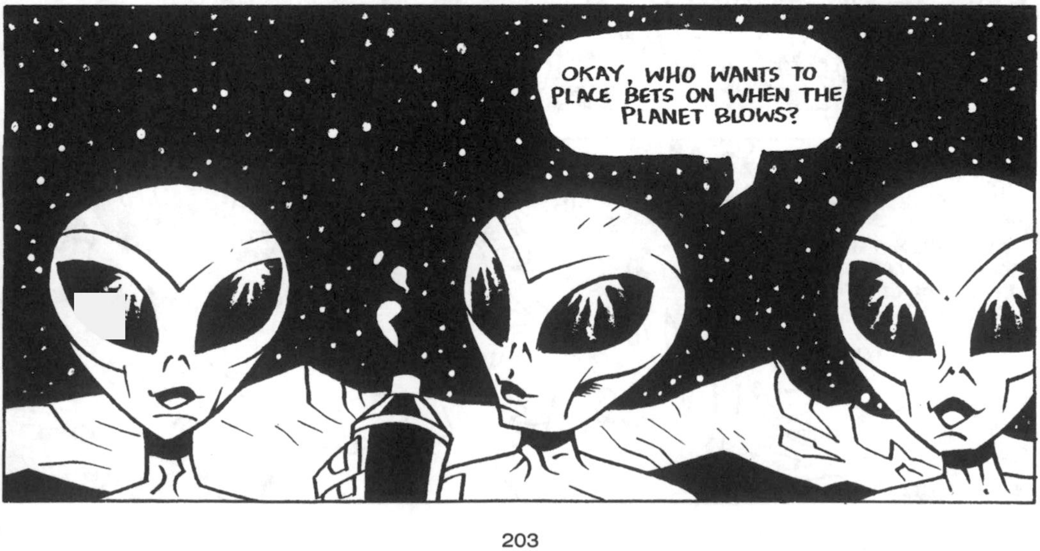
OKAY, WHO WANTS TO PLACE BETS ON WHEN THE PLANET BLOWS?

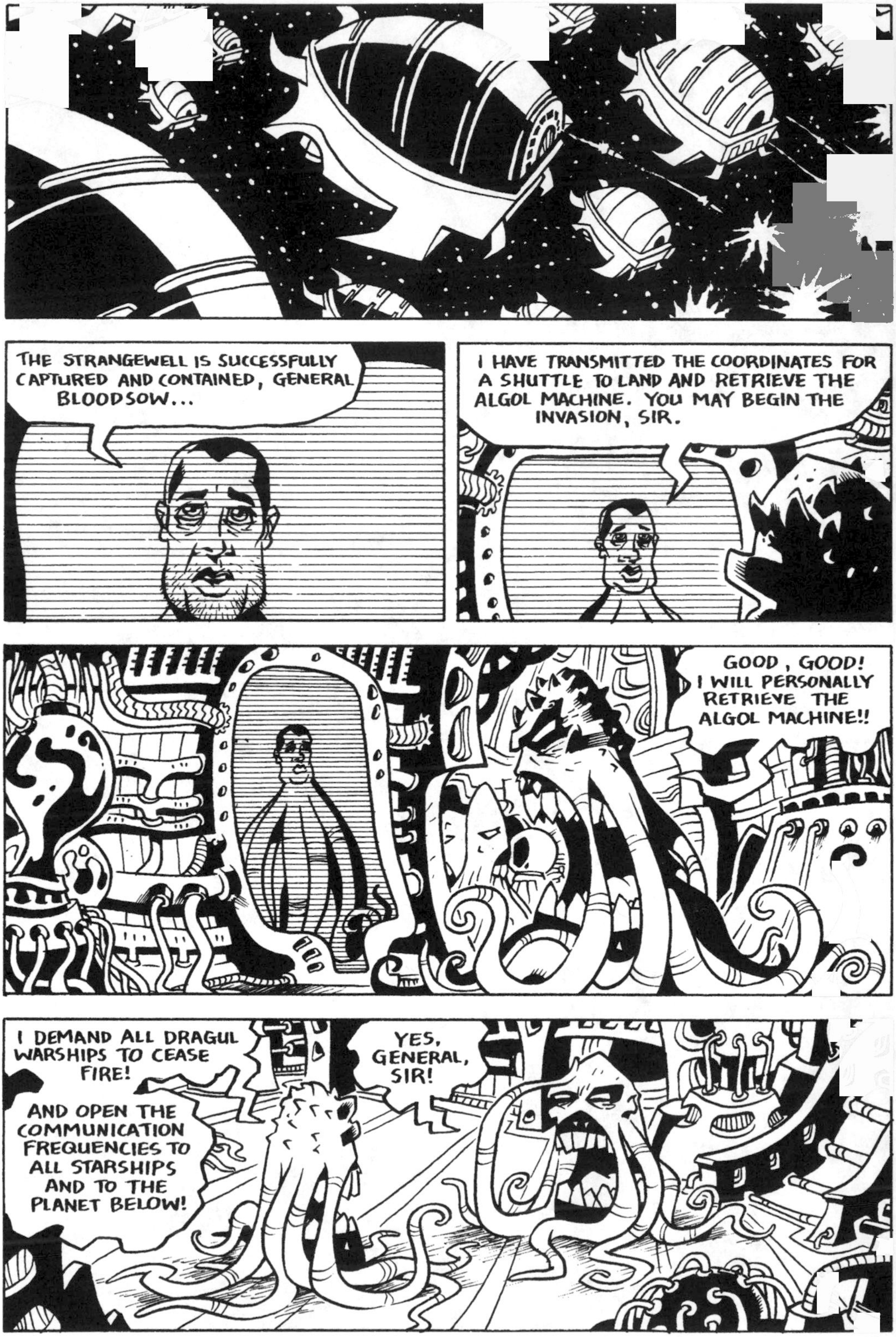
THE STRANGEWELL IS SUCCESSFULLY CAPTURED AND CONTAINED, GENERAL BLOODSOW...
I HAVE TRANSMITTED THE COORDINATES FOR A SHUTTLE TO LAND AND RETRIEVE THE ALGOL MACHINE. YOU MAY BEGIN THE INVASION, SIR.
GOOD, GOOD! I WILL PERSONALLY RETRIEVE THE ALGOL MACHINE!!
I DEMAND ALL DRAGUL WARSHIPS TO CEASE FIRE!
AND OPEN THE COMMUNICATION FREQUENCIES TO ALL STARSHIPS AND TO THE PLANET BELOW!
YES, GENERAL, SIR!

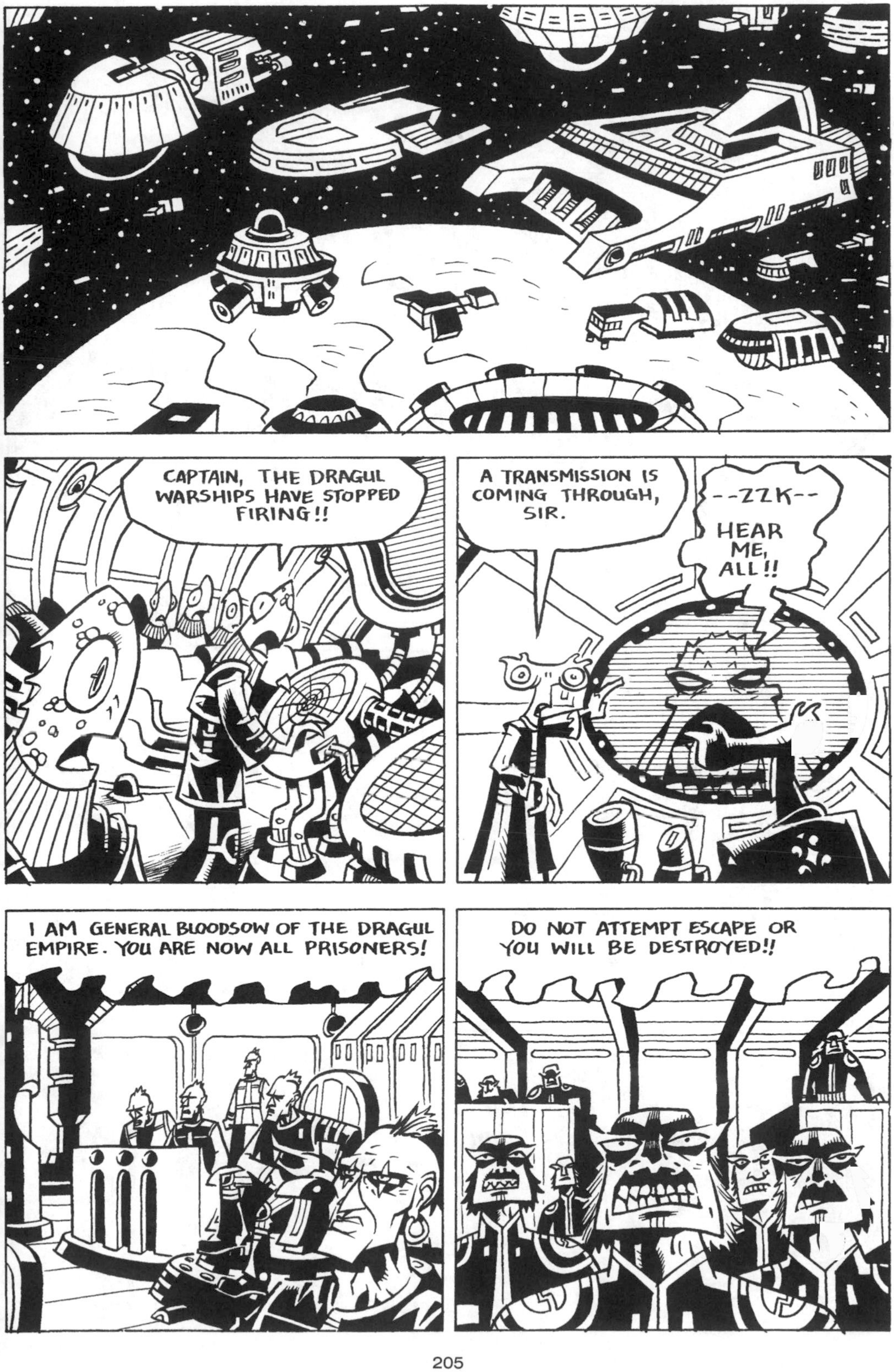
CAPTAIN, THE DRAGUL WARSHIPS HAVE STOPPED FIRING!!
A TRANSMISSION IS COMING THROUGH, SIR.
--ZZK-- HEAR ME, ALL!!
I AM GENERAL BLOODSOW OF THE DRAGUL EMPIRE. YOU ARE NOW ALL PRISONERS!
DO NOT ATTEMPT ESCAPE OR YOU WILL BE DESTROYED!!

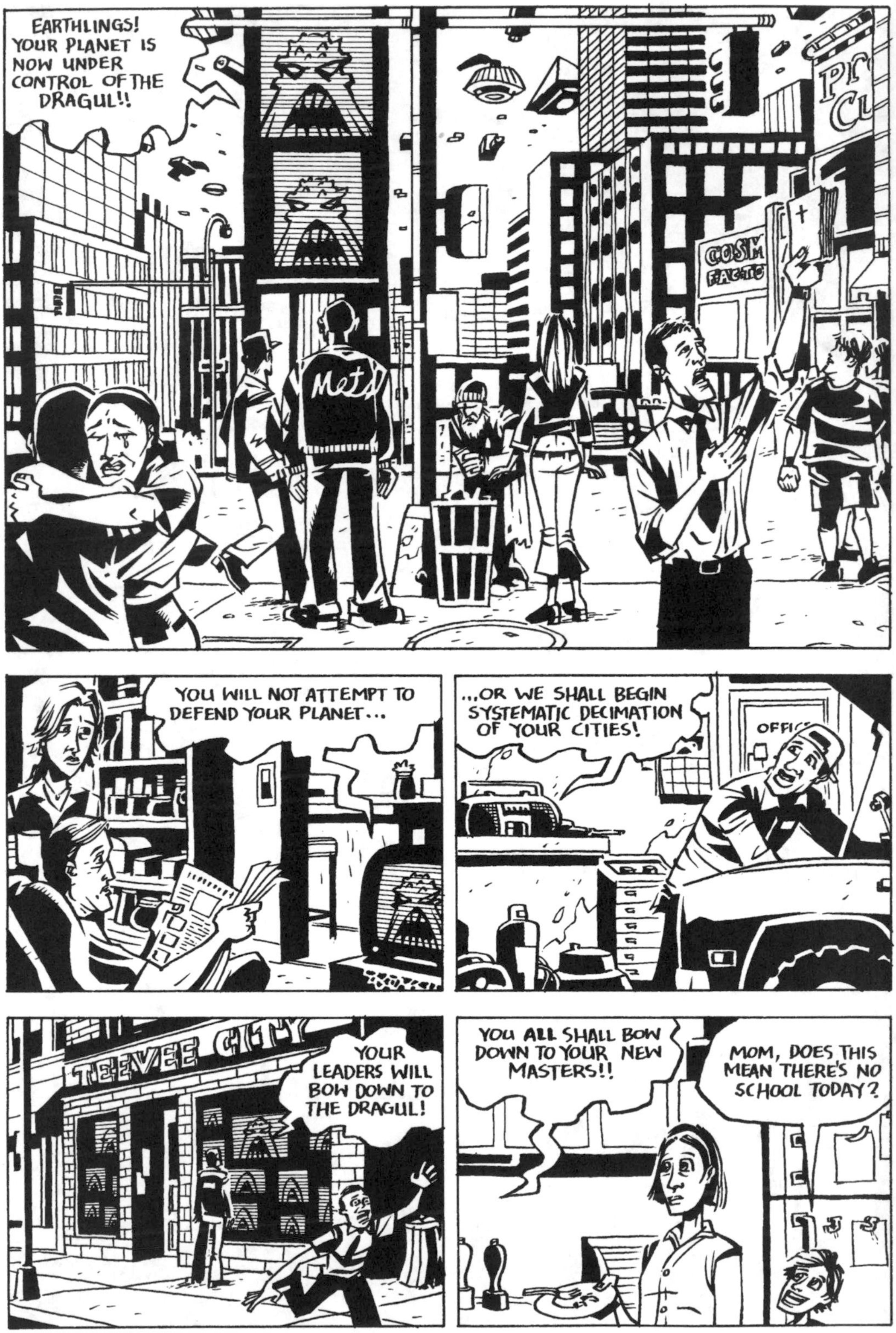
EARTHLINGS! YOUR PLANET IS NOW UNDER CONTROL OF THE DRAGUL!!
Mets
YOU WILL NOT ATTEMPT TO DEFEND YOUR PLANET...
...OR WE SHALL BEGIN SYSTEMATIC DECIMATION OF YOUR CITIES!
TEEVEE CITY
YOUR LEADERS WILL BOW DOWN TO THE DRAGUL!
YOU ALL SHALL BOW DOWN TO YOUR NEW MASTERS!!
MOM, DOES THIS MEAN THERE'S NO SCHOOL TODAY?

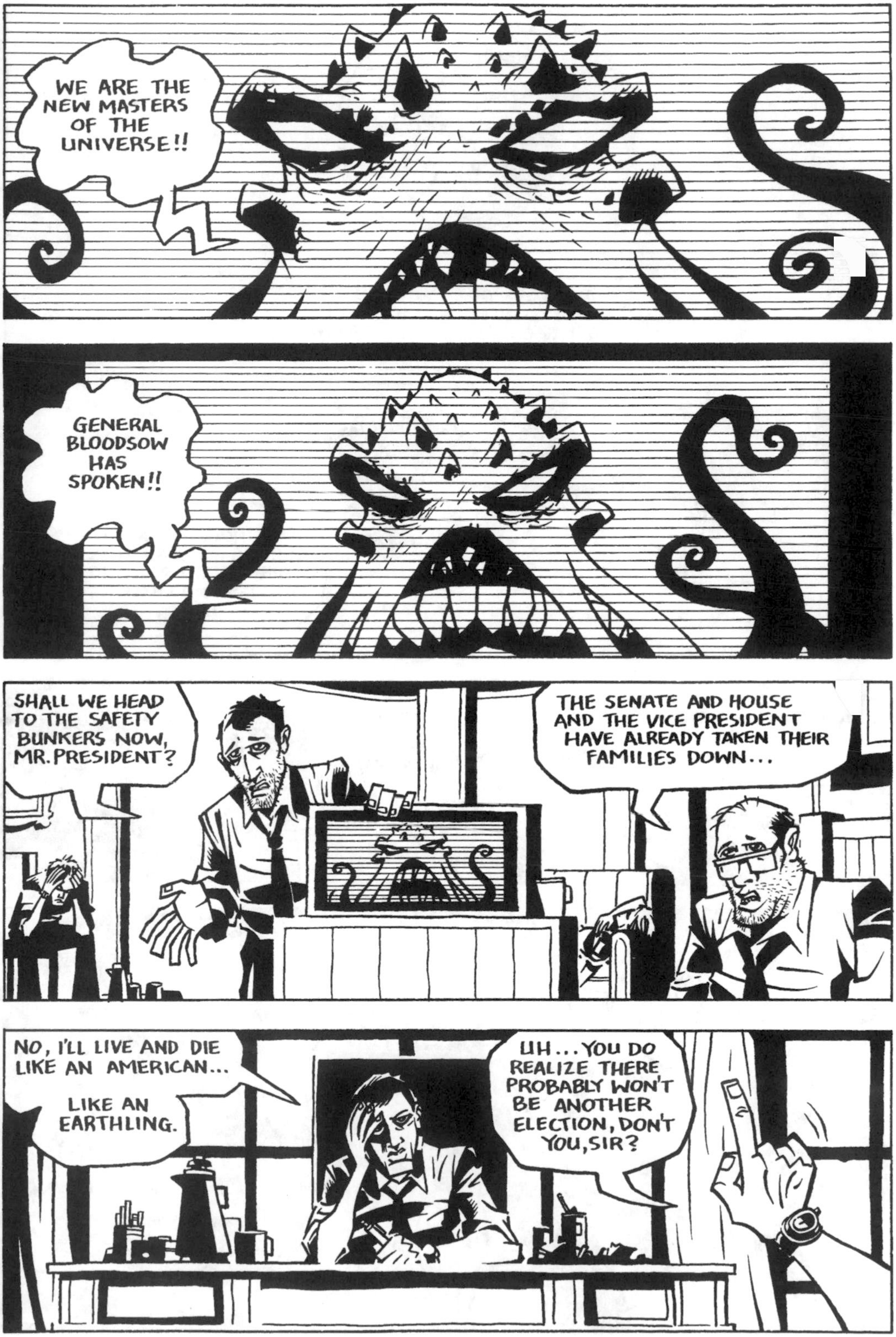
WE ARE THE NEW MASTERS OF THE UNIVERSE!!
GENERAL BLOODSOW HAS SPOKEN!!
SHALL WE HEAD TO THE SAFETY BUNKERS NOW, MR. PRESIDENT?
THE SENATE AND HOUSE AND THE VICE PRESIDENT HAVE ALREADY TAKEN THEIR FAMILIES DOWN...
NO, I'LL LIVE AND DIE LIKE AN AMERICAN...
LIKE AN EARTHLING.
UH... YOU DO REALIZE THERE PROBABLY WON'T BE ANOTHER ELECTION, DON'T YOU, SIR?

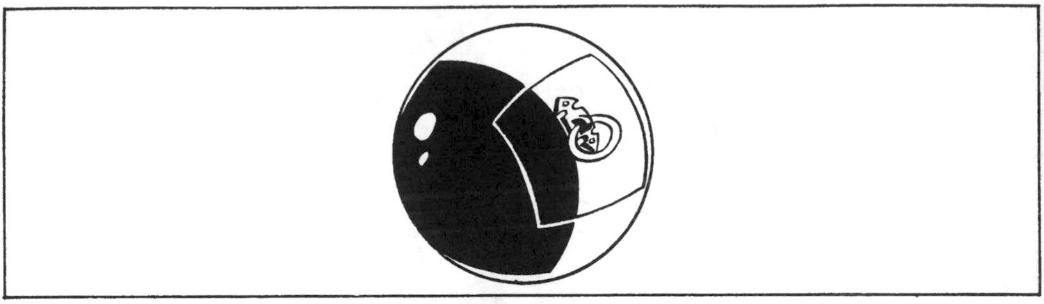

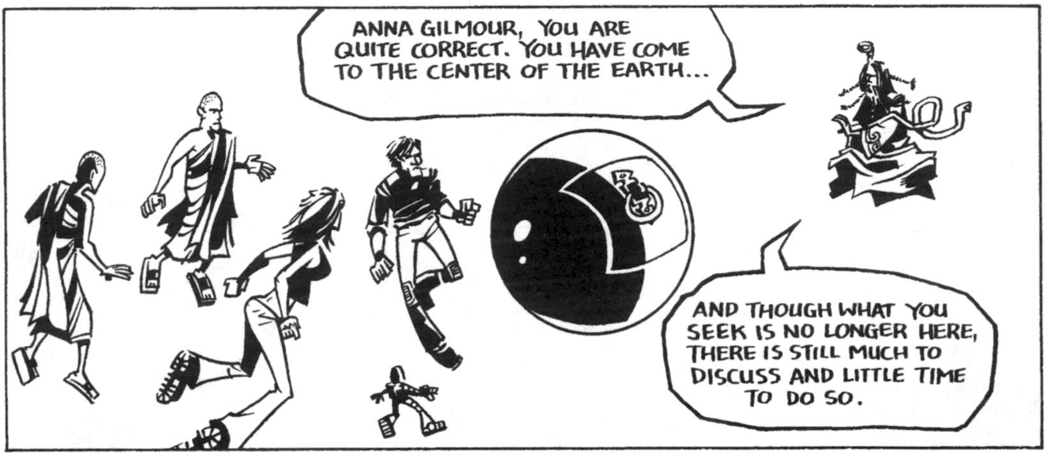
ANNA GILMOUR, YOU ARE QUITE CORRECT. YOU HAVE COME TO THE CENTER OF THE EARTH...
AND THOUGH WHAT YOU SEEK IS NO LONGER HERE, THERE IS STILL MUCH TO DISCUSS AND LITTLE TIME TO DO SO.

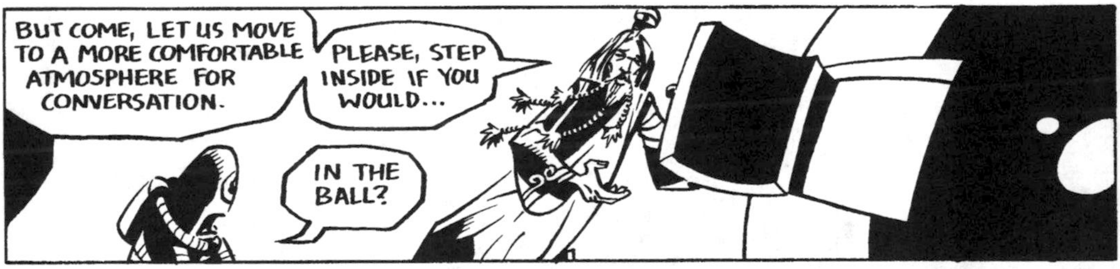
BUT COME, LET US MOVE TO A MORE COMFORTABLE ATMOSPHERE FOR CONVERSATION.
PLEASE, STEP INSIDE IF YOU WOULD...
IN THE BALL?

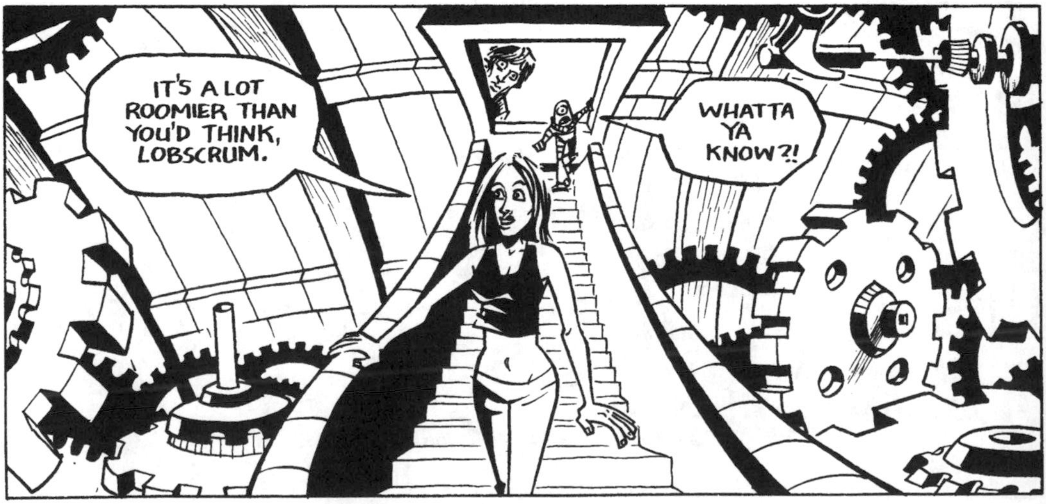
IT'S A LOT ROOMIER THAN YOU'D THINK, LOBSCRUM.
WHATTA YA KNOW?!

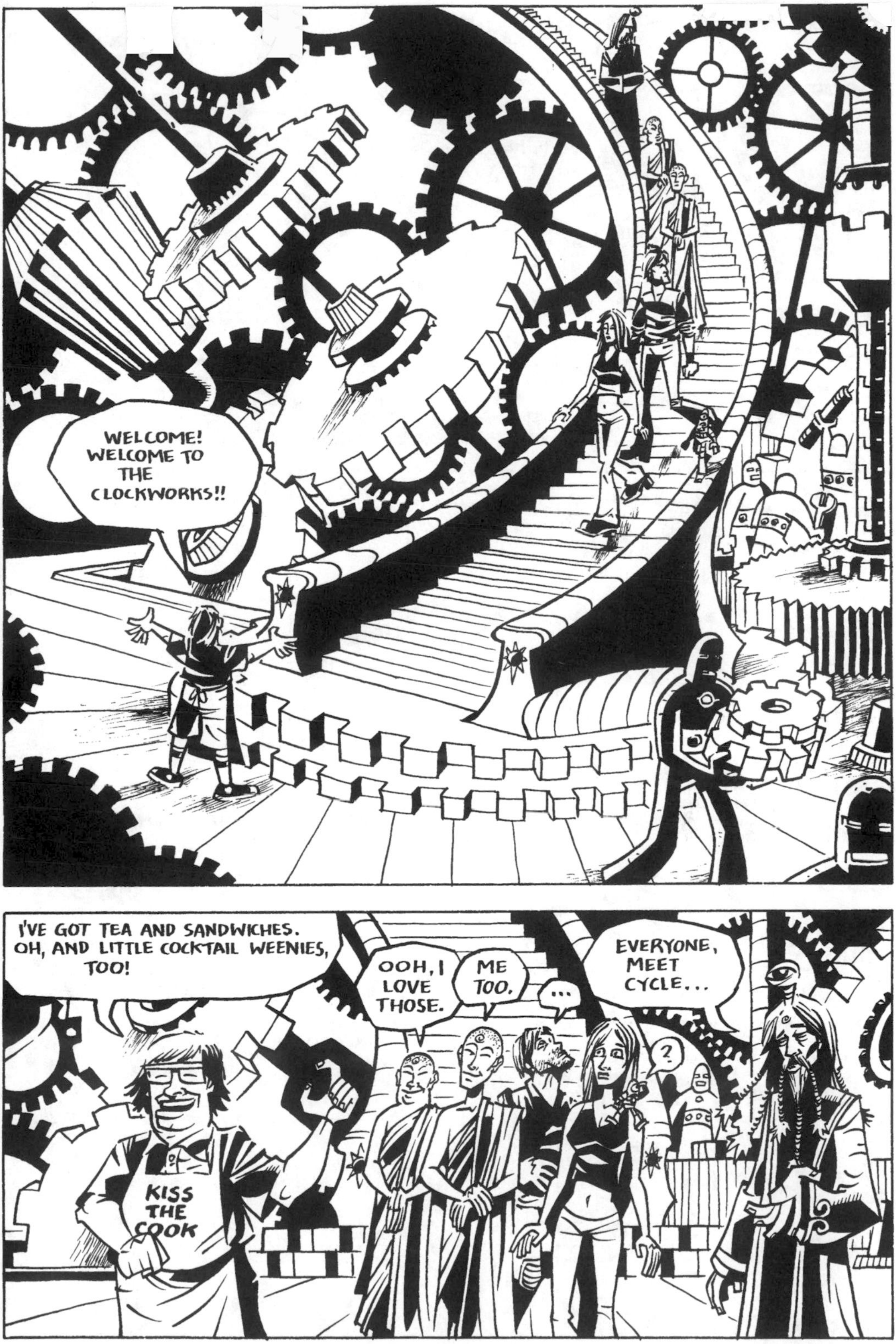
WELCOME! WELCOME TO THE CLOCKWORKS!!
I'VE GOT TEA AND SANDWICHES. OH, AND LITTLE COCKTAIL WEENIES, TOO!
OOH, I LOVE THOSE.
ME TOO.
...
?
EVERYONE, MEET CYCLE...
KISS THE COOK

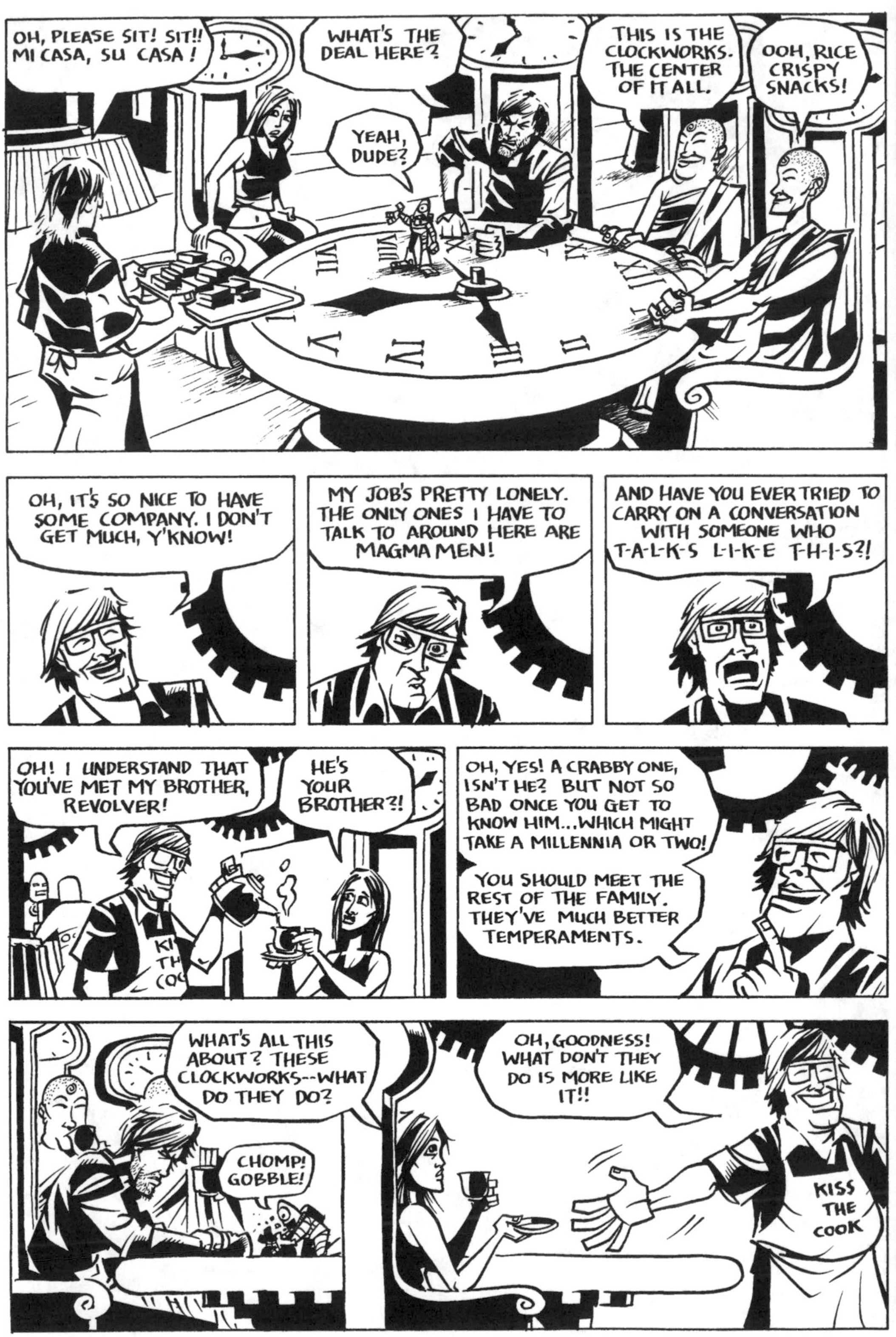
OH, PLEASE SIT! SIT!! MI CASA, SU CASA!
WHAT'S THE DEAL HERE?
YEAH, DUDE?
THIS IS THE CLOCKWORKS. THE CENTER OF IT ALL.
OOH, RICE CRISPY SNACKS!
OH, IT'S SO NICE TO HAVE SOME COMPANY. I DON'T GET MUCH, Y'KNOW!
MY JOB'S PRETTY LONELY. THE ONLY ONES I HAVE TO TALK TO AROUND HERE ARE MAGMA MEN!
AND HAVE YOU EVER TRIED TO CARRY ON A CONVERSATION WITH SOMEONE WHO T-A-L-K-S L-I-K-E T-H-I-S?!
OH! I UNDERSTAND THAT YOU'VE MET MY BROTHER, REVOLVER!
HE'S YOUR BROTHER?!
OH, YES! A CRABBY ONE, ISN'T HE? BUT NOT SO BAD ONCE YOU GET TO KNOW HIM...WHICH MIGHT TAKE A MILLENNIA OR TWO!
YOU SHOULD MEET THE REST OF THE FAMILY. THEY'VE MUCH BETTER TEMPERAMENTS.
WHAT'S ALL THIS ABOUT? THESE CLOCKWORKS--WHAT DO THEY DO?
CHOMP! GOBBLE!
OH, GOODNESS! WHAT DON'T THEY DO IS MORE LIKE IT!!
KISS THE COOK

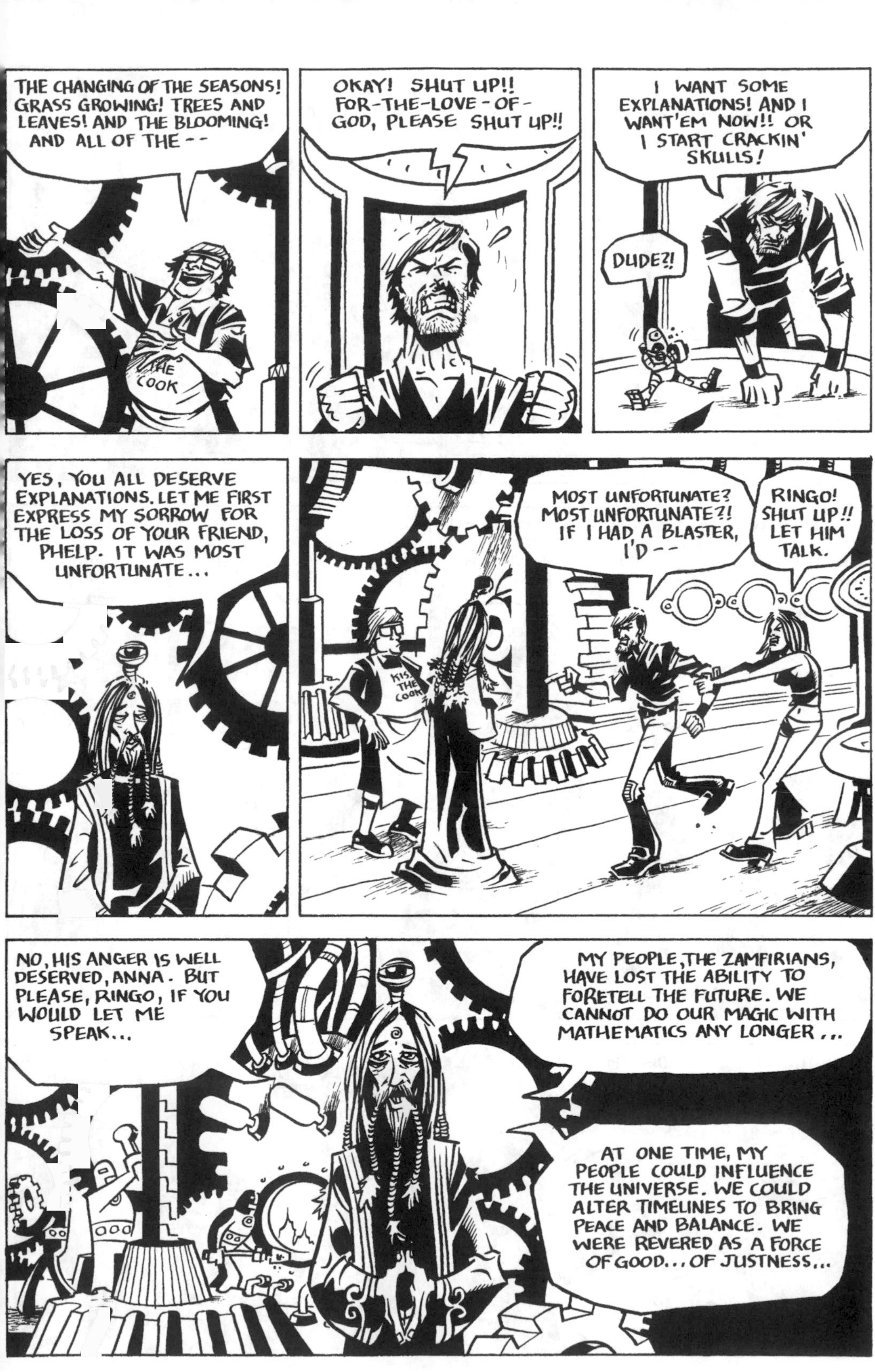
THE CHANGING OF THE SEASONS! GRASS GROWING! TREES AND LEAVES! AND THE BLOOMING! AND ALL OF THE --
KISS THE COOK
OKAY! SHUT UP!! FOR-THE-LOVE-OF-GOD, PLEASE SHUT UP!!
I WANT SOME EXPLANATIONS! AND I WANT'EM NOW!! OR I START CRACKIN' SKULLS!
DUDE?!
YES, YOU ALL DESERVE EXPLANATIONS. LET ME FIRST EXPRESS MY SORROW FOR THE LOSS OF YOUR FRIEND, PHELP. IT WAS MOST UNFORTUNATE...
MOST UNFORTUNATE? MOST UNFORTUNATE?! IF I HAD A BLASTER, I'D --
RINGO! SHUT UP!! LET HIM TALK.
NO, HIS ANGER IS WELL DESERVED, ANNA. BUT PLEASE, RINGO, IF YOU WOULD LET ME SPEAK...
MY PEOPLE, THE ZAMFIRIANS, HAVE LOST THE ABILITY TO FORETELL THE FUTURE. WE CANNOT DO OUR MAGIC WITH MATHEMATICS ANY LONGER...
AT ONE TIME, MY PEOPLE COULD INFLUENCE THE UNIVERSE. WE COULD ALTER TIMELINES TO BRING PEACE AND BALANCE. WE WERE REVERED AS A FORCE OF GOOD... OF JUSTNESS...

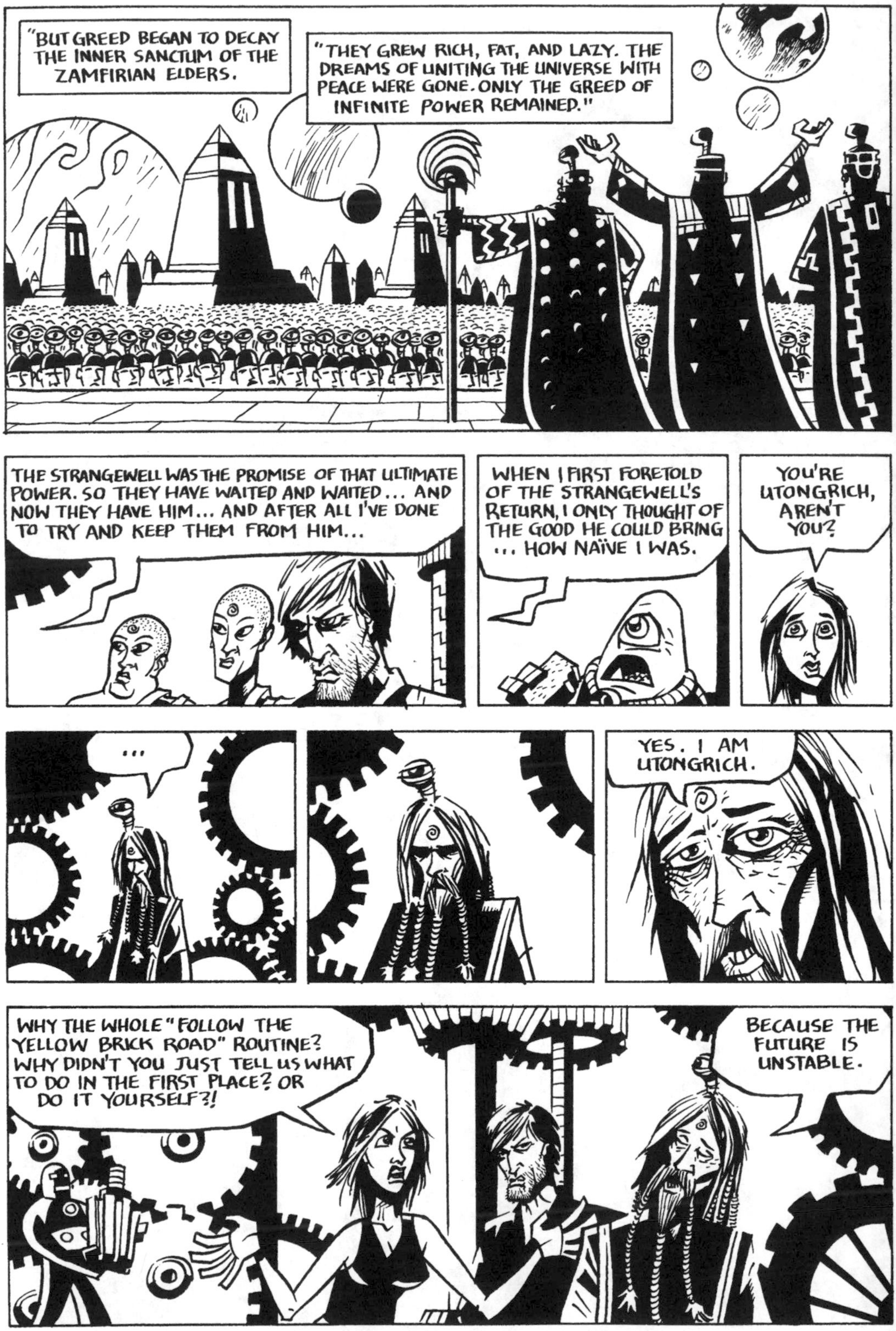

"BUT GREED BEGAN TO DECAY THE INNER SANCTUM OF THE ZAMFIRIAN ELDERS.
"THEY GREW RICH, FAT, AND LAZY. THE DREAMS OF UNITING THE UNIVERSE WITH PEACE WERE GONE. ONLY THE GREED OF INFINITE POWER REMAINED."
THE STRANGEWELL WAS THE PROMISE OF THAT ULTIMATE POWER. SO THEY HAVE WAITED AND WAITED ... AND NOW THEY HAVE HIM ... AND AFTER ALL I'VE DONE TO TRY AND KEEP THEM FROM HIM...
WHEN I FIRST FORETOLD OF THE STRANGEWELL'S RETURN, I ONLY THOUGHT OF THE GOOD HE COULD BRING ... HOW NAÏVE I WAS.
YOU'RE UTONGRICH, AREN'T YOU?
...
YES. I AM UTONGRICH.
WHY THE WHOLE "FOLLOW THE YELLOW BRICK ROAD" ROUTINE? WHY DIDN'T YOU JUST TELL US WHAT TO DO IN THE FIRST PLACE? OR DO IT YOURSELF?!
BECAUSE THE FUTURE IS UNSTABLE.

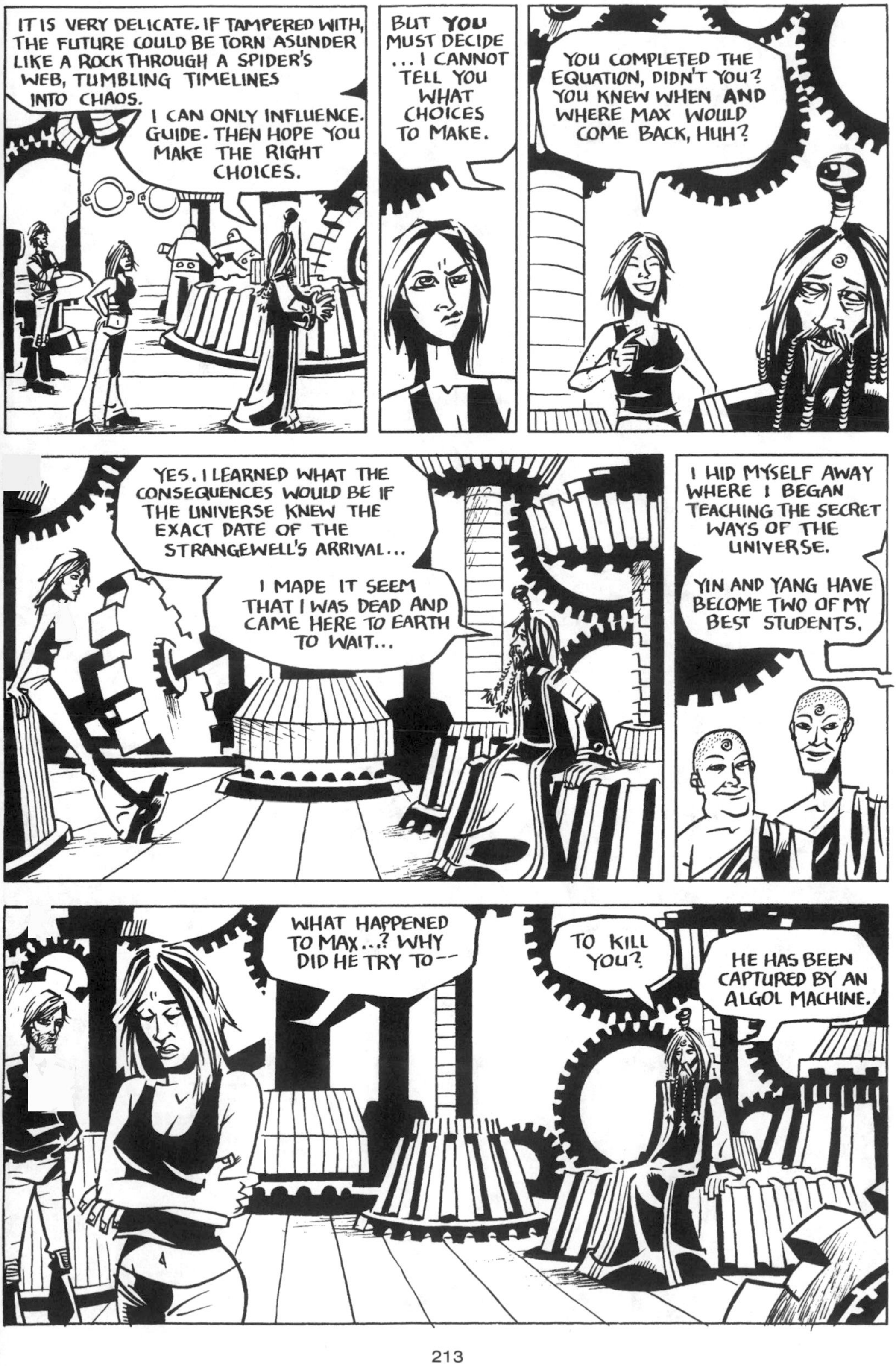

IT IS VERY DELICATE. IF TAMPERED WITH, THE FUTURE COULD BE TORN ASUNDER LIKE A ROCK THROUGH A SPIDER'S WEB, TUMBLING TIMELINES INTO CHAOS.
I CAN ONLY INFLUENCE. GUIDE. THEN HOPE YOU MAKE THE RIGHT CHOICES.
BUT YOU MUST DECIDE ...I CANNOT TELL YOU WHAT CHOICES TO MAKE.
YOU COMPLETED THE EQUATION, DIDN'T YOU? YOU KNEW WHEN AND WHERE MAX WOULD COME BACK, HUH?
YES. I LEARNED WHAT THE CONSEQUENCES WOULD BE IF THE UNIVERSE KNEW THE EXACT DATE OF THE STRANGEWELL'S ARRIVAL...
I MADE IT SEEM THAT I WAS DEAD AND CAME HERE TO EARTH TO WAIT...
I HID MYSELF AWAY WHERE I BEGAN TEACHING THE SECRET WAYS OF THE UNIVERSE.
YIN AND YANG HAVE BECOME TWO OF MY BEST STUDENTS.
WHAT HAPPENED TO MAX...? WHY DID HE TRY TO--
TO KILL YOU?
HE HAS BEEN CAPTURED BY AN ALGOL MACHINE.

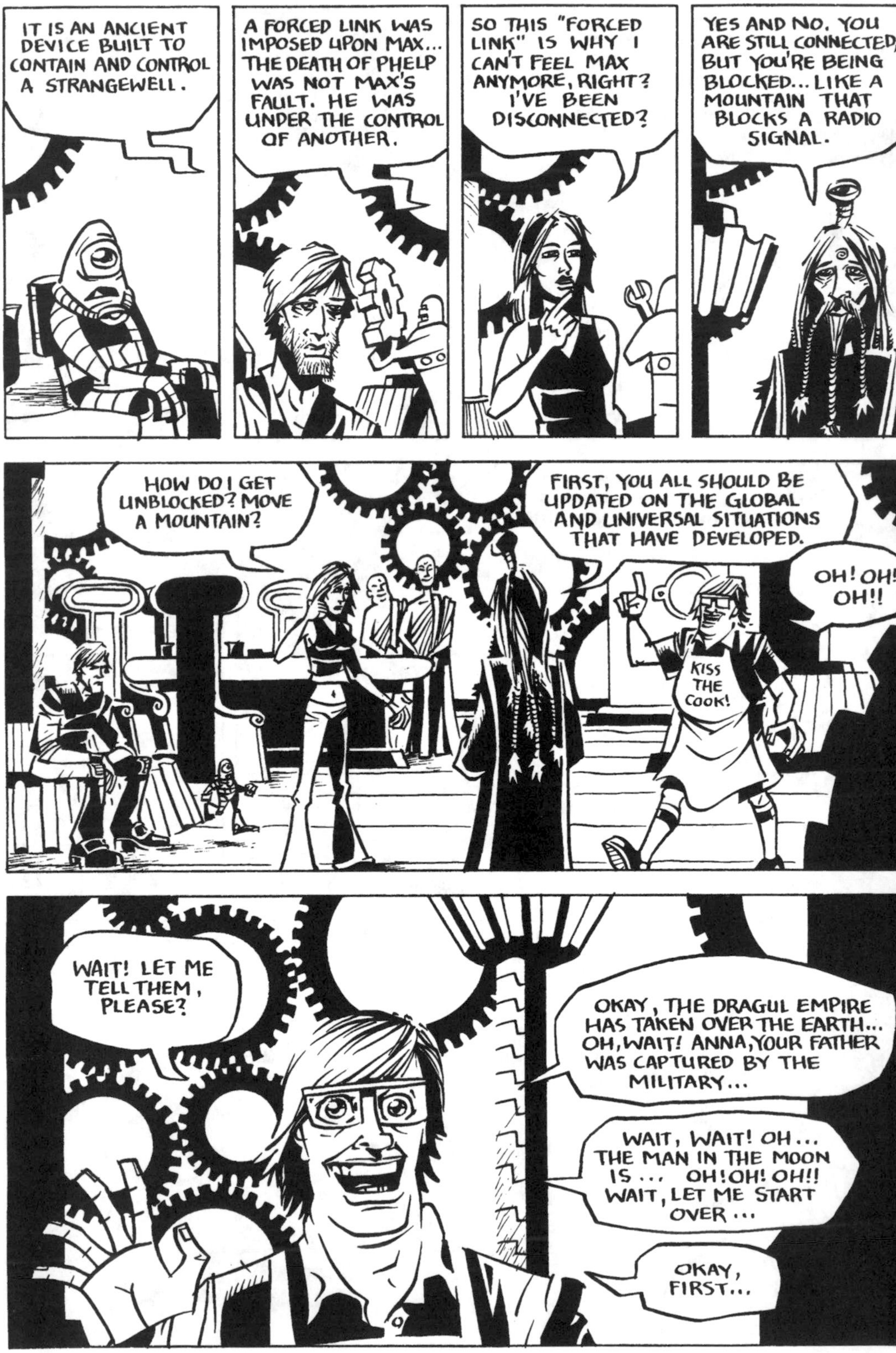
IT IS AN ANCIENT DEVICE BUILT TO CONTAIN AND CONTROL A STRANGEWELL.
A FORCED LINK WAS IMPOSED UPON MAX... THE DEATH OF PHELP WAS NOT MAX'S FAULT. HE WAS UNDER THE CONTROL OF ANOTHER.
SO THIS "FORCED LINK" IS WHY I CAN'T FEEL MAX ANYMORE, RIGHT? I'VE BEEN DISCONNECTED?
YES AND NO. YOU ARE STILL CONNECTED, BUT YOU'RE BEING BLOCKED... LIKE A MOUNTAIN THAT BLOCKS A RADIO SIGNAL.
HOW DO I GET UNBLOCKED? MOVE A MOUNTAIN?
FIRST, YOU ALL SHOULD BE UPDATED ON THE GLOBAL AND UNIVERSAL SITUATIONS THAT HAVE DEVELOPED.
OH! OH! OH!!
KISS THE COOK!
WAIT! LET ME TELL THEM, PLEASE?
OKAY, THE DRAGUL EMPIRE HAS TAKEN OVER THE EARTH... OH, WAIT! ANNA, YOUR FATHER WAS CAPTURED BY THE MILITARY...
WAIT, WAIT! OH... THE MAN IN THE MOON IS... OH! OH! OH!! WAIT, LET ME START OVER...
OKAY, FIRST...

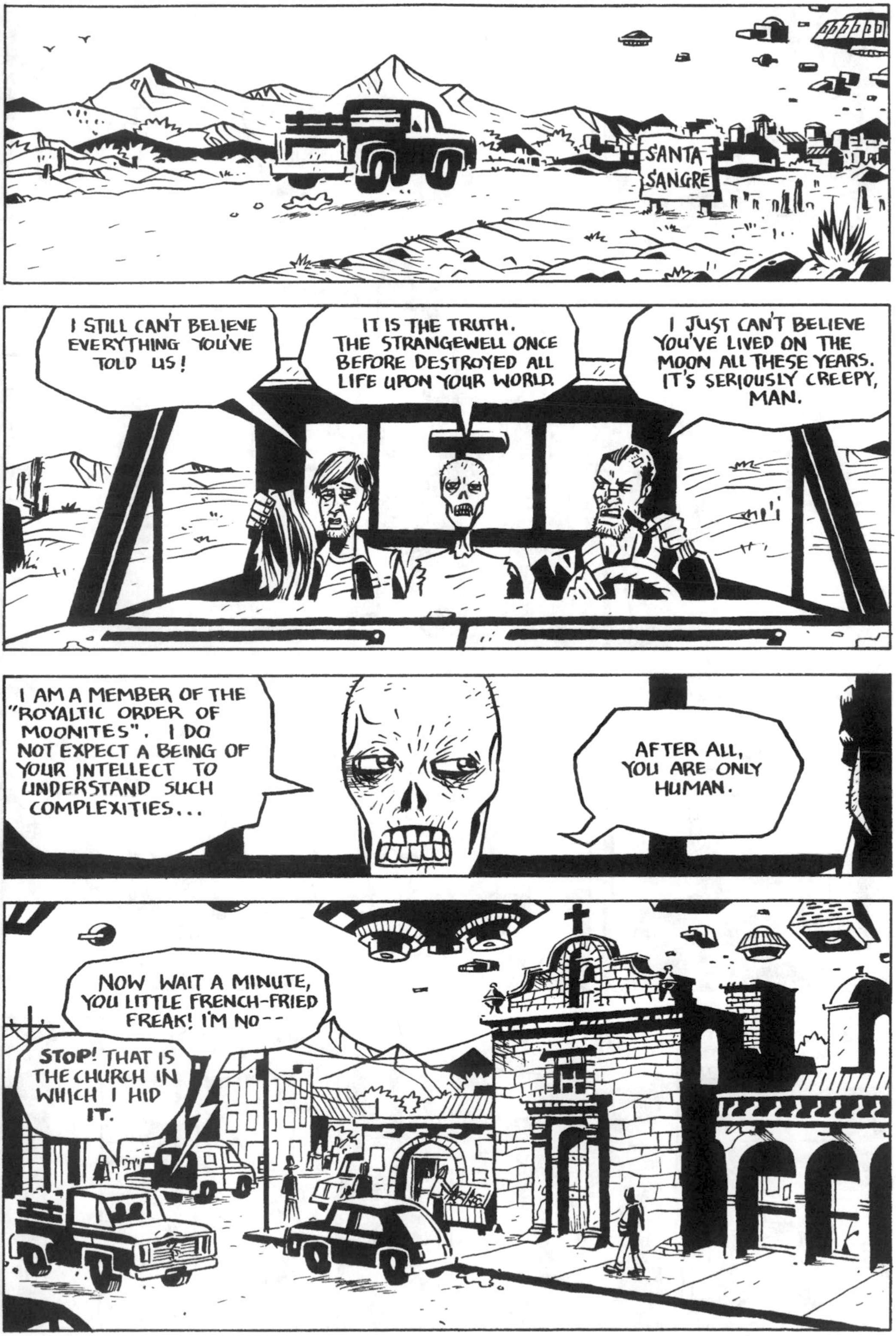
SANTA SANGRE
I STILL CAN'T BELIEVE EVERYTHING YOU'VE TOLD US!
IT IS THE TRUTH. THE STRANGEWELL ONCE BEFORE DESTROYED ALL LIFE UPON YOUR WORLD.
I JUST CAN'T BELIEVE YOU'VE LIVED ON THE MOON ALL THESE YEARS. IT'S SERIOUSLY CREEPY, MAN.
I AM A MEMBER OF THE "ROYALTIC ORDER OF MOONITES". I DO NOT EXPECT A BEING OF YOUR INTELLECT TO UNDERSTAND SUCH COMPLEXITIES...
AFTER ALL, YOU ARE ONLY HUMAN.
NOW WAIT A MINUTE, YOU LITTLE FRENCH-FRIED FREAK! I'M NO--
STOP! THAT IS THE CHURCH IN WHICH I HID IT.

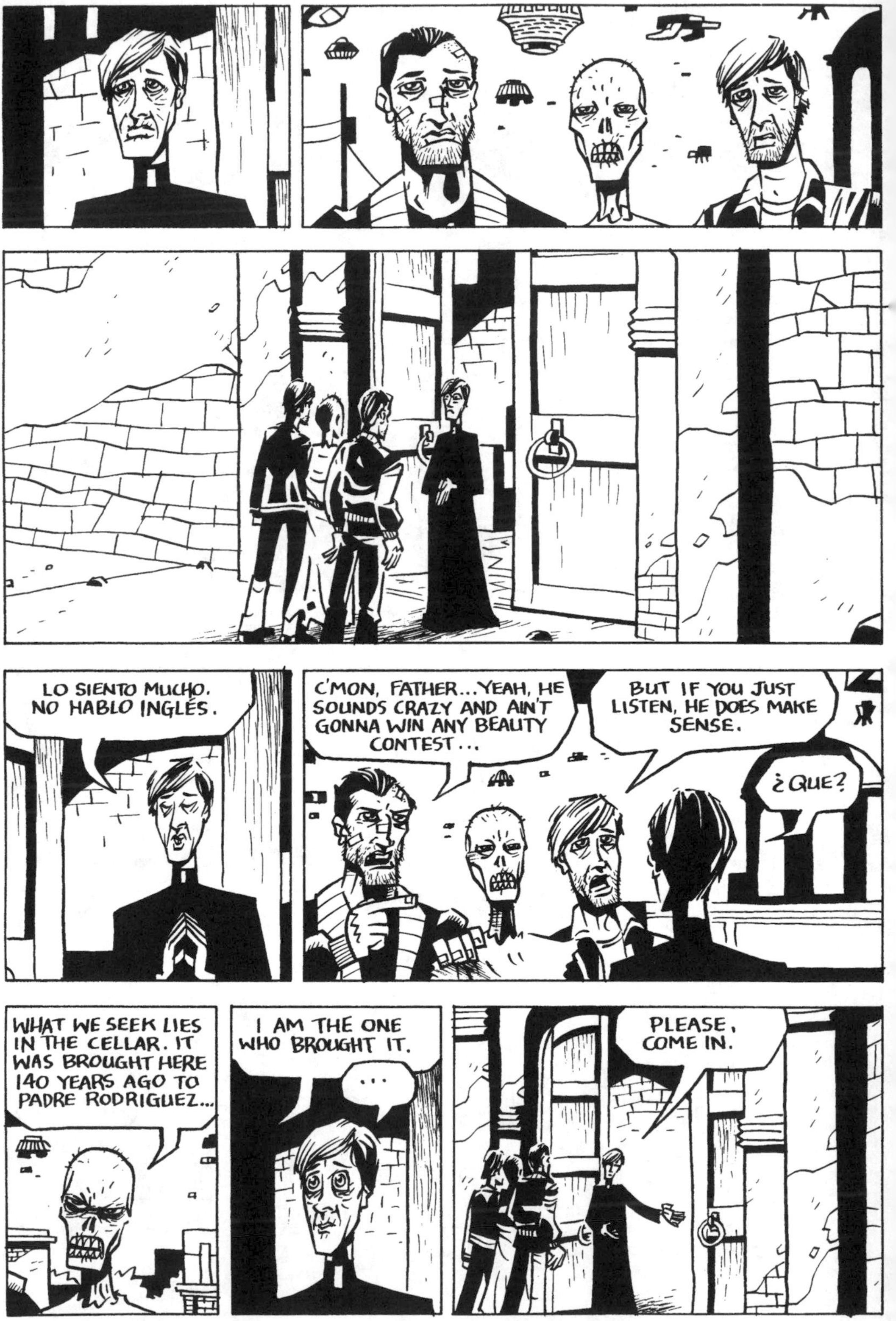

LO SIENTO MUCHO. NO HABLO INGLÉS.
C'MON, FATHER... YEAH, HE SOUNDS CRAZY AND AIN'T GONNA WIN ANY BEAUTY CONTEST...
BUT IF YOU JUST LISTEN, HE DOES MAKE SENSE.
¿QUE?
WHAT WE SEEK LIES IN THE CELLAR. IT WAS BROUGHT HERE 140 YEARS AGO TO PADRE RODRIGUEZ...
I AM THE ONE WHO BROUGHT IT.
...
PLEASE, COME IN.

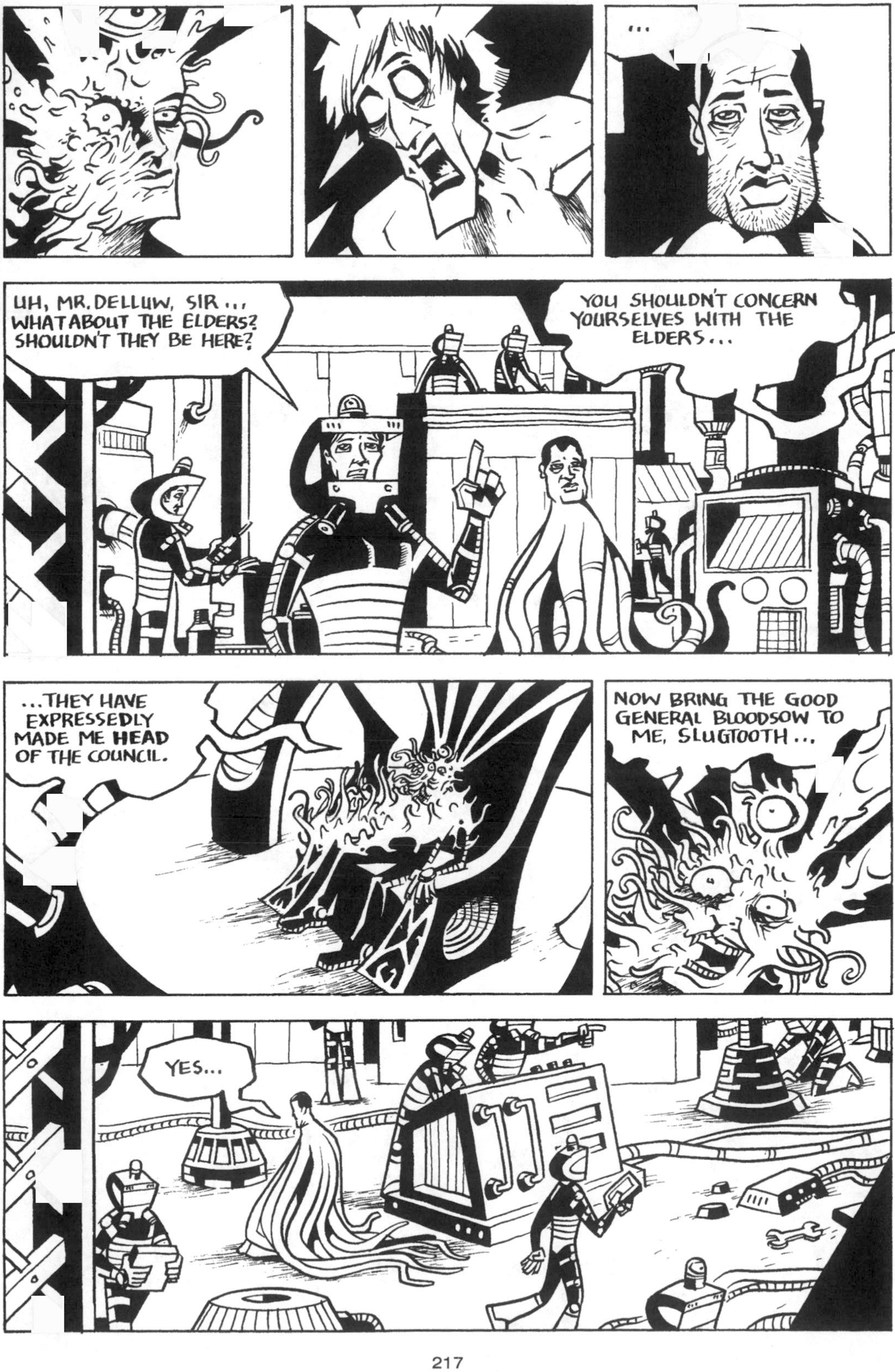
...
UH, MR. DELLUW, SIR...,
WHATABOUT THE ELDERS?
SHOULDN'T THEY BE HERE?
YOU SHOULDN'T CONCERN YOURSELVES WITH THE ELDERS...
...THEY HAVE EXPRESSEDLY MADE ME HEAD OF THE COUNCIL.
NOW BRING THE GOOD GENERAL BLOODSOW TO ME, SLUGTOOTH...
YES...

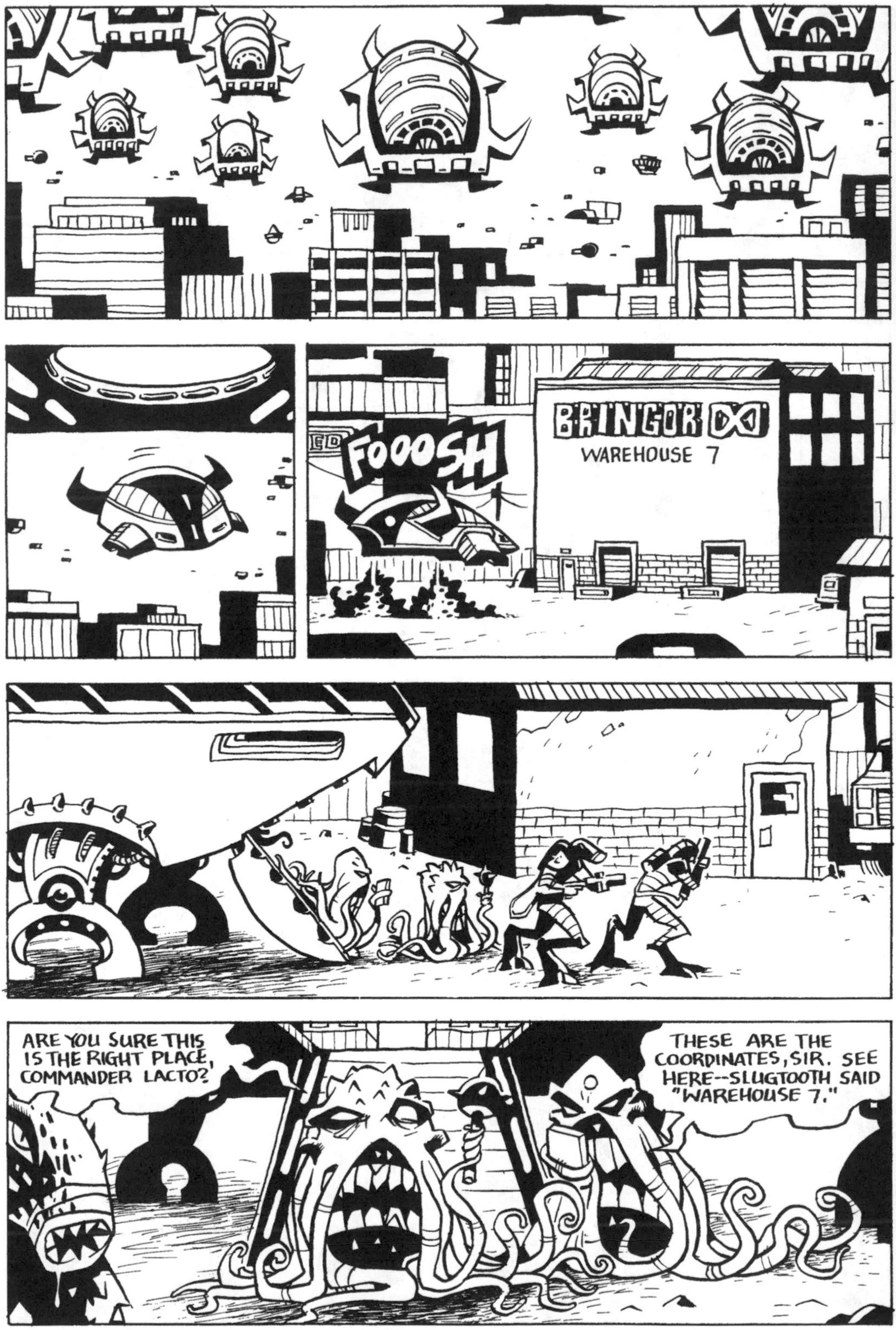
FOOOSH
BRINGOR
WAREHOUSE 7
ARE YOU SURE THIS IS THE RIGHT PLACE, COMMANDER LACTO?
THESE ARE THE COORDINATES, SIR. SEE HERE--SLUGTOOTH SAID "WAREHOUSE 7."

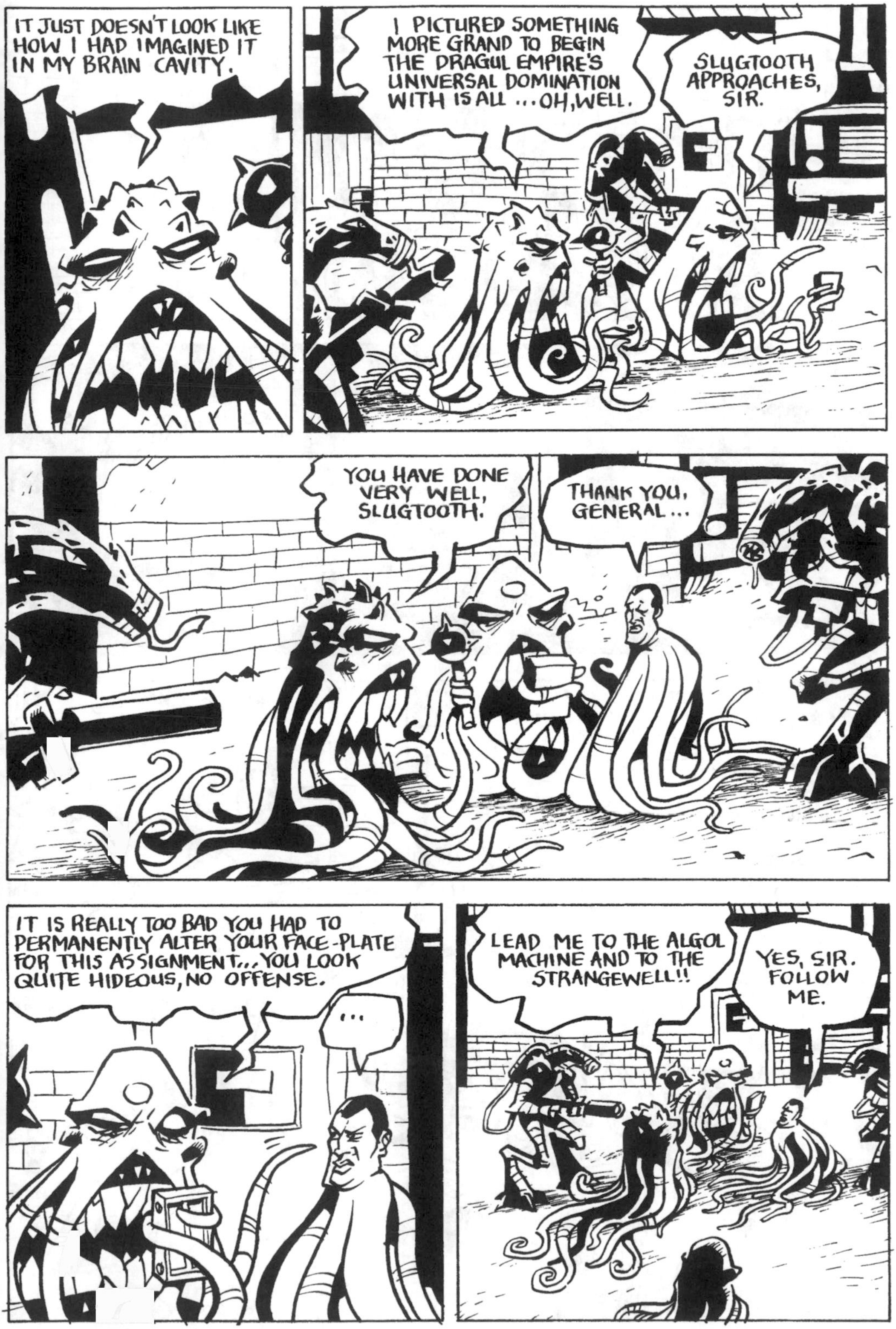
IT JUST DOESN'T LOOK LIKE HOW I HAD IMAGINED IT IN MY BRAIN CAVITY.
I PICTURED SOMETHING MORE GRAND TO BEGIN THE DRAGUL EMPIRE'S UNIVERSAL DOMINATION WITH IS ALL ... OH, WELL.
SLUGTOOTH APPROACHES, SIR.
YOU HAVE DONE VERY WELL, SLUGTOOTH.
THANK YOU, GENERAL...
IT IS REALLY TOO BAD YOU HAD TO PERMANENTLY ALTER YOUR FACE-PLATE FOR THIS ASSIGNMENT... YOU LOOK QUITE HIDEOUS, NO OFFENSE.
...
LEAD ME TO THE ALGOL MACHINE AND TO THE STRANGEWELL!!
YES, SIR. FOLLOW ME.

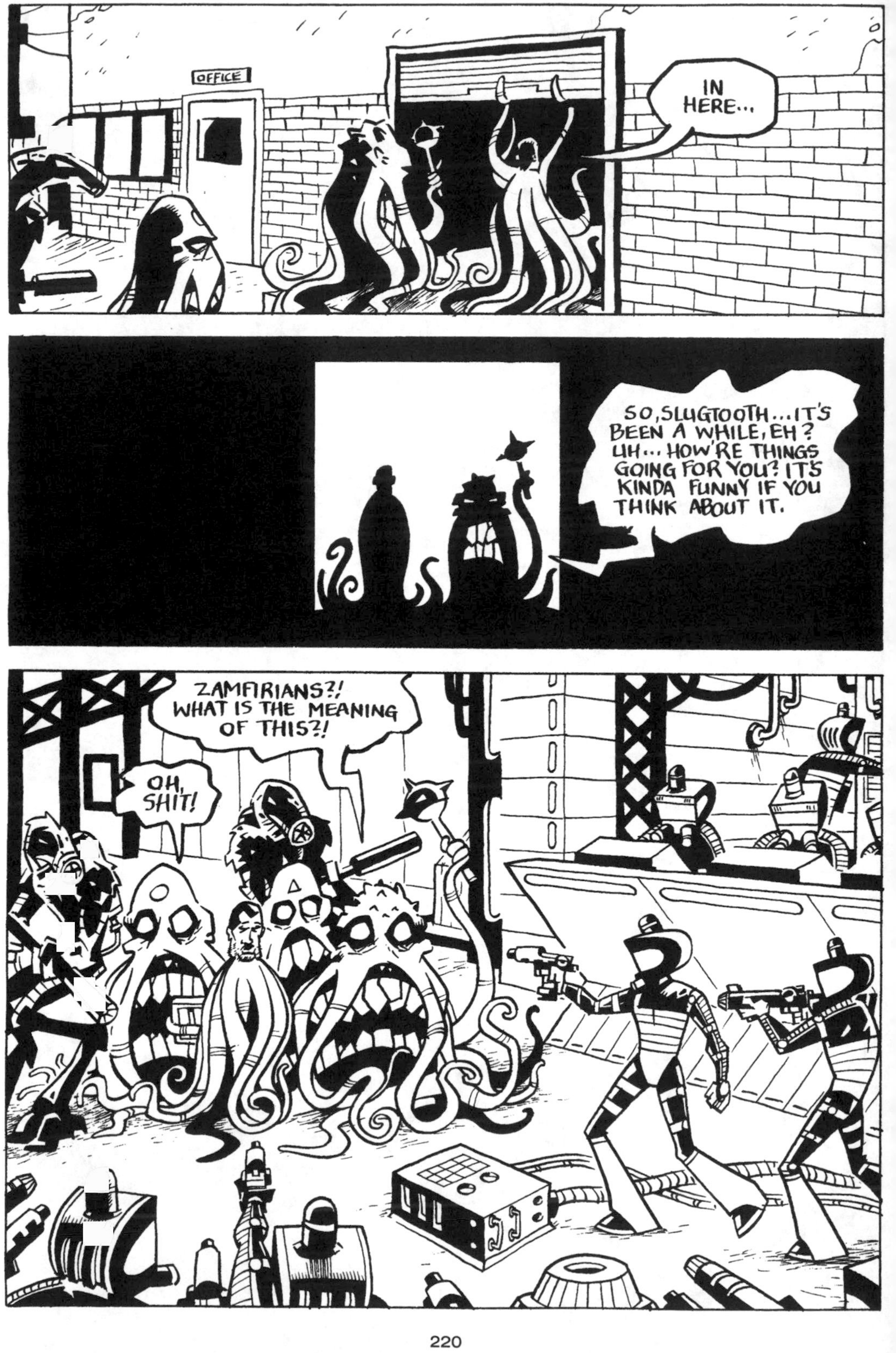

OFFICE
IN HERE...
SO, SLUGTOOTH...IT'S BEEN A WHILE, EH? UH... HOW'RE THINGS GOING FOR YOU? IT'S KINDA FUNNY IF YOU THINK ABOUT IT.
ZAMFIRIANS?! WHAT IS THE MEANING OF THIS?!
OH, SHIT!

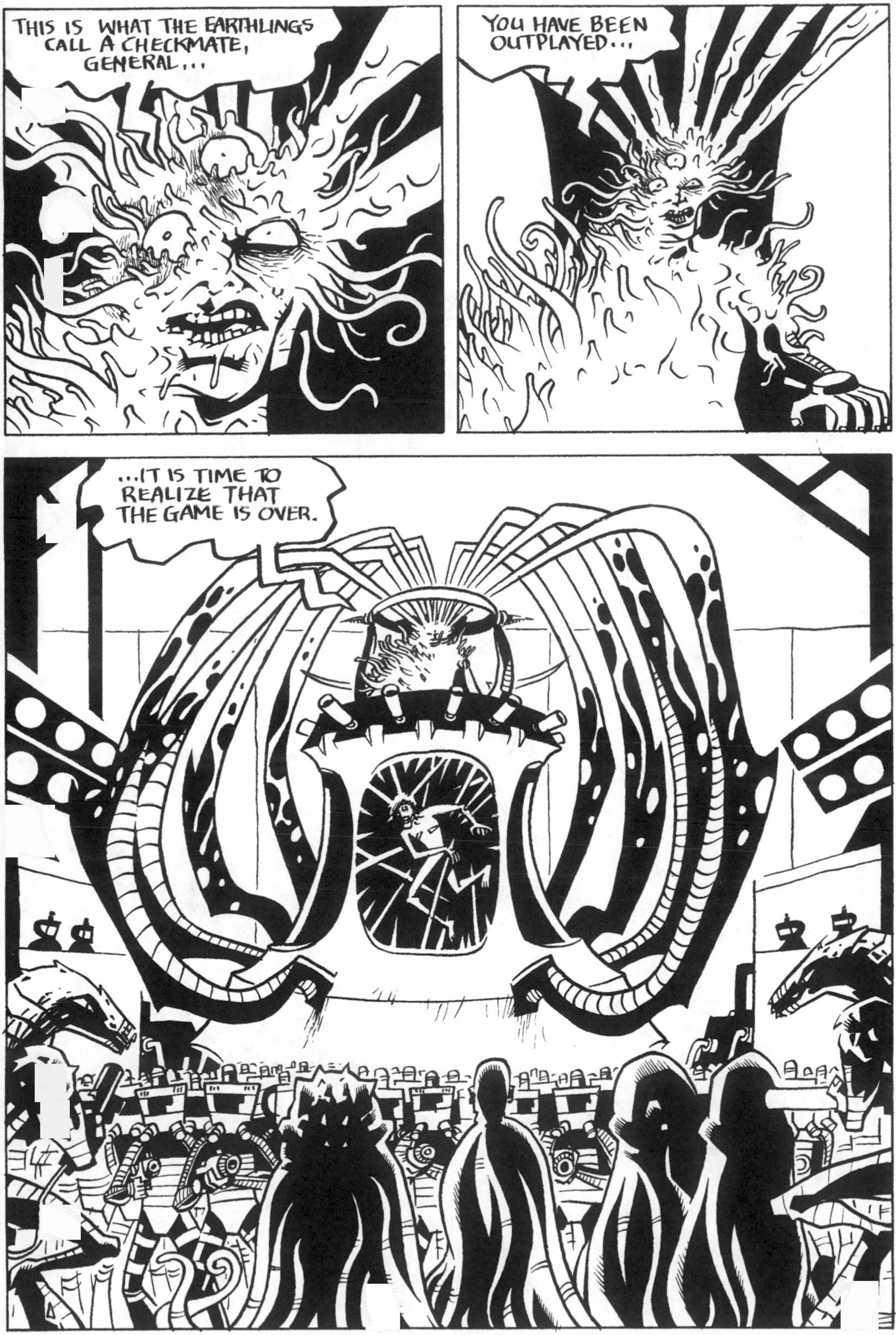
THIS IS WHAT THE EARTHLINGS CALL A CHECKMATE, GENERAL...
YOU HAVE BEEN OUTPLAYED...
...IT IS TIME TO REALIZE THAT THE GAME IS OVER.

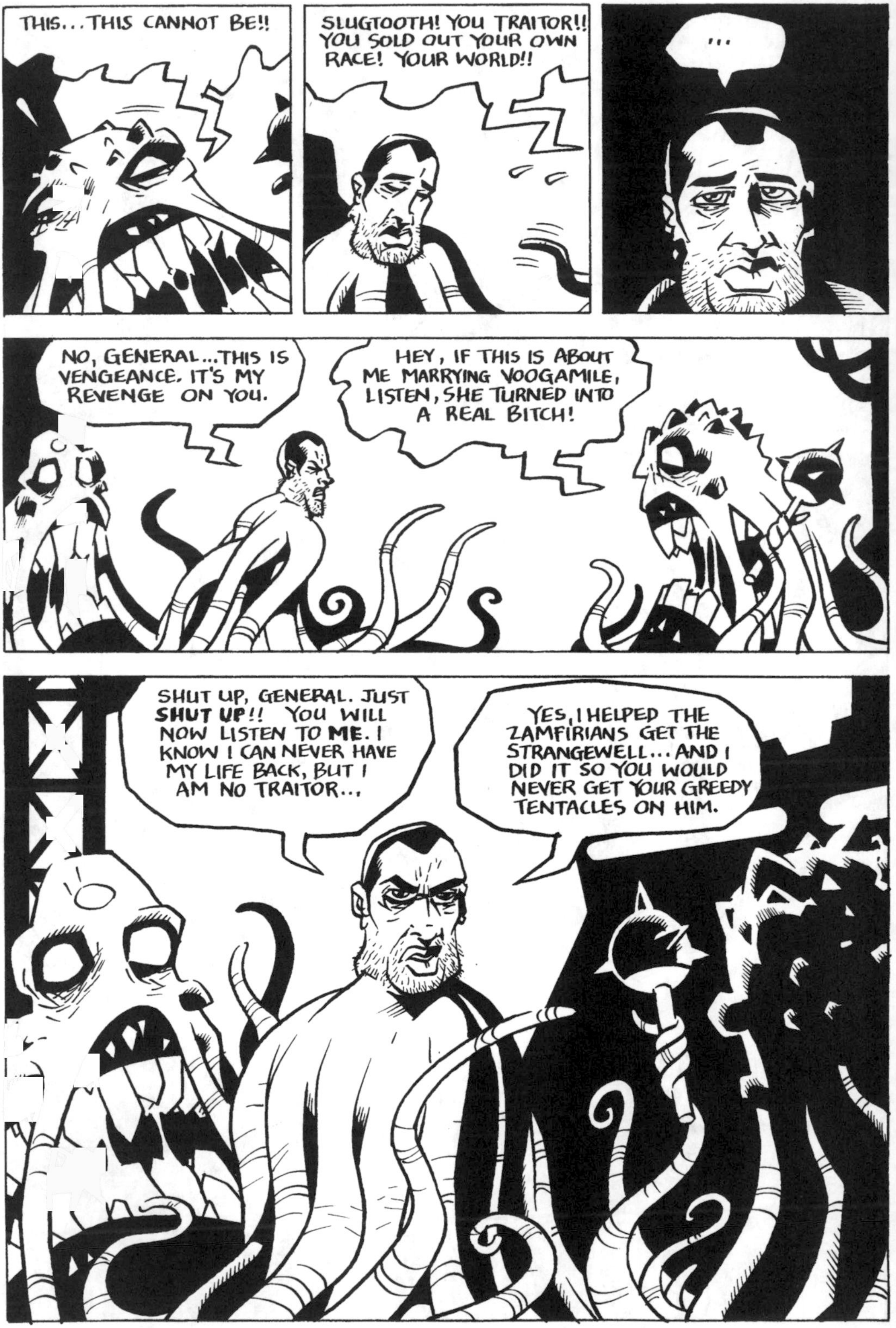
THIS...THIS CANNOT BE!!
SLUGTOOTH! YOU TRAITOR!! YOU SOLD OUT YOUR OWN RACE! YOUR WORLD!!
...
NO, GENERAL...THIS IS VENGEANCE. IT'S MY REVENGE ON YOU.
HEY, IF THIS IS ABOUT ME MARRYING VOOGAMILE, LISTEN, SHE TURNED INTO A REAL BITCH!
SHUT UP, GENERAL. JUST SHUT UP!! YOU WILL NOW LISTEN TO ME. I KNOW I CAN NEVER HAVE MY LIFE BACK, BUT I AM NO TRAITOR...
YES, I HELPED THE ZAMFIRIANS GET THE STRANGEWELL...AND I DID IT SO YOU WOULD NEVER GET YOUR GREEDY TENTACLES ON HIM.

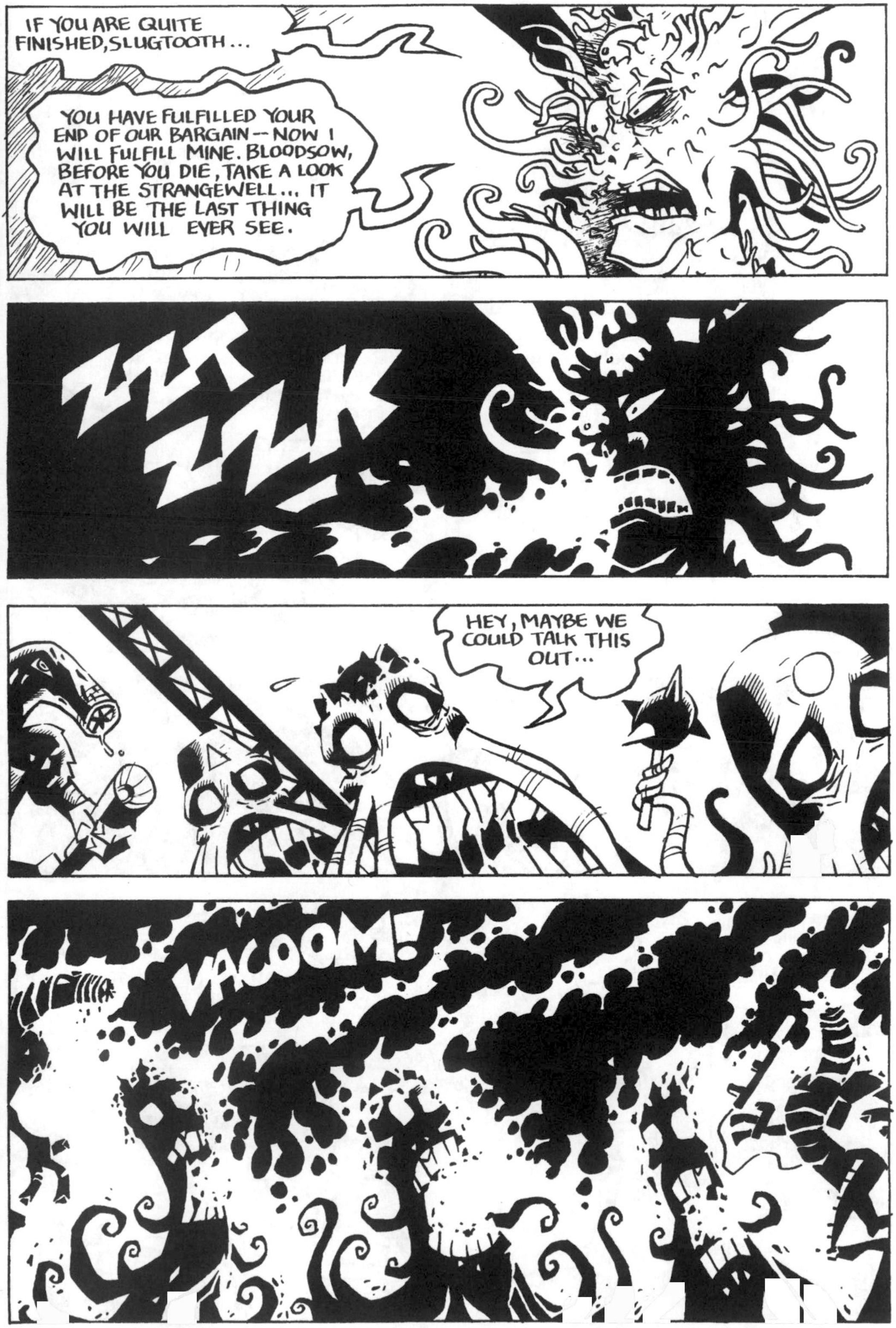

IF YOU ARE QUITE FINISHED, SLUGTOOTH...
YOU HAVE FULFILLED YOUR END OF OUR BARGAIN-- NOW I WILL FULFILL MINE. BLOODSOW, BEFORE YOU DIE, TAKE A LOOK AT THE STRANGEWELL... IT WILL BE THE LAST THING YOU WILL EVER SEE.
ZZT ZZK
HEY, MAYBE WE COULD TALK THIS OUT...
VACOOM!

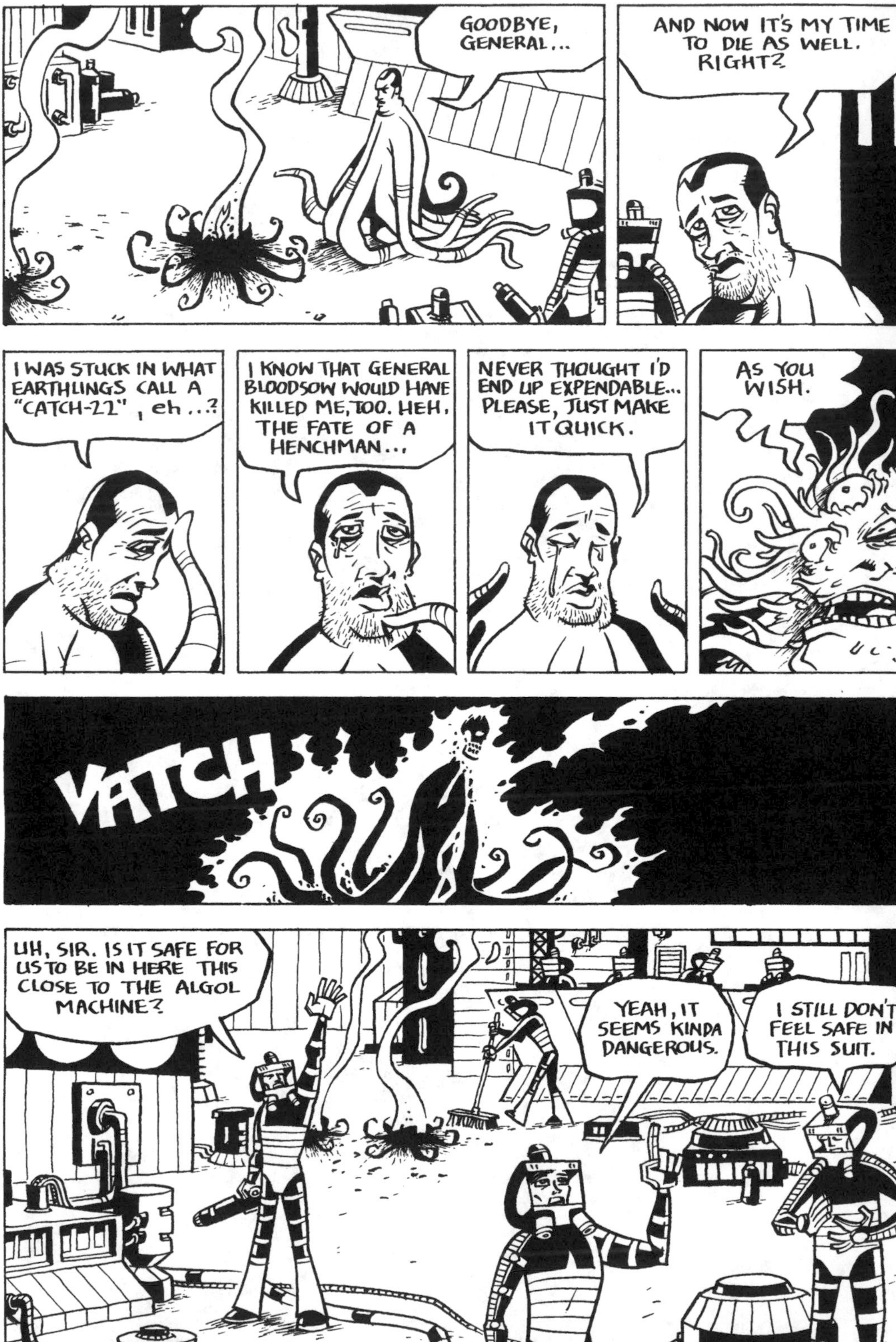
GOODBYE, GENERAL...
AND NOW IT'S MY TIME TO DIE AS WELL. RIGHT?
I WAS STUCK IN WHAT EARTHLINGS CALL A "CATCH-22", eh...?
I KNOW THAT GENERAL BLOODSOW WOULD HAVE KILLED ME, TOO. HEH. THE FATE OF A HENCHMAN...
NEVER THOUGHT I'D END UP EXPENDABLE... PLEASE, JUST MAKE IT QUICK.
AS YOU WISH.
VATCH
UH, SIR. IS IT SAFE FOR US TO BE IN HERE THIS CLOSE TO THE ALGOL MACHINE?
YEAH, IT SEEMS KINDA DANGEROUS.
I STILL DON'T FEEL SAFE IN THIS SUIT.

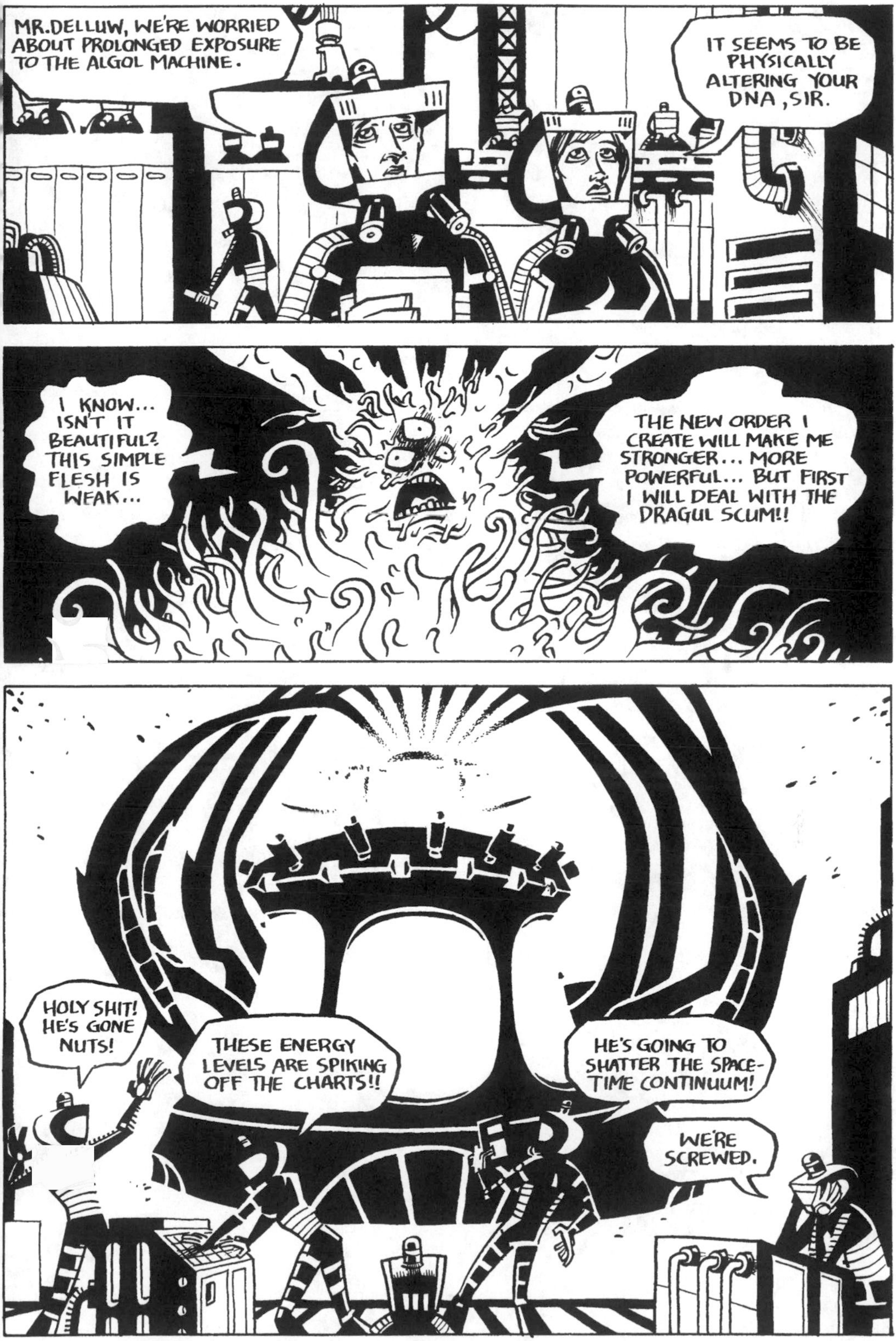
MR.DELLUW, WE'RE WORRIED ABOUT PROLONGED EXPOSURE TO THE ALGOL MACHINE.
IT SEEMS TO BE PHYSICALLY ALTERING YOUR DNA ,SIR.
I KNOW... ISN'T IT BEAUTIFUL? THIS SIMPLE FLESH IS WEAK...
THE NEW ORDER I CREATE WILL MAKE ME STRONGER... MORE POWERFUL... BUT FIRST I WILL DEAL WITH THE DRAGUL SCUM!!
HOLY SHIT! HE'S GONE NUTS!
THESE ENERGY LEVELS ARE SPIKING OFF THE CHARTS!!
HE'S GOING TO SHATTER THE SPACE-TIME CONTINUUM!
WE'RE SCREWED.

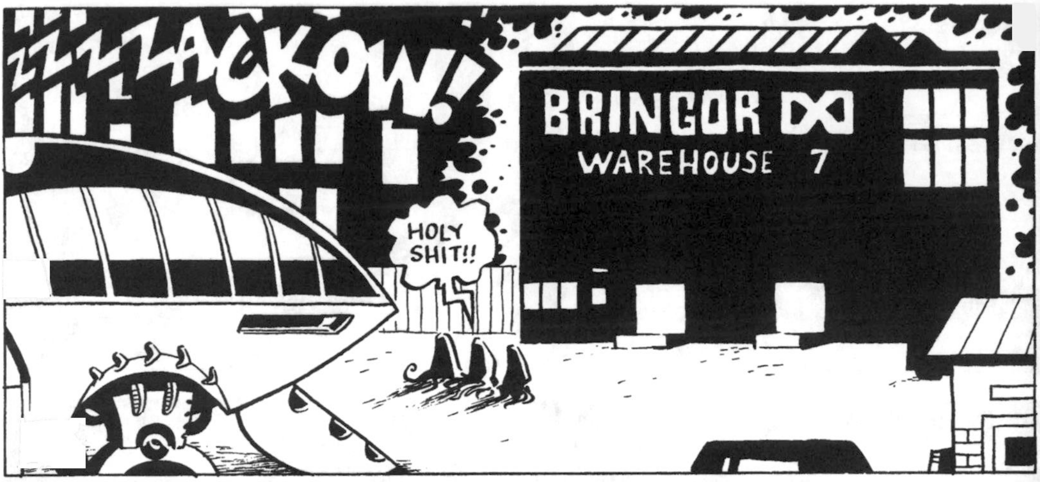
ZZZZZACKOW!!
BRINGOR
WAREHOUSE 7
HOLY SHIT!!

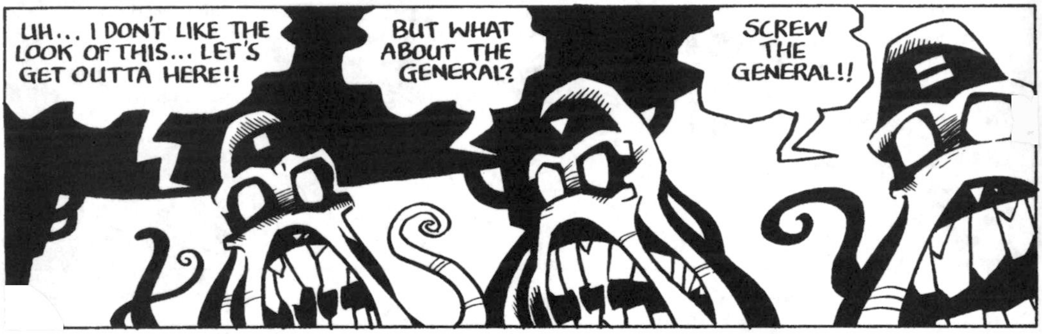
UH... I DON'T LIKE THE LOOK OF THIS... LET'S GET OUTTA HERE!!
BUT WHAT ABOUT THE GENERAL?
SCREW THE GENERAL!!

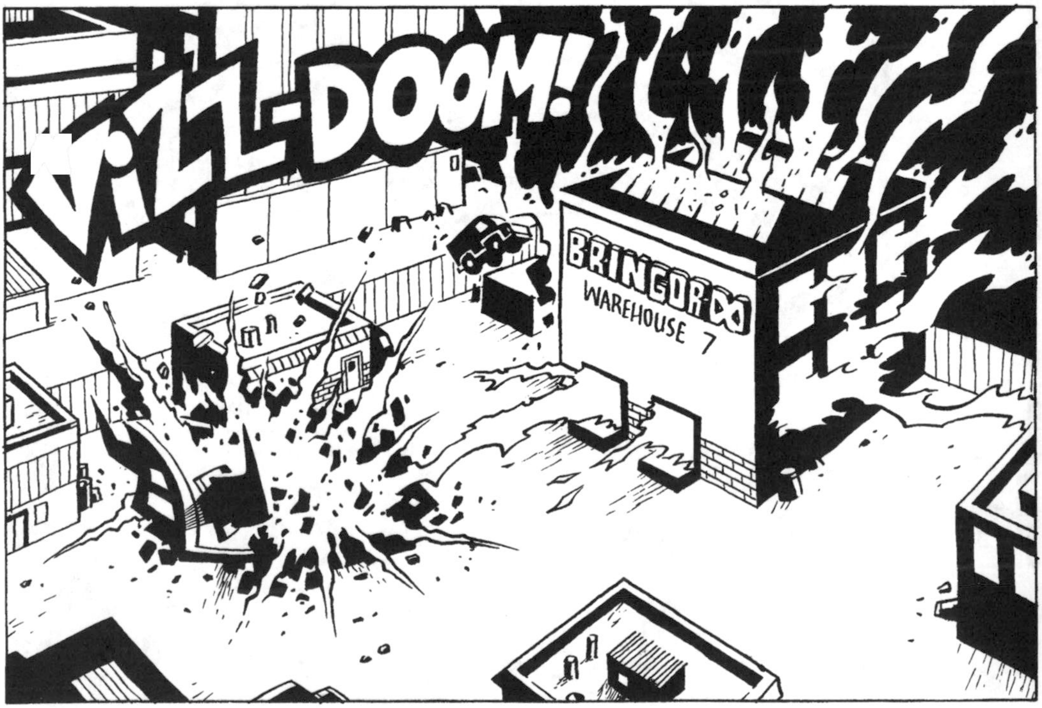
VIZZ-DOOM!
BRINGOR
WAREHOUSE 7

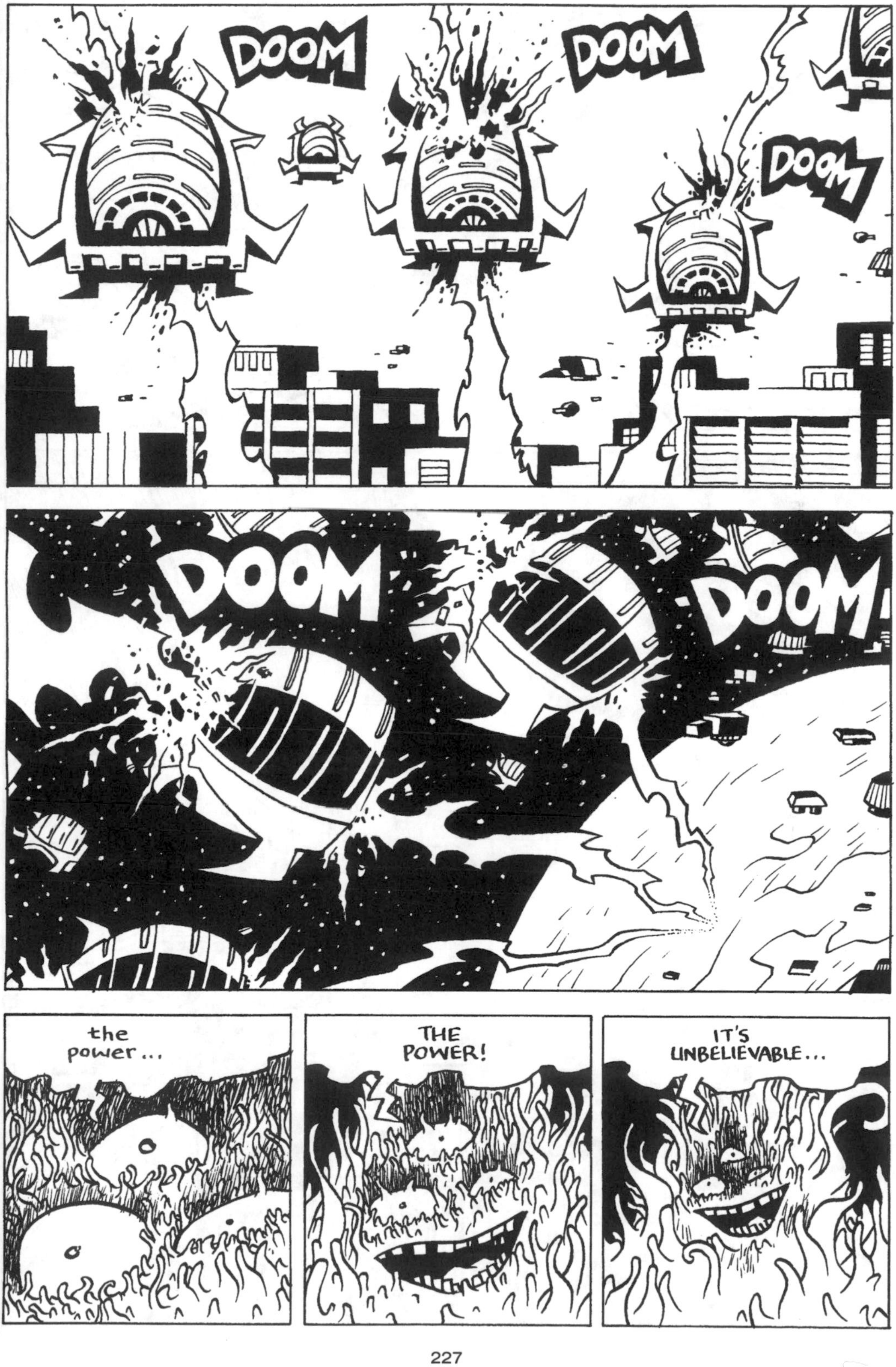
DOOM
DOOM
DOOM
DOOM
DOOM
the power...
THE POWER!
IT'S UNBELIEVABLE...

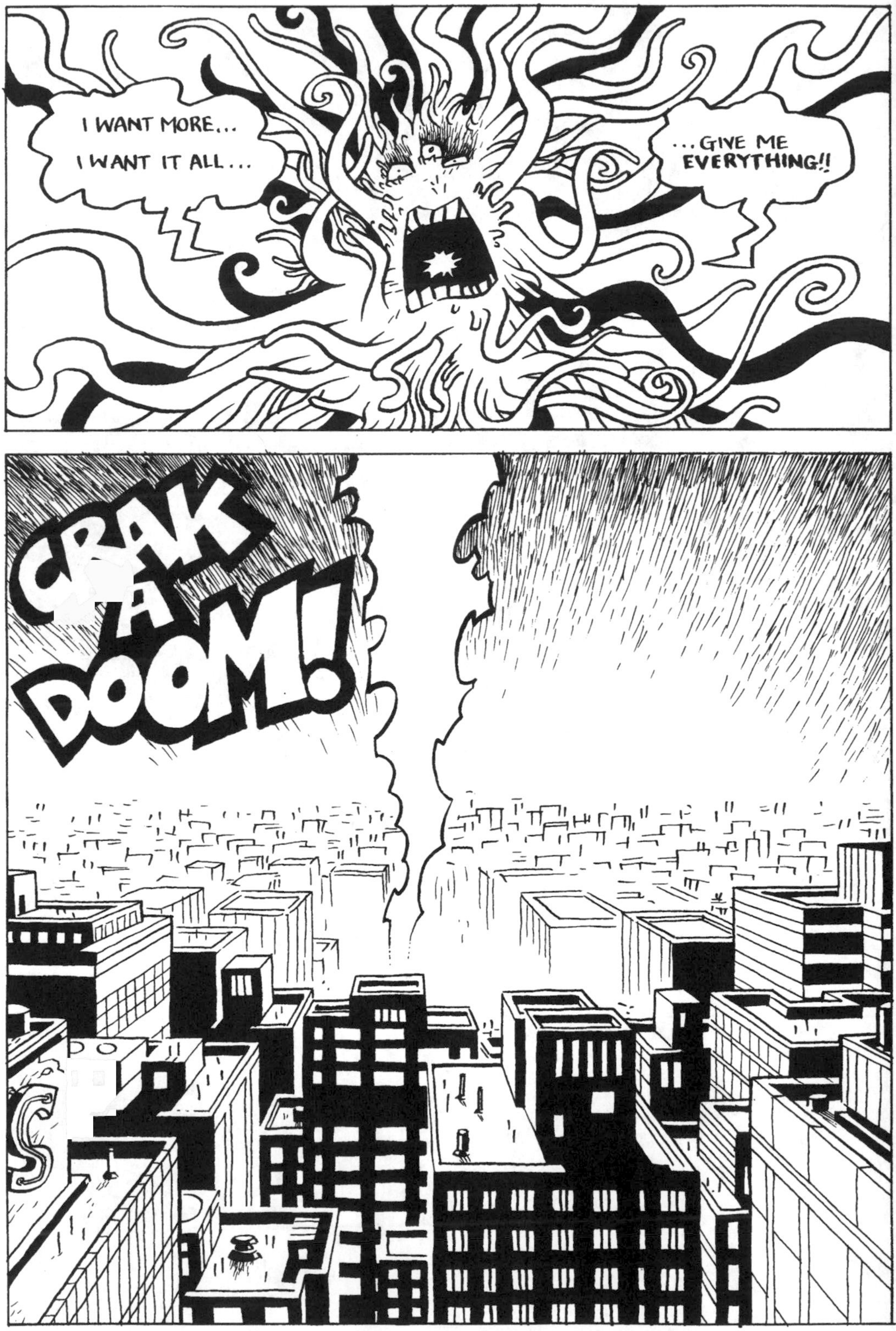
I WANT MORE...
I WANT IT ALL...
...GIVE ME **EVERYTHING!!**
CRAK A DOOM!

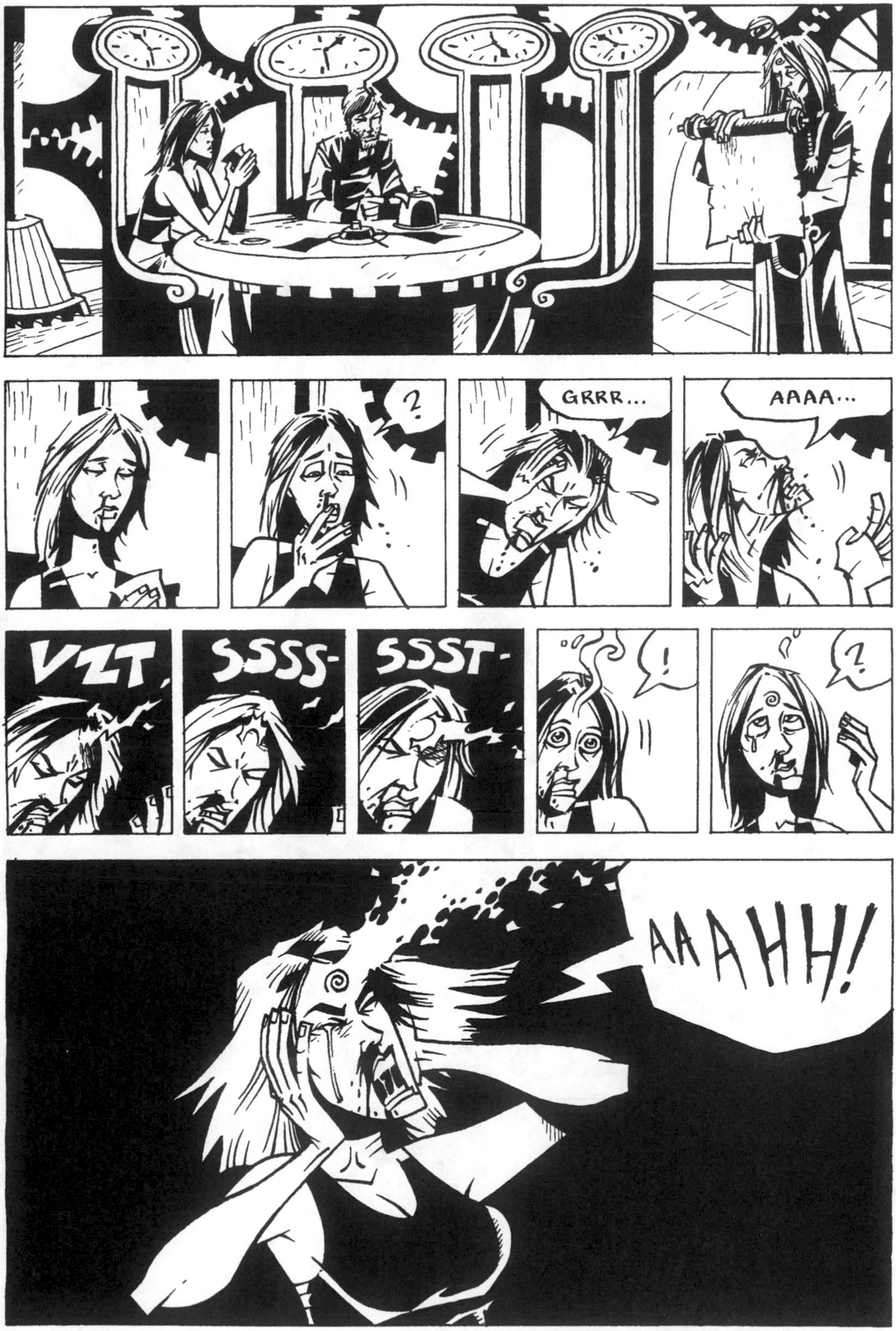
?
GRRR...
AAAA...
VZT
SSSS-
SSST-
!
?
AAAHH!

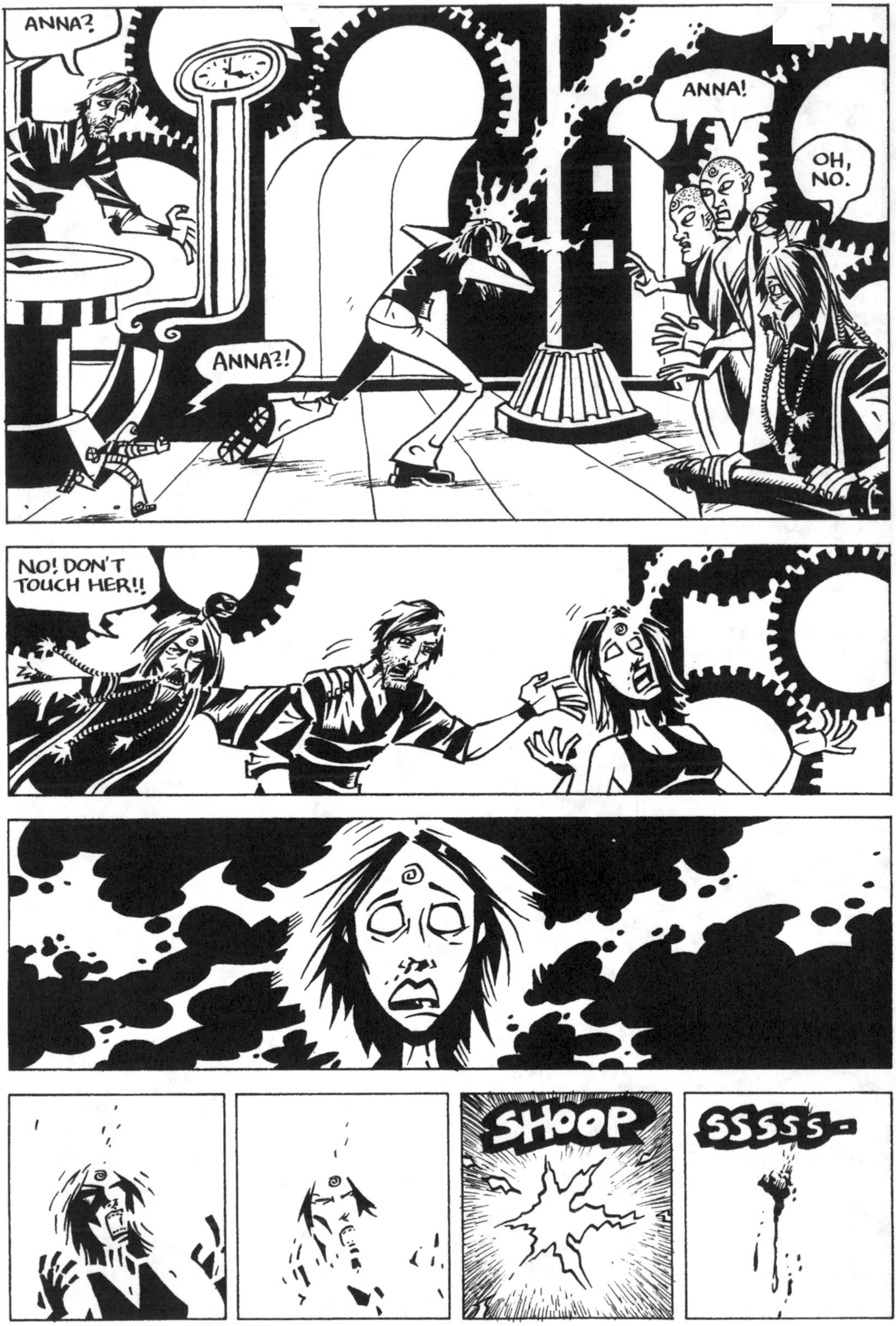
ANNA?
ANNA!
OH, NO.
ANNA?!
NO! DON'T TOUCH HER!!
SHOOP
SSSSS-

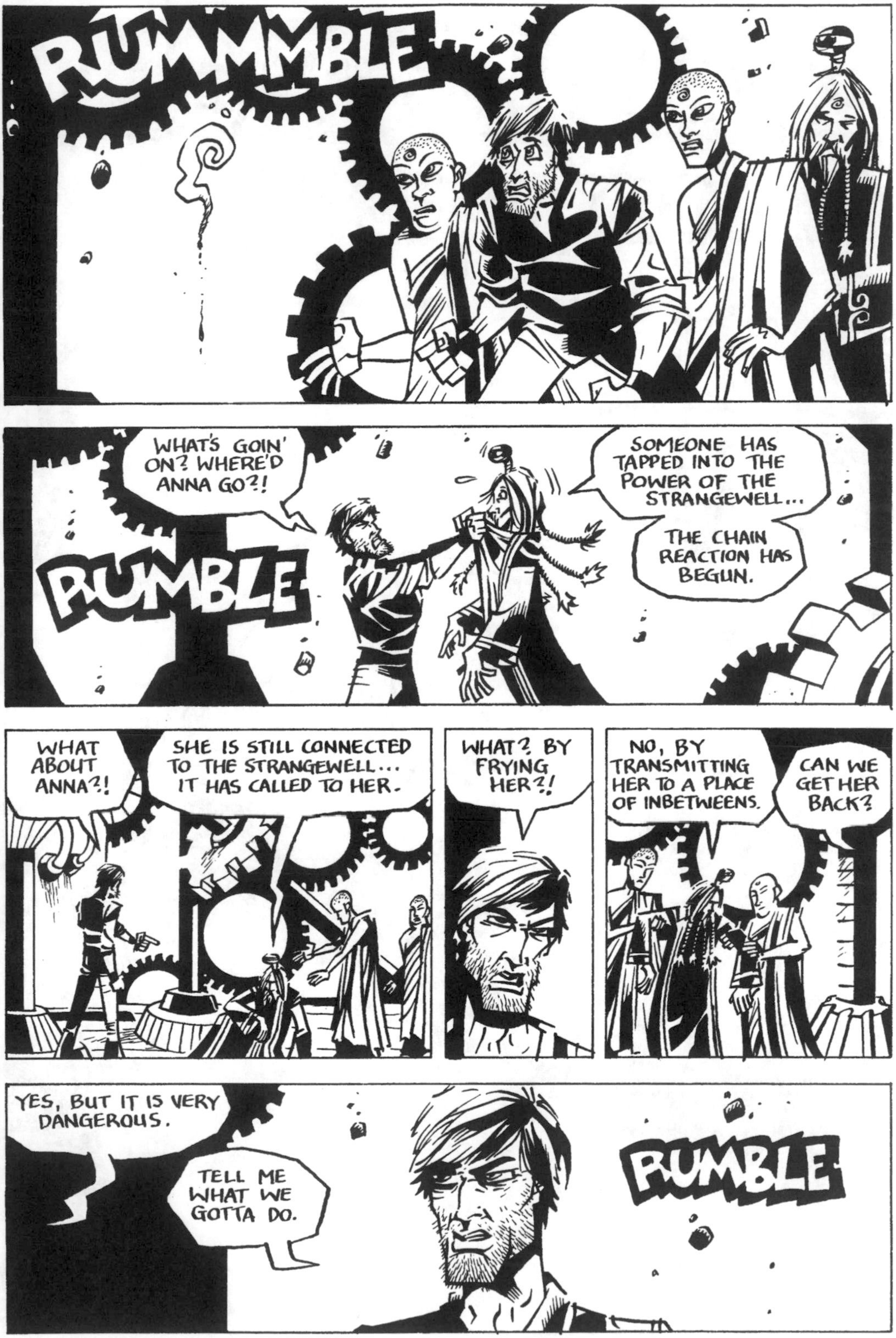
RUMMMBLE
WHAT'S GOIN' ON? WHERE'D ANNA GO?!
SOMEONE HAS TAPPED INTO THE POWER OF THE STRANGEWELL...
THE CHAIN REACTION HAS BEGUN.
RUMBLE
WHAT ABOUT ANNA?!
SHE IS STILL CONNECTED TO THE STRANGEWELL... IT HAS CALLED TO HER.
WHAT? BY FRYING HER?!
NO, BY TRANSMITTING HER TO A PLACE OF INBETWEENS.
CAN WE GET HER BACK?
YES, BUT IT IS VERY DANGEROUS.
TELL ME WHAT WE GOTTA DO.
RUMBLE

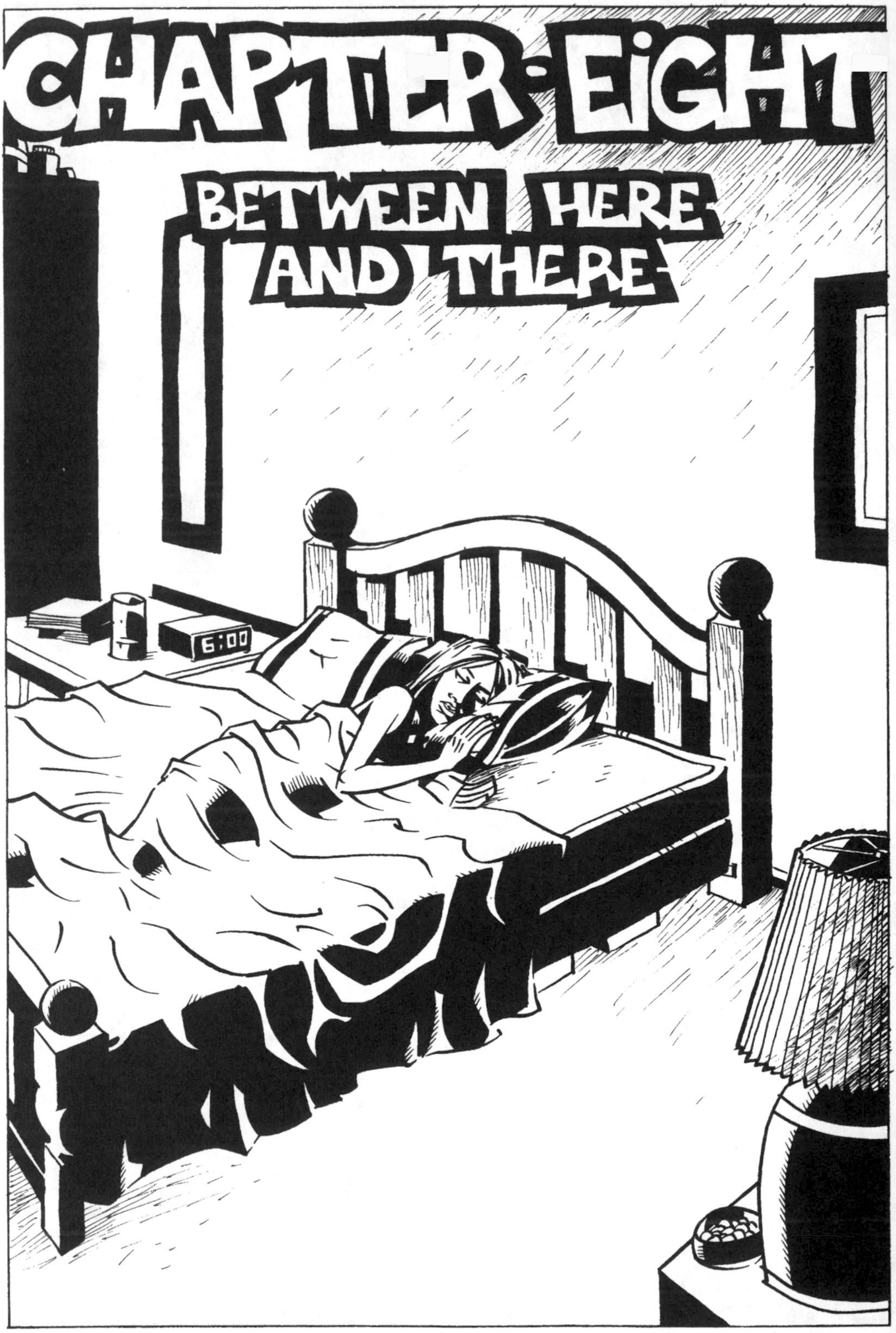
CHAPTER EIGHT
BETWEEN HERE AND THERE
6:00

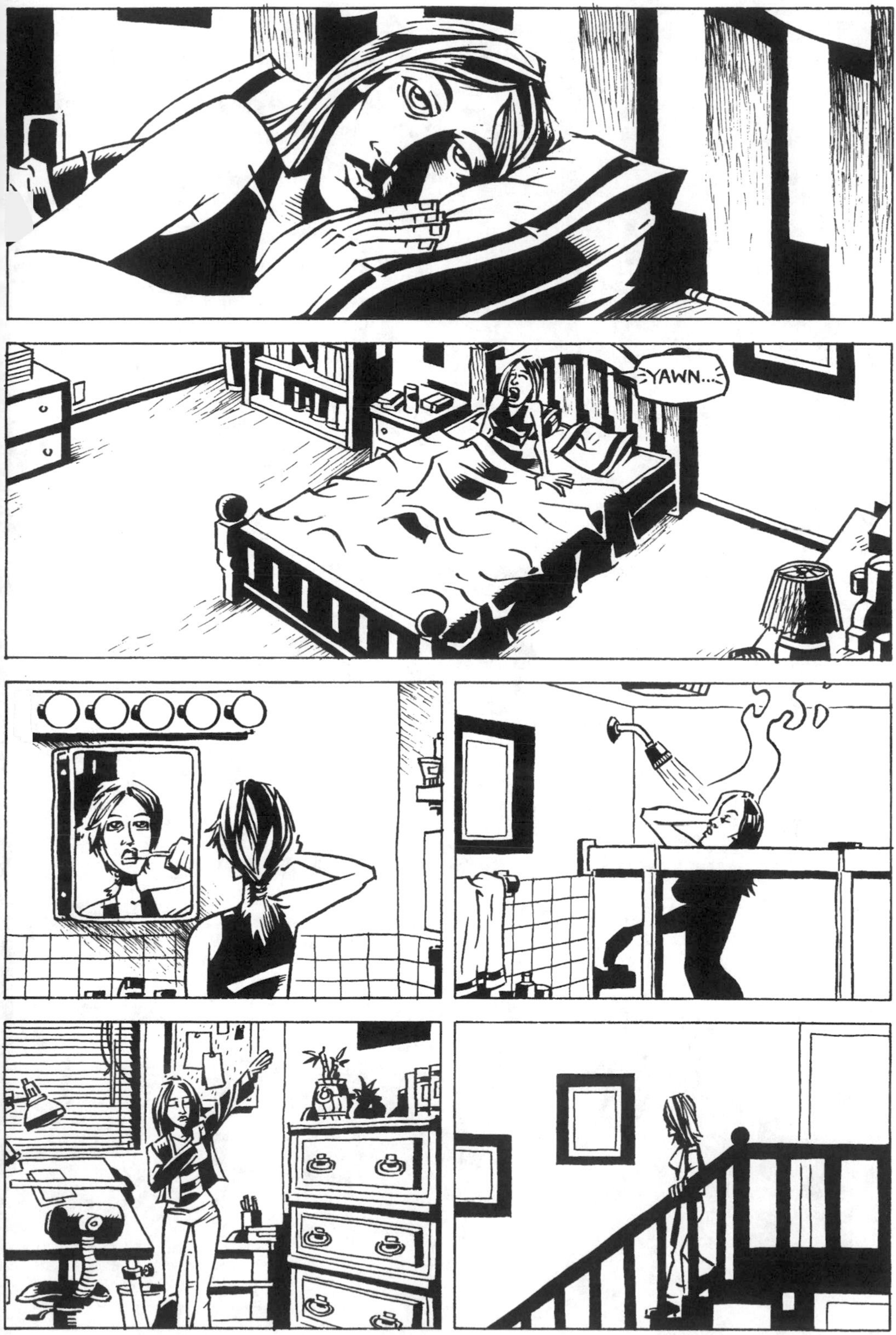
YAWN...

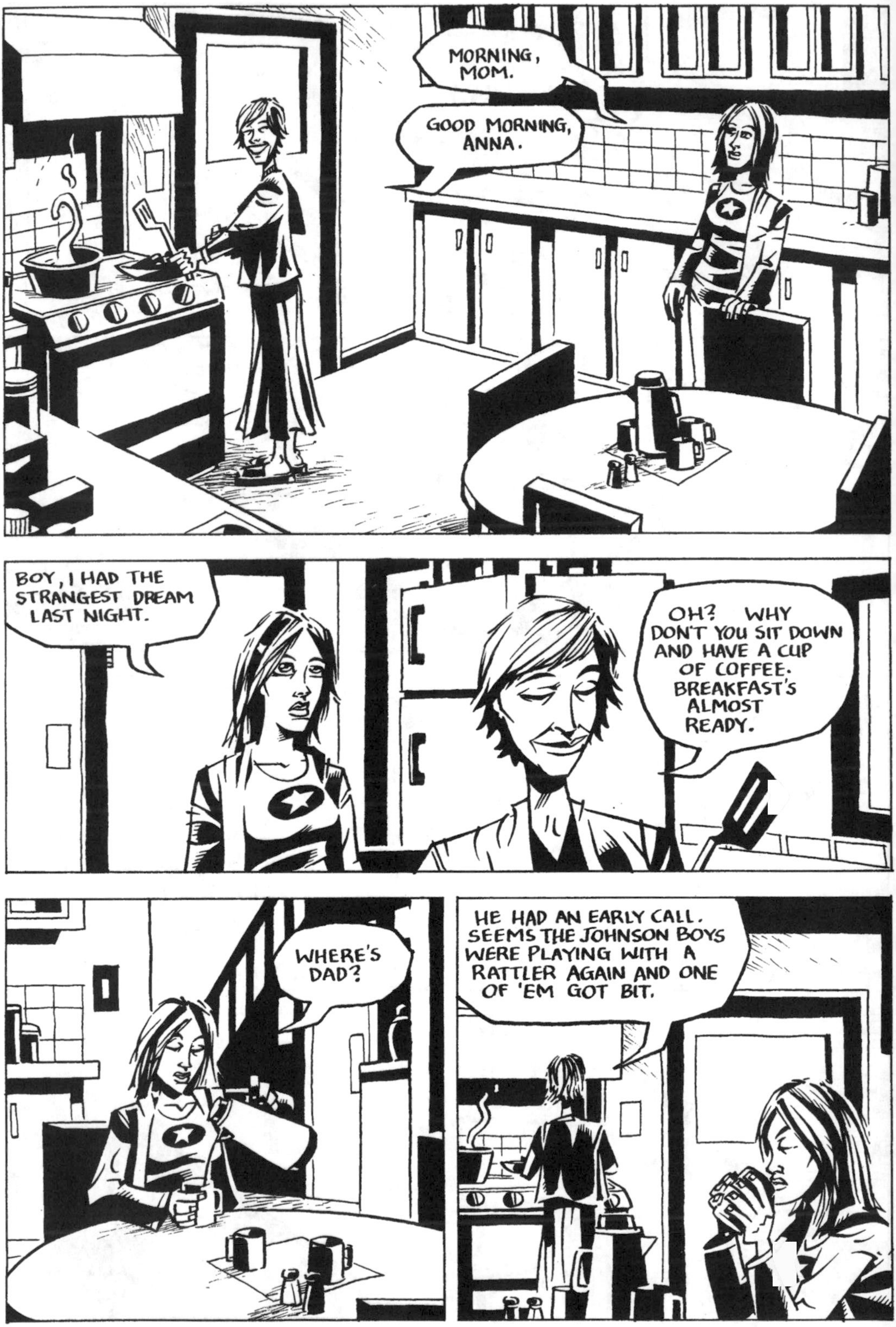
MORNING, MOM.
GOOD MORNING, ANNA.
BOY, I HAD THE STRANGEST DREAM LAST NIGHT.
OH? WHY DON'T YOU SIT DOWN AND HAVE A CUP OF COFFEE. BREAKFAST'S ALMOST READY.
WHERE'S DAD?
HE HAD AN EARLY CALL. SEEMS THE JOHNSON BOYS WERE PLAYING WITH A RATTLER AGAIN AND ONE OF 'EM GOT BIT.

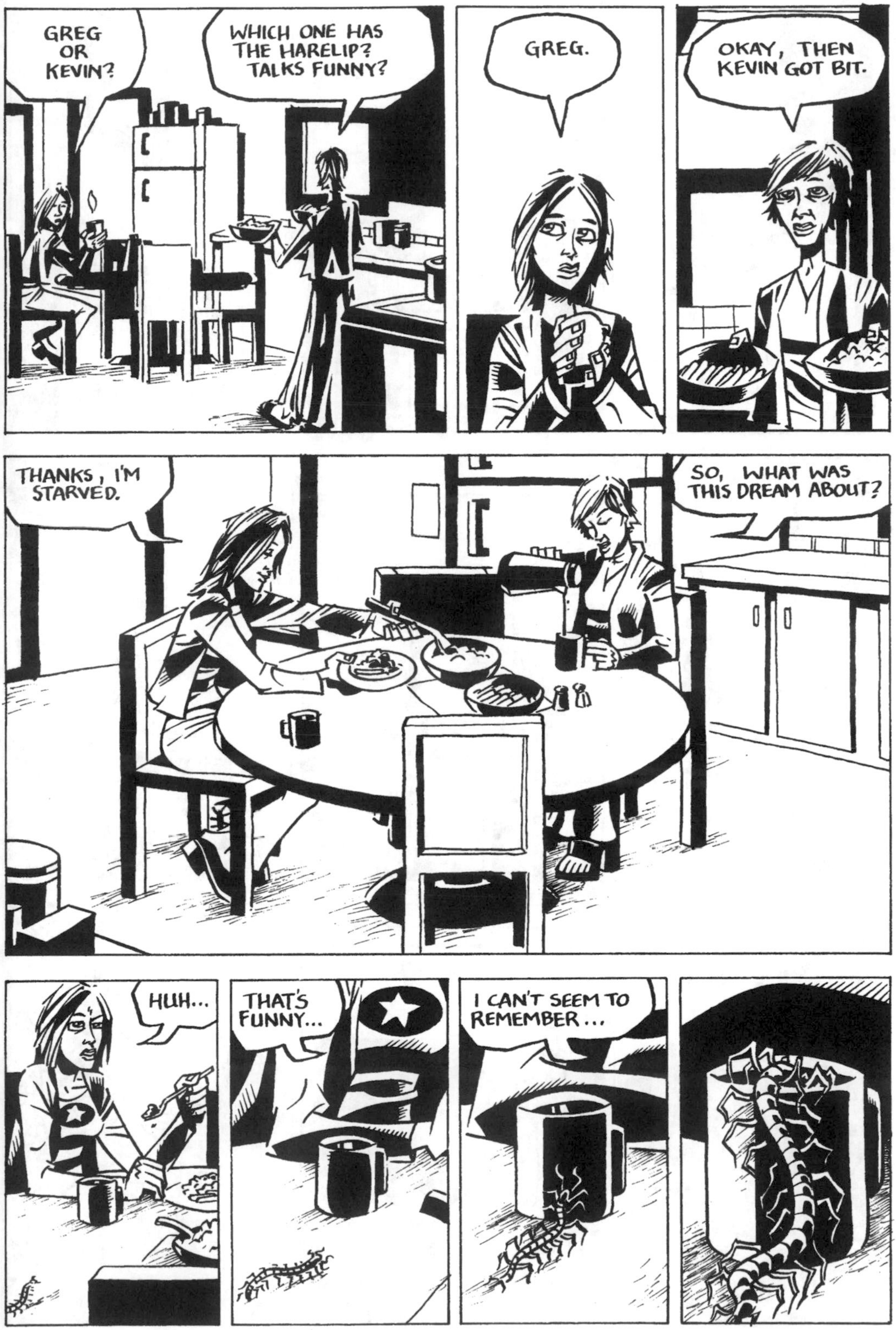
GREG OR KEVIN?
WHICH ONE HAS THE HARELIP? TALKS FUNNY?
GREG.
OKAY, THEN KEVIN GOT BIT.
THANKS, I'M STARVED.
SO, WHAT WAS THIS DREAM ABOUT?
HUH...
THAT'S FUNNY...
I CAN'T SEEM TO REMEMBER...

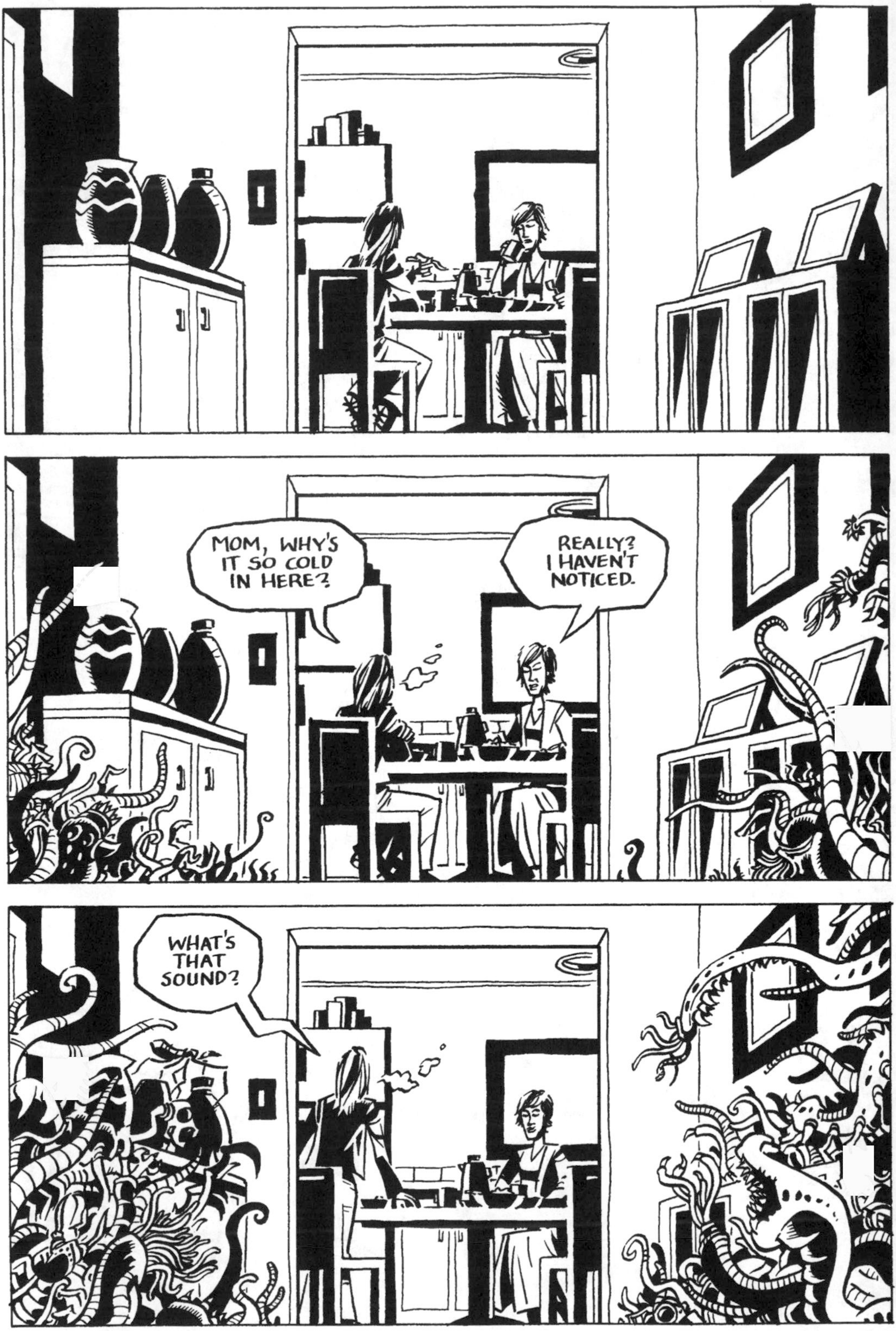
MOM, WHY'S IT SO COLD IN HERE?
REALLY? I HAVEN'T NOTICED.
WHAT'S THAT SOUND?

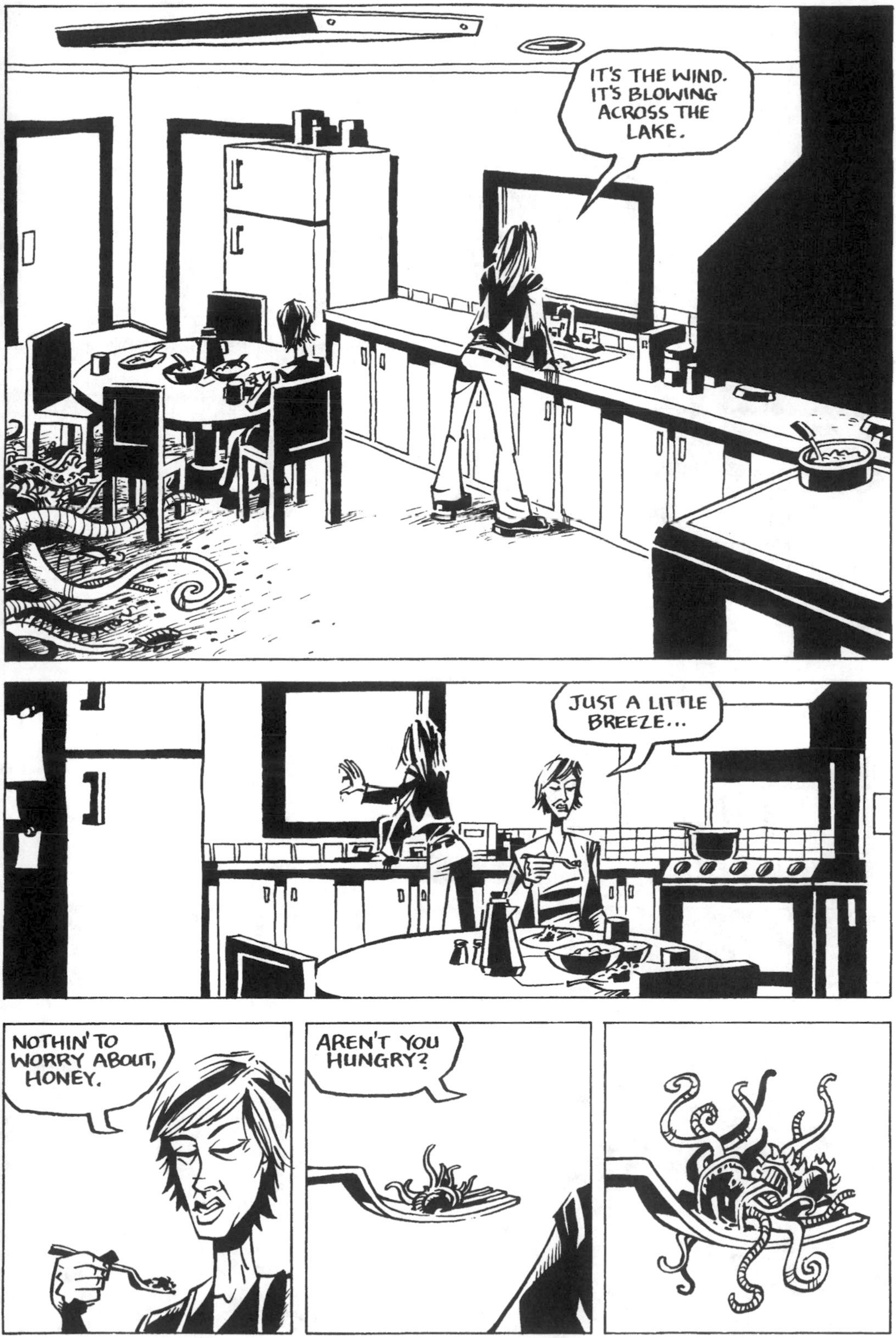
IT'S THE WIND. IT'S BLOWING ACROSS THE LAKE.
JUST A LITTLE BREEZE...
NOTHIN' TO WORRY ABOUT, HONEY.
AREN'T YOU HUNGRY?

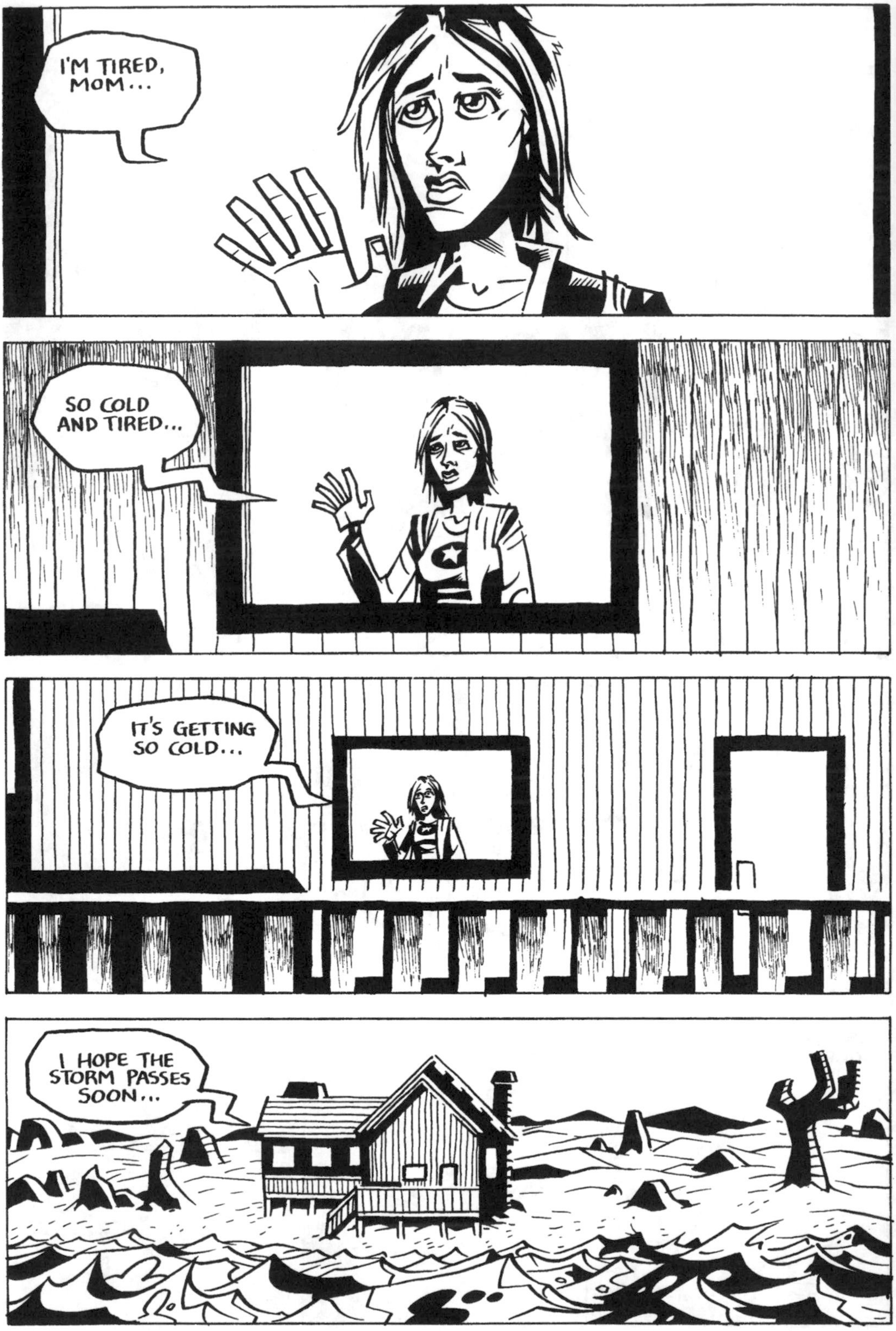
I'M TIRED, MOM...
SO COLD AND TIRED...
IT'S GETTING SO COLD...
I HOPE THE STORM PASSES SOON...

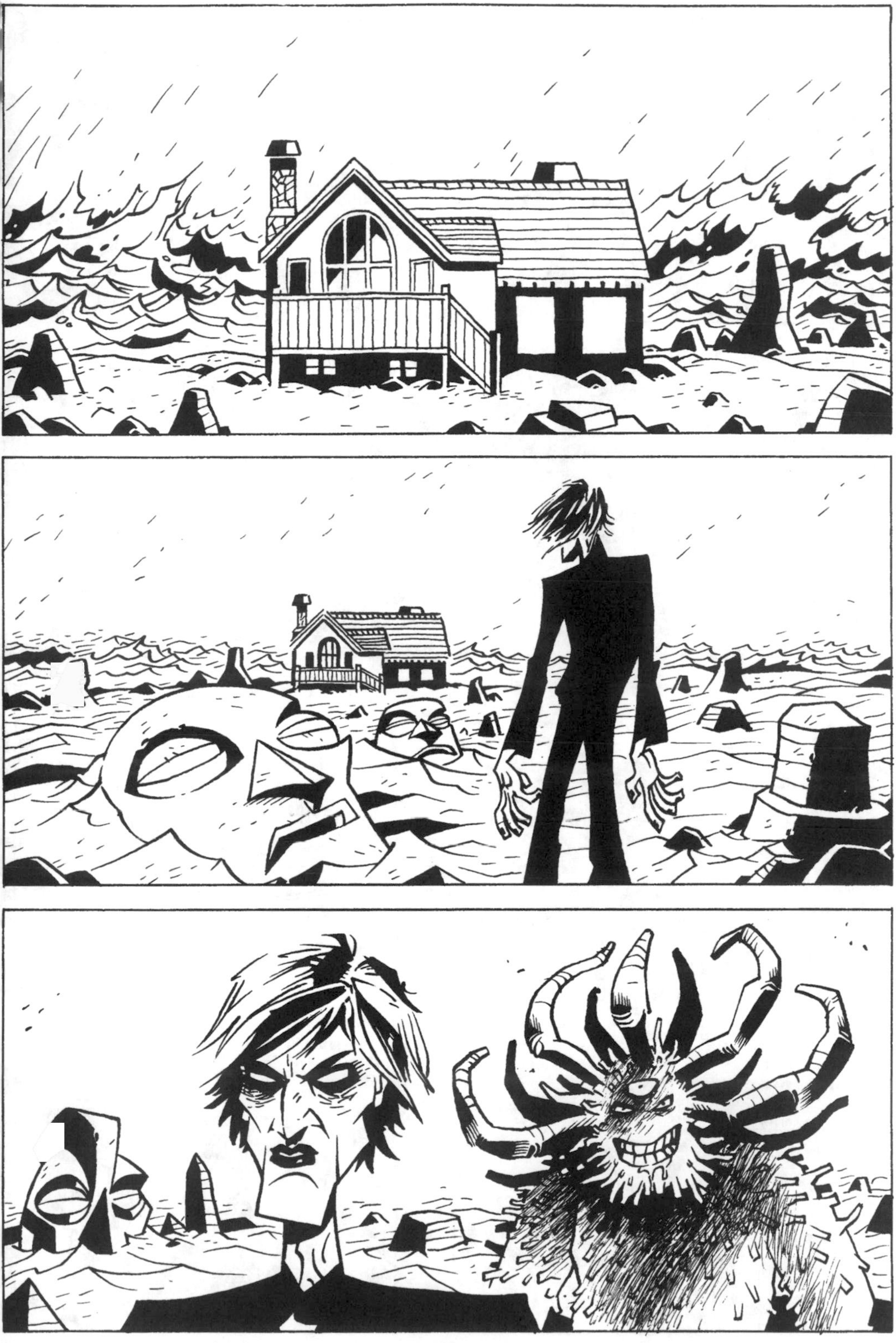

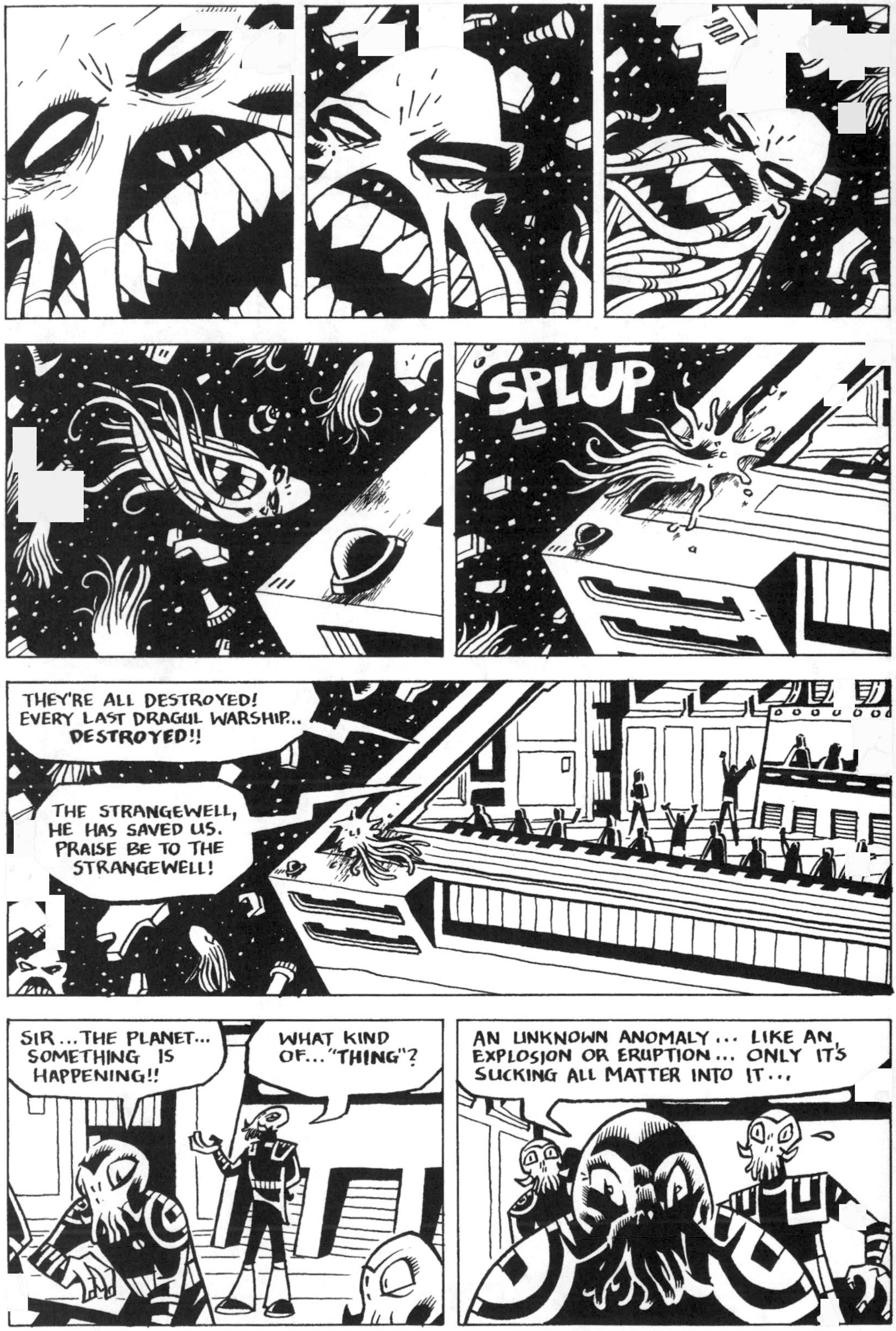
SPLUP
THEY'RE ALL DESTROYED! EVERY LAST DRAGUL WARSHIP... DESTROYED!!
THE STRANGEWELL, HE HAS SAVED US. PRAISE BE TO THE STRANGEWELL!
SIR... THE PLANET... SOMETHING IS HAPPENING!!
WHAT KIND OF... "THING"?
AN UNKNOWN ANOMALY... LIKE AN EXPLOSION OR ERUPTION... ONLY IT'S SUCKING ALL MATTER INTO IT...

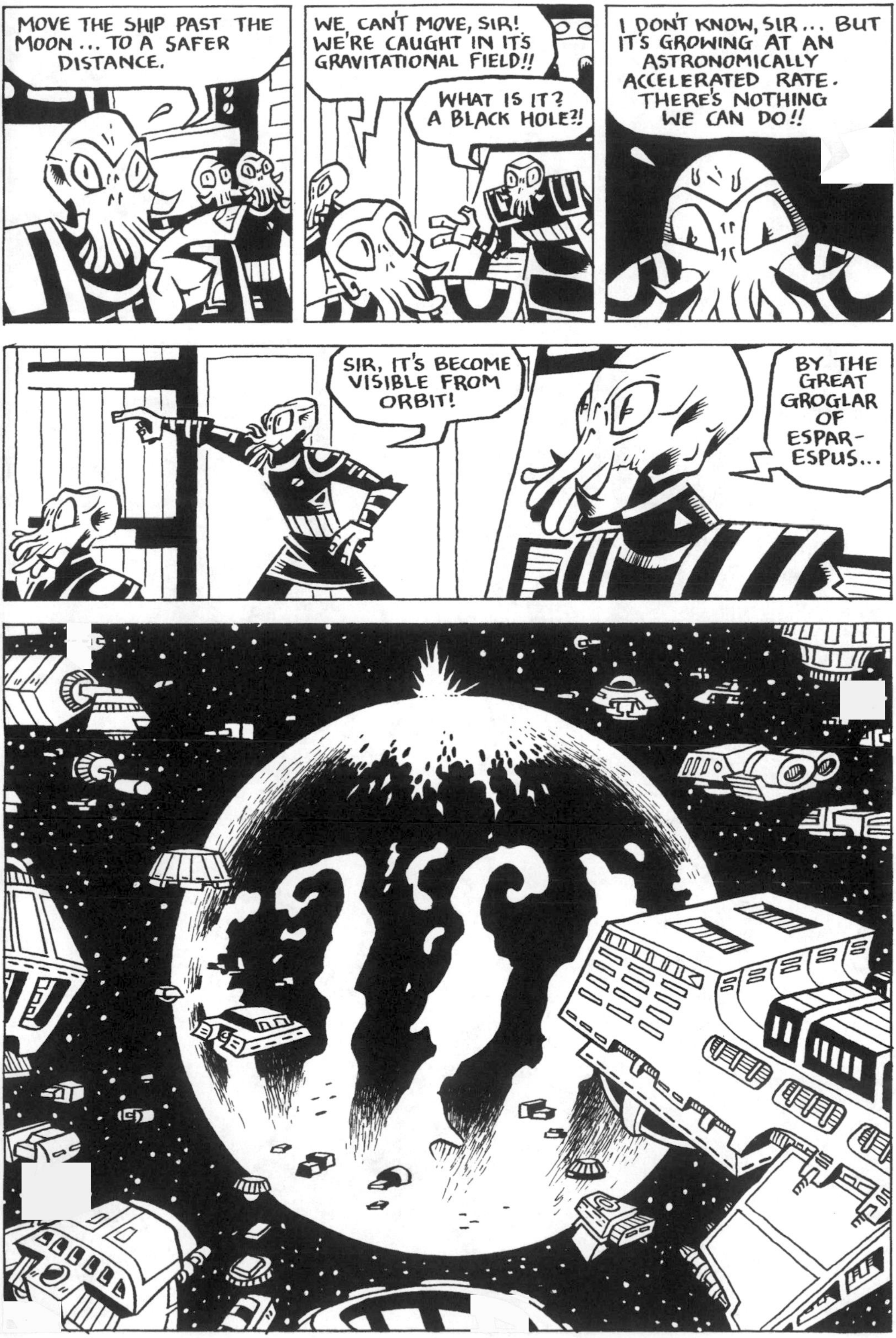
MOVE THE SHIP PAST THE MOON ... TO A SAFER DISTANCE.
WE CAN'T MOVE, SIR! WE'RE CAUGHT IN IT'S GRAVITATIONAL FIELD!!
WHAT IS IT? A BLACK HOLE?!
I DON'T KNOW, SIR ... BUT IT'S GROWING AT AN ASTRONOMICALLY ACCELERATED RATE. THERE'S NOTHING WE CAN DO!!
SIR, IT'S BECOME VISIBLE FROM ORBIT!
BY THE GREAT GROGLAR OF ESPAR-ESPUS...

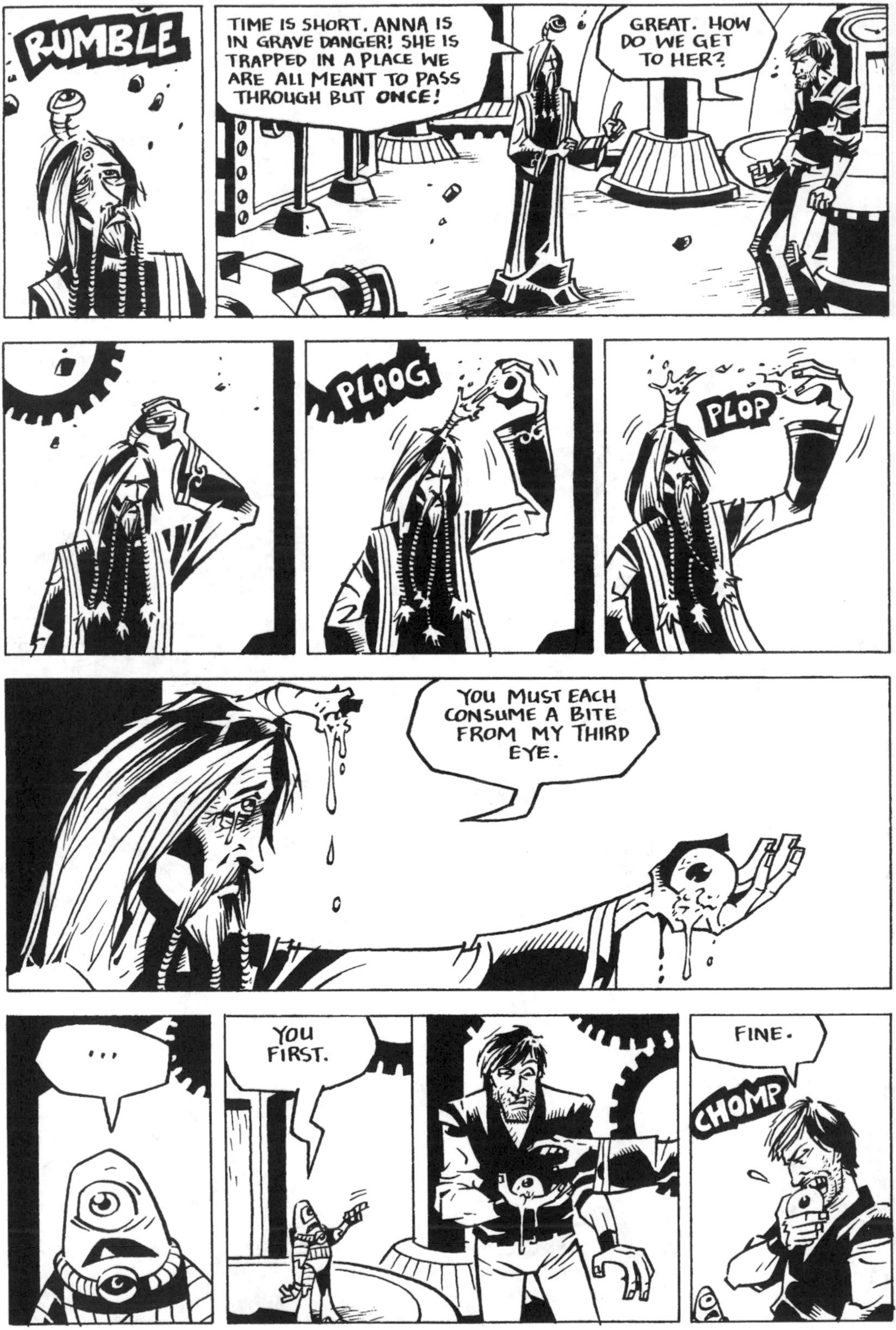
RUMBLE
TIME IS SHORT. ANNA IS IN GRAVE DANGER! SHE IS TRAPPED IN A PLACE WE ARE ALL MEANT TO PASS THROUGH BUT ONCE!
GREAT. HOW DO WE GET TO HER?
PLOOG
PLOP
YOU MUST EACH CONSUME A BITE FROM MY THIRD EYE.
...
YOU FIRST.
FINE.
CHOMP

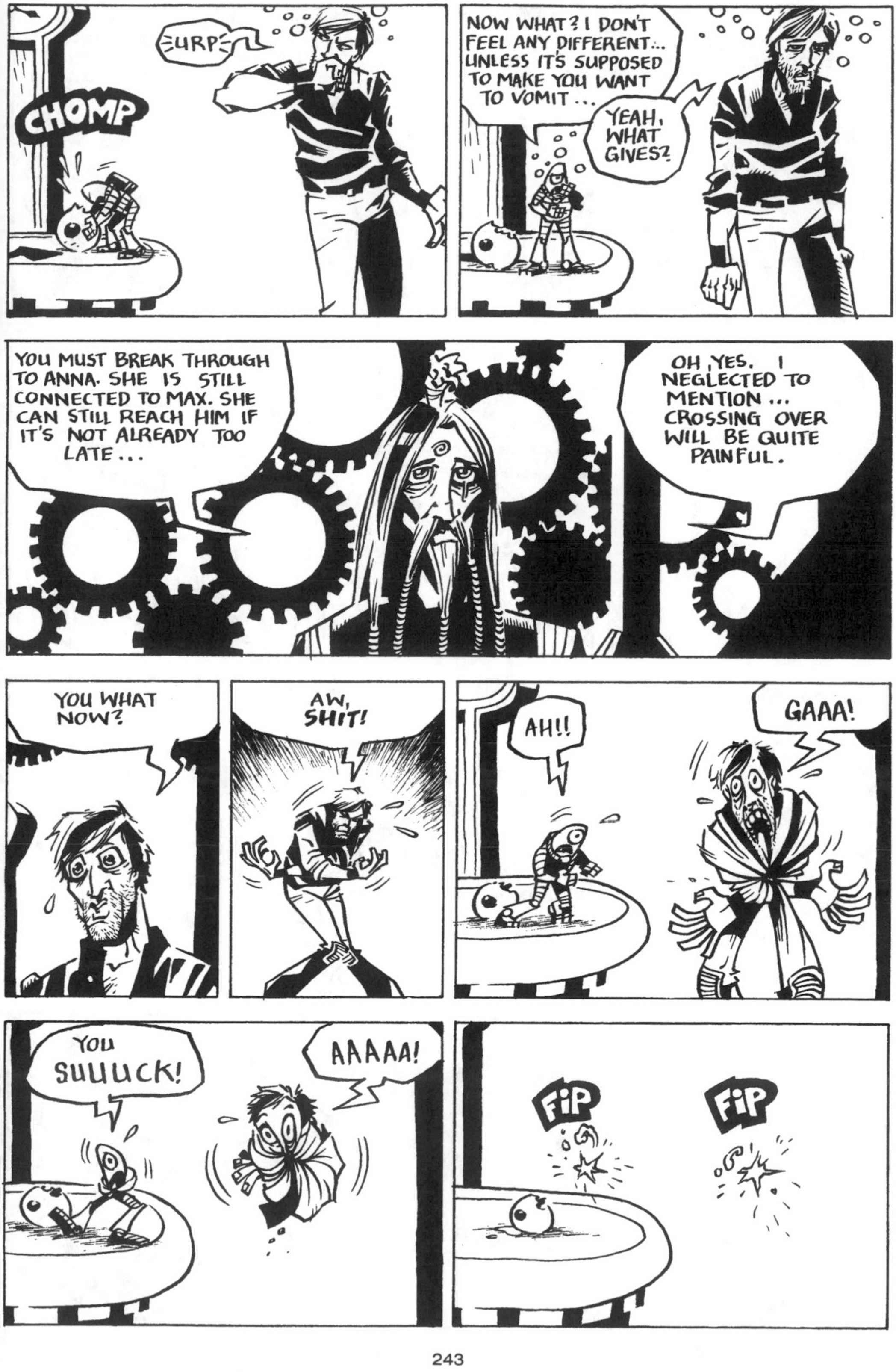
URP
CHOMP
NOW WHAT? I DON'T FEEL ANY DIFFERENT... UNLESS IT'S SUPPOSED TO MAKE YOU WANT TO VOMIT...
YEAH, WHAT GIVES?
YOU MUST BREAK THROUGH TO ANNA. SHE IS STILL CONNECTED TO MAX. SHE CAN STILL REACH HIM IF IT'S NOT ALREADY TOO LATE...
OH, YES. I NEGLECTED TO MENTION... CROSSING OVER WILL BE QUITE PAINFUL.
YOU WHAT NOW?
AW, SHIT!
AH!!
GAAA!
YOU SUUUCK!
AAAAA!
FIP
FIP

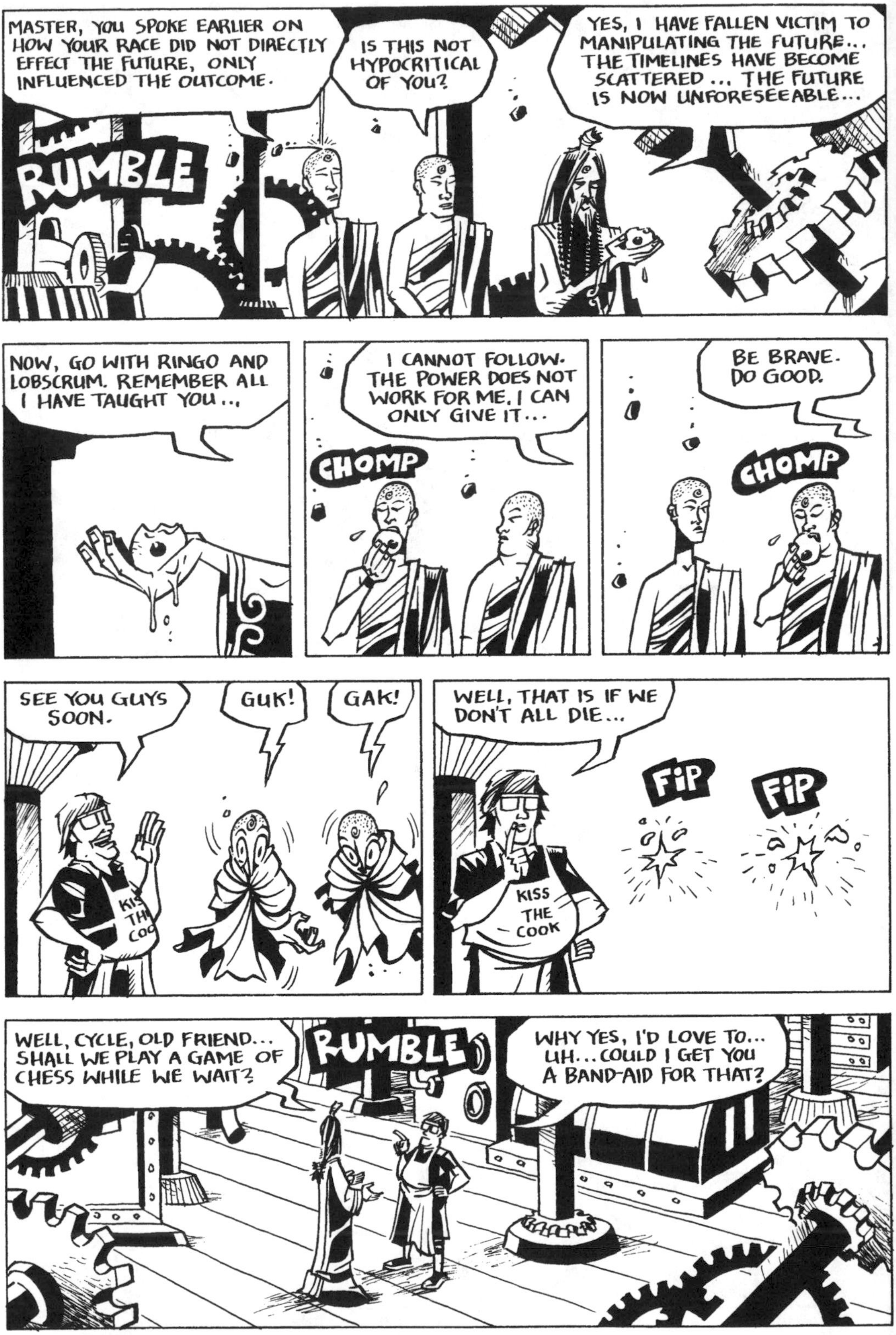

MASTER, YOU SPOKE EARLIER ON HOW YOUR RACE DID NOT DIRECTLY EFFECT THE FUTURE, ONLY INFLUENCED THE OUTCOME.
IS THIS NOT HYPOCRITICAL OF YOU?
RUMBLE
YES, I HAVE FALLEN VICTIM TO MANIPULATING THE FUTURE... THE TIMELINES HAVE BECOME SCATTERED ... THE FUTURE IS NOW UNFORESEEABLE...
NOW, GO WITH RINGO AND LOBSCRUM. REMEMBER ALL I HAVE TAUGHT YOU...
I CANNOT FOLLOW. THE POWER DOES NOT WORK FOR ME. I CAN ONLY GIVE IT...
CHOMP
BE BRAVE. DO GOOD.
CHOMP
SEE YOU GUYS SOON.
GUK!
GAK!
KISS THE COOK
WELL, THAT IS IF WE DON'T ALL DIE...
KISS THE COOK
FIP
FIP
WELL, CYCLE, OLD FRIEND... SHALL WE PLAY A GAME OF CHESS WHILE WE WAIT?
RUMBLE
WHY YES, I'D LOVE TO... UH... COULD I GET YOU A BAND-AID FOR THAT?

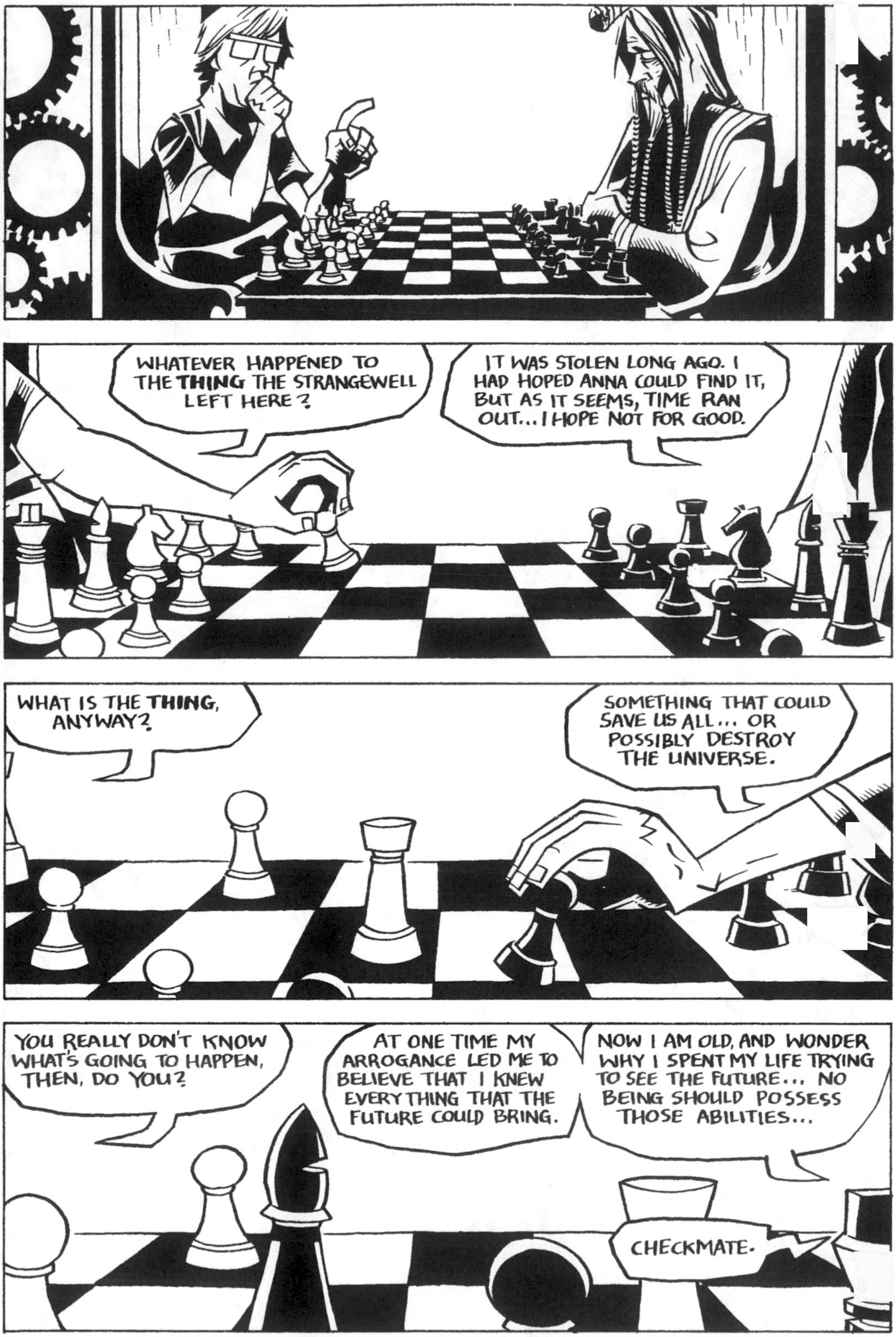
WHATEVER HAPPENED TO THE THING THE STRANGEWELL LEFT HERE?
IT WAS STOLEN LONG AGO. I HAD HOPED ANNA COULD FIND IT, BUT AS IT SEEMS, TIME RAN OUT... I HOPE NOT FOR GOOD.
WHAT IS THE THING, ANYWAY?
SOMETHING THAT COULD SAVE US ALL... OR POSSIBLY DESTROY THE UNIVERSE.
YOU REALLY DON'T KNOW WHAT'S GOING TO HAPPEN, THEN, DO YOU?
AT ONE TIME MY ARROGANCE LED ME TO BELIEVE THAT I KNEW EVERYTHING THAT THE FUTURE COULD BRING.
NOW I AM OLD, AND WONDER WHY I SPENT MY LIFE TRYING TO SEE THE FUTURE... NO BEING SHOULD POSSESS THOSE ABILITIES...
CHECKMATE.

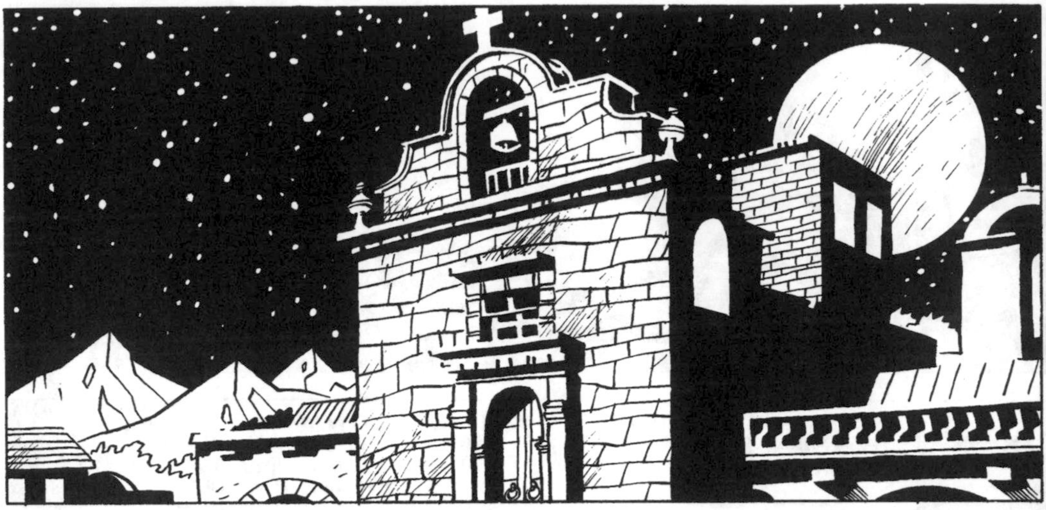

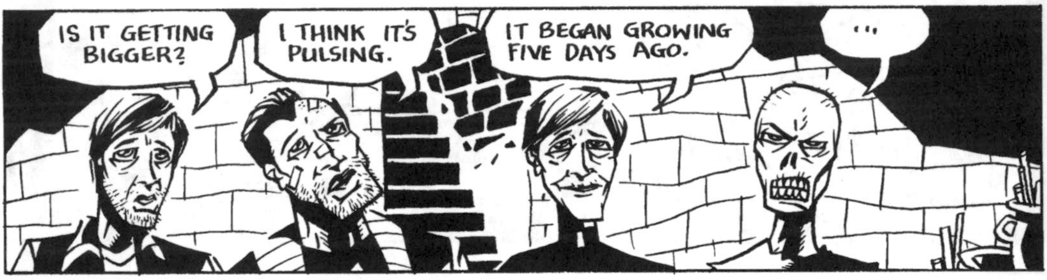
IS IT GETTING BIGGER?
I THINK IT'S PULSING.
IT BEGAN GROWING FIVE DAYS AGO.
...

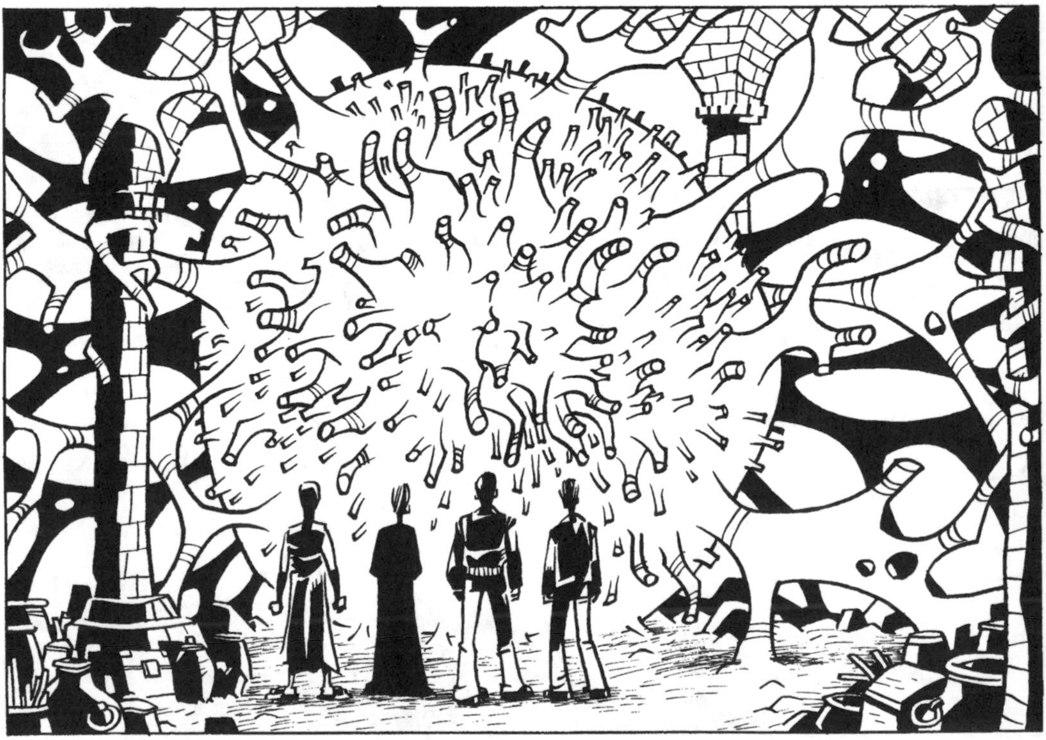

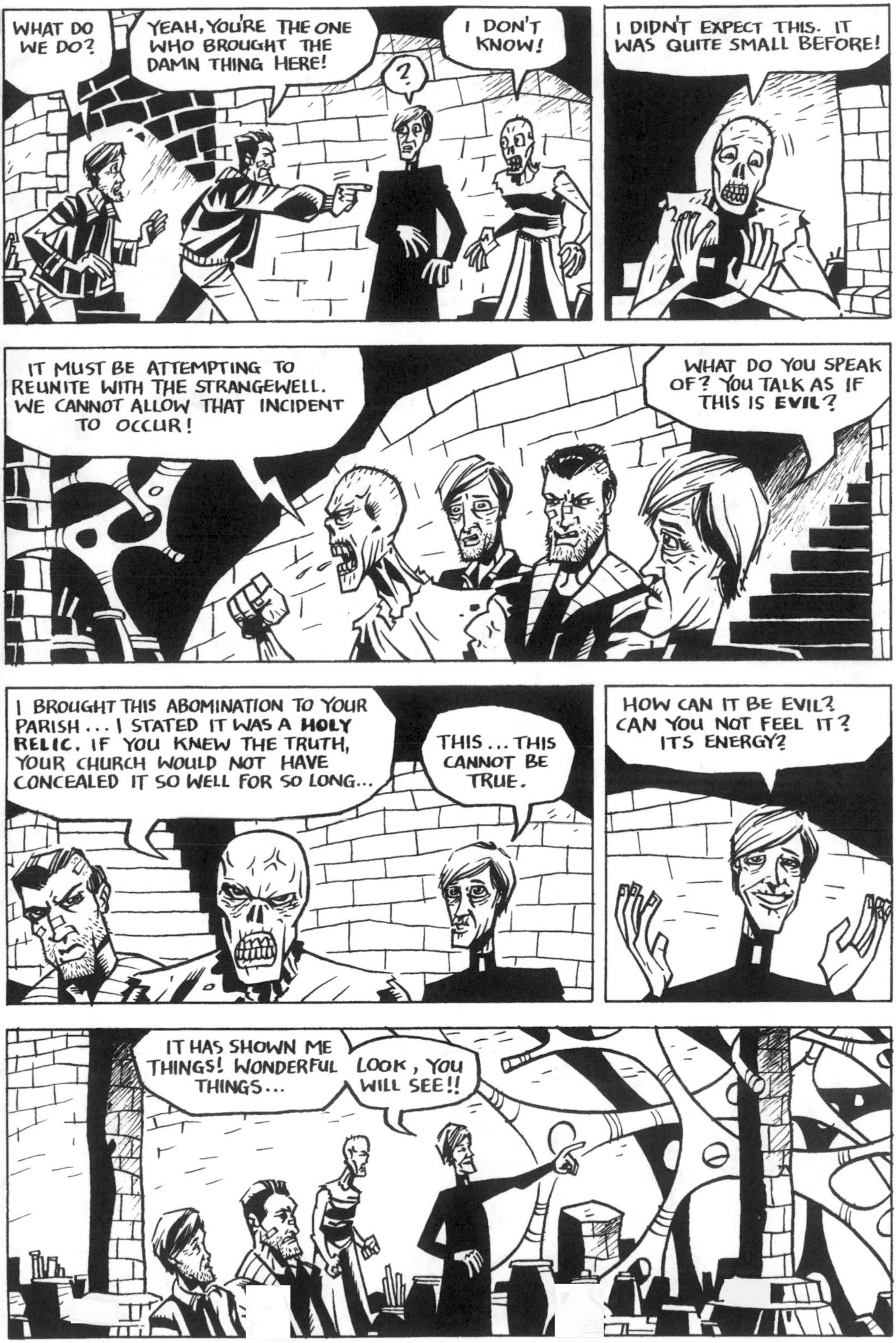
WHAT DO WE DO?
YEAH, YOU'RE THE ONE WHO BROUGHT THE DAMN THING HERE!
?
I DON'T KNOW!
I DIDN'T EXPECT THIS. IT WAS QUITE SMALL BEFORE!
IT MUST BE ATTEMPTING TO REUNITE WITH THE STRANGEWELL. WE CANNOT ALLOW THAT INCIDENT TO OCCUR!
WHAT DO YOU SPEAK OF? YOU TALK AS IF THIS IS EVIL?
I BROUGHT THIS ABOMINATION TO YOUR PARISH... I STATED IT WAS A HOLY RELIC. IF YOU KNEW THE TRUTH, YOUR CHURCH WOULD NOT HAVE CONCEALED IT SO WELL FOR SO LONG...
THIS... THIS CANNOT BE TRUE.
HOW CAN IT BE EVIL? CAN YOU NOT FEEL IT? ITS ENERGY?
IT HAS SHOWN ME THINGS! WONDERFUL THINGS...
LOOK, YOU WILL SEE!!

WHAT'S IT DOING?

DON'T BE ALARMED. IT WON'T HURT YOU...

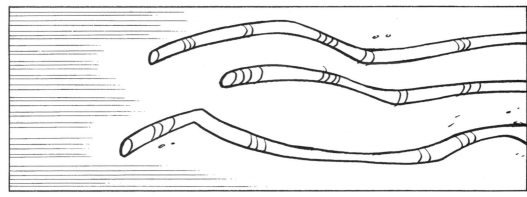

BOK

BOK

BOK

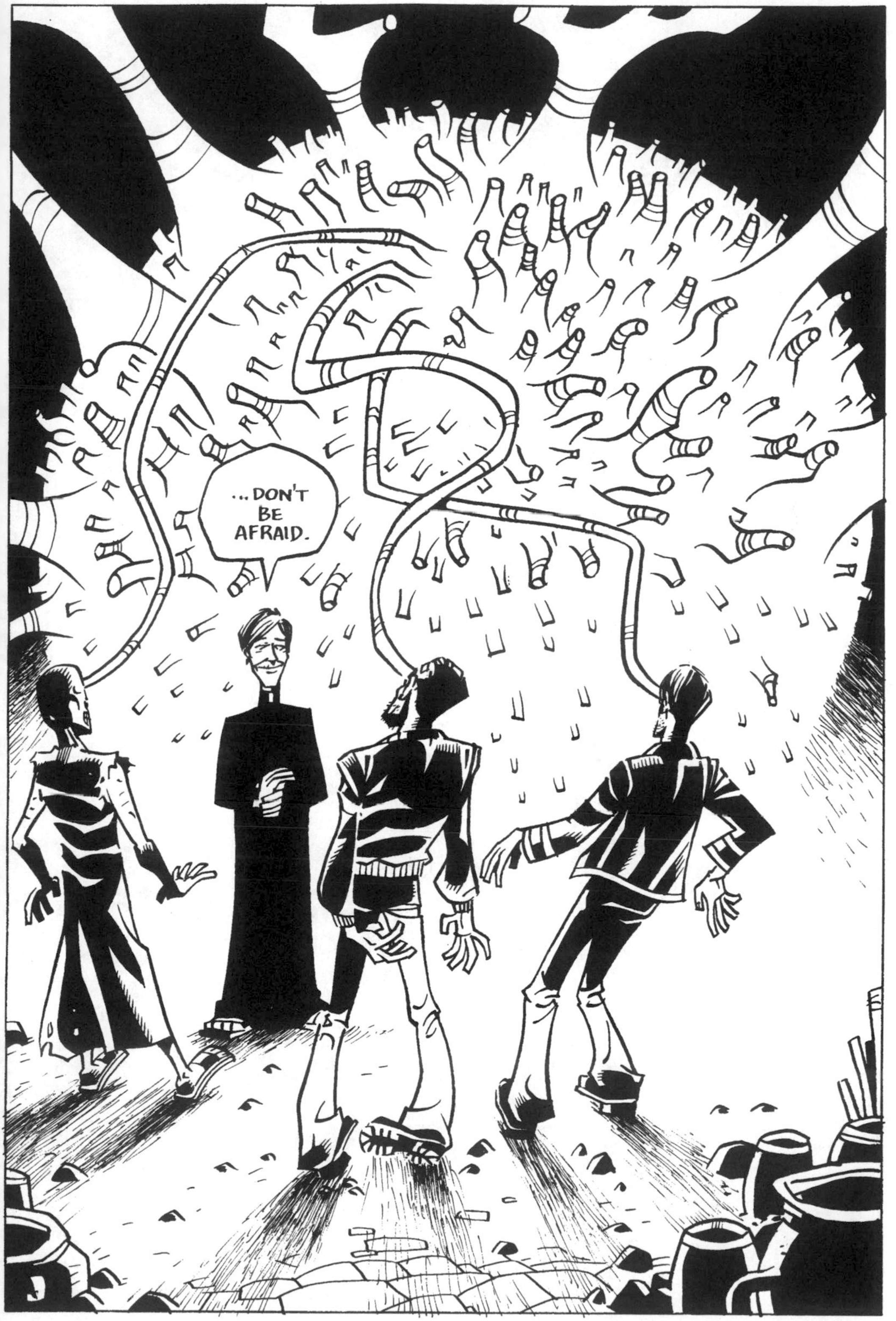
...DON'T BE AFRAID.

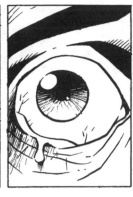

WHAT AN ADORABLE BABY! AND HIS NAME IS--

PAUL! STOP LEAVING YOUR TOYS OUT. YOU'RE A BIG BOY NOW, YOU--

GONNA START CRYING NOW? HUH? I'D--

LOVE TO GO TO HOMECOMING WITH YOU, PAUL. I'VE BEEN WAITING--

FOR A MEDIC FOR HOURS NOW! IT'S ABOUT GODDAMN TIME YOUR--

GOING TO BE A DOCTOR? AND YOU THINK THAT WILL IMPRESS ME? YOU KNOW, OF COURSE--

I'LL MARRY YOU, PAUL! I'M SO HAPPY. IT'S WHAT I'VE ALWAYS--

WANTED A DAUGHTER ...SO HOW DOES IT FEEL TO BE A--

DADDY! AMY STARTED THE FIGHT! I KNOW--

I'VE BEEN A BIT FLAKY ABOUT SCHOOL, DAD, BUT I'M GOING BACK TO STUDY PHOTOGRAPHY. AND--

I'M SO SORRY, DOCTOR GILMOUR, BUT IT'S MALIGNANT. THERE'S NOT MUCH TIME... SIX--

MONTHS, PAUL... PLEASE, I JUST WANT TO GO HOME. I DON'T WANT TO DIE IN A HOSPITAL.

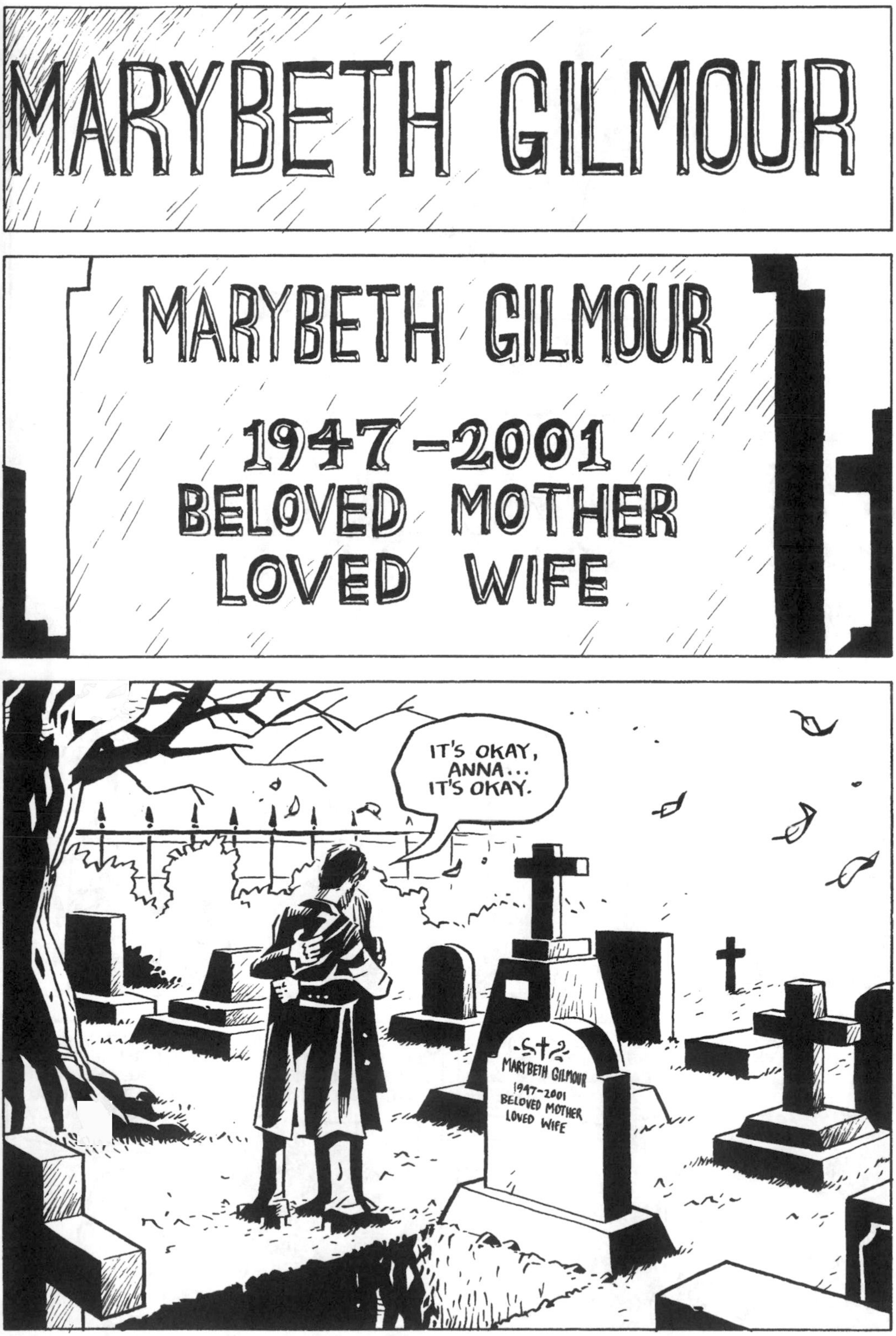
MARYBETH GILMOUR
MARYBETH GILMOUR
1947-2001
BELOVED MOTHER
LOVED WIFE
IT'S OKAY, ANNA... IT'S OKAY.
MARYBETH GILMOUR
1947-2001
BELOVED MOTHER
LOVED WIFE

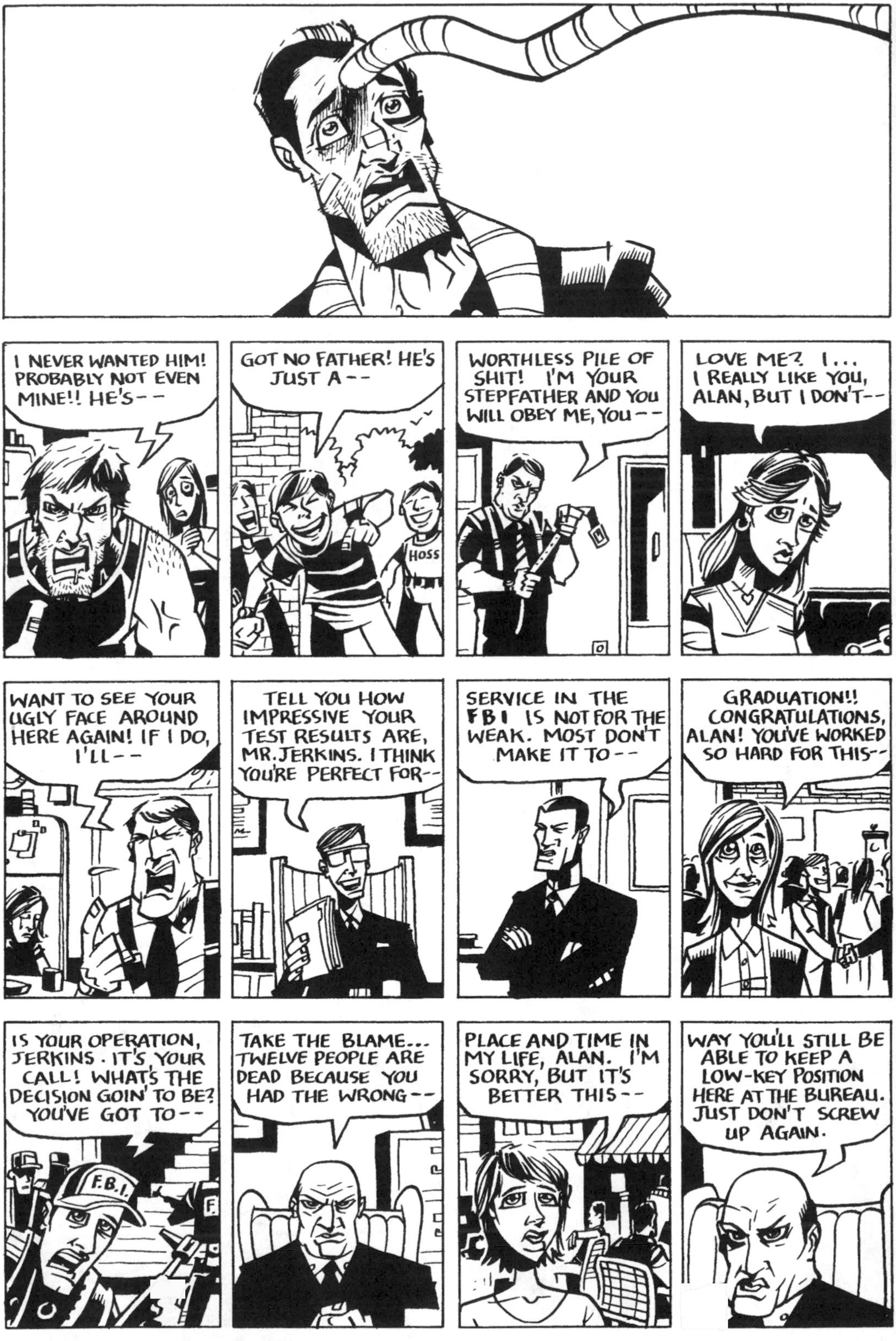
I NEVER WANTED HIM! PROBABLY NOT EVEN MINE!! HE'S--
GOT NO FATHER! HE'S JUST A--
WORTHLESS PILE OF SHIT! I'M YOUR STEPFATHER AND YOU WILL OBEY ME, YOU--
LOVE ME? I... I REALLY LIKE YOU, ALAN, BUT I DON'T--
HOSS
WANT TO SEE YOUR UGLY FACE AROUND HERE AGAIN! IF I DO, I'LL--
TELL YOU HOW IMPRESSIVE YOUR TEST RESULTS ARE, MR. JERKINS. I THINK YOU'RE PERFECT FOR--
SERVICE IN THE FBI IS NOT FOR THE WEAK. MOST DON'T MAKE IT TO--
GRADUATION!! CONGRATULATIONS, ALAN! YOU'VE WORKED SO HARD FOR THIS--
IS YOUR OPERATION, JERKINS. IT'S YOUR CALL! WHAT'S THE DECISION GOIN' TO BE? YOU'VE GOT TO--
F.B.I.
TAKE THE BLAME... TWELVE PEOPLE ARE DEAD BECAUSE YOU HAD THE WRONG--
PLACE AND TIME IN MY LIFE, ALAN. I'M SORRY, BUT IT'S BETTER THIS--
WAY YOU'LL STILL BE ABLE TO KEEP A LOW-KEY POSITION HERE AT THE BUREAU. JUST DON'T SCREW UP AGAIN.

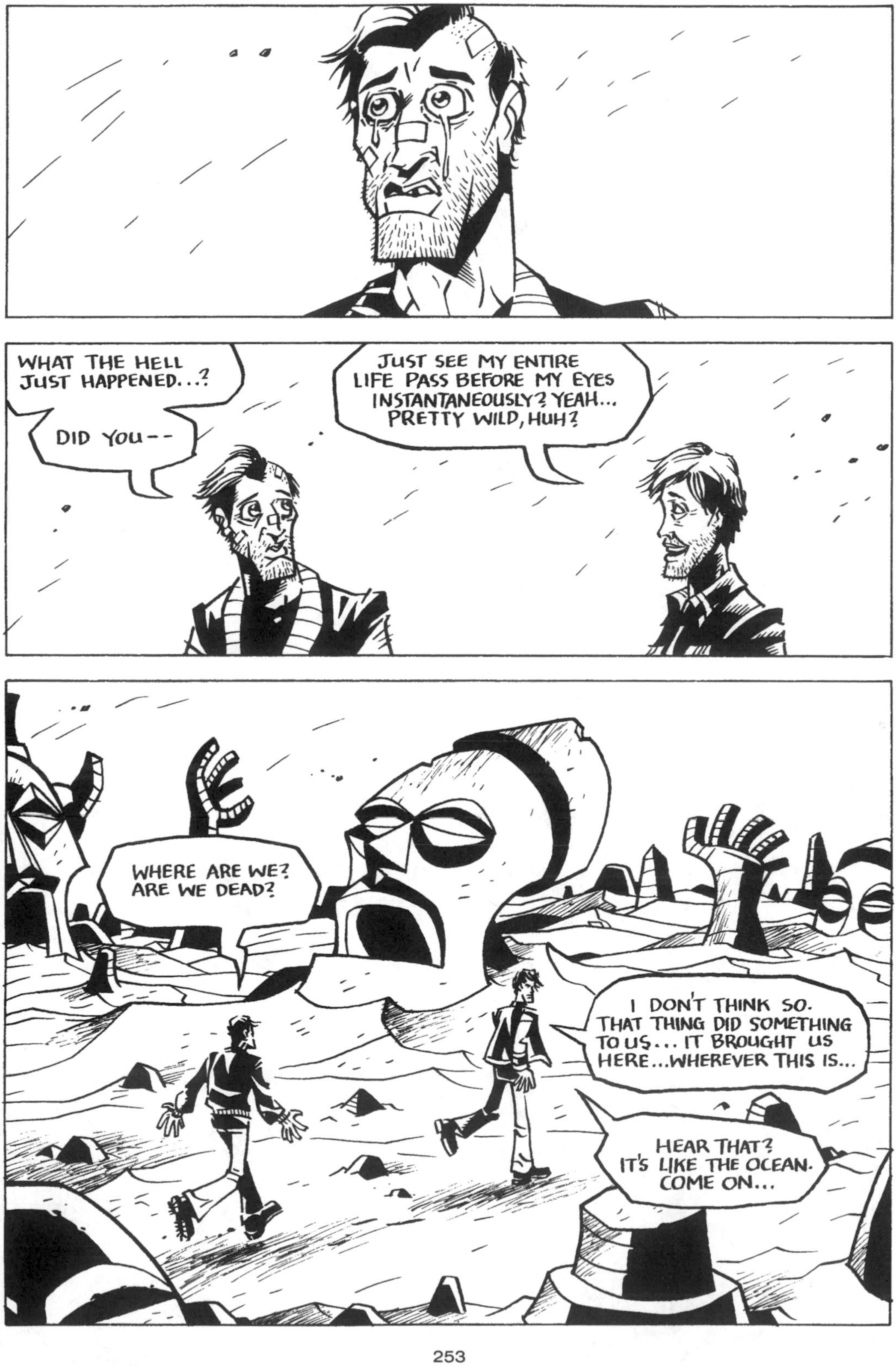
WHAT THE HELL JUST HAPPENED...?
DID YOU--
JUST SEE MY ENTIRE LIFE PASS BEFORE MY EYES INSTANTANEOUSLY? YEAH... PRETTY WILD, HUH?
WHERE ARE WE? ARE WE DEAD?
I DON'T THINK SO. THAT THING DID SOMETHING TO US... IT BROUGHT US HERE...WHEREVER THIS IS...
HEAR THAT? IT'S LIKE THE OCEAN. COME ON...

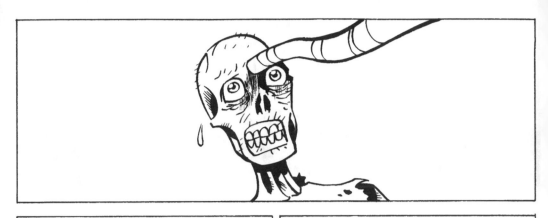

YOU HAVE BEEN SELECTED TO JOIN THE ROYALTIC ORDER OF MOONITES. SAY GOODBYE TO YOUR FAMILY. YOU WILL NEVER SEE THEM --

AGAIN?! MUST I INFORM YOU AGAIN, RODUIBEN? THERE WILL BE ABSOLUTELY NO FRATERNIZING WITH OTHER BEINGS FOR THE FIRST THOUSAND YEARS OF YOUR STUDIES. AND YOU--

WILL BE SELECTED A NEWLY-FORMED PLANET ON THE OUTER EDGES OF THE KNOWN UNIVERSE. IT IS ONLY A GAS BALL AT THE MOMENT, BUT SOON --

YOU WILL STUDY YOUR PLANET. KEEP FULL NOTES OF EVERY OCCURENCE. ONCE EACH MILLENNIA A SURVEYOR WILL COME FOR YOUR FULL REPORT FOR THE MOONITE ARCHIVES. FURTHERMORE --

NEVER MUST YOU INTERFERE WITH YOUR SELECTED PLANET'S EVOLUTION --

NO!

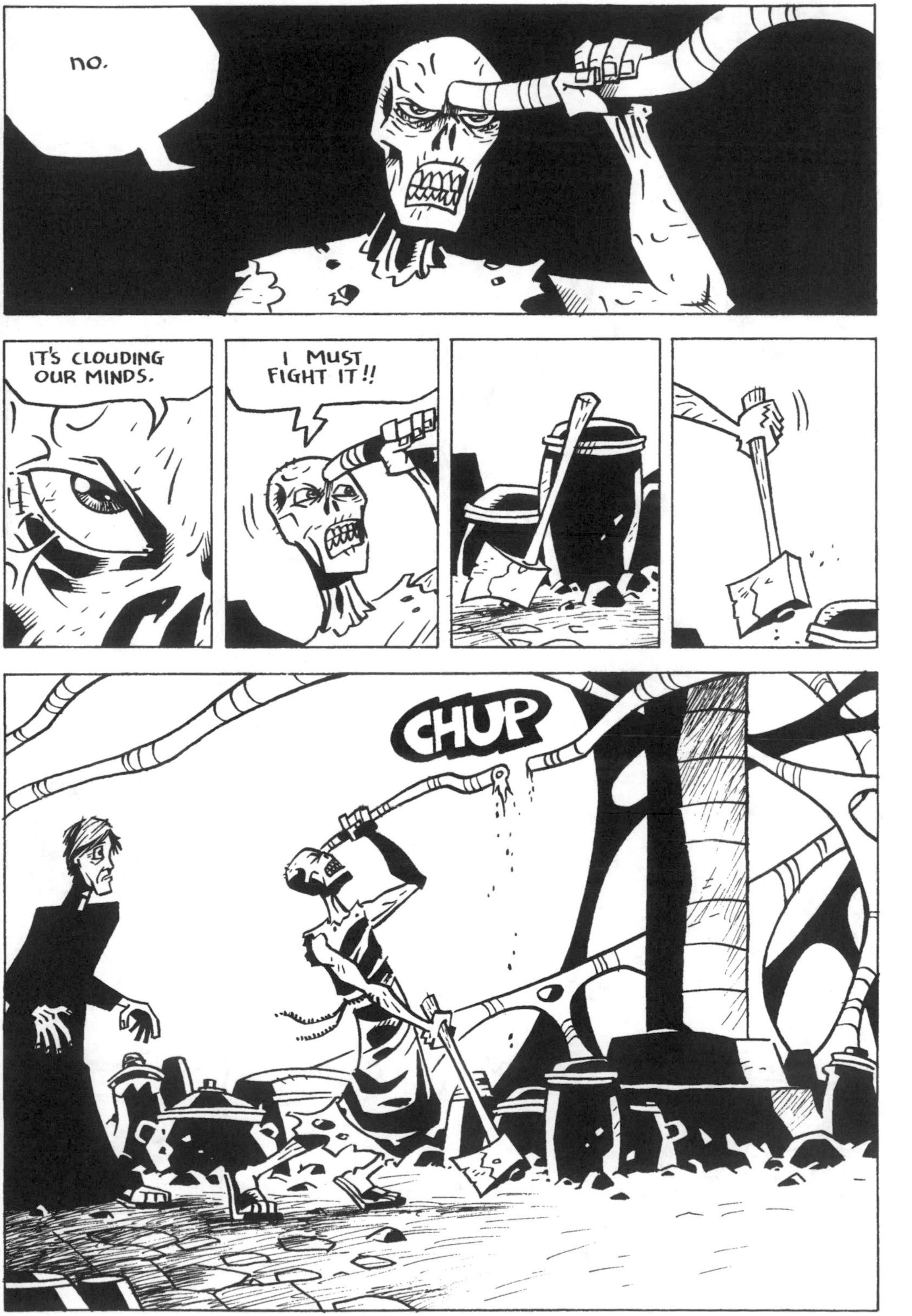

no.
IT'S CLOUDING OUR MINDS.
I MUST FIGHT IT!!
CHUP

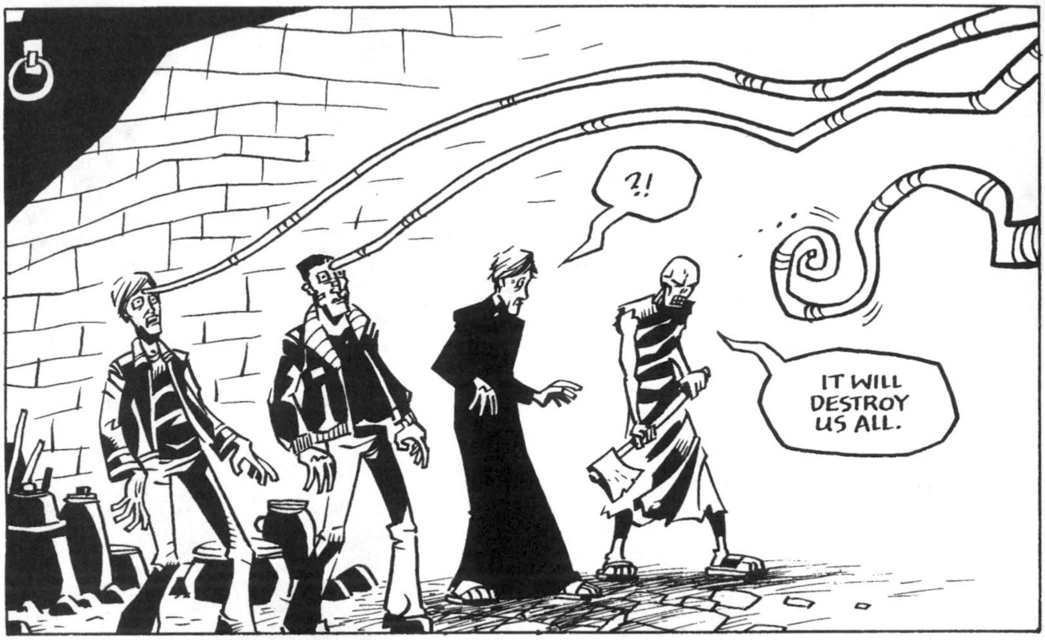
?!
IT WILL DESTROY US ALL.

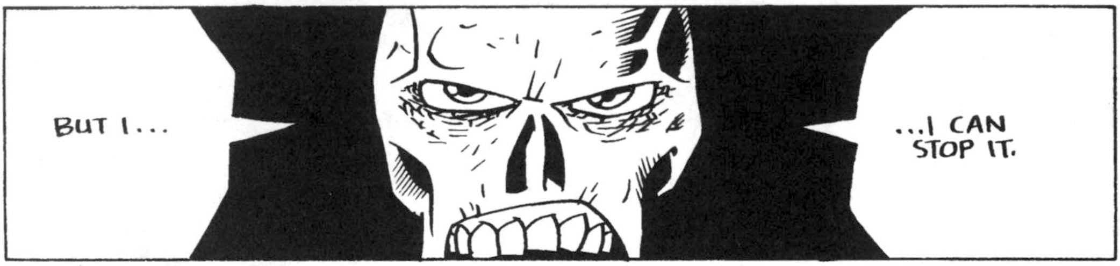
BUT I...
...I CAN STOP IT.

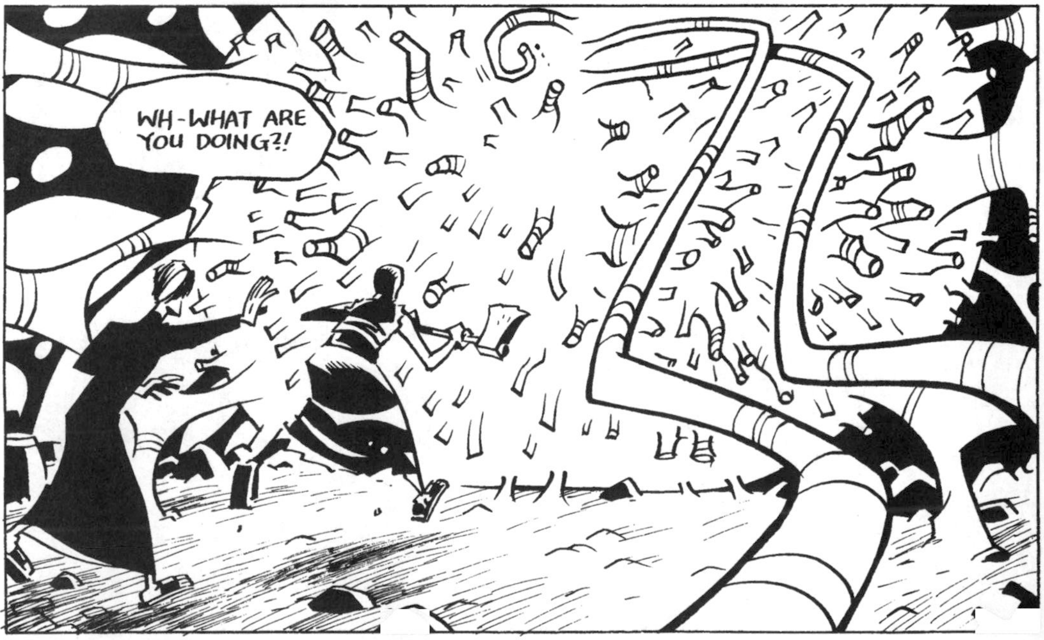
WH-WHAT ARE YOU DOING?!

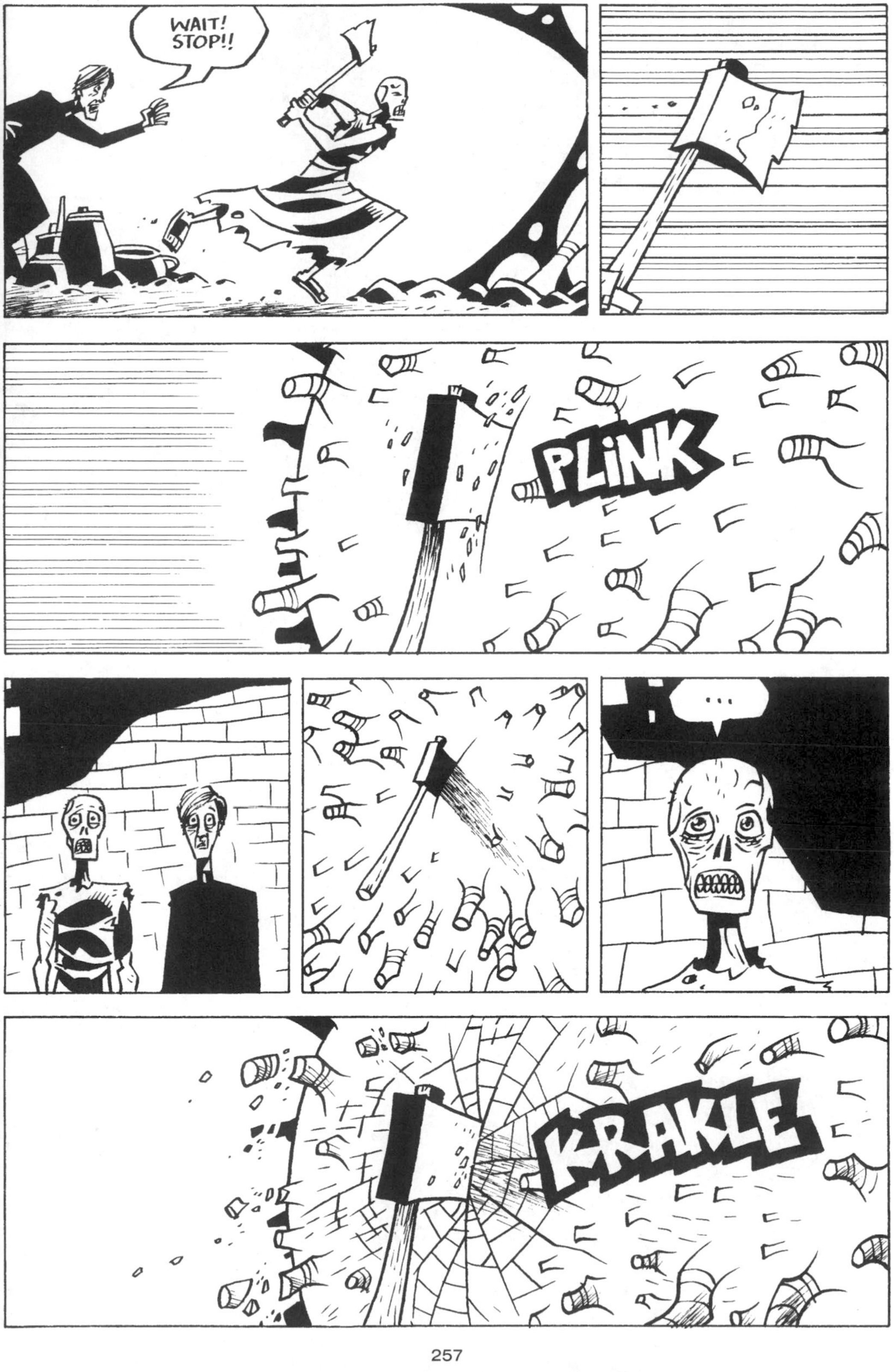
WAIT! STOP!!
PLINK
...
KRAKLE

WHAT HAVE
I DONE?
KISH
VACOOM!

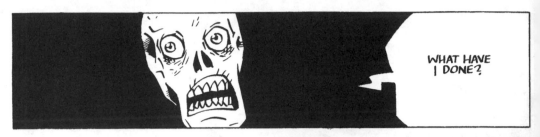

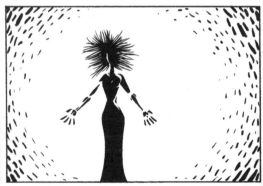

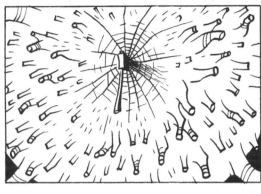

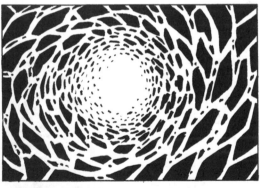

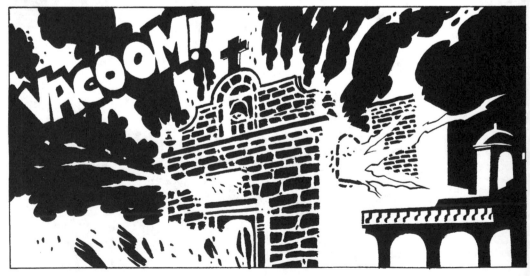

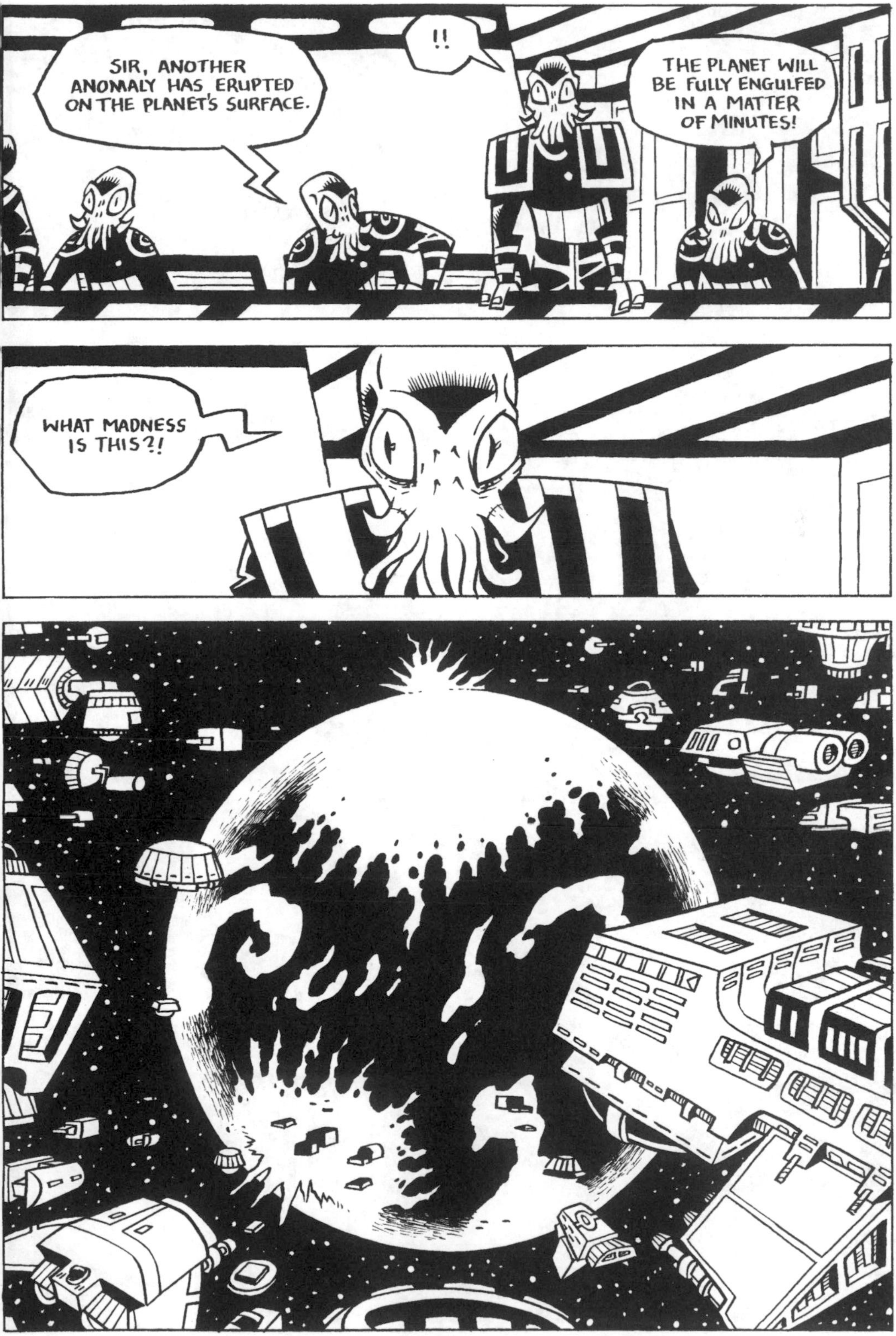
SIR, ANOTHER ANOMALY HAS ERUPTED ON THE PLANET'S SURFACE.
!!
THE PLANET WILL BE FULLY ENGULFED IN A MATTER OF MINUTES!
WHAT MADNESS IS THIS?!

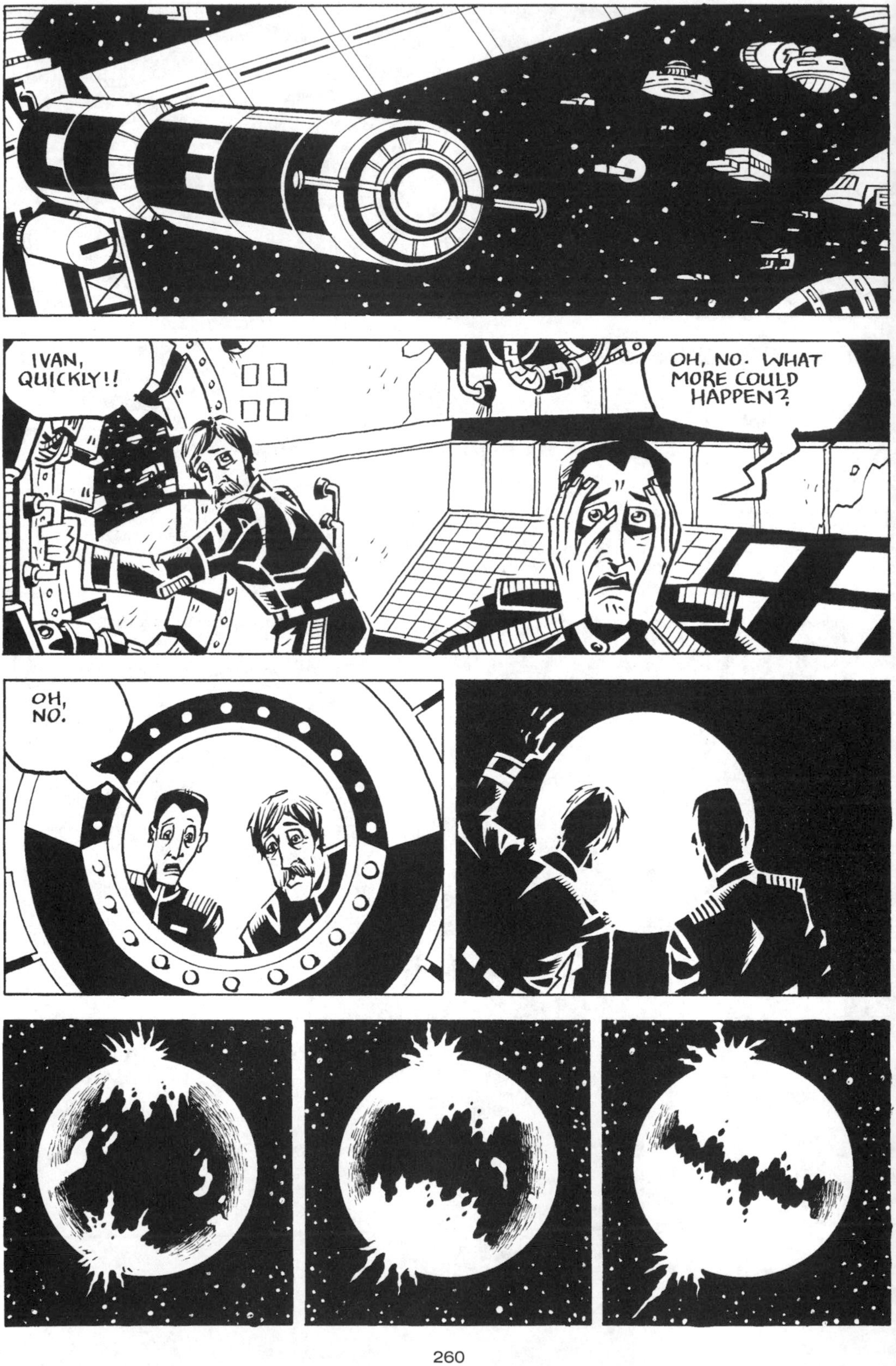
IVAN, QUICKLY!!
OH, NO. WHAT MORE COULD HAPPEN?
OH, NO.

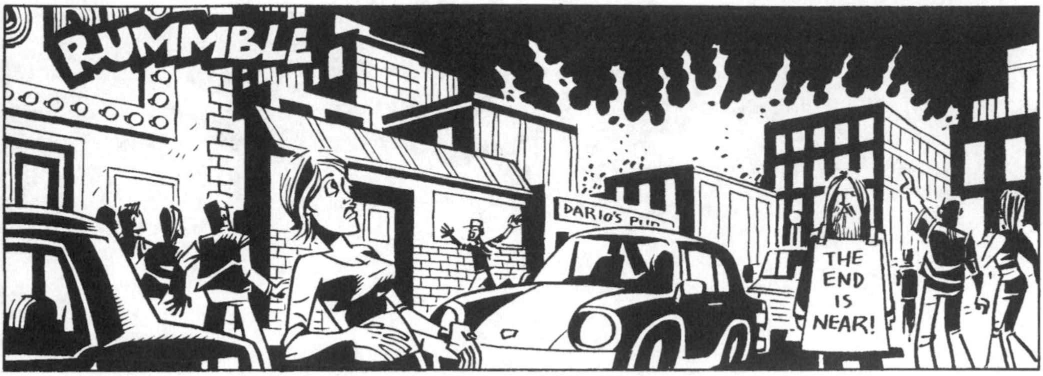
RUMMBLE
DARIO'S PUB
THE END IS NEAR!

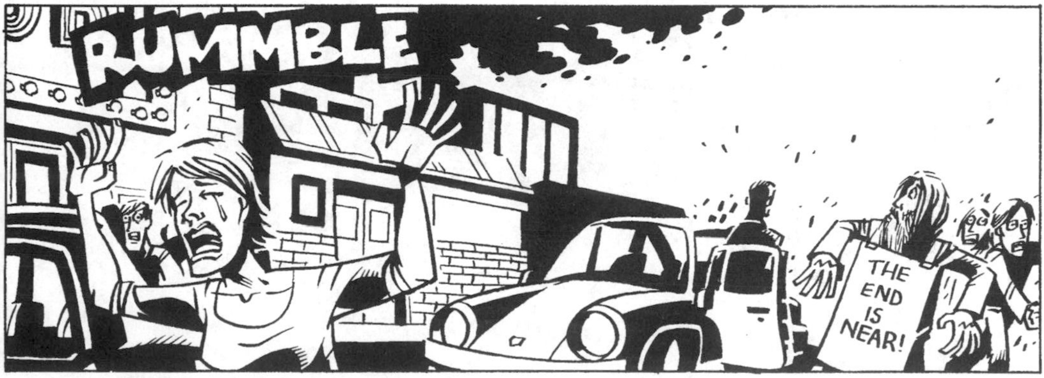
RUMMBLE
THE END IS NEAR!

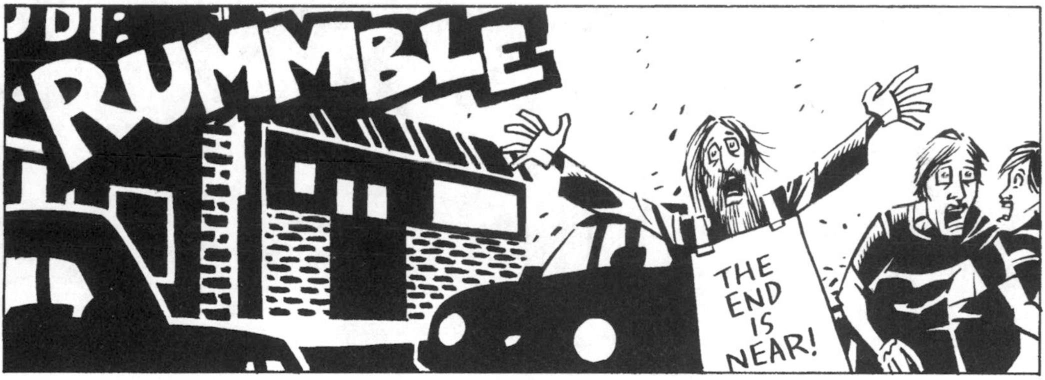
RUMMBLE
THE END IS NEAR!

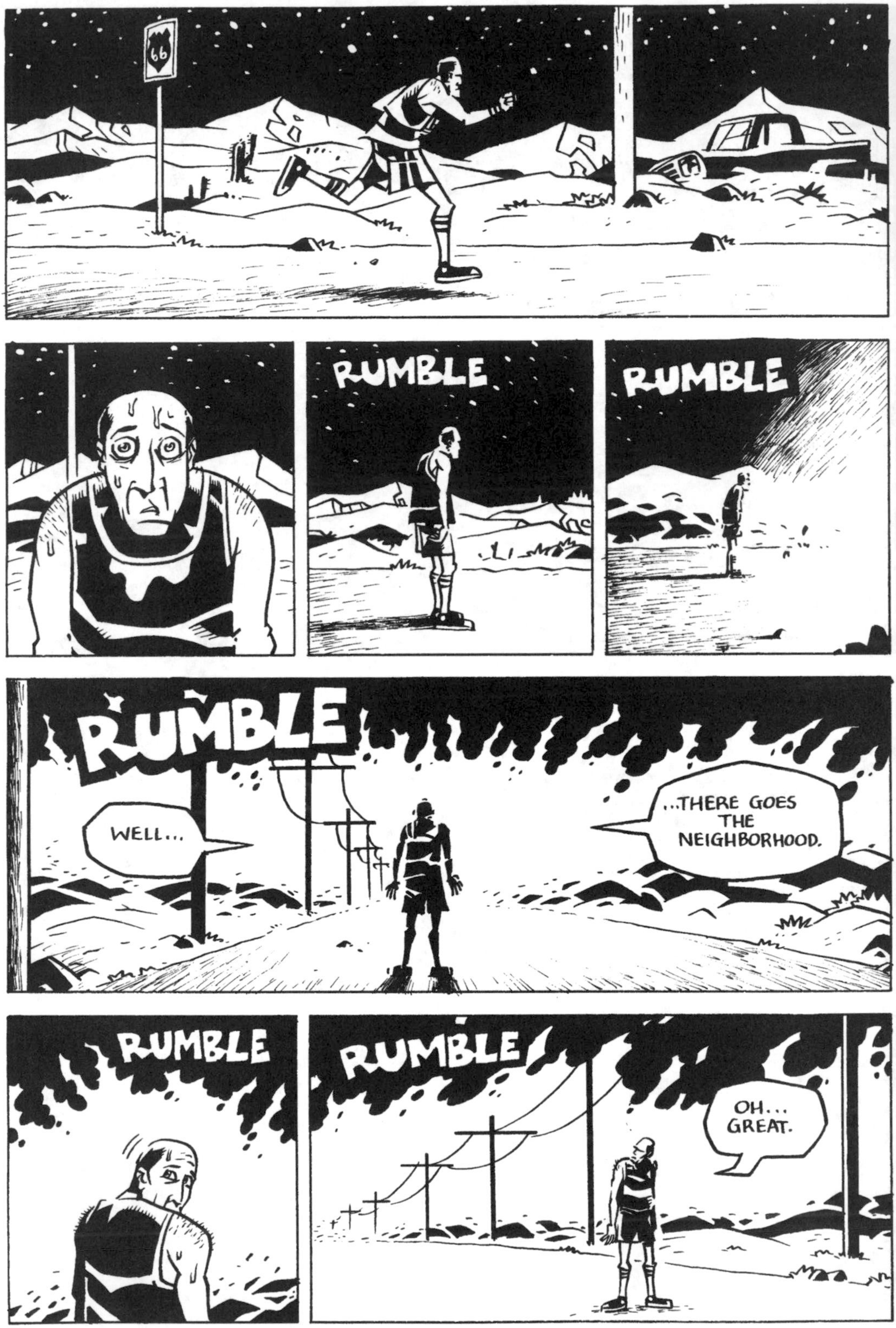
66
RUMBLE
RUMBLE
RUMBLE
WELL...
...THERE GOES THE NEIGHBORHOOD.
RUMBLE
RUMBLE
OH... GREAT.

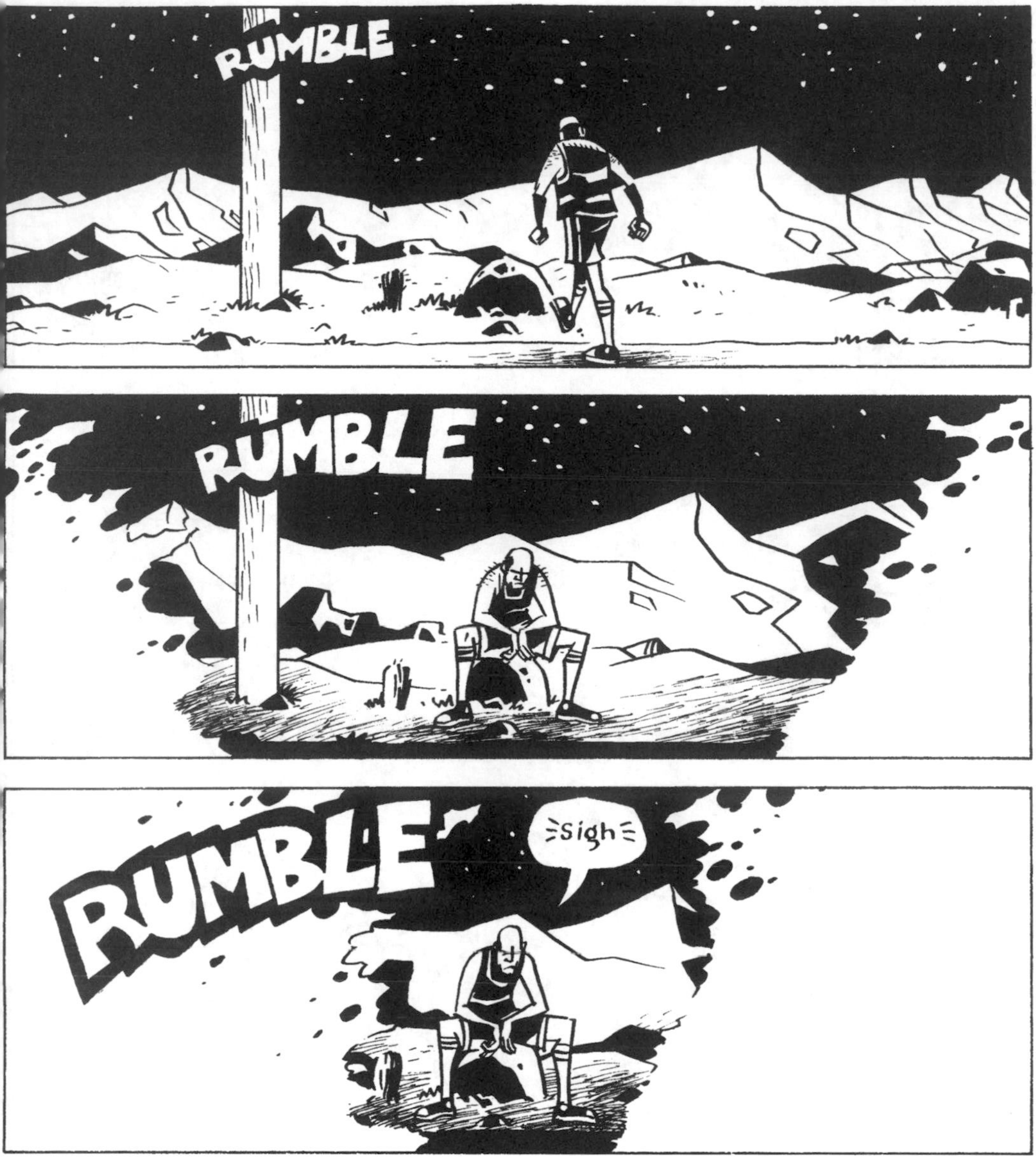
RUMBLE
RUMBLE
RUMBLE
Sigh

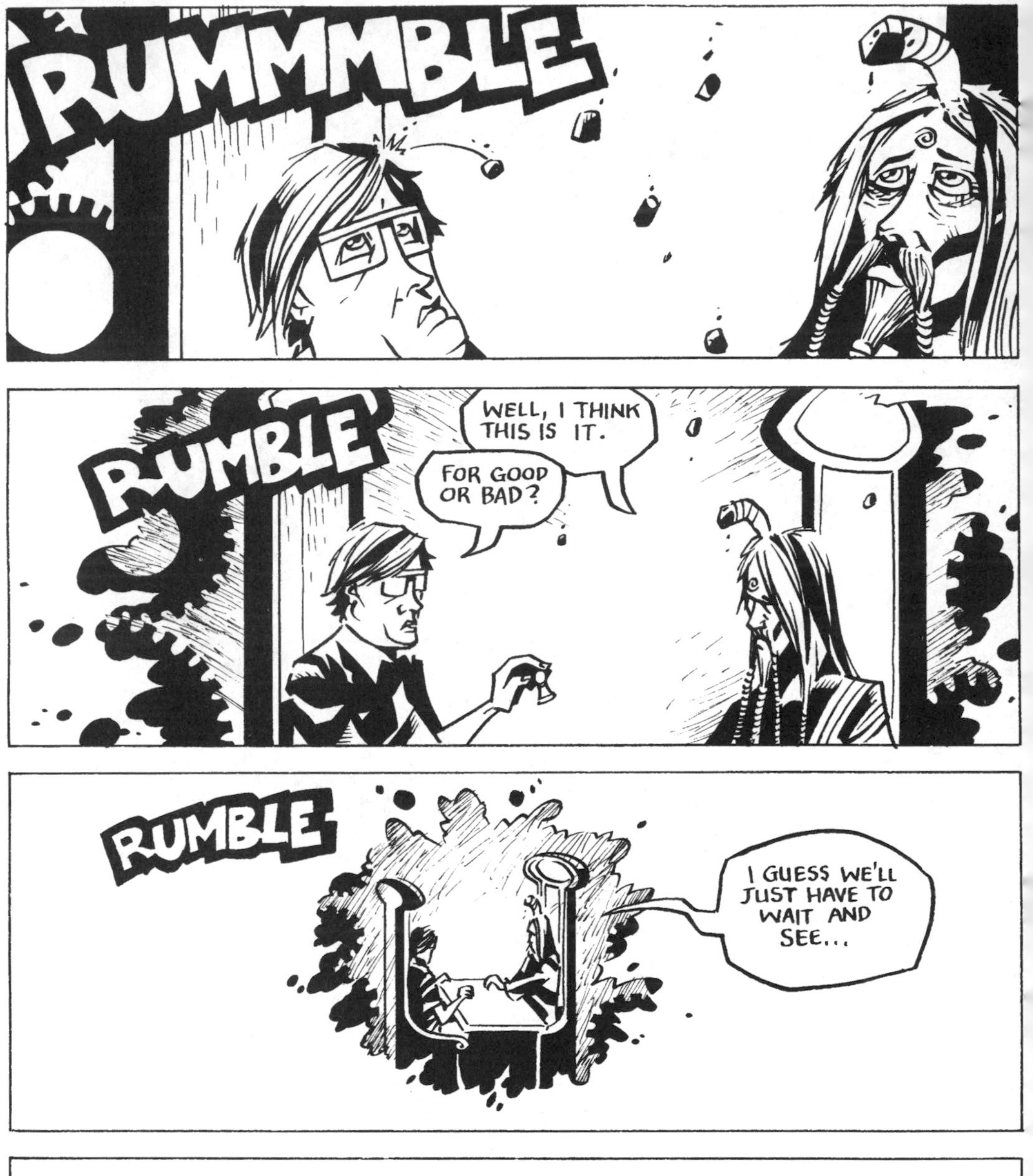
RUMMMBLE
RUMBLE
WELL, I THINK THIS IS IT.
FOR GOOD OR BAD?
RUMBLE
I GUESS WE'LL JUST HAVE TO WAIT AND SEE...

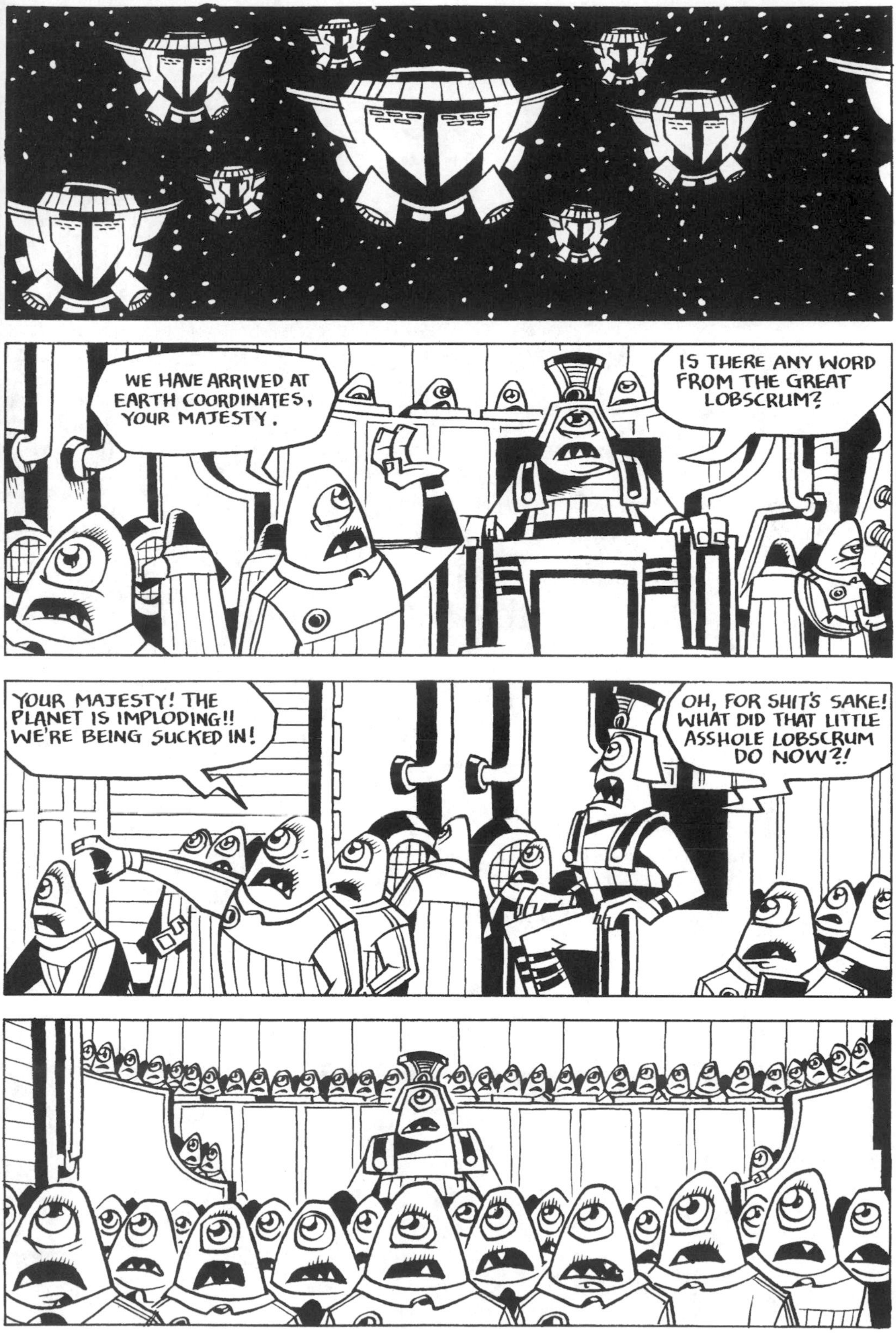
WE HAVE ARRIVED AT EARTH COORDINATES, YOUR MAJESTY.
IS THERE ANY WORD FROM THE GREAT LOBSCRUM?
YOUR MAJESTY! THE PLANET IS IMPLODING!! WE'RE BEING SUCKED IN!
OH, FOR SHIT'S SAKE! WHAT DID THAT LITTLE ASSHOLE LOBSCRUM DO NOW?!

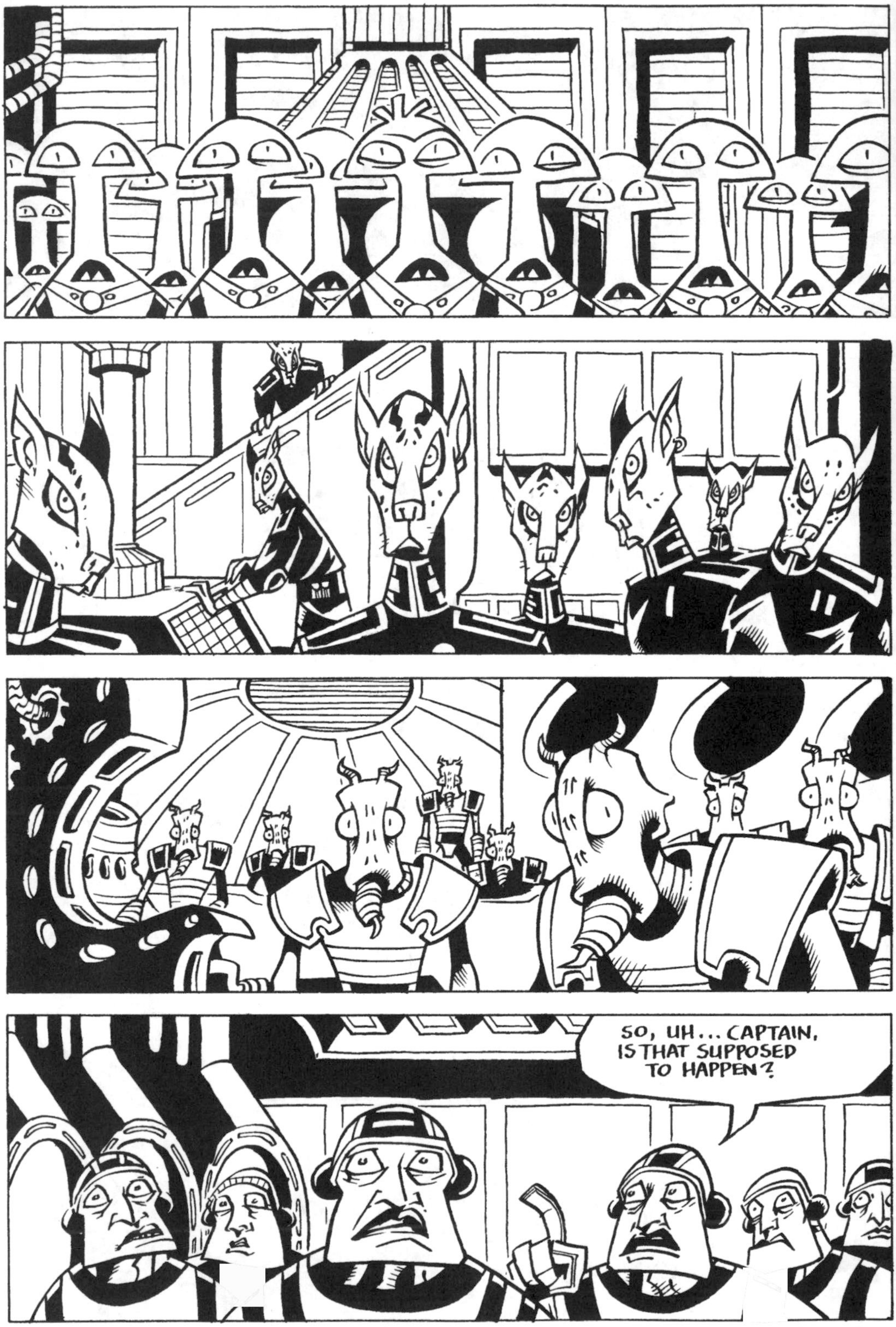
SO, UH... CAPTAIN, IS THAT SUPPOSED TO HAPPEN?

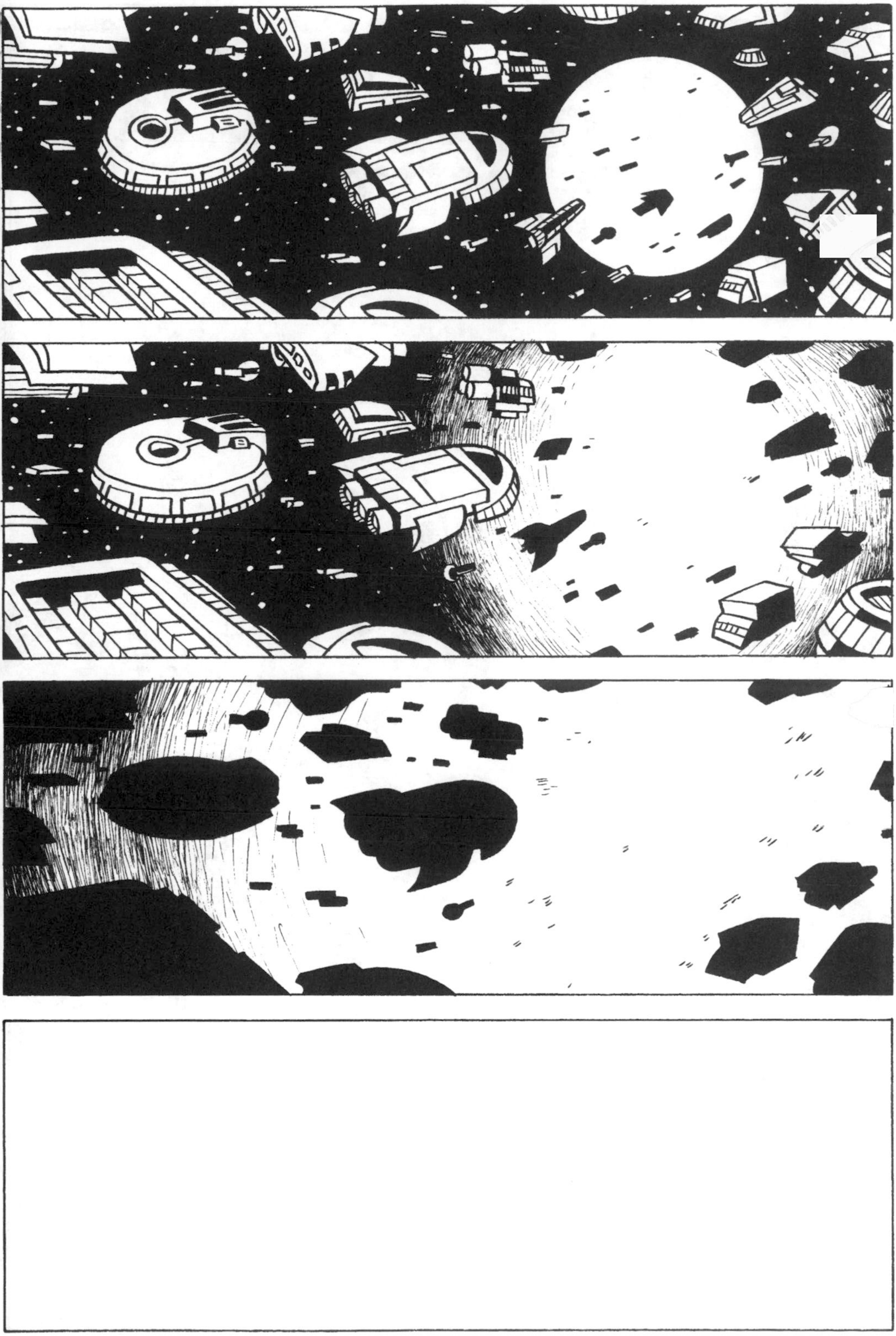

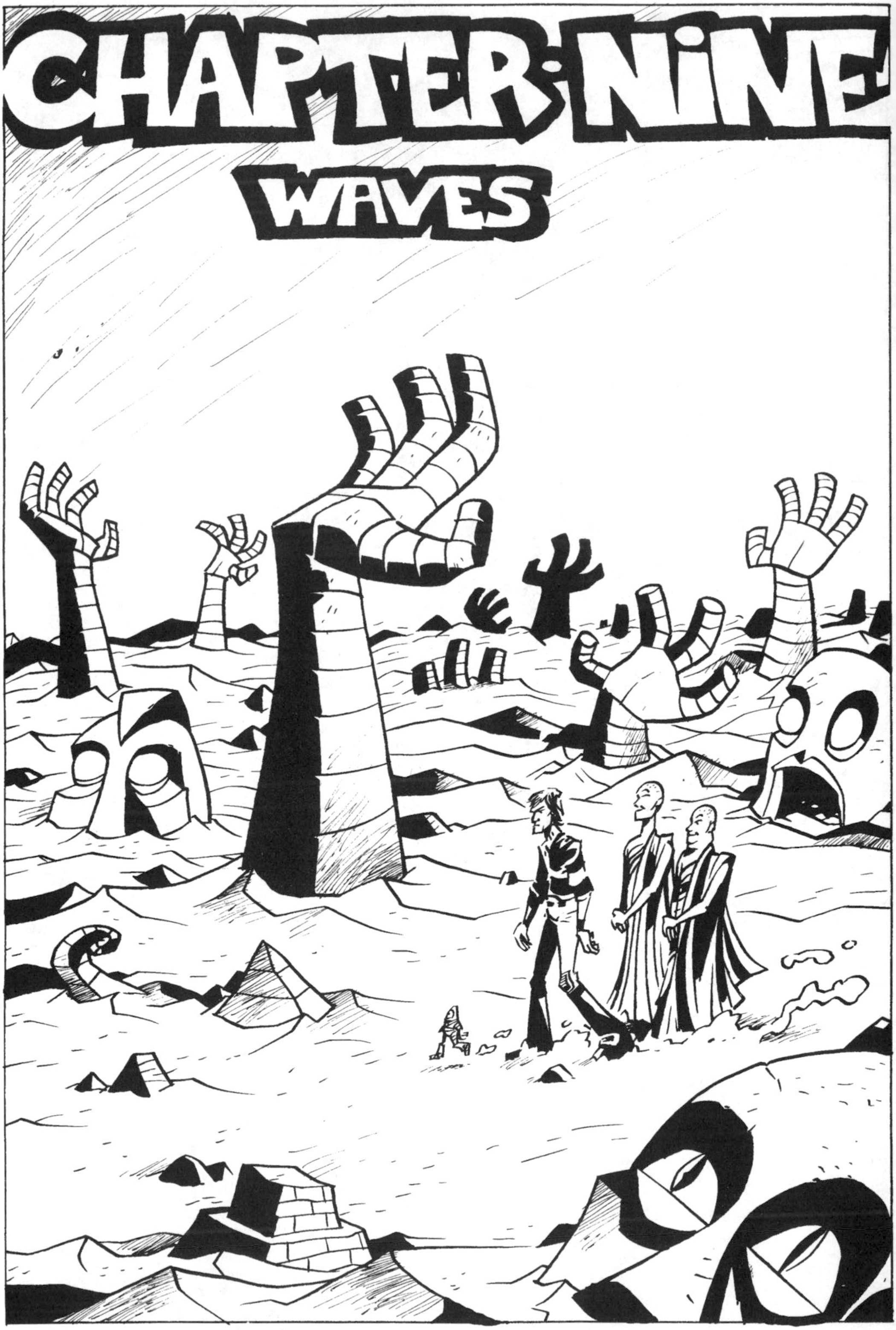
CHAPTER NINE:
WAVES

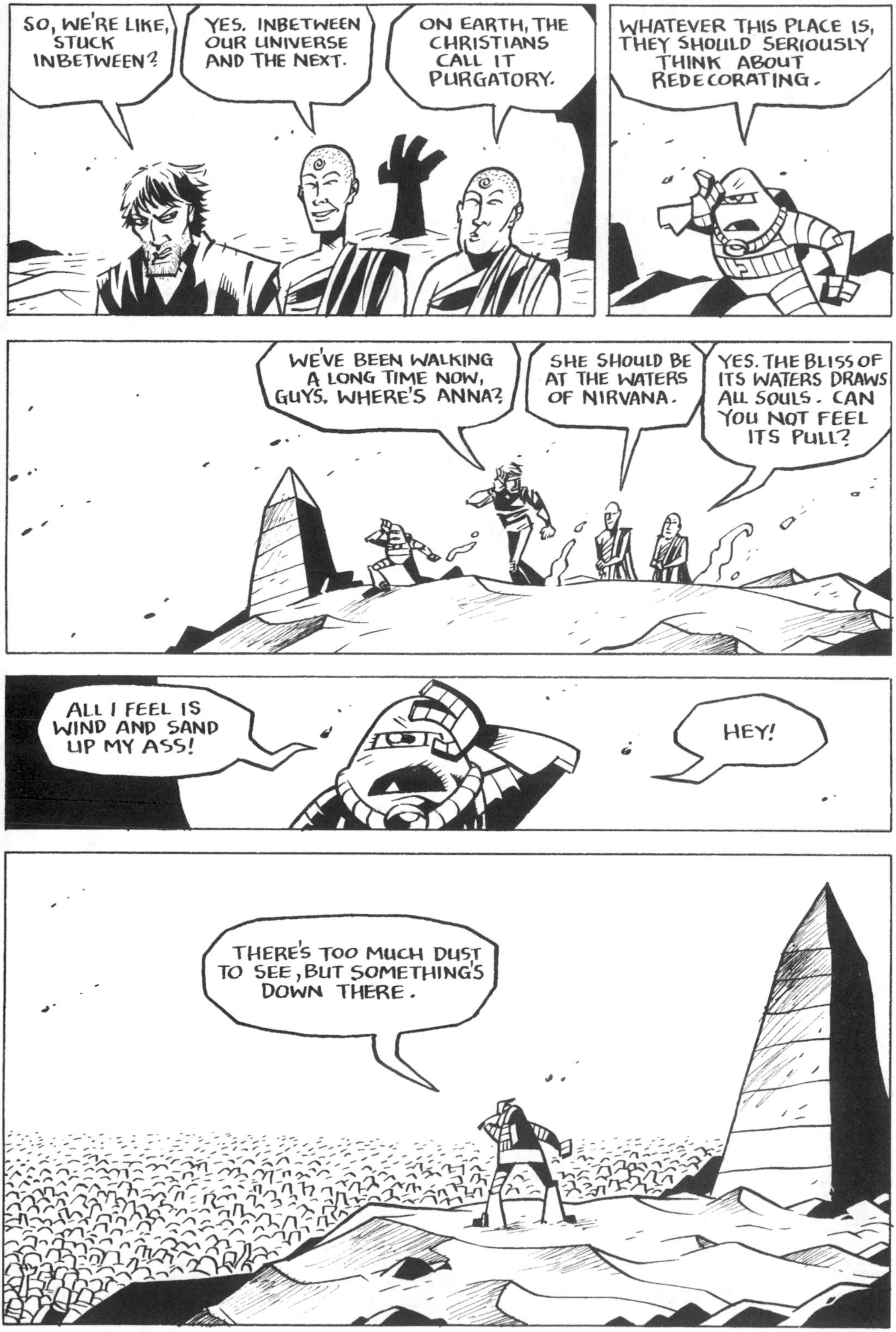
SO, WE'RE LIKE, STUCK INBETWEEN?
YES. INBETWEEN OUR UNIVERSE AND THE NEXT.
ON EARTH, THE CHRISTIANS CALL IT PURGATORY.
WHATEVER THIS PLACE IS, THEY SHOULD SERIOUSLY THINK ABOUT REDECORATING.
WE'VE BEEN WALKING A LONG TIME NOW, GUYS. WHERE'S ANNA?
SHE SHOULD BE AT THE WATERS OF NIRVANA.
YES. THE BLISS OF ITS WATERS DRAWS ALL SOULS. CAN YOU NOT FEEL ITS PULL?
ALL I FEEL IS WIND AND SAND UP MY ASS!
HEY!
THERE'S TOO MUCH DUST TO SEE, BUT SOMETHING'S DOWN THERE.

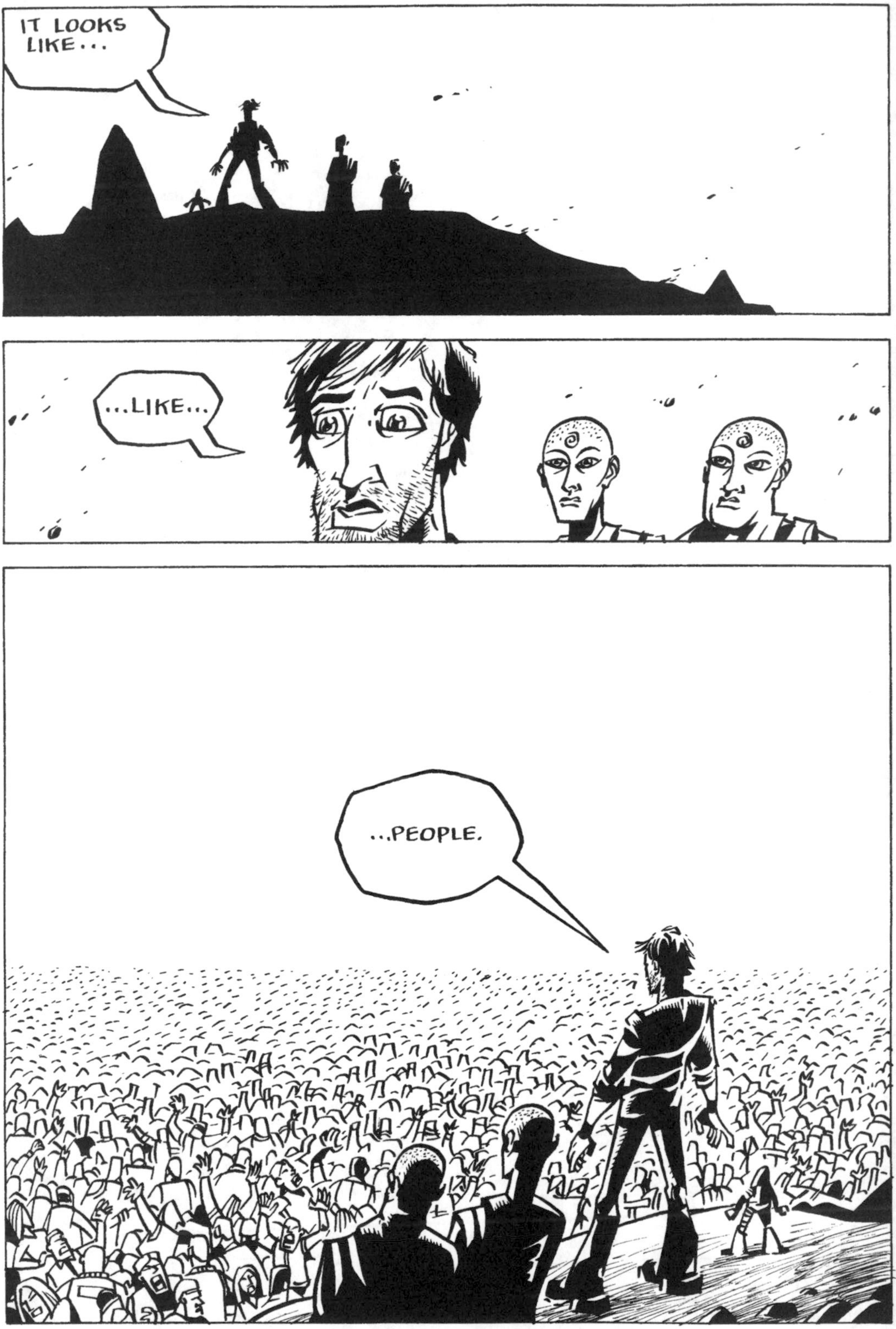
IT LOOKS LIKE...
...LIKE...
...PEOPLE.

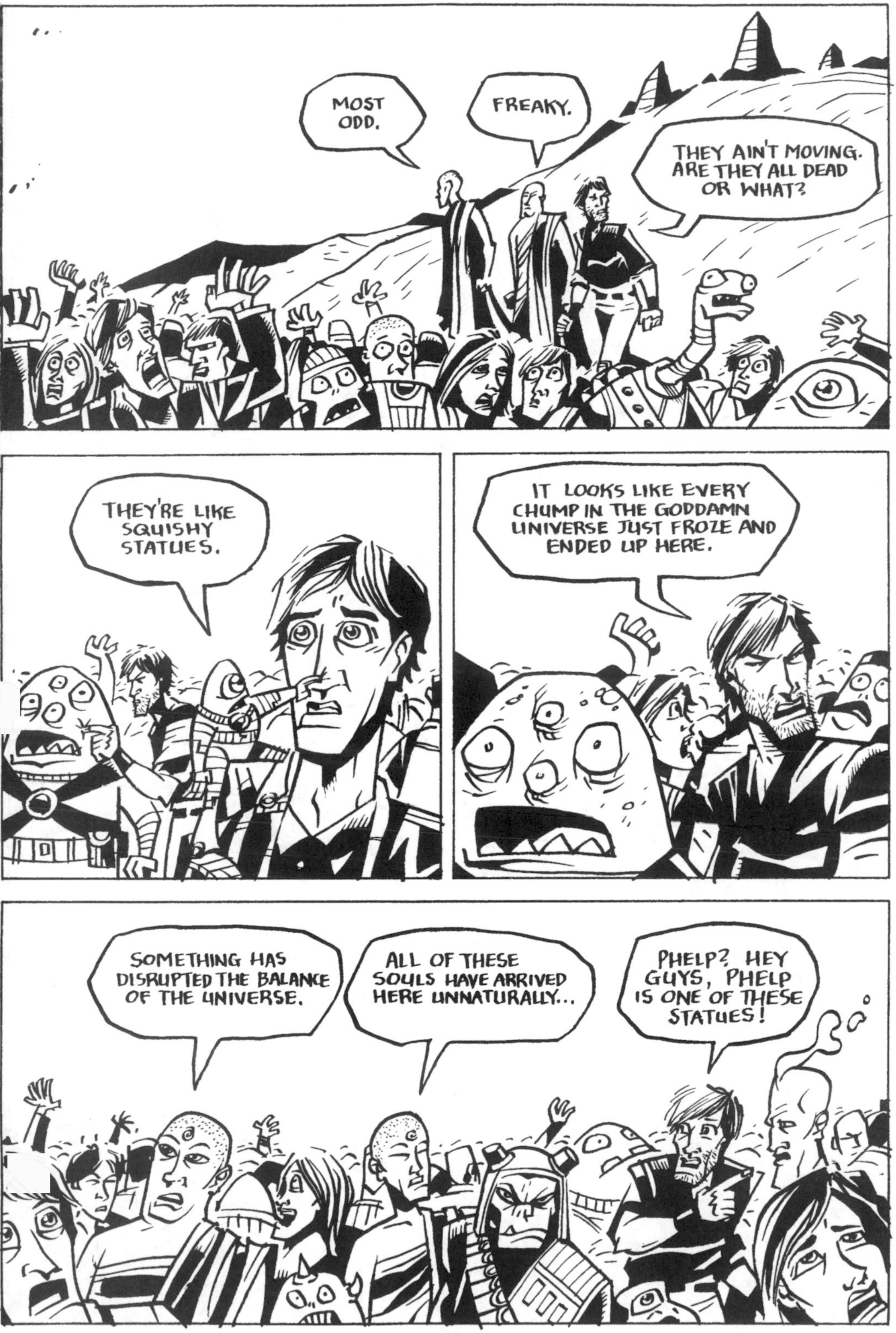
MOST ODD.
FREAKY.
THEY AIN'T MOVING. ARE THEY ALL DEAD OR WHAT?
THEY'RE LIKE SQUISHY STATUES.
IT LOOKS LIKE EVERY CHUMP IN THE GODDAMN UNIVERSE JUST FROZE AND ENDED UP HERE.
SOMETHING HAS DISRUPTED THE BALANCE OF THE UNIVERSE.
ALL OF THESE SOULS HAVE ARRIVED HERE UNNATURALLY...
PHELP? HEY GUYS, PHELP IS ONE OF THESE STATUES!

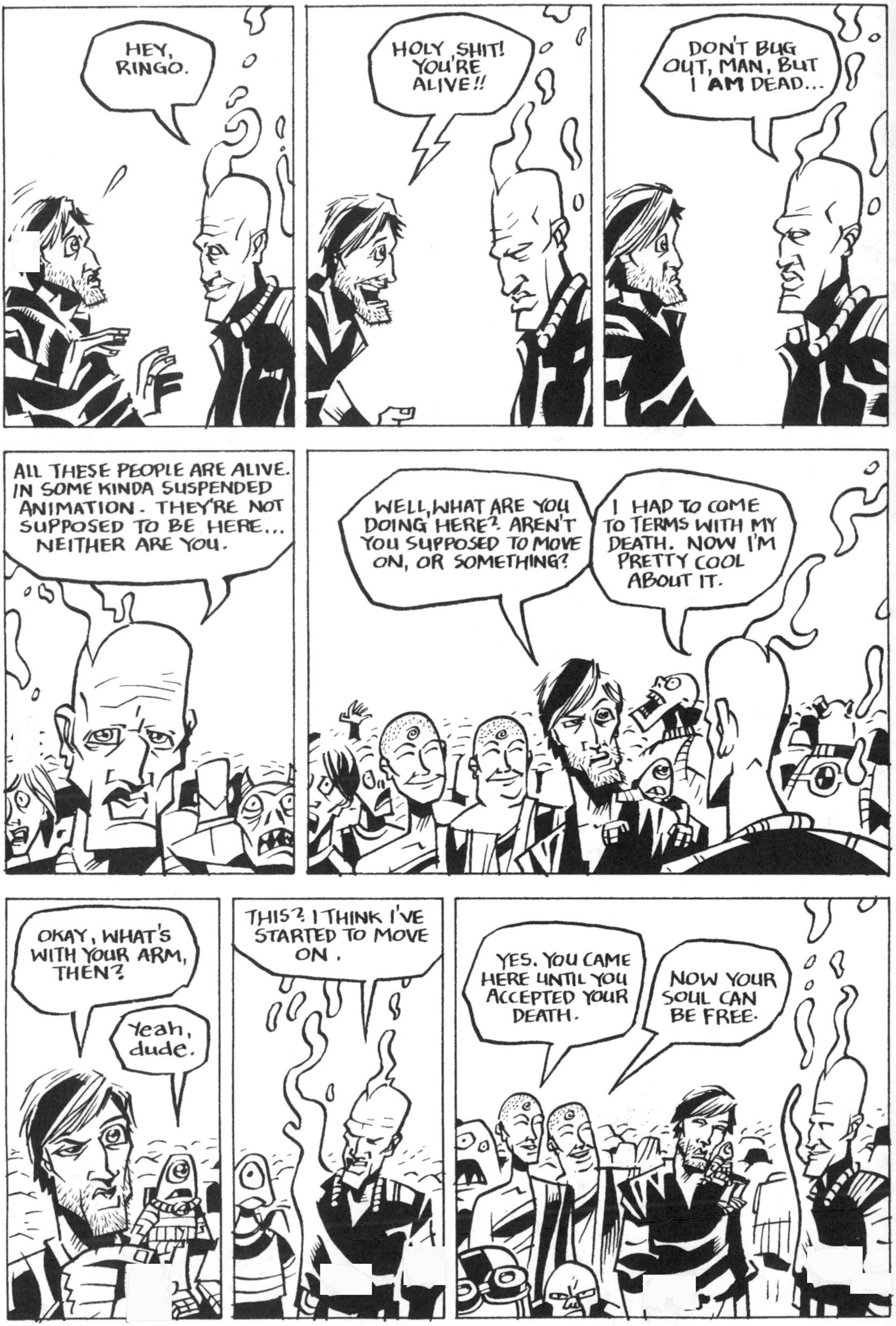
HEY, RINGO.
HOLY SHIT! YOU'RE ALIVE!!
DON'T BUG OUT, MAN, BUT I **AM** DEAD...
ALL THESE PEOPLE ARE ALIVE. IN SOME KINDA SUSPENDED ANIMATION. THEY'RE NOT SUPPOSED TO BE HERE... NEITHER ARE YOU.
WELL, WHAT ARE YOU DOING HERE? AREN'T YOU SUPPOSED TO MOVE ON, OR SOMETHING?
I HAD TO COME TO TERMS WITH MY DEATH. NOW I'M PRETTY COOL ABOUT IT.
OKAY, WHAT'S WITH YOUR ARM, THEN?
Yeah, dude.
THIS? I THINK I'VE STARTED TO MOVE ON.
YES. YOU CAME HERE UNTIL YOU ACCEPTED YOUR DEATH.
NOW YOUR SOUL CAN BE FREE.

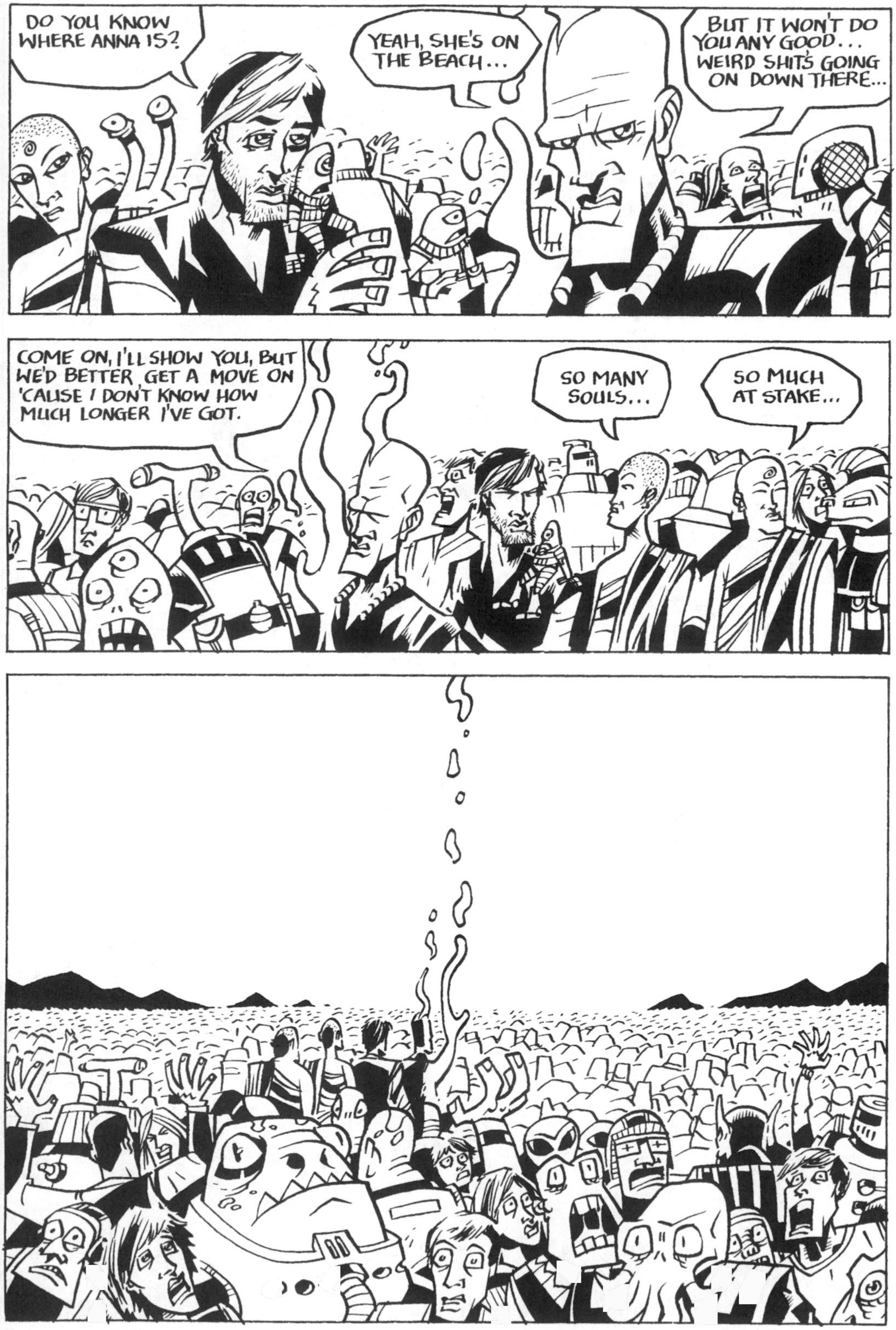
DO YOU KNOW WHERE ANNA IS?
YEAH, SHE'S ON THE BEACH...
BUT IT WON'T DO YOU ANY GOOD... WEIRD SHIT'S GOING ON DOWN THERE...
COME ON, I'LL SHOW YOU, BUT WE'D BETTER GET A MOVE ON 'CAUSE I DON'T KNOW HOW MUCH LONGER I'VE GOT.
SO MANY SOULS...
SO MUCH AT STAKE...

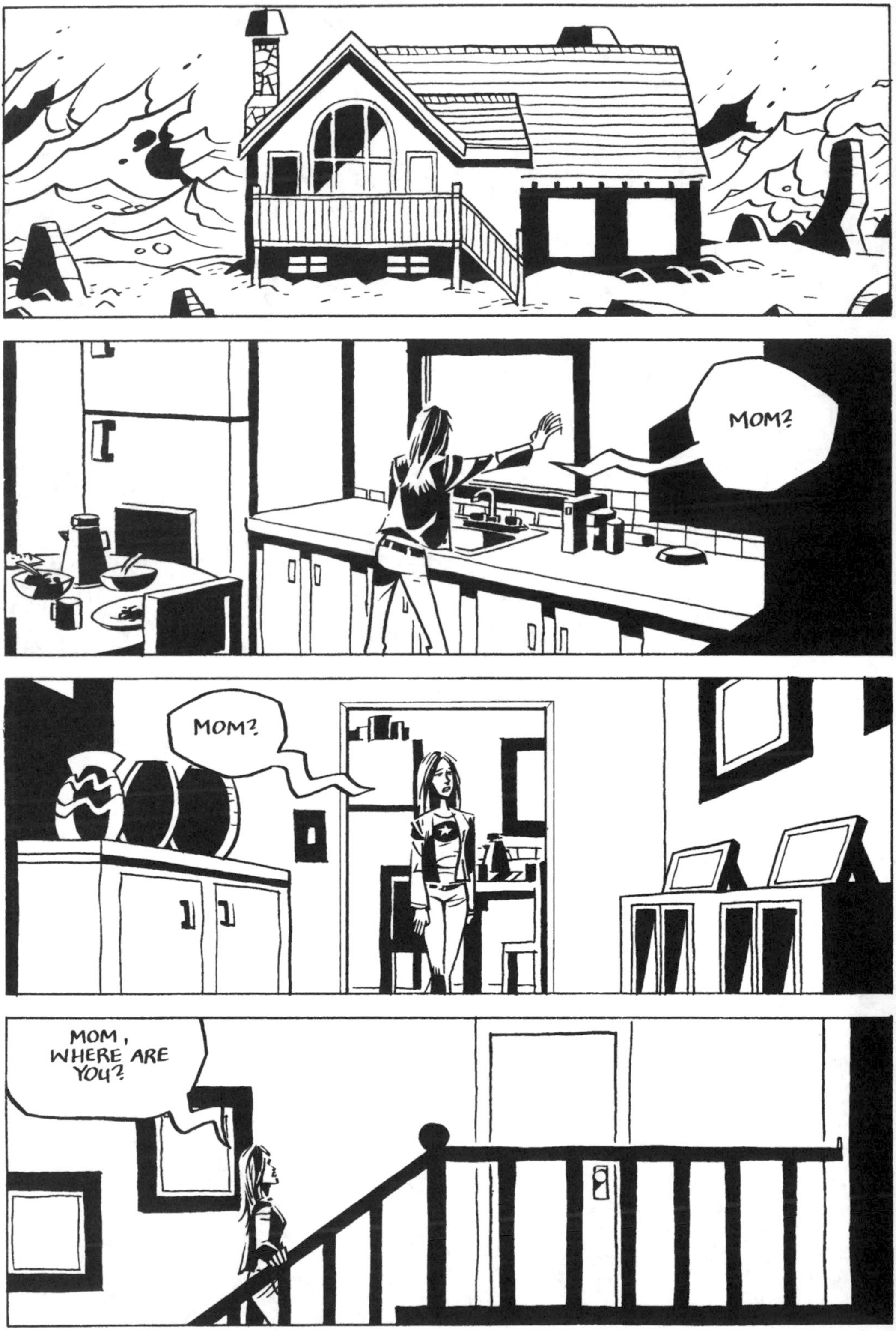
MOM?
MOM?
MOM, WHERE ARE YOU?

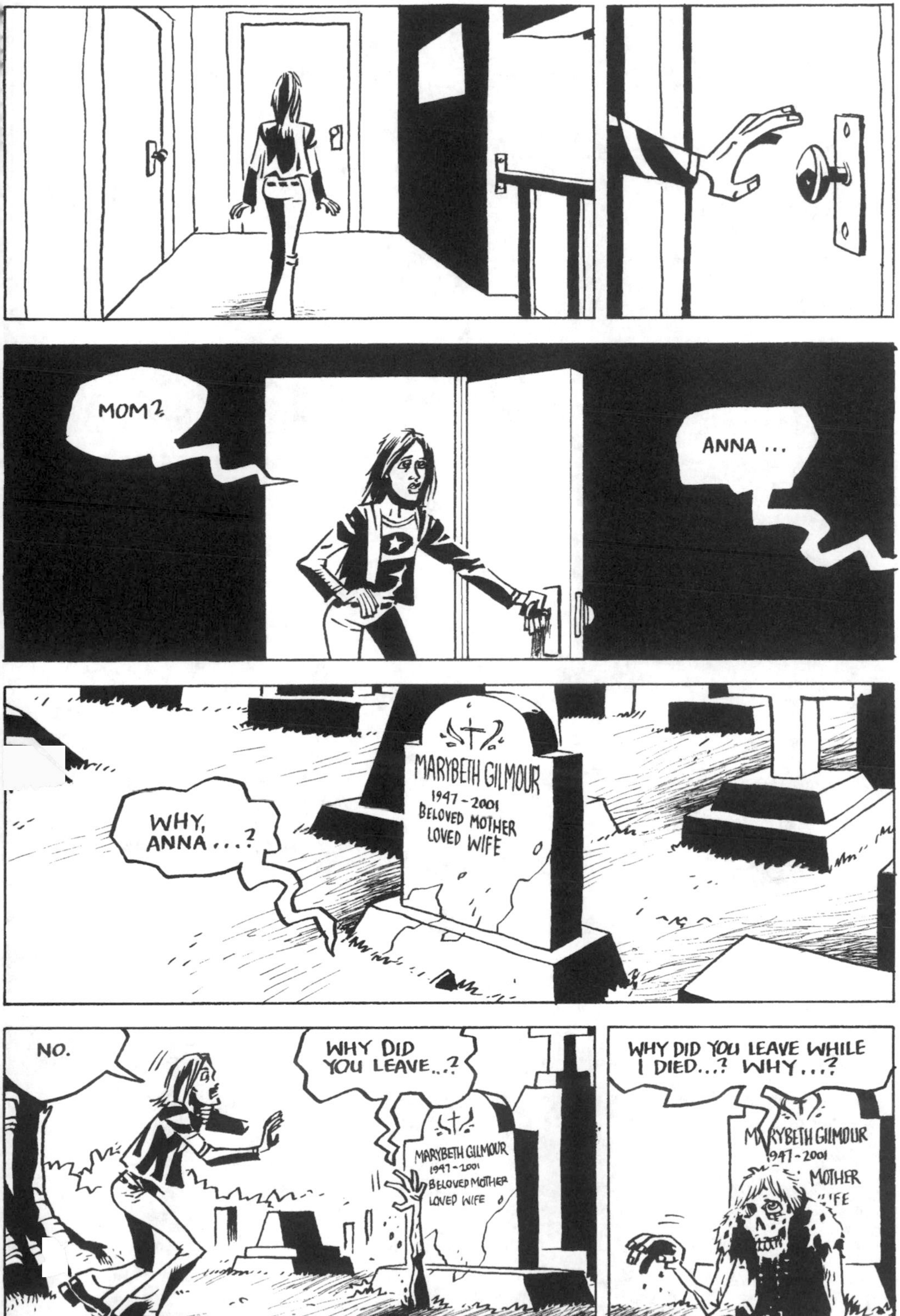
MOM?
ANNA ...
MARYBETH GILMOUR
1947 - 2001
BELOVED MOTHER
LOVED WIFE
WHY, ANNA ...?
NO.
WHY DID YOU LEAVE...?
MARYBETH GILMOUR
1947 - 2001
BELOVED MOTHER
LOVED WIFE
WHY DID YOU LEAVE WHILE I DIED...? WHY...?

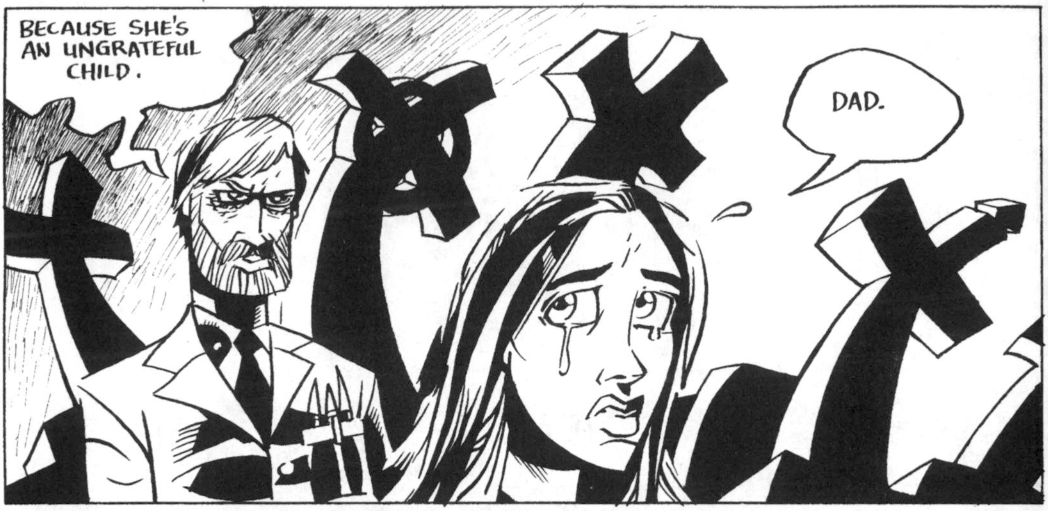
BECAUSE SHE'S AN UNGRATEFUL CHILD.
DAD.

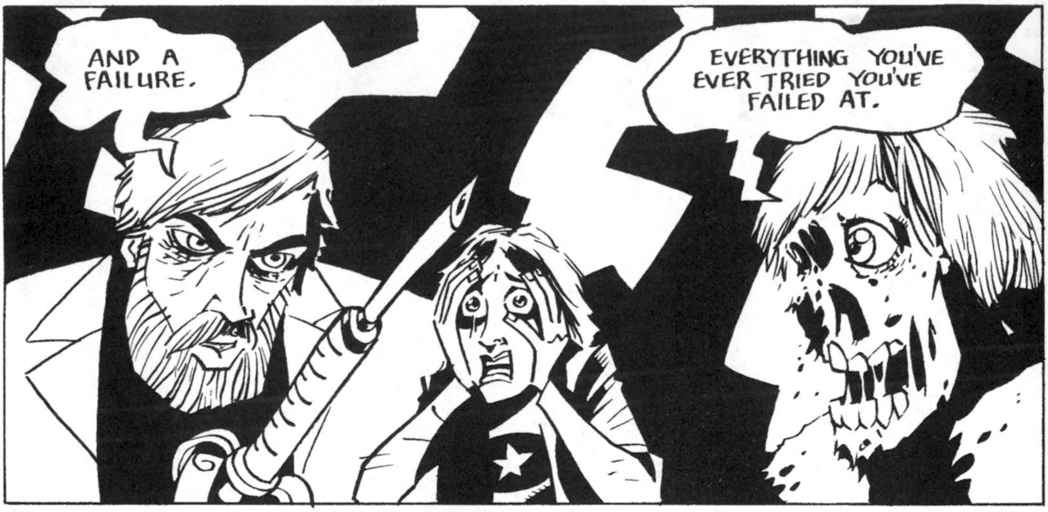
AND A FAILURE.
EVERYTHING YOU'VE EVER TRIED YOU'VE FAILED AT.

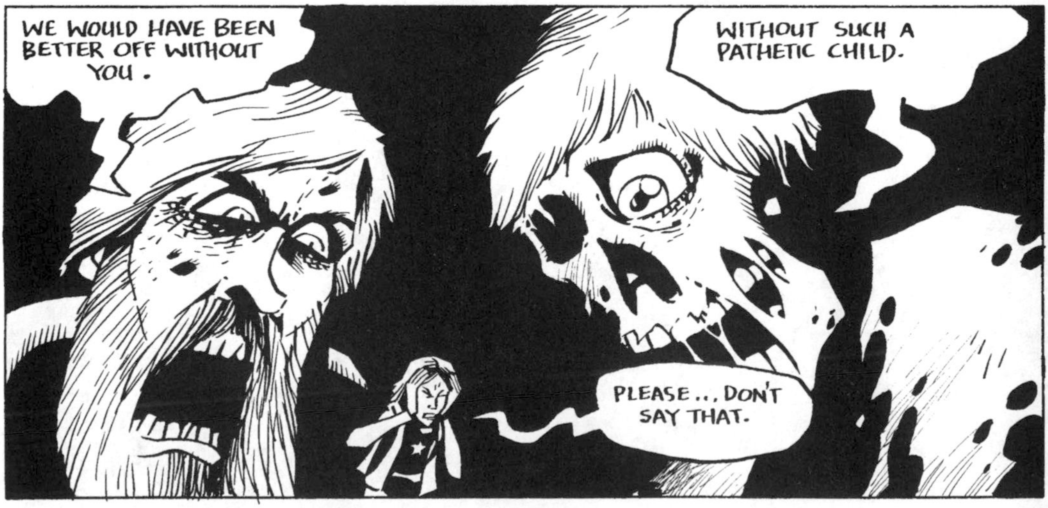
WE WOULD HAVE BEEN BETTER OFF WITHOUT YOU.
WITHOUT SUCH A PATHETIC CHILD.
PLEASE... DON'T SAY THAT.

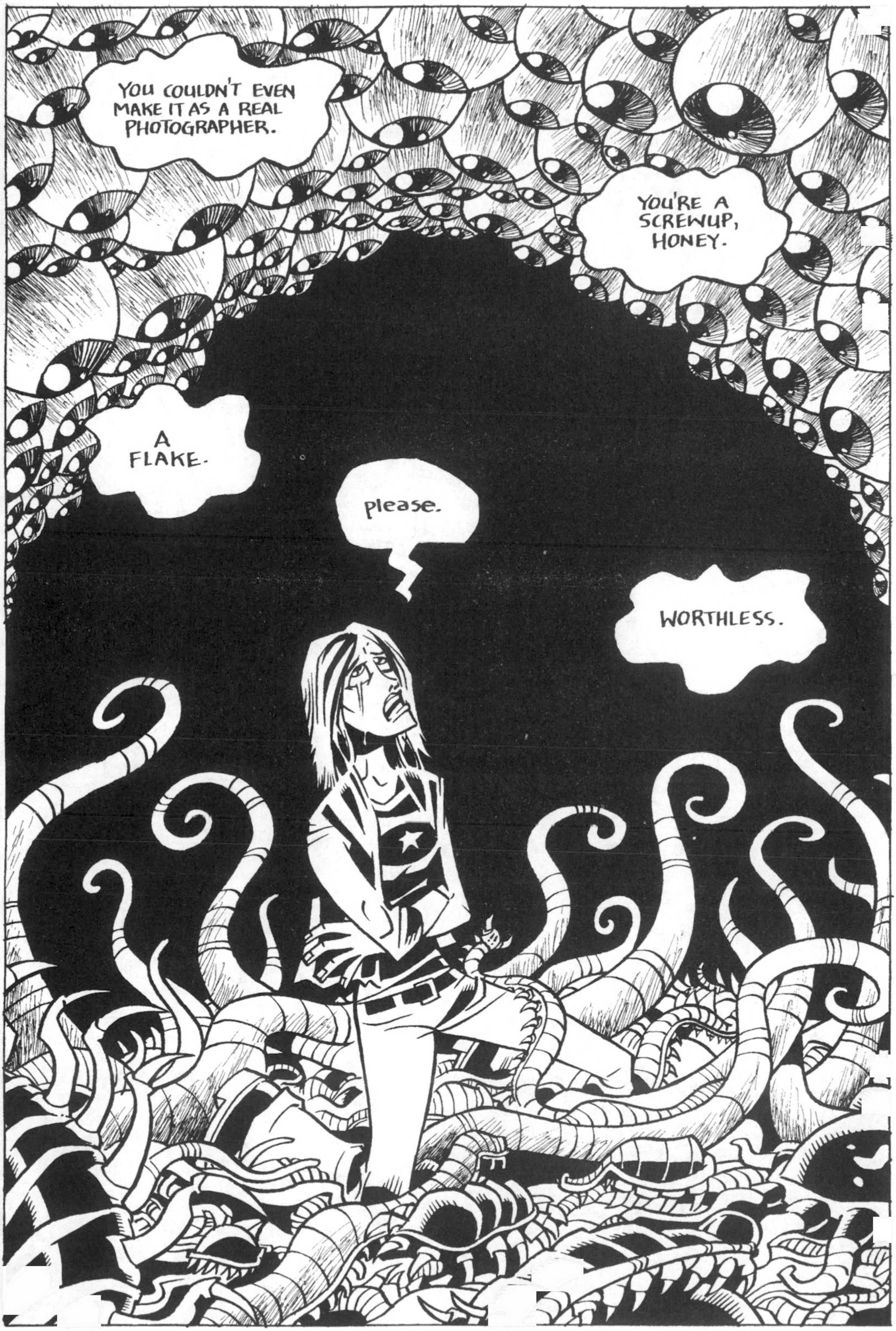
YOU COULDN'T EVEN MAKE IT AS A REAL PHOTOGRAPHER.
YOU'RE A SCREWUP, HONEY.
A FLAKE.
please.
WORTHLESS.

I WAS SIMPLY GOING TO KILL HER, BUT PLAYING WITH HER LIKE THIS IS MUCH TOO FUN... LIKE PULLING THE WINGS FROM A FLY...

HER MIND IS RIFE WITH GUILT... HA! THE PITIFUL FRAILTIES OF HUMAN EMOTION ARE ENDLESS.

SO EASY TO MANIPULATE... TO CONTROL. SO SUITING FOR HER TO WASTE AWAY IN THE PRISON OF HER OWN MIND.

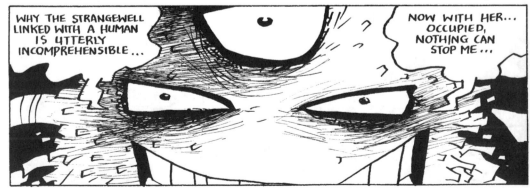

WHY THE STRANGEWELL LINKED WITH A HUMAN IS UTTERLY INCOMPREHENSIBLE...

NOW WITH HER... OCCUPIED, NOTHING CAN STOP ME...

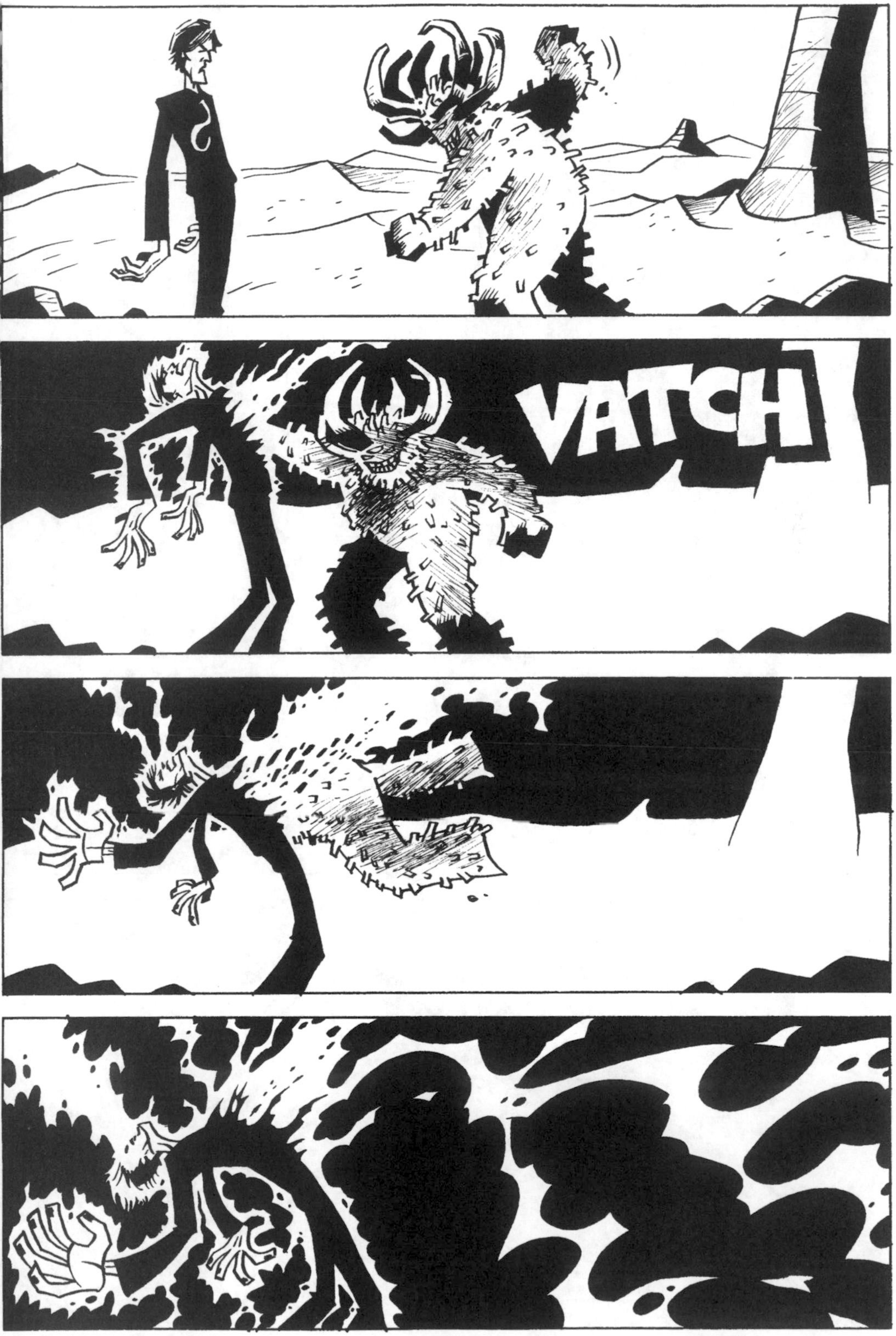
VATCH

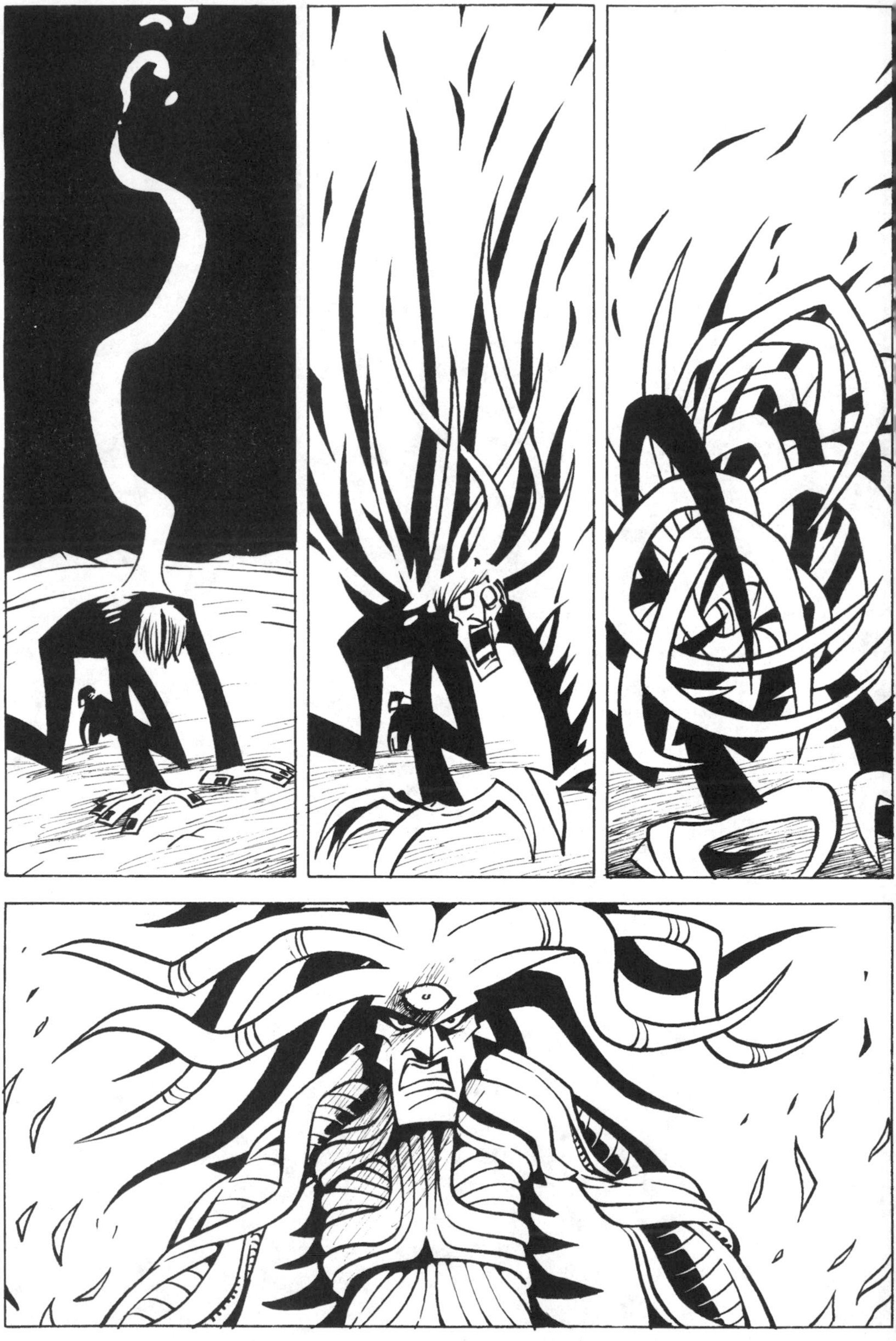

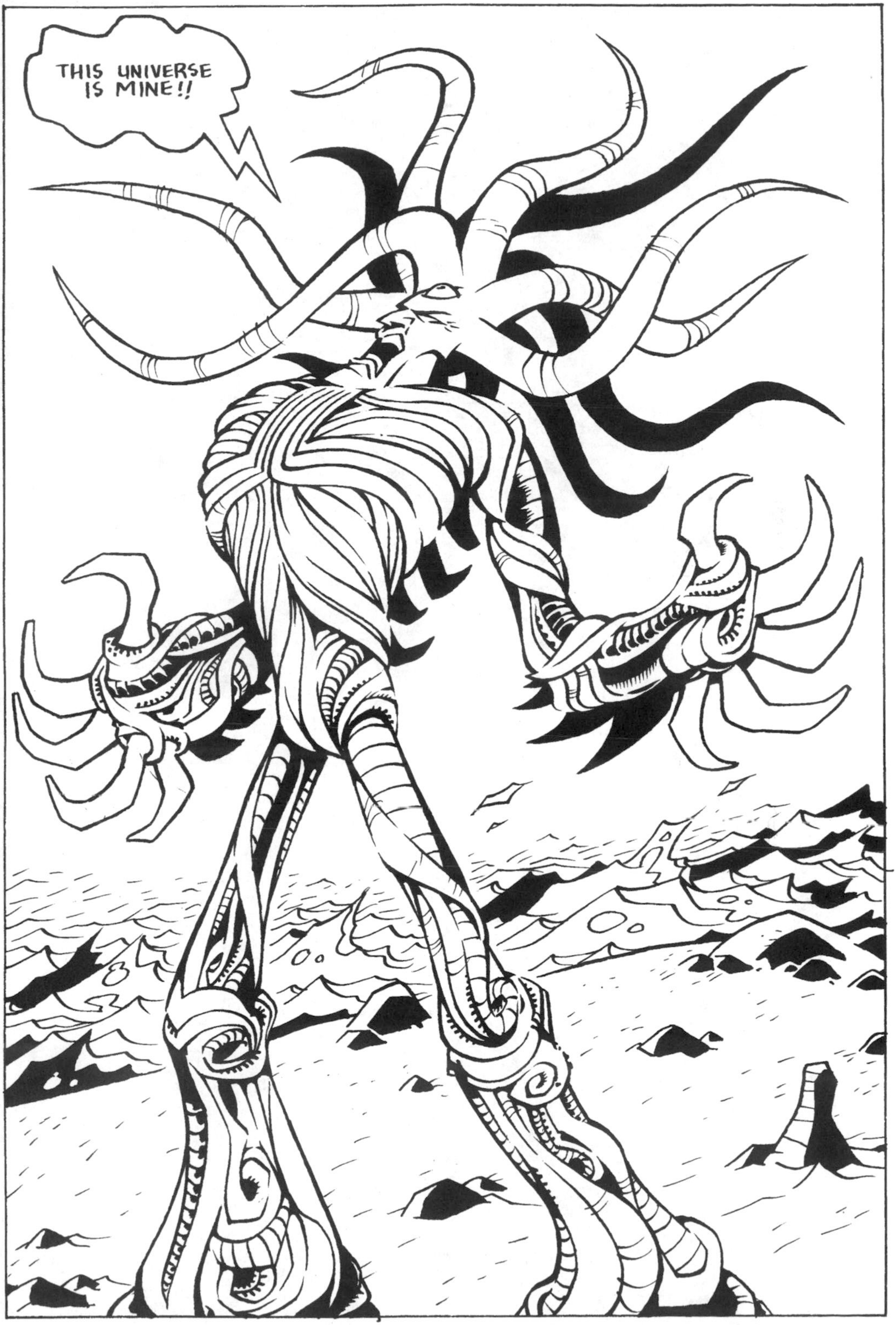
THIS UNIVERSE IS MINE!!

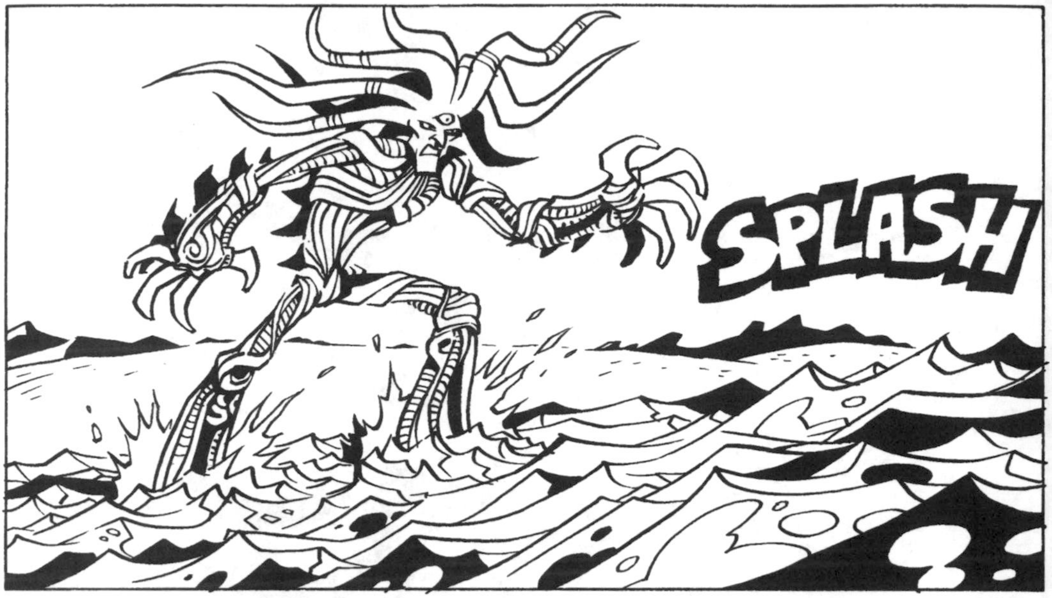
SPLASH

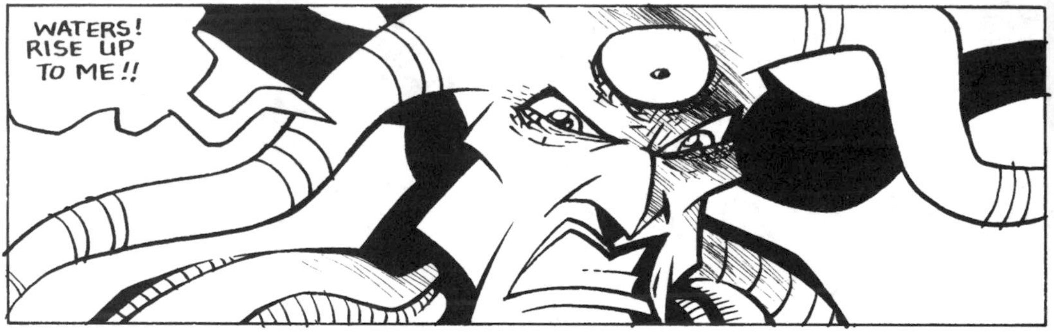
WATERS! RISE UP TO ME!!

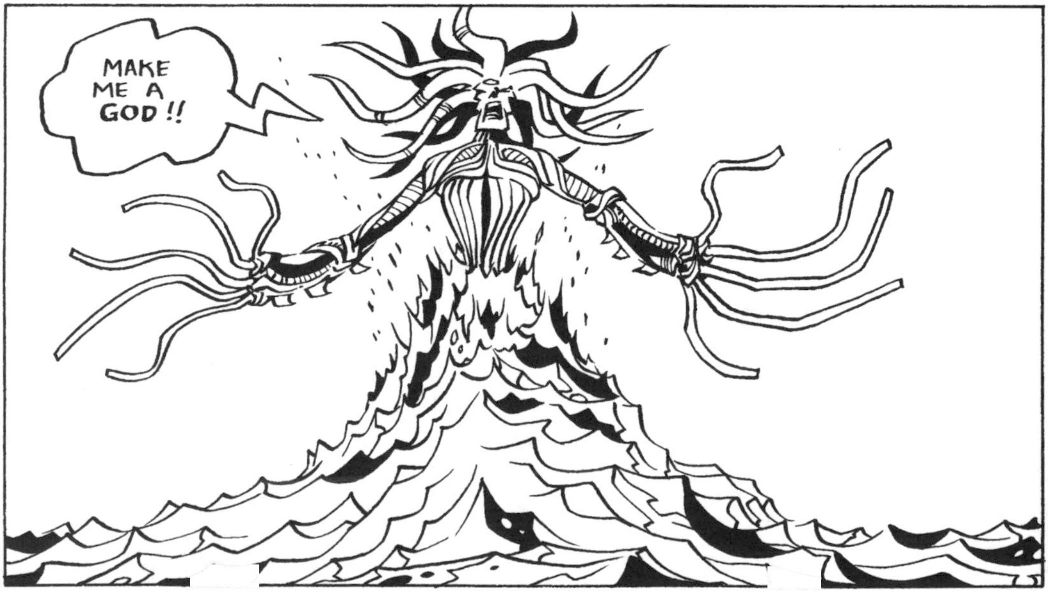
MAKE ME A GOD!!

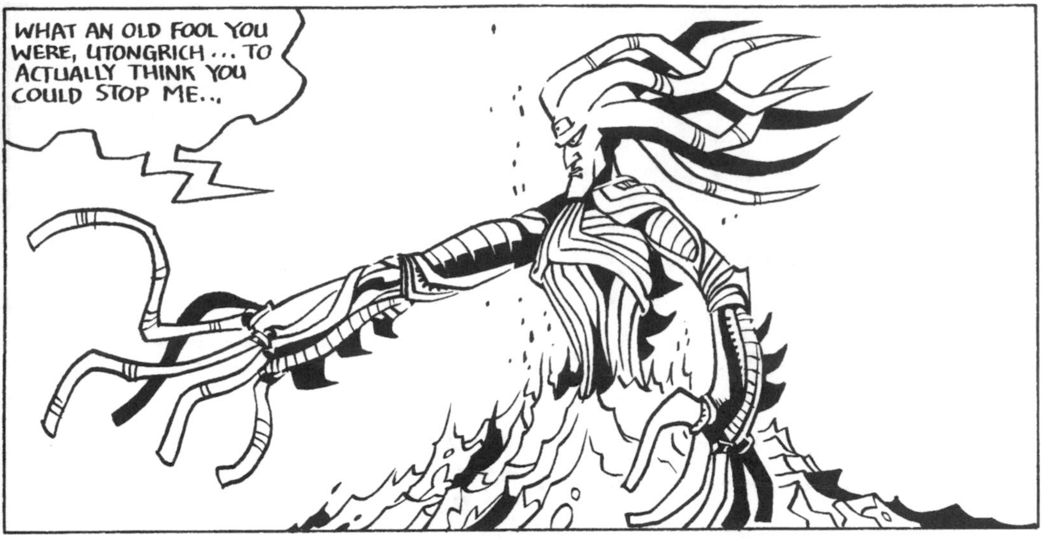
WHAT AN OLD FOOL YOU WERE, UTONGRICH... TO ACTUALLY THINK YOU COULD STOP ME...

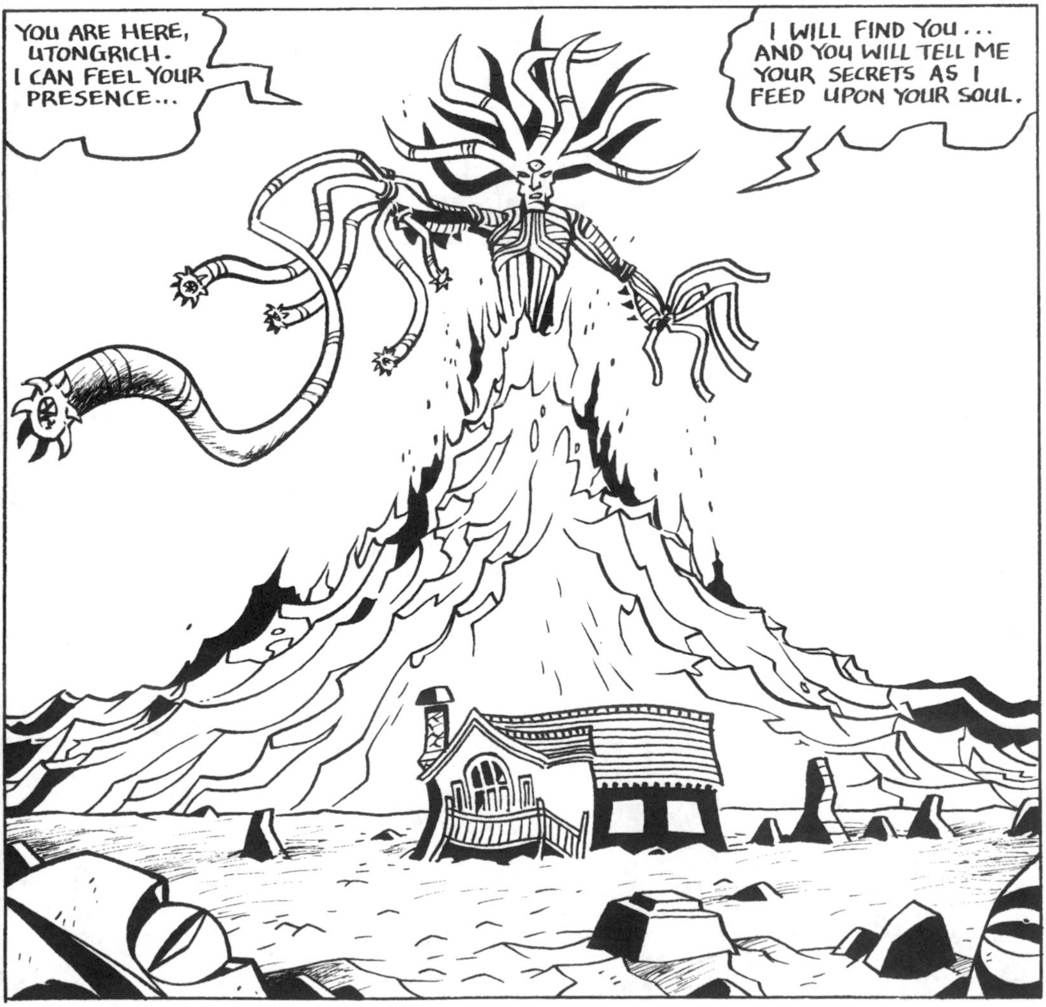
YOU ARE HERE, UTONGRICH. I CAN FEEL YOUR PRESENCE...
I WILL FIND YOU... AND YOU WILL TELL ME YOUR SECRETS AS I FEED UPON YOUR SOUL.

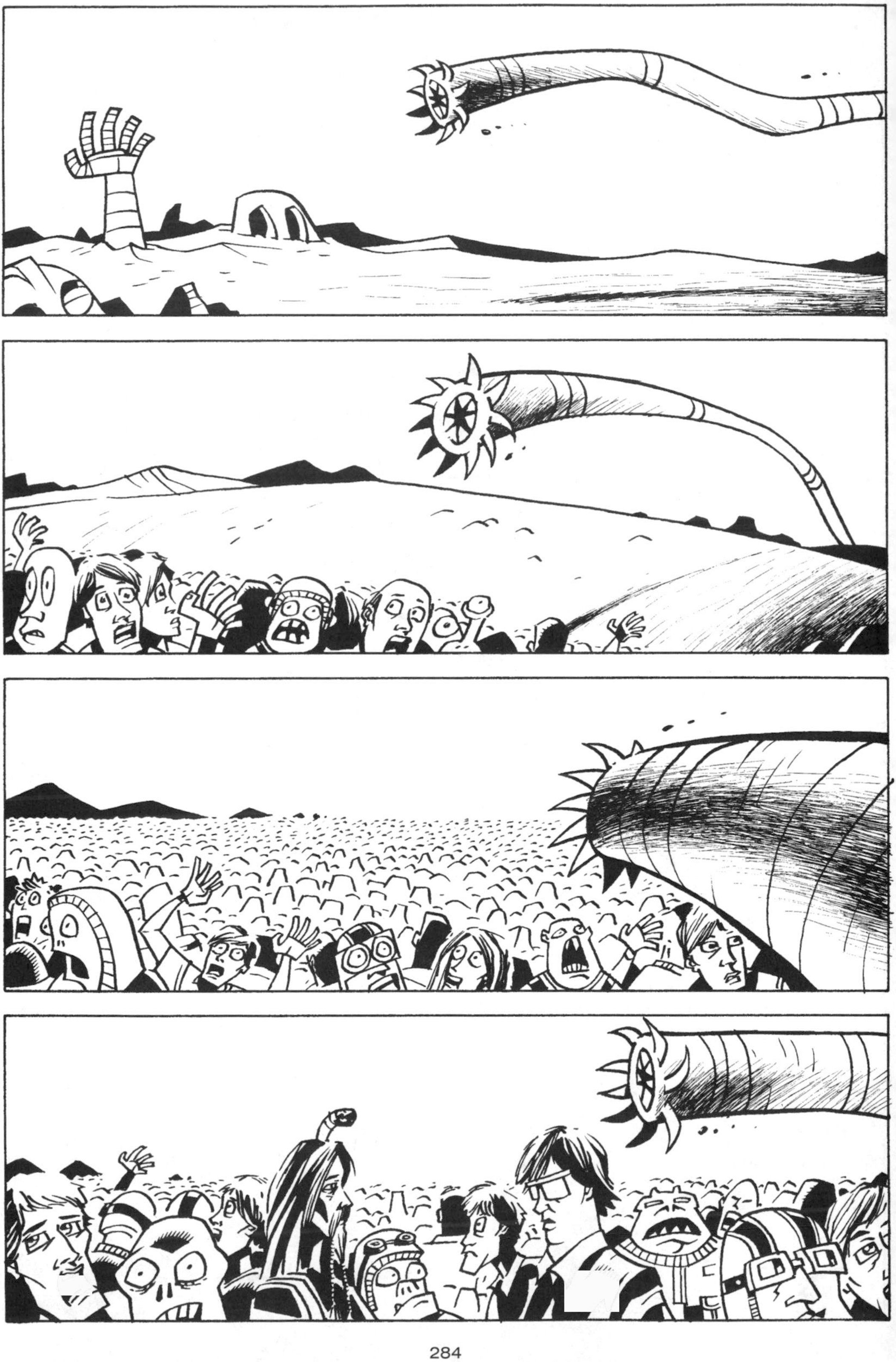

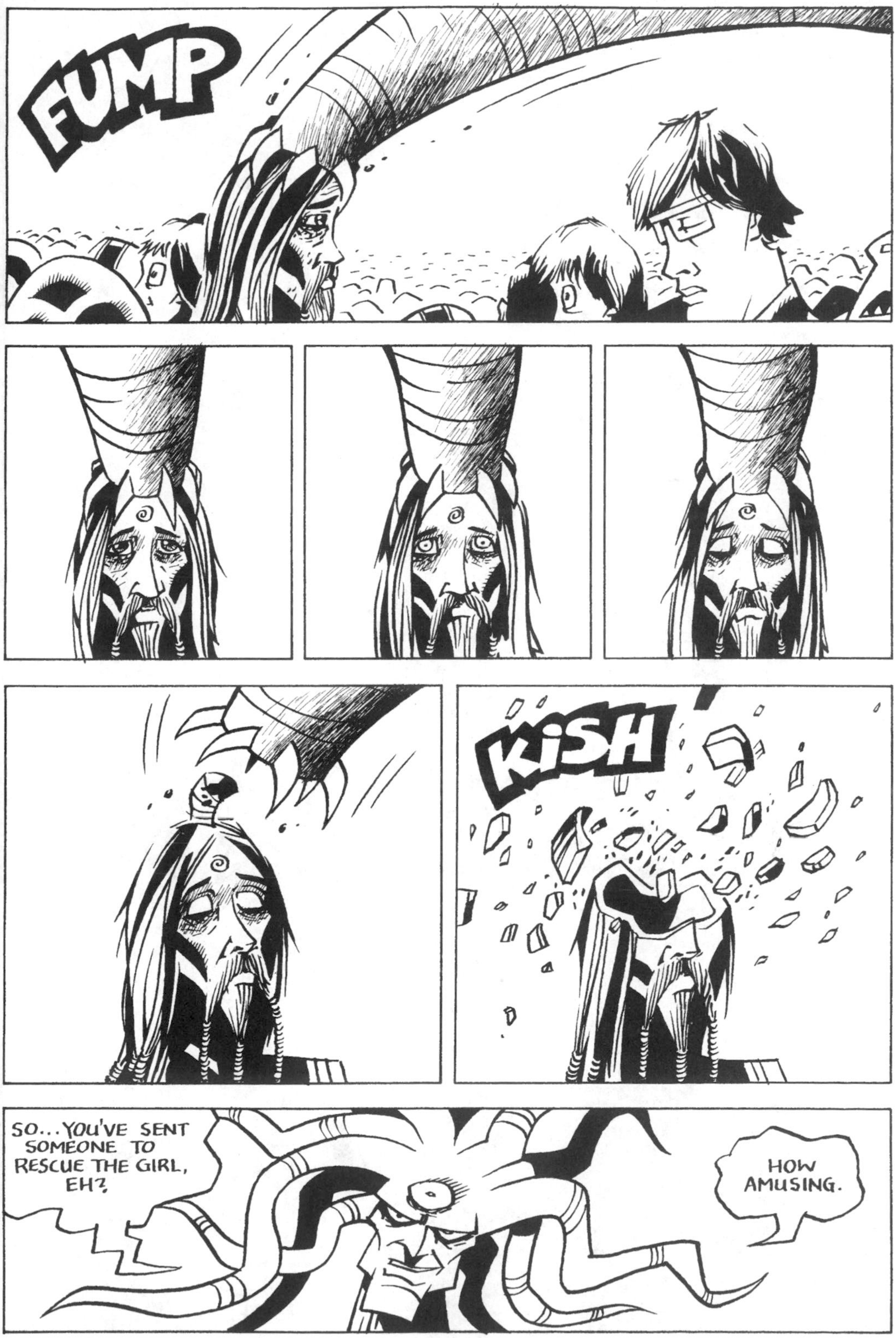
FUMP
KISH
SO... YOU'VE SENT SOMEONE TO RESCUE THE GIRL, EH?
HOW AMUSING.

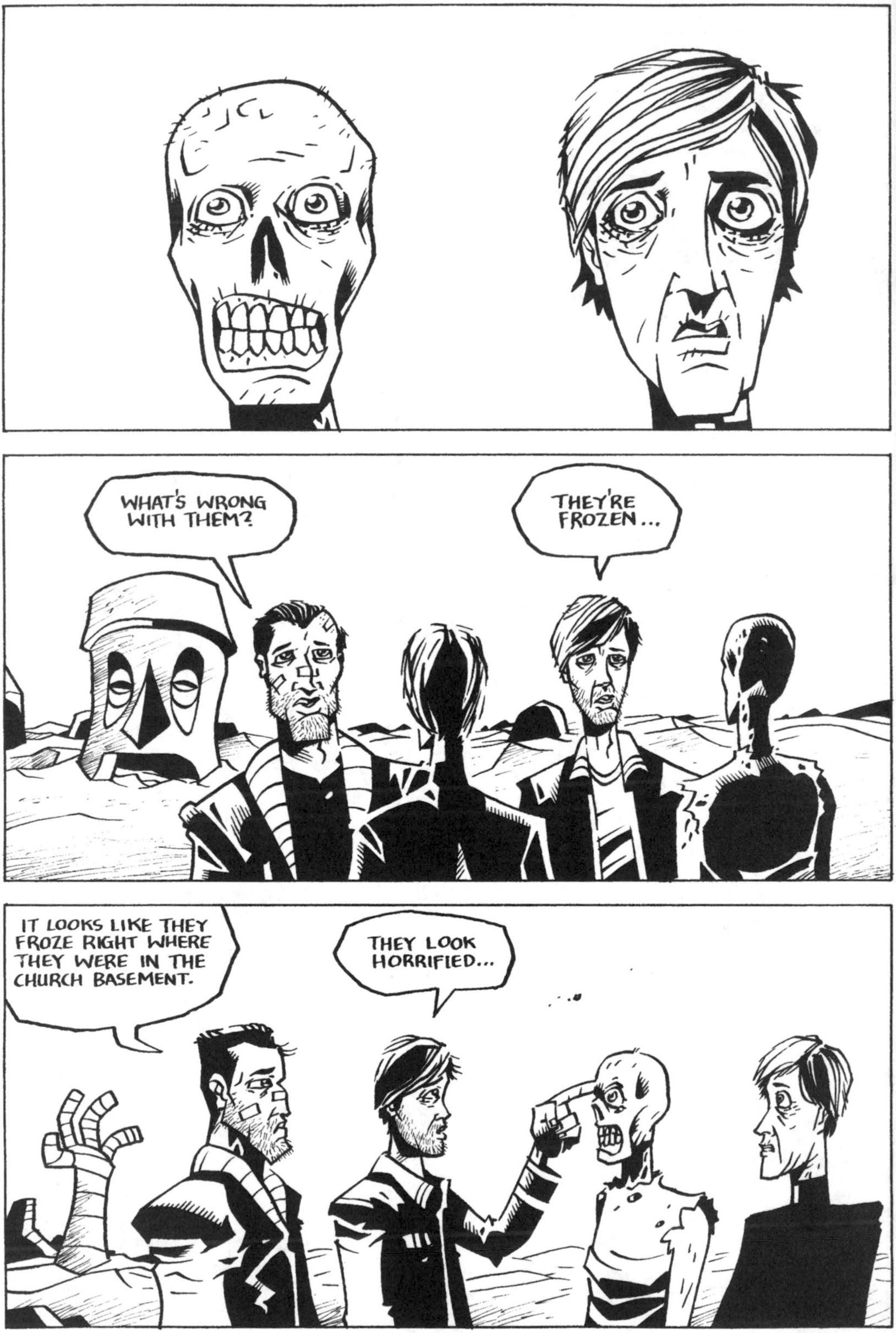
WHAT'S WRONG WITH THEM?
THEY'RE FROZEN...
IT LOOKS LIKE THEY FROZE RIGHT WHERE THEY WERE IN THE CHURCH BASEMENT.
THEY LOOK HORRIFIED...

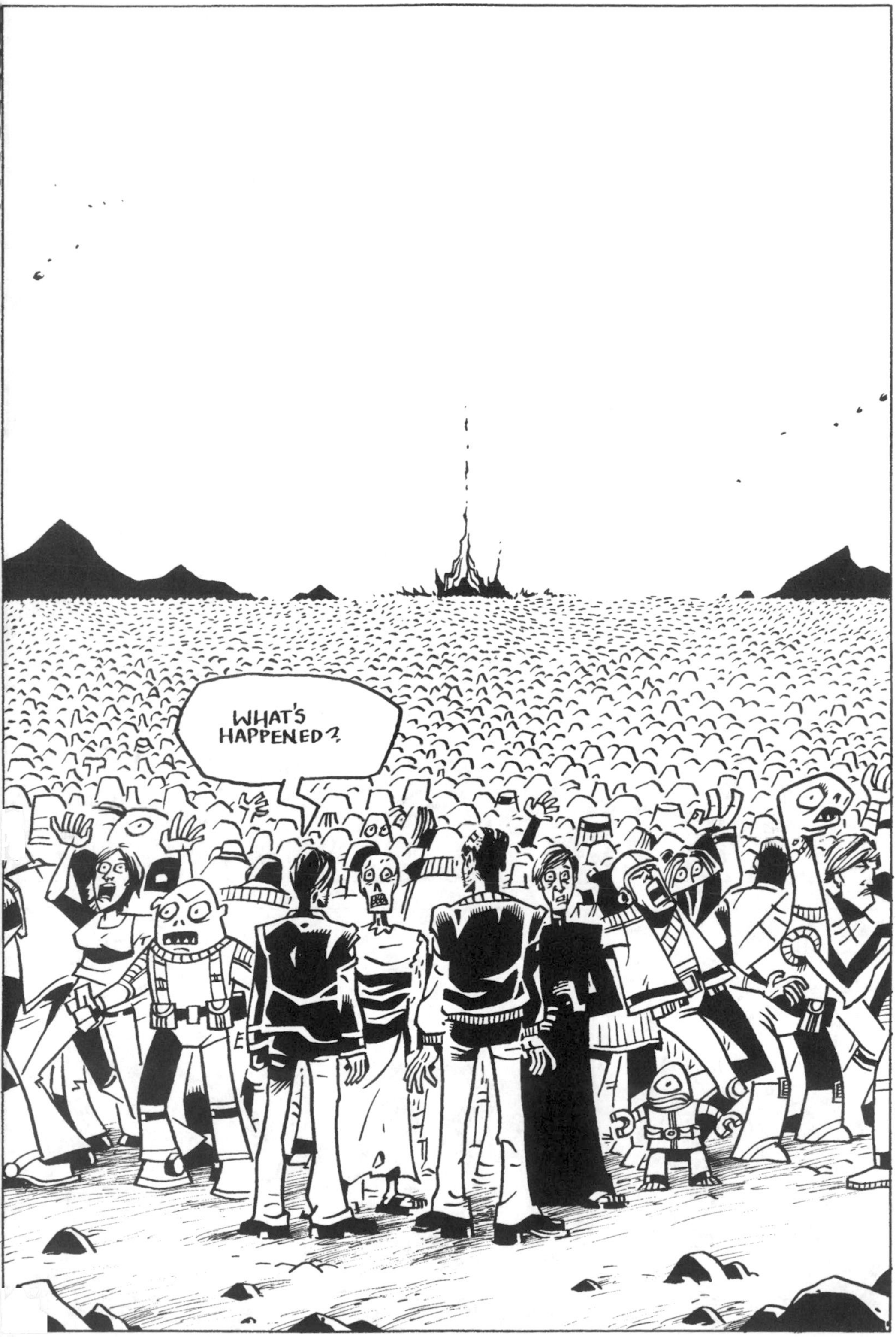
WHAT'S HAPPENED?

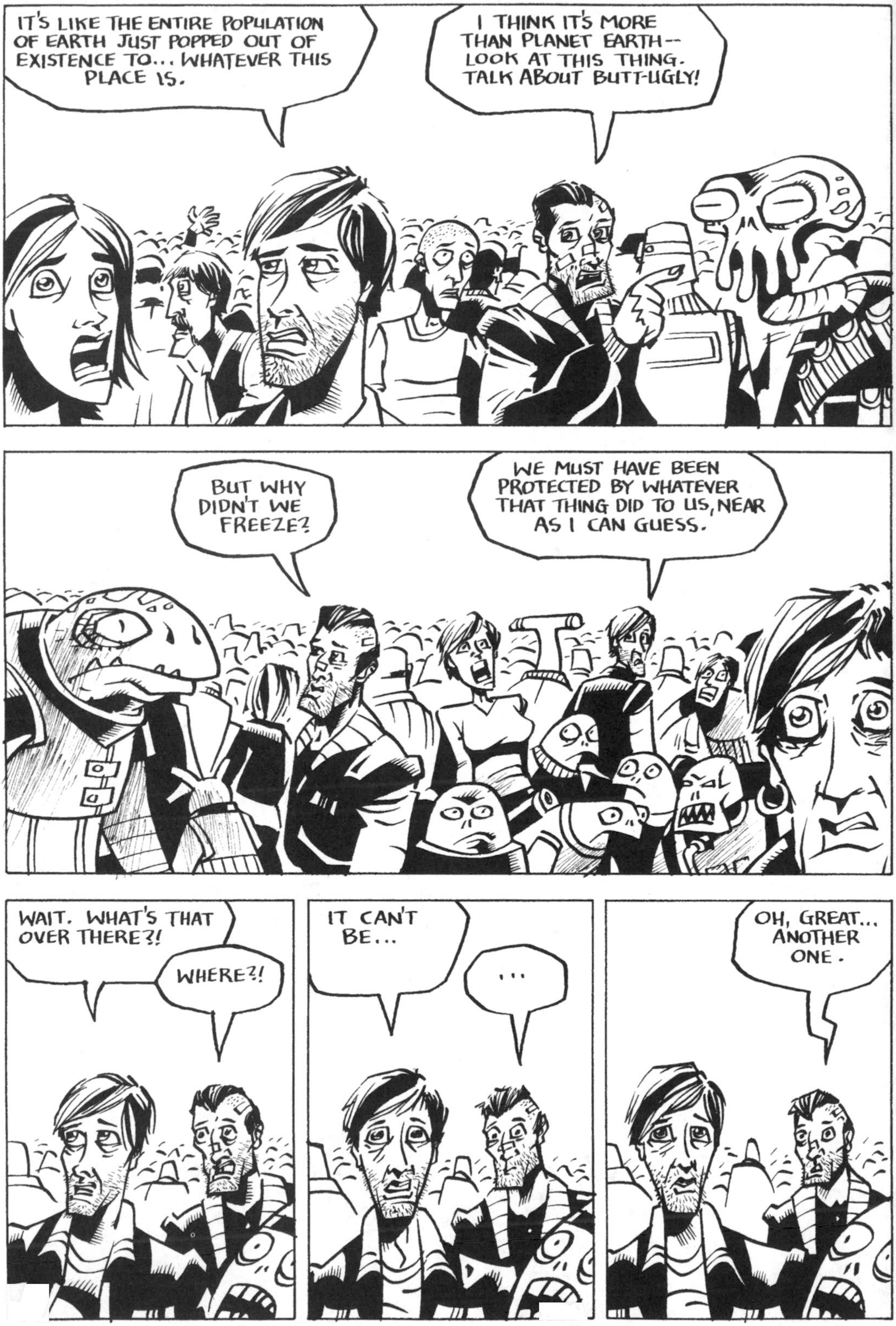
IT'S LIKE THE ENTIRE POPULATION OF EARTH JUST POPPED OUT OF EXISTENCE TO... WHATEVER THIS PLACE IS.
I THINK IT'S MORE THAN PLANET EARTH-- LOOK AT THIS THING. TALK ABOUT BUTT-UGLY!
BUT WHY DIDN'T WE FREEZE?
WE MUST HAVE BEEN PROTECTED BY WHATEVER THAT THING DID TO US, NEAR AS I CAN GUESS.
WAIT. WHAT'S THAT OVER THERE?!
WHERE?!
IT CAN'T BE...
...
OH, GREAT... ANOTHER ONE.

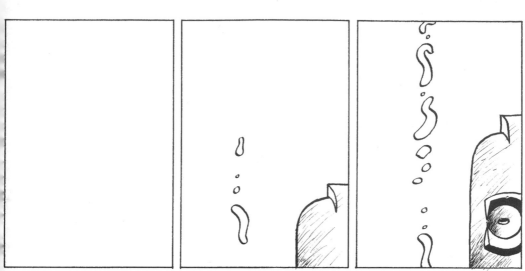

PHELP, WHAT'S IT LIKE BEING DEAD?

KINDA LIKE A DREAM, I GUESS. DISORIENTING AT FIRST, BUT THEN YOU GO WITH THE FLOW.

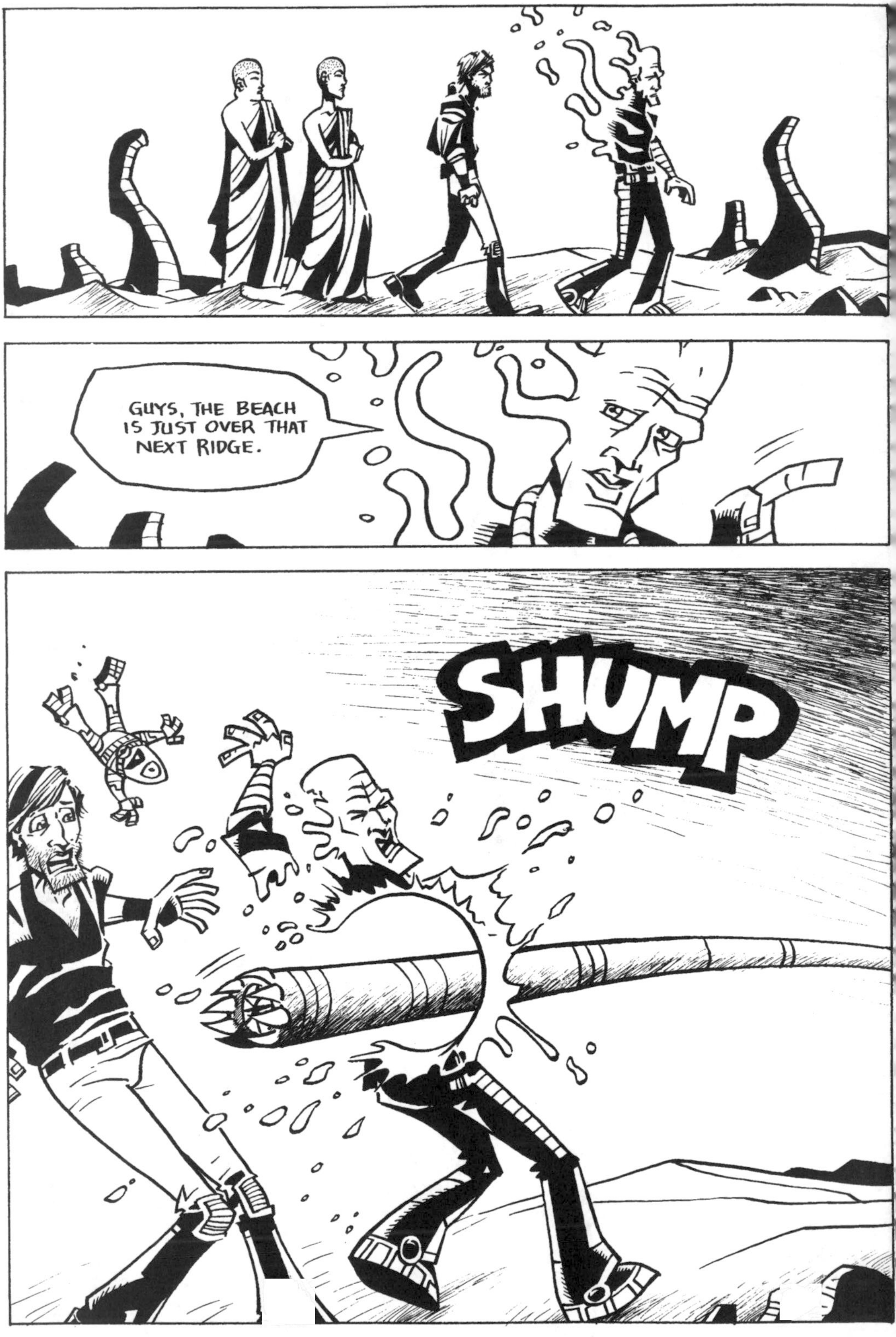
GUYS, THE BEACH IS JUST OVER THAT NEXT RIDGE.
SHUMP

SHIT!
GAH!
CHUNK
CHUP
CHUP
HOLD STILL.

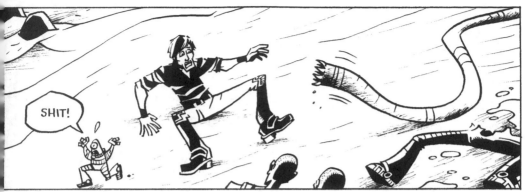

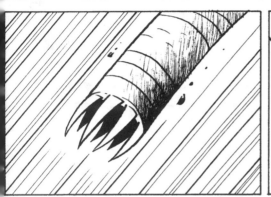

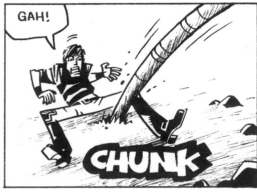

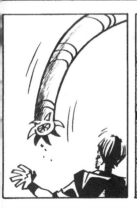

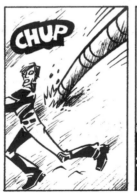

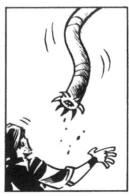

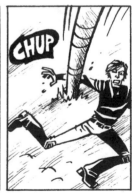

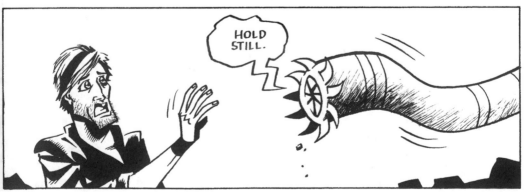

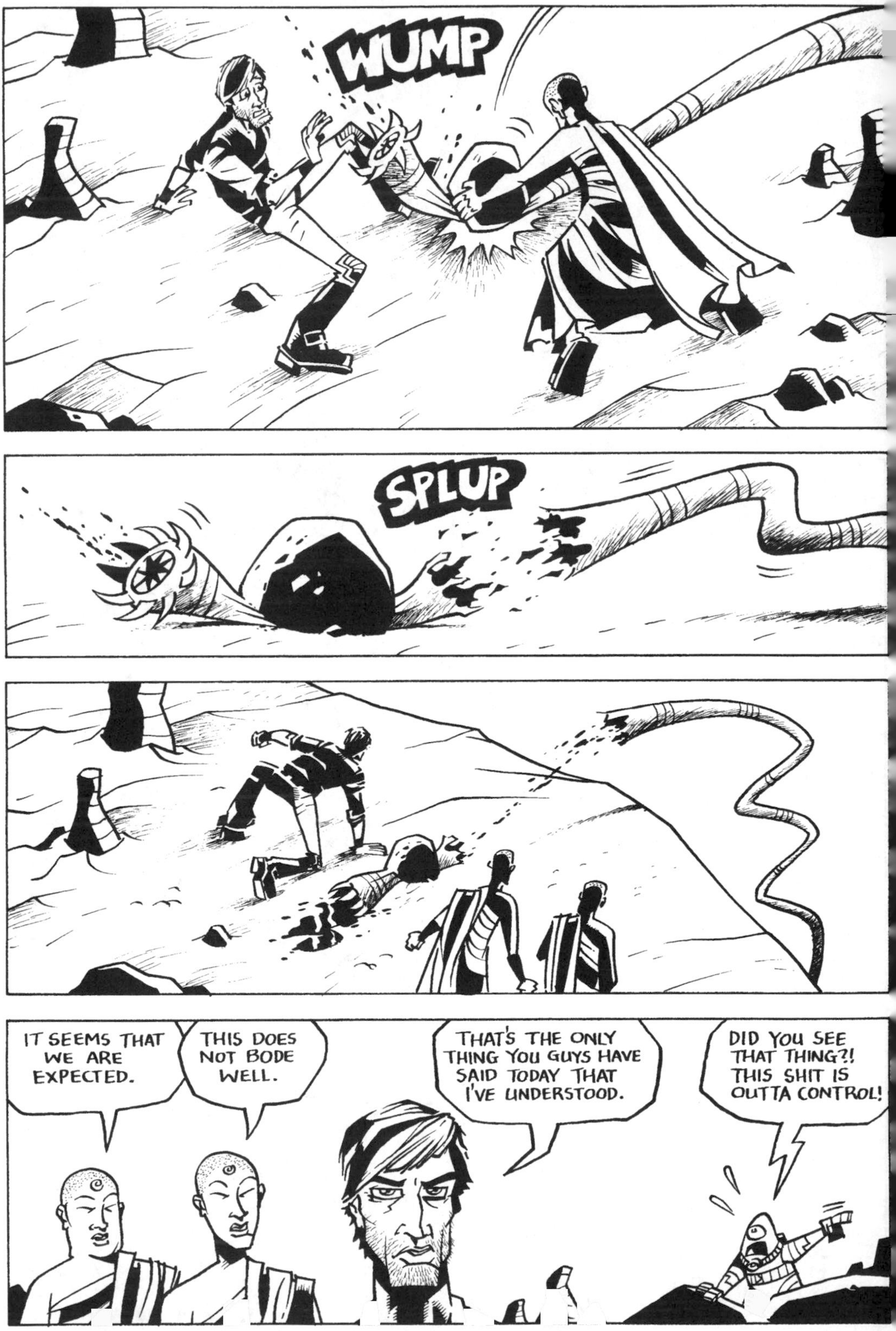
WUMP
SPLUP
IT SEEMS THAT WE ARE EXPECTED.
THIS DOES NOT BODE WELL.
THAT'S THE ONLY THING YOU GUYS HAVE SAID TODAY THAT I'VE UNDERSTOOD.
DID YOU SEE THAT THING?! THIS SHIT IS OUTTA CONTROL!

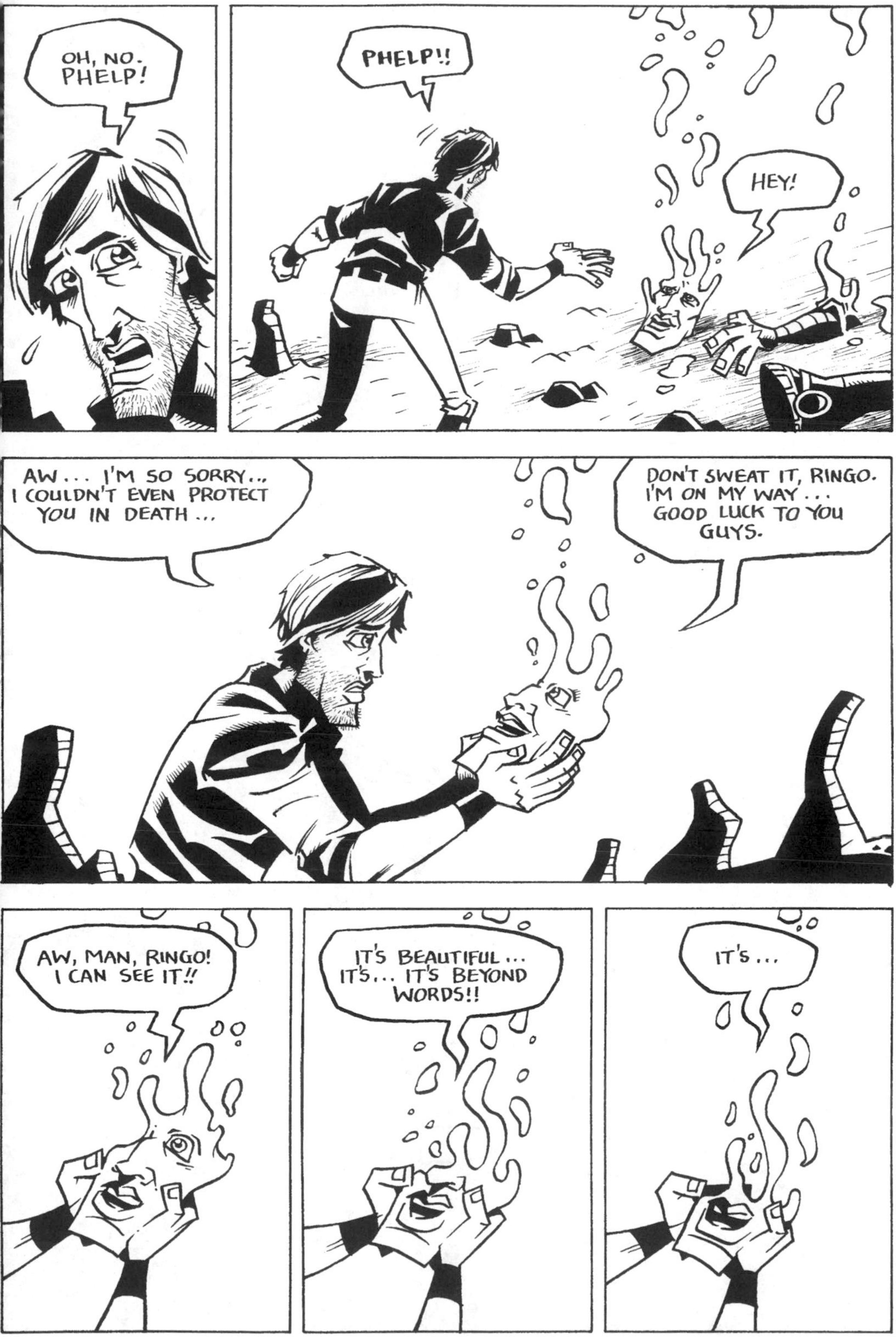
OH, NO. PHELP!
PHELP!!
HEY!
AW... I'M SO SORRY.., I COULDN'T EVEN PROTECT YOU IN DEATH...
DON'T SWEAT IT, RINGO. I'M ON MY WAY... GOOD LUCK TO YOU GUYS.
AW, MAN, RINGO! I CAN SEE IT!!
IT'S BEAUTIFUL... IT'S... IT'S BEYOND WORDS!!
IT'S...

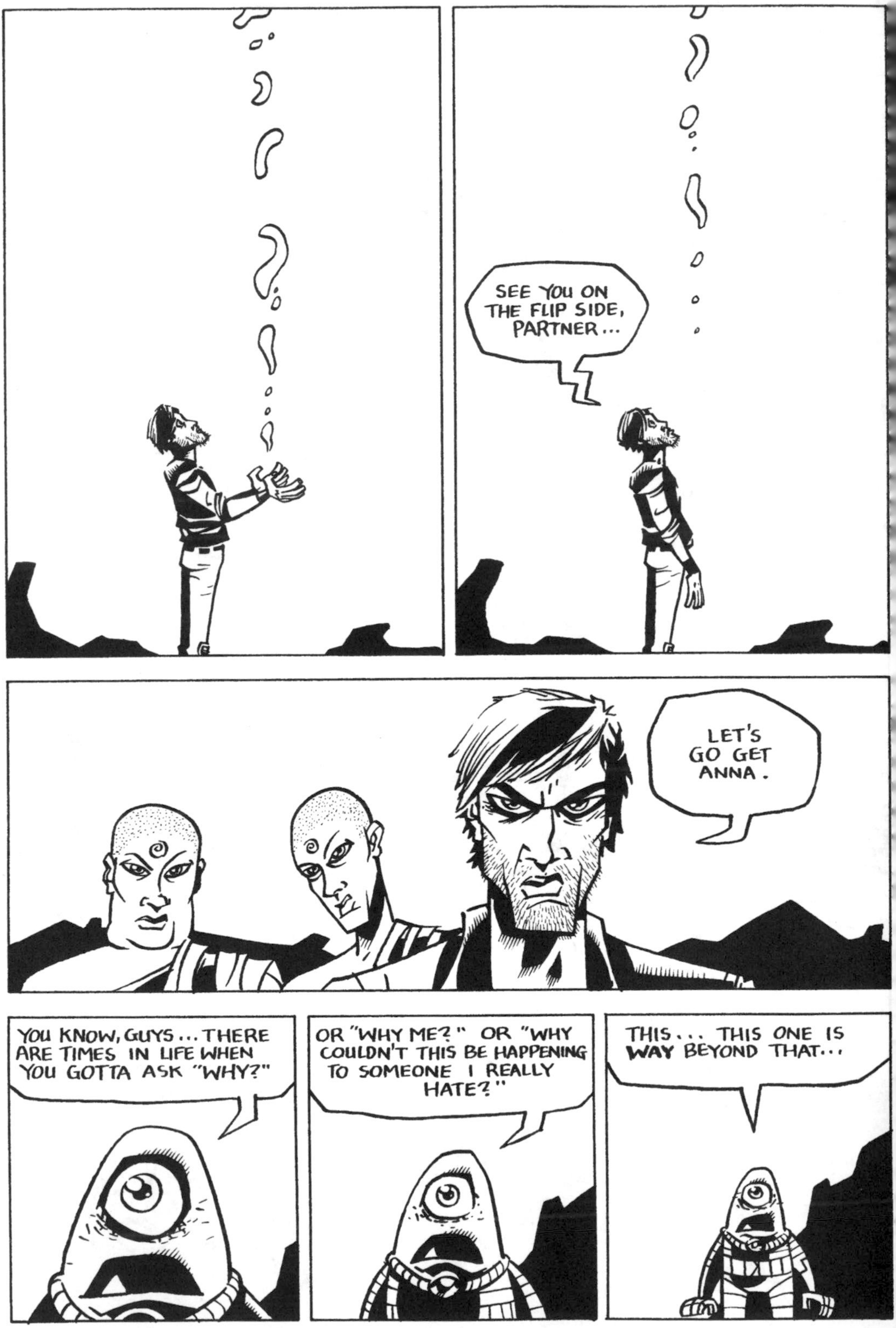
SEE YOU ON THE FLIP SIDE, PARTNER...
LET'S GO GET ANNA.
YOU KNOW, GUYS... THERE ARE TIMES IN LIFE WHEN YOU GOTTA ASK "WHY?"
OR "WHY ME?" OR "WHY COULDN'T THIS BE HAPPENING TO SOMEONE I REALLY HATE?"
THIS... THIS ONE IS **WAY** BEYOND THAT...

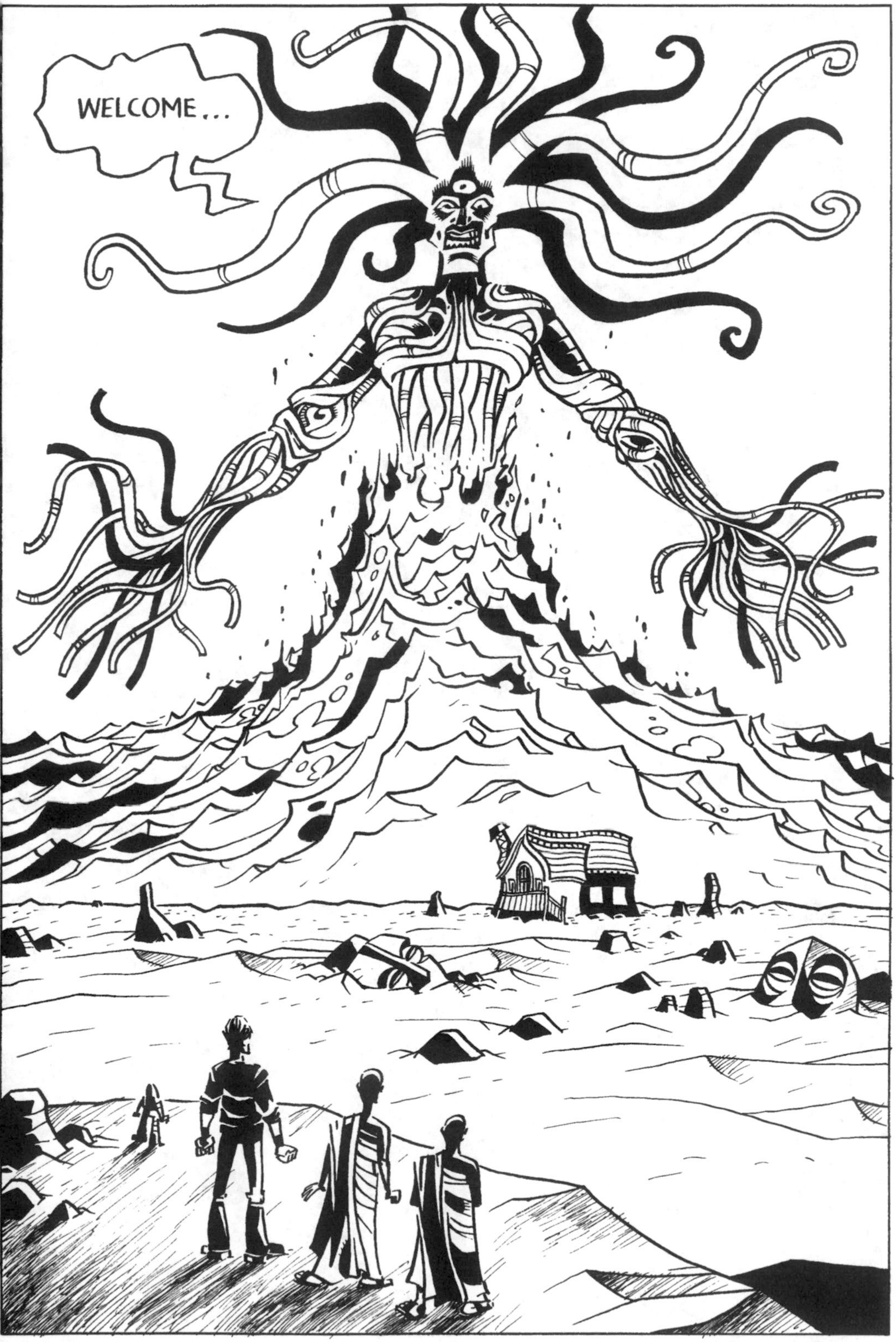
WELCOME...

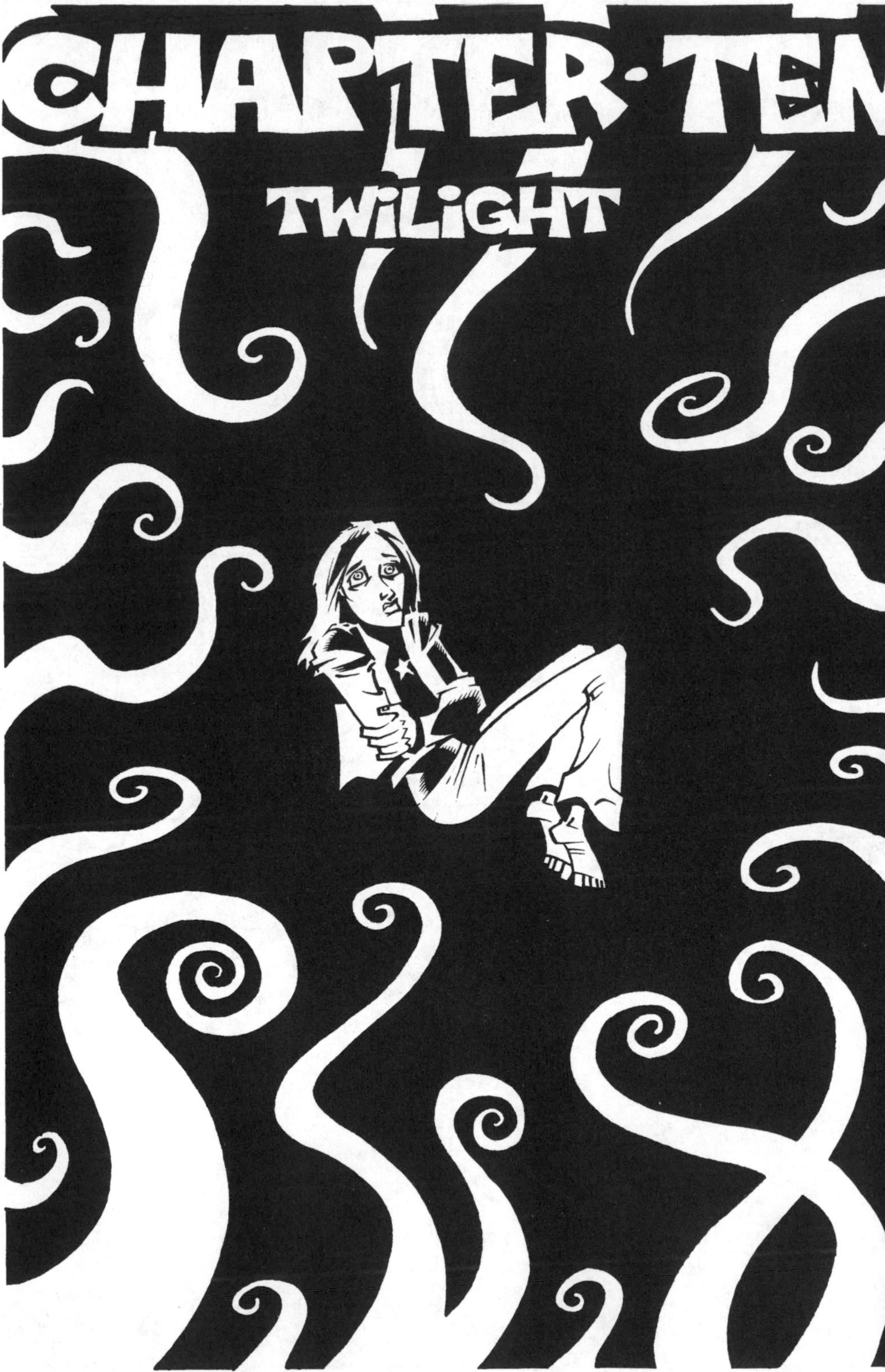
CHAPTER·TEN
TWILIGHT

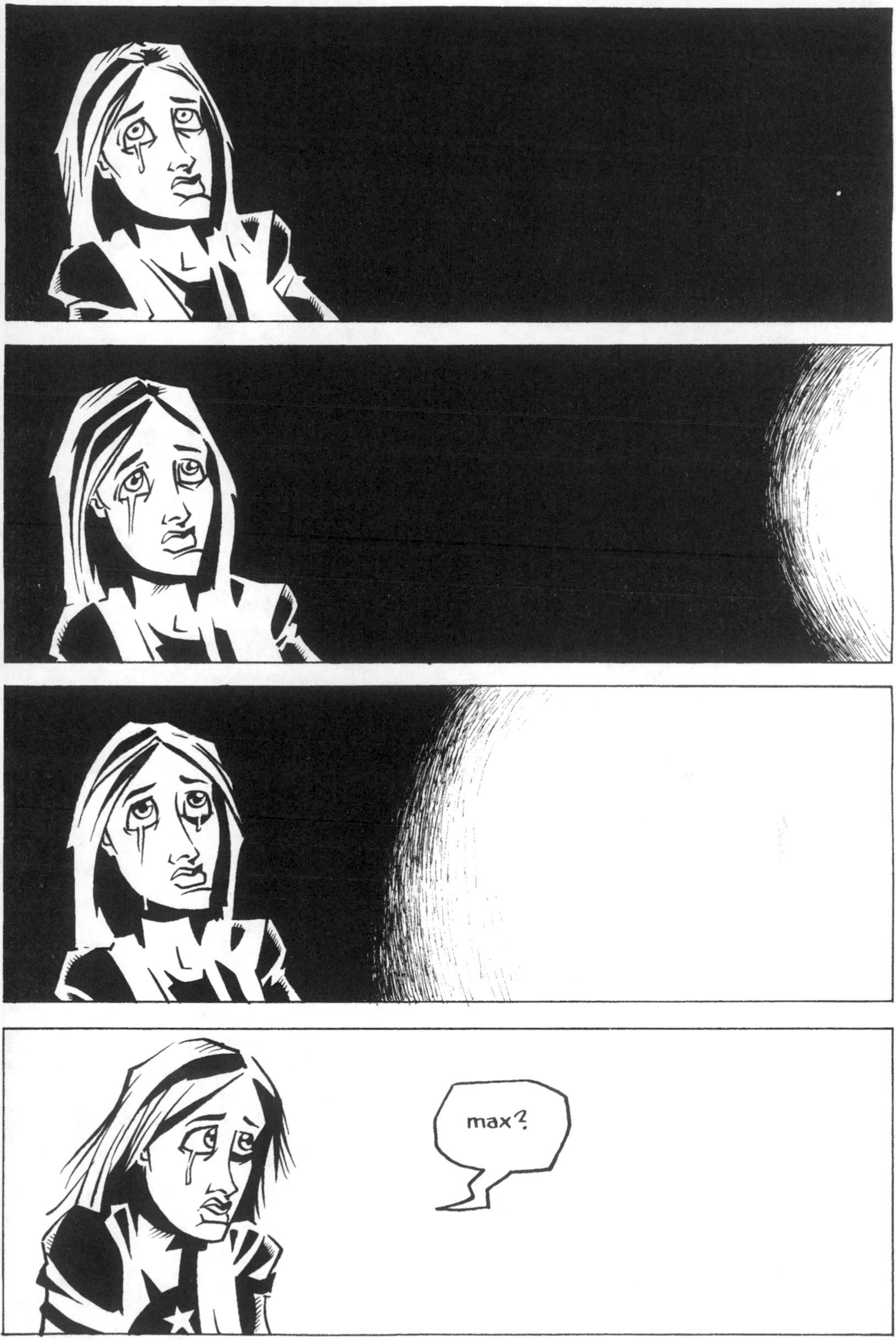
max?

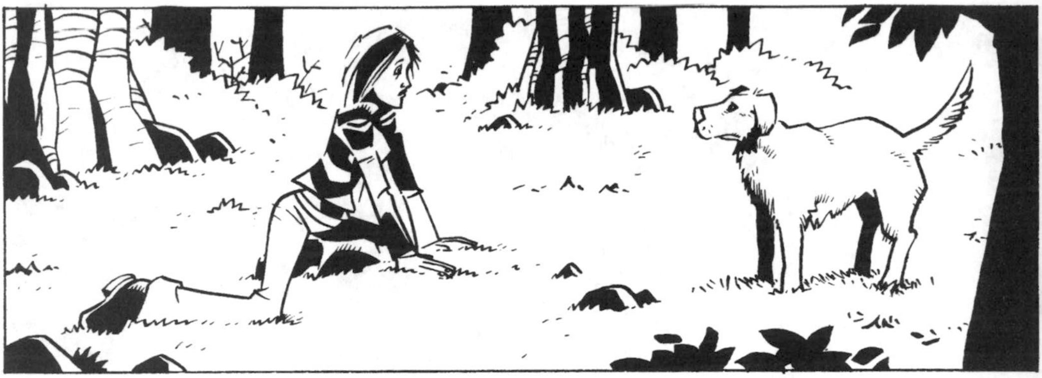

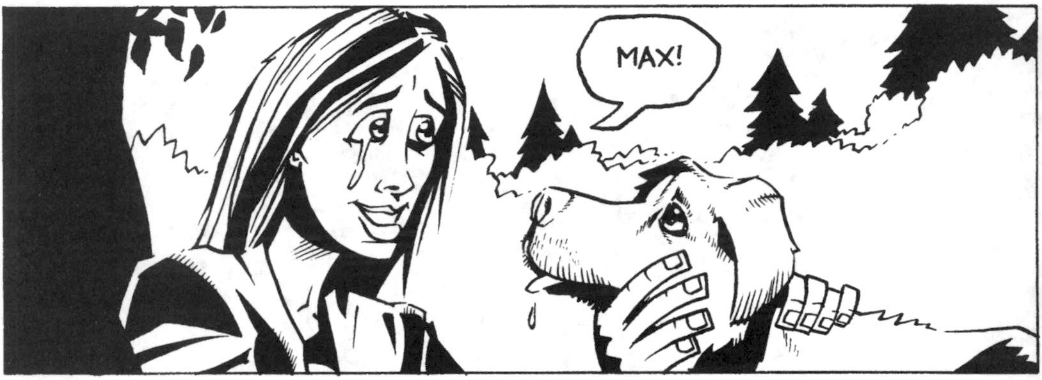
MAX!

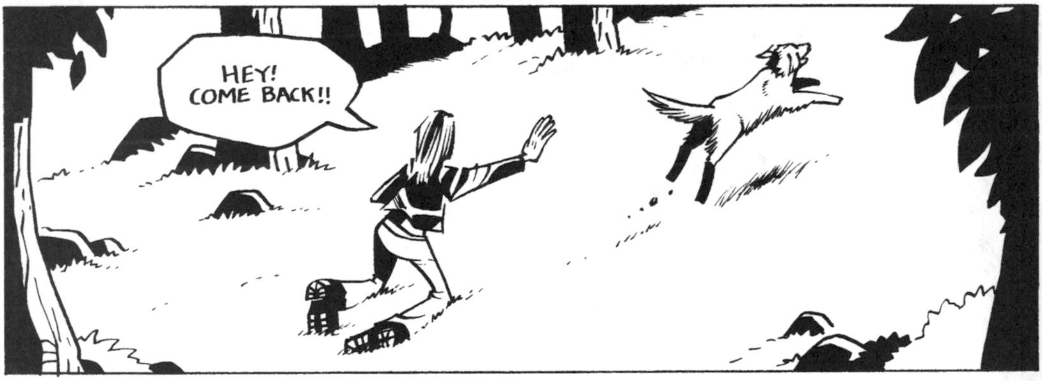
HEY!
COME BACK!!

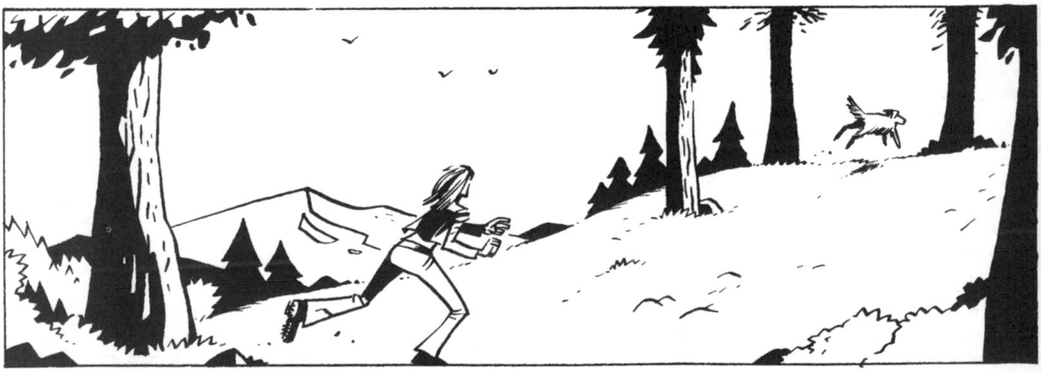

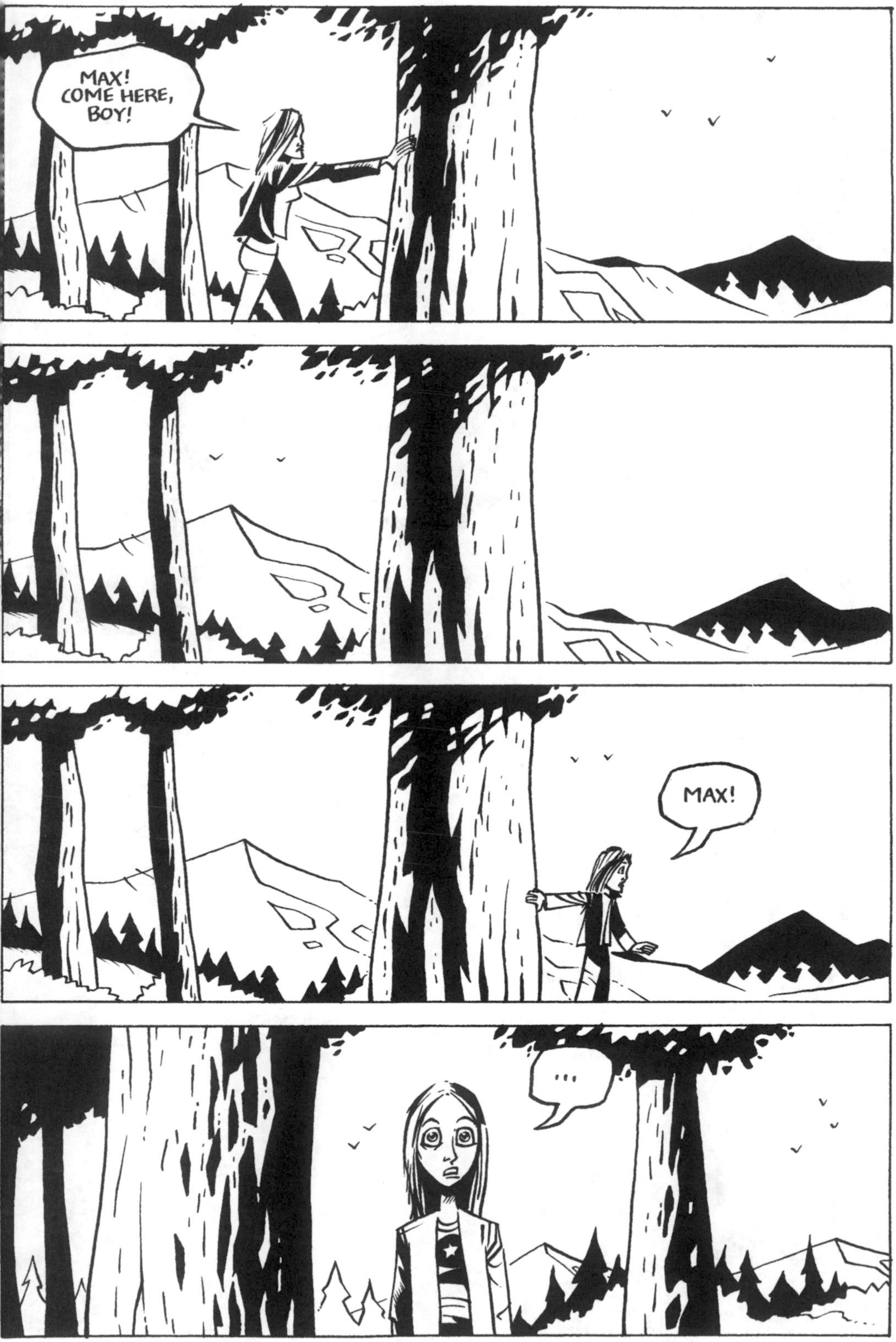
MAX! COME HERE, BOY!
MAX!
...

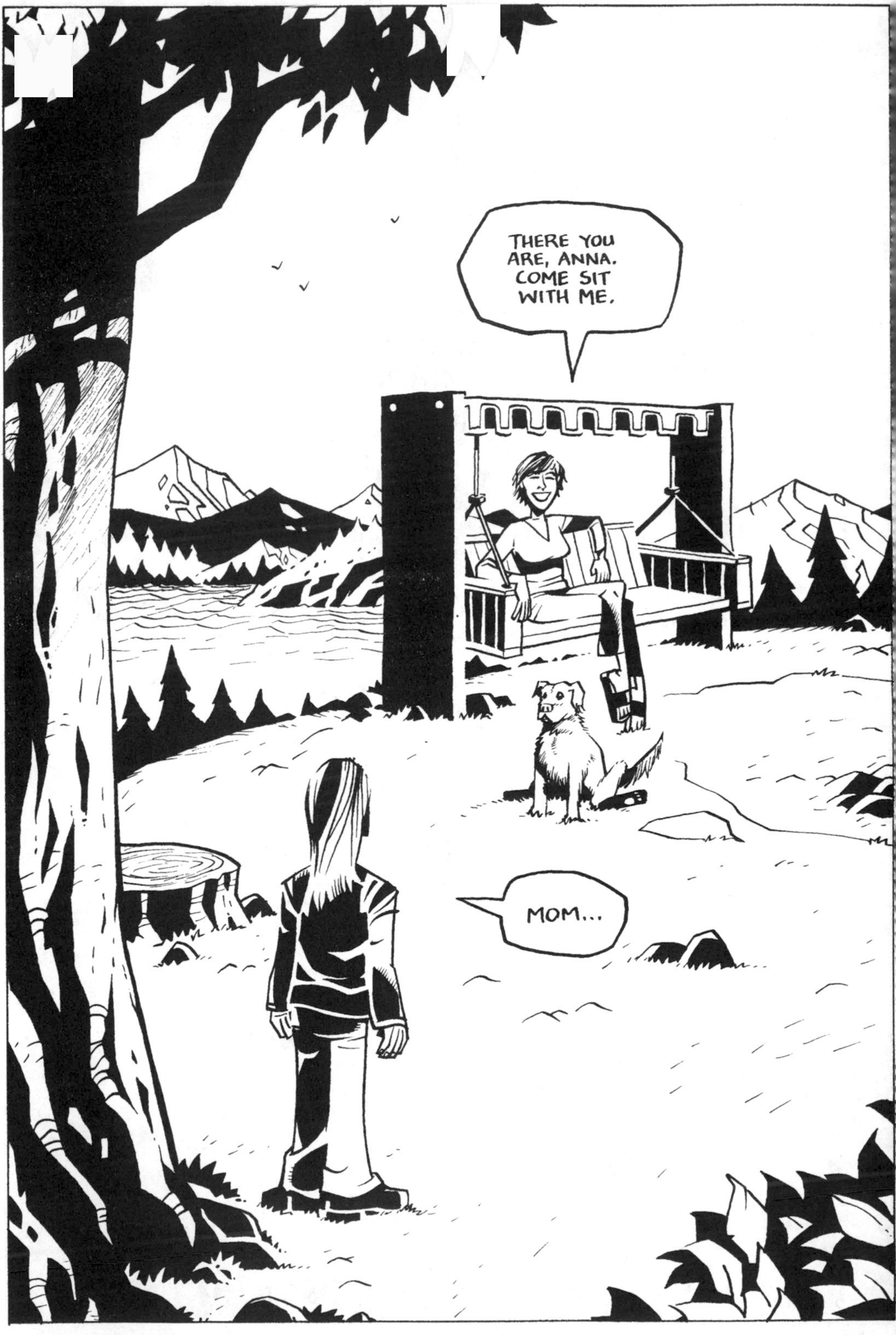
THERE YOU ARE, ANNA. COME SIT WITH ME.
MOM...

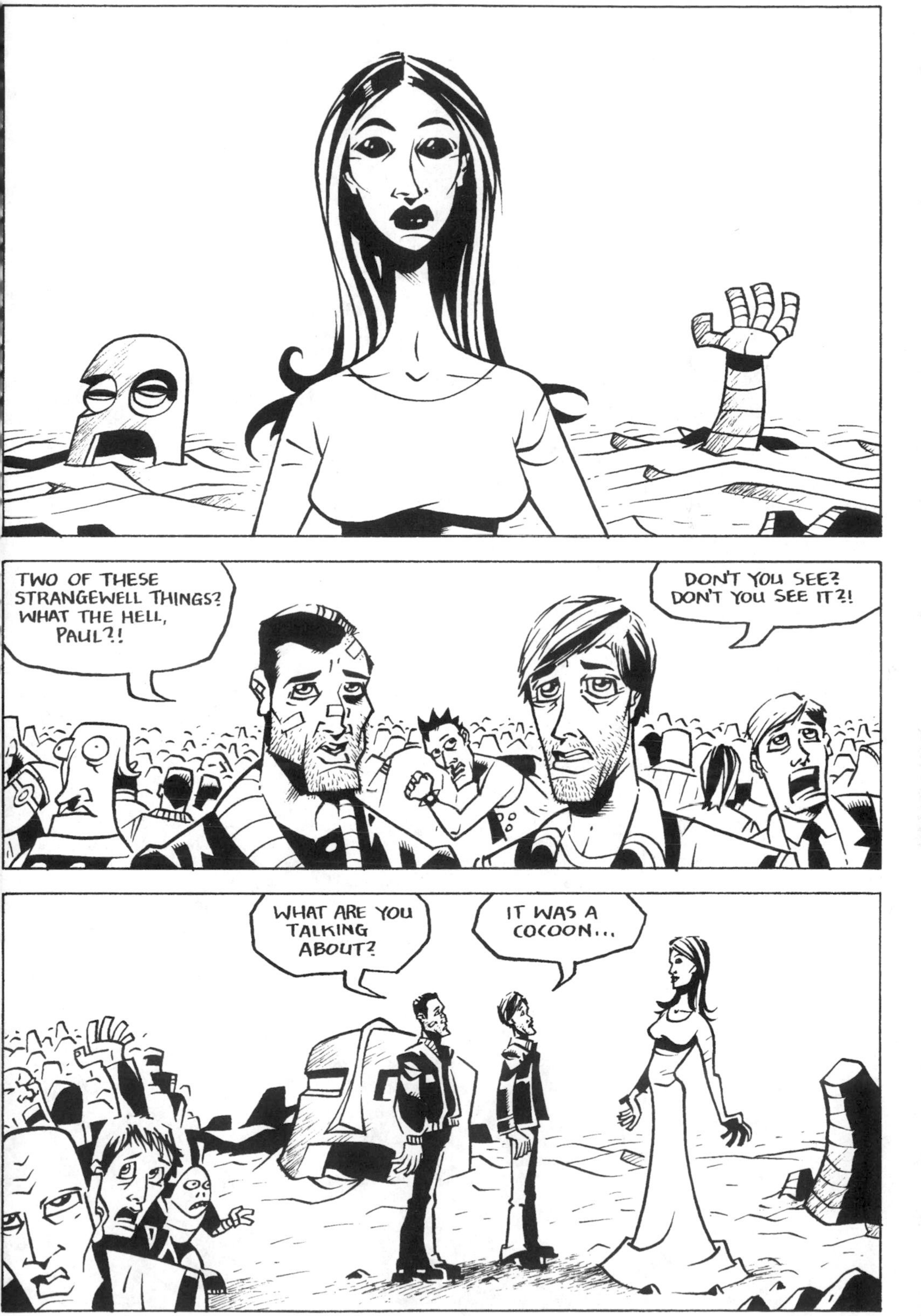
TWO OF THESE STRANGEWELL THINGS? WHAT THE HELL, PAUL?!
DON'T YOU SEE? DON'T YOU SEE IT?!
WHAT ARE YOU TALKING ABOUT?
IT WAS A COCOON...

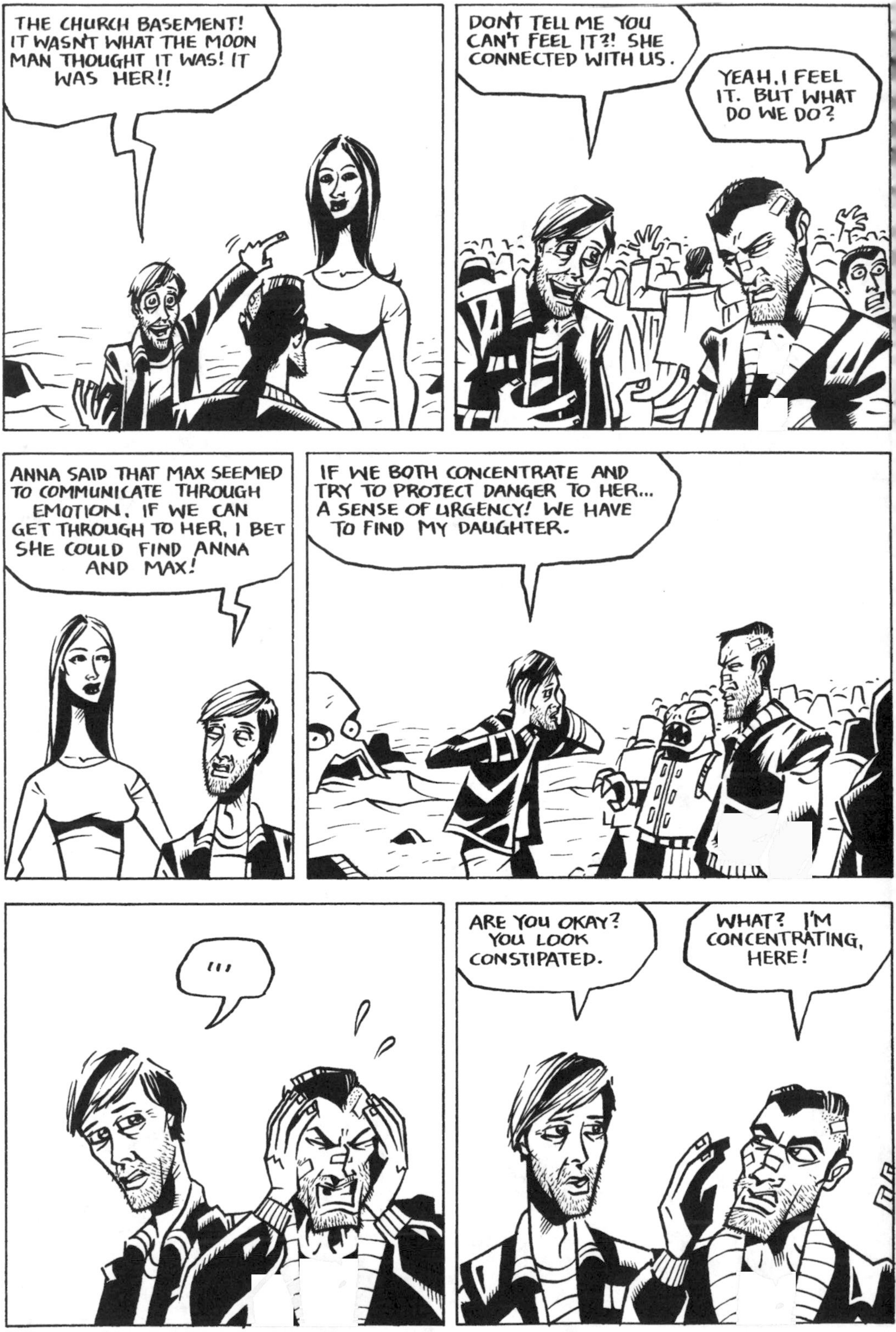
THE CHURCH BASEMENT! IT WASN'T WHAT THE MOON MAN THOUGHT IT WAS! IT WAS HER!!
DON'T TELL ME YOU CAN'T FEEL IT?! SHE CONNECTED WITH US.
YEAH, I FEEL IT. BUT WHAT DO WE DO?
ANNA SAID THAT MAX SEEMED TO COMMUNICATE THROUGH EMOTION. IF WE CAN GET THROUGH TO HER, I BET SHE COULD FIND ANNA AND MAX!
IF WE BOTH CONCENTRATE AND TRY TO PROJECT DANGER TO HER... A SENSE OF URGENCY! WE HAVE TO FIND MY DAUGHTER.
...
ARE YOU OKAY? YOU LOOK CONSTIPATED.
WHAT? I'M CONCENTRATING, HERE!

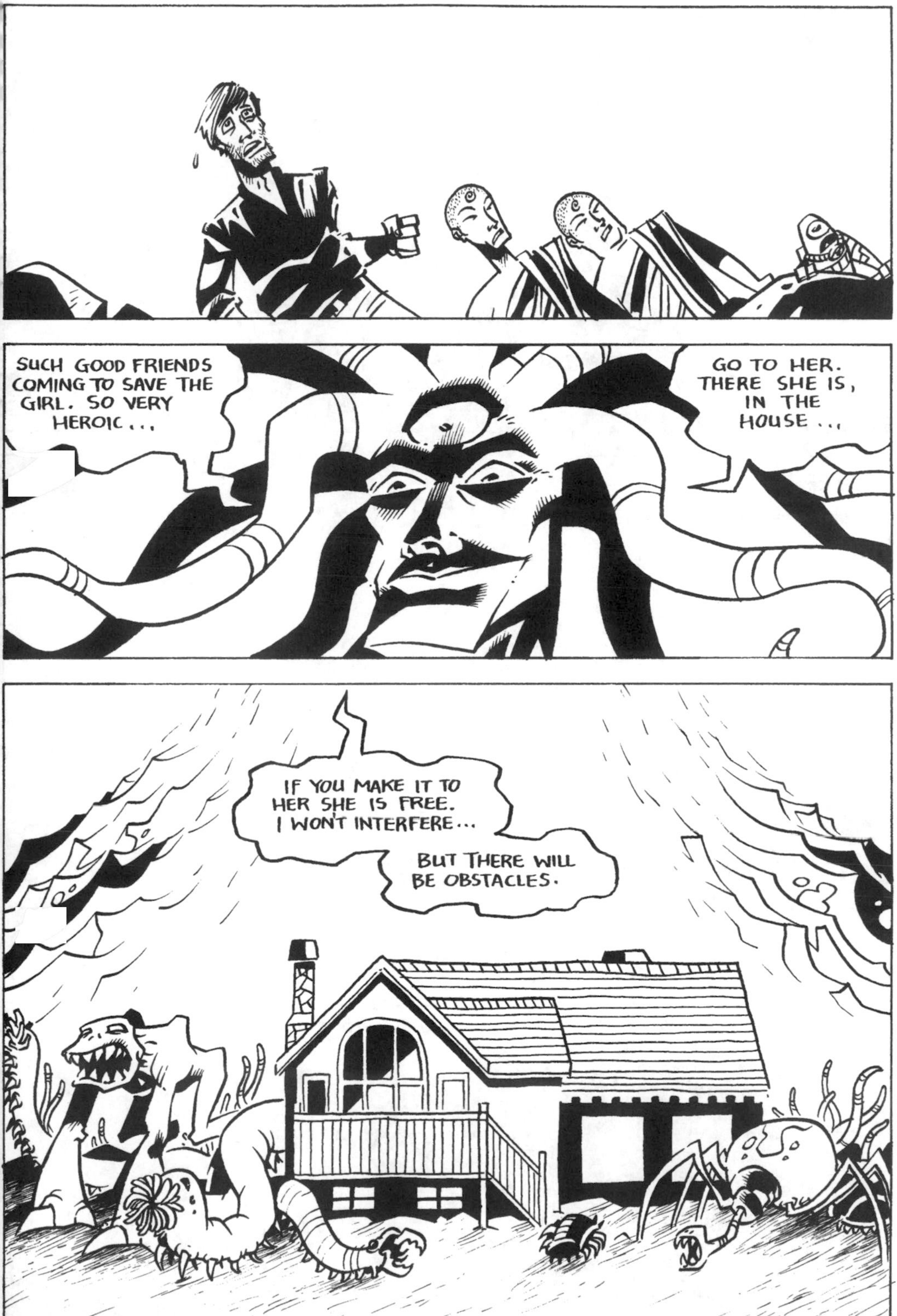
SUCH GOOD FRIENDS COMING TO SAVE THE GIRL. SO VERY HEROIC...
GO TO HER. THERE SHE IS, IN THE HOUSE...
IF YOU MAKE IT TO HER SHE IS FREE. I WON'T INTERFERE...
BUT THERE WILL BE OBSTACLES.

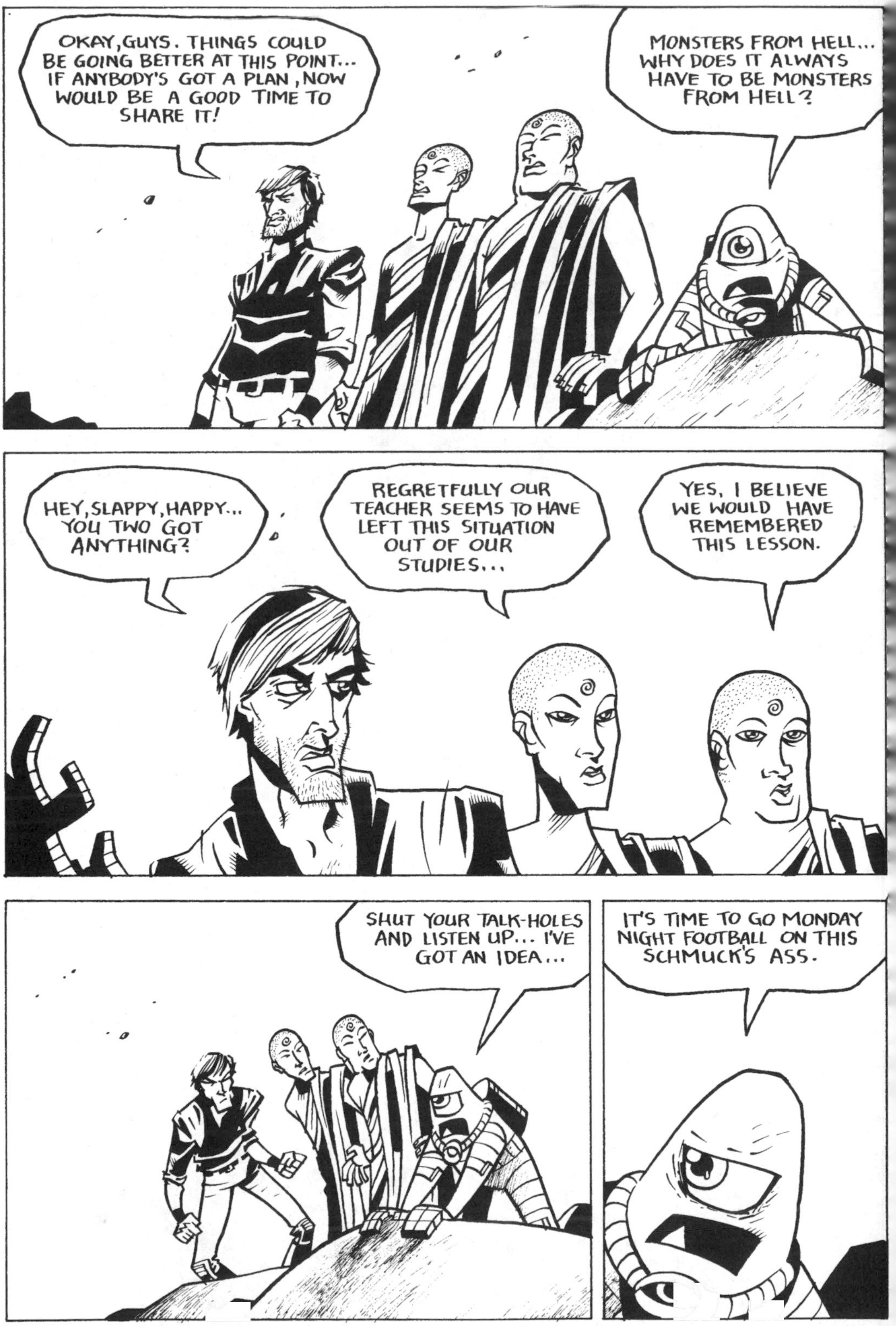
OKAY, GUYS. THINGS COULD BE GOING BETTER AT THIS POINT... IF ANYBODY'S GOT A PLAN, NOW WOULD BE A GOOD TIME TO SHARE IT!
MONSTERS FROM HELL... WHY DOES IT ALWAYS HAVE TO BE MONSTERS FROM HELL?
HEY, SLAPPY, HAPPY... YOU TWO GOT ANYTHING?
REGRETFULLY OUR TEACHER SEEMS TO HAVE LEFT THIS SITUATION OUT OF OUR STUDIES...
YES, I BELIEVE WE WOULD HAVE REMEMBERED THIS LESSON.
SHUT YOUR TALK-HOLES AND LISTEN UP... I'VE GOT AN IDEA...
IT'S TIME TO GO MONDAY NIGHT FOOTBALL ON THIS SCHMUCK'S ASS.

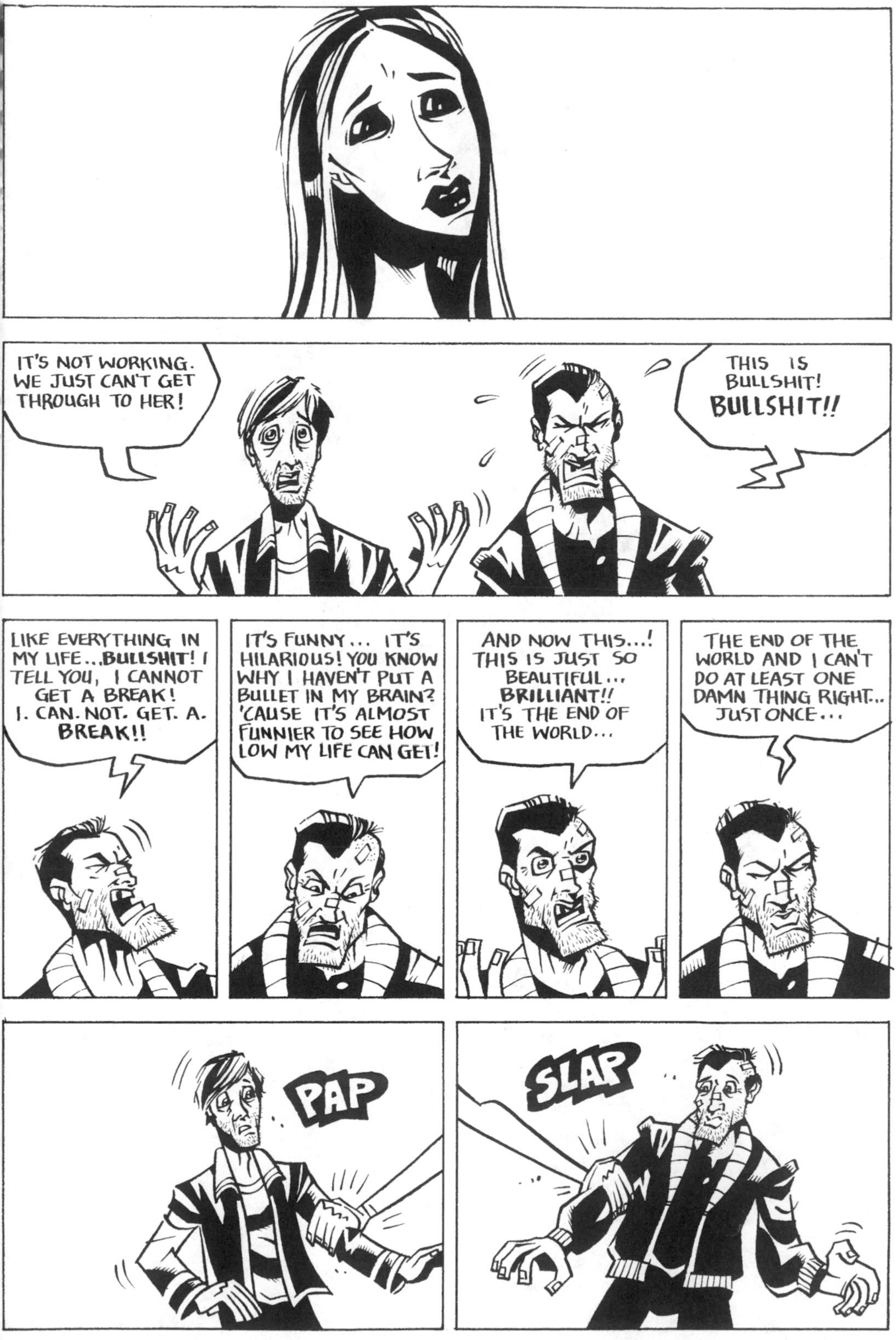
IT'S NOT WORKING. WE JUST CAN'T GET THROUGH TO HER!
THIS IS BULLSHIT! BULLSHIT!!
LIKE EVERYTHING IN MY LIFE... BULLSHIT! I TELL YOU, I CANNOT GET A BREAK! I. CAN. NOT. GET. A. BREAK!!
IT'S FUNNY... IT'S HILARIOUS! YOU KNOW WHY I HAVEN'T PUT A BULLET IN MY BRAIN? 'CAUSE IT'S ALMOST FUNNIER TO SEE HOW LOW MY LIFE CAN GET!
AND NOW THIS...! THIS IS JUST SO BEAUTIFUL... BRILLIANT!! IT'S THE END OF THE WORLD...
THE END OF THE WORLD AND I CAN'T DO AT LEAST ONE DAMN THING RIGHT... JUST ONCE...
PAP
SLAP

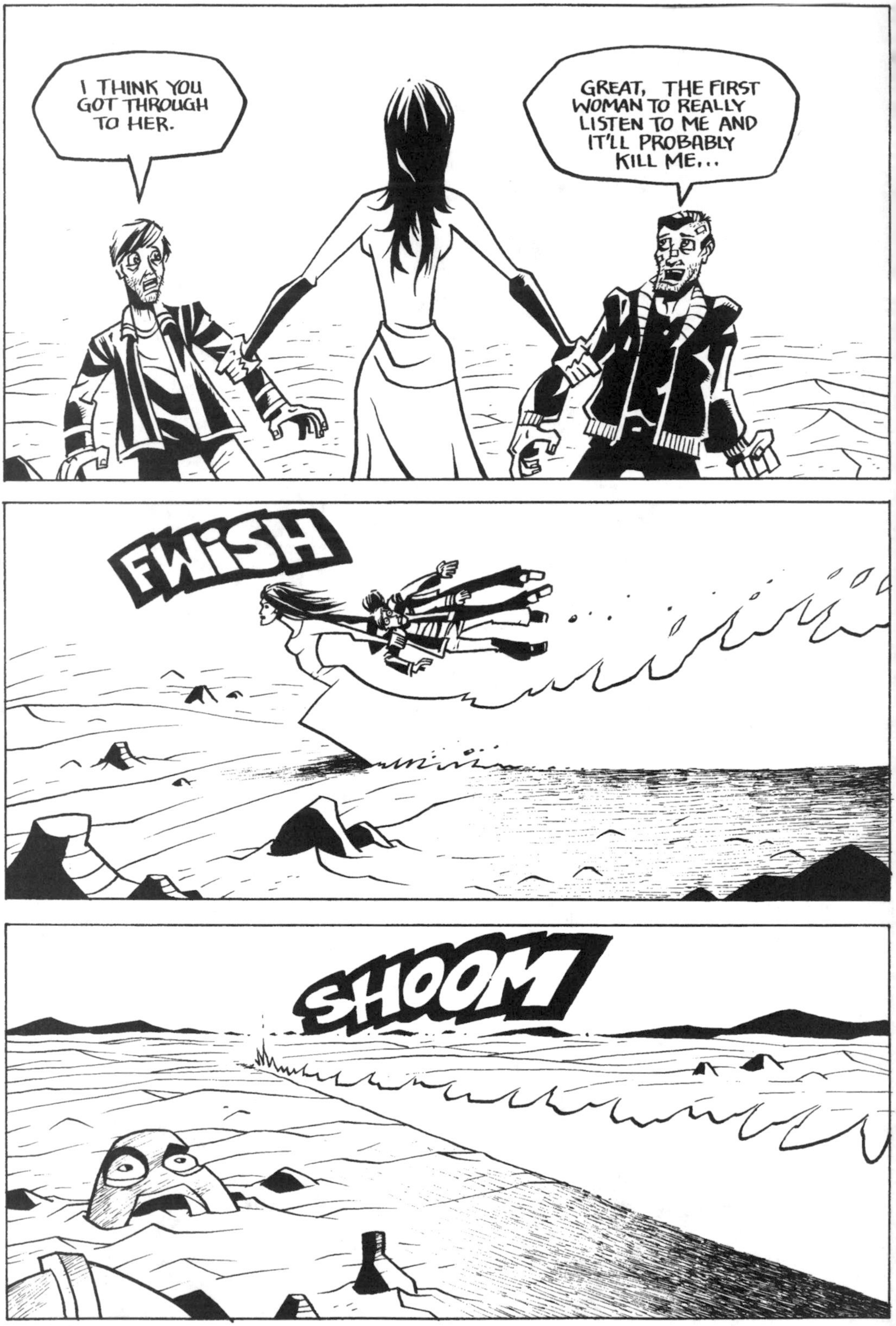
I THINK YOU GOT THROUGH TO HER.
GREAT, THE FIRST WOMAN TO REALLY LISTEN TO ME AND IT'LL PROBABLY KILL ME...
FWiSH
SHOOM

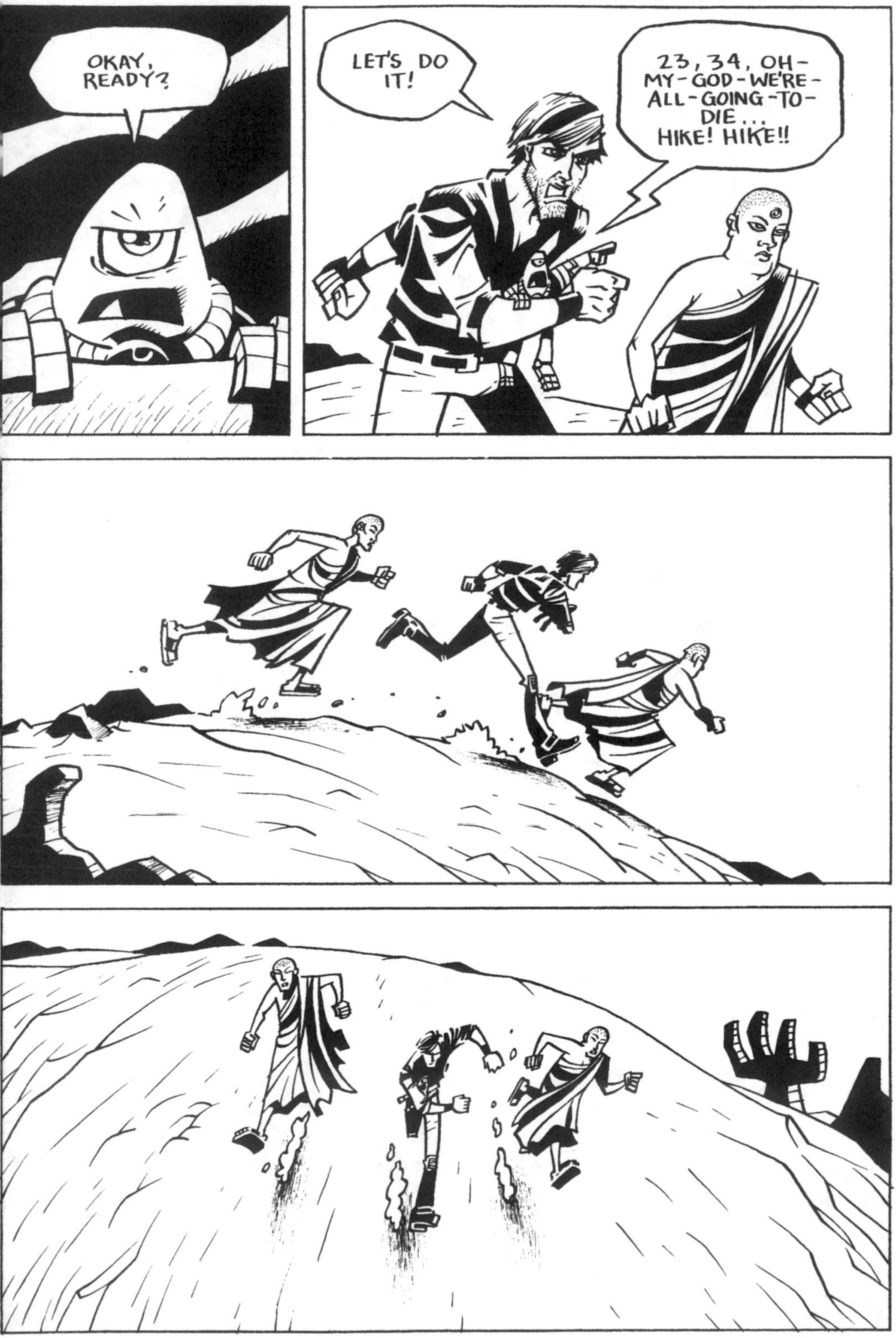
OKAY, READY?
LET'S DO IT!
23, 34, OH- MY-GOD-WE'RE-ALL-GOING-TO-DIE... HIKE! HIKE!!

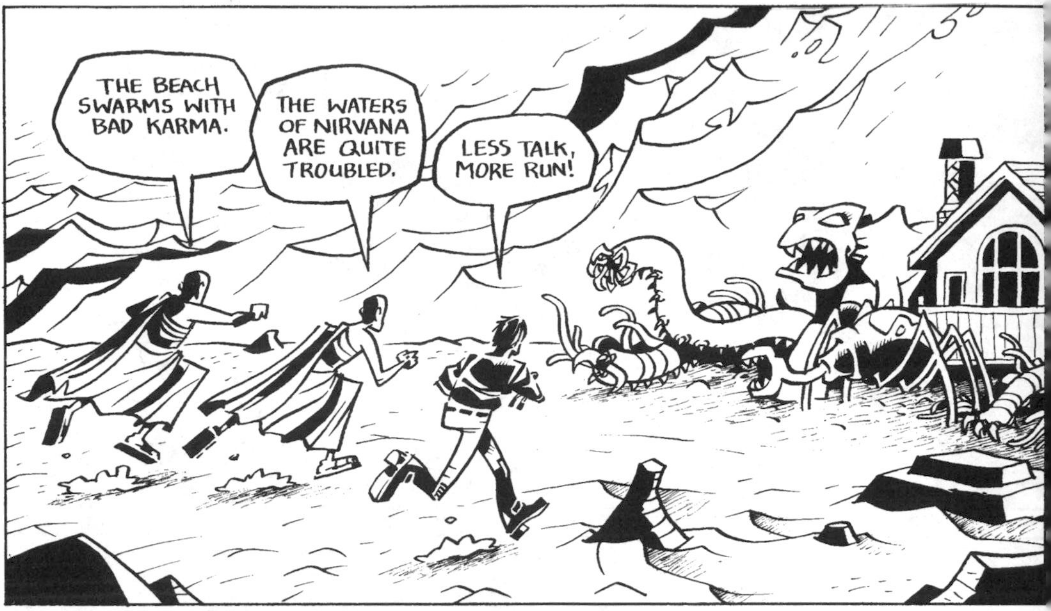
THE BEACH SWARMS WITH BAD KARMA.
THE WATERS OF NIRVANA ARE QUITE TROUBLED.
LESS TALK, MORE RUN!

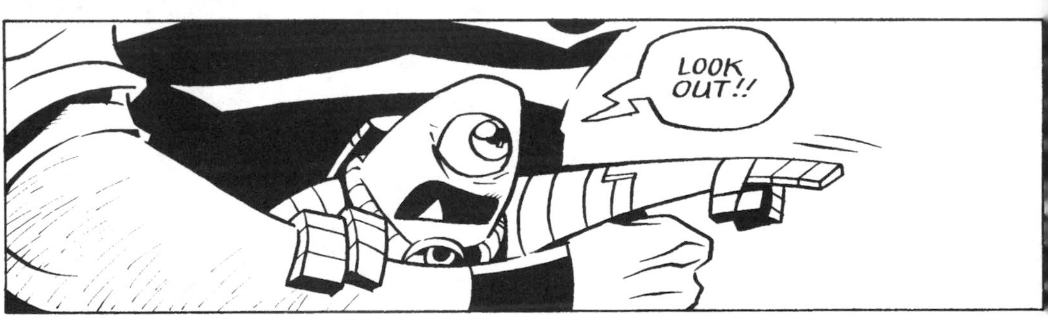
LOOK OUT!!

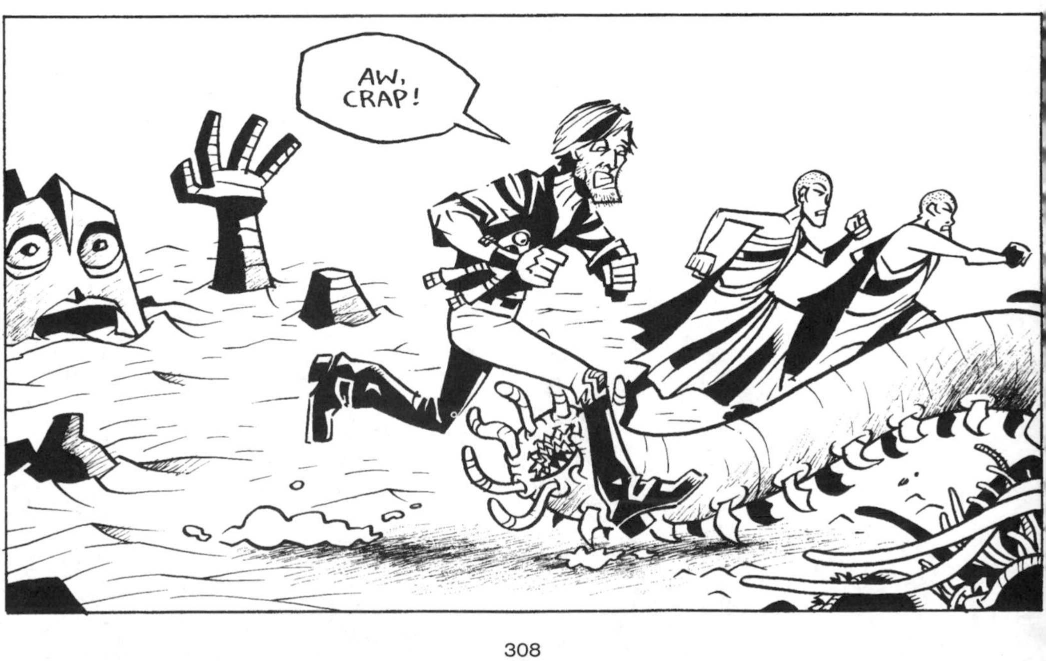
AW, CRAP!

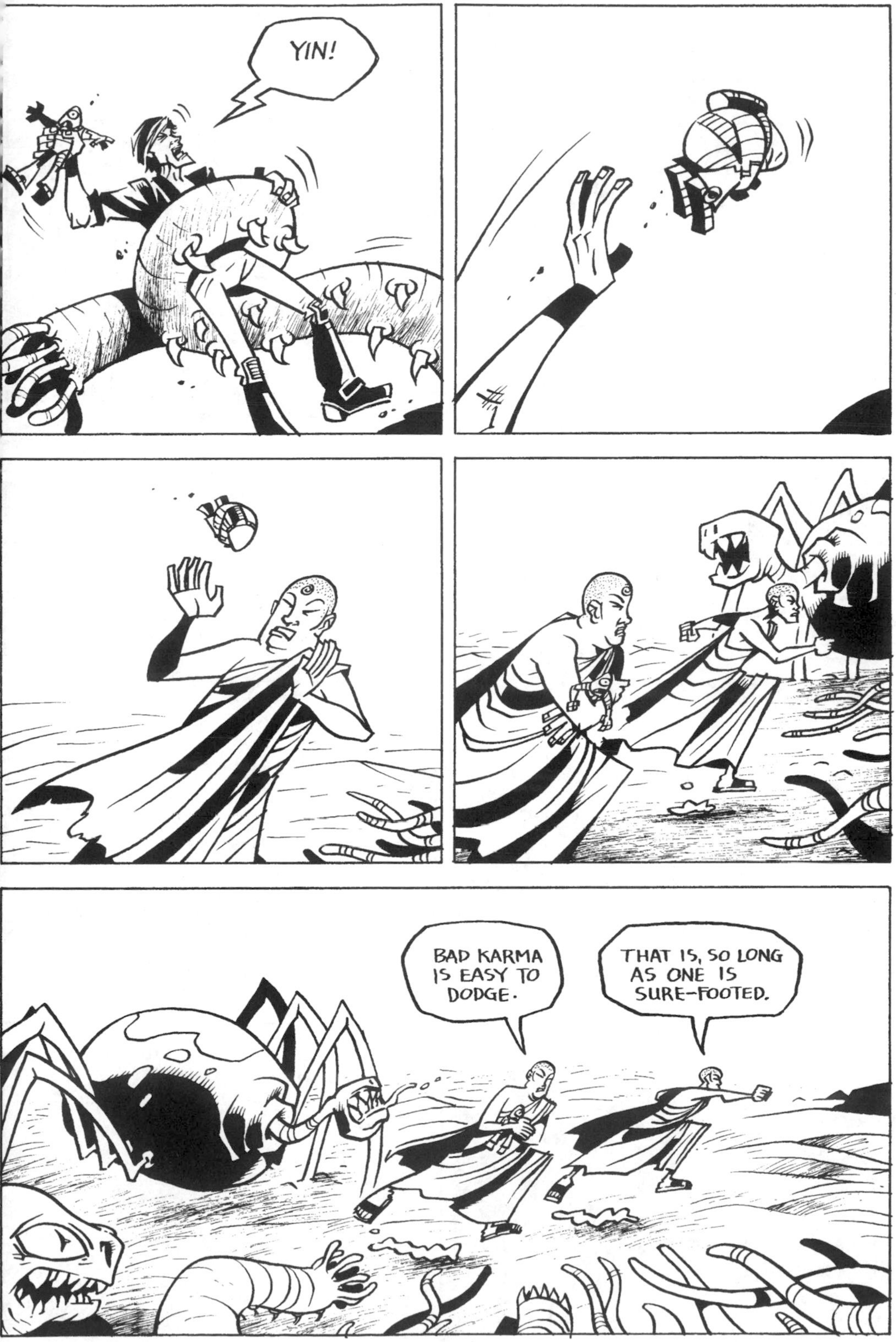
YIN!
BAD KARMA IS EASY TO DODGE.
THAT IS, SO LONG AS ONE IS SURE-FOOTED.

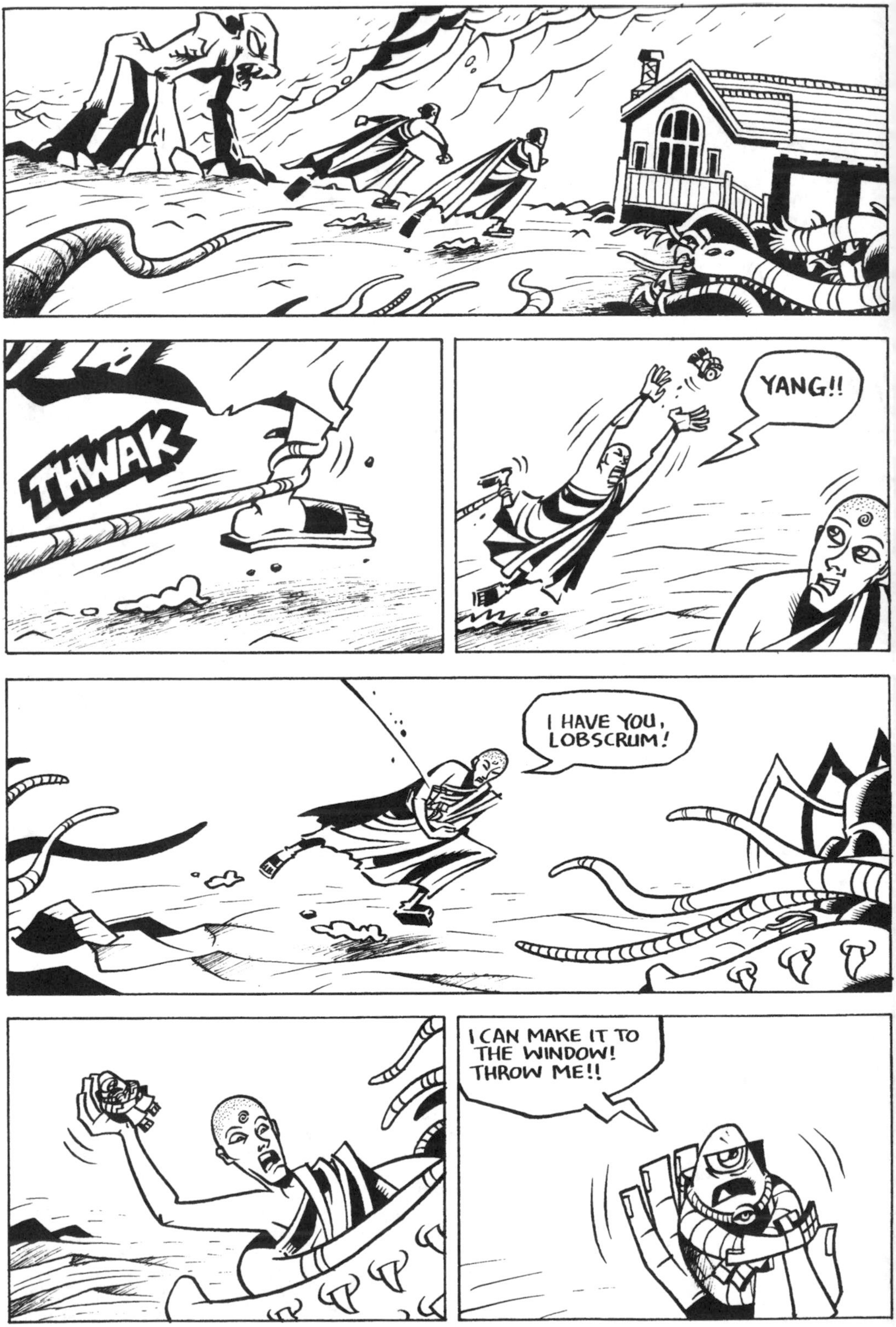
THWAK
YANG!!
I HAVE YOU, LOBSCRUM!
I CAN MAKE IT TO THE WINDOW! THROW ME!!

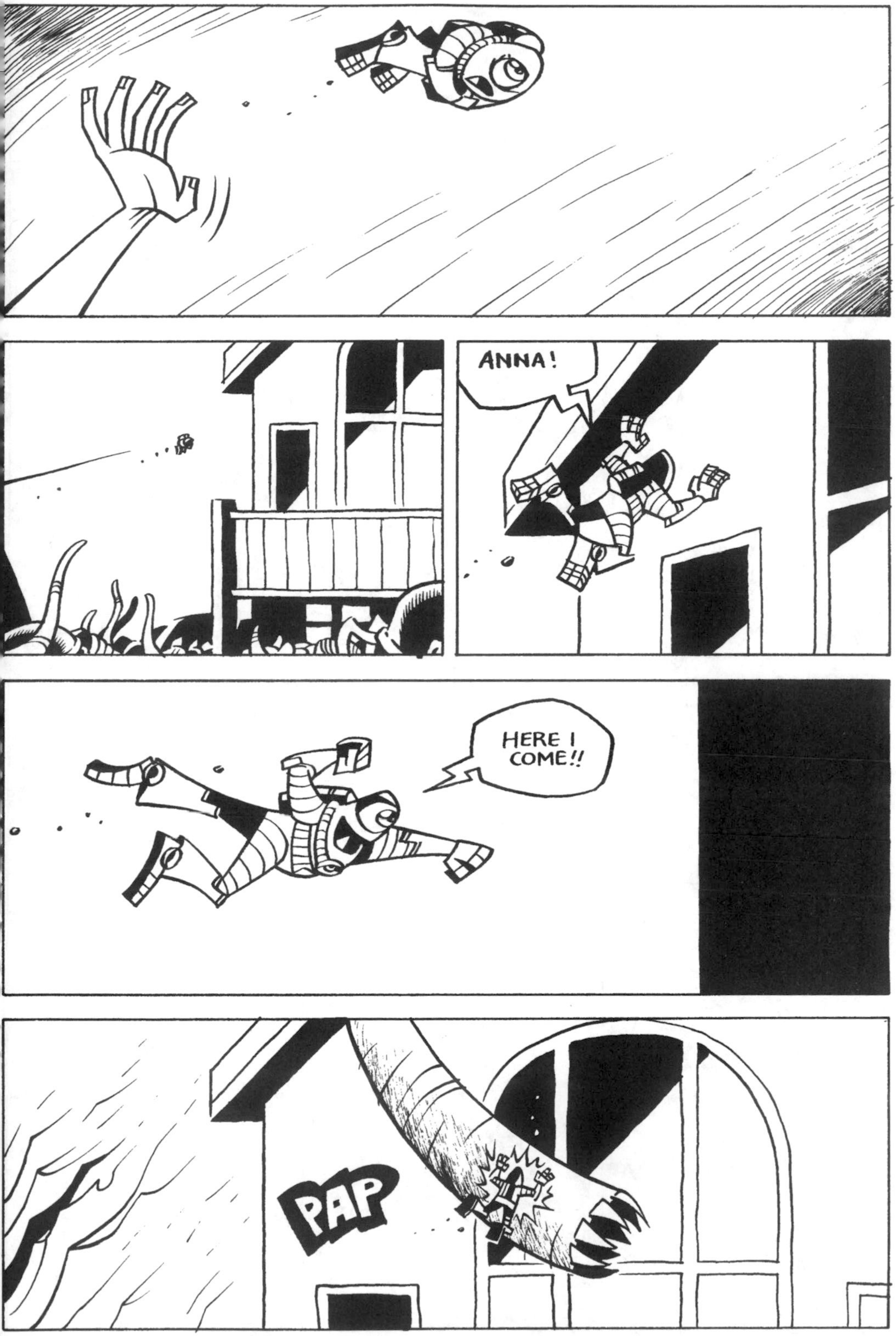
ANNA!
HERE I COME!!
PAP

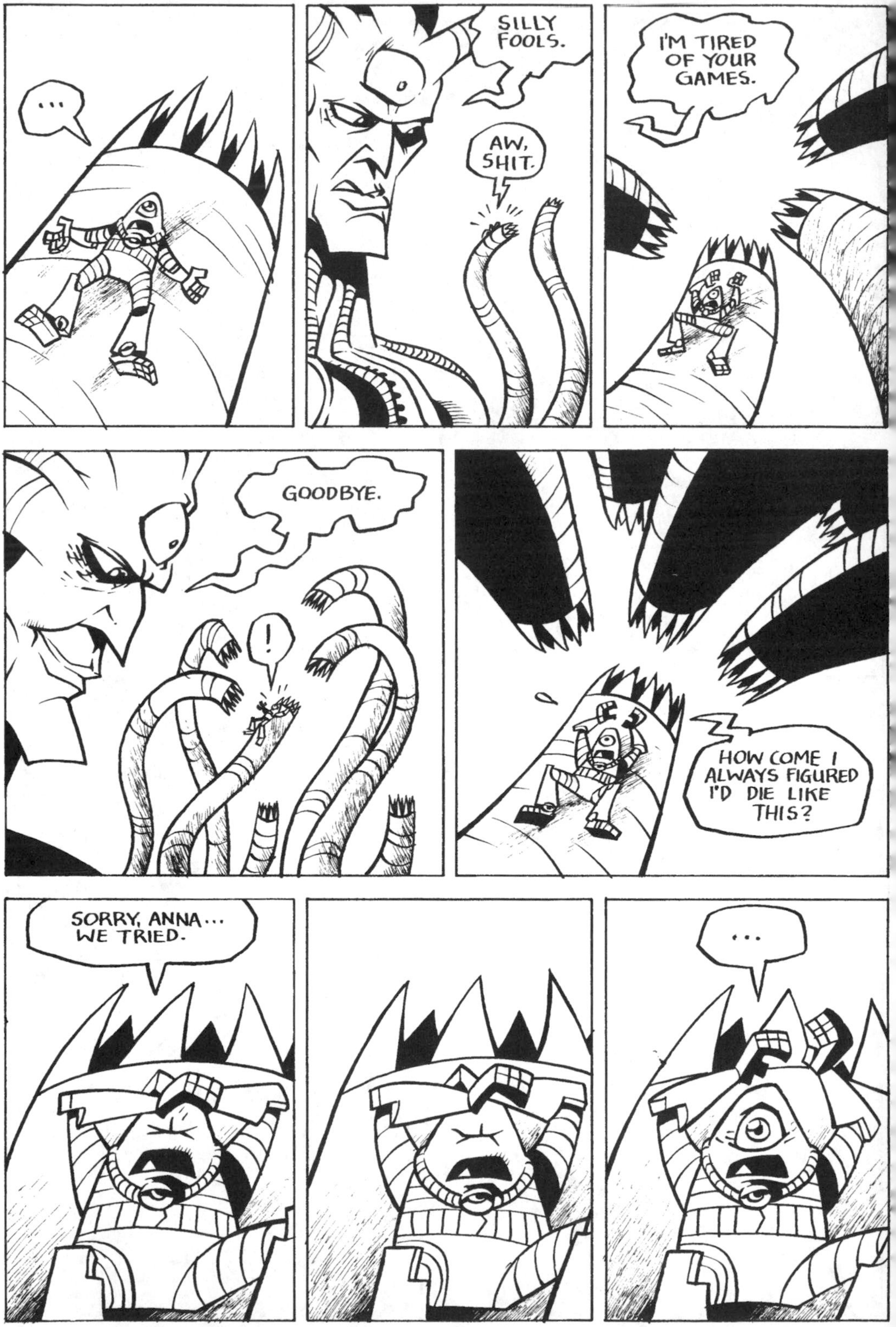
...
SILLY FOOLS.
AW, SHIT.
I'M TIRED OF YOUR GAMES.
GOODBYE.
!
HOW COME I ALWAYS FIGURED I'D DIE LIKE THIS?
SORRY, ANNA... WE TRIED.
...

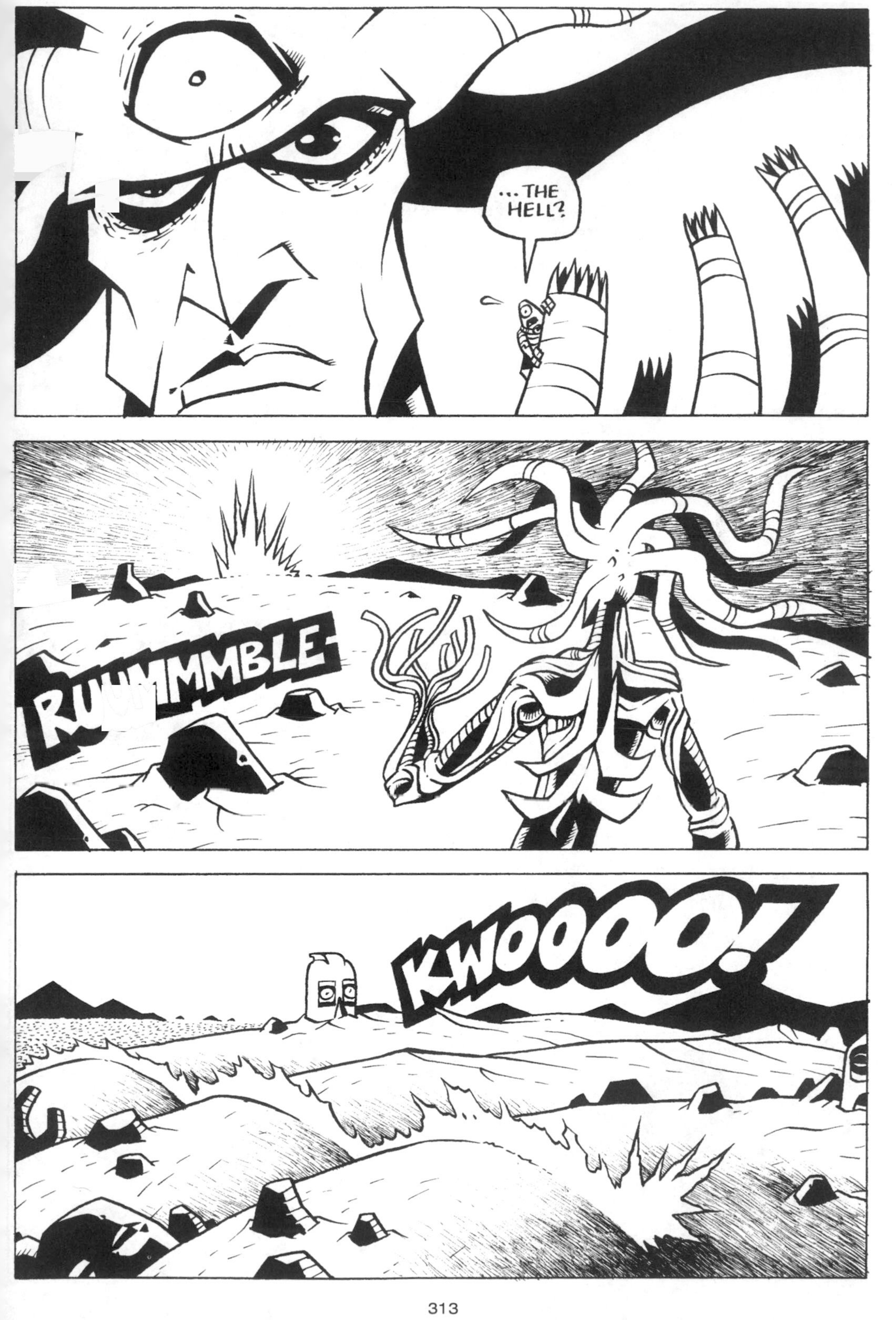

...THE HELL?
RUMMMMBLE
KWOOOOO!

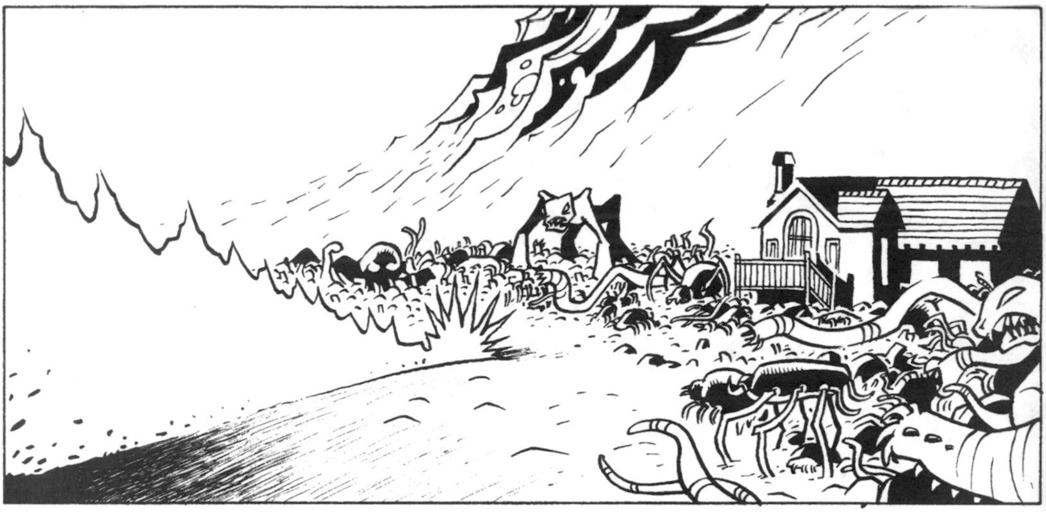

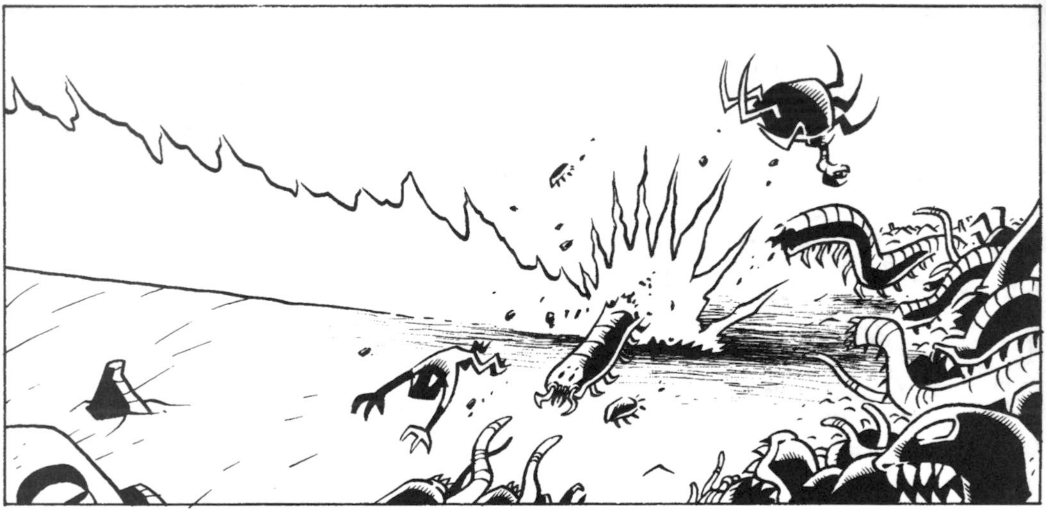

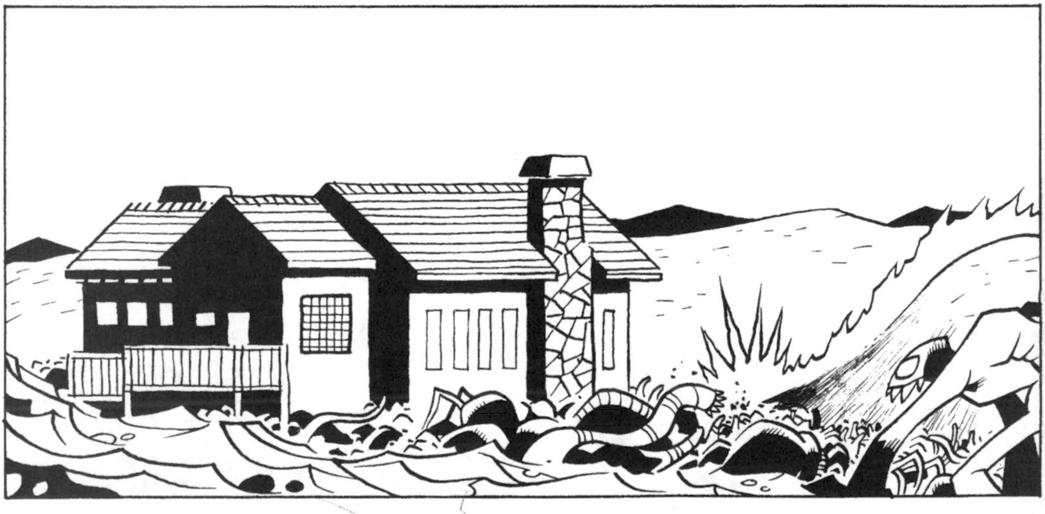

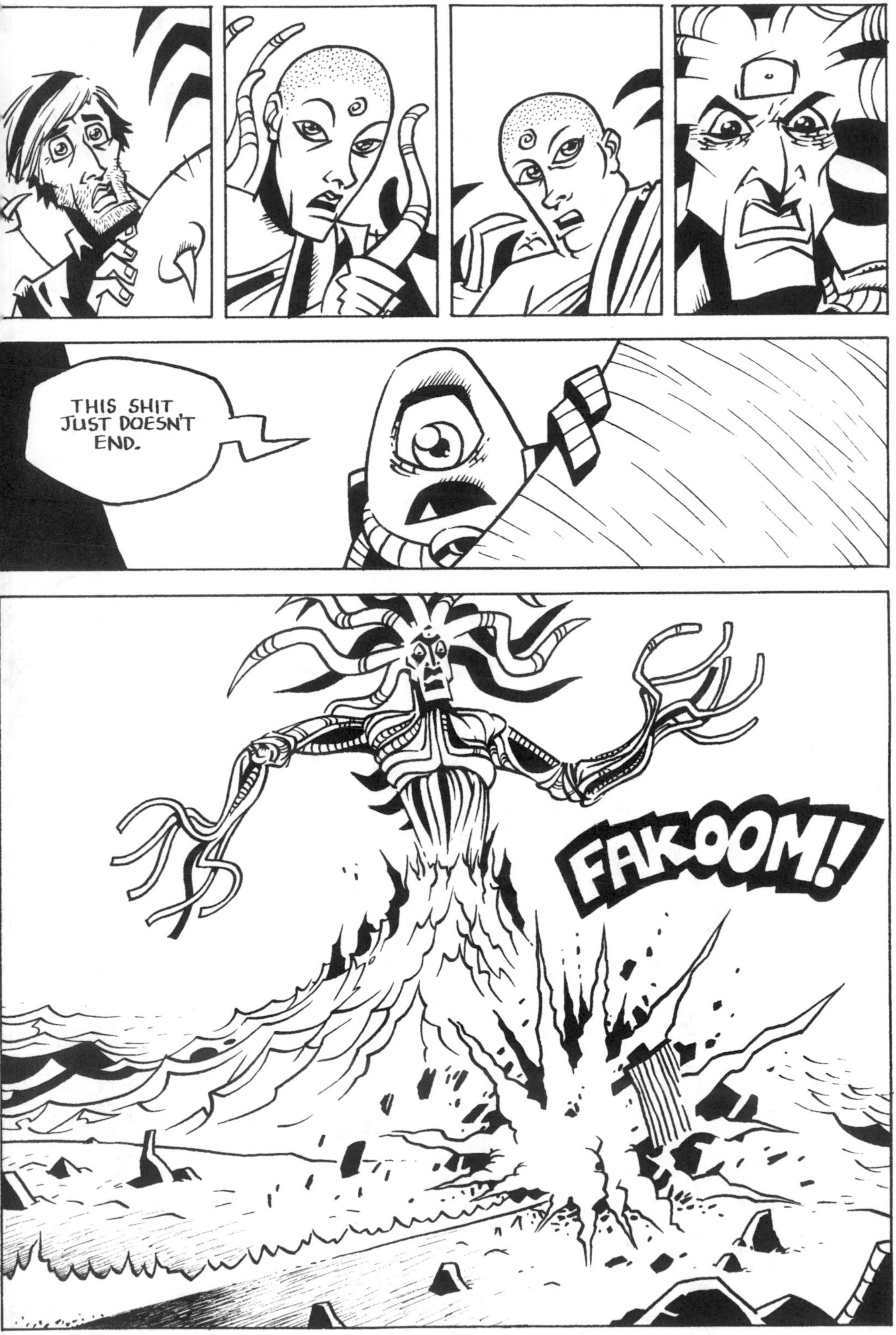
THIS SHIT JUST DOESN'T END.
FAKOOM!

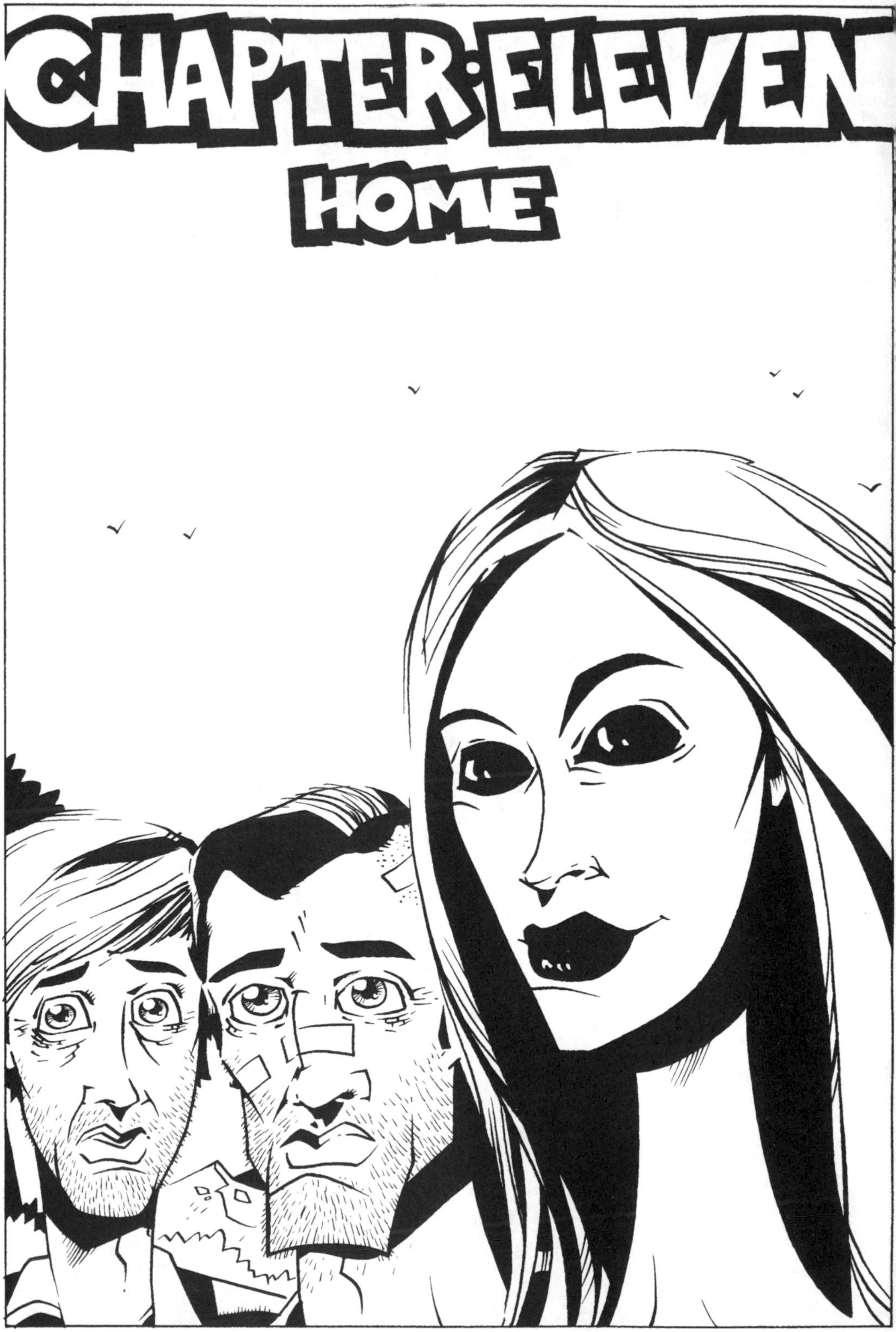
CHAPTER ELEVEN
HOME

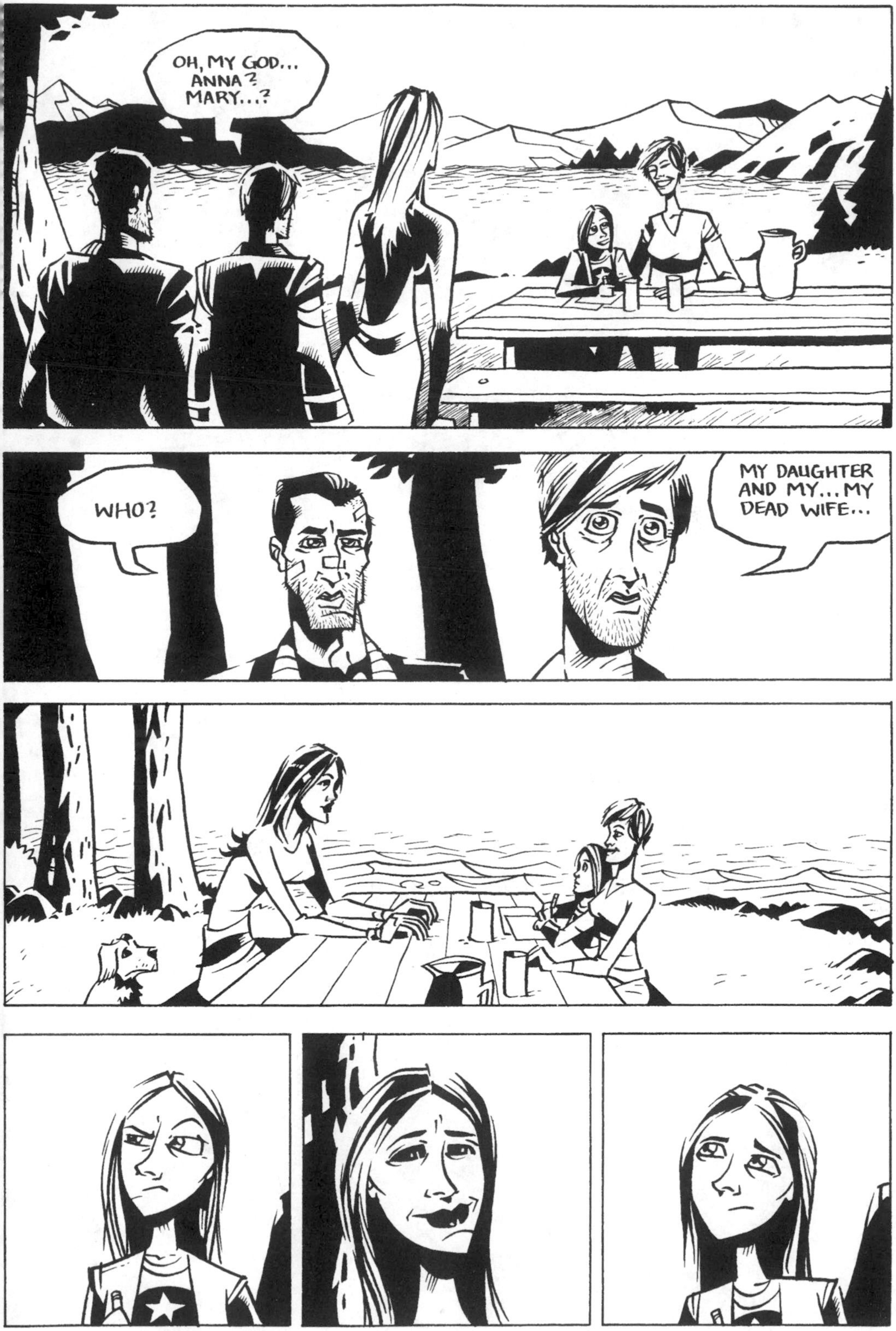
OH, MY GOD...
ANNA?
MARY...?
WHO?
MY DAUGHTER AND MY... MY DEAD WIFE...

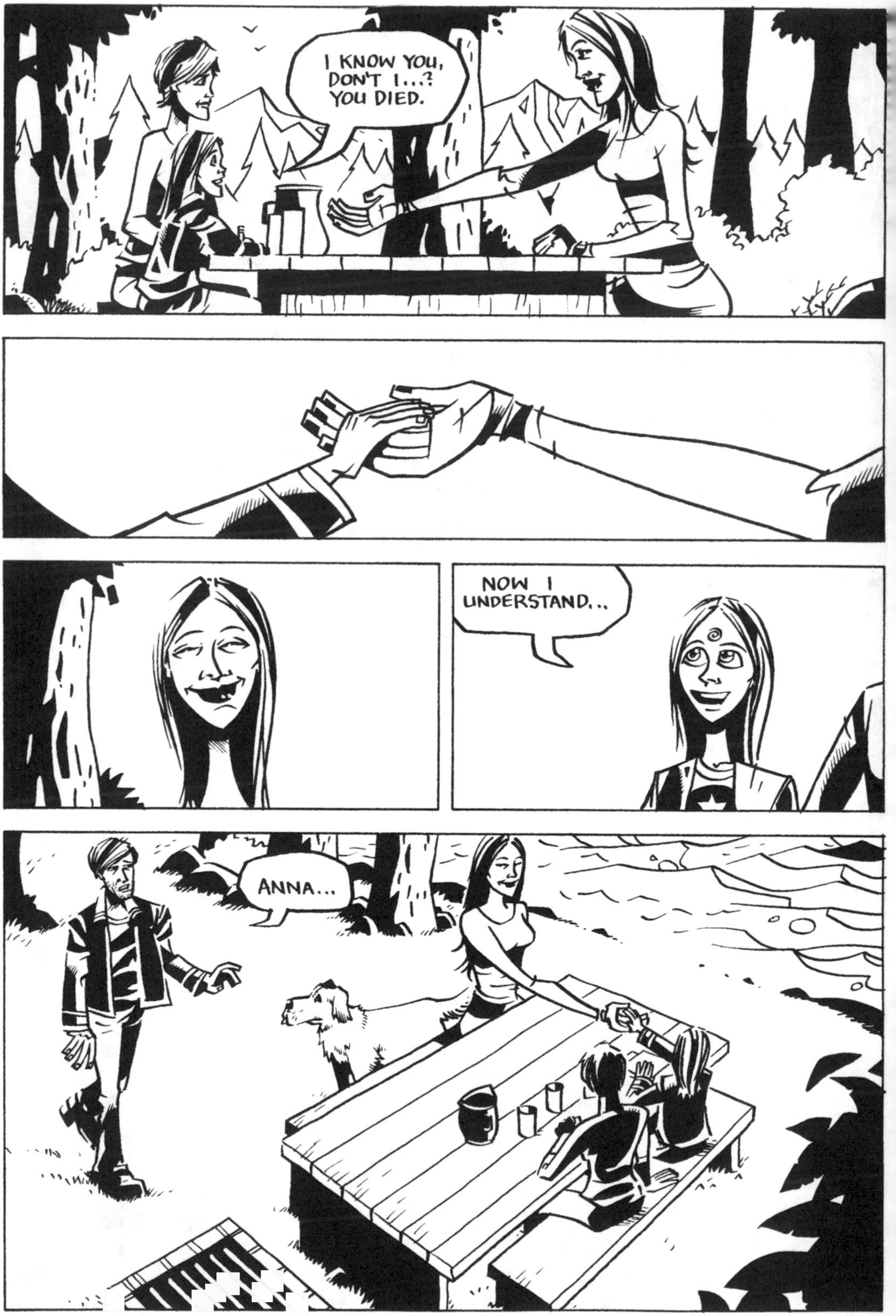
I KNOW YOU,
DON'T I...?
YOU DIED.
NOW I UNDERSTAND...
ANNA...

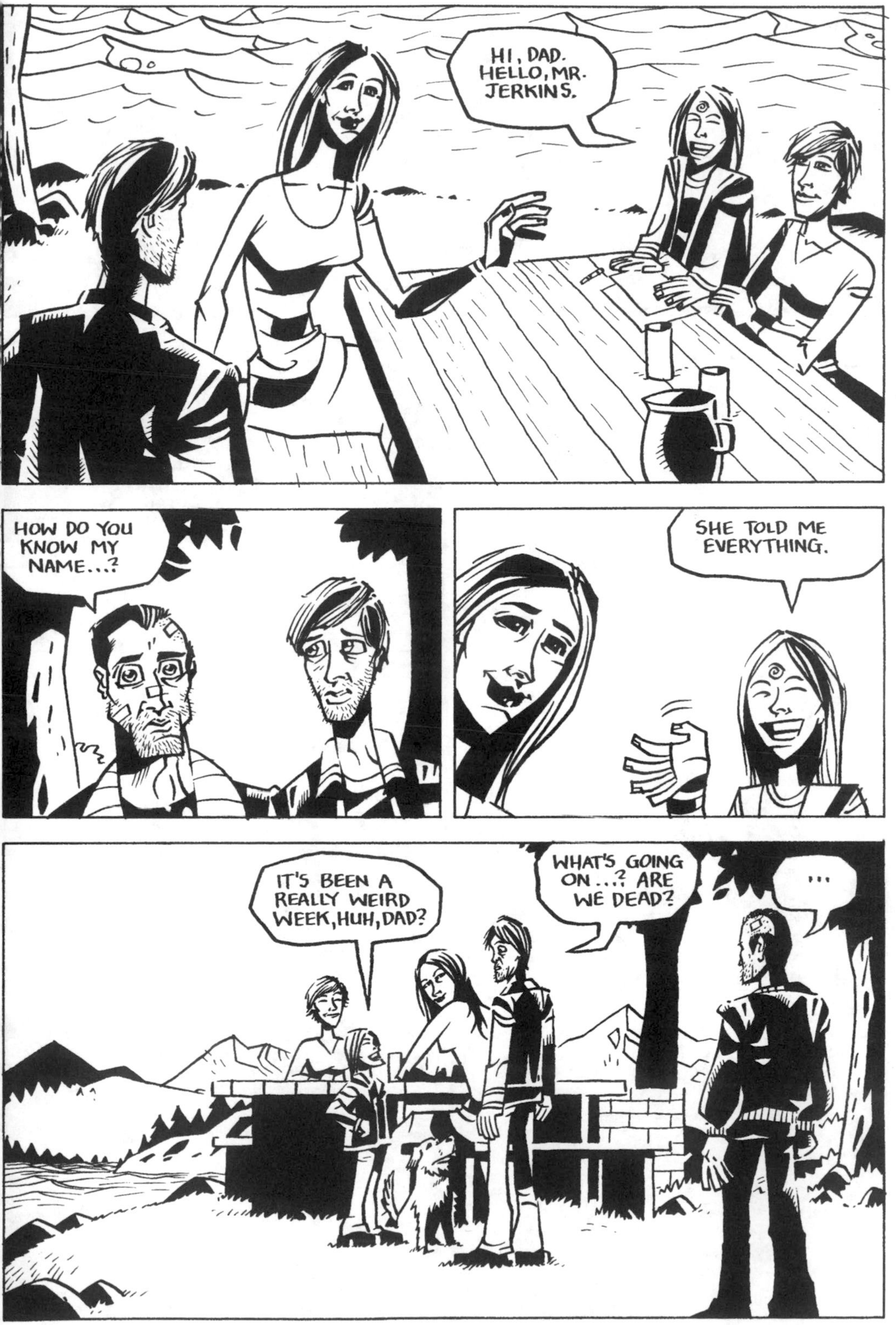
HI, DAD. HELLO, MR. JERKINS.
HOW DO YOU KNOW MY NAME...?
SHE TOLD ME EVERYTHING.
IT'S BEEN A REALLY WEIRD WEEK, HUH, DAD?
WHAT'S GOING ON...? ARE WE DEAD?
...

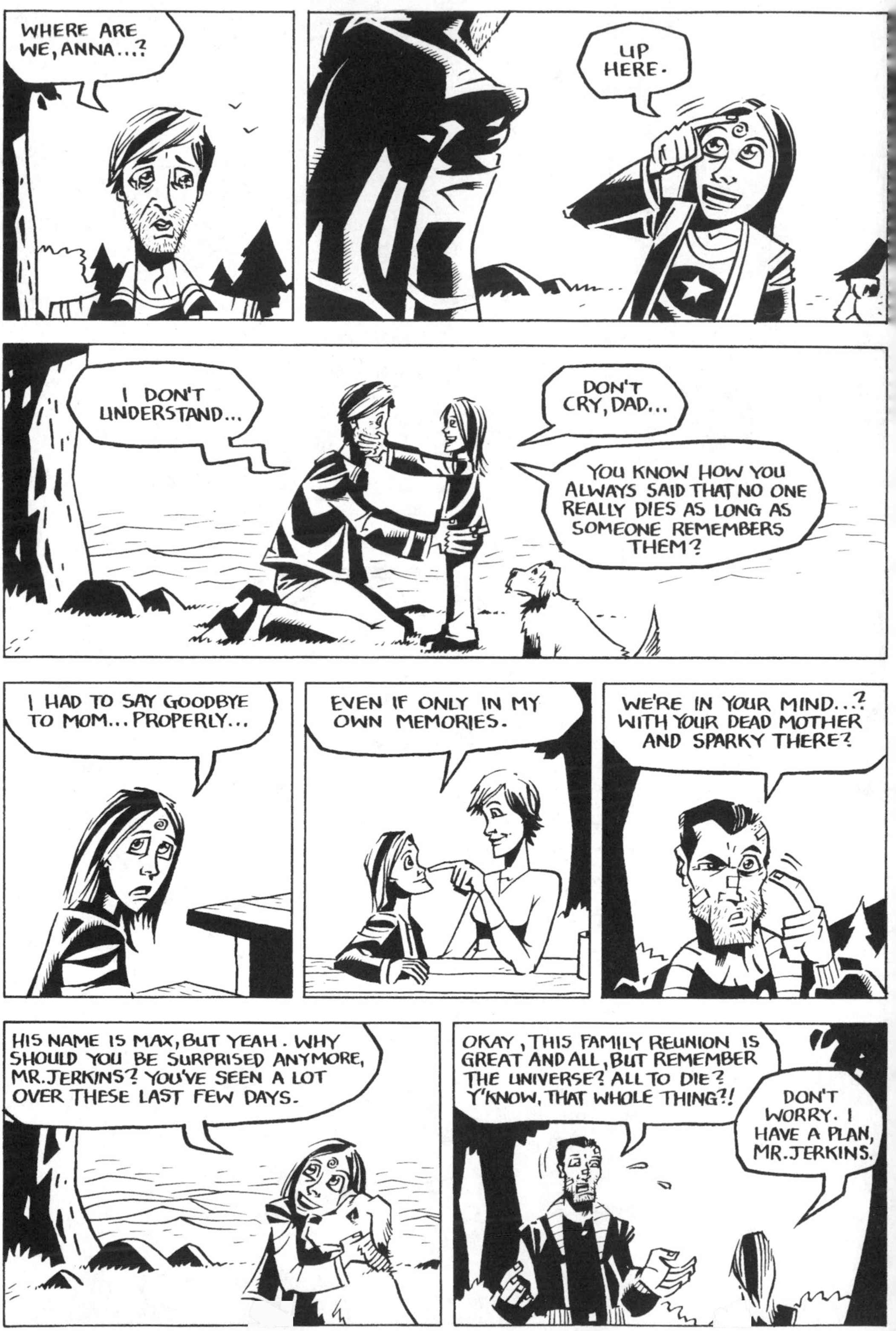
WHERE ARE WE, ANNA...?
UP HERE.
I DON'T UNDERSTAND...
DON'T CRY, DAD...
YOU KNOW HOW YOU ALWAYS SAID THAT NO ONE REALLY DIES AS LONG AS SOMEONE REMEMBERS THEM?
I HAD TO SAY GOODBYE TO MOM... PROPERLY...
EVEN IF ONLY IN MY OWN MEMORIES.
WE'RE IN YOUR MIND...? WITH YOUR DEAD MOTHER AND SPARKY THERE?
HIS NAME IS MAX, BUT YEAH. WHY SHOULD YOU BE SURPRISED ANYMORE, MR. JERKINS? YOU'VE SEEN A LOT OVER THESE LAST FEW DAYS.
OKAY, THIS FAMILY REUNION IS GREAT AND ALL, BUT REMEMBER THE UNIVERSE? ALL TO DIE? Y'KNOW, THAT WHOLE THING?!
DON'T WORRY. I HAVE A PLAN, MR. JERKINS.

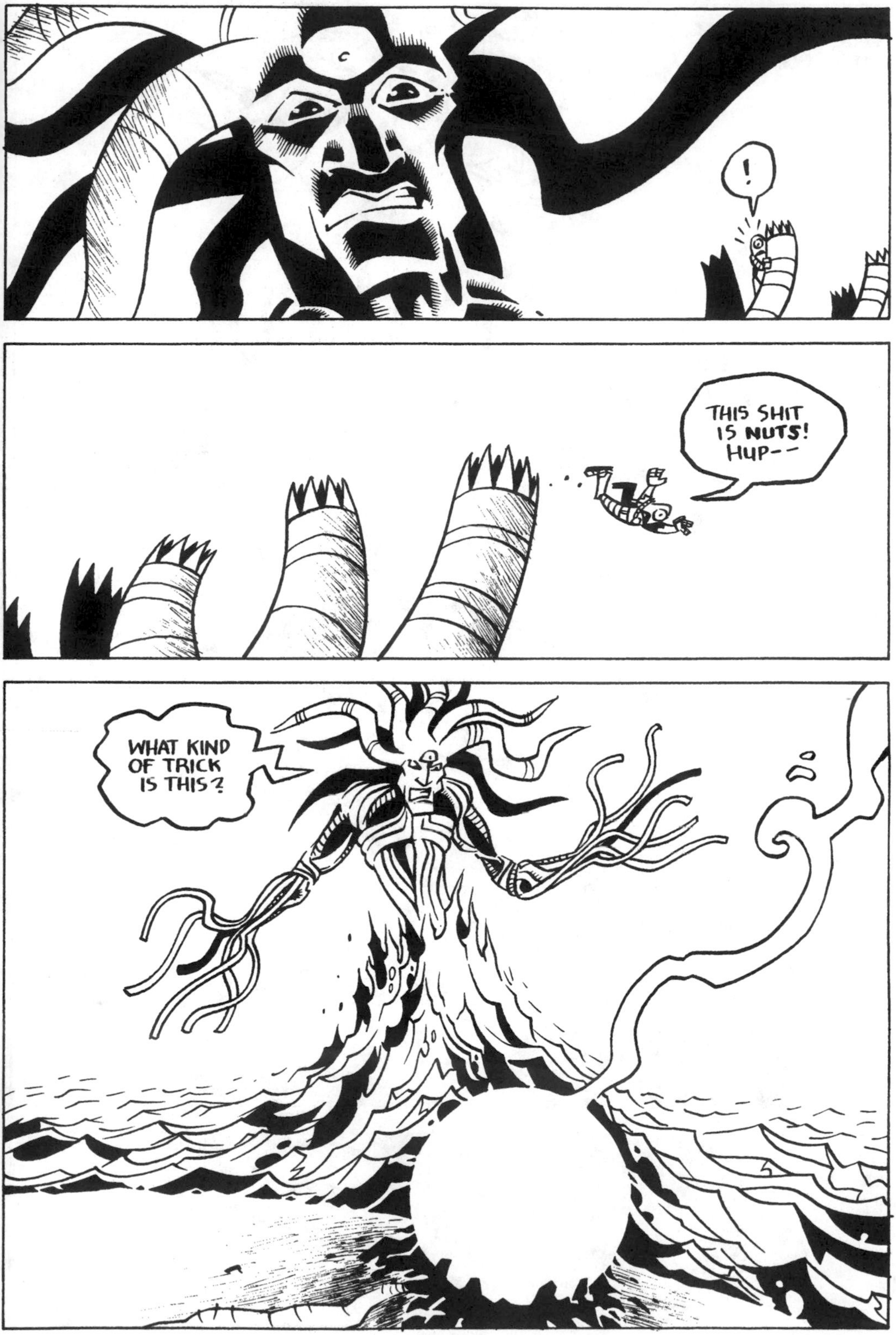
!
THIS SHIT IS NUTS! HUP--
WHAT KIND OF TRICK IS THIS?

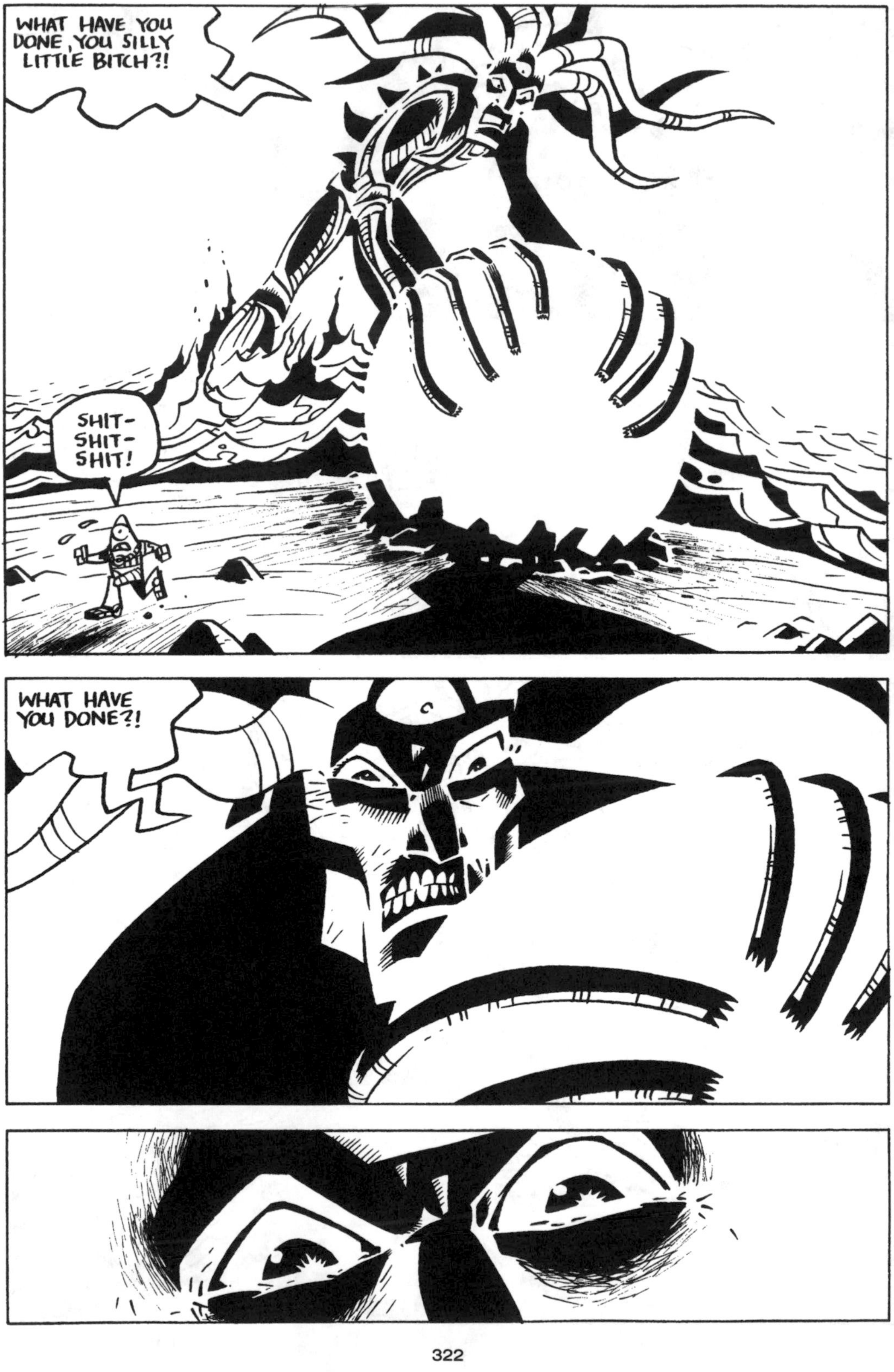
WHAT HAVE YOU DONE, YOU SILLY LITTLE BITCH?!
SHIT-SHIT-SHIT!
WHAT HAVE YOU DONE?!

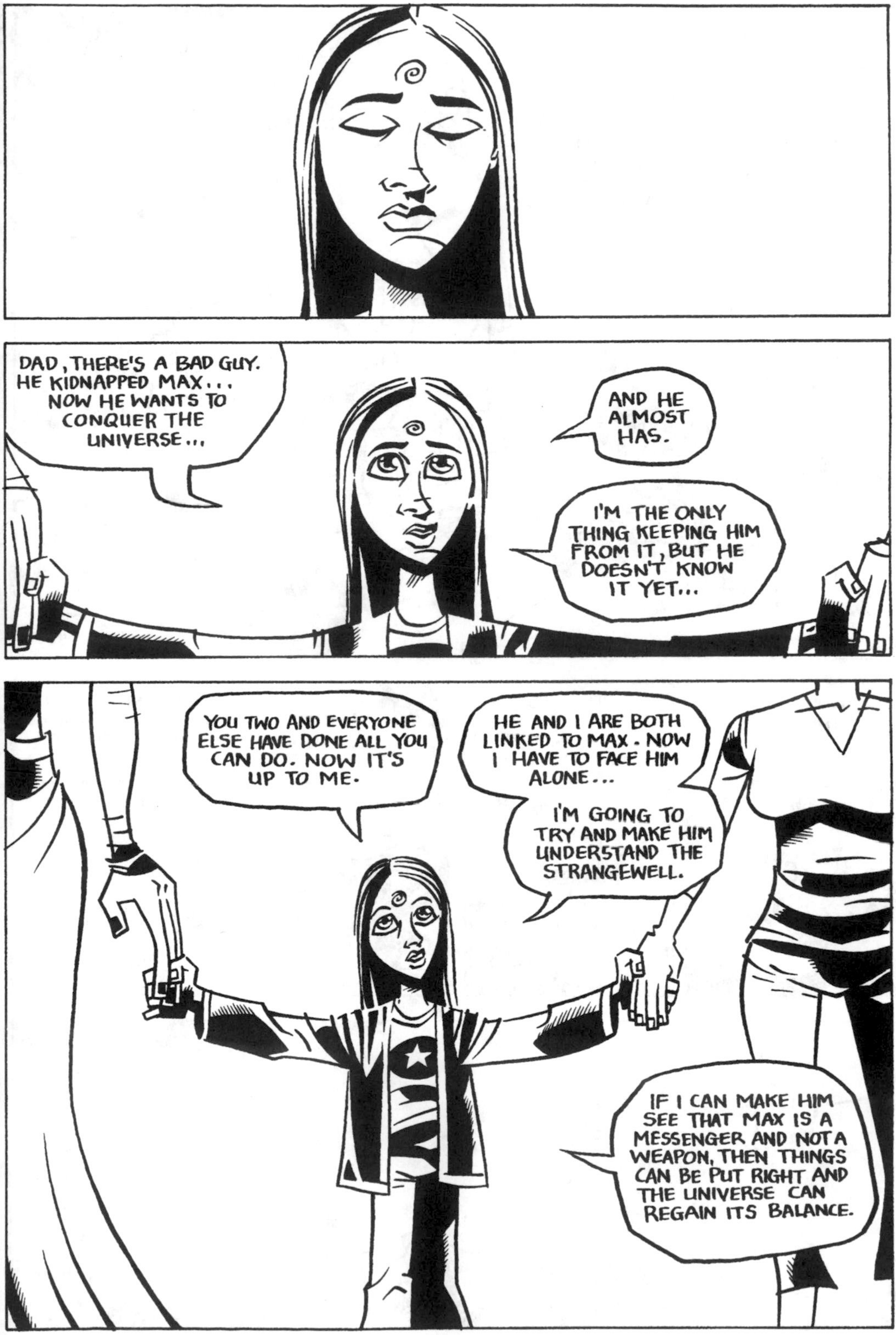
DAD, THERE'S A BAD GUY. HE KIDNAPPED MAX... NOW HE WANTS TO CONQUER THE UNIVERSE...
AND HE ALMOST HAS.
I'M THE ONLY THING KEEPING HIM FROM IT, BUT HE DOESN'T KNOW IT YET...
YOU TWO AND EVERYONE ELSE HAVE DONE ALL YOU CAN DO. NOW IT'S UP TO ME.
HE AND I ARE BOTH LINKED TO MAX. NOW I HAVE TO FACE HIM ALONE...
I'M GOING TO TRY AND MAKE HIM UNDERSTAND THE STRANGEWELL.
IF I CAN MAKE HIM SEE THAT MAX IS A MESSENGER AND NOT A WEAPON, THEN THINGS CAN BE PUT RIGHT AND THE UNIVERSE CAN REGAIN ITS BALANCE.

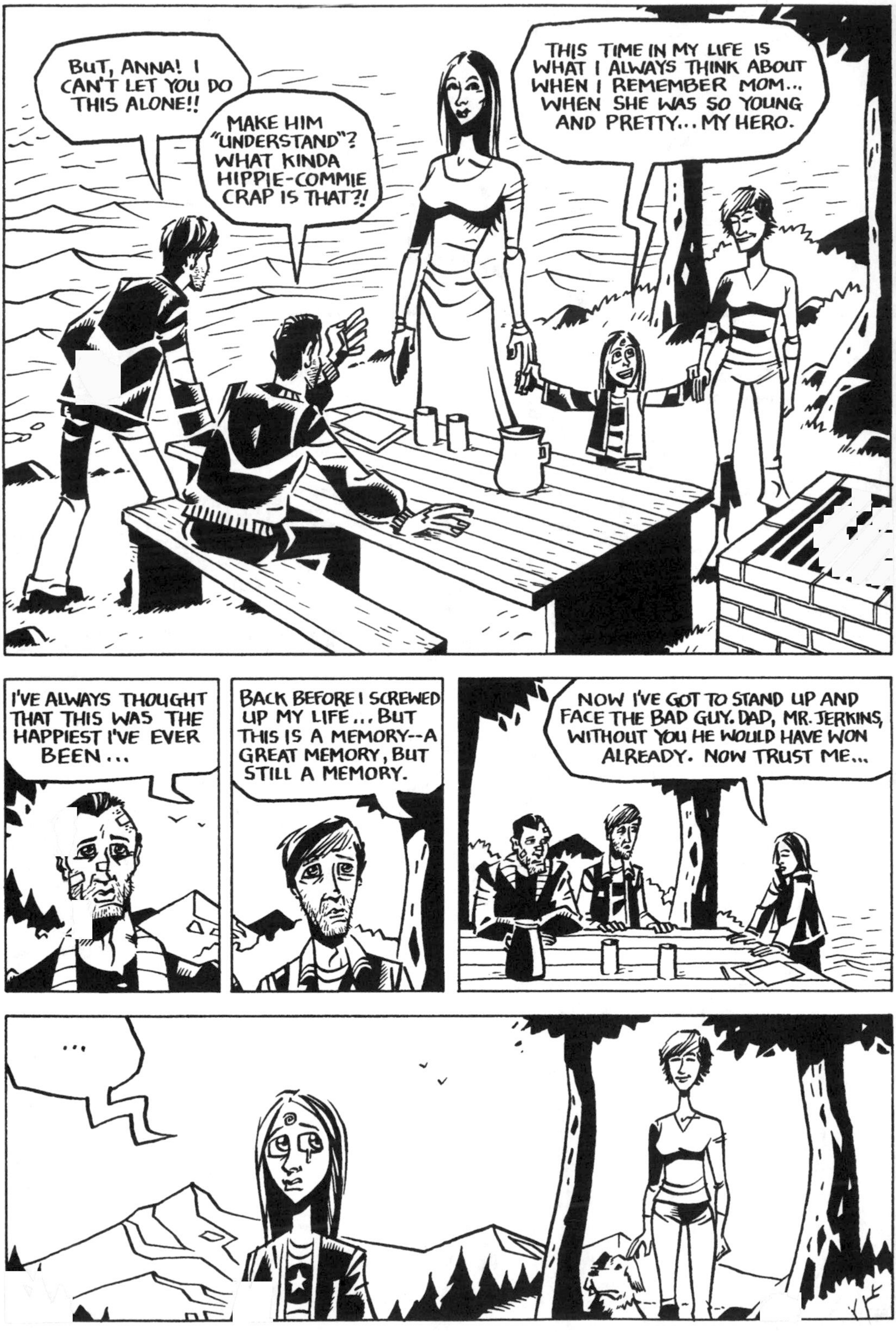
BUT, ANNA! I CAN'T LET YOU DO THIS ALONE!!
MAKE HIM "UNDERSTAND"? WHAT KINDA HIPPIE-COMMIE CRAP IS THAT?!
THIS TIME IN MY LIFE IS WHAT I ALWAYS THINK ABOUT WHEN I REMEMBER MOM... WHEN SHE WAS SO YOUNG AND PRETTY... MY HERO.
I'VE ALWAYS THOUGHT THAT THIS WAS THE HAPPIEST I'VE EVER BEEN...
BACK BEFORE I SCREWED UP MY LIFE... BUT THIS IS A MEMORY--A GREAT MEMORY, BUT STILL A MEMORY.
NOW I'VE GOT TO STAND UP AND FACE THE BAD GUY. DAD, MR. JERKINS, WITHOUT YOU HE WOULD HAVE WON ALREADY. NOW TRUST ME...
...

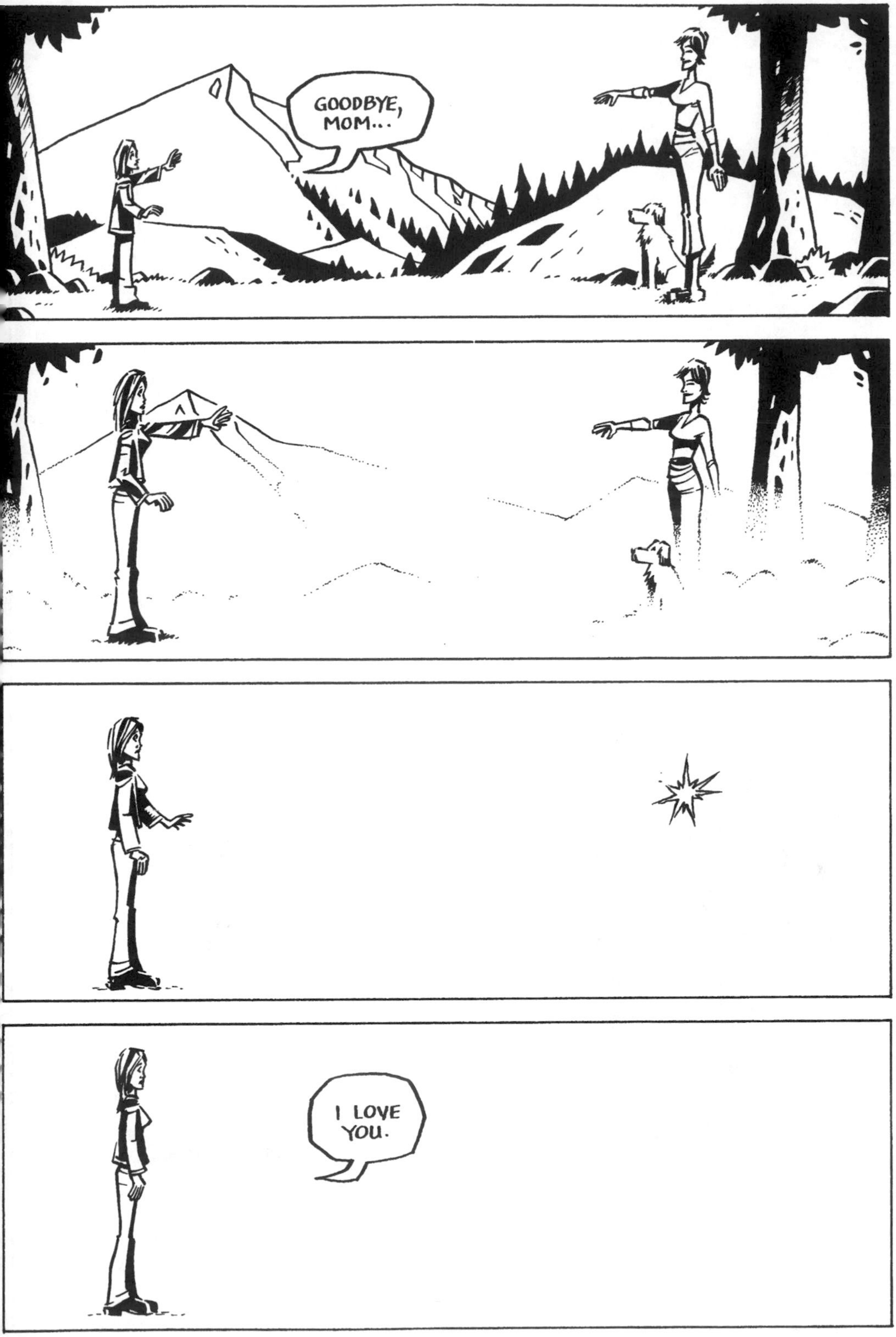
GOODBYE, MOM...
I LOVE YOU.

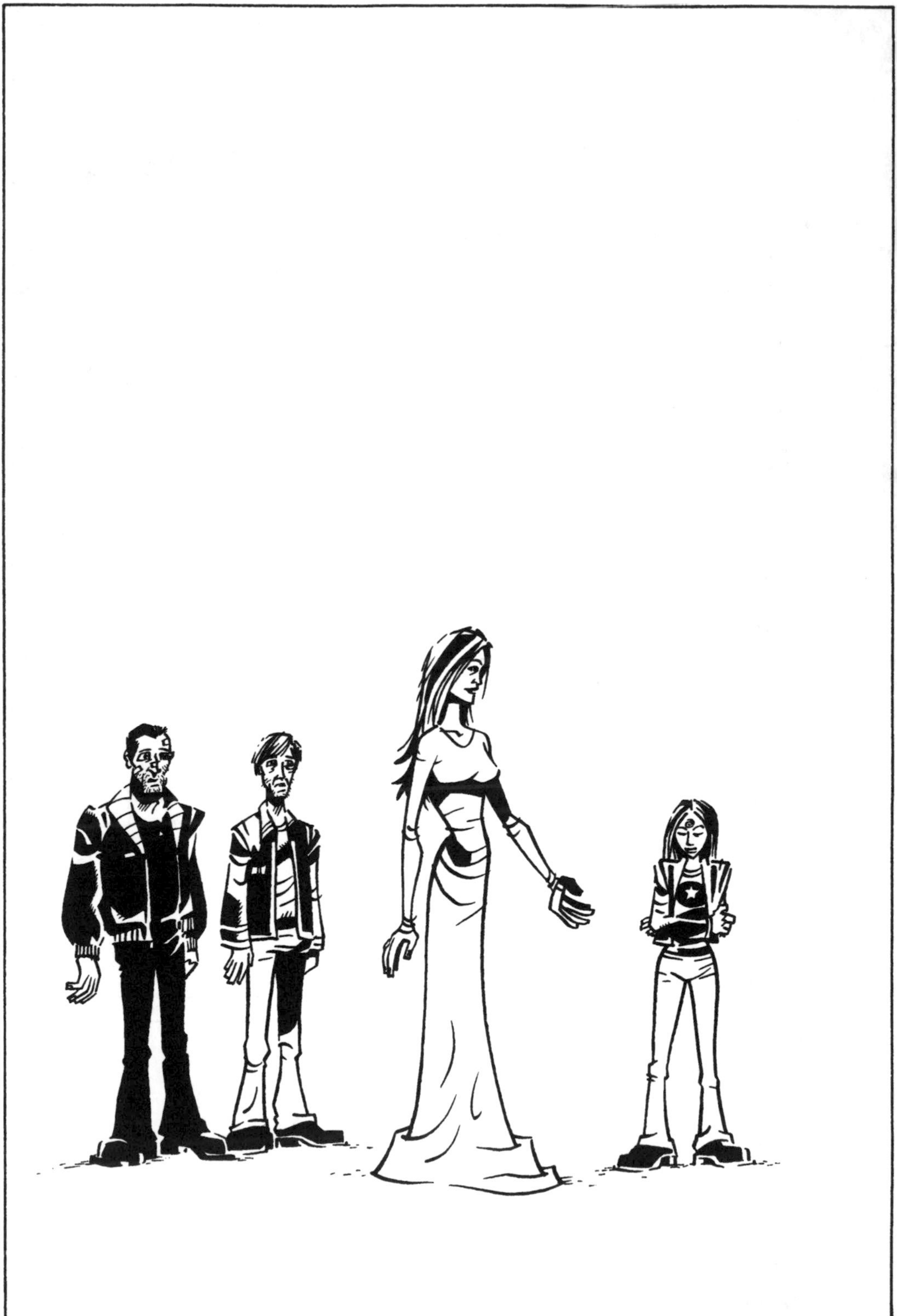

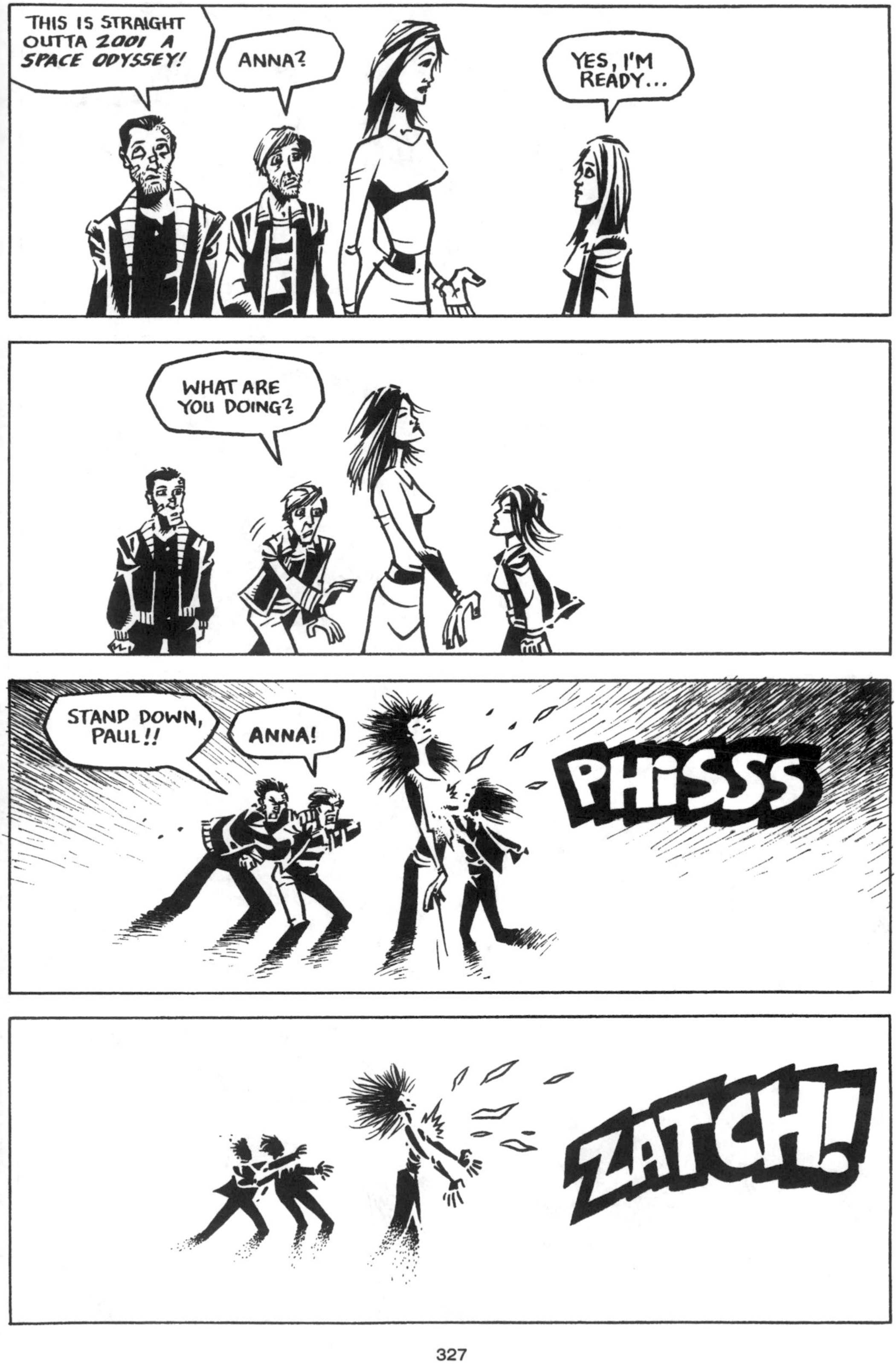
THIS IS STRAIGHT OUTTA 2001 A SPACE ODYSSEY!
ANNA?
YES, I'M READY...
WHAT ARE YOU DOING?
STAND DOWN, PAUL!!
ANNA!
PHiSSS
ZATCH!

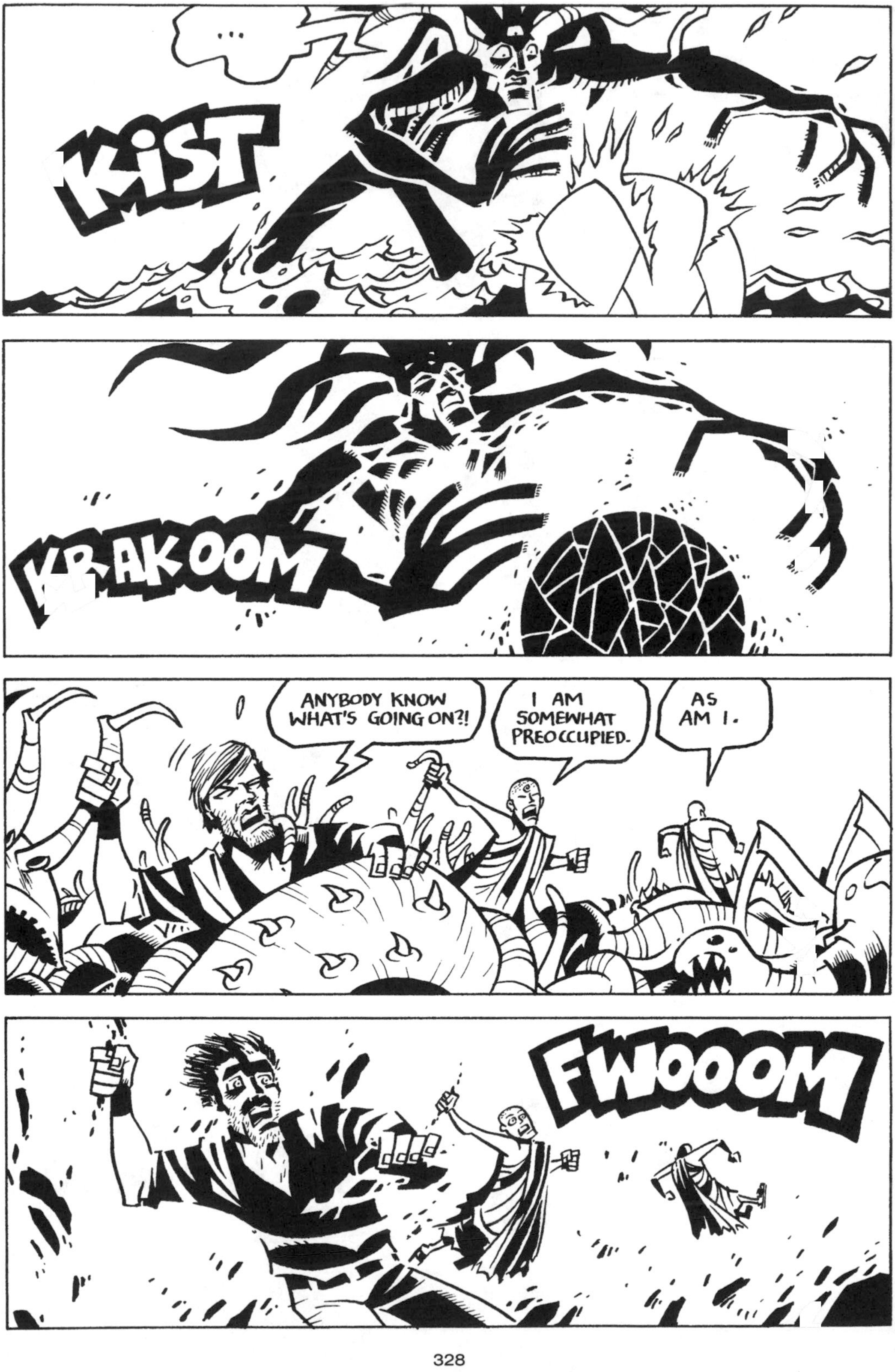
...
KiST
KRAKOOM
ANYBODY KNOW WHAT'S GOING ON?!
I AM SOMEWHAT PREOCCUPIED.
AS AM I.
FWOOOM

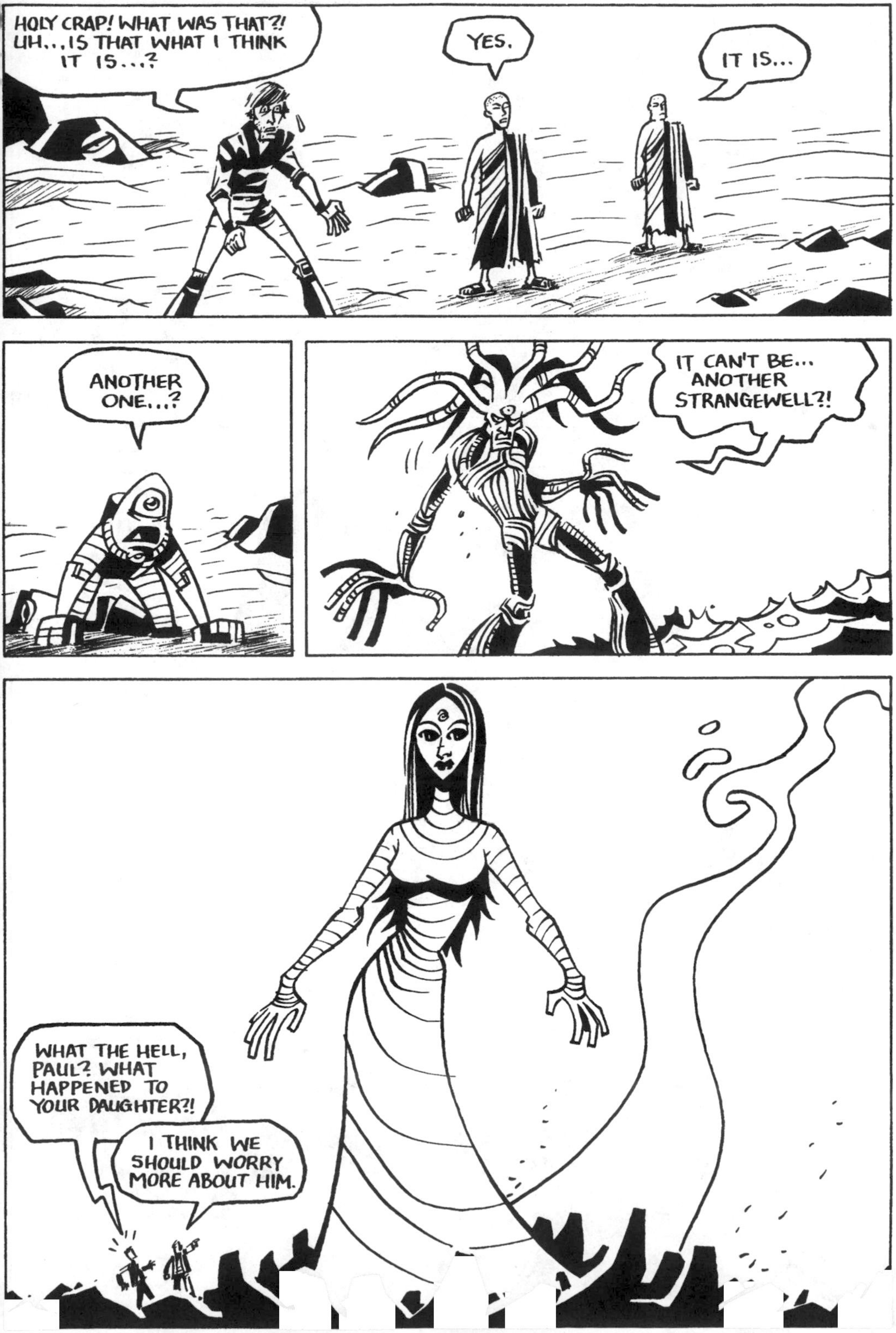
HOLY CRAP! WHAT WAS THAT?! UH...IS THAT WHAT I THINK IT IS...?
YES.
IT IS...
ANOTHER ONE...?
IT CAN'T BE... ANOTHER STRANGEWELL?!
WHAT THE HELL, PAUL? WHAT HAPPENED TO YOUR DAUGHTER?!
I THINK WE SHOULD WORRY MORE ABOUT HIM.

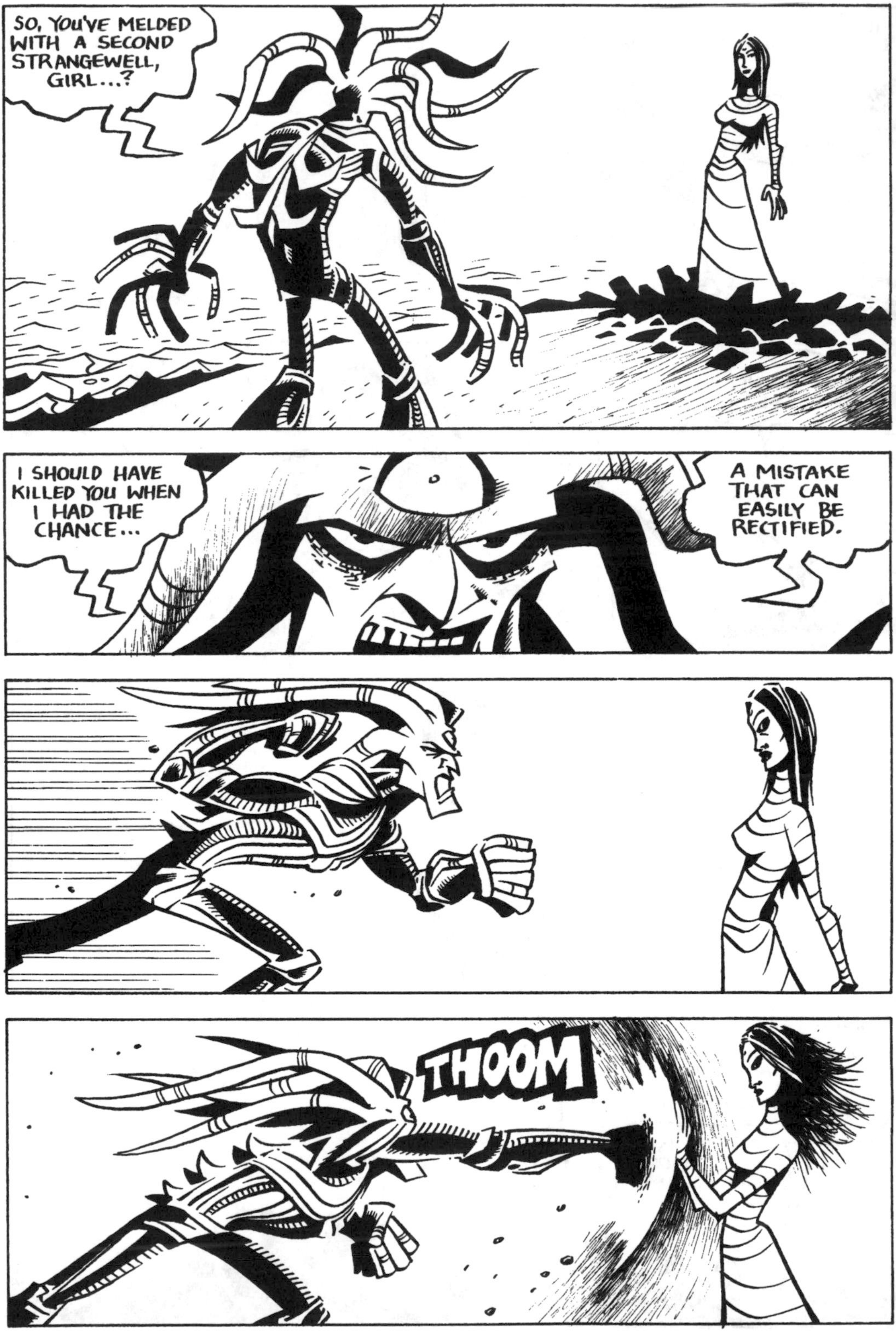
SO, YOU'VE MELDED WITH A SECOND STRANGEWELL, GIRL...?
I SHOULD HAVE KILLED YOU WHEN I HAD THE CHANCE...
A MISTAKE THAT CAN EASILY BE RECTIFIED.
THOOM

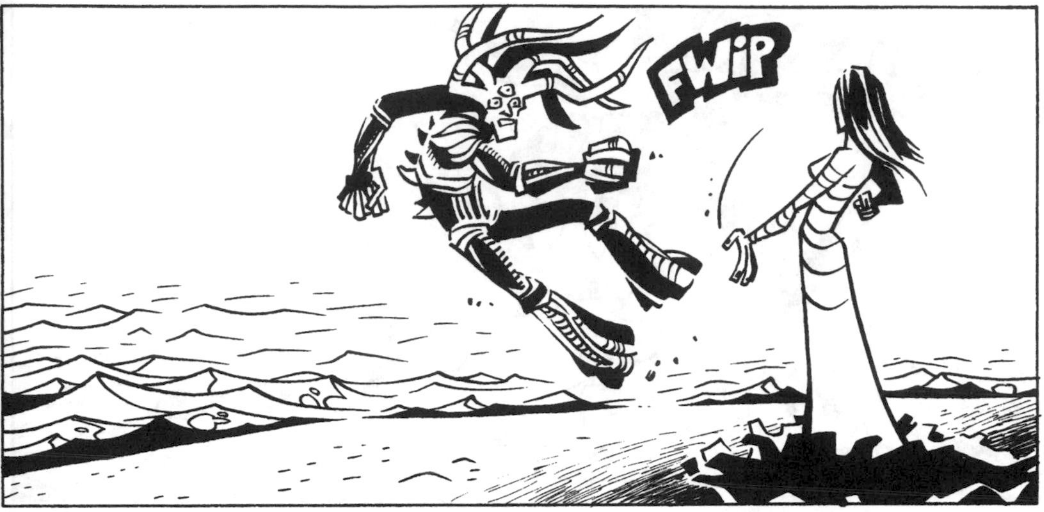
FWIP

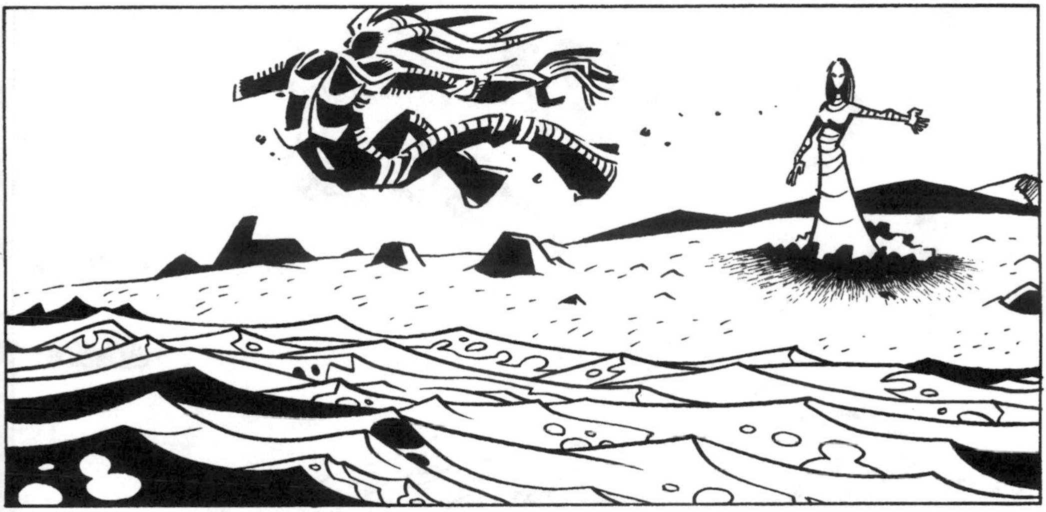

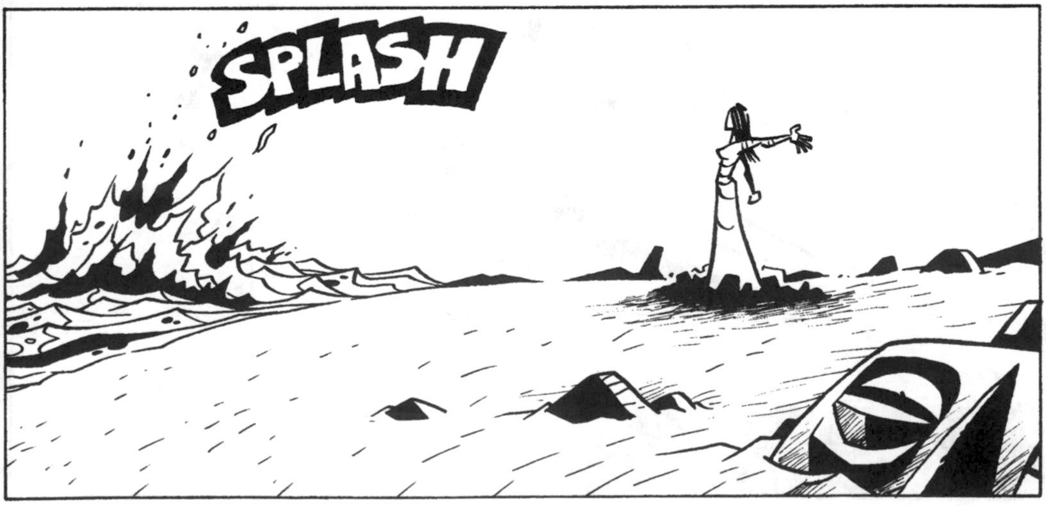
SPLASH

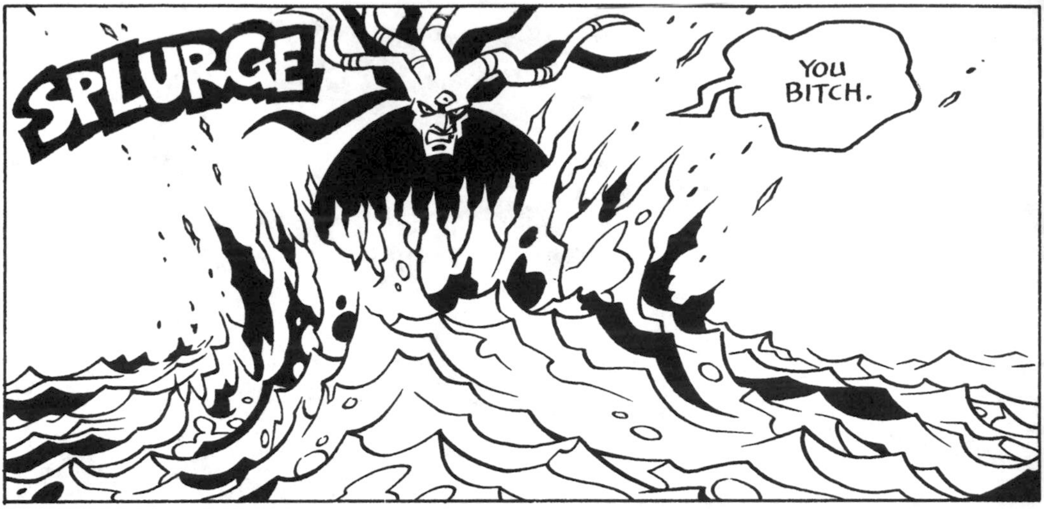
SPLURGE
YOU BITCH.
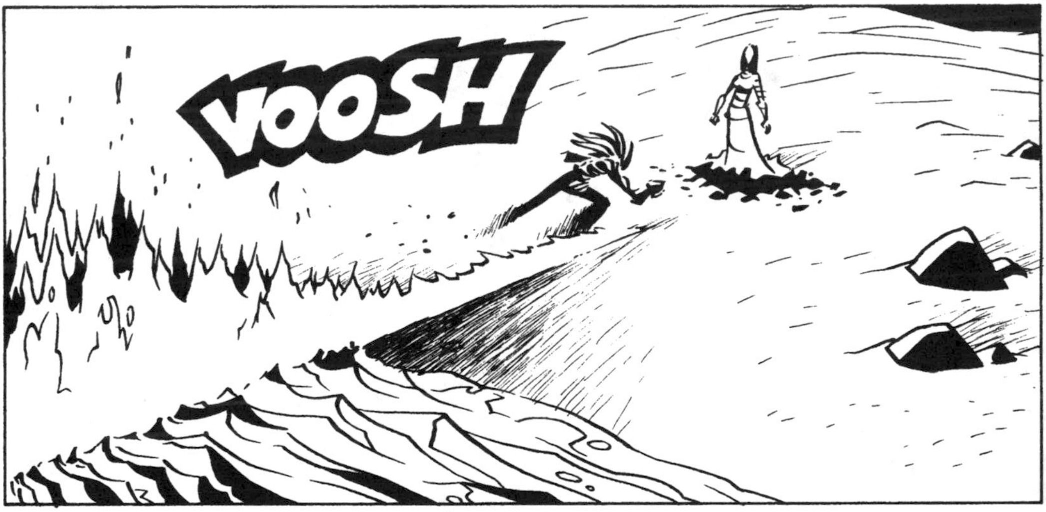
VOOSH
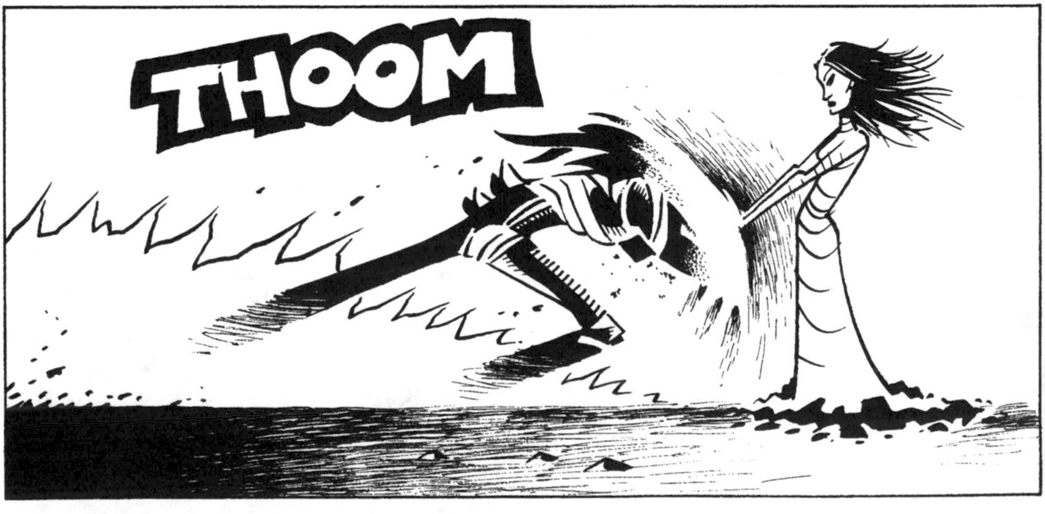
THOOM

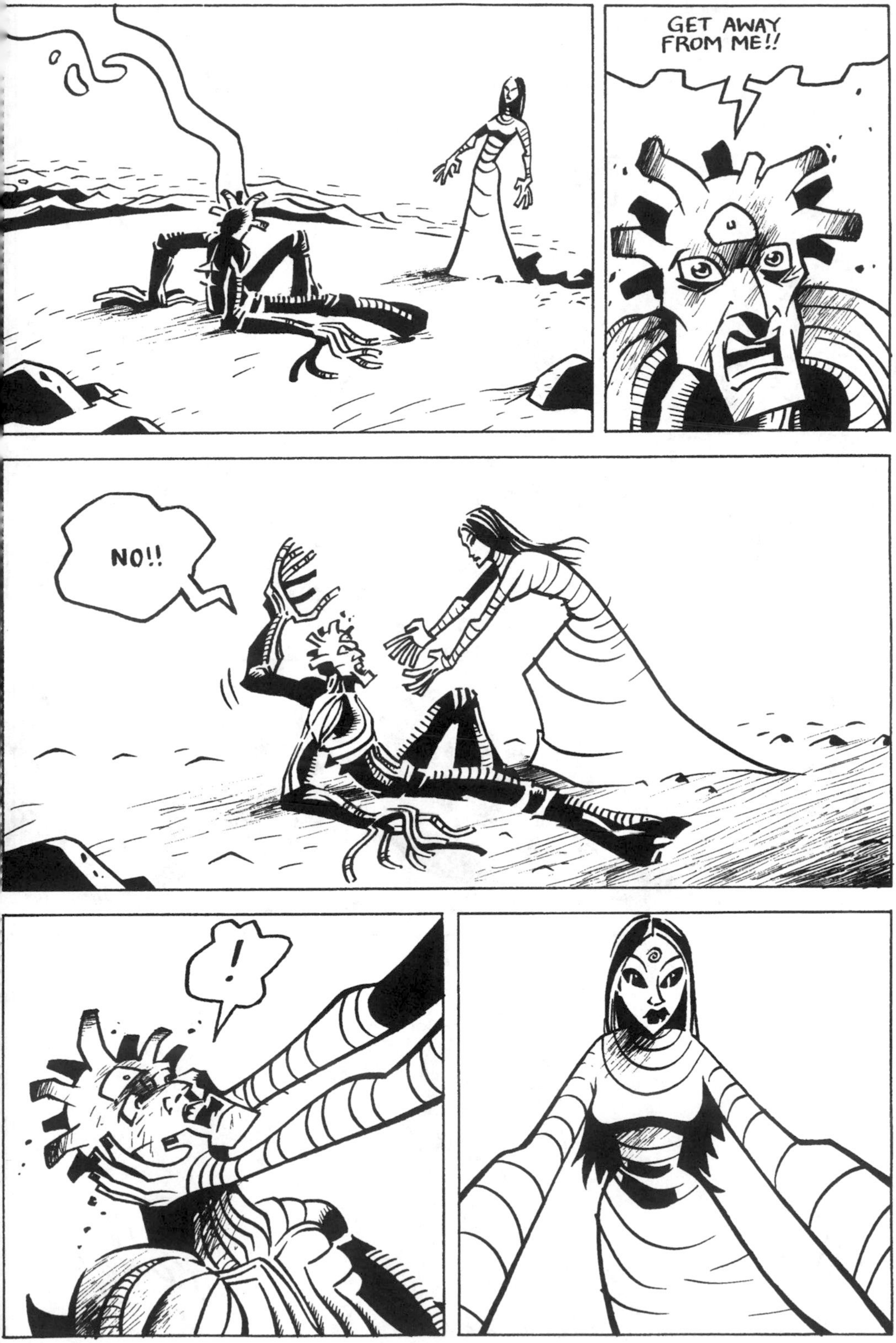
GET AWAY FROM ME!!
NO!!
!

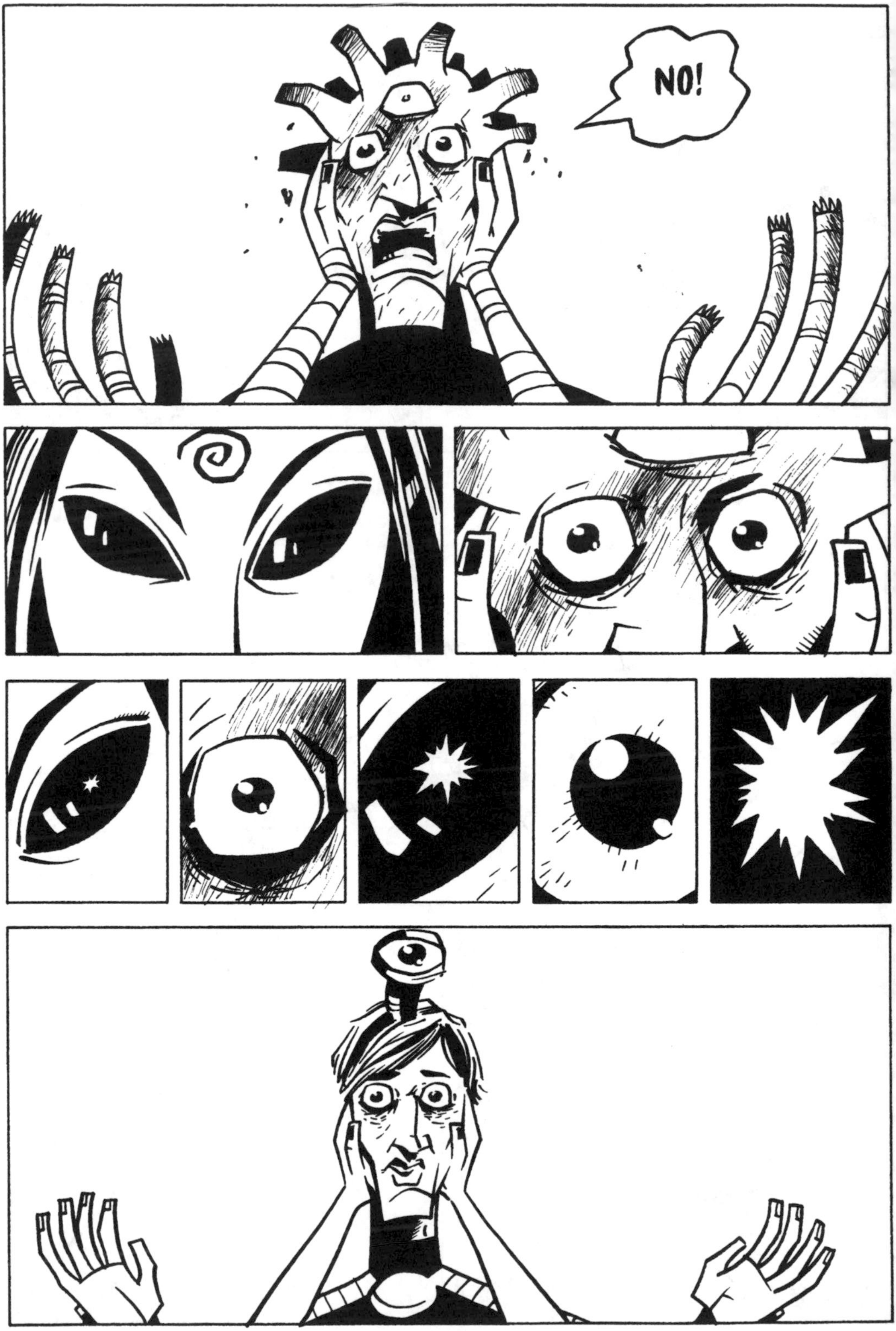
NO!

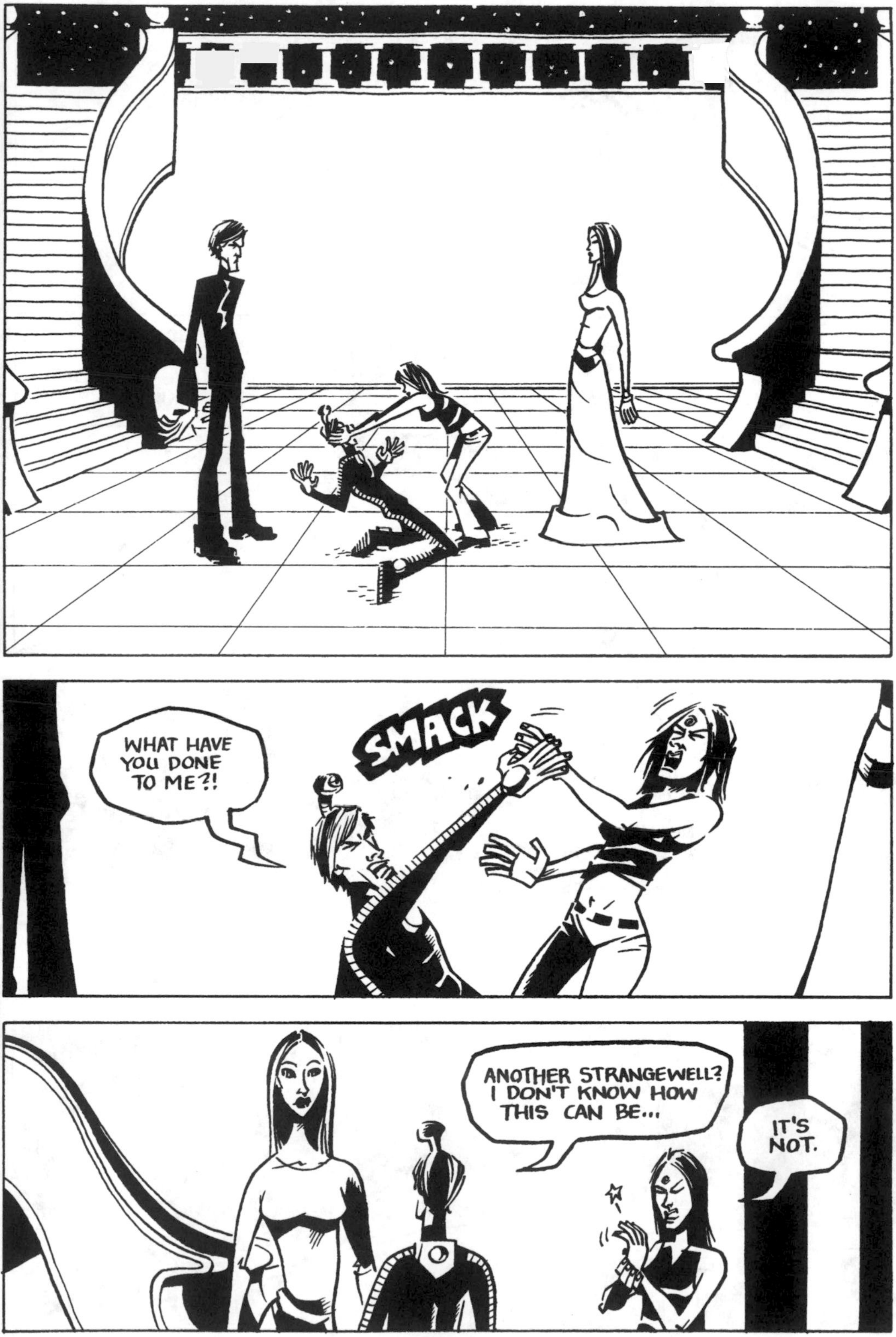
WHAT HAVE YOU DONE TO ME?!
SMACK
ANOTHER STRANGEWELL? I DON'T KNOW HOW THIS CAN BE...
IT'S NOT.

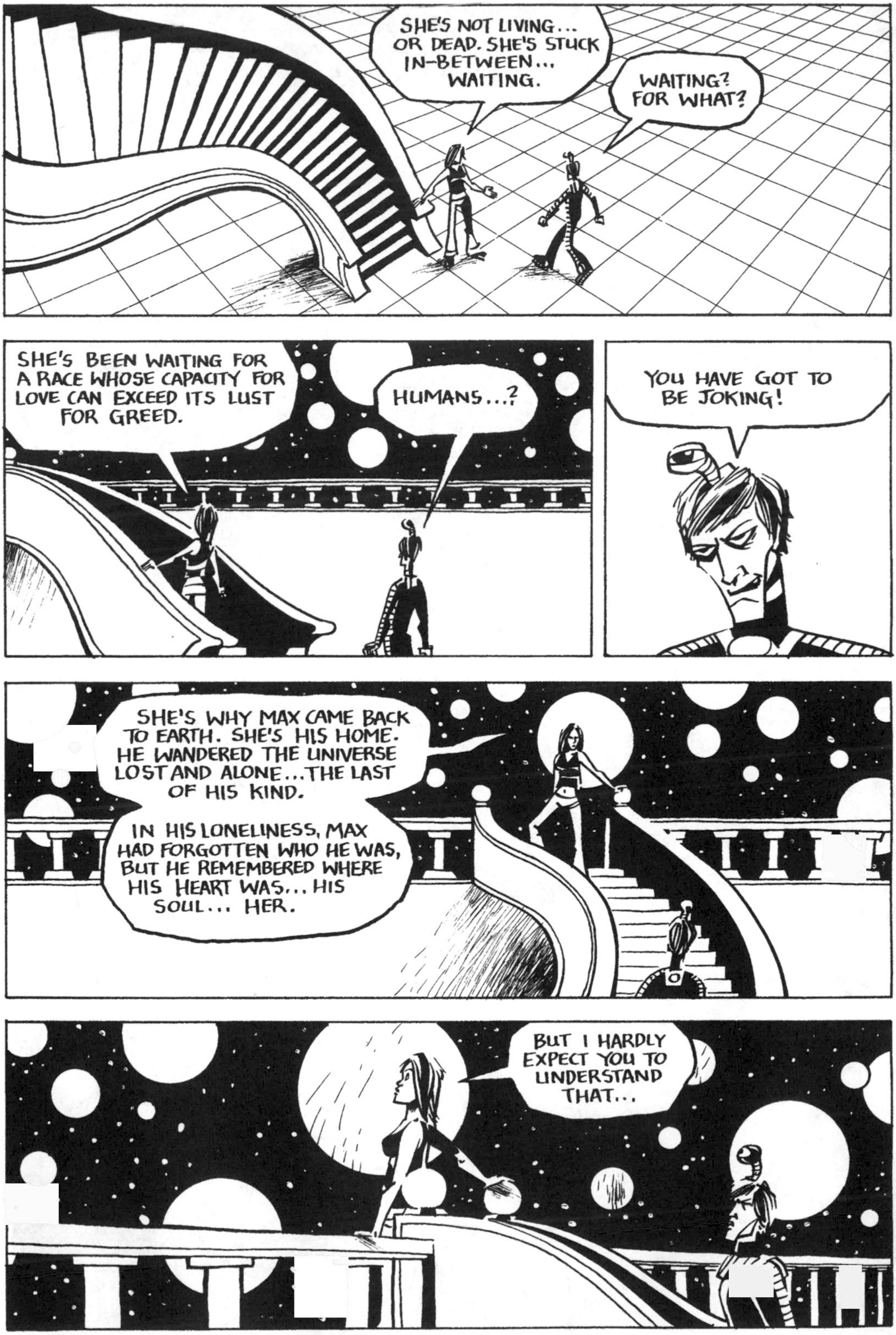
SHE'S NOT LIVING... OR DEAD. SHE'S STUCK IN-BETWEEN... WAITING.
WAITING? FOR WHAT?
SHE'S BEEN WAITING FOR A RACE WHOSE CAPACITY FOR LOVE CAN EXCEED ITS LUST FOR GREED.
HUMANS...?
YOU HAVE GOT TO BE JOKING!
SHE'S WHY MAX CAME BACK TO EARTH. SHE'S HIS HOME. HE WANDERED THE UNIVERSE LOST AND ALONE... THE LAST OF HIS KIND.
IN HIS LONELINESS, MAX HAD FORGOTTEN WHO HE WAS, BUT HE REMEMBERED WHERE HIS HEART WAS... HIS SOUL... HER.
BUT I HARDLY EXPECT YOU TO UNDERSTAND THAT...

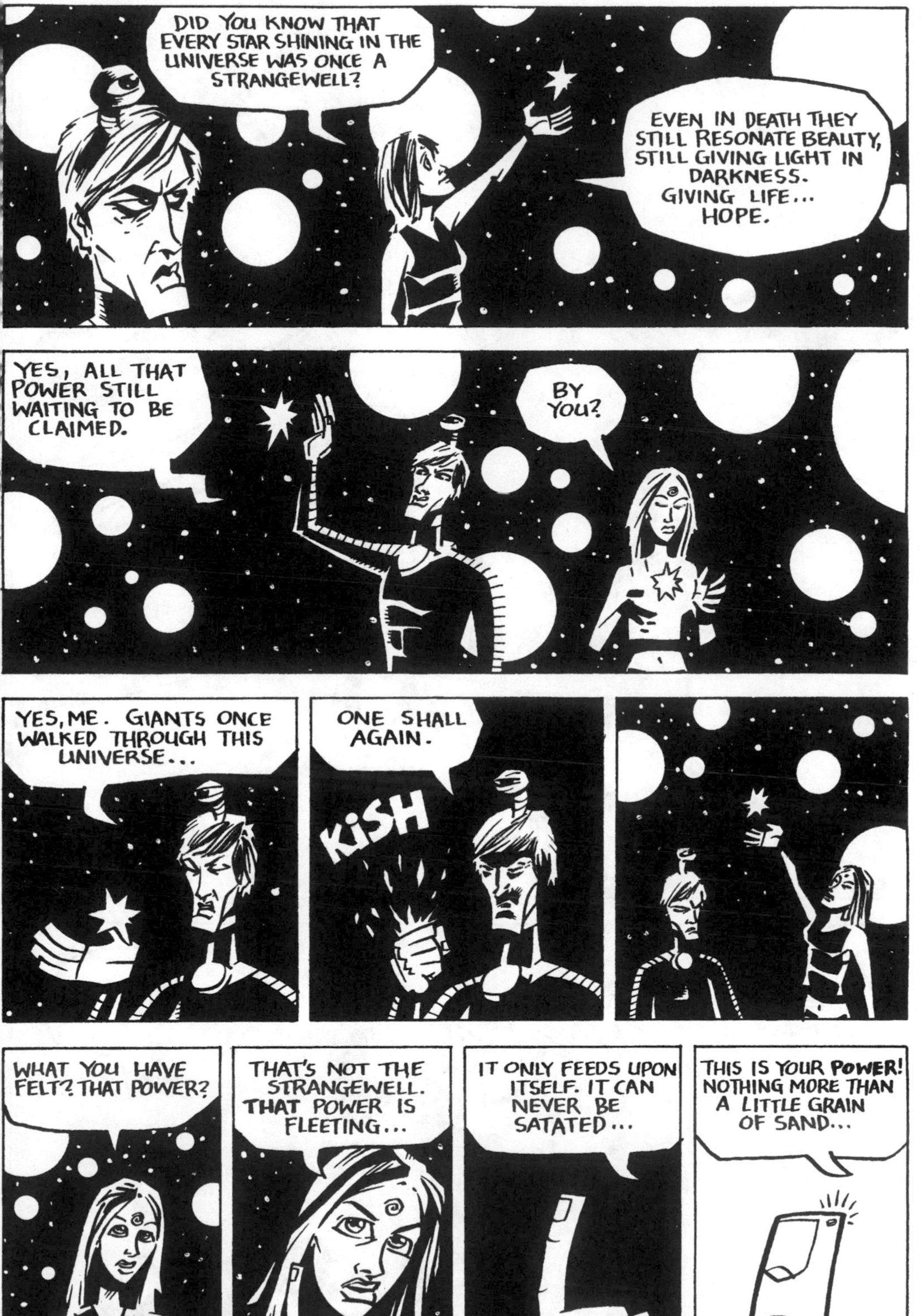
DID YOU KNOW THAT EVERY STAR SHINING IN THE UNIVERSE WAS ONCE A STRANGEWELL?
EVEN IN DEATH THEY STILL RESONATE BEAUTY, STILL GIVING LIGHT IN DARKNESS. GIVING LIFE... HOPE.
YES, ALL THAT POWER STILL WAITING TO BE CLAIMED.
BY YOU?
YES, ME. GIANTS ONCE WALKED THROUGH THIS UNIVERSE...
ONE SHALL AGAIN.
KISH
WHAT YOU HAVE FELT? THAT POWER?
THAT'S NOT THE STRANGEWELL. THAT POWER IS FLEETING...
IT ONLY FEEDS UPON ITSELF. IT CAN NEVER BE SATATED...
THIS IS YOUR POWER! NOTHING MORE THAN A LITTLE GRAIN OF SAND...

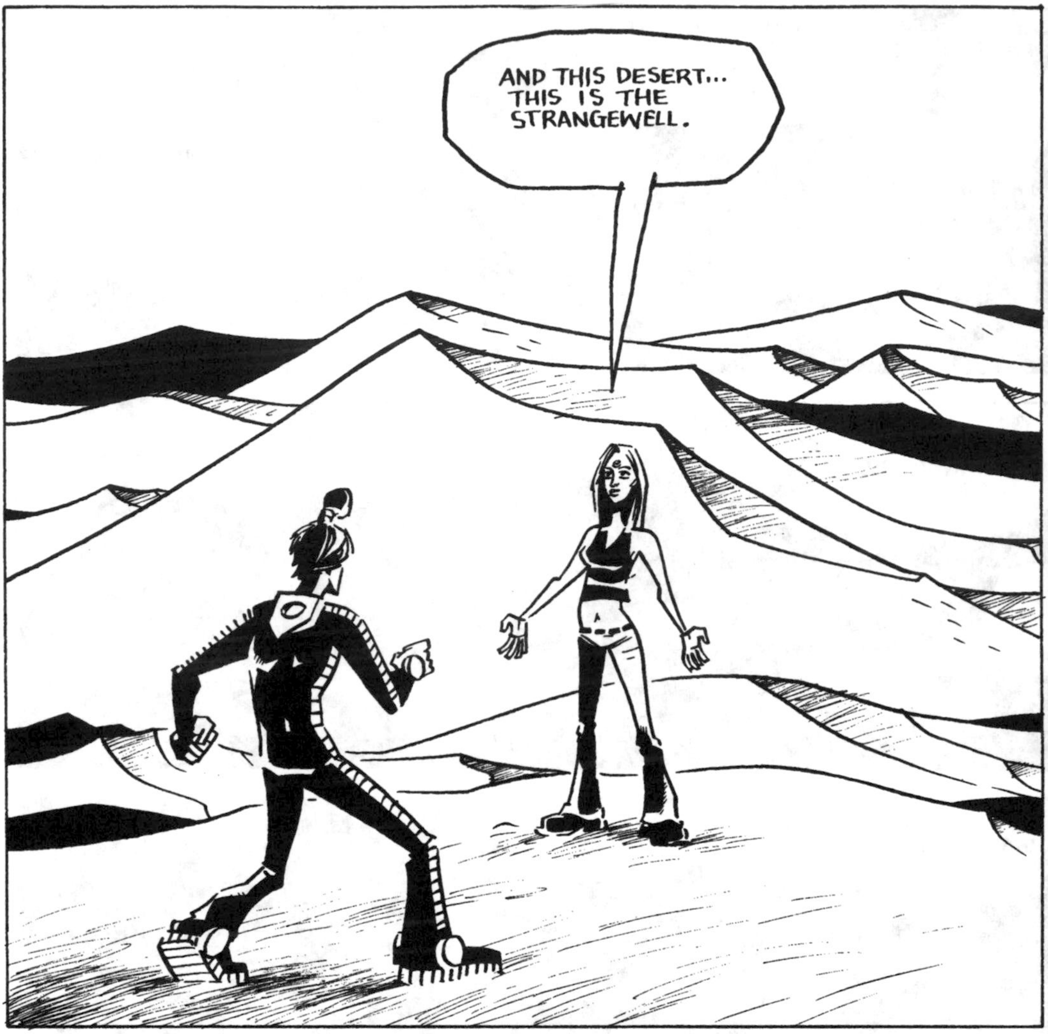
AND THIS DESERT...
THIS IS THE
STRANGEWELL.

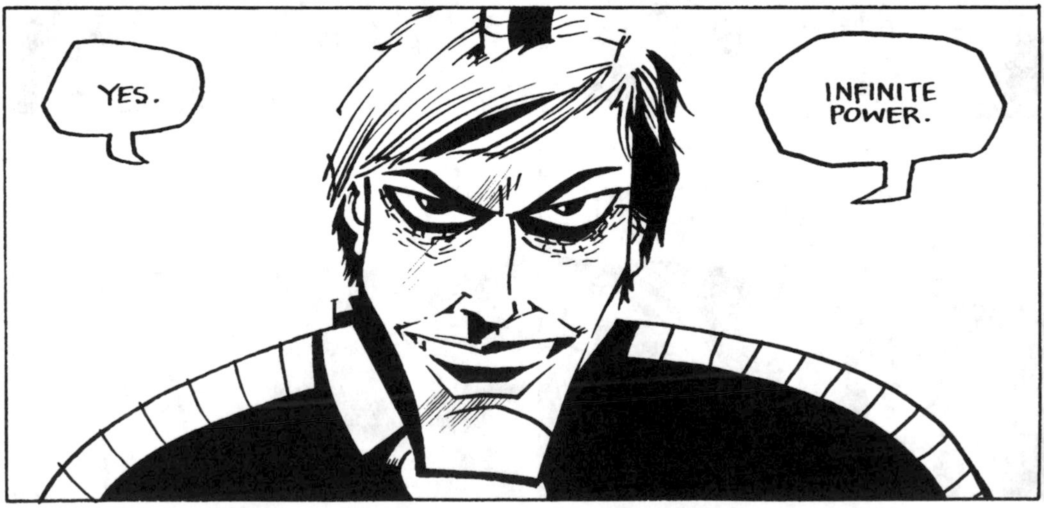
YES.
INFINITE
POWER.

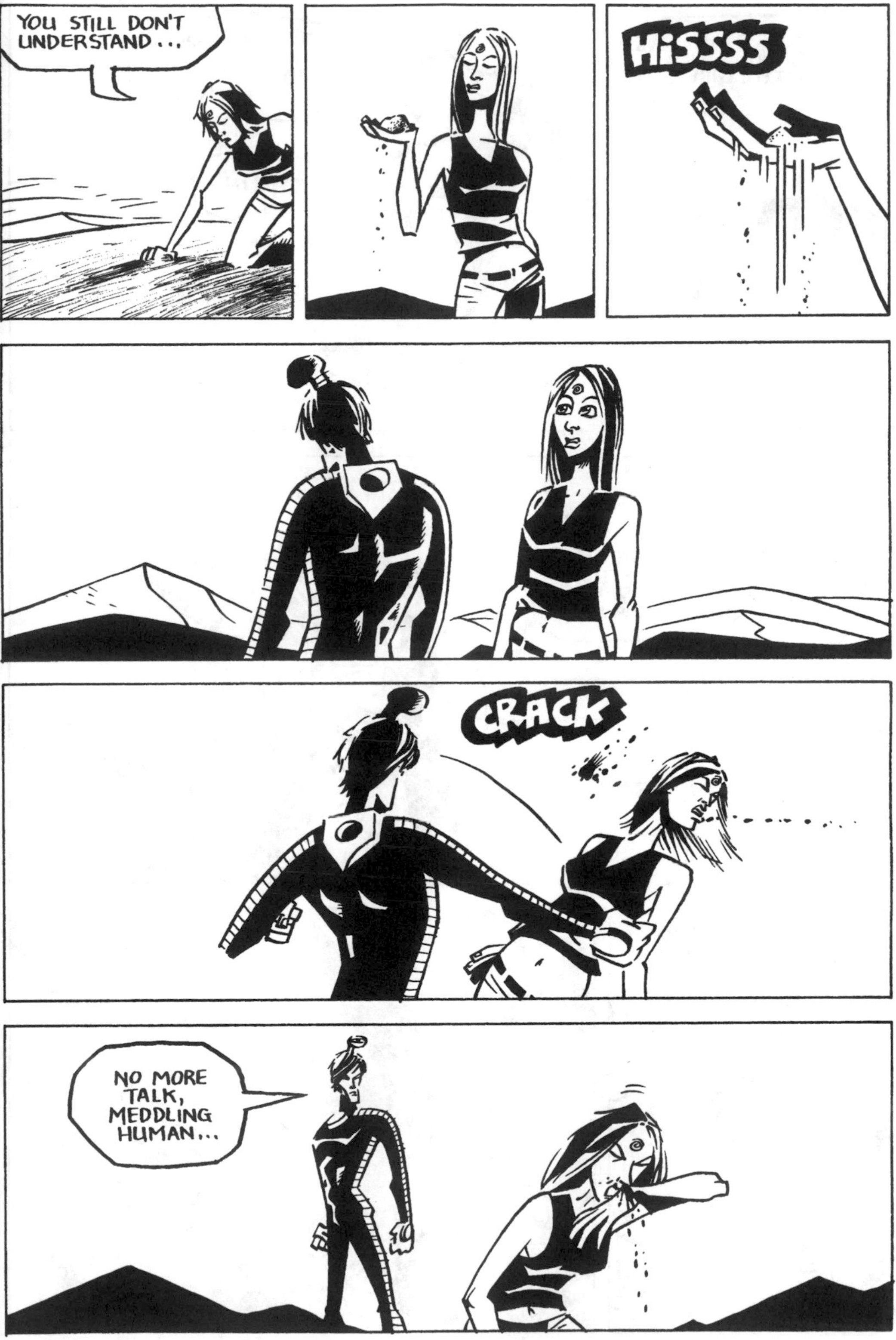
YOU STILL DON'T UNDERSTAND...
HiSSSS
CRACK
NO MORE TALK, MEDDLING HUMAN...

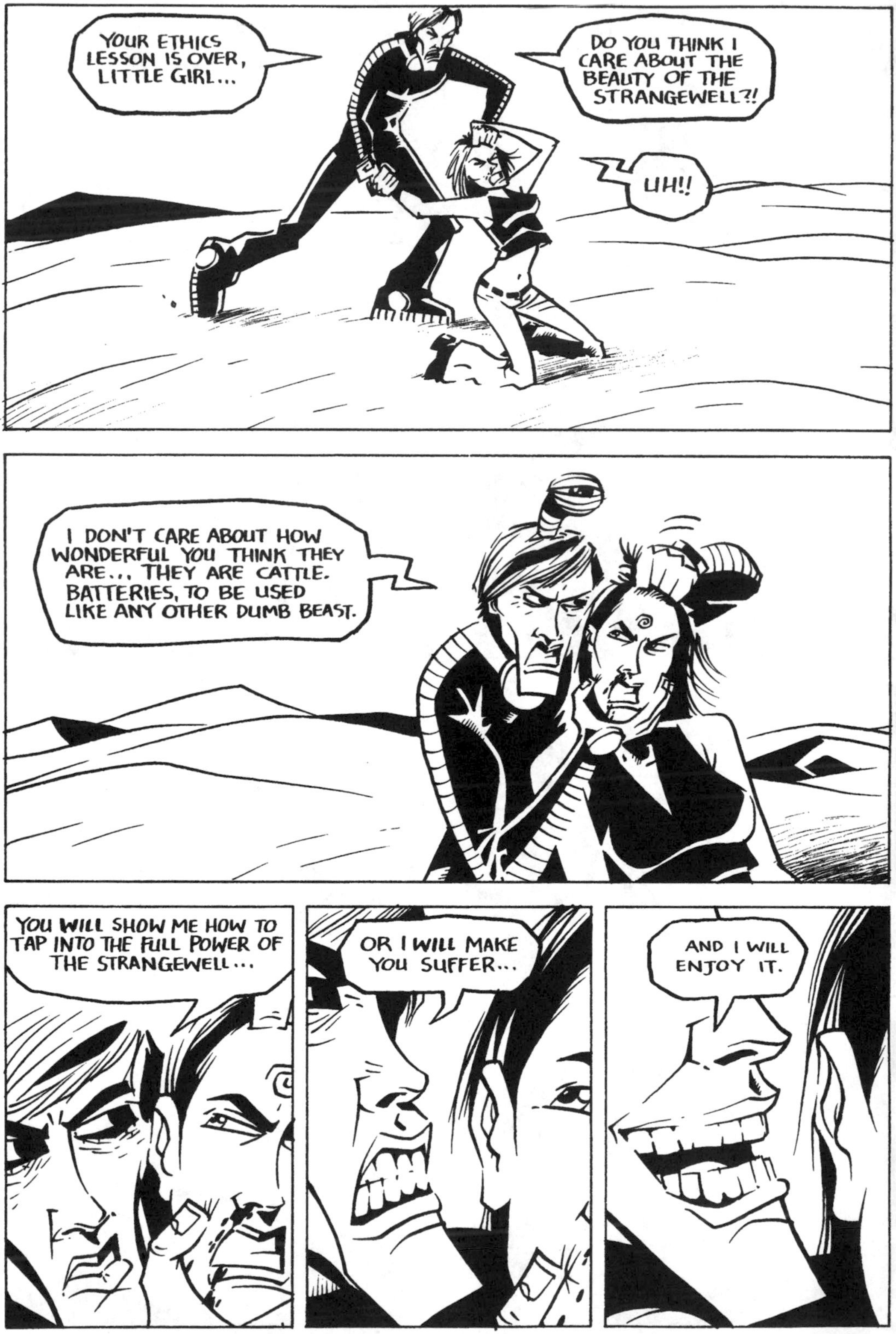
YOUR ETHICS LESSON IS OVER, LITTLE GIRL...
DO YOU THINK I CARE ABOUT THE BEAUTY OF THE STRANGEWELL?!
UH!!
I DON'T CARE ABOUT HOW WONDERFUL YOU THINK THEY ARE.., THEY ARE CATTLE. BATTERIES, TO BE USED LIKE ANY OTHER DUMB BEAST.
YOU WILL SHOW ME HOW TO TAP INTO THE FULL POWER OF THE STRANGEWELL...
OR I WILL MAKE YOU SUFFER...
AND I WILL ENJOY IT.

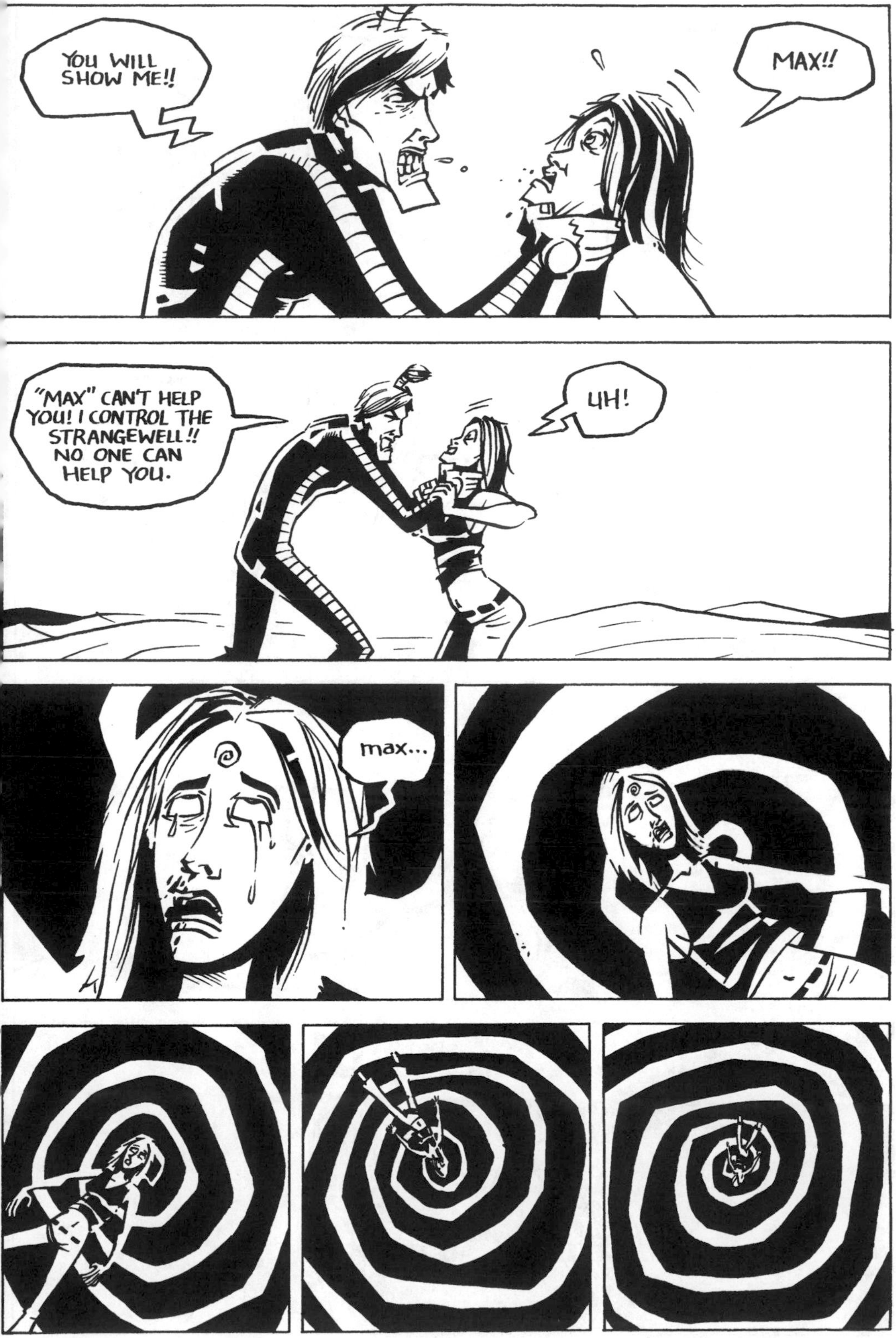
YOU WILL SHOW ME!!
MAX!!
"MAX" CAN'T HELP YOU! I CONTROL THE STRANGEWELL!! NO ONE CAN HELP YOU.
UH!
max...

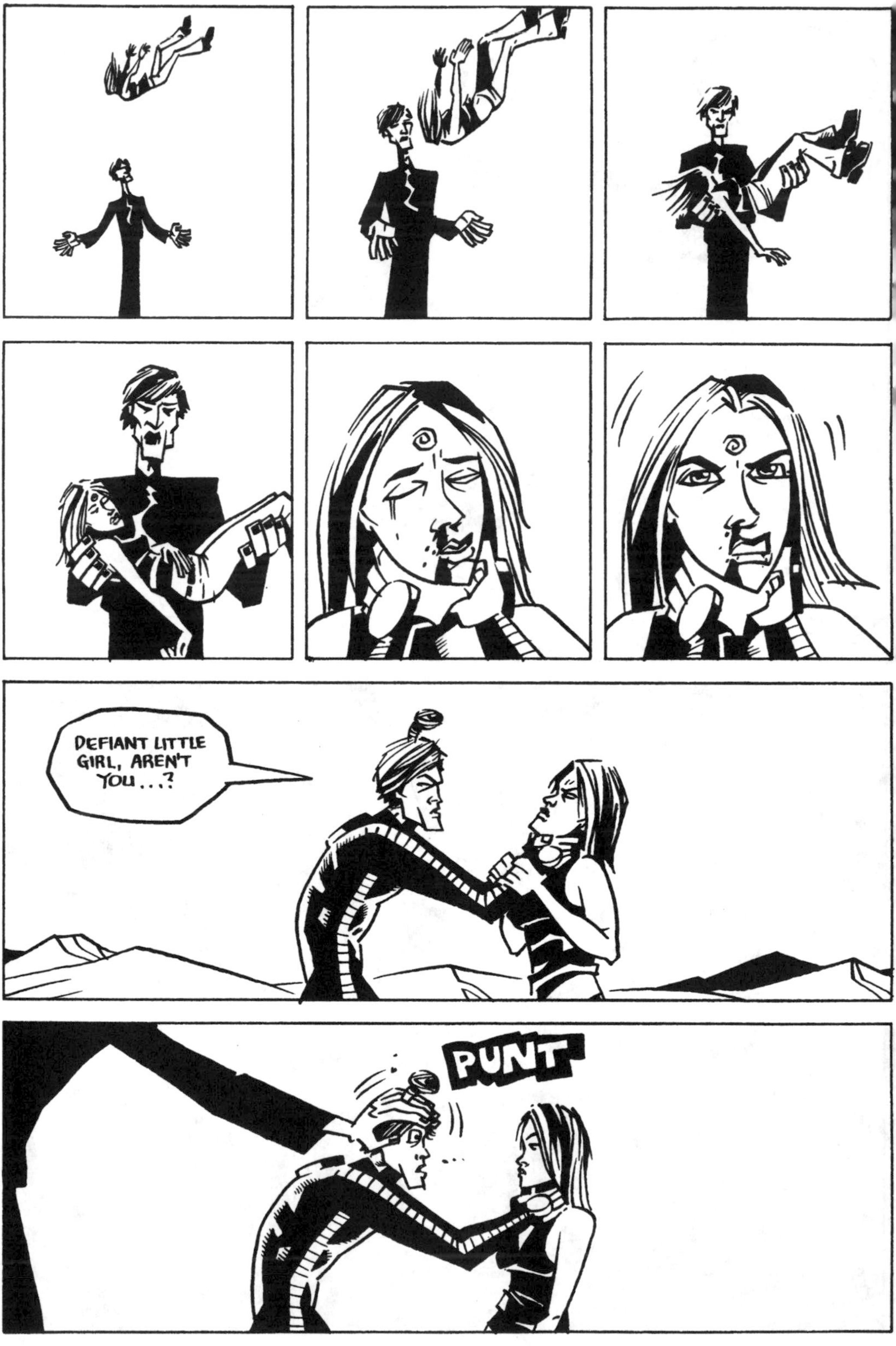
DEFIANT LITTLE GIRL, AREN'T YOU...?
PUNT

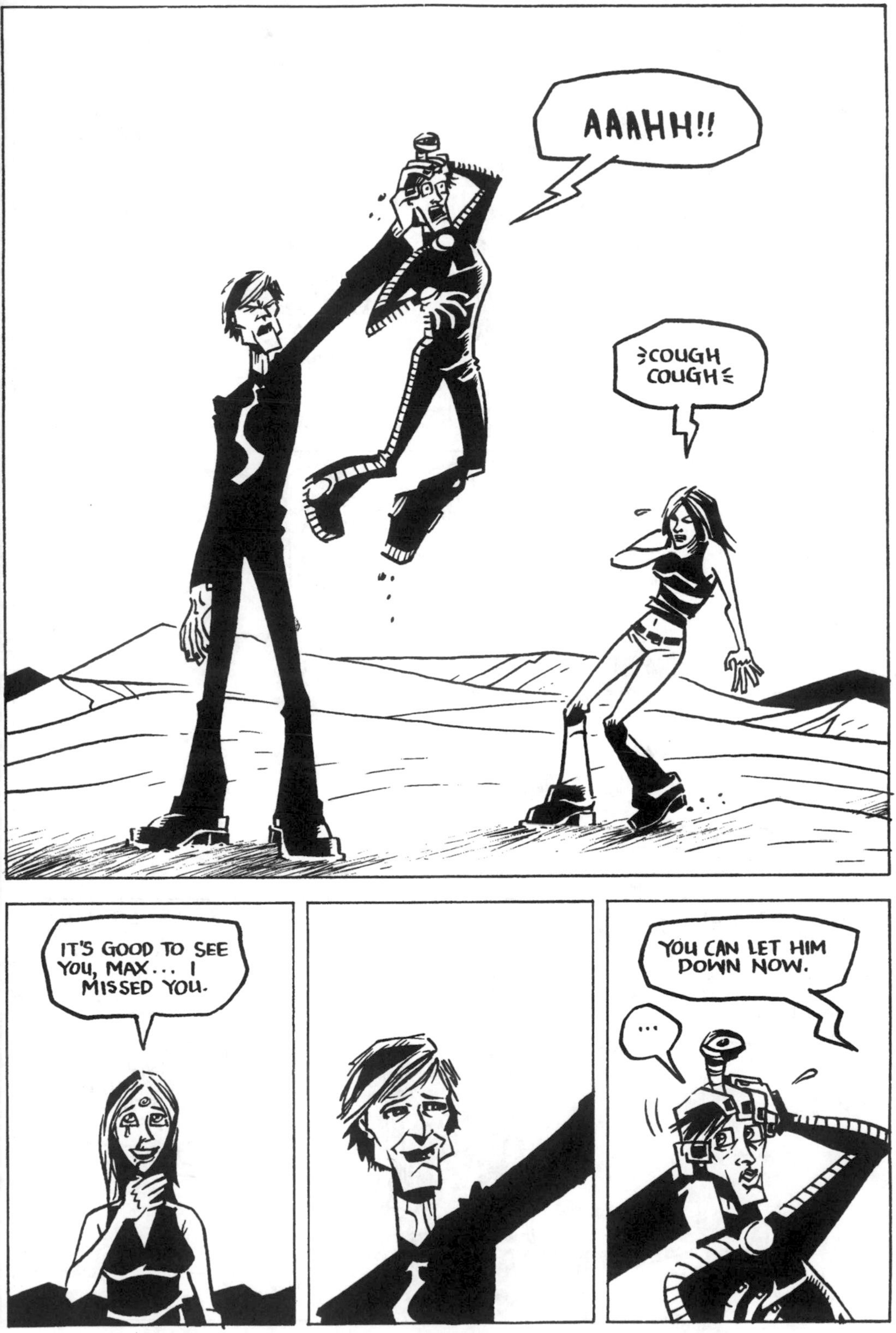
AAAHH!!
COUGH COUGH
IT'S GOOD TO SEE YOU, MAX... I MISSED YOU.
YOU CAN LET HIM DOWN NOW.
...

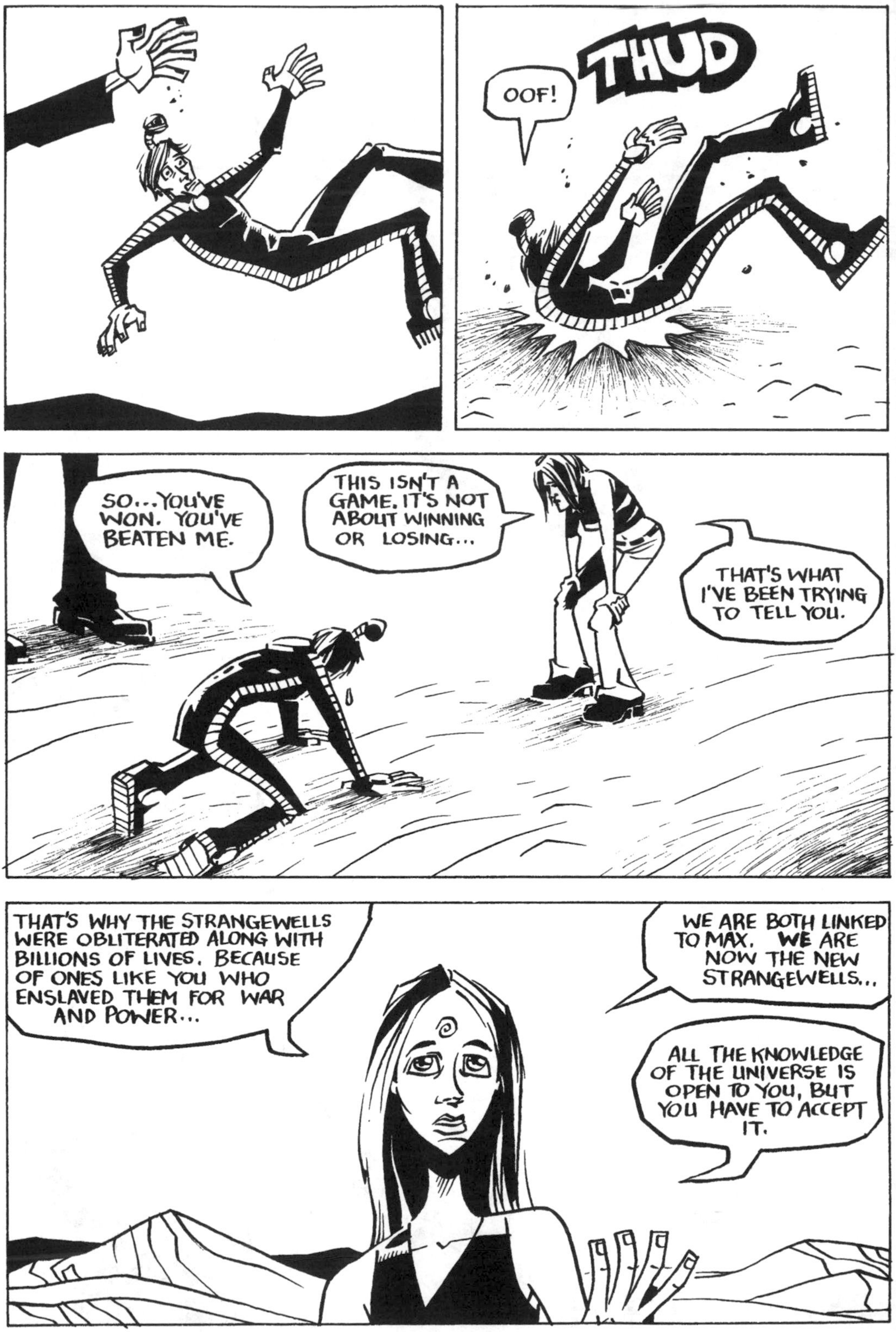
OOF!
THUD
SO...YOU'VE WON. YOU'VE BEATEN ME.
THIS ISN'T A GAME. IT'S NOT ABOUT WINNING OR LOSING...
THAT'S WHAT I'VE BEEN TRYING TO TELL YOU.
THAT'S WHY THE STRANGEWELLS WERE OBLITERATED ALONG WITH BILLIONS OF LIVES. BECAUSE OF ONES LIKE YOU WHO ENSLAVED THEM FOR WAR AND POWER...
WE ARE BOTH LINKED TO MAX. WE ARE NOW THE NEW STRANGEWELLS...
ALL THE KNOWLEDGE OF THE UNIVERSE IS OPEN TO YOU, BUT YOU HAVE TO ACCEPT IT.

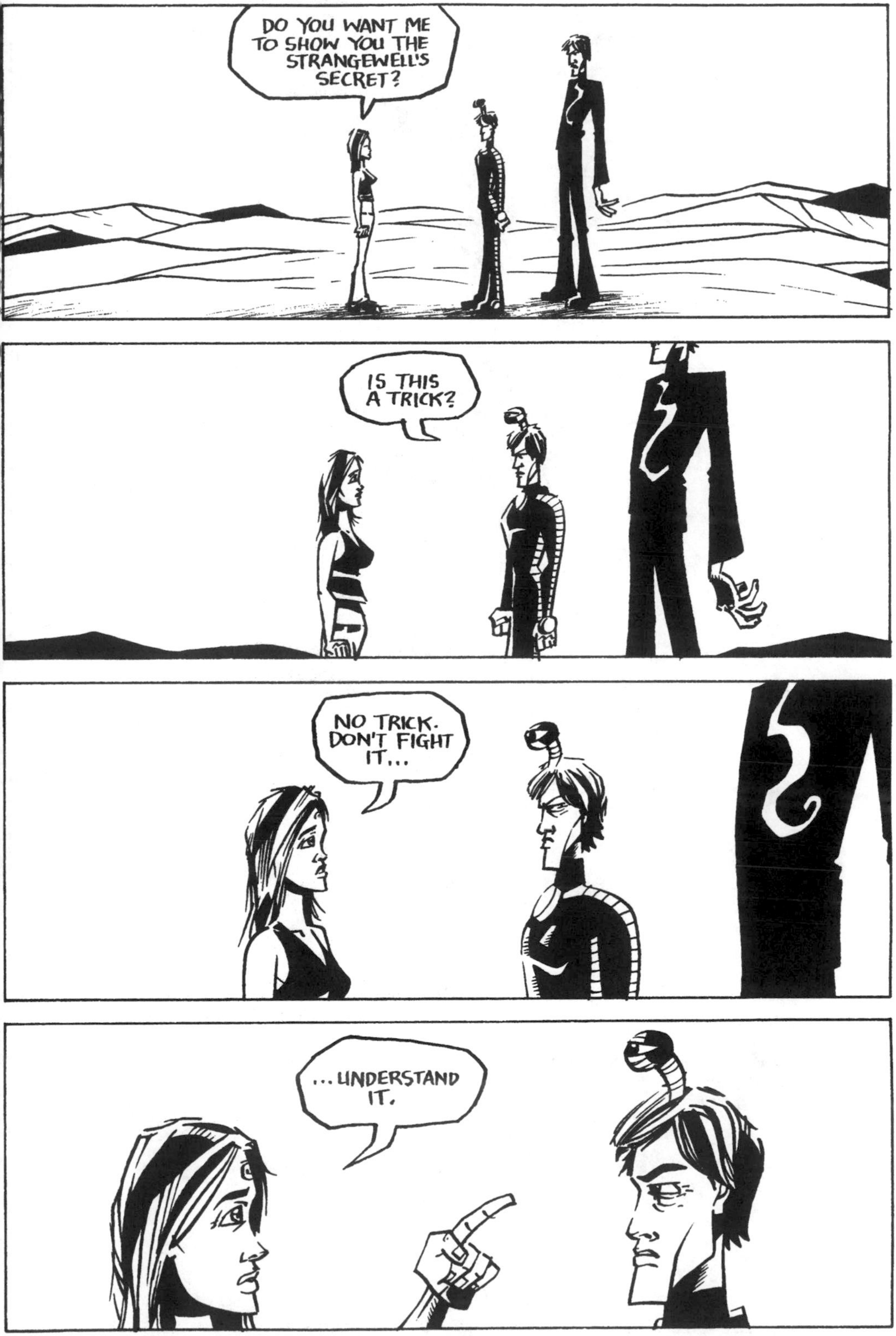
DO YOU WANT ME TO SHOW YOU THE STRANGEWELL'S SECRET?
IS THIS A TRICK?
NO TRICK. DON'T FIGHT IT...
...UNDERSTAND IT.

ZUP
FIP

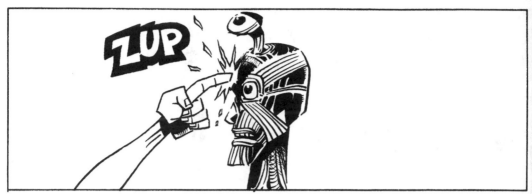

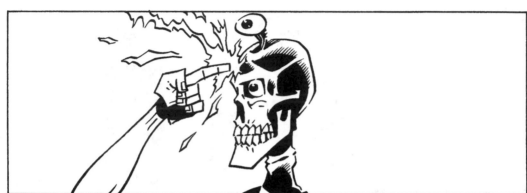

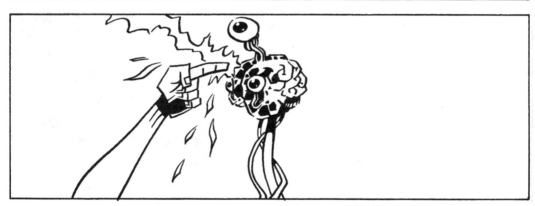

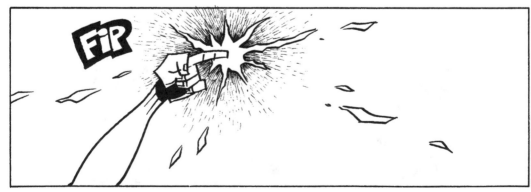

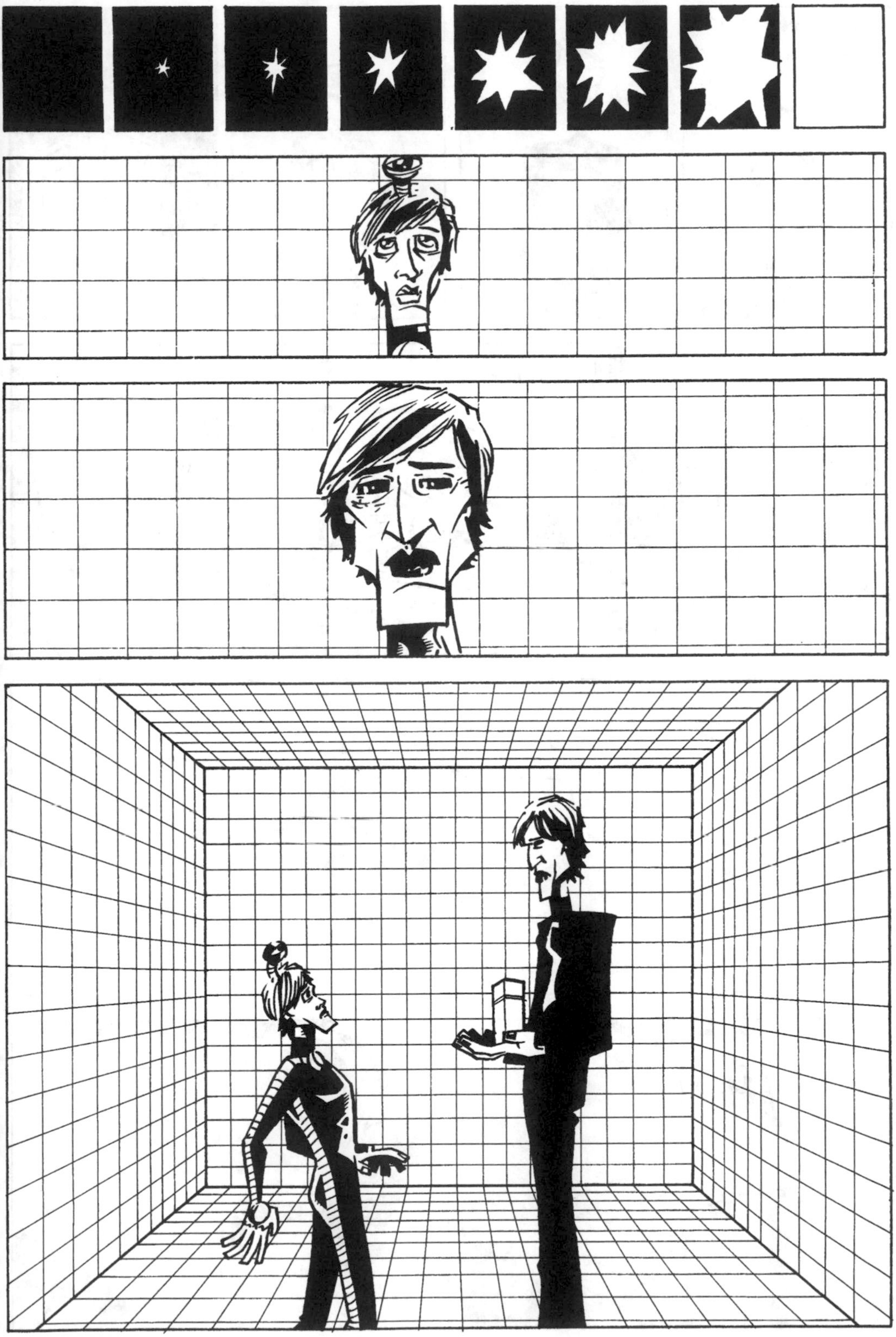

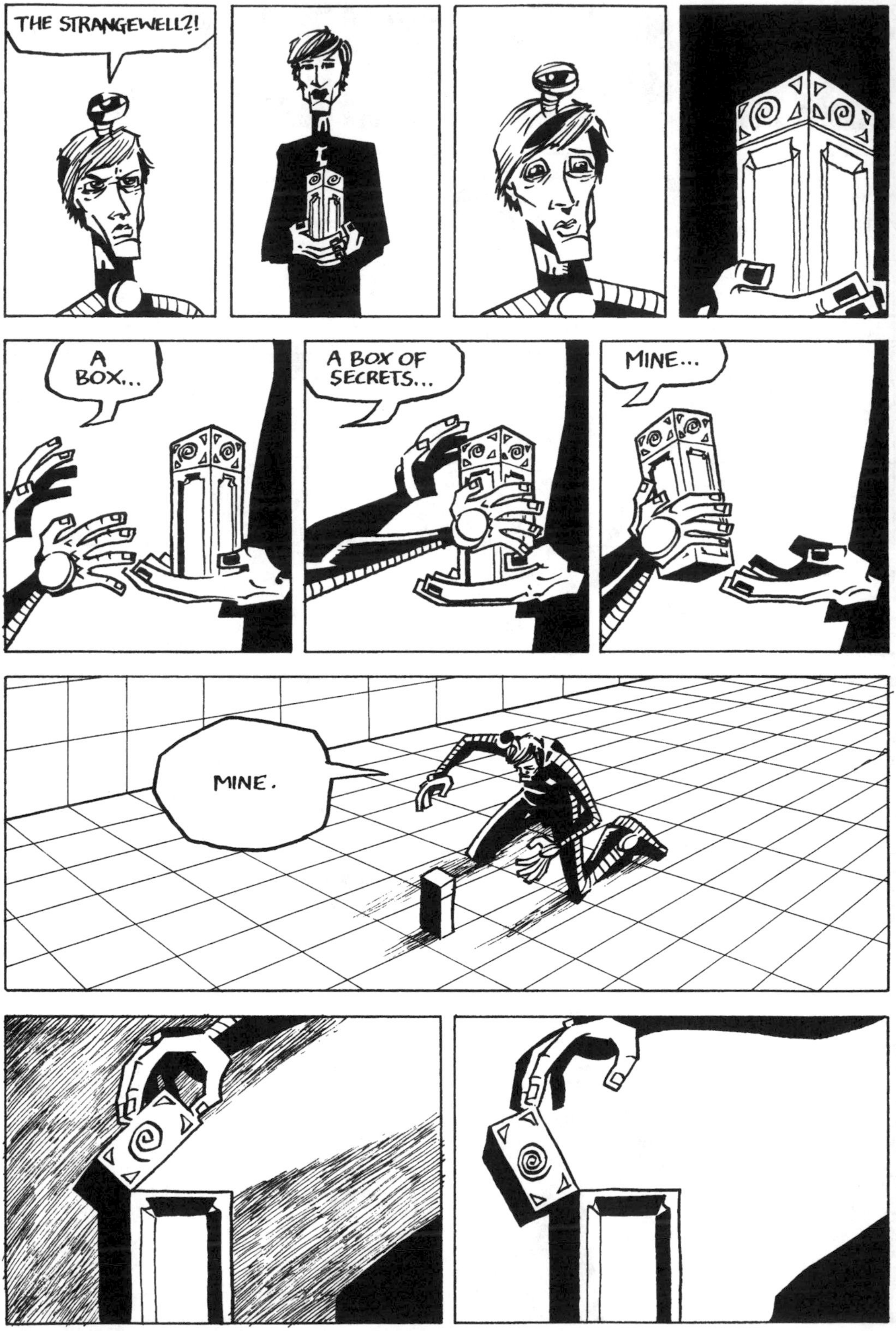
THE STRANGEWELL?!
A BOX...
A BOX OF SECRETS...
MINE...
MINE.

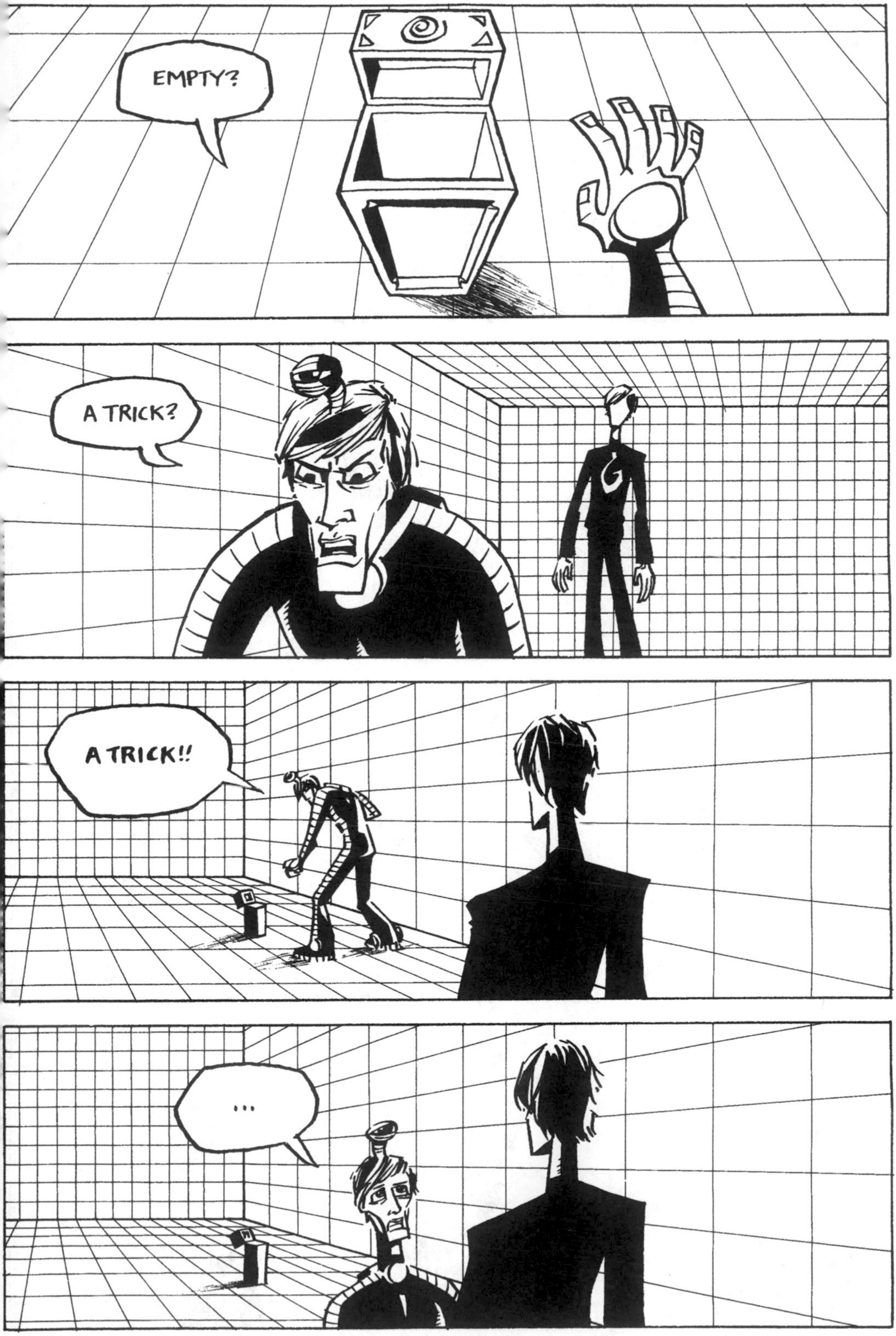
EMPTY?
A TRICK?
A TRICK!!
...

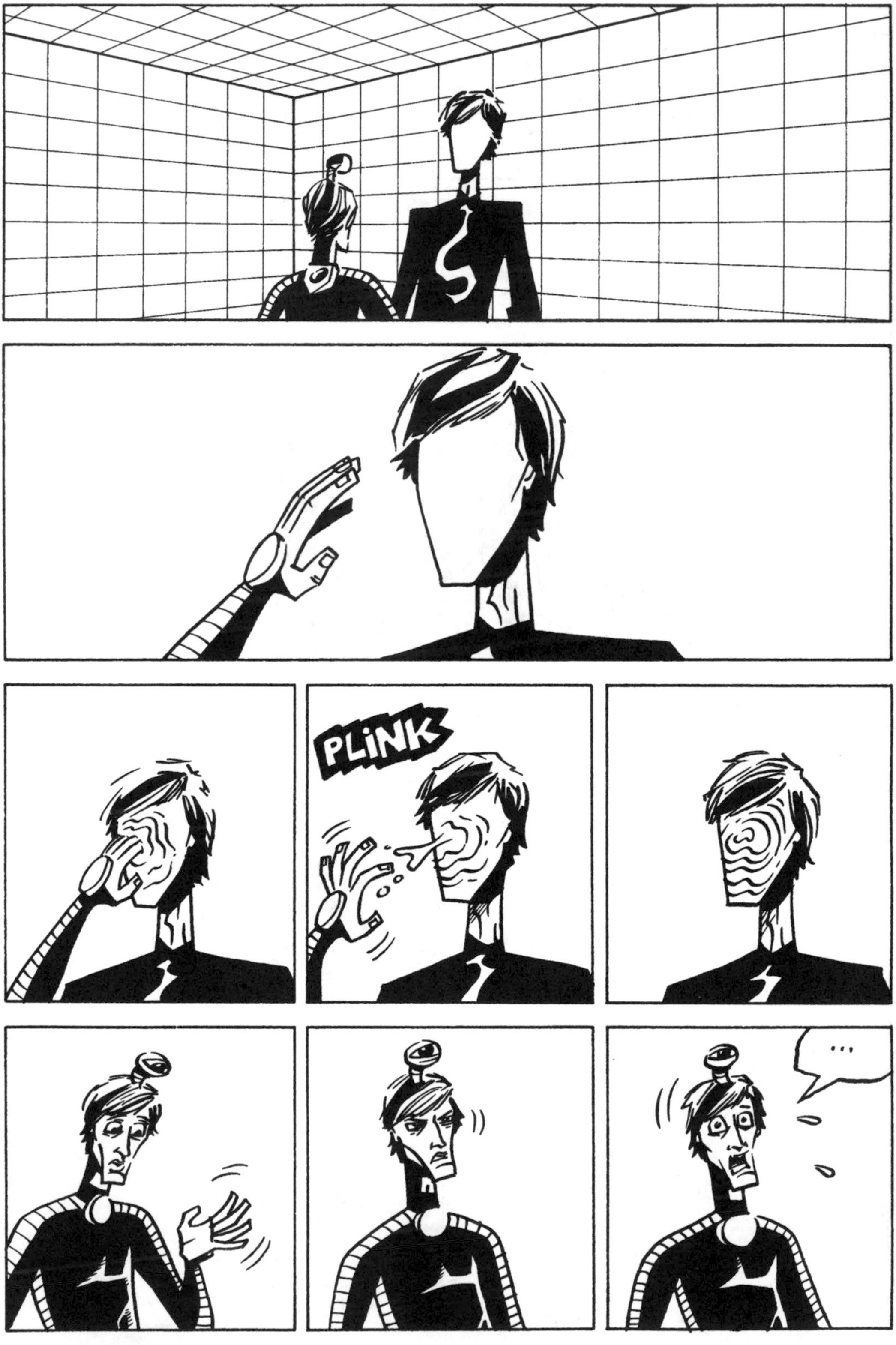
PLINK
...

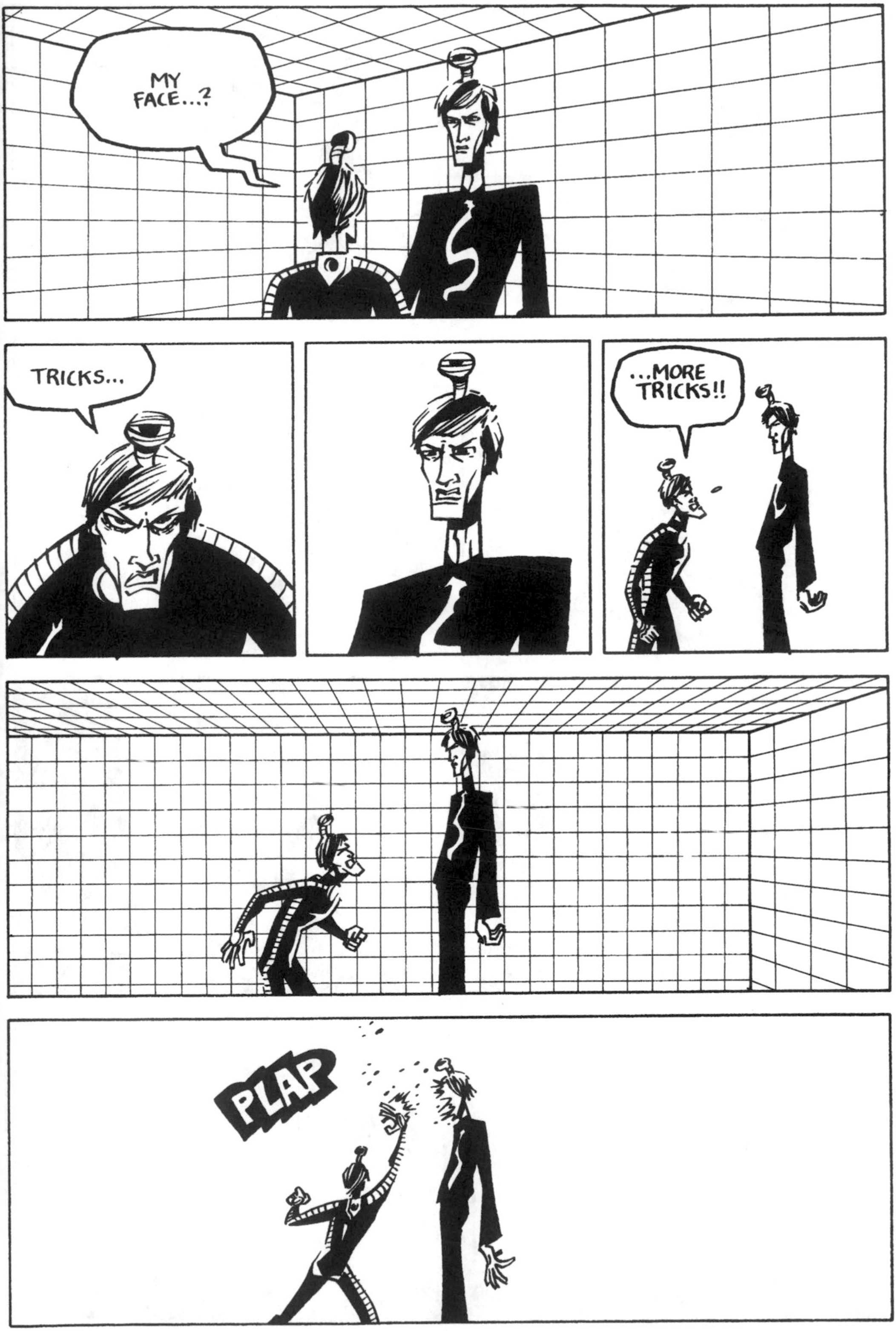
MY FACE...?
TRICKS...
...MORE TRICKS!!
PLAP

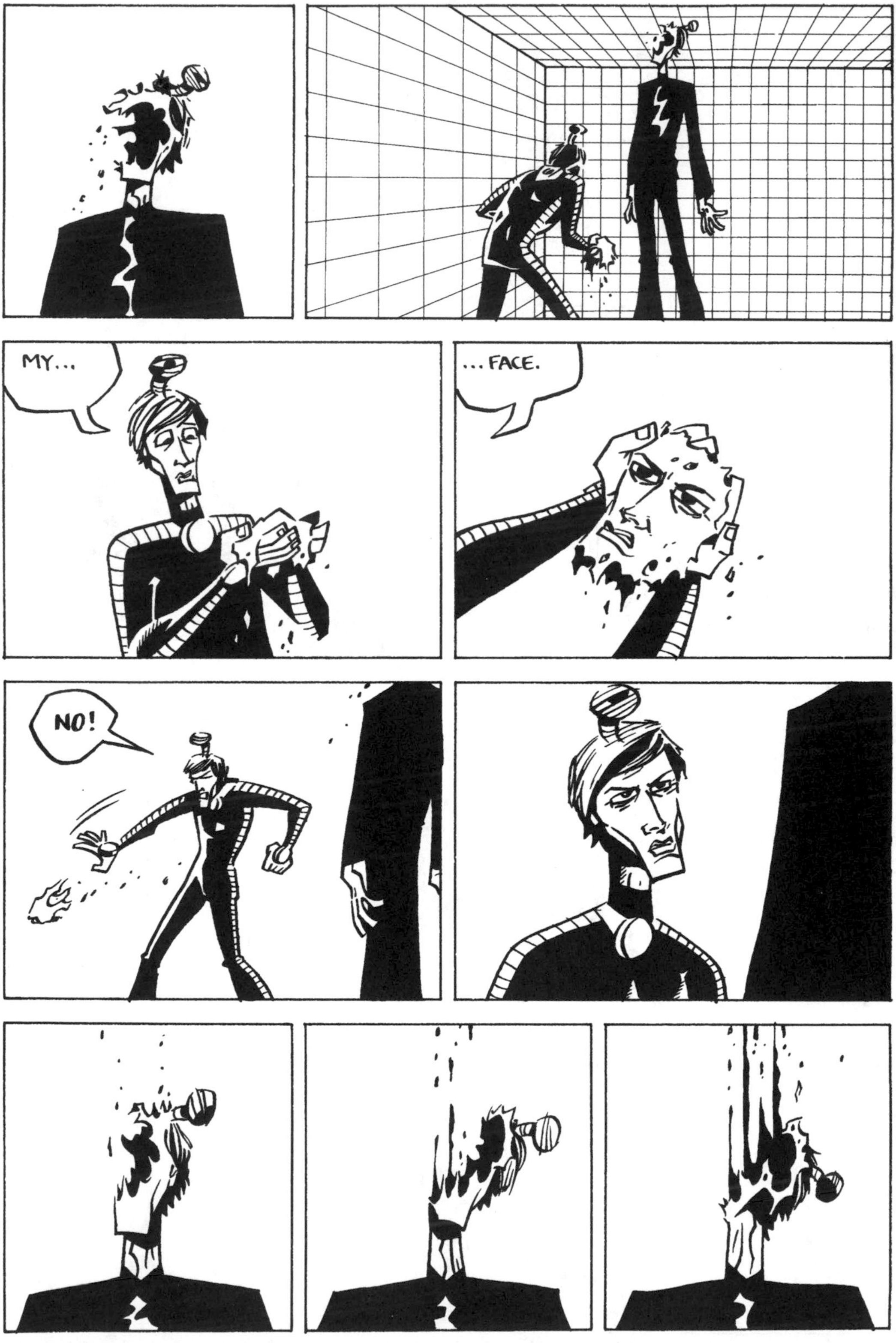
MY...
...FACE.
NO!

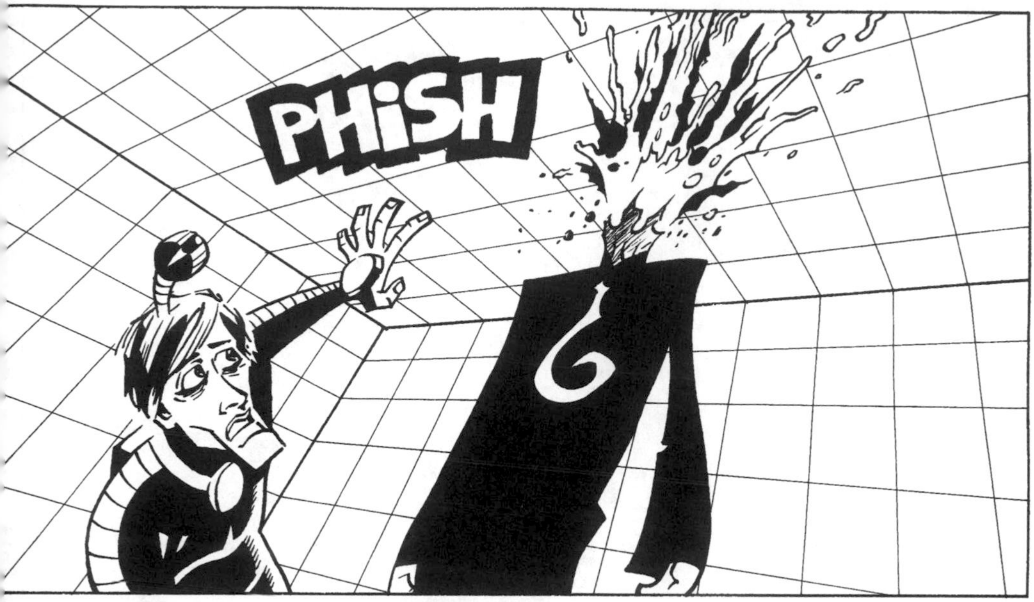
PHISH

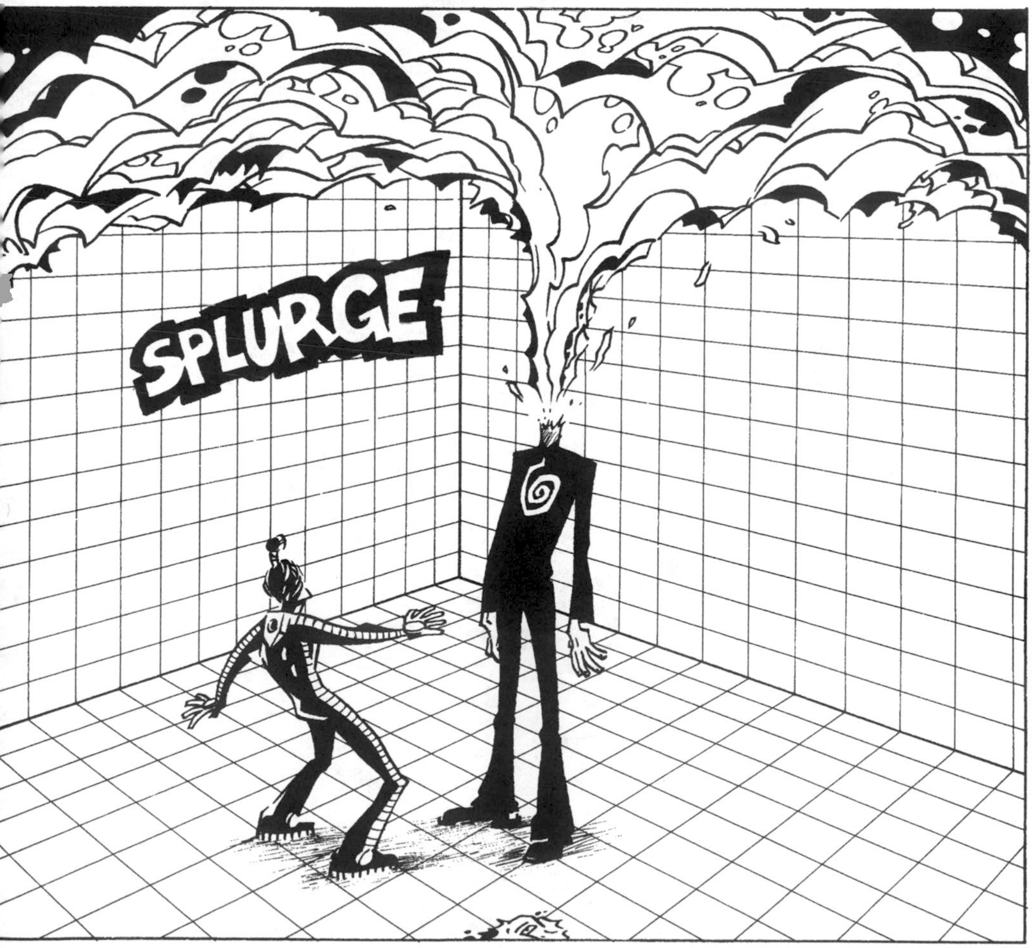
SPLURGE

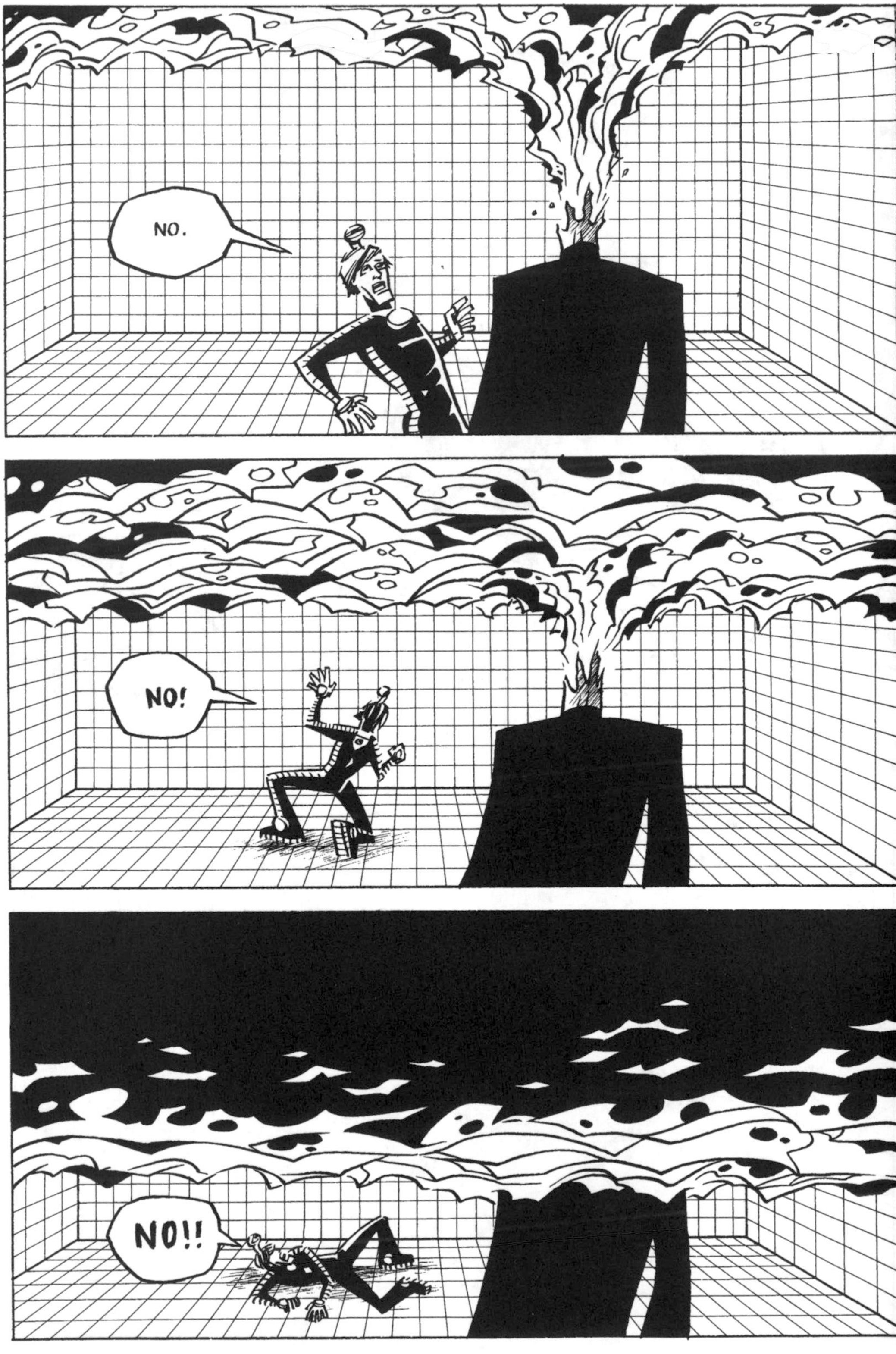
NO.
NO!
NO!!

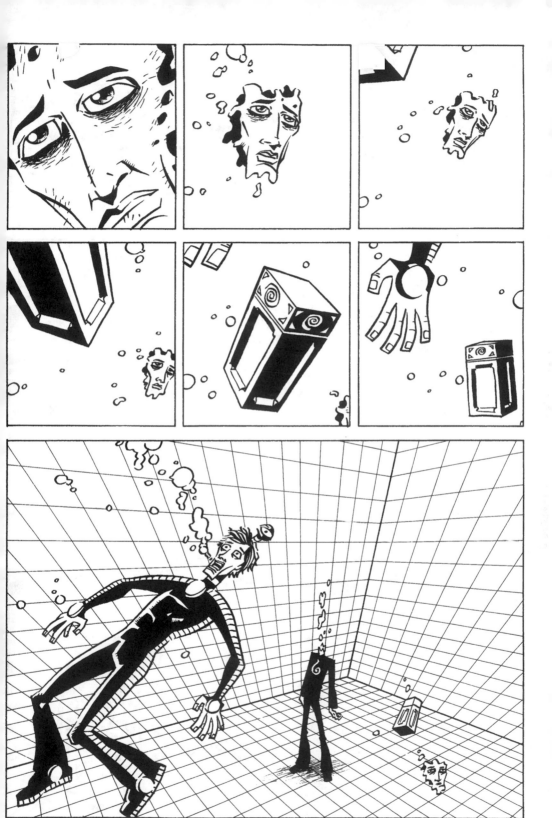

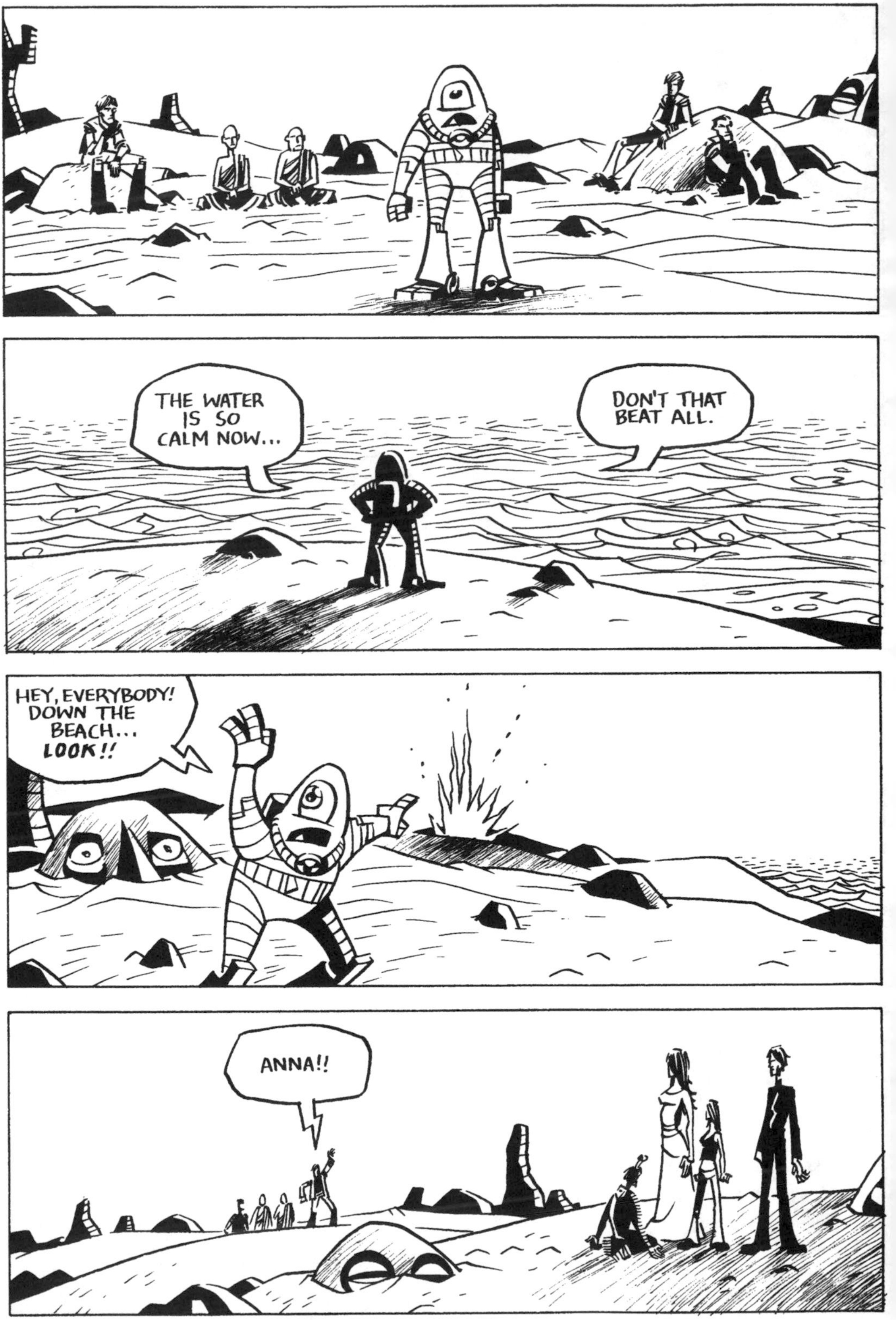
THE WATER IS SO CALM NOW...
DON'T THAT BEAT ALL.
HEY, EVERYBODY! DOWN THE BEACH... **LOOK!!**
ANNA!!

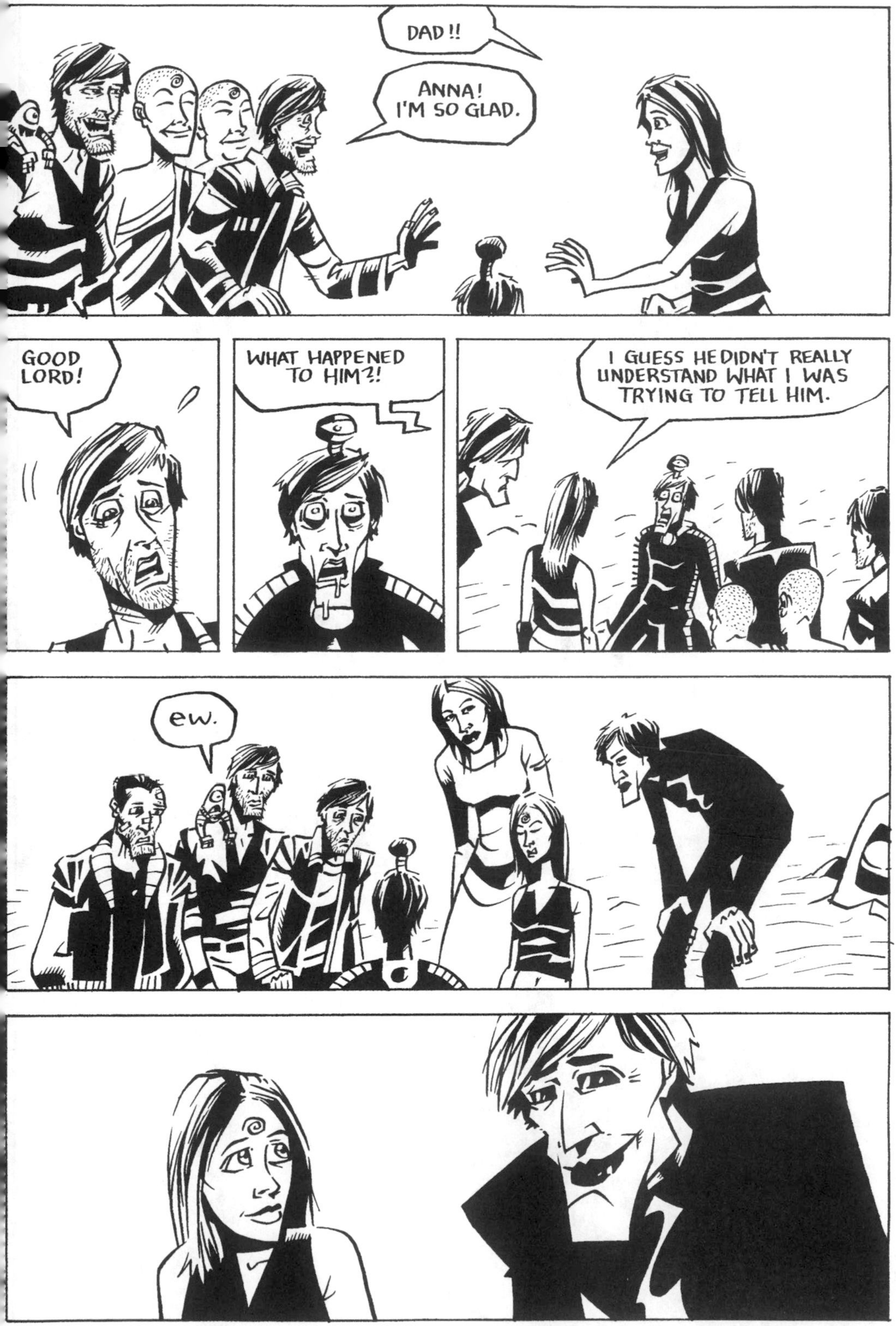
DAD!!
ANNA! I'M SO GLAD.
GOOD LORD!
WHAT HAPPENED TO HIM?!
I GUESS HE DIDN'T REALLY UNDERSTAND WHAT I WAS TRYING TO TELL HIM.
ew.

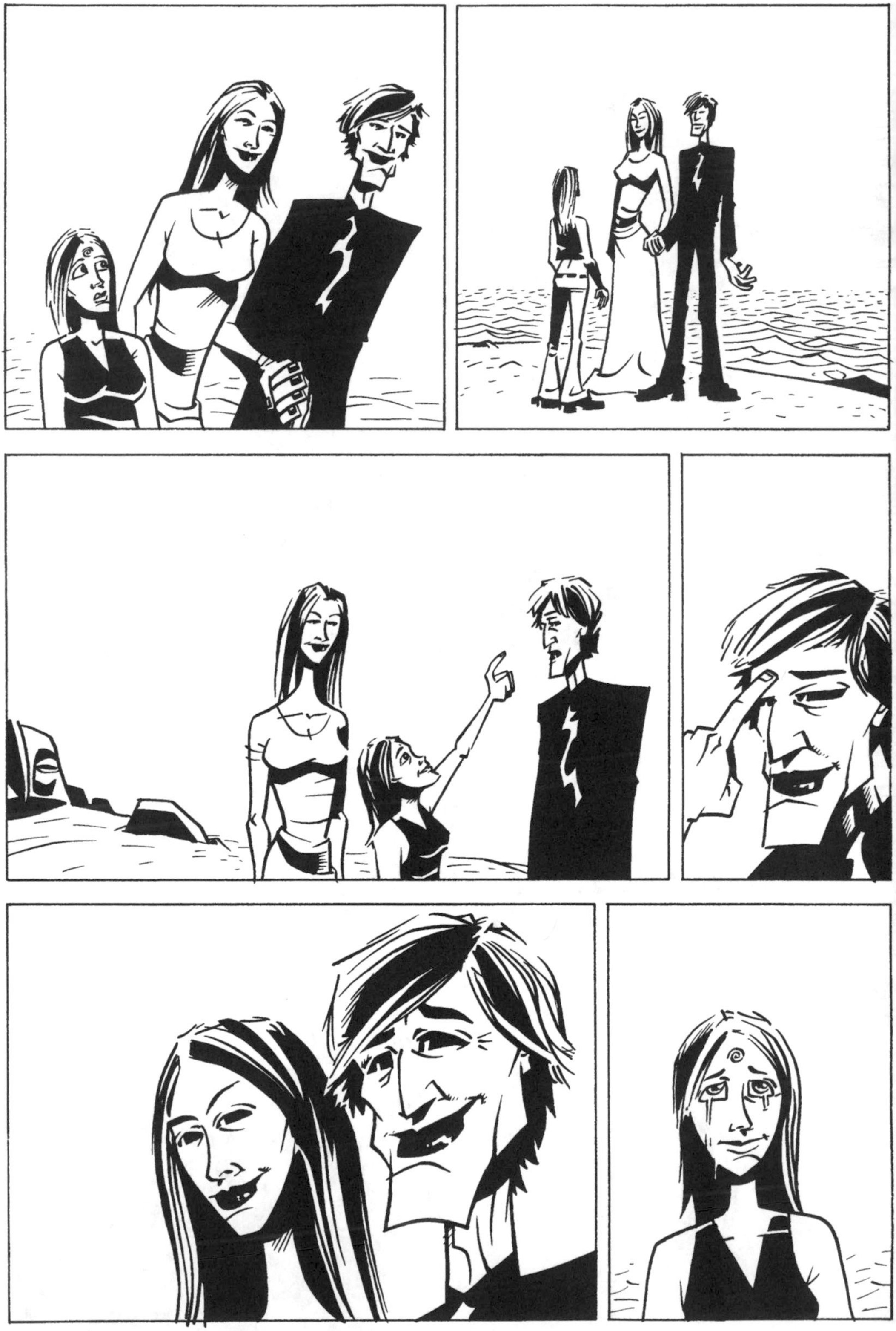

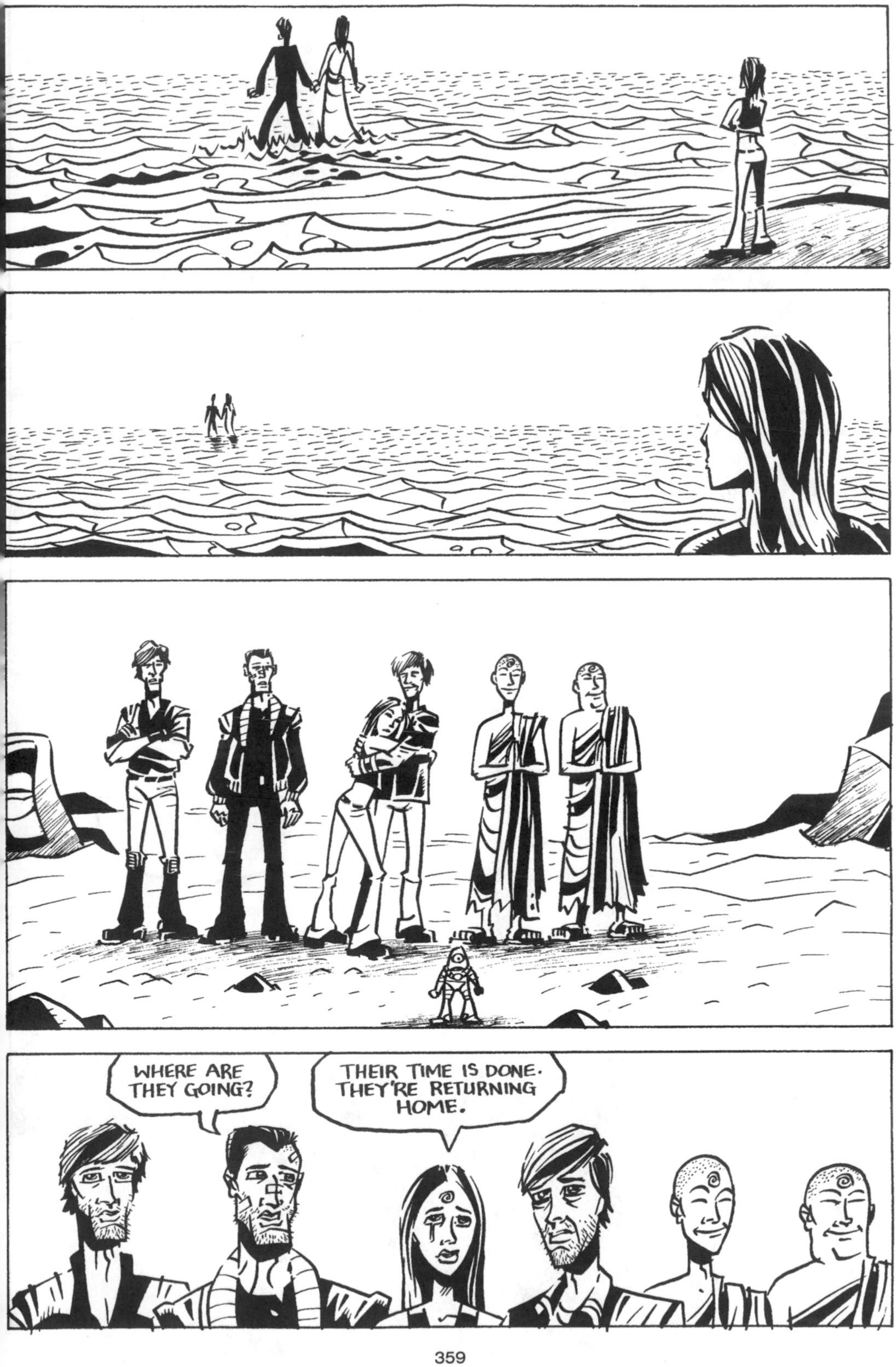
WHERE ARE THEY GOING?
THEIR TIME IS DONE. THEY'RE RETURNING HOME.

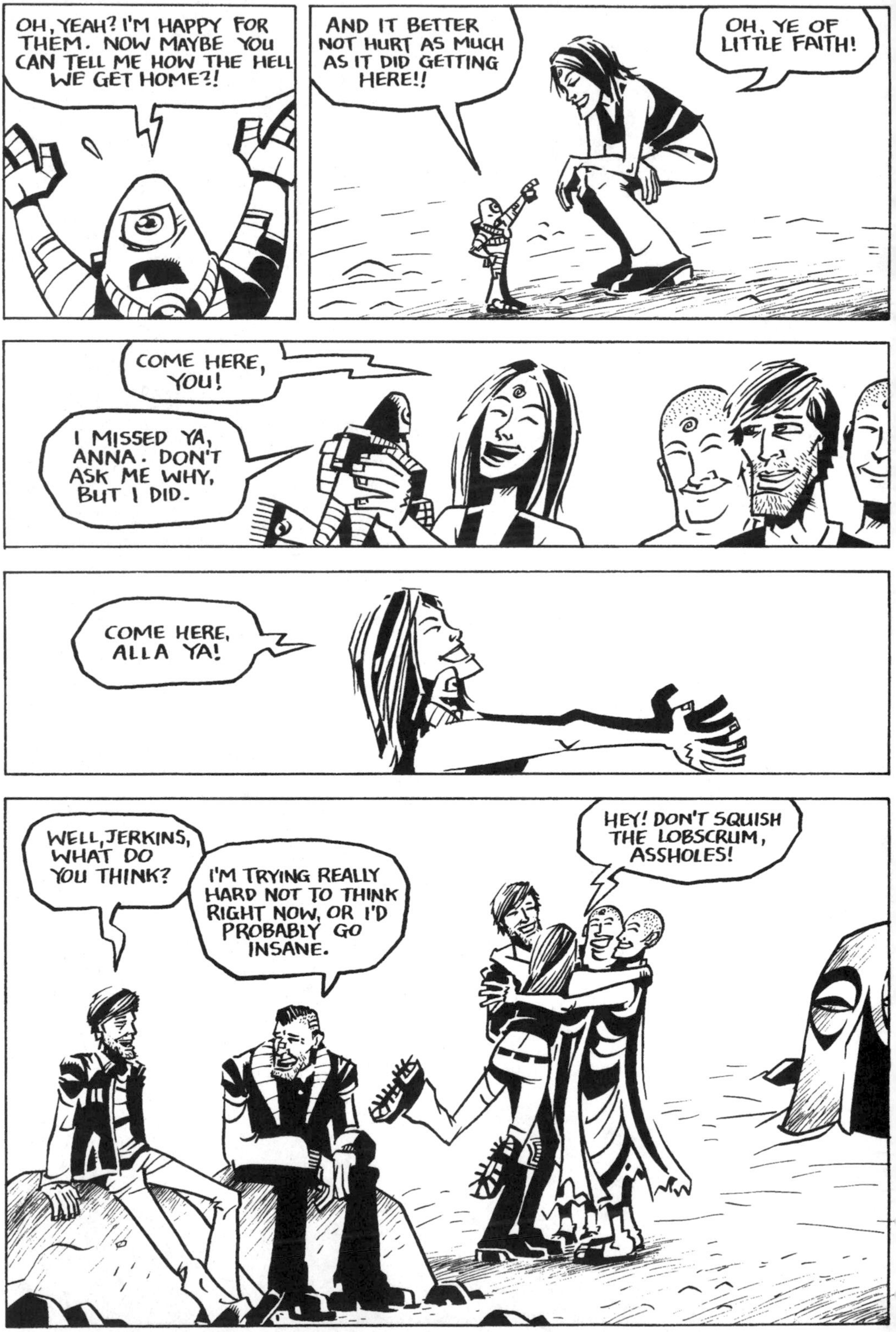

OH, YEAH?! I'M HAPPY FOR THEM. NOW MAYBE YOU CAN TELL ME HOW THE HELL WE GET HOME?!
AND IT BETTER NOT HURT AS MUCH AS IT DID GETTING HERE!!
OH, YE OF LITTLE FAITH!
COME HERE, YOU!
I MISSED YA, ANNA. DON'T ASK ME WHY, BUT I DID.
COME HERE, ALLA YA!
WELL, JERKINS, WHAT DO YOU THINK?
I'M TRYING REALLY HARD NOT TO THINK RIGHT NOW, OR I'D PROBABLY GO INSANE.
HEY! DON'T SQUISH THE LOBSCRUM, ASSHOLES!

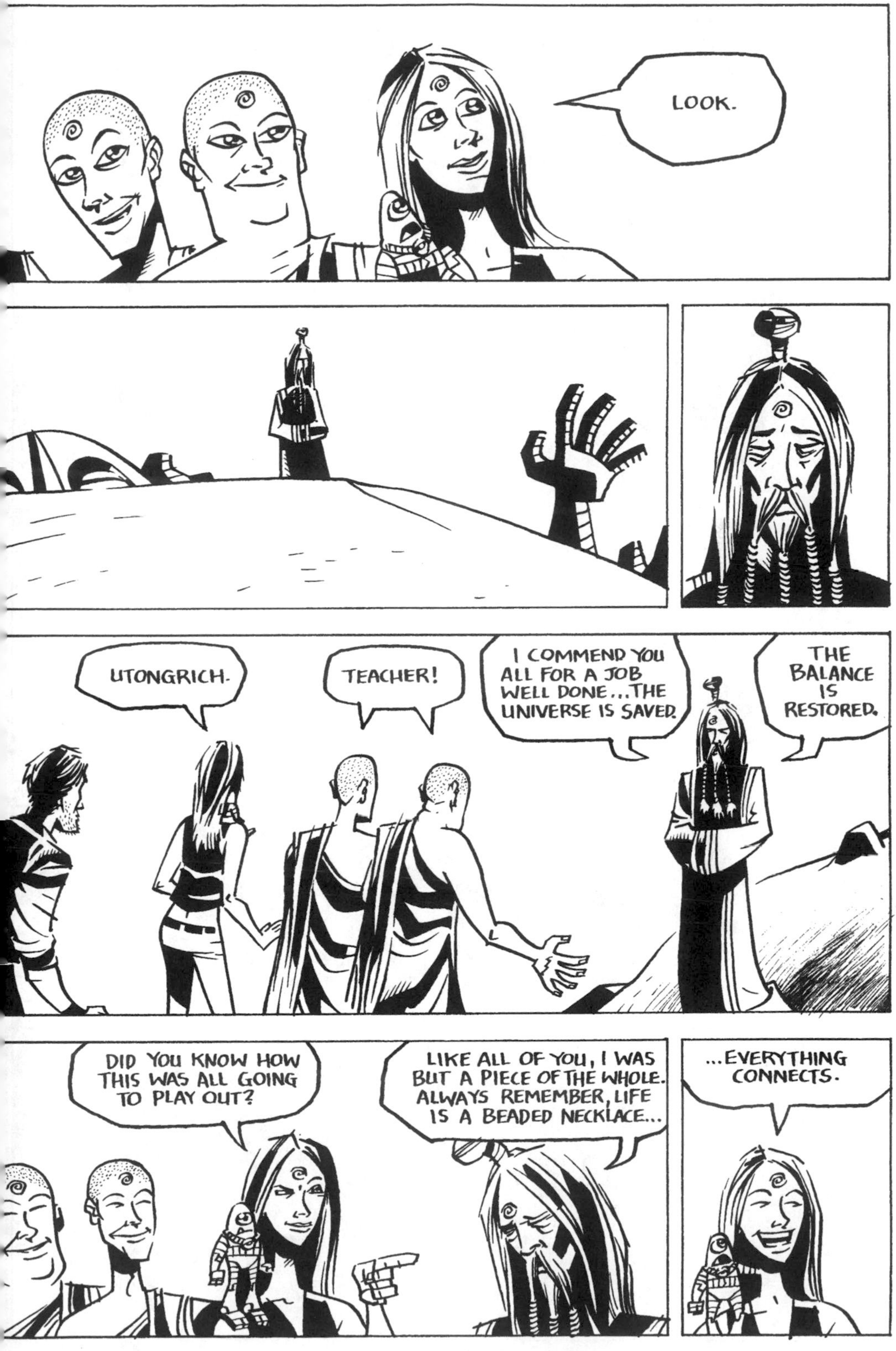
LOOK.
UTONGRICH.
TEACHER!
I COMMEND YOU ALL FOR A JOB WELL DONE...THE UNIVERSE IS SAVED.
THE BALANCE IS RESTORED.
DID YOU KNOW HOW THIS WAS ALL GOING TO PLAY OUT?
LIKE ALL OF YOU, I WAS BUT A PIECE OF THE WHOLE. ALWAYS REMEMBER, LIFE IS A BEADED NECKLACE...
...EVERYTHING CONNECTS.

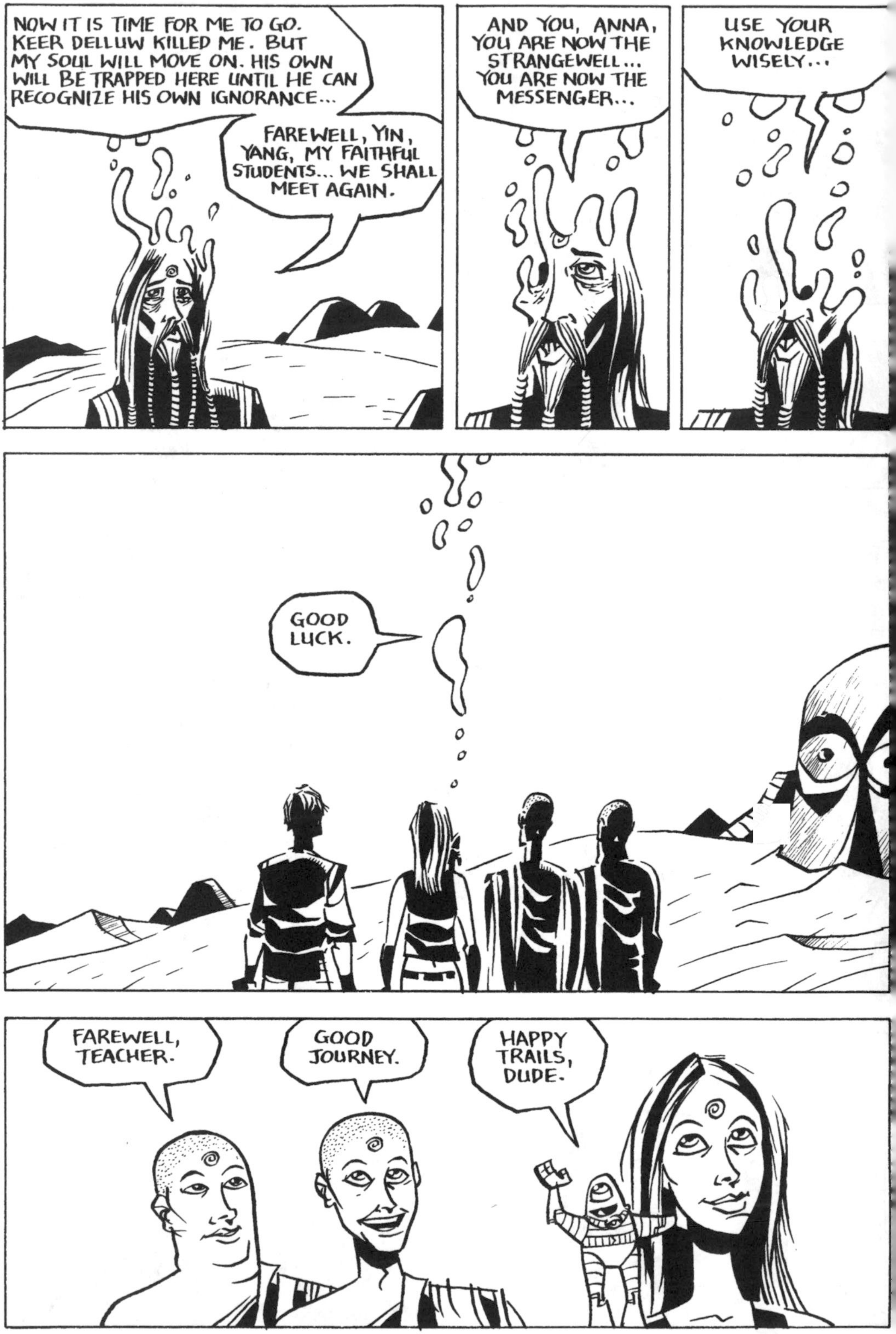
NOW IT IS TIME FOR ME TO GO. KEER DELLUW KILLED ME. BUT MY SOUL WILL MOVE ON. HIS OWN WILL BE TRAPPED HERE UNTIL HE CAN RECOGNIZE HIS OWN IGNORANCE...
FAREWELL, YIN, YANG, MY FAITHFUL STUDENTS... WE SHALL MEET AGAIN.
AND YOU, ANNA, YOU ARE NOW THE STRANGEWELL... YOU ARE NOW THE MESSENGER...
USE YOUR KNOWLEDGE WISELY...
GOOD LUCK.
FAREWELL, TEACHER.
GOOD JOURNEY.
HAPPY TRAILS, DUDE.

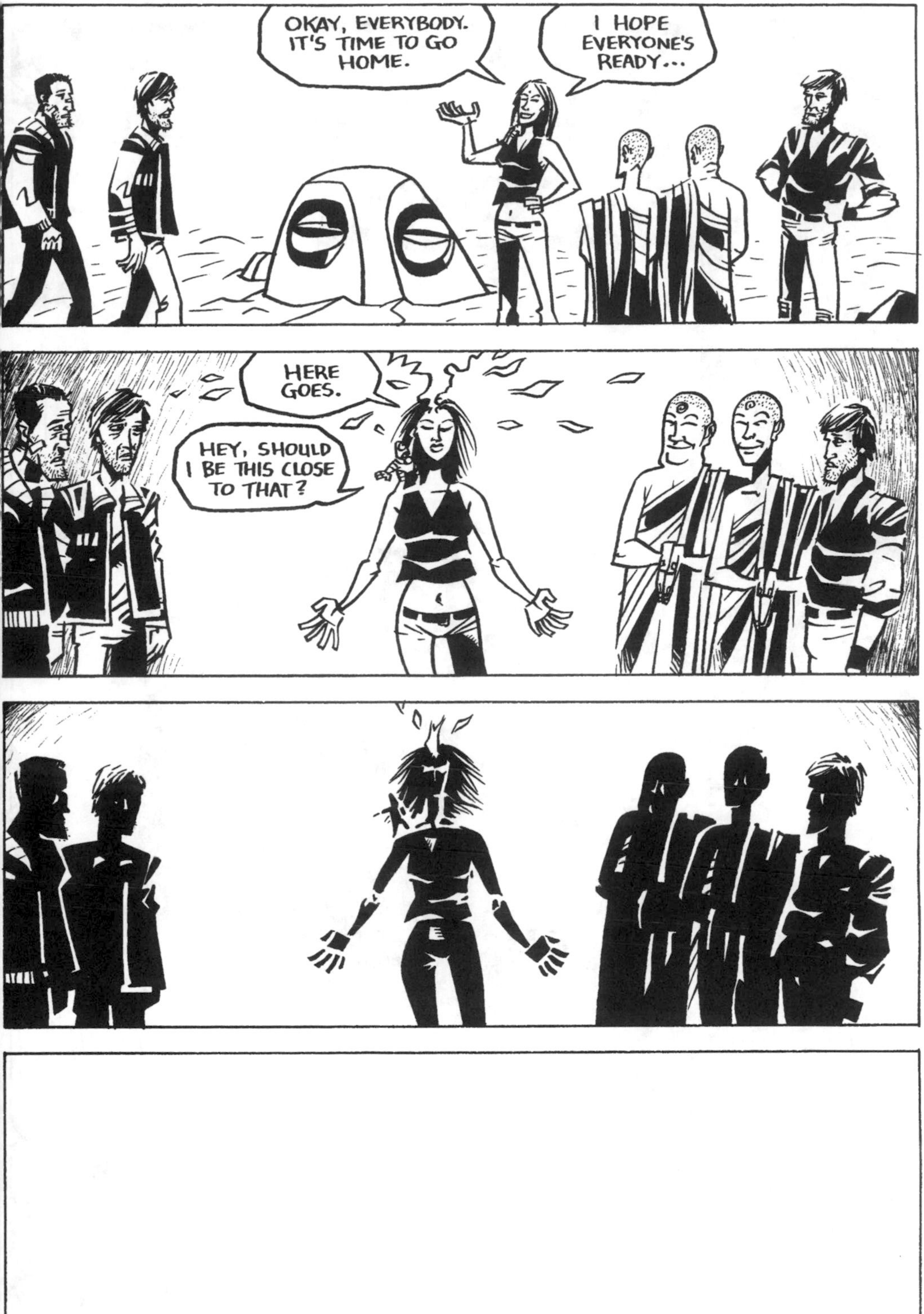
OKAY, EVERYBODY. IT'S TIME TO GO HOME.
I HOPE EVERYONE'S READY...
HERE GOES.
HEY, SHOULD I BE THIS CLOSE TO THAT?

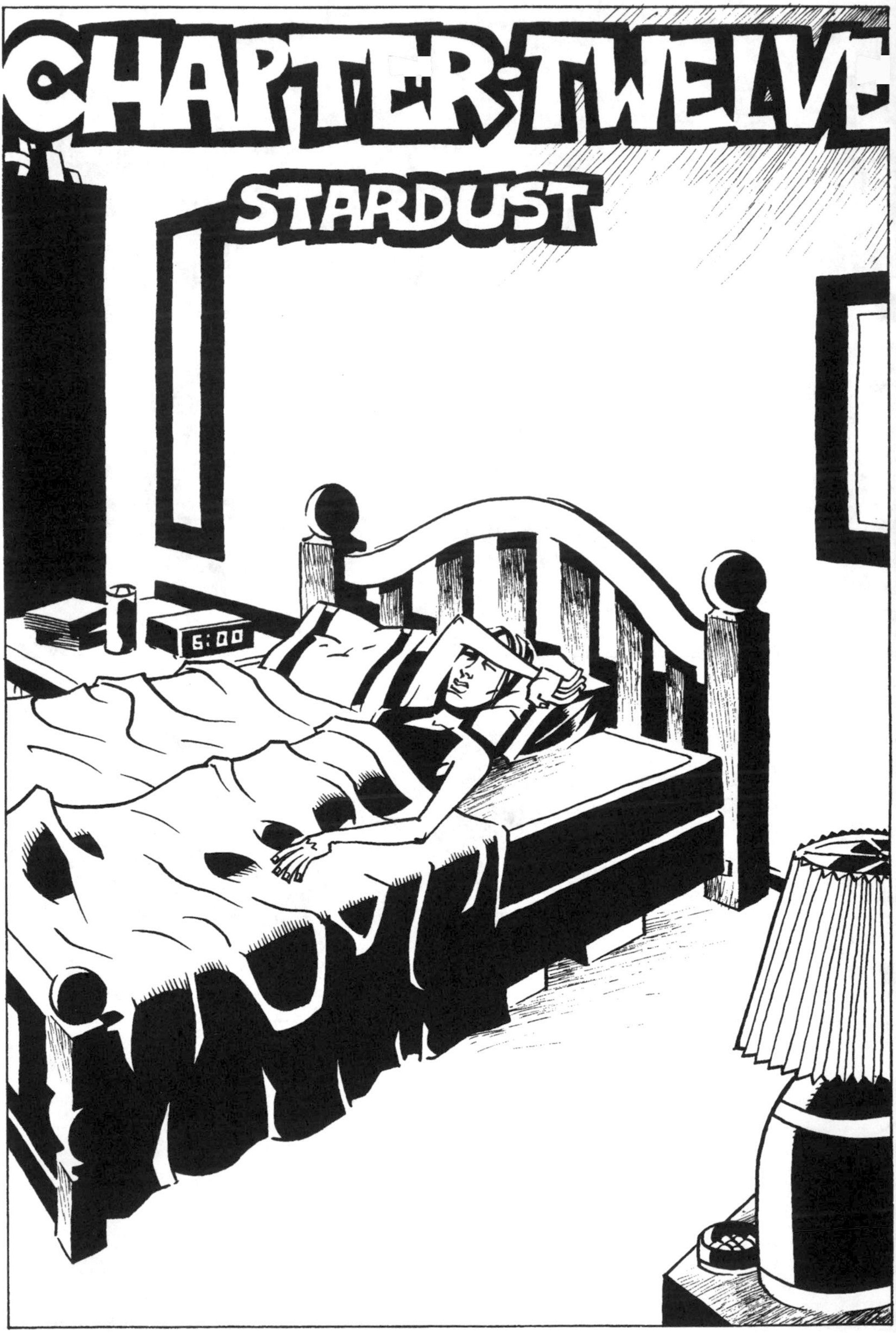

CHAPTER TWELVE
STARDUST
6:00

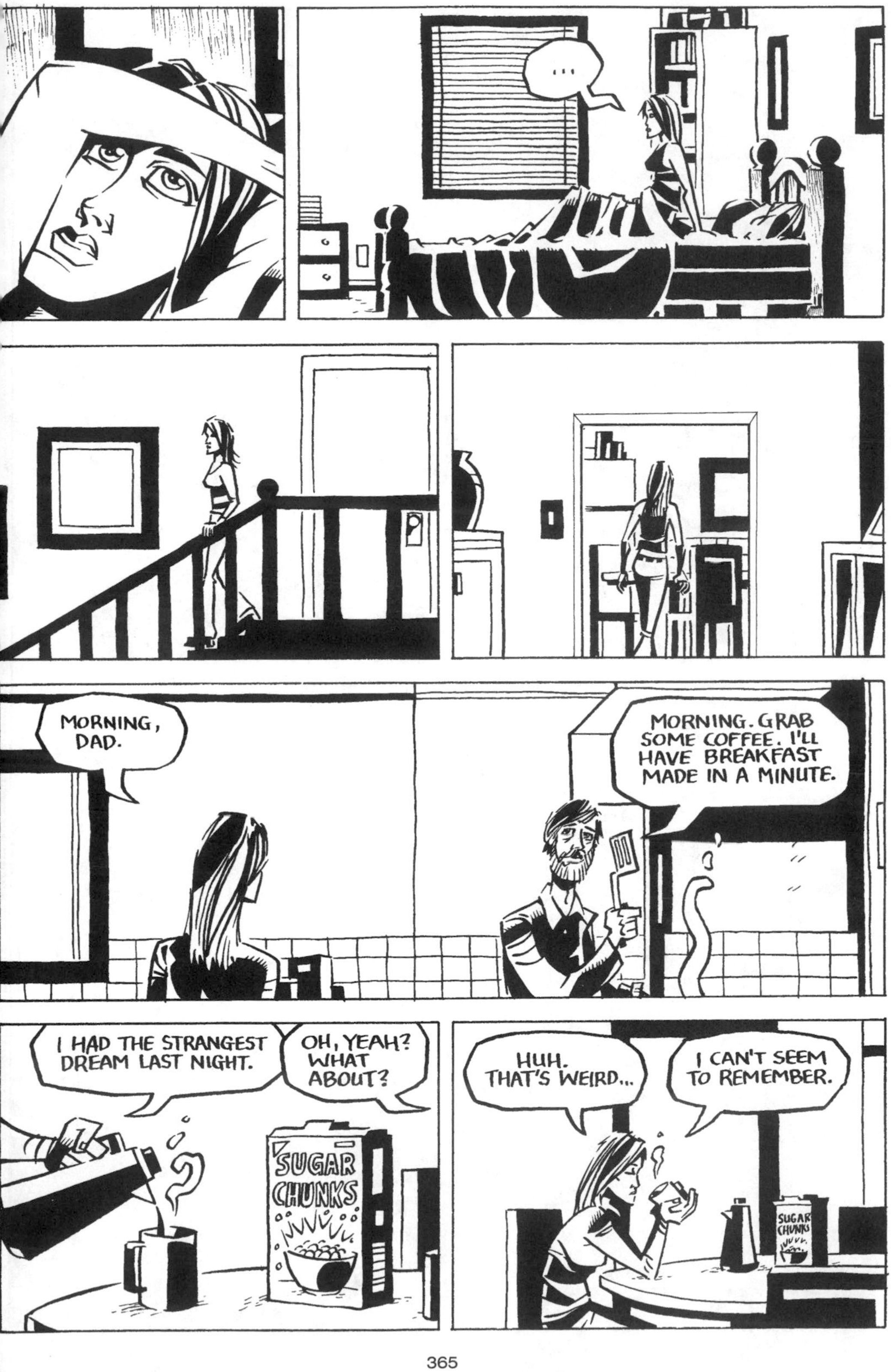
...
MORNING, DAD.
MORNING. GRAB SOME COFFEE. I'LL HAVE BREAKFAST MADE IN A MINUTE.
I HAD THE STRANGEST DREAM LAST NIGHT.
OH, YEAH? WHAT ABOUT?
SUGAR CHUNKS
HUH. THAT'S WEIRD...
I CAN'T SEEM TO REMEMBER.
SUGAR CHUNKS

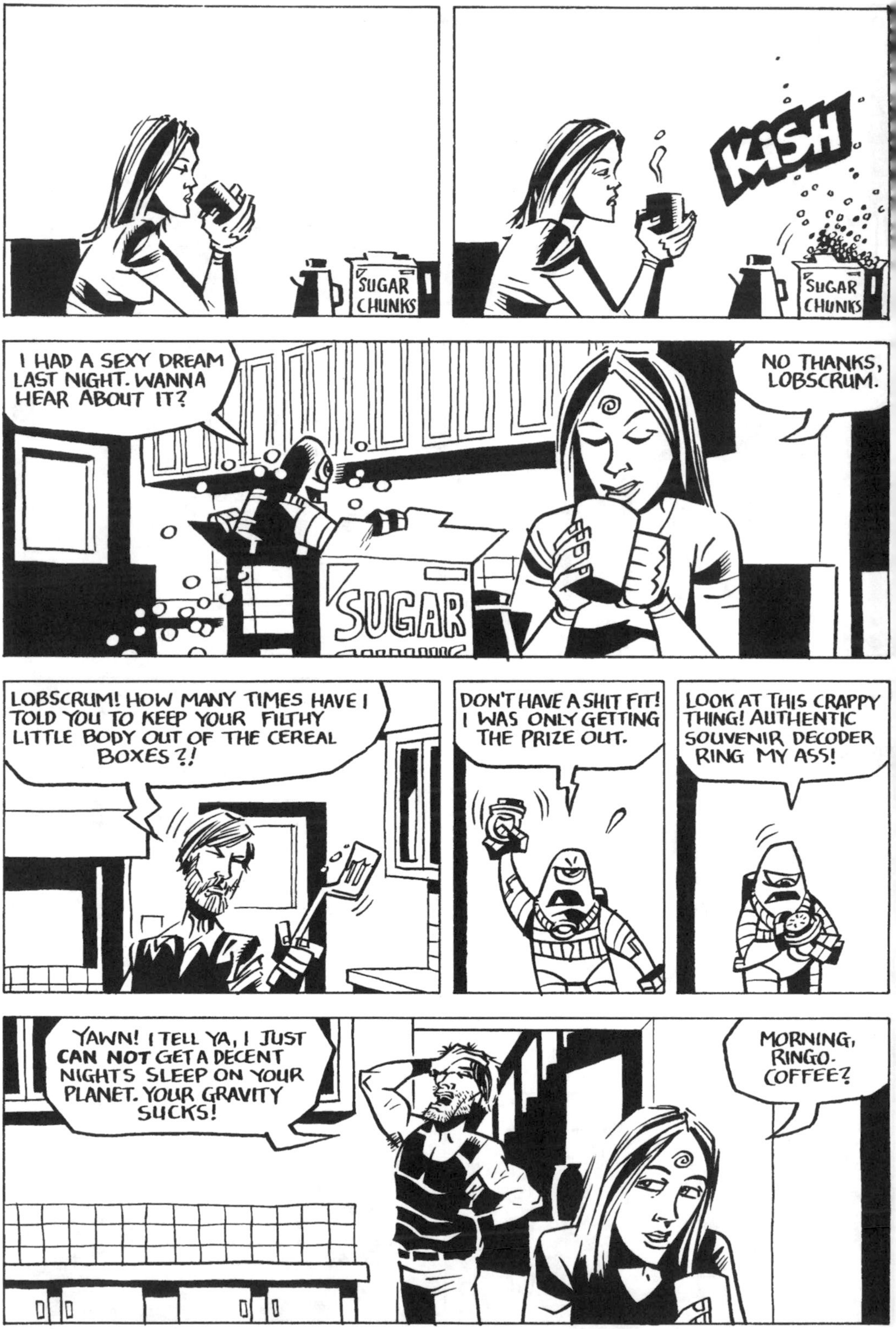
SUGAR CHUNKS
KiSH
SUGAR CHUNKS
I HAD A SEXY DREAM LAST NIGHT. WANNA HEAR ABOUT IT?
NO THANKS, LOBSCRUM.
SUGAR
LOBSCRUM! HOW MANY TIMES HAVE I TOLD YOU TO KEEP YOUR FILTHY LITTLE BODY OUT OF THE CEREAL BOXES?!
DON'T HAVE A SHIT FIT! I WAS ONLY GETTING THE PRIZE OUT.
LOOK AT THIS CRAPPY THING! AUTHENTIC SOUVENIR DECODER RING MY ASS!
YAWN! I TELL YA, I JUST CAN NOT GET A DECENT NIGHTS SLEEP ON YOUR PLANET. YOUR GRAVITY SUCKS!
MORNING, RINGO. COFFEE?

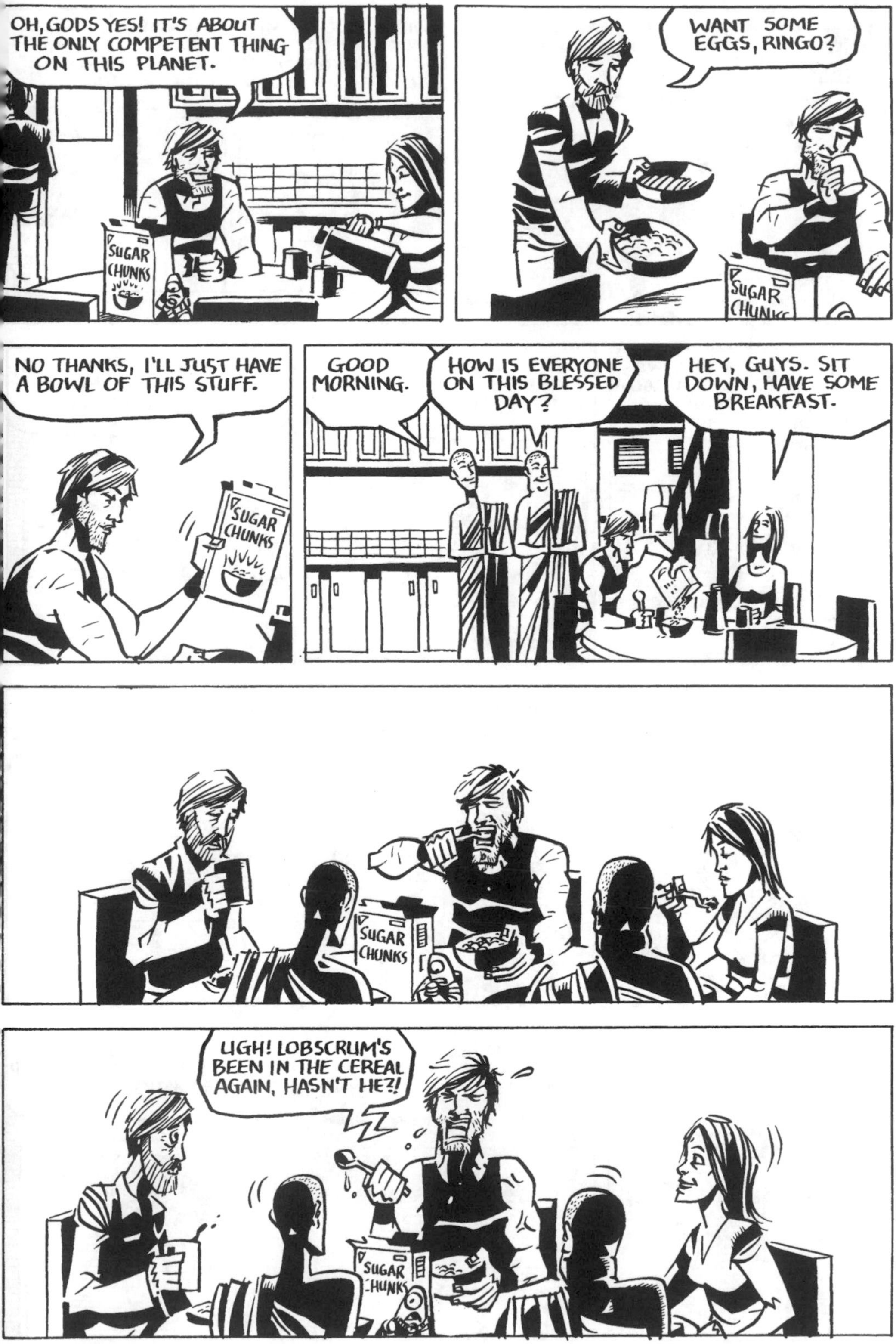
OH, GODS YES! IT'S ABOUT THE ONLY COMPETENT THING ON THIS PLANET.
SUGAR CHUNKS
WANT SOME EGGS, RINGO?
SUGAR CHUNKS
NO THANKS, I'LL JUST HAVE A BOWL OF THIS STUFF.
SUGAR CHUNKS
GOOD MORNING.
HOW IS EVERYONE ON THIS BLESSED DAY?
HEY, GUYS. SIT DOWN, HAVE SOME BREAKFAST.
SUGAR CHUNKS
UGH! LOBSCRUM'S BEEN IN THE CEREAL AGAIN, HASN'T HE?!
SUGAR CHUNKS

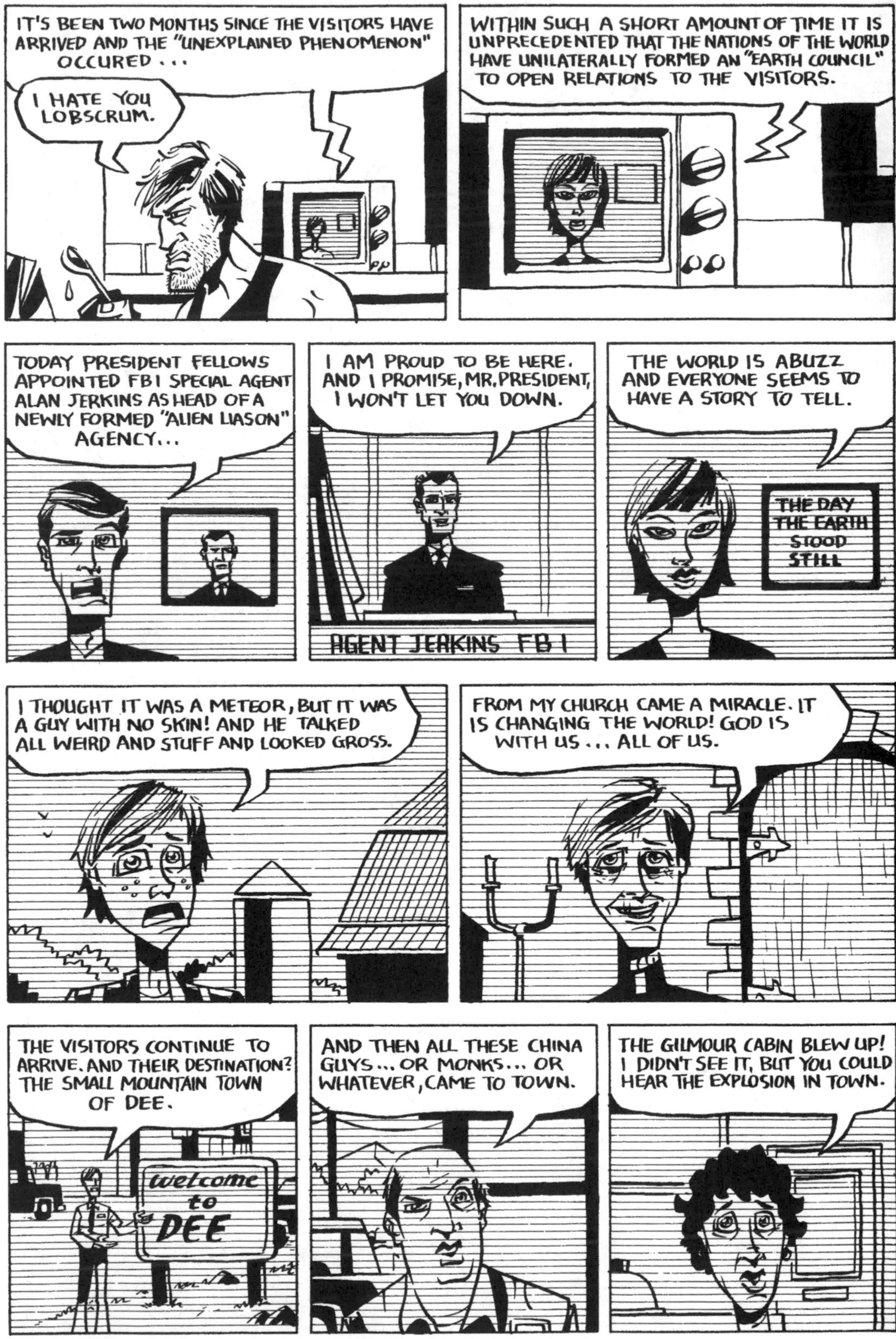
IT'S BEEN TWO MONTHS SINCE THE VISITORS HAVE ARRIVED AND THE "UNEXPLAINED PHENOMENON" OCCURED . . .
I HATE YOU LOBSCRUM.
WITHIN SUCH A SHORT AMOUNT OF TIME IT IS UNPRECEDENTED THAT THE NATIONS OF THE WORLD HAVE UNILATERALLY FORMED AN "EARTH COUNCIL" TO OPEN RELATIONS TO THE VISITORS.
TODAY PRESIDENT FELLOWS APPOINTED FBI SPECIAL AGENT ALAN JERKINS AS HEAD OF A NEWLY FORMED "ALIEN LIASON" AGENCY...
I AM PROUD TO BE HERE. AND I PROMISE, MR. PRESIDENT, I WON'T LET YOU DOWN.
AGENT JERKINS FBI
THE WORLD IS ABUZZ AND EVERYONE SEEMS TO HAVE A STORY TO TELL.
THE DAY THE EARTH STOOD STILL
I THOUGHT IT WAS A METEOR, BUT IT WAS A GUY WITH NO SKIN! AND HE TALKED ALL WEIRD AND STUFF AND LOOKED GROSS.
FROM MY CHURCH CAME A MIRACLE. IT IS CHANGING THE WORLD! GOD IS WITH US . . . ALL OF US.
THE VISITORS CONTINUE TO ARRIVE. AND THEIR DESTINATION? THE SMALL MOUNTAIN TOWN OF DEE.
welcome to DEE
AND THEN ALL THESE CHINA GUYS ... OR MONKS ... OR WHATEVER, CAME TO TOWN.
THE GILMOUR CABIN BLEW UP! I DIDN'T SEE IT, BUT YOU COULD HEAR THE EXPLOSION IN TOWN.

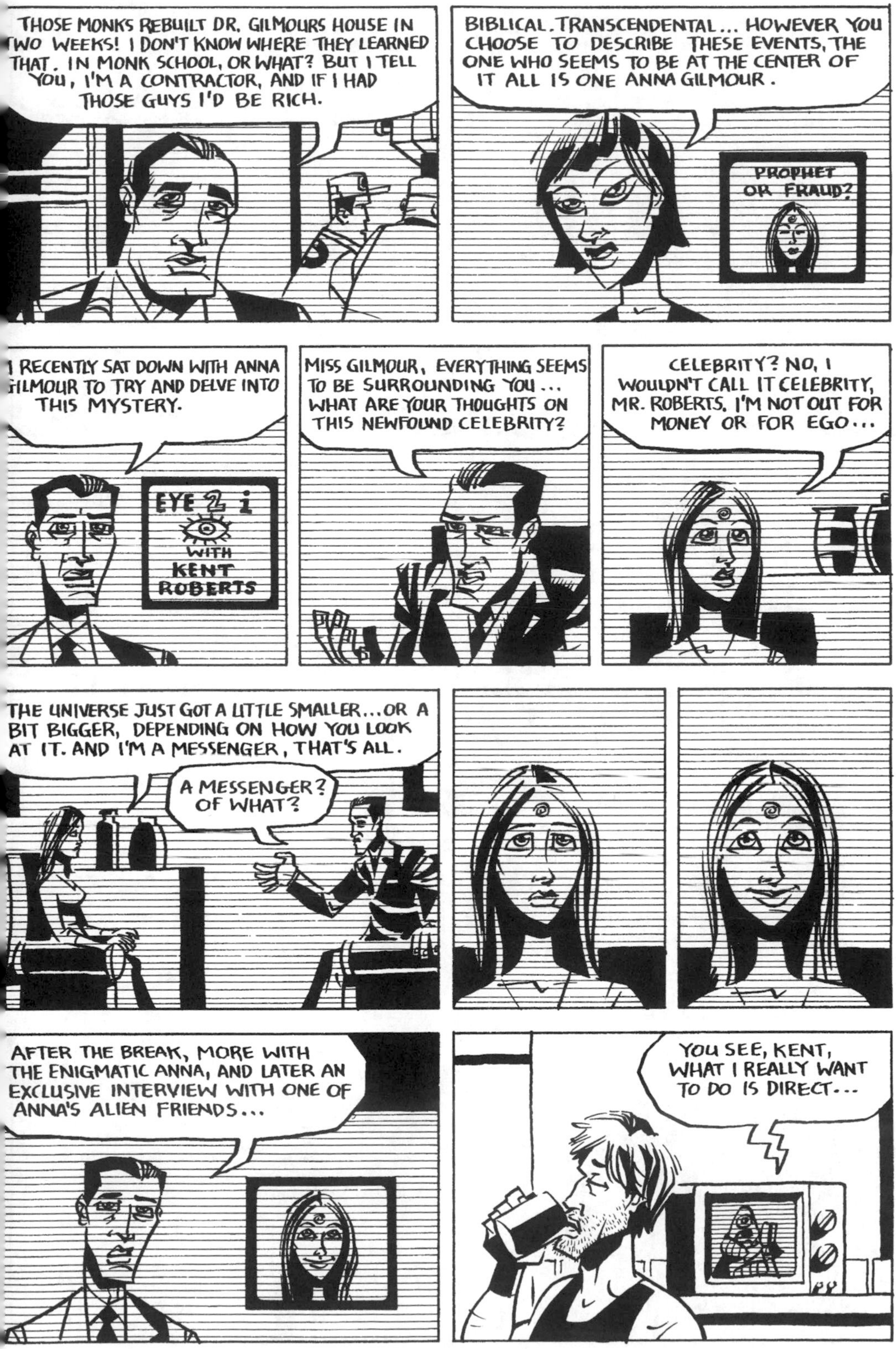
THOSE MONKS REBUILT DR. GILMOURS HOUSE IN TWO WEEKS! I DON'T KNOW WHERE THEY LEARNED THAT. IN MONK SCHOOL, OR WHAT? BUT I TELL YOU, I'M A CONTRACTOR, AND IF I HAD THOSE GUYS I'D BE RICH.
BIBLICAL. TRANSCENDENTAL... HOWEVER YOU CHOOSE TO DESCRIBE THESE EVENTS, THE ONE WHO SEEMS TO BE AT THE CENTER OF IT ALL IS ONE ANNA GILMOUR.
PROPHET OR FRAUD?
I RECENTLY SAT DOWN WITH ANNA GILMOUR TO TRY AND DELVE INTO THIS MYSTERY.
EYE 2 i
WITH KENT ROBERTS
MISS GILMOUR, EVERYTHING SEEMS TO BE SURROUNDING YOU... WHAT ARE YOUR THOUGHTS ON THIS NEWFOUND CELEBRITY?
CELEBRITY? NO, I WOULDN'T CALL IT CELEBRITY, MR. ROBERTS. I'M NOT OUT FOR MONEY OR FOR EGO...
THE UNIVERSE JUST GOT A LITTLE SMALLER... OR A BIT BIGGER, DEPENDING ON HOW YOU LOOK AT IT. AND I'M A MESSENGER, THAT'S ALL.
A MESSENGER? OF WHAT?
AFTER THE BREAK, MORE WITH THE ENIGMATIC ANNA, AND LATER AN EXCLUSIVE INTERVIEW WITH ONE OF ANNA'S ALIEN FRIENDS...
YOU SEE, KENT, WHAT I REALLY WANT TO DO IS DIRECT...

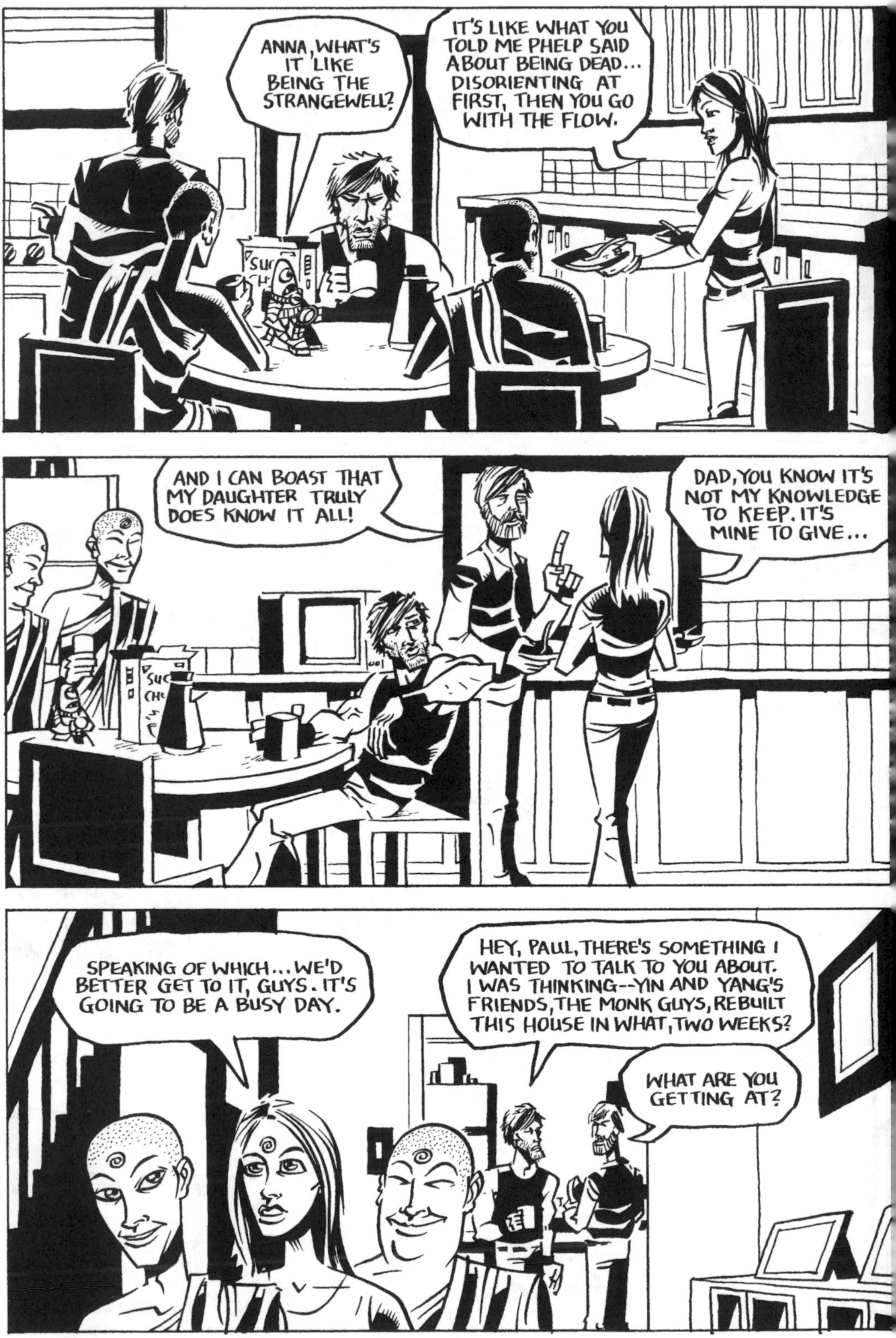
ANNA, WHAT'S IT LIKE BEING THE STRANGEWELL?
IT'S LIKE WHAT YOU TOLD ME PHELP SAID ABOUT BEING DEAD... DISORIENTING AT FIRST, THEN YOU GO WITH THE FLOW.
AND I CAN BOAST THAT MY DAUGHTER TRULY DOES KNOW IT ALL!
DAD, YOU KNOW IT'S NOT MY KNOWLEDGE TO KEEP. IT'S MINE TO GIVE...
SPEAKING OF WHICH... WE'D BETTER GET TO IT, GUYS. IT'S GOING TO BE A BUSY DAY.
HEY, PAUL, THERE'S SOMETHING I WANTED TO TALK TO YOU ABOUT. I WAS THINKING--YIN AND YANG'S FRIENDS, THE MONK GUYS, REBUILT THIS HOUSE IN WHAT, TWO WEEKS?
WHAT ARE YOU GETTING AT?

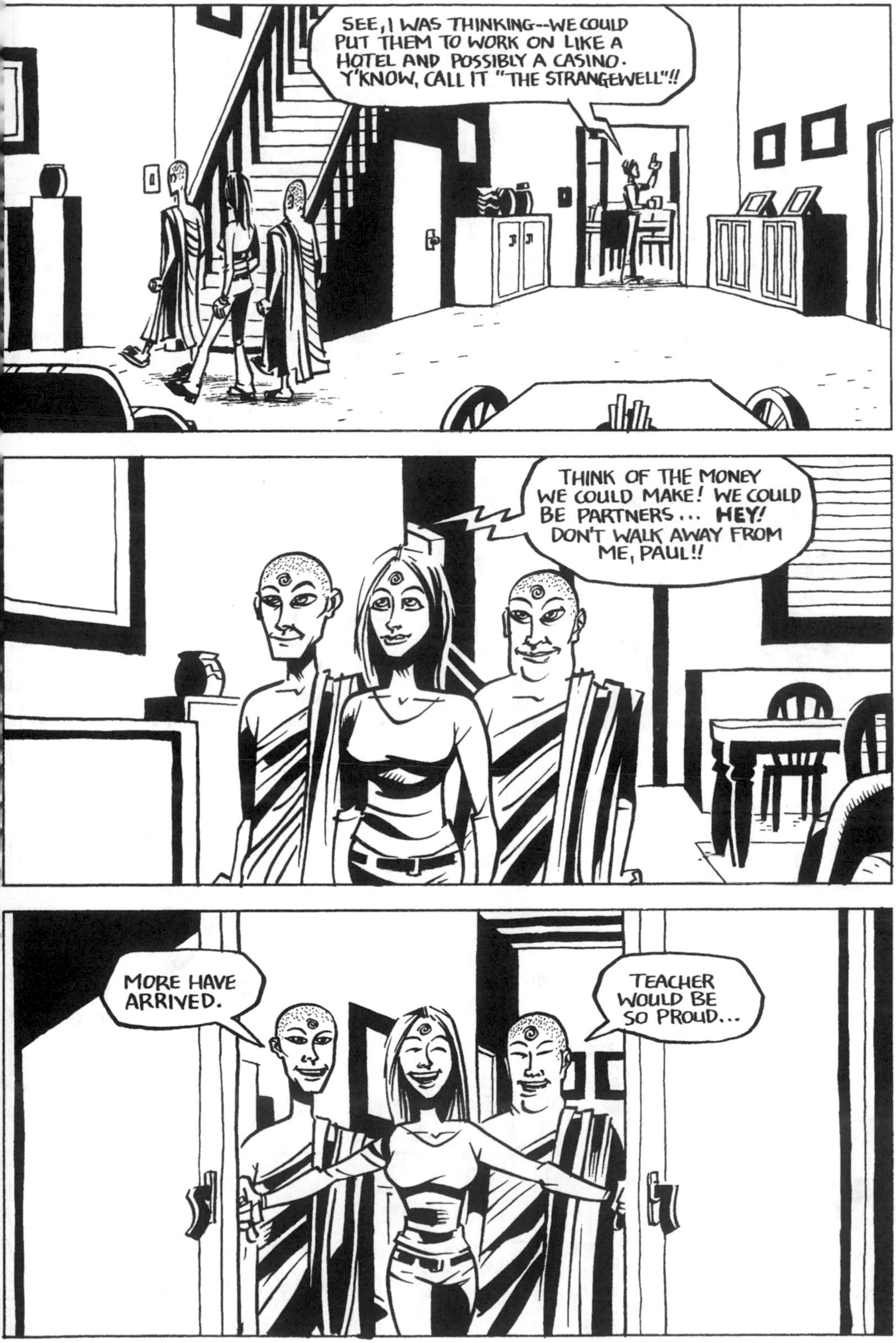
SEE, I WAS THINKING--WE COULD PUT THEM TO WORK ON LIKE A HOTEL AND POSSIBLY A CASINO. Y'KNOW, CALL IT "THE STRANGEWELL"!!
THINK OF THE MONEY WE COULD MAKE! WE COULD BE PARTNERS... HEY! DON'T WALK AWAY FROM ME, PAUL!!
MORE HAVE ARRIVED.
TEACHER WOULD BE SO PROUD...

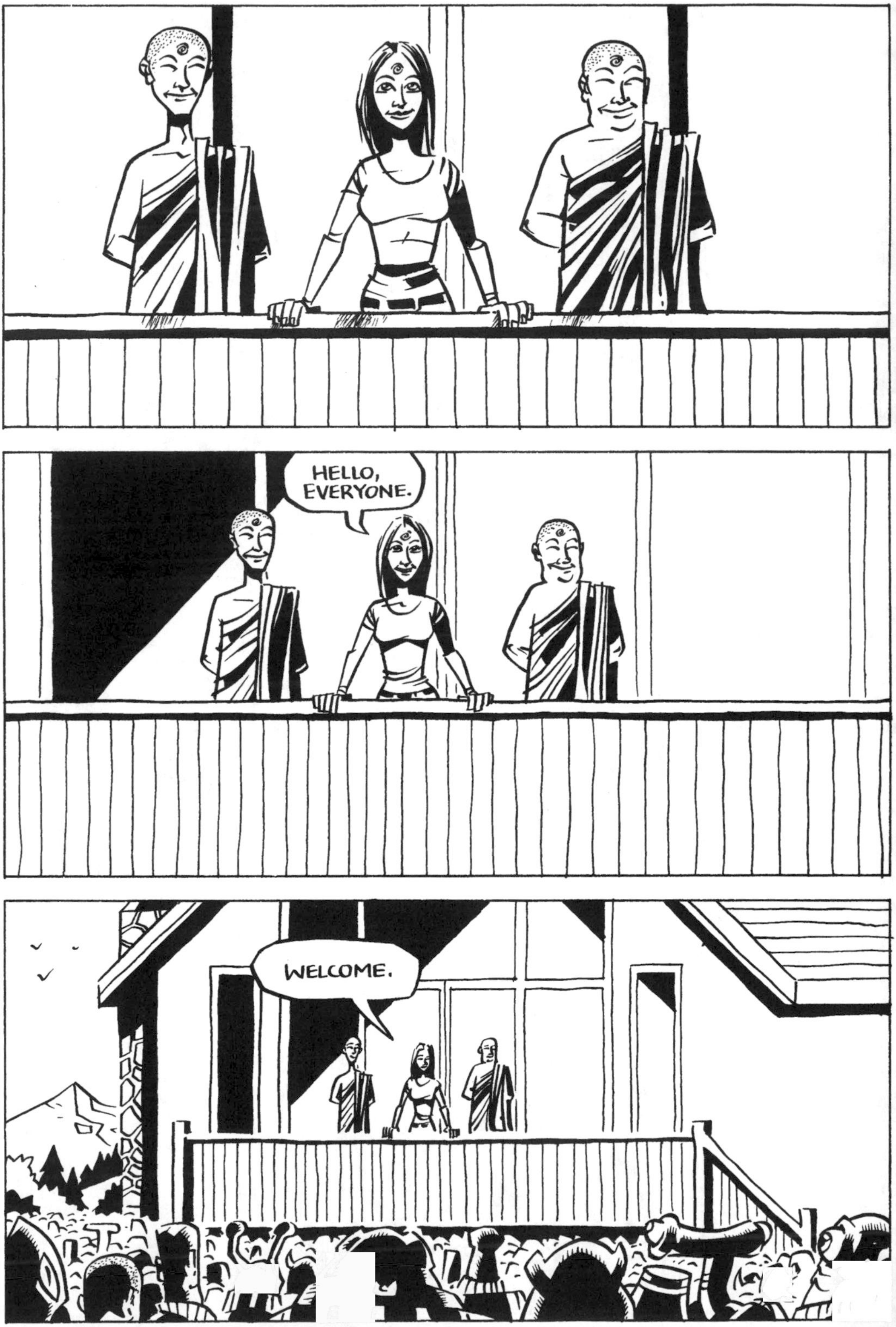
HELLO, EVERYONE.
WELCOME.

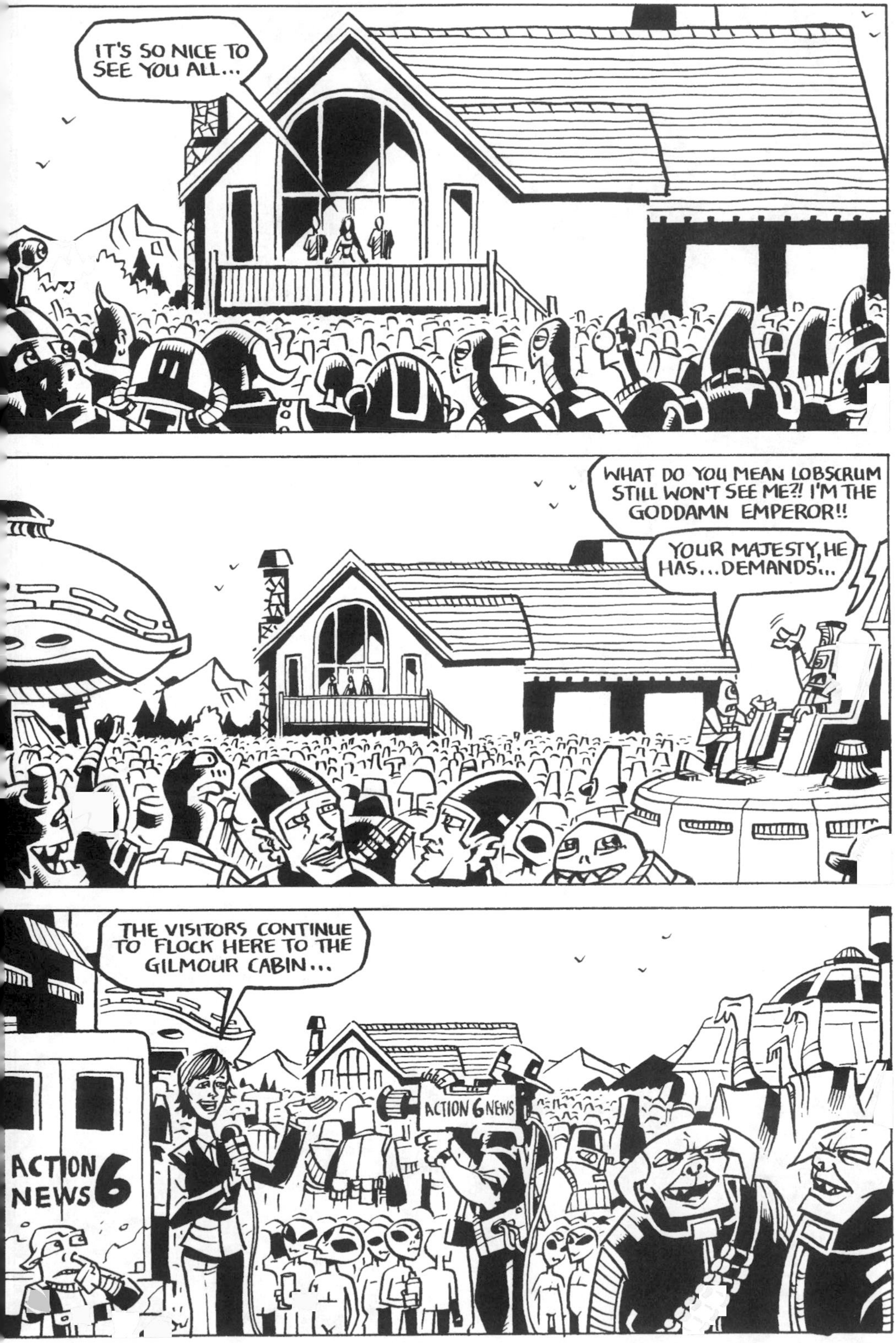
IT'S SO NICE TO SEE YOU ALL...
WHAT DO YOU MEAN LOBSCRUM STILL WON'T SEE ME?! I'M THE GODDAMN EMPEROR!!
YOUR MAJESTY, HE HAS...DEMANDS...
THE VISITORS CONTINUE TO FLOCK HERE TO THE GILMOUR CABIN...
ACTION 6 NEWS
ACTION NEWS 6

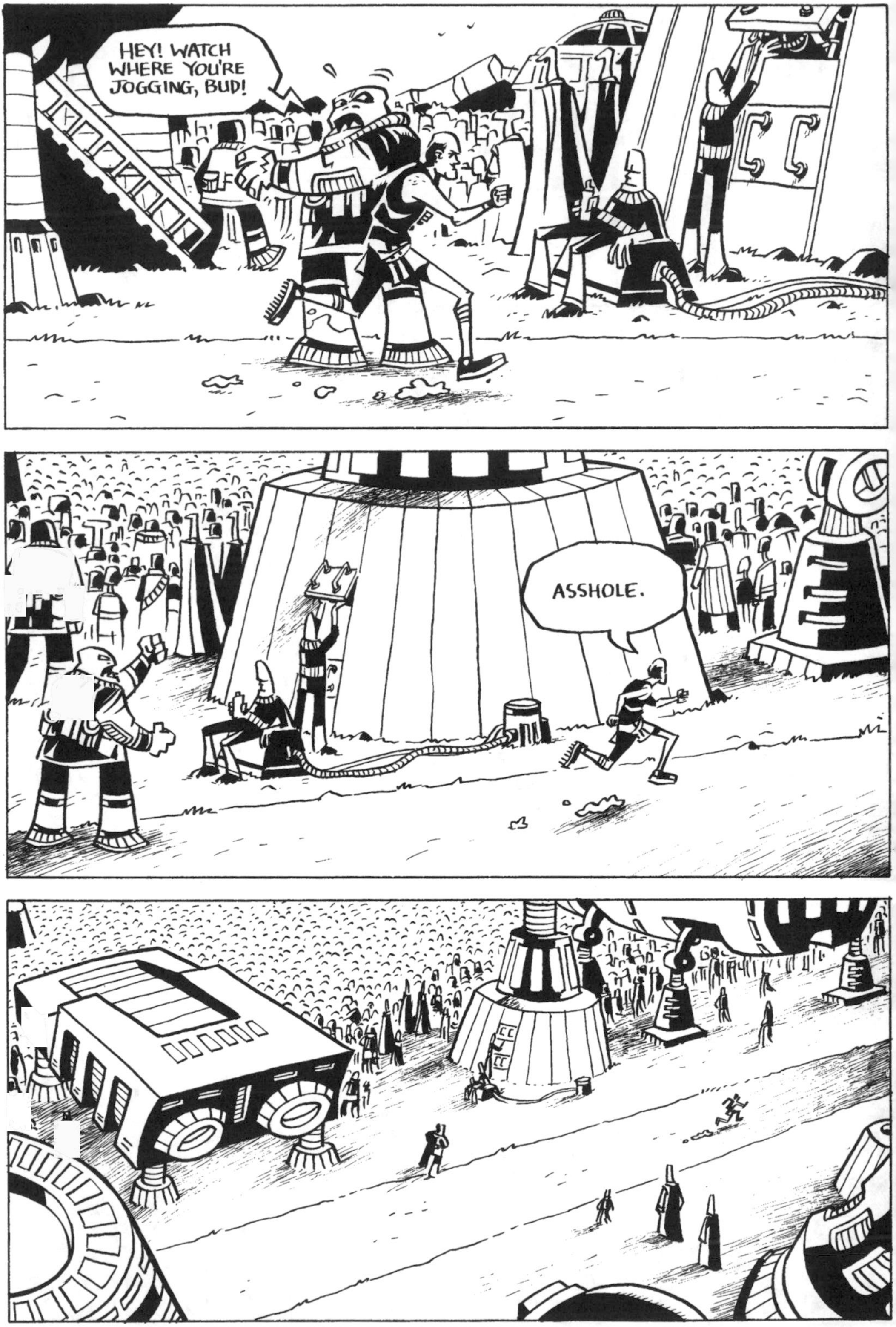
HEY! WATCH WHERE YOU'RE JOGGING, BUD!
ASSHOLE.

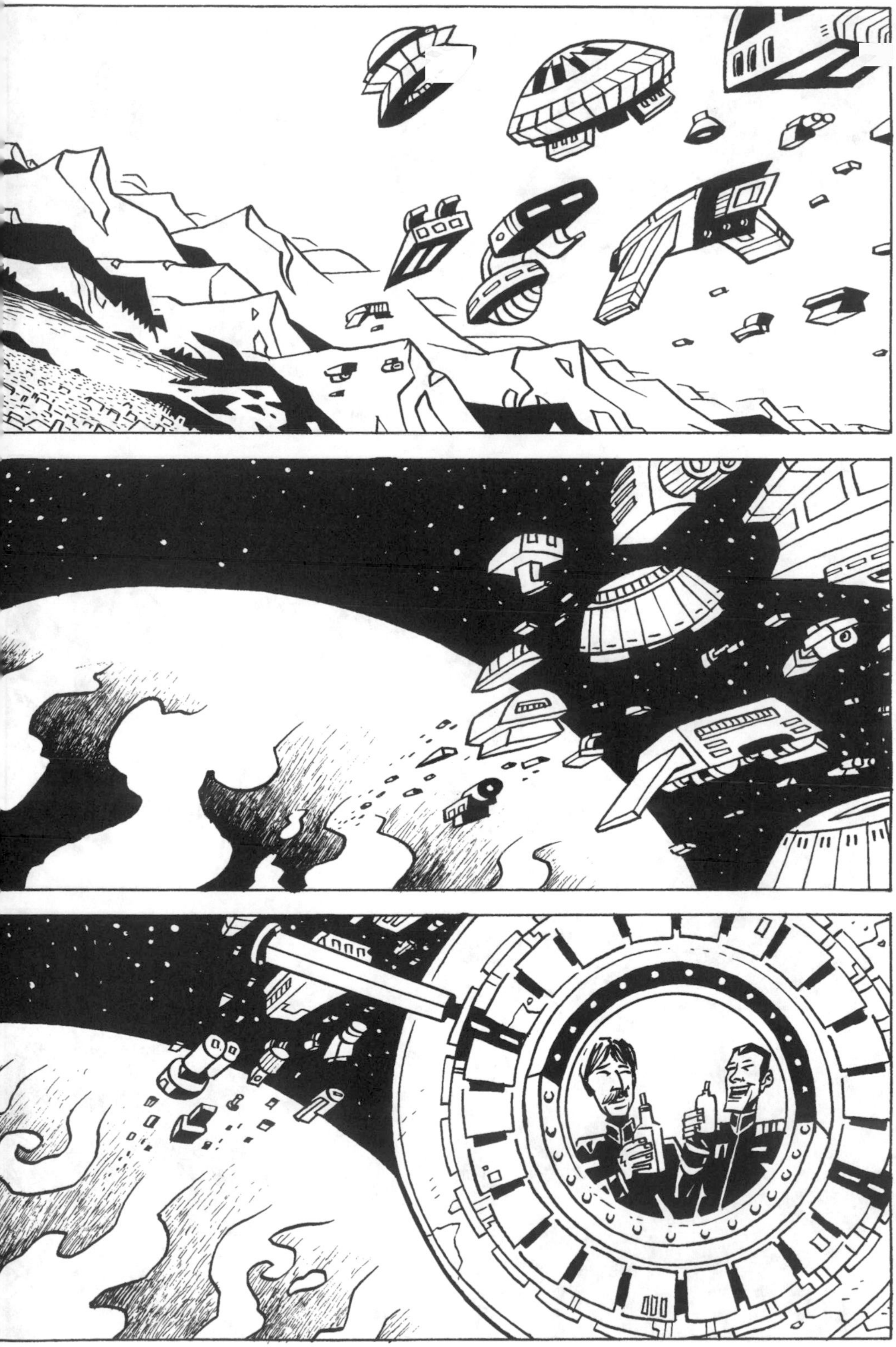

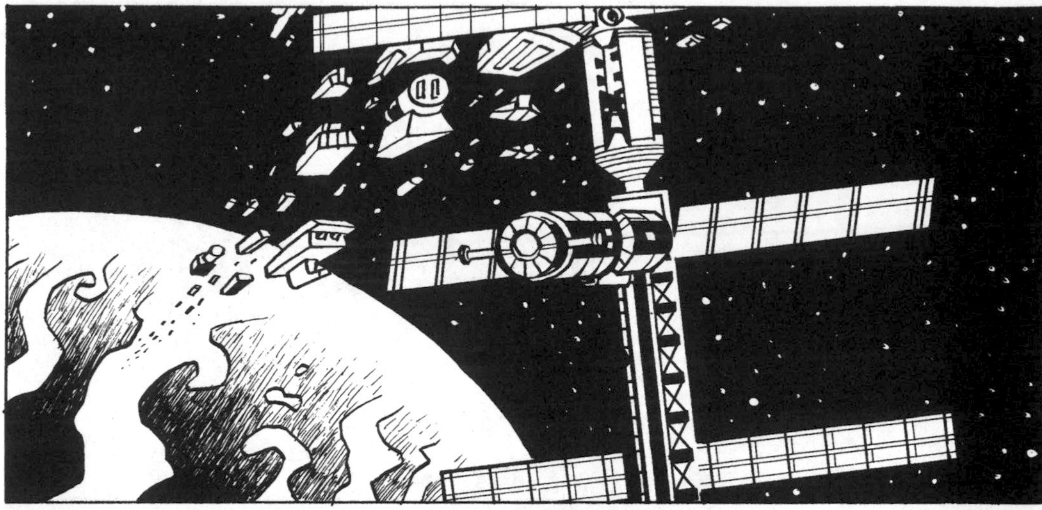

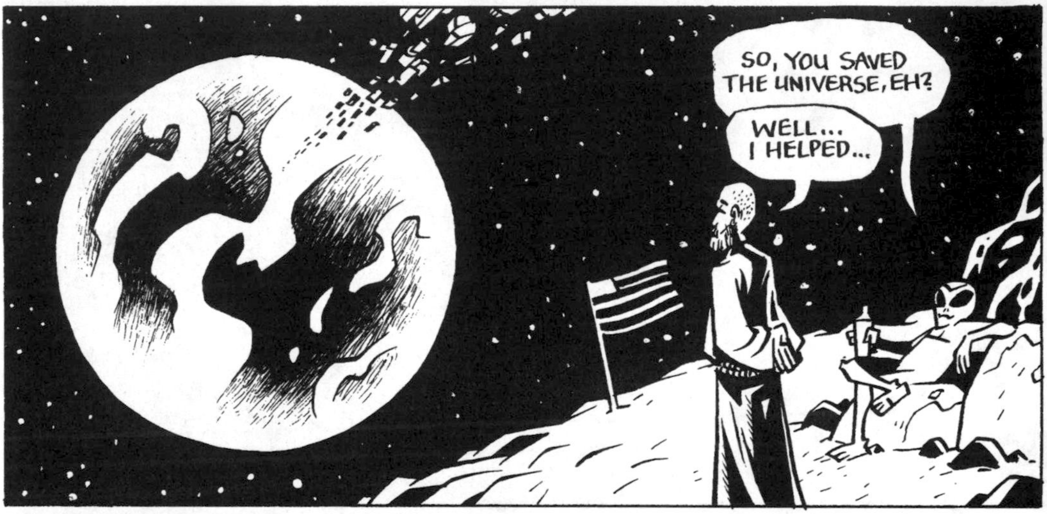
SO, YOU SAVED THE UNIVERSE, EH?
WELL... I HELPED...

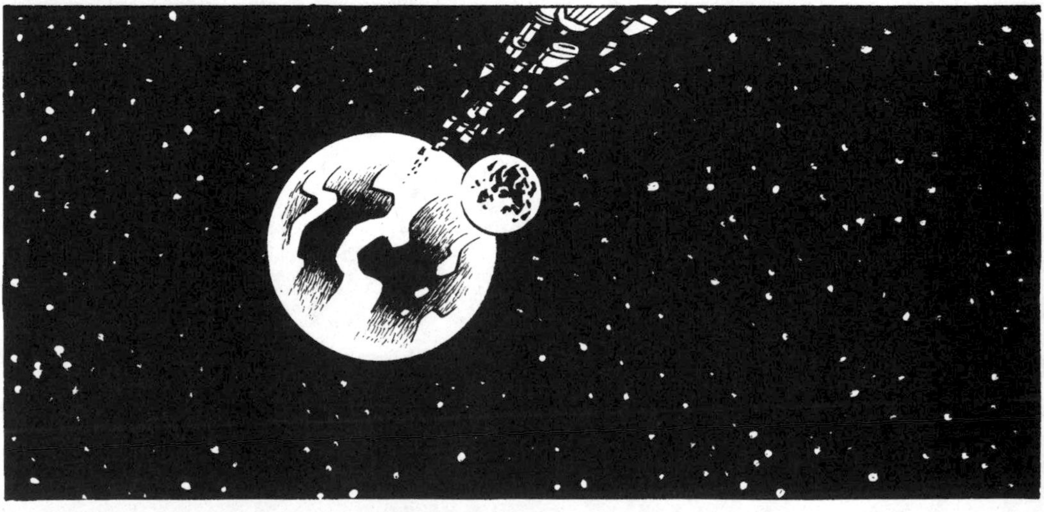

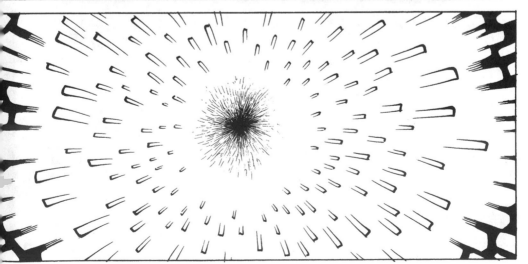

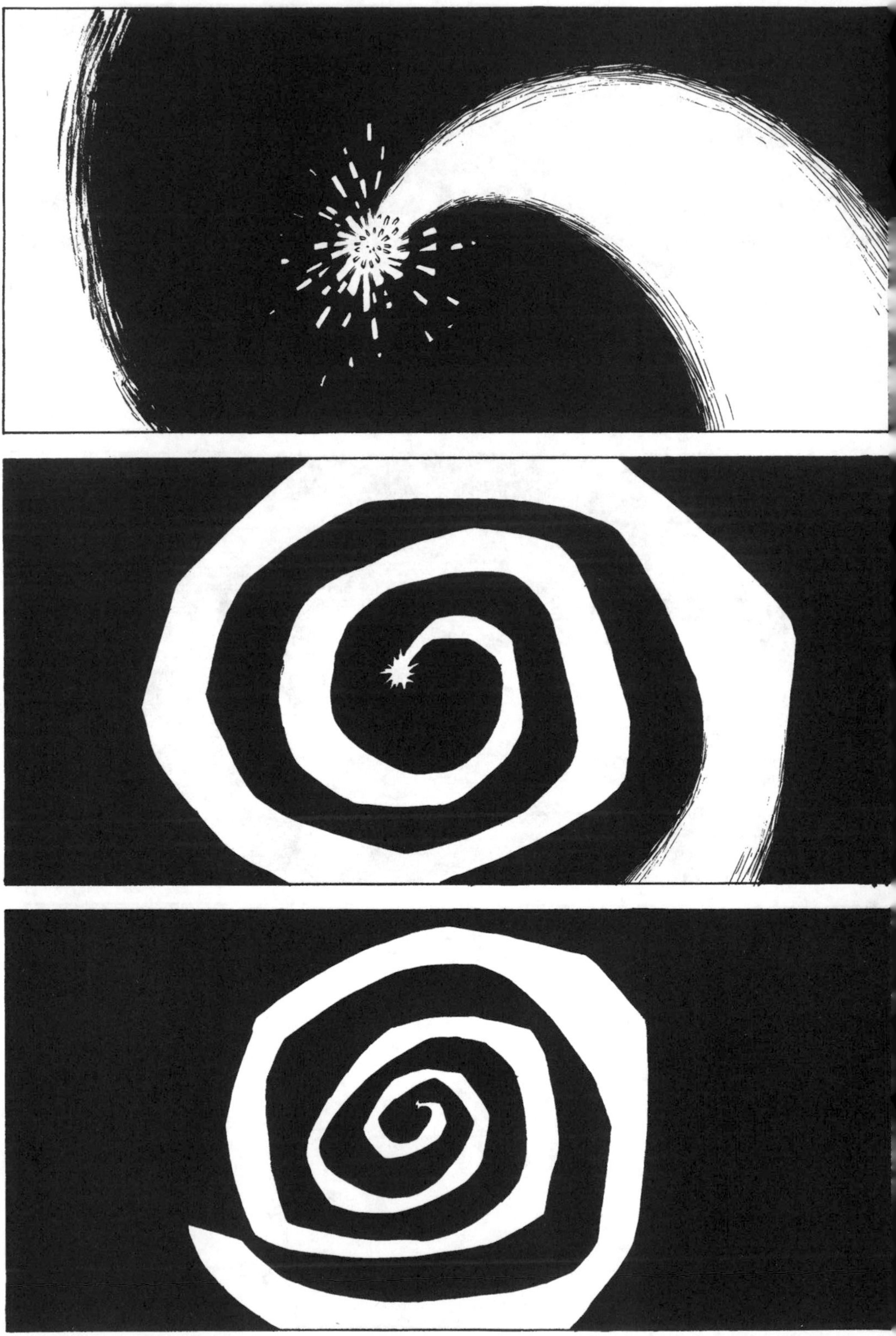

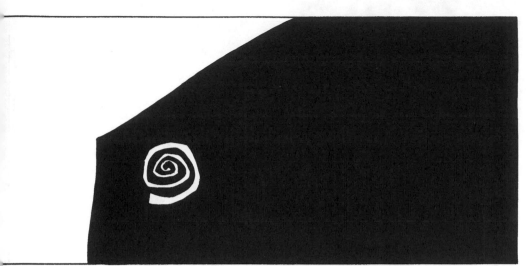

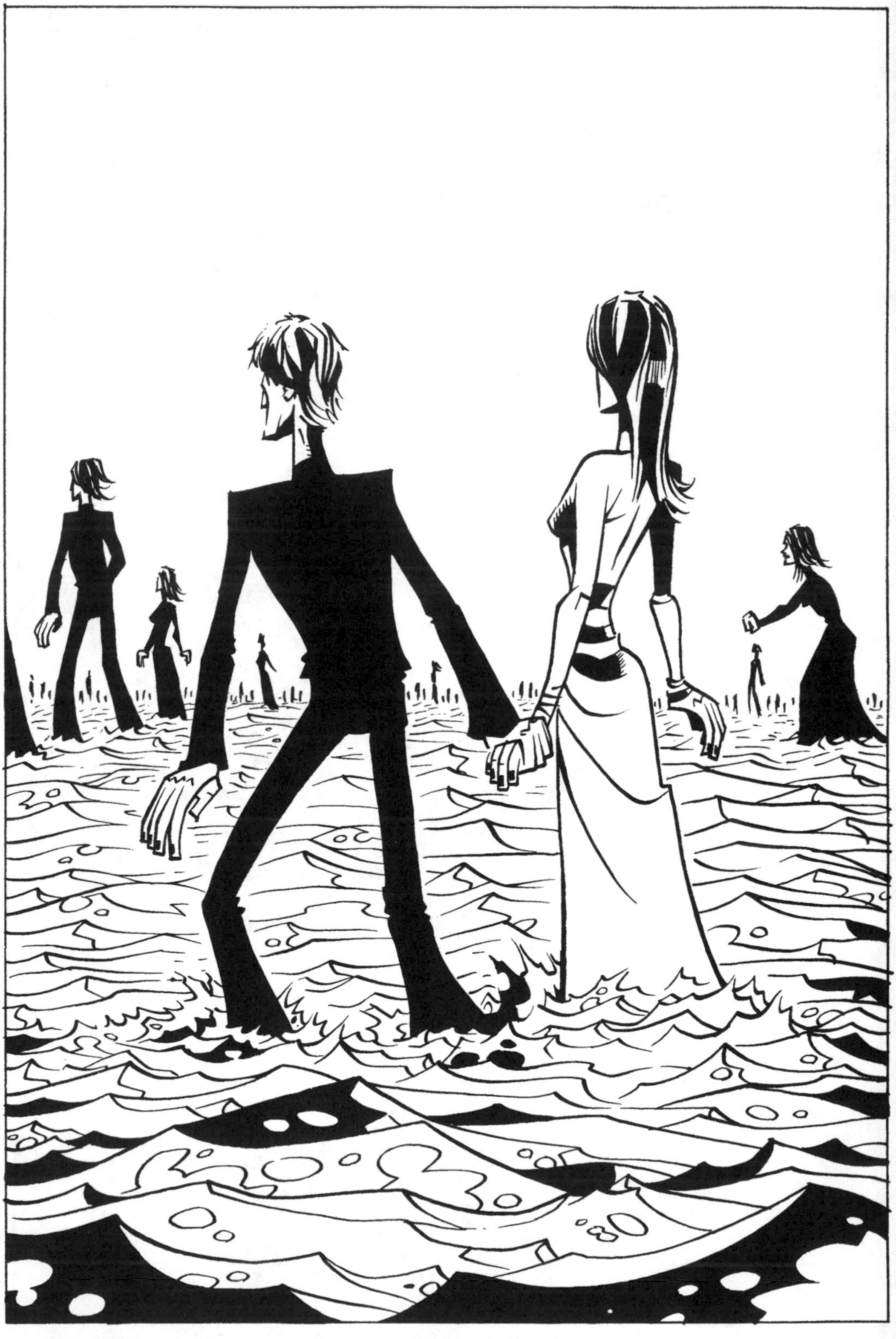

THE
END

WRITTEN
AND
DIRECTED
BY
THE
FILLBÄCH
BROTHERS

LOVE EVERYBODY

AND HELP SOMEBODY iF YOU CAN

FOR
MARY PRICE
AND
DEE PRICE

2007